RODGERS AND HAMMERSTEIN

FACT BOOK

Richard Rodgers and Oscar Hammerstein II

RODGERS AND HAMMERSTEIN

FACT BOOK

A Record of Their Works Together and with Other Collaborators

Edited by

STANLEY GREEN

The Lynn Farnol Group, Inc.
New York

Richard Rodgers died in New York on December 30, 1979. He is survived by his wife Dorothy Feiner Rodgers; two daughters, Mary Rodgers Guettel, and Linda Rodgers Breckir; six grandchildren, Richard Rodgers Beaty (Tod), Linda Beaty (Nina), Constance Beaty (Kim), Peter Melnick, Adam Guettel and Alexander Guettel.

DESIGNED AND MANUFACTURED IN THE UNITED STATES
OF AMERICA BY GANIS AND HARRIS, INC., NEW YORK

Contents

Oscar Hammerstein II

RICHARD RODGERS

Vivienne Segal and Gene Kelly singing "Den of Iniquity" in "Pal Joey" (1940).

BIOGRAPHICAL FACT SHEET

RICHARD RODGERS

BORN: New York, N.Y., June 28, 1902.

PARENTS: William and Mamie (Levy) Rodgers.

FATHER'S PROFESSION: Doctor.

EDUCATION: Townsend Harris Hall (1916); DeWitt Clinton High School (1916-19); Columbia University (1919-21); Institute of Musical Art (Juilliard) (1921-23).

MARRIED: Dorothy Feiner, March 5, 1930.

CHILDREN: Mary, Linda.

FIRST SONGS: *Dear Old Wigwam* and *Camp-Fire Days* (written at Camp Wigwam, Harrison, Maine, 1916).

FIRST COPYRIGHT SONG: *Auto Show Girl,* lyric by David Dyrenforth (June 30, 1917).

FIRST SCORE (music and part lyrics): *One Minute, Please* (amateur, 1917).

FIRST PUBLISHED SONGS (music and lyrics): *Twinkling Eyes, Asiatic Angles, Butterfly Love, Love Is Not in Vain, Love Me by Parcel Post* (lyric by Mortimer Rodgers, brother), all in *Up Stage and Down* (amateur, 1919).

FIRST PROFESSIONAL SONG WITH LORENZ HART: *Any Old Place with You,* in *A Lonely Romeo* (copyright, December 19, 1919).

FIRST SCORE WITH MR. HART: *You'd Be Surprised* (amateur, 1920).

FIRST PROFESSIONAL SCORE WITH MR. HART: *Poor Little Ritz Girl* (1920).

FIRST SONGS WITH MR. HAMMERSTEIN: *Weaknesses, Can It* and *There's Always Room for One More,* all in *Up Stage and Down* (amateur, 1919).

FIRST PROFESSIONAL SONG WITH MR. HAMMERSTEIN: *Oh, What a Beautiful Mornin'* in *Oklahoma!* (1943).

FIRST PROFESSIONAL SCORE WITH MR. HAMMERSTEIN: *Oklahoma!*

FIRST PROFESSIONAL SCORE WITH OWN LYRICS: *No Strings* (1962).

LYRICIST COLLABORATORS BESIDES MR. HAMMERSTEIN:

Lorenz Hart (1895-1943), 29 stage scores, 9 film scores
Stephen Sondheim (born 1930), 1 stage score
Martin Charnin (born 1934), 2 stage scores
Sheldon Harnick (born 1924), 1 stage score

STAGE AND FILM WORKS TO DATE:

40 Broadway musicals (26 with Hart; 9 with Hammerstein; 1 alone; 1 with Sondheim; 2 with Charnin; 1 with Harnick)

1 Broadway play (with Hart and Herbert Fields)
3 London musicals (with Hart)
10 film musicals (9 with Hart; 1 with Hammerstein)
2 television musicals (1 with Hammerstein; 1 alone)
2 television documentaries
1 night club revue (with Hart)
1 ballet

PERFORMANCE STATISTICS:
The number of performances achieved by all of Mr. Rodgers' Broadway stage works to date—including revivals—totals 18,126. On the basis of eight performances per week, this is equivalent to almost 2,266 weeks—or an unbroken run of almost 43½ years.

PROFESSIONAL POSITIONS: Partner, Rodgers and Hammerstein productions; partner, Williamson Music, Inc.; president and producing director, Music Theater of Lincoln Center (1962-69).

PROFESSIONAL ASSOCIATIONS: American Society of Composers, Authors and Publishers (ASCAP) (director, 1941-47, 1960-74); Authors League of America; Dramatists Guild (president, 1943-47); National Association of American Composers and Conductors; Actors Fund of America (trustee, 1949-); American Guild of Authors and Composers.

BOARD MEMBERSHIPS: American Theatre Wing (1941-); Barnard College (1953-1966); Philharmonic-Symphony Society of New York (1954-); Juilliard School of Music (1959-); Founding member, John F. Kennedy Center for the Performing Arts (1964-); National Council on the Arts (1965-1968).

ENDOWMENTS: Permanent Scholarship, Juilliard (1953); Max Dreyfus Annual Scholarship, Juilliard (endowed with Mr. Hammerstein) (1954); 2 scholarships, American Theatre Wing (Rodgers and Hammerstein Foundation) (1955); Rodgers and Hammerstein annual award to individual who has done the most for the theatre in the Boston area (1959); Rodgers and Hammerstein annual award to individual who has done the most for the theatre in the Southwest (1960); Mt. Morris Park Amphitheatre (1970); Professional Children's School Award (1974); Richard Rodgers Production Award, musical-theatre production award established through the American Academy and Institute of Arts and Letters (1978); Rodgers and Hammerstein Archives of Recorded Sound, Lincoln Center (Rodgers and Hammerstein Foundation).

PERSONAL HONORS AND AWARDS *(awards for specific works are found under stage and film productions)*

1949 Columbia University Medal for Excellence
Drury College honorary LL.D.
1950 100 Year Association Gold Medal
1951 Connecticut State Bar Assn. Distinguished Public Service Award
1952 Columbia College Outstanding Achievement Award
U.S. Navy Distinguished Public Service Medal
1954 Columbia University honorary Mus.D.
University of Massachusetts honorary DHL
1955 Elected to membership National Institute of Arts and Letters, Department of Music (now American Academy and Institute of Arts and Letters)
1956 Columbia College Alexander Hamilton Medal
1957 Dutch Treat Club Distinguished Achievement Award
1959 National Conference of Christians and Jews Human Relations Award
New England Theatre Conference Award
1960 Advertising Federation of America Award
Poor Richard Club Gold Medal
Texas Music Educators Award
1961 Broadway Association Gold Medal
1962 American Theatre Wing Special "Tony" Award
University of Bridgeport honorary Mus.D.
University of Maryland honorary Mus.D.
1963 Holland Society Gold Medal
1964 Mary MacArthur Memorial Fund Award
1965 City of Boston Distinguished Achievement Award
Brandeis University honorary Mus.D.
Hamilton College honorary Mus.D.
1966 B'nai B'rith National Performing Arts Award
Sam S. Shubert Foundation Award
1967 City of New York Handel Medallion
1968 Fairfield University honorary Mus.D.
Brandeis University Creative Arts Award
Lambs Club Award
1971 New York University honorary Mus.D.
Actors Fund Medal
Elected to Songwriters Hall of Fame
1972 Elected to Theatre Hall of Fame
League of N.Y. Theatres Special "Tony" Award

1975 Dance Educators of America Award
Elected to Entertainment Hall of Fame
1976 The New England Conservatory of Music honorary Mus.D.
American Music Conference National Music Award
1978 Stereo Review Certificate of Merit
Barnard Medal of Distinction
Kennedy Center Honors
1979 Philadelphia College of the Performing Arts honorary Mus.D.
The Lawrence Langner "Tony" Award for Distinguished Lifetime Achievement in the Theater

AMATEUR PRODUCTIONS

1917
One Minute Please
A musical comedy with book by Ralph G. Engelsman; music by Richard C. Rodgers; lyrics by Messrs. Engelsman and Rodgers. Presented by the Akron Club for the benefit of the *New York Sun* Tobacco Fund; directed by Milton G. Bender. NEW YORK RUN: Plaza Hotel Grand Ballroom, December 29, 1917.
MUSICAL NUMBERS: *I'm a Vampire; My Camera Man; At the Movies* (by Dr. Bender); *Whispers; He Stole the Heart of a Vamp; Auto Show Girl* (lyric by David Dyrenforth); *Lest We Forget; When They Rub Noses in Alaska; They've Got Nothing on Us "Over There."*

1919
Up Stage And Down
A musical comedy with book by Myron D. Rosenthal; music and lyrics by Richard C. Rodgers. Presented by the Infants Relief Society; directed by Harry A. Goldberg; choreography by Sydney Oberfelder; music director, Mr. Rodgers. NEW YORK RUN: Waldorf-Astoria Hotel Grand Ballroom, March 8, 1919.
MUSICAL NUMBERS: *Love Me By Parcel Post* (lyric by Mortimer W. Rodgers); *Wild Women's Wiles; Twinkling Eyes; Weaknesses* (lyric by Oscar Hammerstein II); *Asiatic Angles; Love Is Not in Vain; Out of a Job; There's Always Room for One More* (lyric by Mr. Hammerstein); *Ali Baba; Prisms, Plums and Prunes* (lyric by Benjamin Kaye); *Butterfly Love; Now Listen, Dearie; Can It* (lyric by Mr. Hammerstein); *Loving Cup; Japanese Jazz; Advertise.*
NOTE: On May 18, 1919, musical was reopened under title *Twinkling Eyes* at the 44th Street Theatre. This production was presented by the Brooklyn YMHA for the benefit of the Soldiers and Sailors

Welfare Fund, with book now credited to Harry Lea Strong and Mr. Rosenthal, and with Lorenz M. Hart as director. One new song, *I'm So Shy* was added; *Asiatic Angles, Out of a Job, Now Listen, Dearie,* and *Advertise* were dropped.

1920

You'd Be Surprised

An "atrocious musical comedy" with book by Milton G. Bender; music by Richard C. Rodgers; lyrics by Lorenz M. Hart and Dr. Bender. Presented by the Akron Club; directed by Dr. Bender; professional assistance by Lew Fields; music director, Mr. Rodgers. Cast included Dorothy Fields. NEW YORK RUN: Plaza Hotel Grand Ballroom.

MUSICAL NUMBERS: *Don't Love Me Like Othello; Spain; You Don't Have to Be a Toreador; Poor Fish; College Baby* (lyric by Robert A. Simon); *Kid, I Love You; My World of Romance; The Boomerang; China; That Boy of Mine* (lyric by Oscar Hammerstein II); *When We Are Married; Princess of the Willow Tree; Aphrodite; Mary, Queen of Scots* (lyric by Herbert L. Fields); *Breath of Spring.*

Fly With Me

A musical comedy with book by Milton Kroopf and Philip Leavitt, adapted by Lorenz M. Hart; music by Richard C. Rodgers; lyrics by Mr. Hart. Presented by the Columbia University Players as the Varsity Show of 1920; directed by Ralph Bunker; choreography by Herbert L. Fields; music director, Mr. Rodgers. NEW YORK RUN: Astor Hotel Grand Ballroom, March 24-27, 1920.

MUSICAL NUMBERS: *Gone Are the Days; A Penny for Your Thoughts; Another Melody in F; Working for the Government; Inspiration; Don't Love Me Like Othello; Peek in Peking; Dreaming True; A College on Broadway; The Moon and You; There's Always Room for One More* (lyric by Oscar Hammerstein II); *If I Only Were a Boy; Kid, I Love You; If I Were You; Weaknesses* (lyric by Mr. Hammerstein); *Gunga Dhin.*

1921

Say Mama

A musical comedy with music by Richard C. Rodgers; lyrics by Lorenz M. Hart. Presented by the Akron Club for the Oppenheim Collins Mutual Aid Association and the *New York Mail* Save-a-Home Fund; directed by Herbert L. Fields. Cast included Dorothy Fields. NEW YORK RUN: Plaza Hotel Grand Ballroom, February 12; Academy of Music, February 21, 1921.

MUSICAL NUMBERS: *Chorus Girl Blues; Watch Yourself; Wake Up; Poor Little Model; First Love; I Surrender!; Show Him the Way; Under the Mistletoe; Jack and Jill.*

You'll Never Know

A musical comedy with book by Herman A. Axelrod and Henry William Hanemann; music by Richard C. Rodgers; lyrics by Lorenz M. Hart. Presented by the Columbia University Players as the Varsity Show of 1921; directed by Oscar Hammerstein II, and Messrs. Axelrod and Hanemann; choreography by Herbert Fields; settings by Joseph Physioc; music director, Mr. Rodgers. NEW YORK RUN: Astor Hotel Grand Ballroom, April 20-23, 1921.

MUSICAL NUMBERS: *Virtue Wins the Day; I'm Broke; When I Go on the Stage; Will You Forgive Me?; Just a Little Lie; You'll Never Know; Let Me Drink in Your Eyes; Your Lullaby; Watch Yourself; Chorus Girl Blues; Jumping Jack.*

Say It With Jazz

"A Coq-d'Orian Fantasy" with book by Dorothy Crowthers, Frank Hunter, Maurice Lieberman; music by Richard C. Rodgers; lyrics by Lorenz M. Hart and Mr. Hunter. Presented by the Institute of Musical Art. NEW YORK RUN: June 1-2, 1921.

MUSICAL NUMBERS: *Just Remember Coq d'Or; See the Golden Rooster; If I Knew* (by Gerald Warburg); *Your Lullaby; Don't Love Me Like Othello; Weaknesses* (lyric by Oscar Hammerstein II); *Working for the Institute; Hindoo Moon* (by William Kroll); *Hymn to the Moon; The Moon and You; Dreaming True; Something Like Me; Chorus Girl Blues; Just a Little Lie; Oh, Harold.*

1922

The Chinese Lantern

Play by Laurence Housman; music by Richard C. Rodgers. Presented by the Benjamin School for Girls. Cast included Dorothy Fields. NEW YORK RUN: Benjamin School, May 7, 1922.

MUSICAL NUMBERS: *Anywhere; Partners; Wee China Rose; I Want to Be a Grocer.*

Jazz a la Carte

A musical comedy with book by Dorothy Crowthers; music by Richard C. Rodgers; lyrics by Frank Hunter. Presented by the Institute of Musical Art; directed by Herbert Fields and Mr. Rodgers; music director, William Kroll. NEW YORK RUN: June 2-3, 1922.

MUSICAL NUMBERS: *Another Melody in F* (lyric by Lorenz M. Hart);

The Poster Girl; What Ragtime Did to Business; Breath of Spring (lyric by Mr. Hart); *Waiting* (music by Gerald Warburg); *There's Always Room for One More* (lyric by Oscar Hammerstein II); *Another Mad Scene* (music by William Kroll); *Moonlight and You; Everytime I Think of You* (music by Mr. Warburg); *Mary, Queen of Scots* (lyric by Herbert L. Fields); *Every Girlie Wants to Be a Sally; My Prince of Wales* (music by Gerald Warburg); *That Pathetique Melody* (music by Sigmund Krumgold).

1923

If I Were King

A musical comedy with music by Richard C. Rodgers; lyrics by Lorenz M. Hart. Presented by the Benjamin School for Girls for benefit Free Scholarship Fund of New York Child Labor Comm.; directed by Herbert L. Fields; music director, Mr. Rodgers. NEW YORK RUN: Thirty-Ninth Street Theatre, March 25, 1923.
MUSICAL NUMBERS: *The Band of the Ne'er Do Wells; If I Were King; Sextette; March Louis XI; Minuet Waltz; Courtly Etiquette.*

A Danish Yankee in King Tut's Court

A musical comedy with book and lyrics by Dorothy Crowthers, Herbert L. Fields, Richard C. Rodgers; music by Mr. Rodgers. Presented by the Institute of Musical Art; directed by Mr. Fields; music director, Mr. Rodgers. NEW YORK RUN: Institute, May 31-June 1, 1923.
MUSICAL NUMBERS: *King Tut's Birthday; My Cleopatra; Send for Nielsen; Will You Forgive Me?* (lyric by Lorenz M. Hart); *Egyptian Night* (music by Sigmund Krumgold); *If You're Single* (lyric by Mr. Hart); *If I Were King* (lyric by Mr. Hart); *College Baby* (lyric by Robert A. Simon); *Hermits* (lyric by Mr. Hart); *Bob-o-Link; Song of the Moon; Wake Up Miss Aida.*

1924

Temple Bells

A one-act musical comedy with book and music by Richard C. Rodgers; lyrics by Lorenz M. Hart. Presented by the Park Avenue Synagogue as Purim Entertainment; directed by Herbert L. Fields; music director Mr. Rodgers. NEW YORK RUN: Park Avenue Synagogue, March 20, 1924.
MUSICAL NUMBERS: *Just a Little Lie; Bob-o-Link* (lyric by Dorothy Crowthers); *A Penny for Your Thoughts; Hermits.*

The Prisoner of Zenda

A musical comedy with music by Richard C. Rodgers; lyrics by Herbert L. Fields. Presented by the Benjamin School for Girls for Free Scholarship Fund of New York Child Labor Comm.; directed by Mr. Fields; music director, Mr. Rodgers. Cast included Dorothy Fields in title role. NEW YORK RUN: Selwyn Theatre, March 23, 1924. MUSICAL NUMBERS: *My King Can Do No Wrong; This Is a Situation; Oh, Dear!; Farewell to Rudolph; Make Way; Without Love; The Worst of Friends; Song of Russia; When Men Are in Love.*

1925

Bad Habits of 1925

A revue—"The Kind of Show that Men Forget"—with music by Richard C. Rodgers; lyrics by Lorenz M. Hart. Presented for benefit of Evelyn Goldsmith Home for Crippled Children; directed by Mr. Hart and Irving Strouse; choreography by Gene Richard and Sydney Oberfelder; music director, Mr. Rodgers. NEW YORK RUN: Children's Theatre, Heckscher Foundation, February 8, 1925. MUSICAL NUMBERS: *The Merrie Merrie; In Gingham; Across the Garden Wall; Mah Jong Maid; Darling Will Not Grow Older; If I Were King; I'd Like to Take You Home; College Baby* (lyric by Robert A. Simon).

POOR LITTLE RITZ GIRL

(1920)

A musical comedy with book by George Campbell and Lew Fields; music by Richard C. Rodgers and Sigmund Romberg; lyrics by Lorenz M. Hart and Alex Gerber.

Presented by Mr. Fields
Directed and lighted by Ned Wayburn
Choreography by David Bennett
Settings by Robert H. Law Studios
Costumes by Cora Macgeachy, Marie Cook and Anna Spencer
Music director, Charles Previn

Tryout

(book originally by Henry B. Stillman and William J. O'Neil)
Shubert-Wilbur Theatre, Boston, May 28-July 14, 1920
Stamford Theatre, Stamford, Conn., July 16-17, 1920
Nixon Theatre, Atlantic City, July 18-23, 1920

New York Run

Central Theatre, July 28-October 16, 1920
119 performances

The Story

Barbara Arden, an unsophisticated girl from the South, comes to New York to dance in the chorus of *Poor Little Ritz Girl.* She rents an apartment from an unscrupulous janitor, with embarrassing situations arising when the apartment's true owner, Billy Pembroke, returns. The confusion is abated when Barbara and Billy fall in love, thereby settling their problem by getting married.

The Cast

BARBARA ARDEN, Eleanor Griffith
MADGE MERRIL, Lulu McConnell
LILLIAN LAWRENCE, Aileen Poe
ANNIE FARRELL (SWEETIE), Florence Webber
WILLIAM PEMBROKE (BILLY), *a wealthy bachelor,* Charles Purcell
DR. RUSSELL STEVENS, *his bachelor "pal,"* Andrew Tombes
JANE DE PUYSTER, *Billy's aunt,* Eugenie Blair
DOROTHY ARDEN, *Barbara's sister,* Ardelle Cleaves
TEDDIE BURNS, *a leading juvenile,* Donald Kerr
HELEN BOND, *a dancer,* Elise Bonwit

MARGUERITE, *another,* Ruth Hale
MLLE. LOVA, *première, danseuse,* Dolly Clements
M. MORDKY, *her partner,* Michael Cunningham
STAGE MANAGER, Grant Simpson
ENSEMBLE: Muriel Manners, Bobbie Beckwith, Julie Anderson, Madeline Smith, DeSacia Crandell, Dore Lighton, Frisco Devere, Mabel Pierson, Nan Phillips, Betty Warlow, Vivian White, Mary Phillips, Josephine Rolfe, Peggy Walsh, Mabel Hastings, Lee Smith

NOTE: During Boston tryout, BARBARA played by Aileen Poe, BILLY by Victor Morley, RUSSELL by Roy Atwell, LILLIAN by Alma Adaire, DOROTHY by Eleanor Griffith. During Stamford tryout, BARBARA played by Gertrude Vanderbilt. In October, Mr. Purcell succeeded by Frederic Santley.

Musical Numbers

ACT I

SCENE ONE—STAGE OF FRIVOLITY THEATRE, BROADWAY, DURING DRESS REHEARSAL
Poor Little Ritz Girl (Romberg-Gerber), ENSEMBLE
Mary, Queen of Scots (Rodgers-Herbert Fields), MADGE

SCENE TWO—APARTMENT OF WILLIAM PEMBROKE ON RIVERSIDE DRIVE
Love Will Call (Rodgers-Hart), BARBARA

SCENE THREE—STAGE OF FRIVOLITY THEATRE, DURING A PERFORMANCE
Pretty Ming Toy (Romberg-Gerber), ANNIE and ENSEMBLE

SCENE FOUR—APARTMENT OF WILLIAM PEMBROKE
I Love to Say Hello to the Girls (Romberg-Gerber), RUSSELL
When I Found You (Romberg-Gerber), BILLY

ACT II

SCENE ONE—APARTMENT OF WILLIAM PEMBROKE
You Can't Fool Your Dreams (Rodgers-Hart), BARBARA, BILLY, DOC

SCENE TWO—STAGE DOOR OF FRIVOLITY THEATRE
What Happened Nobody Knows (Rodgers-Hart), MADGE, LILLIAN, ANNIE
My Violin (Romberg-Gerber), DOROTHY

SCENE THREE—APARTMENT OF WILLIAM PEMBROKE
All You Need to Be a Star (Rodgers-Hart), BARBARA, DOROTHY, BILLY, DOC
Love's Intense in Tents (Rodgers-Hart), DOROTHY and DOC

SCENE FOUR—STAGE OF FRIVOLITY THEATRE, DURING OPENING NIGHT PERFORMANCE
The Daisy and the Lark (Rodgers-Hart), ANNIE, HELEN and ENSEMBLE
In the Land of Yesterday (Romberg-Gerber), DOROTHY, HELEN and ENSEMBLE
The Phantom Waltz (Romberg), danced by MLLE. LOVA and M. MORDKY
The Bombay Bombashay (Romberg-Gerber), TEDDIE, HELEN, MARGUERITE and ENSEMBLE

SCENE FIVE—APARTMENT OF WILLIAM PEMBROKE
Finale, COMPANY

NOTE: As originally presented at the Shubert-Wilbur Theatre, Boston, the entire score of the musical was written by Rodgers and Hart alone. It consisted of the following numbers:

ACT I
Poor Little Ritz Girl, IRENE, HELEN and ENSEMBLE
The Midnight Supper, BARBARA, MADGE, LILLIAN, ANNIE
Lady Raffles—Behave, BARBARA and BILLY
The Gown Is Mightier than the Sword, LILLIAN and ENSEMBLE
Let Me Drink in Your Eyes, IRENE, HELEN and ENSEMBLE
Will You Forgive Me?, BARBARA and BILLY
Souvenir, BILLY

ACT II
Call the Doc, DOC
You Can't Fool Your Dreams, BARBARA, BILLY, DOC
The Lord Only Knows, MADGE, LILLIAN, ANNIE
The Boomerang, IRENE, HELEN and ENSEMBLE
Love Will Call, DOROTHY
All You Need to Be a Star, BARBARA, DOROTHY, DOC, BILLY
Love's Intense in Tents, DOROTHY and DOC
The Daisy and the Lark, LILLIAN, ANNIE, IRENE, HELEN and CHORUS
Mary, Queen of Scots (lyric by Herbert Fields), MADGE
I Surrender, BARBARA, BILLY and ENSEMBLE
Finale, COMPANY

NOTE: *You Can't Fool Your Dreams* has same music as *Don't Love Me Like Othello (Fly with Me, You'd Be Surprised); Love Will Call* same as *Dreaming True (Fly with Me, Say It With Jazz); Love's Intense in Tents* same as *Peek in Pekin (Fly with Me).*

Reviews

New York Times
". . . contains much that is above the average of musical comedy as well as a good deal that is just average . . . considerable of it is broadly amusing in a more or less stereotyped fashion . . ."

Heywood Broun—*New York Tribune*
". . . stands heads and shoulders above any of its recent rivals because the producer has taken the pains to add a few jokes . . . The neglected lyric also gets more of its due than usual, for *Mary, Queen of Scots* seems to us the most rollicking ballad we have heard in a twelvemonth. It is perhaps fitting to mention that Richard C. Rodgers composed the music for this ditty as well as that for another excellent song, *What Happened Nobody Knows.* The more serious songs are from Sigmund Romberg, and they are pleasing, but hardly as striking as the lighter numbers . . ."

New York World
"... rich in everything that goes to make a successful entertainment of the girl and music type. It has a real plot, humor, a good looking chorus, and a tuneful score . . . so dexterously blended that the farce does not interfere with the musical comedy and the musical numbers are never allowed to interfere with the progress of the plot . . ."

Alan Dale—*New York American*
"... one song, *Mary, Queen of Scots,* was worth the price of admission . . . Some of the profanity could be advantageously deleted. H---! is no longer funny. It is merely silly . . ."

McElliott—*New York Daily News*
"... a chromatic, plotty and deft revue. Funny it is certainly, although sometimes it descends to obvious crudities for this effect . . . nothing amazingly original in the story . . . All of the tunes, though pretty, must in all truth be labelled 'reminiscent' . . ."

Charles Pike Sawyer—*New York Post*
"... as good as it is new. From beginning to end, dull moments are rare . . . an intelligent plot, well worked out, and the fun, action and music are never lugged in . . . nothing particularly inspired in the music, but it has a pleasant lilt, that by Romberg being in his best Viennese waltz style, while Rodgers has written some good numbers . . . above and beyond all, there is never a suggestive line or gesture . . ."

New York Sun
"... has a plot that makes an occasional appearance when costumes and tenors are getting ready to appear . . . There are some attractive ensemble numbers, a humorous song now and then, and the usual dancing numbers common to all the shows that bloom in the summer . . ."

Kenneth Macgowan—*New York Globe*
"... a cross between a revue and an American musical comedy with a plot. The plot is rather short and not too husky, and there aren't a great many revue scenes, but the two together make a rather odd and satisfactory entertainment . . . The music is about equally divided between Rodgers' hard, brisk tunes and Romberg's rich and syrupy melodies . . ."

Jack Pulaski (Ibee.)—*Variety,* August 6, 1920
"... has considerable novelty which should weigh nicely in swinging the piece into the list of successes . . ."

Louis R. Reid—*New York Dramatic Mirror,* August 7, 1920
". . . well above the average in many respects . . . naively told, naively acted story, but sufficient for musical-comedy purposes during the dog days . . ."

Arthur Hornblow—*Theatre Magazine,* October, 1920
". . . unusually good entertainment . . . flimsy plot . . . rich in hilarious lines and clever tunes . . ."

Tour

Poli's Theatre, Washington, December 5, 1920 (record incomplete)

Bibliography

Seventeen-Year-Old Composer —*Variety,* May 21, 1920

THE MELODY MAN

(1924)

A comedy by Herbert Richard Lorenz (pseudonym for Herbert Fields, Richard Rodgers and Lorenz Hart).

Presented by Lew Fields
Directed by Lawrence Marston and Alexander Leftwich

Tryout
(known as "The Jazz King")
Kurtz Theatre, Bethlehem, Pa., March 24-29, 1924
Orpheum Theatre, Harrisburg, March 25, 1924
Cambria Theatre, Johnstown, March 26, 1924
Auditorium, Wheeling, March 27, 1924
Auditorium, Toledo, March 28-29, 1924
Garrick Theatre, Detroit, March 30-April 5, 1924
Hanna Theatre, Cleveland, April 7-12, 1924
(known as "Henky")
LaSalle Theatre, Chicago, April 21-May 3, 1924
Teller's Shubert Theatre, Brooklyn, May 5-10, 1924

New York Run
Ritz Theatre, May 13-31, 1924
Forty-Ninth Street Theatre, June 2-28, 1924
56 performances

The Story
Austrian composer Franz Henkel struggles to win recognition in America. Finally, he gets a job as an arranger for the Al Tyler Music Publishing Company, for which he performs many unpleasant tasks. He is particularly enraged when Tyler rearranges his serious composition, the *Dresden Sonata,* and calls it *Moonlight Mama.* In the end, Elsa, Henkel's daughter, marries Tyler, and the old man is free to compose the kind of music he loves.

The Cast
JESSIE SANDS, *the telephone girl,* Eleanor Rowe
SIDNEY, *the office boy,* Jerry Devine

THE SAXOPHONE THE CORONET THE TROMBONE THE PIANO THE DRUMS	Joseph B. Franklin's Revellers	Fred Starwer Joe Lindwurm Dave Stryker Al Schenck Bill Tucker

RUTH DAVIS, *a small-time ballad singer,* Louise Kelley
STELLA MALLORY, *manager of the Al Tyler Music Publishing Company,* Eva Puck
AL TYLER, *owner of the Al Tyler Music Publishing Company,* Donald Gallaher

RITA LAMARR BERT HACKETT	*a married vaudeville team*	Renee Noel Sam White

ELSA HENKEL, *Al Tyler's secretary,* Betty Weston
DONALD CLEMENS, *a student violinst,* Fredric March
FRANZ HENKEL, *arranger of music with the company,* Lew Fields
DAVE LOEB, *a police court lawyer,* Jules Jordan
A CHAUFFEUR, Joseph Torpey
A MAID, Sara Chapelle
A PIANO PLAYER, Jimmy Kapper

ACT I—THE AL TYLER MUSIC PUBLISHING COMPANY
ACT II—FRANZ HENKEL'S FLAT
ACT III—AL TYLER'S APARTMENT ON RIVERSIDE DRIVE

Musical Numbers
Moonlight Mama and *I'd Like to Poison Ivy* sung by Eva Puck and Sam White in Act I. Songs credited to "Herbert Richard Lorenz."

Reviews
John Corbin—*New York Times*
". . . something on the pattern of *The Music Master* . . . neither the best nor the worst of its kind. The only question of importance with regard to it is just how easy it is to amuse those who are easily amused . . ."

Percy Hammond—*New York Tribune*
". . . Pretty poor stuff for a player of Mr. Fields' caliber. It belongs among the trundle bedtime stories, feeble, immature and meandering. Now and then it is lighted by flashes of Mr. Fields' underdog humor and pathos . . . the comedy itself is a hopeless sham, sully of ancient devices unskillfully contrived . . ."

Quinn Martin—*New York World*
". . . must be regarded as one of the surprises of this dramatic season. No comedy in the closing winter's long list has found itself more heartily or more continuously laughed at on opening night. It deserved everything it got. It is a tremendously funny show . . ."

Gene Fowler—*New York American*
"... Lew Fields gave out fun in large portions last night and he did it without ceasing to be human about it . . . *The Melody Man* is comedy that does not tarnish . . ."

New York Post
". . . a riot of laughter, full of home-brewed heart throbs, and cramjammed with the latest Broadway nifties . . ."

Alexander Woollcott—*New York Sun*
". . . has enormously comic interludes. One would hesitate to say that the play is uncommonly funny in its own right, but there are moments when it seems to recede discreetly and leave one or two highly entertaining individuals to do their best undisturbed by the throbbing of its audible machinery . . ."

Robert Benchley—*Life,* May 13, 1924
". . . full of good old corned-beef which made our fathers the hardy race they were. But it does have some pretty funny wise-cracks, and plenty of chance for Lew Fields to be Lew Fields, which is almost enough for any show to have at this time of year . . ."

Abel Green—*Variety,* May 14, 1924
". . . The first act starts with a zip, the second sags and the last act is a little better . . . not a hit possibility . . ."

George Jean Nathan—*Judge,* May 15, 1924
"*Plot Deutsch* . . . a couple of well-drawn characters and some humorous scenes and dialect dialogue . . . But the plot is not only enough to ruin the play; it is enough—and I feel I may say it without fear of contradiction—to ruin even *Hamlet* . . ."

Time, May 26, 1924
". . . seems to be a jumble of *The Music Master, The Show Shop,* and *Potash and Perlmutter,* cemented by the unshakable popularity of Lew Fields."

THE MELODY MAN

(Film Version—1930)

A Columbia Picture
Produced by Harry Cohn
Directed by R. William Neill
Screenplay by Howard J. Green
Photographed by Ted Tetzlaff

Release Date
February 16, 1930

The Story
Eighteen years before the film begins, Austrian composer Otto Kemper killed his faithless wife and her lover, and took his infant daughter with him to America where he becomes a musician at a Broadway restaurant. His daughter grows up to become an arranger for a dance band, which takes Kemper's place in the restaurant. When the bandleader needs new music for a concert appearance, Kemper's daughter rearranges one of her father's classical pieces. Upon hearing the music, the Austrian police are led to Kemper, and arrest him for the murders.

The Cast
OTTO KEMPER, John St. Polis
KEMPER'S DAUGHTER, Alice Day
BAND LEADER, William Collier, Jr.
Albert Conti
Johnny Walker
Mildred Harris
Tennen Holtz
Lee Kohlmar
Bertram Marburgh
Anton Vazerka
Major Nichols

Musical Number
Broken Dreams (music by Arthur Johnston; lyric by Ballard MacDonald)

Reviews
Variety, February 23, 1930
". . . Columbia has managed to strengthen the continuity and music. That it doesn't make the top grade lies mainly in the subject matter . . . For the sticks . . ."

THE GARRICK GAIETIES

(1925)

A musical revue with sketches by Benjamin M. Kaye, Arthur Sullivan, Morrie Ryskind, Louis Sorin, Sam Jaffe, Howard J. Green and Edith Meiser; music by Richard Rodgers; lyrics by Lorenz Hart.

Presented by the Theatre Guild
Directed by Philip Loeb
Choreography by Herbert Fields
Settings and costumes by Carolyn Hancock
Stage manager, Harold E. Clurman
Music Director, Mr. Rodgers

New York Run

Garrick Theatre, May 17, 24, 26, 27, 29, June 3, 5 (special performances); June 8-November 28, 1925 (regular schedule of performances)
211 performances

The Cast

THE THEATRE GUILD JUNIOR PLAYERS

Sterling Holloway
Romney Brent
Betty Starbuck
Philip Loeb
John McGovern
Stanley Lindahl
Willard Tobias
Barbara Wilson
Edward Hogan
Hildegarde Halliday
Louis Richardson
Paul Jones
Starr Jones
Sally Bates
Jack Quigley
Mary Marsh
James Norris
June Cochrane
Edith Meiser
Eleanor Shaler
Carolyn Hancock
Felix Jacoves
Harold W. Conklin
House Jamieson
Peggy Conway
Lee Strasberg
Frances Hyde
Rose Rolanda
Elisabeth (Libby) Holman
Alvah Bessie
Henry Geiger
Sanford Meisner

Musical Numbers and Sketches

ACT I

Soliciting Subscriptions, Sterling Holloway, James Norris, Romney Brent, June Cochrane

Gilding the Guild, Betty Starbuck and Chorus

The Guardsman (sketch by Benjamin M. Kaye)

ALFRED LUNT, *the actor,* Romney Brent

LYNN FONTANNE, *the actress,* Edith Meiser

DUDLEY DIGGES, *the critic,* Philip Loeb

Butcher, Baker, Candle-Stick Maker (music by Mana-Zucca; lyric by Benjamin M. Kaye; staged by Edith Meiser)

SINGER, Harold W. Conklin

MARIE, Carolyn Hancock

THE BUTCHER, Stanley Lindahl

THE BAKER, Felix Jacoves

THE CANDLE-MAKER, James Norris

THE LITTLE MAN, Willard Tobias

The Theatre Guild Enters Heaven (sketch written and staged by Edith Meiser)

ST. PETER, Romney Brent

JURORS, Sanford Meisner, Henry Geiger, Alvah Bessie, Jack Quigley

THE GUARDSMAN'S WIFE, Edith Meiser

AMY, Peggy Conway

ST. JOAN, Mary Marsh

SADIE COHEN, Hildegarde Halliday

TWO CHERUBS, Willard Tobias, Lee Strasberg

Working With a Scarf, dance by Eleanor Shaler

Sh! Shh! ((sketch by Louis Sorin and Sam Jaffe)

MABEL, Frances Hyde

HER HUSBAND, House Jamieson

JACK, Edward Hogan

MAID, Peggy Conway

An Old-Fashioned Girl (music by Mr. Rodgers; lyric by Edith Meiser), Edith Meiser

April Fool, Betty Starbuck, Romney Brent and Chorus

They Didn't Know What They Were Getting (sketch by Benjamin M. Kaye)

TONY, John McGovern

AMY, Peggy Conway

JOE, Edward Hogan

THE DOCTOR, Alvah Bessie

Stage Managers' Chorus (lyric by Dudley Digges and Mr. Hart), Willard Tobias, Sterling Holloway, Romney Brent, Lee Strasberg, Stanley Lindahl, Frances Hyde, Starr Jones, Edward Hogan

Ruth Draper, impersonated by Hildegarde Halliday

The Joy Spreader ("An American Jazz Opera with music by Mr. Rodgers; libretto by Mr. Hart; inspiration by Gilbert Seldes, who is therefore primarily responsible for this outrage.")

JEREMIAH PRICE, *owner of Price's Big Store,* Edward Hogan
MARY BROWN, Betty Starbuck
TOM JONES, Romney Brent
STELLA MALLOY, June Cochrane
DOORMEN, Willard Tobias, Lee Strasberg
FLOORWALKERS, Starr Jones, Felix Jacoves
MRS. KATZ, *a customer,* Frances Hyde
EMPLOYEES, SHOPPERS
SETTING IS THE MAIN FLOOR OF PRICE'S BIG STORE
SCENE ONE—CLOSING TIME
SCENE TWO—OPENING TIME

ACT II

Rancho Mexicano (music by Tatanacho; settings and costumes by Miguel Covarrubias)

TWO DRUNKARDS, Lee Strasberg, House Jamieson
TWO WOMEN SINGING, Louise Richardson, Frances Hyde
THREE MEN SINGING, Lee Strasberg, Edward Hogan, Harold W. Conklin
A POLICEMAN, Paul Jones
TWO DANCERS, Rose Rolanda, Starr Jones

Ladies of the Boxoffice, Betty Starbuck, Elisabeth (Libby) Holman, June Cochrane

Mr. and Mrs. (sketch by Arthur Sullivan and Morrie Ryskind)

MRS. COOLIDGE, Edith Meiser
PRESIDENT COOLIDGE, John McGovern

Manhattan, June Cochrane and Sterling Holloway

Where Credit is Due (sketch by Howard J. Green)

JULIA, Peggy Conway
JIM, Lee Strasberg
FRED, Starr Jones
MARIE, *a maid,* Sally Bates

The Three Musketeers, Romney Brent, Sterling Holloway, Philip Loeb

Do You Love Me?, Louise Richardson; danced by Rose Rolanda and Chorus

Black and White, Elisabeth (Libby) Holman and Chorus; danced by Eleanor Shaler and Willard Tobias

Fate in the Morning (sketch)

MISS EMILY STEVENS (MATHILDE), Sterling Holloway
MR. MORGAN FARLEY (GEORGE), James Norris
THE DOGS! THE DOGS!, Romney Brent

The Guild Gilded, SIX DIRECTORS (Peggy Conway, Edward Hogan, Edith Meiser, Jack Quigley, Alvah Bessie, Lee Strasberg) and Company

NOTE: For regular run in June, *The Theatre Guild Enters Heaven, Stage Managers' Chorus, The Joy Spreader,* and *Black and White* were dropped.

Following musical numbers and sketches added in June:
Sentimental Me, June Cochrane, James Norris, Edith Meiser, Sterling Holloway
And Thereby Hangs a Tail (sketch by Morrie Ryskind and Philip Loeb; lyrics by Mr. Hart)
JUDGE, Lee Strasberg
DISTRICT ATTORNEY, Edward Norris
DEFENDANT, Sterling Holloway
SPECIAL COUNSEL, Philip Loeb
SCENE: AN AFRICAN COURTHOUSE
On With the Dance, June Cochrane and Chorus; danced by Eleanor Shaler

NOTE: *And Thereby Hangs a Tail dropped in August; The Guardsman* and *The Guild Gilded* dropped in October.

Following musical numbers and sketches added in October:
Subway Manners (sketch by Benjamin M. Kaye)
THE AGENT, House Jamieson
THE LADY, Peggy Conway
FIRST PASSENGER, T. Brewster Board
SECOND PASSENGER, William Johnstone
OTHER PASSENGERS: Lee Strasberg, Edward Hogan, Alvah Bessie, Sanford Meisner, Hildegarde Halliday, Jack Quigley, Romney Brent, Patricia Barclay, Eleanor Shaler
BOOTBLACK, Willard Tobias
ANNOUNCER,Henry Geiger
One of the Finest (sketch by Newman Levy)
CHIEF OF POLICE, Philip Loeb
A LADY, Edith Meiser
TRAFFIC OFFICER, Edward Hogan
SERGEANT, Romney Brent
FOUR POLICEMEN, James Norris, William Johnstone, Lee Strasberg, Harold W. Conklin
CIVILIANS, Alvah Bessie, T. Brewster Board, Henry Geiger, Jack Quigley, Sanford Meisner, Willard Tobias
TAXICABS, Patricia Barclay, Gladys Laird, Frances Hyde, Sylvia Shear, Eleanor Shaler, Marjorie Warden
The Green Derby (sketch by Benjamin M. Kaye)
IRIS MARCH, Edith Meiser
GERALD MARCH, Romney Brent
NAPIER HARPENDEN, Sterling Holloway
SIR MAURICE HARPENDEN, Edward Hogan

HILARY, House Jamieson
BOY FENWICK, James Norris
VENICE, Betty Starbuck
HOTEL PROPRIETOR, Lee Strasberg
MAID, Hildegarde Halliday
AN AUTHOR, Philip Loeb
A PRODUCER, William Johnstone

Finale

G.B.S., Philip Loeb
BLUNTCHLI, James Norris
RAINA, Edith Meiser
ST. JOAN, Betty Starbuck
DICK DUDGEON, Romney Brent
CAESAR, Sterling Holloway
CLEOPATRA, June Cochrane

Reviews

New York Times
". . . What there is in the Grand Street manner is very, very good, and what there is in the Winter Garden tradition is only fair . . . All the sketches were funny . . . The lyrics were mature and intelligently contrived. Rodgers' music was tuneful and well adapted to the needs of the entertainment."

Ward Morehouse—*New York Herald Tribune*
". . . brisk, refreshing and generally entertaining . . . most of the lyrics are particularly bright, and the music is appealingly sprightly . . ."

Wells Root—*New York World*
". . . The show had a good deal of difficulty going into its dance now and then and it needs tightening, but it has a decided personality and a good many laughs . . . The witnesses testified fervent approval. It is probably one of those programs that will be dug up from nowhere in ten years and conned with reminiscent chuckles . . . Everybody acted as though he or she was glad that school was out and that Art's ribs were for the moment free digging."

M. L.—*New York Daily News*
". . . excellent material . . . The music and the lyrics were well above the average Broadway ouput. *Manhattan* and *April Fool* were the numbers the audience seemed to like best . . . even grander than *The Grand Street Follies*."

Robert Coleman—*New York Daily Mirror*
". . . a spirited, tuneful revue . . . its sparkling wit and colorful movement is enhanced considerably by its lack of surface polish and

its irrepressible spontaneity . . . one of the most enjoyable numbers is *An Old Fashioned Girl* . . . *The Joy Spreader* is a droll satire . . ."

New York Graphic
". . . the show always flows nicely, has pretty chorus girls, some lovely ensemble numbers with hit music which would be used in any Broadway revue . . . sophisticated entertainment and very contemporary in its Guildish way . . . there's no greater bargain or bet in town."

E. W. Osborn—*New York Evening World*
"Listen! The newest thing in town, and the gayest, is called *The Garrick Gaieties,* which opened tentatively, continued joyfully, and closed triumphantly . . . new in every last meaning of the term. Which is to say it is absolutely fresh in word, song, dance, skit and bit of skittishness . . . the lyrics are real ones, having wit, rhyme and reason . . ."

Gilbert W. Gabriel—*New York Telegram*
". . . a witty, boisterous, athletic chowchow they have cooked up, its ingredients sometimes fully as sharp and tasty as those which celebrate the season rites on Grand Street, and preserved in a similar spirit of impromptu. Their scripts are the best of fun, their music fitting and enlivening . . . a crackling of good lyrics . . ."

Alexander Woollcott—*New York Sun*
". . . all of it is fresh, spirited and engaging; some of it is bright with the brightness of something new minted . . . a distinct 'varsity show' character to the lyrics. They are the kind invariably written by those who set out to show up the banal sentiments and meager vocabulary of Irving Berlin—rich in sprightly elaborate rhymes and suffering only from the not unimportant qualification that they do not sing well . . . the elders of the Guild must know now the acute discomfort of parenthood when one finds that one's prodigy are almost embarrassingly bright."

Bernard Simon—*New York Morning Telegraph*
". . . as spontaneous and quick moving a show as is to be found in town . . . a thing of wit and engaging lack of polish . . . The distinguishing feature of the whole performance was the zest and enthusiasm with which the players played . . . several songs of a tunefulness which insures their being whistled for many months to come . . ."

Robert F. Sisk—*Variety,* May 27, 1925
". . . Although it held some dull stuff and also some amateurish cutups, it qualifies as a corking revue, holding some fine music and

several lyrical pieces worthy of $5 notice . . . Rodgers and Hart's stuff clicked here like a colonel's heels at attention . . ."

Richard Watts, Jr.—*New York Herald Tribune,* June 9, 1925
". . . bright and engaging . . . Its gaiety, high spirits and cleverness, combined with a certain quality that makes the spectator feel that he is a guest at a party, proves once more that here is the ideal summer fare . . . The music is pleasant and the lyrics serviceable, if frequently obvious . . ."

Rozella McDevitt (a stenographer of Ft. Wadsworth, Staten Island)—*New York Graphic,* June 9, 1925
". . . a very grown-up wit and a most sophisticated tang to the merrymaking . . . The music is excellent and the songs are delightful. You will go away whistling . . ."

H. R.—*ibid.*
"If Broadway produced in a year three songs as captivating as those Rodgers has written, we haven't heard them. His music is a complete delight and the lyrics are all the talk, as well they should be . . ."

John Anderson—*New York Post,* June 9, 1925
"To all the lightness of heart and all the nimble grace and good fun that go to make up *The Garrick Gaieties* this paean of praise is sung . . . one is refreshed at the lack of June-moon in the lyrics, the best of them being *Ladies of the Box Office.* The music is pleasant and tinkly enough, but rather lacking in rhythmic variety . . ."

Robert Littell—*The New Republic,* July 1, 1925
". . . At its best, the bill is uproariously funny (particularly the crazy burlesque of *Fata Morgana*), on the average it is gay, light and trim, with awful spots like the tasteless, stupid travesty of President and Mrs. Coolidge . . . The words of the songs are far beyond normally intelligent for such a show, but the music is not up to them . . ."

George Jean Nathan—*Judge,* July 4, 1925
". . . contains one amusing sketch called *Mr. and Mrs.* (a lampoon of Cal Coolidge and *frau*) and one fairly diverting song called *Butcher, Baker, Candle-Stick Maker.* But aside from these, and for all a Homeric striving, it contains nothing that Ziegfeld, White and Charlot do not do fifty times better. Its singing is bad; its comedy is poor; its dancing is commonplace; its pictorial quality is nil . . ."

Herman J. Mankiewicz—*The New Yorker,* July 4, 1925
". . . amusing in a casual way and has several high spots that would

fit well into its more ambitious rivals . . . The outstanding features are the imitations of Pauline Lord and Ruth Draper, and the songs . . ."

Joseph Wood Krutch—*The Nation,* July 8, 1925
". . . the youth, gaiety and impudence of the entertainment more than make up for its relative deficiencies in smoothness, splendor and expenditure . . ."

Frank Sullivan—*New York World,* July 14, 1925
". . . I liked *The Garrick Gaieties* for its gay celebration. I liked the lyrics and still do, despite the criticism of a close friend of mine that they are clever but unsingable. I think there is a soupcon of tosh to that argument, although I did not say so in so many words to him. I simply told him he was crazy . . ."

John Mason Brown—*Theatre Arts Monthly,* August, 1925
". . . Rodgers' score gives a continuous zest to the performance . . . The show relies on the music and the dancing for the major part of its enjoyment, and succeeds most when it steers clear of parody . . . much of the humor is cheap and much is tedious . . . *An Old Fashioned Girl* is the high point of the performance . . . *The Butcher, the Baker, the Candlestick Maker* and *Manhattan* are witty and charming . . ."

Robert Benchley—*Life,* November 26, 1925
". . . by miles the cleverest and most civilized show in town. Messrs. Rodgers and Hart's music and lyrics, together with the burlesque sketches and the playing by half a dozen hitherto unknown youngsters, should be a standing taunt and source of chagrin to those uptown revue managers who keep putting on the same old thing each year."

Bibliography

How the Theatre Guild Put on Its Music Revue —*New York World,* May 17, 1925

Flaunting Youth —*New York Telegram,* June 12, 1925

A Unique, Youthful Revue —*New York Sun,* June 26, 1925

DEAREST ENEMY

(1925)

A musical comedy with book by Herbert Fields; music by Richard Rodgers; lyrics by Lorenz Hart.

Presented by George Ford
Production directed by John Murray Anderson
Book directed by Charles Sinclair and Harry Ford
Choreography by Carl Hemmer
Settings by Clark Robinson
First act costumes by Mark Mooring and Hubert Davis
Second and third act costumes by James Reynolds
Intermission curtain by Reginald Marsh
Music director, Mr. Rodgers
Orchestrations by Emil Gerstenberger

Tryout
(known as "Dear Enemy")
Colonial Theatre, Akron, Ohio, July 20, 1925
(known as "Dearest Enemy")
Ford's Opera House, Baltimore, September 7-12, 1925

New York Run
Knickerbocker Theatre, September 18, 1925-May 22, 1926
286 performances

The Story
In order to give General Putnam enough time to join General Washington's forces during the American Revolution, Mrs. Robert Murray holds a ball for General Howe and his English troops. Her niece, Betsy, falls in love with Captain Copeland, an aide to General Howe. All is righted, however, after the war.

The Cast
MRS. ROBERT MURRAY, Flavia Arcaro
CAROLINE, Alden Gay
ANNABELLE, Marian Williams
PEG, Jane Overton

JANE MURRAY, Helen Spring
JIMMY BURKE, Andrew Lawlor, Jr.
CAPTAIN HENRY TRYON, John Seymour
GENERAL HENRY CLINTON, William Evill
LIEUTENANT SUDSBY, Arthur Brown
GENERAL JOHN TRYON, Detmar Poppen
CAPTAIN SIR JOHN COPELAND, Charles Purcell
BETSY BURKE, Helen Ford
GENERAL ISRAEL PUTNAM, Percy Woodley
MAJOR AARON BURR, James Cushman
MORGAN SCOUTS: Jack Shannon, Mark Truscott, Percy French
ENVOY, Frank Lambert
GENERAL GEORGE WASHINGTON, H. E. Eldridge
LADIES OF THE ENSEMBLE: Betty Linn, Rachel Chester, Marion Dabney, Roberta Curry, Mabel Zpeckler, Polly Williams, Josephine Payne, Peggy Bancroft, Elizabeth North, Marita Dennis, Joy Leitch, Devah Worrell, Gloria Faye, Geneva Price, Mildred Mann, Lucille Smyser, Eugenia Renon
GENTLEMEN OF THE ENSEMBLE: George Harold, John Valentine, Burton McEvilly, Louis Gomez, Walter T. Burke, Edward Larkin, Conrad Gordon, James Cushman, Don Knobloch

NOTE: During Akron tryout, CAPTAIN SIR JOHN COPELAND played by Joseph Mendelsohn, MRS. ROBERT MURRAY by Marguerite Wolfe.

Musical Numbers

ACT I—THE MURRAY MANSION, MURRAY HILL, NEW YORK, 1776
Heigh-Ho, Lackaday, MRS. MURRAY and GIRLS
War Is War, MRS. MURRAY and GIRLS
I Beg Your Pardon, JANE and HARRY
Cheerio, SIR JOHN and OFFICERS
Full Blown Roses, MRS. MURRAY, OFFICERS and GIRLS
The Hermits, MRS. MURRAY and GEN. TRYON
Here in My Arms, BETSY and SIR JOHN
Finale, ENSEMBLE

ACT II—DRAWING ROOM AT THE MURRAY MANSION
Gavotte (arranged by John Murray Anderson), OFFICERS and GIRLS
I'd Like to Hide It, BETSY and GIRLS
Where the Hudson River Flows, MRS. MURRAY, GEN. TRYON, GEN. HOWE, and OFFICERS
Bye and Bye, BETSY and SIR JOHN
Old Enough to Love, GEN. TRYON and GIRLS
Sweet Peter, JANE, HENRY, OFFICERS and GIRLS
Here's a Kiss, BETSY and SIR JOHN

ACT III—THE MURRAY MANSION AFTER THE WAR
Opening, ENSEMBLE
Reprise, *Here in My Arms,* BETSY
Finale, COMPANY

NOTE: *Ale, Ale, Ale, The Pipes of Pansy* and *Dear Me* cut before New York opening.

Reviews

New York Times

". . . by reason of the full-toned quality of the music and the richly colored design of the plot, it is operetta, with more than a chance flavor of Gilbert and Sullivan . . . If the settings please the eye, the music pleases the ear no less. The martial swing of *Cheerio,* the dainty *Here In My Arms,* the humorous *Old Enough to Love,* the *Gavotte,* and several others are compositions of genuine musical quality. Here we have duets, trios and chorals that blend with the entire production. They are as uncommon as most of them are beautiful . . ."

Percy Hammond—*New York Herald Tribune*

". . . a baby-grand opera . . . polite, sentimental and prettily embroidered . . . Smart and delicate libretto . . . The music was modest and perhaps a bit too tranquil to beat time to for today's audience. The verse rippled and was humorously polysyllabic . . . a deluxe kindergarten, planned for those who like sweet amusements."

Alexander Woollcott—*New York World*

". . . a befrilled and be-furbelowed romance . . . though its score is fresh and pleasing, it remains a feast for the eyes rather than the ears, a gay, gentle, gracious spectacle of little, young New York . . ."

Alan Dale—*New York American*

". . . singularly tuneful, artistic and agreeable . . . I'd award the lion's share of the glory to Mr. Rodgers. His music was charming, full of melody, pep and imagination . . . a delectable score, minus molasses and devoid of that insipid saccharinity so in vogue today . . ."

Burns Mantle—*New York Daily News*

". . . mannerly, melodious, sane and charming . . . Lorenz Hart and Richard Rodgers are responsible for most of *Dearest Enemy.* I thank them for it . . ."

E. W. Osborn—*New York Evening World*

". . . a book which is wise and truly witty and genuinely romantic; verses that take ripplingly to every lyrical mood and turn; melodies that laugh and sing and dance and love without bringing up on the listening ear even a touch of that heard-that-before feeling . . ."

Frank Vreeland—*New York Telegram*
". . . not even a furtive breath of jazz in Rodgers' score . . . He continues to improve markedly with every score, and he has such a fecund store of catchy tunes and has obviously mastered so well the peculiar technique of arranging them for popular consumption that he will go far as a composer . . . he seems ideally teamed with Lorenz Hart and Herbert Fields . . . We have a glimmering notion that someday they will form the American counterpart of the once-great triumvirate of Bolton, Wodehouse and Kern . . ."

Gilbert W. Gabriel—*New York Sun*
". . . simple hearted nimble minded delights . . . Its songs are the better part of *Dearest Enemy* . . . a here and there ingratiating melody . . . As for the lyrics, they are no less than excellent. Any gentleman capable of rhyming 'radiant' with 'lady aunt' deserves the whole hoorahs . . ."

Ed Barry—*Variety,* September 23, 1925
". . . a mildly interesting piece which will provide entertainment for many despite the inability to qualify in the success division . . . sparkles but lacks that seemingly elusive wallop which puts a show over . . . lyrics that are gems, and a commendable score in which *Bye and Bye* and *Here's a Kiss* look like the outstanders . . . a good buy at $3.30."

Wells Root—*Time,* October 5, 1925
". . . the costumes, the music and Helen Ford are decidedly first rate although humor and interest drag a bit through the middle and final sections."

Herman J. Mankiewicz—*The New Yorker,* October 17, 1925
". . . the book, in short, is dull. The lyrics and the music are fascinating, however, and there is tasteful and inventive direction . . ."

George Jean Nathan—*Judge,* October 17, 1925
". . . some pleasing melodies and some attractive stage pictures, but the comedy has been completely overlooked. As a result, what might have been a tasty exhibit turns out to be an only moderately entertaining one . . ."

Arthur Hornblow—*Theatre Magazine,* December, 1925
"Something very akin to a genuine comic opera . . . a very graceful

libretto—pruning will help—and Hart's lyrics are not only singable but pregnant with genuine wit. The score is really delightful, combining as it does refinement and genuinely sustained melody throughout . . ."

Robert Benchley—*Life,* January 7, 1926
". . . another musical show that comes under the heading of 'nice.' Whatever it lacks in humor is more than made up for by the beauty of its costumes and settings, the charm of Helen Ford, and the music and lyrics by that God-given team of Rodgers and Hart . . ."

Tour

Shubert Theatre, Newark, May 24, 1926—Hartman Theatre, Columbus, November 27, 1926 (12 cities).

Selected Revival

Goodspeed Opera House, East Haddam, Conn., May 4-June 20, 1976
Jeanne Lehman (BETSY); Kenneth Cory (JOHN); Nancy Andrews (MRS. MURRAY); Louis Edmonds (HOWE).

Television Production

NBC Network, November 26, 1955
Produced and directed by Max Liebman; adaptation by William Friedberg and Neil Simon; book directed by Milton Lyon; choreography by James Starbuck; music director, Charles Sanford; choral director, Clay Warnick; sponsored by Oldsmobile. *Cast:* Anne Jeffreys (BETSY); Robert Sterling (JOHN); Cornelia Otis Skinner (MRS. MURRAY); Cyril Ritchard (HOWE); Donald Burr (CORNWALLIS); Donn Driver (COURIER); Wynne Miller (CLARA).

THE FIFTH AVENUE FOLLIES

(Night Club—1926)

A revue with sketches by Harold Atteridge and Ballard MacDonald; music by Richard Rodgers; lyrics by Lorenz Hart.

Presented by Billy Rose
Production conceived and directed by Seymour Felix
Settings and costumes by Booth, Willoughby and Jones
Lighting by L. A. Nestler
Music director, Reginald Childs
conducting Harry Archer's Orchestra

New York Run
Fifth Avenue Club, January, 1926

The Cast
Cecil Cunningham
Doris Canfield
Edith Babson
Johnne Clare
Elizabeth Brown
Mignon Laird
Oscar Herman
Dorothy Deeder
Maryland Jarboe
Fifth Avenue Girls
Bert Hanlon
Bobbie Clif
Richard Bennett
Albert Burke
Dan McCarthy
Mable Olsen
Harry Weil
Helen Sheperd
Ednor Frilling
Third Avenue Girls

Musical Numbers and Sketches

ACT I
Do You Notice Anything?, Cecil Cunningham, Doris Canfield, Bert Hanlon, and the Fifth Avenue Girls
In the Name of Art, Cecil Cunningham, Doris Canfield, Bert Hanlon
Fatigue (sketch by Harold Atteridge)
COMMERE, Bobbie Clif
THE HUSBAND, Bert Hanlon
THE OTHER WOMAN, Doris Canfield
THE WIFE, Cecil Cunningham
Reprise, *Do You Notice Anything?,* Fifth Avenue Girls
The Morning After (sketch)
THE LADY, Edith Babson
THE GENTLEMAN, Richard Bennett

Maybe It's Me, Johnne Clare, Albert Burke and Fifth Avenue Girls; danced by Elizabeth Brown and Dan McCarthy
An Olive (by Bert Hanlon), Bert Hanlon
Mammy's Knee (by Jack Donahue), Bert Hanlon
Harp dance, Mignon Laird
Reprise, *Do You Notice Anything?,* Fifth Avenue Girls
Literally Speaking (sketch by Harold Atteridge)
COMMÈRE, Mable Olsen
THE FATHER, Oscar Herman
THE UNCLE, Bert Hanlon
THE WOMAN, Cecil Cunningham
THE SON, Albert Burke
THE BOOTLEGGER, Harry Weil
A City Flat, Bert Hanlon and Cecil Cunningham
Reprise, *Do You Notice Anything?,* Fifth Avenue Girls
Mike, Cecil Cunningham
So Does Your Old Mandarin (by Adler, Weil and Herman), Adler, Weil and Herman
High Hats, Adler, Weil and Herman
Finale, Company

ACT II
Lillie, Lawrence and Jack, Cecil Cunningham, Doris Canfield, Bert Hanlon
Where's That Little Girl?, Albert Burke, Adler, Weil and Herman, Bert Hanlon, Johnne Clare, Elizabeth Brown, Doris Canfield, and Fifth Avenue Girls
Gloves (sketch by Ballard MacDonald)
THE HUSBAND, Bert Hanlon
THE FRIEND, Harry Weil
THE CRIMINOLOGIST, Albert Burke
THE WIFE, Cecil Cunningham
Reprise, *Do You Notice Anything?,* Elizabeth Brown, Edith Babson, Johnne Clare, Fifth Avenue Girls
Susie, Doris Canfield
FLO, Cecil Cunningham
BELLE, Mable Olsen
LULU, Bobbie Clif
GERTIE, Dorothy Deeder
BILLIE, Helen Sheperd
MAY, Maryland Jarboe
FRITZIE, Ednor Frilling
Fifth Avenue Girls
Third Avenue Girls
Finale, reprise, *Do You Notice Anything?,* Fifth Avenue Girls

NOTE: *Maybe It's Me* has same music as *I'm Crazy 'Bout the Charleston (Cochran's Revue of 1926).*

Reviews

Walter Winchell—*New York Graphic*
". . . possesses all of the necessary essentials for a successful song-and-dance affair, with laugh-provoking skits . . ."

Abel Green—*Variety,* February 3, 1926
"Quite an ambitious entertainment, but a question whether just the thing for a supper club . . . in these pro-prohibition benighted states one wonders whether the clever Lorenz Hart lyrics aren't wasted on the $5 couvert charges . . . The show is a bear for ideas and cleverness . . . *Maybe It's Me* is one of the best numbers in it . . ."

M. H. Shapiro—*Billboard,* February 6, 1926
". . . every bit of it sparkling with brilliant talent, comedy, singing and dancing . . . Each number was not only an effort to be different but a distinct hit . . ."

Lois Long (Lipstick)—*The New Yorker,* February 6, 1926
". . . it lasts—actually—well over an hour, but it did not bore me. Its charm probably lies in the fact that all the performers appear to be having a swell time and that the show moves along at such a rapid pace, shunning all attempts at sentimental ballads . . ."

THE GIRL FRIEND

(1926)

A musical comedy with book by Herbert Fields; music by Richard Rodgers; lyrics by Lorenz Hart.

Presented by Lew Fields
Directed by John Harwood
Choreography by Jack Haskell
Settings by P. Dodd Ackerman
Costumes by Booth, Willoughby and Jones
Music director, Ernest Cutting
Orchestrations by Maurice de Packh

Tryout
Apollo Theatre, Atlantic City, March 8-13, 1926

New York Run
Vanderbilt Theatre, March 17-December 4, 1926
301 performances

The Story
Leonard Silver, a young Long Island dairyman, hopes to become a great six-day bicycle rider. His girl friend, Mollie Farrell, is his trainer, his manager, and his promoter. Arthur Spencer, a professional manager, and his designing sister, Wynn, try to get the dairyman to ride for them. But honesty and true love win out.

The Cast
FANNY SILVER, Eva Condon
ELLEN, Dorothy Barber
LEONARD SILVER, Sammy White
MOLLIE FARRELL, Eva Puck
THOMAS LARSON, John Hundley
ARTHUR SPENCER, Frank Doane
WYNN SPENCER, Evelyn Cavanaugh
IRENE COVEL, June Cochrane
DONALD LITT, Francis X. Donegan
ANN, Silvia Shawn
MIKE, *a trainer,* Jack Kogan
DUFFY, *another trainer,* Walter Bigelow

JANE TALBOT, Dorothy Barber
MME. RUBY DE LILLY, Jan Moore
A BUTLER, Ainsley Lambert
EDDIE, Leon Rose
FRANK, Joel Duroe

JIM	Leon Rose's Band	Paul Sabin
HENRY		Herman Newman
WALTER		William Marshall
BILL		Sanford Wolf

GIRLS: Gypsy Mooney, Olive Peebe, Eve Marie Gray, Helen Shepard, Dorothy Brown, Evelyn Ruh Urilda, Elizabeth Mears, Alice Kosta, Dorothy Roy, Virginia Otis, Carol Lynne, Gertrude Cole

BOYS: Roy Clements, Eddie Leslie, Austin Clarke, Arthur C. Budd, K. Smith Stanley, A. Goodrich

Musical Numbers

ACT I

SCENE ONE—BACKYARD OF THE SILVER DAIRY, LONG ISLAND

Hey!Hey!, ENSEMBLE
The Simple Life, ENSEMBLE
The Girl Friend, MOLLIE and LEONARD

SCENE TWO—RAILROAD STATION, MAPLE VILLA, LONG ISLAND

Goodbye, Lennie!, ENSEMBLE

SCENE THREE—ENTRANCE HALL OF THE BLUE GRASS, LONG ISLAND

The Blue Room, MOLLIE and LEONARD
Cabarets, ENSEMBLE
Why Do I?, IRENE, DONALD and ENSEMBLE
The Damsel Who Done All the Dirt, MOLLIE
He's a Winner, SPENCER and ENSEMBLE

SCENE FOUR—ON THE ROAD

SCENE FIVE—BEFORE THE SPENCER ESTATE, ARDSLEY-ON-HUDSON, N.Y.

Town Hall Tonight, MOLLIE, IRENE, DONALD, LEONARD and ENSEMBLE
Good Fellow, Mine, WYNN, LARSON and ENSEMBLE
Finale, ENSEMBLE

ACT II

BEFORE THE SPENCER ESTATE, ARDSLEY-ON-HUDSON, N.Y.

Creole Crooning Song, LARSON and ENSEMBLE; danced by ELLEN
I'd Like to Take You Home, IRENE and DONALD
What Is It?, SPENCER and ENSEMBLE; danced by ELLEN
Dance, LEONARD
Finale, COMPANY

NOTE: *Sleepyhead* and *The Pipes of Pansy* cut before New York opening.

Reviews

New York Times

". . . generally captivating . . . Pleasant tunes, a satisfactory number of comical moments, a chorus of genuine merit, and above all, the circumstance that it serves to restore Eva Puck to Manhattan's theatrical attractions, combined to provide a diverting evening . . . a number of very agreeable tunes that contain, probably, what is known as a song hit or two, and adroit and well fashioned lyrics . . ."

Charles Belmont Davis—*New York Herald Tribune*

". . . a novel and appetizing blend of those ingredients necessary to this particular form of entertainment. There are lilting tunes aplenty, good dancing, comedy, plot enough but not too much . . . The words were in the well known manner of the facile and tricky, but, to us, not always humorous lyricist, Lorenz Hart . . . the speed of the piece was superlative and breathless . . ."

Wells Root—*New York World*

". . . Particularly notable, as in their earlier shows, was the lyric facility of Mr. Hart. The best song is *The Blue Room* . . . eminently good enough."

Alan Dale—*New York American*

". . . a show with gumption in it . . . But what I liked best was its music. This WAS music, instead of molasses. There was a ditty called *The Blue Room* which should be sung to exhaustion, whilst *The Girl Friend* has melody, quaint orchestration and decided lilt . . . a nice, cosy evening . . ."

New York Daily News

". . . bright, clean and pleasant . . . boasts tunes that have a hit-like swing, notably the title song. The lyrics are intelligent and above the average in cleverness . . ."

New York Post

". . . the surrounding performance is quite immaterial and superfluous so long as such rhymes are on the stage as 'The end'll soon/Be a Mendelssohn/Wedding March for me.' . . . the music has a made-to-order ring about it. *Why Do I?* is a melody with a fresh rhythmic twist, and *The Blue Room* has soothing saccharine melodiousness, but the rest are disappointing . . . The plot has authority which is lent by age . . ."

Bide Dudley—*New York Evening World*
". . . a so-so light-weight musical comedy. The music and lyrics are pleasing, but the story, when it can be located, is inconsequential . . . With all its faults, however, the show is quite entertaining now and then . . ."

Gilbert W. Gabriel—*New York Sun*
". . . Musically and lyrically it is as dainty and sprightly as anything the season of such entertainment has managed to put together. It has its lacks, but also its lilts to make up for them . . . Between them, Rodgers and Hart have concocted some things to whistle impatiently until the sheet music arrives . . . call it a successful entertainment."

Garrick—*New York Journal*
". . . humor that has the naturalness of youth, music that is crisply refreshing, and lyrics that are so superior that most others seem merely words to songs that might well be disregarded . . ."

Abel Green—*Variety,* March 24, 1926
". . . a winner . . . The book is the best libretto Fields has contributed so far and is only parred by the songs with ultra smart lyrics and oddly rhythmed and fetching tunes . . . considerably more is anticipated from Rodgers and Hart, who are touted as an American Gilbert and Sullivan . . . The title number is the hit of the show . . . *What Is It?* was a show-stopper . . ."

Gilbert W. Gabriel—*The New Yorker*
". . . a pleasant and particularly tuneful affair wherewith to pass the time . . . Two or three ingratiating little songs, as good in lyrics as they are in lilt, are the chief assets . . ."

Wells Root—*Time,* March 29, 1926
". . . not guaranteed unconditionally, but it offers a consistently agreeable display. It has good music and unquestionably the best lyrics in town. It has a sound enough set of jokes and more than the usual allotment of brisk dancing . . ."

Robert Benchley—*Life,* April 8, 1926
". . . those of us calamity howlers who have been worrying about the low state of musical comedy ought to take up quite a lot of space in hailing young Mr. Hart . . . a very satisfactory show . . ."

Arthur Hornblow—*Theatre Magazine,* June, 1926
". . . tuneful and breezy . . . decidedly entertaining although the book lacks humor . . . *The Blue Room* and *Town Hall Tonight* are easily the hits of this ideal hot weather entertainment . . ."

Tour

Lyceum Theatre, Paterson, October 11, 1926—Adelphi Theatre, Philadelphia, February 26, 1927 (8 cities).

THE GARRICK GAIETIES

(1926)

A musical revue with sketches by Benjamin M. Kaye, Newman Levy, Marion Page Johnson, Herbert Fields, Chester D. Heywood, Edward Hope and Philip Lord; music by Richard Rodgers; lyrics by Lorenz Hart.

Presented by the Theatre Guild
Directed by Philip Loeb
Choreography by Herbert Fields
Settings and costumes by Carolyn Hancock
Stage manager, Lee Strasberg
Music director, Roy Webb
Opening-night conductor, Mr. Rodgers

New York Run
Garrick Theatre, May 10-October 9, 1926
174 performances

The Cast

THE THEATRE GUILD STUDIO

Philip Loeb
Blanche Fleming
Romney Brent
Edith Meiser
Hardwick Nevin
John McGovern
George Frierson
Ruth Morris
William Johnstone
Tommy Law
Sylvia Shear
Ann Moss
Jean Crittendon
Mary Jordan
Philip Jones
John Richards
Betty Starbuck
Jack Edwards
William M. Griffith
Sterling Holloway
Edward Hogan
Bobbie Perkins
Hildegarde Halliday
Eleanor Shaler
Helen Ramsey
Dorothy Jordan
Gladys Rodgers
Gladys Laird
Dorothea Chard
Marta Keys
Felix Jacoves
Alex Tiers

Musical Numbers and Sketches

ACT I

Six Little Plays

UNDERTAKER, Philip Loeb
ARMS AND THE MAN, Betty Starbuck
THE GLASS SLIPPER, Blanche Fleming
MERCHANTS OF GLORY, Jack Edwards
ANDROCLES AND THE LION, Romney Brent
GOAT SONG, William M. Griffith
THE CHIEF THING, Edith Meiser
THE GARRICK GAIETIES, Sterling Holloway and Company

DeBock Song (sketch by Benjamin M. Kaye)

STUDENT, Romney Brent
GIRL, Blanche Fleming
FIRST MAN, Jack Edwards
SECOND MAN, Hardwick Nevin
THIRD MAN, Edward Hogan
HIGH PRIEST, Philip Loeb
SPEAKER, John McGovern
FATHER, William M. Griffith

Mountain Greenery, Bobbie Perkins and Sterling Holloway

Burglary à la Mode (sketch by Newman Levy)

MISS ANNABELLE VAN BLENKINSOP, Edith Meiser
JEVONS, *the butler,* Romney Brent
SCHUYLER WIFFLE, Philip Loeb
MR. VAN BLENKINSOP, John McGovern

L'Après Midi d'un Papillon, danced by Eleanor Shaler

Keys to Heaven, Bobbie Perkins, George Frierson, Blanche Fleming, and Company

Home Sweet Home (sketch by Marion Page Johnson)

PA HOSKINS, William M. Griffith
MA HOSKINS, Hildegarde Halliday
HECTOR HOSKINS, William Johnstone
CLYTEMNESTRA HOSKINS, Ruth Morris

Sleepyhead, Sterling Holloway

Rose of Arizona (book by Herbert Fields)

ROSABELLE, Eleanor Shaler
GLORIA VAN DYKE, Blanche Fleming
GUSTAVE VAN DYKE, Philip Loeb
ALLAN STERLING, Jack Edwards
CASABA CARAMBA, Romney Brent
PIMENTO, Edith Meiser
MRS. VAN DYKE, Ruth Morris
MCFADDEN, John McGovern
ANNOUNCER, William M. Griffith

FLOWERS:
BLUE BELL, Helen Ramsey
LILY, Hildegarde Halliday
TULIP, Tommy Law
ORCHID, Dorothy Jordan
POPPY, Sylvia Shear
VIOLET, Gladys Rodgers
CHRYSANTHEMUM, Ann Moss
ROSE, Gladys Laird

ENSEMBLE: Jean Crittendon, Dorothea Chard, Ann Moss, Hildegarde Halliday, Dorothy Jordan, Mary Jordan, Marta Keys, Gladys Laird, Helen Ramsey, Gladys Rodgers, Sylvia Shear, Tommy Law

SOLDIERS: George Frierson, Philip Jones, Felix Jacoves, William Johnstone, John Richards, Alex Tiers

SCENE: THE TERRACE OF THE ROSA RAISA HOTEL ON THE BORDERLINE OF MEXICO AND ARIZONA.

ACT II

Viennese (music by Ladislas Kun)
SPECIALTY DANCERS, Betty Starbuck and George Frierson
FLOWER GIRL, Blanche Fleming
BARON, William M. Griffith
PROPRIETOR, Edward Hogan
WALTZERS, GYPSY GIRLS, MEN

Tennis Champs
HELEN WILLS, Romney Brent
BILL TILDEN, Edith Meiser
SUZANNE LENGLEN, Philip Loeb

Green Chartreuse (sketch by Chester D. Heywood)
SIR GEORGE PANCKENHAM, Hardwick Nevin
BROOKE, *his manservant,* John McGovern
THE MAN, Philip Loeb

Reprise, *Mountain Greenery,* Dorothy Jordan, Betty Starbuck, Gladys Laird, Bobbie Perkins

Addled, or the Psychopathetic Ward (sketch by Edward Hope)
DOCTOR, John McGovern
INTERNE, Hardwick Nevin
NURSE, Ruth Morris
PATIENT, Romney Brent

What's the Use of Talking?, Betty Starbuck and Sterling Holloway

Idles of the King
KING ARTHUR, Romney Brent
SIR LANCELOT, Edward Hogan
SIR GALAHAD, Philip Loeb

Gigolo, Betty Starbuck and Company

Queen Elizabeth, Edith Meiser
Finale
JUDGE, Romney Brent
JURY:
JOHANN STRAUSS, Edward Hogan
SIR ARTHUR SULLIVAN, Hardwick Nevin
W. S. GILBERT, Jack Edwards
IRVING BERLIN, Philip Loeb
THE GARRICK GAIETIES, Sterling Holloway and Company

NOTE: *Little Souvenir* cut before opening. *Sleepyhead* dropped shortly after opening, with following musical numbers and sketches added:

"Allez-Up," Betty Starbuck, Bobby Perkins, Sterling Holloway
Washington and the Spy (sketch by Newman Levy)
GEN. GEORGE WASHINGTON, John McGovern
GEN. GRANT, Philip Loeb
MARY, QUEEN OF SCOTS, Edith Meiser
NAPOLEON, Romney Brent
GUARD, James Norris
ANNOUNCER, William M. Griffith
Crossing the Avenue (sketch by Sally Humason)
USHER, Knox Herold
MADGE, Edith Meiser
TOM, John McGovern
ETHEL, Hildegarde Halliday
STEWARD, William M. Griffith
SANDWICHMAN, John Richards
MESSENGER BOY, Jack Edwards
BRIDE, Harriet Woodruff
BRIDEGROOM, Edward Hogan
GIRL, Blance Fleming
BOY, William Johnstone
POLICEMAN, Felix Jacoves

Reviews

J. Brooks Atkinson—*New York Times*
". . . Although it opens with several uncommonly clever travesties and topical thrusts, it slumps badly in the second half . . . Nevertheless, it is the most intelligent revue in town, sparing none of the gravest art theatres in its satire, buoyant for the most part, and well staged . . . This year Rodgers and Hart's score seems inferior in quality . . ."

Percy Hammond—*New York Herald Tribune*
". . . quite a sturdy weanling now, and it excels in wit, humor and song any of Broadway's current and similar dissipations. Last year it

seemed to be saying 'Ain't I cute, I'm only six'; which it was. But this time it is a wise and flippant ingenue, well versed in the ways of the world, though a bit awkward in pursuing them . . . a good semi-pro exhibition . . ."

Alexander Woollcott—*New York World*
". . . after most of the rather laborious high jinks which were breathlessly indugled in, I see no reason for postponing so long this lamentation about the dear old *Garrick Gaieties* not being what they used to be, but perhaps it should be explained that these are merely the sentiments of one who has always suspected they never were . . . one really delightful episode was a burlesque called *Rose of Arizona* . . ."

Alan Dale—*New York American*
". . . most attractive and singularly free from the curse of the average revue . . . filled with good features, all varied and pungent . . . The music was far above the average and several of the melodies were charming . . ."

Burns Mantle—*New York Daily News*
". . . a lively combination of intelligent humor and pleasing songs . . . The score is pretty sure to be one of the most popular of the summer . . ."

Robert Coleman—*New York Daily Mirror*
"*Gay In Name Only* . . . The lines are 'blue.' Very 'blue.' And seldom clever . . . The lyrics and the score are pleasing to jaded ears . . ."

Walter Winchell—*New York Graphic*
". . . below the standard of the first . . . But it is pretty good entertainment . . . The chief fault is that it lacks zip . . . Hart and Rodgers served a brand of material less illuminating than they offered last season . . ."

John Anderson—*New York Post*
"Something that was a little brash, a little gay, unstudiedly amusing and intimate has become a trifle labored and unsteady . . . Talented, literate and vivacious, it seems to suffer mainly from the fear that last year's spontaneous success was staring reproachfully over its shoulder . . . Hart twirled the convolutions of his rhymes too often past the point of pleasant freshness . . . amiable music . . . not as good as last year but good enough. Take it and be thankful."

E. W. Osborn—*New York Evening World*
". . . The *Gaieties* of 1926 are as good as those of 1925—and then

some! . . . a fetching musical score. Once again there came swinging to the ear the characteristically quaint lyrics of Lorenz Hart . . ."

Frank Vreeland—*New York Telegram*
". . . The verve and dash of the first chukker of the affair was buoyed up by Rodgers' delightfully prattling score. In fact, his tunes held up unflaggingly, with great gusto and enchantment, even when the rest of the show began to run down and buzz somewhat painfully toward the end. Rodgers more than fulfilled the promise of yesteryear, radiating melodies that would be hard to beat . . . In the freshness and spontaniety of his work he is the most auspicious young composer for musical comedy now in our midst, and should develop into the Irving Berlin of the future . . ."

Gilbert W. Gabriel—*New York Sun*
". . . not as witty a time as last year's . . . But it is far and away the best of the tribe of young revues in town. What it lacks—and groans in lacking—is in the matter of sketches. The rest of its ingredients are guaranteed delightful. And this rest is furnished by Rodgers and Hart . . . a welcome intimate revue, a bit blotto at times, but maintaining all in all a rather nice sense of what is and isn't intelligent fun . . ."

Robert F. Sisk—*Variety,* May 13, 1926
". . . with no reflection on their proven ability, Rodgers and Hart have turned out quite a few mediocre numbers . . . *Mountain Greenery* is fair but not possessed of much commercial possibilities . . . the show has merit even though it doesn't touch its predecessor . . ."

Gilbert W. Gabriel—*The New Yorker,* May 22, 1926
". . . go to it with guarantees of an intelligently funny, tunefully and brightfully informal evening . . . The songs, written in that excellent flipperty style which is the outcome of the Rodgers and Hart combination are tossed about and danced against with great glee . . ."

Wells Root—*Time,* May 24, 1926
". . . activities were as ingratiating as ever, but perhaps not so brilliantly supplied with material as last year . . . There was perhaps a feeling that the players were too flagrantly depending on their unquestionably charming precocity . . . A compact and generally amusing assembly of impudence. Small favors should perhaps be gratefully received."

Robert Benchley—*Life*, June 3, 1926
". . . the last word in intimate and esoteric kidding . . . original music and high-grade lyrics . . . original comedy sketches which get laughs without recourse to the offal container . . ."

George Jean Nathan—*Judge*, June 5, 1926
"The audience at the opening applauded everything but the hat-holders under the seats . . . The reason for all this jubilation was not quite clear to me, not related to any of the boys and girls . . . The first part is pretty deadly, even for an amateur affair. The second part is fairly good . . . The best melody is that called *Mountain Greenery*."

Edmund Wilson—*The New Republic*, July 28, 1926
"It seems a tragedy that informal revues, after winning their first successes through spontaniety, afterwards tend to become labored. I thought *The Garrick Gaieties* this year seemed rather self-conscious and effortful . . ."

John Mason Brown—*Theatre Arts Monthly*, August, 1926
". . . a fairly entertaining revue that rises to one completely irresistible number called *Rose of Arizona* . . . In its music, as well as its lyrics, it tends on the whole, to fall below its standard of last year. Once again the actual skits have little originality and less wit, and fall back on the regular clichés of their ilk, without any new twists, to enliven them . . ."

Tour

Weiting Theatre, Syracuse, November 1, 1926—Garrick Theatre, Detroit, November 20, 1926 (3 cities). NOTE: Material was taken from both 1925

LIDO LADY

(London—1926)

A musical comedy with book by Ronald Jeans, based on the book by Guy Bolton, Bert Kalmar and Harry Ruby; music by Richard Rodgers; lyrics by Lorenz Hart.

Presented by Jack Hulbert and Paul Murray
Directed by Mr. Hulbert
Costumes mostly by Guy de Gerald and Hoban et Jeanne
Music director, Sydney Baynes

Tryout
Alhambra Theatre, Bradford, October 4-9, 1926
King's Theatre, Southsea, October 11-16, 1926
Royal Theatre, Leeds, October 18-23, 1926
Royal Theatre, Newcastle, October 25-30, 1926
Empire Theatre, Liverpool, November 1-13, 1926
Palace Theatre, Manchester, November 15-27, 1926

London Run
Gaiety Theatre, December 1, 1926-July 23, 1927
259 performances

The Story
Fay Blake, known as the "Lido Lady," is a famous and beautiful tennis champion. Her father, Rufus Blake, is determined that she marry a man who is as brilliant a sportsman as she is. Harry Bassett, one of Fay's suitors, tries tennis, boxing and golf, but fails in all. However, his perseverance finally wins her love and her father's approval.

The Cast
MARJORIE WILSON, Phyl Arnold
MOLLIE DOONE, Muriel Montrose
"PEACHES" STONE, Johnne Clare
BENSON, *Mr. Blake's butler,* Laurence Green
SPENCER WELDON, *Mr. Blake's General Manager,* Harold French
RUFUS BLAKE, *a wealthy sporting goods manufacturer,* Bobby Comber
LUIS VALEZE, Henry de Bray

BILL HARKER, *an American friend of Harry Bassett,* Billy Arlington
RITA, April Harmon
HARRY BASSETT, Jack Hulbert
FAY BLAKE, *Mr. Blake's daughter,* Phyllis Dare
PEGGY BASSETT, *a motion picture actress and cousin of Harry Bassett,* Cicely Courtneidge
MASTER-AT-ARMS, Eddie Garr
DANCERS: Dave Fitzgibbon, Harry White, Frank Tiernan, Joe Gerald, Billy Shaw
VISITORS TO THE LIDO: Marjorie Gascoigne, Myra Bernard, Jessie Fredericksen, Nancy Rigg, Mona D'Elta, Cynthia Carlton, Jeannette Andrews, Lillian Du Roy, Lilian Logan, Vera Budge, Mary de Pury, Marjory Davidson, Erin Burke, Pamela Baxter, Rosamund Gardner, Ella Lowes, Rubie Stewart, Dorice Mason, Marjorie Bell, Molly Neame, Thelma Morland, Vera Smart; Dennis Ray, Donald Aked, Paul French, Charles Ellis, Percy Gage, George Guinness, Arthur Ives

Musical Numbers

ACT I
MR. BLAKE'S VILLA ON THE LIDO
A Cup of Tea, COMPANY
You're on the Lido Now, "PEACHES" and COMPANY
Lido Lady, FAY and COMPANY
A Tiny Flat Near Soho Square, PEGGY and SPENCER
But Not Today (Vincent Scotto-Jean Boyer-Con Conrad), HARRY and COMPANY
Here in My Arms, FAY and HARRY
Finale, COMPANY

ACT II
SCENE ONE—A GALA NIGHT AT THE LIDO SPORTING CLUB ("THE FEAST OF THE QUEEN OF SHEBA")
The Beauty of Another Day, COMPANY
My Heart Is Sheba Bound, PEGGY and HARRY
The Dancer, Dave Fitzgibbon
It All Depends on You (Ray Henderson-Lew Brown-B. G. DeSylva), FAY and COMPANY

SCENE TWO—NEXT DAY AT THE LIDO SPORTING CLUB
The Charleston, danced by FAY, Dave Fitzgibbon, Harry White
Try Again Tomorrow, PEGGY and HARRY
Finale, COMPANY

ACT III

SCENE ONE—PROMENADE DECK OF THE SS FUTURIA

What's the Use, SPENCER, MARJORIE and COMPANY

Cheri-Beri, "PEACHES" and BILL

SCENE TWO—ANOTHER PART OF THE DECK

Atlantic Blues, FAY and GIRLS

SCENE THREE—LOUNGE OF THE SHIP DURING THE SHIP'S CONCERT

I Must Be Going, PEGGY, and DANCERS

Letter dance by HARRY

Finale, COMPANY

NOTE: *I Want a Man, Morning Is Midnight* and *Chuck It!* cut before London opening. *A Tiny Flat Near Soho Square* has same music as *A Little House in Soho (She's My Baby); Atlantic Blues* same as *Blue Ocean Blues (Present Arms).*

Reviews

London Times

". . . essentially British . . . The story is involved but logical and always interesting, and the music is always tuneful . . . it is a pleasure to welcome back humour to our native musical comedy."

London Daily Telegraph

". . . plenty of cheery moments for nearly all of which Mr. Jack Hulbert and Miss Cicely Courtneidge were singly or jointly responsible . . . The music struck one for the most part as rather more commonplace even for the average of its kind . . ."

London Daily Mail

". . . a book which has little distinction; the music for the most part is a compromise between the jazzing and the old-time flowing melody; the lyrics have their own particular lilt . . . the acting of Miss Dare and Miss Courtneidge will be recalled when all else in *Lido Lady* is forgotten

London Morning Post

". . . pride of place goes to Miss Dare . . . a pretty ordinary affair . . . not more than a couple of good tunes . . ."

Hannen Swaffer—*London Express*

". . . much of it was very charming; much of it was very funny . . . Miss Courtneidge is indeed now England's cleverest comedienne . . . Many will regret that two of the authors and the writers of the songs came from America, but you must be in the fashion, I suppose . . ."

London Daily Sketch
"... started out very shakily; neither dresses, scenery, music or humour seemed very bright, but the moment Miss Courtneidge arrived she not only cheered up the audience but also her colleagues ..."

London Evening News
"... most credit must be given to Miss Courtneidge ... There are several good tunes, notably *Here in My Arms* and *Try Again Tomorrow,* which are hammered into the ears of the audience ..."

Philip Page—*London Evening Standard*
"... infinitely the brightest musical entertainment in London ... jolly and cheerful and going to amuse London for a long time."

James Agate—*London Sunday Times,* December 12, 1926
"Happy is the country which has no history, and happier still is that musical comedy about which one can find nothing to say. Thrice blest is he who hath his quarrel just, and three times is that musical piece insured against disaster which has no plot to speak of, no lyrics that count, and no music unduly to strain the musical sense ..."

Herbert Farjeon—*London Sunday Pictorial,* December 12, 1926
"... another example of silliness raised to the high point of efficiency. I think I'd rather have a tooth out myself. But it takes all sorts to make an audience ..."

The Era
"... a brilliant production, full of witty lines and good comedy business ... delightfully jolly music ..."

The Queen, December 15, 1926
"... a thoroughly good show ... The music is pleasantly familiar, but the lyric writer should not have let the composer down by writing of things being 'adorabool' and 'kissabool' and 'deplorabool' ..."

David C. Fairweather—*Theatre World,* January, 1927
"... The music is well above the average and far more skillfully orchestrated than is usual in this type of piece. *Here in My Arms,* which is even broadcast in the foyer during the intervals, appealed least of all ... *Lido Lady* is certainly a winner that deserves to run for at least a year."

PEGGY-ANN

(1926)

A musical comedy with book by Herbert Fields, suggested by the musical comedy "Tillie's Nightmare" by Edgar Smith and A. Baldwin Sloane; music by Richard Rodgers; lyrics by Lorenz Hart.

Presented by Lew Fields and Lyle D. Andrews
Directed by Robert Milton
Choreography by Seymour Felix
Settings by Clark Robinson
Costumes by Mark Mooring
Music director, Roy Webb
Orchestrations by Mr. Webb

Tryout
(known as "Peggy")
Walnut Street Theatre, Philadelphia, December 13-25, 1926

New York Run
Vanderbilt Theatre, December 27, 1926-October 29, 1927
333 performances

The Story
Peggy-Ann lives in her aunt's drab boardinghouse in Glens Falls. After quarrelling with her fiancé, Guy, she falls asleep and dreams of various adventures which take her to New York's Fifth Avenue, a large department store, a yachting trip, and the races in Havana. When she awakens, Guy returns, all is forgiven, and they plan to marry.

The Cast
MRS. FROST, Lulu McConnell
MR. FROST, Grant Simpson
DOLORES BARNES, Edith Meiser
ALICE FROST, Betty Starbuck
GUY PENDLETON, Lester Cole
SALLY DAY, Dorothy Roy
PEGGY-ANN BARNES, Helen Ford
ARNOLD SMALL, Fuller Mellish, Jr.

PATRICIA SEYMOUR, Margaret Breen
FREDDIE SHAWN, Jack Thompson
A POLICEMAN, Patrick Rafferty
MISS FLINT, Marion Traube
A SAILOR, Howard Eames
MR. FISH, Harold Mellish
STEWARD, G. Douglas Evans
GIRLS: Evelyn Ruh, Leda Knapp, Louise Joyce, Valma Valentine, Enes Early, Margaret Miller, Sherry Gale, Grace Connelly, Beth Meredith
BOYS: Barney Jackson, Gordon Phillips, Harold Land, Wally Coyle, Jack Morton

NOTE: In February 1927, Mr. Simpson temporarily replaced by Jack Oakie; in September, Mr. Thompson succeeded by Georgie Hale. During tour, Miss Ford succeeded by Betty Starbuck.

Musical Numbers

ACT I

PROLOGUE—MRS. BARNES' BOARDINGHOUSE, GLENS FALLS, N.Y.
Hello, PATRICIA, FRED and ENSEMBLE
A Tree in the Park, PEGGY-ANN and GUY
Howdy Broadway, ENSEMBLE

SCENE ONE—PEGGY-ANN DREAMS SHE SEES FIFTH AVENUE
A Little Birdie Told Me So, PEGGY-ANN

SCENE TWO—PEGGY-ANN DREAMS OF GUY PENDLETON'S DEPARTMENT STORE
Charming, Charming, ENSEMBLE
Where's That Rainbow?, PEGGY-ANN and BOYS
Finale, COMPANY

ACT II

SCENE ONE—PEGGY-ANN DREAMS SHE OWNS A YACHT
We Pirates from Weehawken, ENSEMBLE
In His Arms, PEGGY-ANN
Chuck It!, FREDDIE and GIRLS
I'm So Humble, PEGGY-ANN and GUY

SCENE TWO—THE OPEN SEA

SCENE THREE—PEGGY-ANN DREAMS SHE VISITS A RACETRACK IN HAVANA
Havana, PATRICIA,FREDDIE and ENSEMBLE
Maybe It's Me, PEGGY-ANN and GUY
Give This Little Girl a Hand, MRS. FROST and ENSEMBLE

SCENE FOUR—MRS. BARNES' BOARDINGHOUSE
Finale, COMPANY

NOTE: *Come and Tell Me, Tramping Along, Paris Is Really Divine* and *The Pipes of Pansy* cut before New York opening. *I'm So Humble* dropped shortly after opening in favor of a reprise of *Chuck It! In His Arms* dropped in July.

Reviews

New York Times

". . . From the beginning, Fields, Rodgers and Hart have brought freshness and ideas to the musical-comedy field, and in the new piece they travel a little further along their road. . . . Most of it is literate and entertaining, and the piece raises high hopes for the three authors . . . Fields' libretto contains frequent flights of imagination, and Hart's lyrics quickly get one into the habit of listening hopefully to each song . . . Rodgers' score contains at least one number, *Where's That Rainbow?*, that lingers after the curtain fell. . . ."

George Goldsmith—*New York Herald Tribune*

". . . None was found, save only the incorrigible mortician whose reservations you are now scanning, to hang even a shred of crepe upon an occasion so joyful . . . The score was utterly without flavor, originality or distinction of any kind . . . in its ingratiating refusal to take itself seriously for a moment, the piece seemed to be rather a shouting sort of thing . . . it moved with rhythm and quick, titillating pace. . . . The lyrics were in Hart's very best manner. . . ."

Peter Vischer—*New York World*

". . . sprightly and imaginative, far from the familiar mould . . . generally quite delightful, at times even hilarious. . . . Its music is quite up to the high standards set by Rodgers in his previous scores. Its lines and rhymes are bright. . . ."

Alan Dale—*New York American*

". . . the daintiest, most whimsical, unusualest and captivatingly concise and imaginative little musical play we've had for some time . . . fruity, frisky, frolicsome, festive, funny, fantastic and fascinating . . . I laughed until tears ran down my honest, reviewsome cheeks . . . The cast hadn't a fleck . . . Some of the music was admirable. It was the work of Richard Rodgers who evidently had an inspiration and not pot-boiling proclivities. . . ."

Burns Mantle—*New York Daily News*

". . . a novel little musical piece . . . never sane and never dull . . . the second act sags briefly . . . Rodgers has a hit of proportions in *A Tree in the Park* . . . Hart's lyrics are good."

Robert Coleman—*New York Daily Mirror*

". . . I hereby go on record as placing this triumvirate in the foremost ranks of our youthful and talented show builders. They bring originality, humor, cleverness and an unbounded enthusiasm for their work . . . witty verses and irresistible tunes . . ."

Walter Winchell—*New York Graphic*
". . . a delightful surprise package . . . Chock full of the good old zip that makes the blood race through your veins, plus a series of contagious tunes and eye-filling maidens . . ."

Bide Dudley—*New York Evening World*
". . . futuristic throughout, and this will make it unique among girl-and-music shows. Primarily, its music is going to be one big reason for the success that undoubtably will come, for Rodgers has written at least two numbers that cannot be forgotten. They are *Where's That Rainbow?* and *A Little Birdie Told Me So* . . ."

New York Telegram
". . . varied from good fun to very bad bathos . . . the lyricist and composer seem to have come to the conclusion that Gilbert and Sullivan knew their business for here and there were Victorian echoes that were unmistakable . . ."

Variety, January 5, 1927
"Another musical hit . . . All of the fantasy business is worked deftly and with an experienced hand . . . deluxe in writing, lyrics, music, scenery, staging, and costumes . . ."

Time, January 10, 1927
"Aided by Gilbertian satire, Broadway slapstick, attractive dancers, the pepper of quick wisecracks, the charm of music, it skipped right up to the head of the class in current musical diversions . . ."

Percy Hammond—*New York Herald Tribune,* January 24, 1927
". . . a chipper entertainment with pretty girls, smart verses, a lovely and animated decor of handsome women, and a story much less maudlin than usual. If I am asked to recommend a musical play that does not appear to be written by twelve-year-olds for twelve-year-olds, I shall wave my hand in the direction of the Vanderbilt . . . The book is really humorous, the music soft and airy, and the verse a crafty lot of rhymes and rhythms. One poem entitled *A Little Birdie Told Me So* is especially bright . . ."

Alexander Woollcott—*New York World,* February 27, 1927
". . . a fine gift for fresh, piquant melody which Rodgers buries in no napkin . . . *Peggy-Ann* is unpretentious, homemade—nutty fudge brought in hot from the kitchen . . . It was all like a chapter out of *Alice in Wonderland.* In singing Carrolls in praise of *Peggy-Ann,* I would fain suggest that here is more of Lewis and less of Earl . . . The tunes are gay and sweet and good, but it is the libretto which arrests attention . . . a really bright piece of nonsense . . ."

Tour

Majestic Theatre, Brooklyn, October 31, 1927—Shubert Theatre, Newark, November 19, 1927 (2 cities).

PEGGY-ANN

(London—1927)

Presented by Lee Ephraim and Jack Buchanan
Directed by Lew Fields
Choreography by Seymour Felix
Settings by Joseph and Phil Harker
Costumes by Doris Zinkeisen and Miss Gordon Conway
Music director, Charles Prentice

Tryout

King's Theatre, Southsea, July 18, 1927

London Run

Daly's Theatre, July 27-November 19, 1927
130 performances

The Cast

MRS. FROST, Maisie Gay
MR. FROST, Frank Hector
DOLORES BARNES, Sylvia Leslie
ALICE FROST, Elsie Randolph
GUY PENDLETON, Oliver McLennon
SALLY DAY, Elvira Henderson
PEGGY-ANN BARNES, Dorothy Dickson
ARNOLD SMALL, Robert Gordon
PATRICIA SEYMOUR, Lalla Collins
FREDDIE SHAWN, Basil Howes
OFFICER JONES, Nat Lewis
MISS FLINT, Marjorie Brooks
SAILOR, Noel Colne
MR. FISH, Stanley Randall
STEWARD, Hindle Edgar

Musical Numbers

Same as original production except that *In His Arms* and *I'm So Humble* were cut, and *Howdy, Broadway* and *We Pirates from Weehawken* changed to *Howdy, London* and *We Are Sea Hawks.* During run, lyric of *A Little Birdie Told Me So* rewritten by Desmond Carter and song then called *Country Mouse.* Locale of story in Act I changed to Hants, England, and London.

Reviews

London Times

". . . interesting because it tells a coherent story . . . No better basis could be imagined for a musical piece, and throughout the author keeps to the logical road that he has set himself . . . The incidents are sometimes incoherent but they fit into the framework and there are at least three very pleasant tunes . . . Dorothy Dickson is better than she has ever been before . . ."

London Daily Telegraph

". . . one was tempted to believe that its happiest moments lay in the uncommon ingenuity of Mr. Fields' production and the inventiveness shown by Mr. Felix in his arrangement of the dances . . . The dancing seemed to us at least as important as the music, though in fairness to the composer, one must admit that his tunes are adequate for their purpose and often effective in their livelier moments, while one quasi-sentimental duet, *A Tree in the Park,* is pretty enough to bear the repetition to which it is subjected . . ."

London Daily Mail

". . . There is music that gets away from the conventional jazz. There are lyrics which have point. There is also some humour. The piece is full of fun and beauty; also it is well sung, well danced and well acted."

Hannen Swaffer—*London Daily Express*

". . . a strange concoction of a few good tunes and some noisy ones— a musical version of *A Kiss for Cinderella* and *Beggar on Horseback,* and now a little bit of *Sleeping Beauty* . . . Unfortunately, one of Miss Dickson's songs, *A Little Birdie Told Me So,* is not suitable for a young-girl character. It should be cut out immediately . . . The best part of the production is the clever dancing . . . Unfortunately, the show is too much of a mixture . . ."

Ibid., July 31, 1927 (follow-up)

"*London's Most Vulgar Musical Show* . . . *Peggy-Ann* killed Daly's reputation for refined amusement . . ."

Edgar Wallace—*London Morning Post*

". . . a most rollicking and spicy entertainment that all the town should go and see . . . I doubt whether there has been anything in London quite so satisfying for a long time . . . Some of the songs would be hits without the punching they receive . . ."

London Daily Mirror

". . . the most novel musical of its kind London playgoers have seen for many a day . . . The play has all the ingredients of success, beautiful settings and colourful dresses, good singing and dancing, and tuneful music . . . Dorothy Dickson gives the best performance of her career . . . goes with a swing from start to finish . . ."

R.S.P.—*London Daily Herald*
". . . Did the songs and dances go well? Was the heroine up to standard? And did the funny people really make us laugh? To all of which the answer is an ear-splitting gallery affirmative . . ."

Philip Page—*London Evening Standard*
". . . half *Cinderella* and half *Beggar on Horseback* . . . Let a play be either English in atmosphere or American. Here Americanisation has been attempted, and the result is a rather irritating hybrid . . . Miss Dickson is the most graceful creature imaginable . . . a farrago of ideas used before, produced with extraordinary splash and efficiency . . ."

A.E.M.—*London Evening News*
". . . rather a shrill affair . . . The music gives the same impression . . . Even the most convinced admirer of the American tradition in musical comedy must have wished for just five minutes of some woman with a voice which is low and modulated and for one tune which could forget trying to be clever and begin trying to be gentle . . . In addition to this steady loudness there is also a definite lack of fine taste . . . *A Little Birdie Told Me So* is more lacking in good taste than any principal song in recent musical comedy . . ."

James Agate—*London Sunday Times*, July 31, 1927
". . . the entertainment was tedious because during all this time humour crept into a mouse-hole and the house languished . . . *Peggy-Ann* was *Cinderella* all over again, and Sir James M. Barrie's *Cinderella* in particular . . . Why should this witless desert be the success of which the gallery became more and more stridently assured? . . . much of the music is commonplace . . . there was a sniggering, distasteful lyric entitled *A Little Birdie Told Me So* . . ."

Bibliography

"Peggy-Ann" —*The Play Pictorial*, February, 1928

BETSY

(1926)

A musical comedy with book by Irving Caesar and David Freedman, revised by William Anthony McGuire; music by Richard Rodgers; lyrics by Lorenz Hart.

Presented by Florenz Ziegfeld
Directed by Mr. McGuire
Choreography by Sammy Lee
First act settings by Frank E. Gates and E. A. Morange
Second act settings (scenes 1 and 2) by Bergman Studios
Second act setting (scene 3) by Joseph Urban
Costumes by Charles LeMaire
Music director, Victor Baravalle

Tryout

National Theatre, Washington, December 20-25, 1926

New York Run

New Amsterdam Theatre, December 28, 1926-January 29, 1927
39 performances

The Story

Betsy Kitzel, living on the lower East Side of New York, is without the prospect of a husband. Mama Kitzel therefore asserts that none of her other children, Louie, Moe, Joe, or Ruth, will get married until Betsy finds a husband. At first it looks like Archie, a bird fancier, but he falls in love with Ruth. However, Betsy's interest in the stage and some clever maneuvering combine to provide a happy ending.

The Cast

STONEWALL MOSKOWITZ, *a social luminary,* Al Shean
MAMA KITZEL, Pauline Hoffman

LOUIE, *a tailor*	*her sons*	Jimmy Hussey
JOE, *a barber*		Ralph Whitehead
MOE, *a chef*		Dan Healy
RUTH	*her daughters*	Belle Baker
BETSY		Bobbie Perkins

ARCHIE, *a pigeon flyer,* Allen Kearns

WINNIE HILL, *rich, but Louie's sweetheart,* Madeleine Cameron
FLORA DALE, *rich, but Joe's sweetheart,* Evelyn Law
MAY MEADOW, *rich, but Moe's sweetheart,* Barbara Newberry
TOM MAGUIRE, *a vaudeville agent,* Ed Hickey
DAN KELLY, Jack White
TEX BROWN, Phil Ryley
MRS. BROWN, Vanita LaNier
Borrah Minevitch's Harmonica Symphony Orchestra
SHOW GIRLS: Jean Yoder, Blanche Satchel, Gertrude Walker, Gertrude MacMahon, Claire Joyce, Molly Green, Gloria Begee, Ina Berline, Ethel Allen, Helene Gardner, Bella Harrison, Mixi, Doris Powell, Virginia Hawkins
DANCERS: Lili Kamari, Aline Drange, Dorothy Patterson, Caryl Bergman, Jean Moore, Clara Blackath, Lillian O'Hara, Katherine Wolf, May Carroll, Dorothy Day, Margaret Shea, Suzanne Conroy, Betty Gayl, Mickey Silden, Olga Royce, Ann Wood, Marjorie Bailey, Beatrice Wilson, Mary Irwin, Dorothy May, Viola Boles, Riffles Covert, Anita Banton, Irene Hamlin, Pauline Bartlett, Nellie Mayer
GENTLEMEN OF THE ENSEMBLE: Harold Ettus, Milton Halpern, Frank Cullen, Lester New, Charles DeBevers, Bernard Hassert, Jay Lagasse, Rosa Burly, George Murray, Edward Mackey, Jack Talbott, Neil Collins

Musical Numbers

ACT I

SCENE ONE—THE ROOF OF AN EAST SIDE SETTLEMENT
Opening:
Characteristic dances, ENSEMBLE
The Kitzel Engagement, STONEWALL, WINNIE, LOUIE, FLORA, JOE, MAY, MOE and ENSEMBLE
My Missus, FLORA, JOE, MAY
Stonewall Moskowitz March (lyric by Mr. Caesar), STONEWALL and ENSEMBLE
One of Us Should Be Two, WINNIE, FLORA, BETSY, MAY
Sing, RUTH, ARCHIE and ENSEMBLE

SCENE TWO—THE FIRE ESCAPE OUTSIDE THE KITZEL FLAT
In Our Parlor on the Third Floor Back, BETSY and ARCHIE

SCENE THREE—THE CLEANERS' DEPARTMENT OF VAUDEVILLE CIRCUIT
This Funny World, RUTH

SCENE FOUR—OUTSIDE KITZEL'S CLOTHING STORE

SCENE FIVE—INSIDE THE CLOTHING STORE
The Tales of Hoffman (by Mr. Caesar and A. Segal), LOUIE

SCENE SIX—LOWER EAST SIDE SQUARE
Follow On, DAUGHTERS OF THE BELLES OF NEW YORK

Borrah Minevitch and his Harmonica Symphony Orchestra
National Dances, ENSEMBLE
Push Around, RUTH
Bugle Blow, WINNIE and ENSEMBLE
Finale, COMPANY

ACT II

SCENE ONE—THE KITZEL CONCESSION, CONEY ISLAND
Cradle of the Deep, FLORA and ENSEMBLE
If I Were You, BETSY and ARCHIE
Blue Skies (specially written for Miss Baker by Irving Berlin), RUTH and ENSEMBLE
Leave It to Levy (by Mr. Caesar), LOUIE and ENSEMBLE
Finaletto, COMPANY

SCENE TWO—OUTSIDE OF SASKATCHEWAN COUNTRY CLUB
Borrah Minevitch's Harmonica Symphony Orchestra

SCENE THREE—THE CLUB GARDENS
Birds on High, ARCHIE and ENSEMBLE
Shuffle, WINNIE and ENSEMBLE
Dance Specialty, FLORA
Song Specialty, RUTH
Finale, COMPANY

NOTE: *Come and Tell Me, Show Me How to Make Love, At the Saskatchewan, Ladies' Home Companion, You're the Mother Type, Six Little Kitzels,* and *In Variety* cut before New York opening. *Don't Believe* (by Caesar and M. Siegel) also cut, but put back latter part of run in place of *The Tales of Hoffman.*

Reviews

J. Brooks Atkinson—*New York Times*

". . . an elaborate, loose-jointed, but withal fairly routine musical comedy, smacking more than a little of the variety halls . . . not a highly successful evening for Rodgers and Hart, two of the brighter and more sophisticated song and dance tunesmiths. Their contributions for the most part were not up to standard . . ."

George Goldsmith—*New York Herald Tribune*

"Mr. Ziegfeld has failed . . . All of his talents for production could not have triumphed over the anemic text . . . No ingenuity for stage effects could make Miss Baker a musical comedy heroine. Nor could the most gorgeous *mise en scène* or the most beautiful chorus atone for the insufficiencies of Mr. Rodgers' music. Really, Mr. Hart deserves a better accompanist for his lyrics . . ."

Jeffrey Holmesdale, Earl of Amherst—*New York World*

". . . once in a while the music and lyrics echoed Rodgers and Hart's former quality and fire, but only once in a while. The hit of the evening was *Blue Skies* . . . The show appeared to be a considerable scramble for all concerned . . ."

Alan Dale—*New York American*
". . . pretty, effective music . . . lively, pep-y and up to the 42nd Street standard, and for that standard the sky is the limit . . ."

Robert Coleman—*New York Daily Mirror*
". . . The loveliness of the production makes one gasp . . . There isn't one dirty, objectionable line or situation in it. It is bright and spotlessly clean . . ."

Walter Winchell—*New York Graphic*
". . . will probably do well in spite of its blemishes . . ."

Stephen Rathbun—*New York Sun*
". . . In spite of the fact that she was handicapped by a book that was dull in spots, Miss Baker triumphed. The peak of her triumph was her rendering of a cheerful little ditty entitled *Blue Skies* . . ."

Sime Silverman—*Variety,* January 5, 1927
"A butchered show. It is a waste of space to give it any attention. All Ziegfeld has is production . . . One of the poorest big produced musicals in years . . ."

Charles Brackett—*The New Yorker,* January 8, 1927
". . . a mess, and if I grant that in regard to girls, costumes, and some settings, it is a pretty mess, I guess I've said as much for it as I can . . ."

George Jean Nathan—*Judge,* January 22, 1927
". . . little save a Keith vaudeville show dolled up for the expensive Broadway trade . . . The best features are a fire escape duet, a good looking balloon chorus number and some expert chorus maneuvers . . . Next, Mr. Ziegfeld?"

ONE DAM THING AFTER ANOTHER

(London—1927)

A musical revue by Ronald Jeans; music by Richard Rodgers; lyrics by Lorenz Hart.

Presented by Charles B. Cochran
Directed by Frank Collins
Choreography by Max Rivers
Settings mostly by Marc Henri
Costumes mostly by Kitty Shannon and Doris Zinkeisen
Music director, J. B. Hastings
Orchestrations by Robert Russell Bennett
Pianist, Leslie Hutchinson

London Run

London Pavilion, May 19-December 10, 1927
237 performances

The Cast

Jessie Matthews
Lance Lister
Mimi Crawford
Edythe Baker
Rich Hayes
Greta Fayne
Richard Dolman
Kate Strudwick
Max Wall
Vivienne Glen
Ian Dudley Hardy
Douglas Byng
Sonnie Hale
Morris Harvey
Melville Cooper
Little Gwen Stella
Joan Clarkson
Ann Stephenson
Art Fowler
Brian Glennie
William Cavanagh
Marjorie Browne

GIRLS: Kathleen Coram, Renee LeMoine, Peter May, Peggy Wynne, Greta Taylor, Nora Olive, Ena Elliott, Decilia Mowbray, Medeline Gibson, Florita Fey, Doreen Austin, Nancy Barnett, Isa Bevan, Sheilah Grahame, Betty Davis

BOYS: Philip Buchel, Richard Haydon, Bob Ralston, Barney Glossop, Jack Delmain, P. C. Murray, Claud Newman

Musical Numbers and Sketches

ACT I

The Election

SANDWICH GIRLS: Nora Olive, Decilia Mowbray, Madeline Gibson, Florita Fey, Doreen Austin, Nancy Barnett

THE ELECTION CLERK, Melville Cooper

MR. MELODRAMA, Douglas Byng

MISS BALLET, Greta Fayne

MISS SHAKESPEARE, Joan Clarkson

MOSS, Lance Lister

STOLL, Richard Dolman

MISS MUSICAL COMEDY, Mimi Crawford

MR. BROADWAY PLAY, Sonnie Hale

MISS MODERN COMEDY, Jessie Matthews

SIGNOR OPERA, Morris Harvey

MISS REVUE, Edythe Baker

PAGES, Betty Oliver, Kate Strudwick

REVUE GIRLS

Shuffle, Edythe Baker and GIRLS and BOYS

A One-Sided Affair (Sketch)

FIRST MAN, Richard Dolman

SECOND MAN, Sonnie Hale

MRS. WATERCRESS, Mimi Crawford

MAID, Jessie Matthews

MR. TILBURY, Lance Lister

BUTLER, Douglas Byng

RICHARD *(who does not appear),* Morris Harvey

A VAMP, Joan Clarkson

GUESTS

Borem, with his Ventriloquial Figure, "Cherry"

Lo Hear the Gentle Lark (Bishop), Little Gwen Stella

Paris (Sketch) (Costumes by Aubrey Hammond and Miss Zinkeisen)

AN AMERICAN TOURIST, Sonnie Hale

A GUIDE, Morris Harvey

AN AMERICAN VISITOR, Joan Clarkson

HER FRIEND, Richard Dolman

A SCOTSMAN, Melville Cooper

HIS WIFE, Ann Stephenson

A COCKNEY VISITOR, Kate Strudwick

AN AMERICAN, Art Fowler

A WAITER, Lance Lister

PROPRIETOR OF THE CAFE, Douglas Byng

SARGENT DE VILLE, Sonnie Hale

A GRANNY, Jessie Matthews

AMERICAN TOURISTS, GRANNIES, GIGOLOS, YOUNG GIRLS

Paris Is Really Divine, Sonnie Hale
Gigolo, Jessie Matthews
The Age of Compromise (Sketch)
MONA, Jessie Matthews
UNCLE GILBERT, Morris Harvey
ETHEL, Mimi Crawford
BUTLER, Lance Lister
Max Wall and Greta Fayne
My Heart Stood Still (Costumes by Maison Arthur, Ltd.)
A GIRL, Jessie Matthews
A YOUTH, Richard Dolman
CHILDREN, Little Gwen Stella, Brian Glennie
FRIENDS
The Lady of the Lake (Sketch)
BENTLEY FORD, Morris Harvey
GREGORY GROUCH, Sonnie Hale
Play Us a Tune (Cole Porter), Edythe Baker, BOYS and GIRLS
Birth of the Blues (Ray Henderson), Miss Baker
Reprise, *My Heart Stood Still,* Miss Baker
Progress (Sketch) (setting by Doris Zinkeisen)
UNCLE JIM, Melville Cooper
JACK, Lance Lister
BILLIE, Jessie Matthews
MONTY, Morris Harvey
CONDUCTOR, Max Wall
LADY BETTY CARSTAIRS, Mimi Crawford
SIR BENJAMIN RIP, Douglas Byng
CHARLES RUFFLE, Sonnie Hale
A SERVANT, Melville Cooper
A FOOL, Richard Dolman
LADY ANNE, Jessie Matthews
MARMADUKE, Lance Lister
BARON, Morris Harvey
GLOOK, Sonnie Hale
ZAB-ZAB, Mimi Crawford
BUNK, Douglas Byng
Make Hey! Make Hey!, Max Wall
Finale, COMPANY

ACT II
Max Wall and the Girls
Lost Souls (Sketch)
THE AUTHOR, Lance Lister
THE STAGE MANAGER, Melville Cooper
MARIGOLD, Jessie Matthews
JULIAN, *her husband,* Sonnie Hale
CHATEAU, *her lover,* Morris Harvey

PARKER, *her maid,* Mimi Crawford
SCENE: MARIGOLD'S APARTMENT IN PARIS
Art Fowler, with his Ukulele
As Others See Us (Sketch)
COMPÈRE, Douglas Byng
POLICEMAN, Melville Cooper
NURSE MAID, Kate Strudwick
THE LADY, Greta Fayne
POLICEMAN, Morris Harvey
COOK, Joan Clarkson
POLICEMAN, Sonnie Hale
WIFE, Mimi Crawford
POLICEMAN, Lance Lister
POLICEMAN, William Cavanagh
REVELLER, Ian Dudley Hardy
I Need Some Cooling Off, Edythe Baker, BOYS and GIRLS
My Lucky Star
CHORUS BOY, Sonnie Hale
CHORUS GIRL, Mimi Crawford
One Dam Thing After Another
MOTHER, Mimi Crawford
FATHER, Lance Lister
BABY, Jessie Matthews
NURSE, Joan Clarkson
Community Singing in the Home (Sketch) (setting by Aubrey Hammond)
SERVANT, Marjorie Browne
ELDERLY LADY, Ann Stephenson
THE MAJOR, Morris Harvey
THE SCHOOL MISTRESS, Grace Wilson
THE TIRED BUSINESSMAN, Sonnie Hale
AN ELDERLY VAMP, Kate Strudwick
A CITY CLERK, Lance Lister
CITY CLERK'S WIFE, Greta Fayne
CITY CLERK'S SON, Brian Glennie
THE LITTLE MAN, Ian Dudley Hardy
MRS. ARROWROOT, *the landlady,* Douglas Byng
Rich Hayes, the Eccentric Juggler
Last Dam Thing of All, COMPANY

NOTE: *Idles of the King* and *Danse Grotesque à la Negre* cut before opening.

Reviews

London Times

". . . a little disappointing. It contains many good ideas but only a few of them are successfully developed. The first half is much better than the second . . . it is in the matter of comedy that *One Dam Thing After Another* proves as weak as its title . . ."

London Daily Telegraph
". . . enough good things in it for Cochran's sumptuously staged revue to insure it effectually against the risk of a temptingly obvious jibe. And yet, one must confess the revue is over-long . . . Not a few of the lyrics are cleverly turned, while the music is often above the revue average, and actually contains one or two tunes that do not sound familiar . . ."

London Daily Mail
". . . Its title sounds a little cheap—as cheap as the seats are dear . . . crowded with those things that make a musical play a success. The book as usual matters little; the music breaks away from the conventional—for once a revue is not overburdened by jazz—and there is some humour contained in the lyrics. But perhaps best of all is the prettiness of the production as a whole and the way in which the revue is acted . . . Altogether, a delightful production . . ."

L'E. F.—*London Morning Post*
". . . What admirable composition of scene and idea! What poise and taste and finish! What excellent essays in up-to-date expression! Here is charm and grace, here is satire at its most sardonic, here is expert poetic movement, here is colour and beauty . . . *My Heart Stood Still* is the best thing of its kind for years . . . A piquant revue in all, from which I could spare least Jessie Matthews and that song."

E. A. Baughan—*London Daily News*
". . . one of the best revues Cochran has given us . . . the whole thing has the fascination of youth . . . The dancers are good and Ronald Jean's book has some witty lines. Much of Rodgers' music is original, and he has invented at least one tune, *My Heart Stood Still,* which will deserve to be played and sung all over London . . ."

Herbert Griffith—*London Evening Standard*
". . . taken by and large, a very good show. A great deal of it was amusing. Some of it was pretty. Only a very little of it was boring . . . The music, rag-time of course, has some good tunes in it, which is unusual . . ."

A.E.M.—*London Evening News*
". . . The impression it leaves is of moderation rather than extravagance, of orderliness rather than excess . . . a definite lack of sparkle about the second half of the programme, and nothing in the first half completely 'lifted' the audience . . . one good song, *My Heart Stood Still* . . . The greatest personal success was scored by Jessie Matthews . . ."

James Agate—*London Sunday Times,* May 22, 1927
". . . many delightful things. There is the delicious scene, *My Heart Stood Still* . . . There is that long sustained piece of irony entitled *Progress* . . . There is a delightful number called *My Lucky Star* . . . I should be delighted to see the revue all over again tomorrow . . ."

St. John Ervine—*London Observer,* May 22, 1927
". . . The first half of the program was immensely better than the second, which rather fell to pieces, but the proportion of good items in it was better than experience had led me to expect in any revue at its first performance, and there is one charming sentimental song, *My Heart Stood Still,* which should become popular but not, I hope, too popular. I do not wish to rue the day I praised it . . . Miss Jessie Matthews is clearly destined to be a very brilliant revue actress . . ."

S.T.H.—*Theatre World,* June, 1927
"Quite the worst part of this revue is its title, which in no way conveys the remotest idea of its cleverness, audacity and charm . . . Above the average are Hart's lyrics, notably in *Paris Is Really Divine,* and some of the songs by Rodgers. Of these, *My Heart Stood Still* and *My Lucky Star* are the most tuneful and original . . ."

Horace Horsnell—*The Outlook,* June 4, 1927
". . . The spirit of the revue is corybantic. It appeals chiefly to the eye and to that susceptibility to rhythm which the best of us share with the untutored savage . . . 'One dam thing' follows another so quickly that one hasn't time to bother much about their varying quality . . ."

Bibliography

The Prince "Dictates" a Fox-Trot
"Teaching the Band 'My Heart Stood Still' "
—*London Evening News,* June 11, 1927

The Cochran Revue: "One Dam Thing After Another"
—*Illustrated Sporting and Dramatic News,* June 11, 1927

A CONNECTICUT YANKEE

(1927)

A musical comedy with book by Herbert Fields, adapted from "A Connecticut Yankee in King Arthur's Court" by Mark Twain; music by Richard Rodgers; lyrics by Lorenz Hart.

Presented by Lew Fields and Lyle D. Andrews
Directed by Alexander Leftwich
Choreography by Busby Berkeley
Settings and costumes by John Hawkins, Jr.
Art director, Herbert Ward
Musical director, Roy Webb
Opening night conductor, Mr. Rodgers
Orchestrations by Mr. Webb

Tryout
Stamford Theatre, Stamford, Conn., September 30-October 1, 1927
Walnut Theatre, Philadelphia, October 3-29, 1927

New York Run
Vanderbilt Theatre, November 3, 1927-October 27, 1928
418 performances

The Story
On the eve of his marriage to Fay Morgan, Martin is visited by Alice, his former fiancée. When Fay discovers them together, she knocks Martin out with a champagne bottle. He dreams that he is back in the days of King Arthur, where he becomes a great favorite at court, falls in love with the Demoiselle Alisande, and is soon put in charge of industrializing the country. The king's evil sister, Queen Morgan Le Fay, has Alisande kidnapped, but Martin rescues her just as he is awakening from his dream. The real-life hero then realizes that it is Alice whom he really loves.

The Cast
IN THE PROLOGUE
ALBERT KAY, Gordon Burby
GERALD LAKE, Jack Thompson

MERLIN, William Norris
MARTIN, William Gaxton
ARTHUR PENDRAGOS, Paul Everton
FAY MORGAN, Nana Bryant
ALICE CARTER, Constance Carpenter
LAWRENCE LAKE, William Roselle

IN THE PLAY
SIR KAY, *the seneschal*, Gordon Burby
THE YANKEE, William Gaxton
THE DEMOISELLE ALISANDE LE CARTELOISE, Constance Carpenter
KING ARTHUR OF BRITAIN, Paul Everton
SIR GALAHAD, *his son*, Jack Thompson
MERLIN, *a mighty magician*, William Norris
MAID ANGELA, *lady-in-waiting to Morgan Le Fay*, Dorothy Roy
MISTRESS EVELYN LA BELLE-ANS, June Cochrane
QUEEN MORGAN LE FAY, Nina Bryant
QUEEN GUINEVERE, Celeste Deuth
SIR BORS, G. Douglas Evans
SIR SAGRAMOR, John Morton
SIR TRISTAN, Chester Bree
MISTRESS PHOEBE SAUCE DE POMMES, Regina Diamond
SLAVES, KNIGHTS, LADIES OF THE COURT, FACTORY HANDS: Olive Bertram, Grace Connelly, Ednor Fulling, Enes Early, Harriet Hamell, Leoda Knapp, Mareta Mackay, Margaret Miller, Dothery Rubino, Kaye Renard, Evelyn Ruh, Valma Valentine; G. Douglas Evans, Chester Bree, Martin Denis, John Creighton, Don Donaldson, George Magis, Jack Morton, Ward Arnold, Vernon Downing, Frank Norton, Jack Baker, Leslie Cooley, Richardson Brown, Frank Bocchetta, Philip Kobe, Lew Douglas

NOTE: During tour, Miss Carpenter succeeded by Mary Adams; Mr. Gaxton by Richard Lane.

Musical Numbers

PROLOGUE—GRAND BALLROOM OF A HOTEL IN HARTFORD, CONN., 1927
A Ladies' Home Companion, FAY, PRINCIPALS, and ENSEMBLE
My Heart Stood Still, MARTIN, SANDY, and ENSEMBLE

THE PLAY
ACT I
SCENE ONE—THE ROAD TO CAMELOT, 528 A.D.
Thou Swell, MARTIN and SANDY

SCENE TWO—COURTYARD OF KING ARTHUR'S CASTLE
At the Round Table, ARTHUR, MERLIN, LAUNCELOT, GALAHAD, KNIGHTS and LADIES
On a Desert Island With Thee, GALAHAD and EVELYN; KNIGHTS and LADIES
Reprise, *My Heart Stood Still*, MARTIN and SANDY
Finale, COMPANY

ACT II

SCENE ONE—CORRIDOR OF A FACTORY
Opening, ENSEMBLE
Nothing's Wrong, SANDY
I Feel at Home With You, GALAHAD, EVELYN and ENSEMBLE
Dance, SANDY and GALAHAD

SCENE TWO—THE ROAD FROM CAMELOT
The Sandwich Men, KNIGHTS

SCENE THREE—PALACE OF MORGAN LE FAY
Evelyn, What Do You Say?, EVELYN and KNIGHTS

SCENE FOUR—GARDENS OF THE HOTEL IN HARTFORD, 1927
Finale, COMPANY

NOTE: *You're What I Need, I Blush, Morgan Le Fay, Someone Should Tell Them* (same music as *There's So Much More* in *America's Sweetheart*), *and Britain's Own Ambassadors* cut before New York opening.

Reviews

J. Brooks Atkinson—*New York Times*
". . . Set to as fresh and lilting songs as we may hope to find, with well turned lyrics and an intelligent book, it makes for novel amusement in the best of taste . . . In his unhackneyed score, Mr. Rodgers composes with genuine feeling and versatility . . . Once he comes perilously close to oratorio. In the lyrics, Mr. Hart continues to write original, intelligent, witty rhyme-schemes . . ."

Percy Hammond—*New York Herald Tribune*
". . . The play was richly pictorial, and it was especially beautified by many lovely dancing girls . . . They, the costumes, and four or five alluring songs from the harmonium of Mr. Rodgers were the nicest things in it . . . what made the book tedious was the constant reiteration of the burlesque lingo of King Arthur."

Alexander Woollcott—*New York World*
". . . It was Richard Rodgers, with his head full of tunes, who made the most valuable contribution . . . The libretto did not seem to me quite as funny as it set out to be . . . Of the individuals, the honors and the opportunities go cheerfully to William Gaxton and Constance Carpenter, a pretty miss who evidently made a careful study of Gertrude Lawrence . . ."

Alan Dale—*New York American*
". . . a poignantly amusing book . . . lovely, quaint, deliciously droll and remarkably cerebral music . . . *My Heart Stood Still* is a melody that will haunt for ages . . . I e'en must congratulate Busby

Berkeley, whose groupings, whose 'business,' and whose artistic perception gave great force to the production . . ."

Burns Mantle—*New York Daily News*
". . . Fool humor it is. It lacks the finer touch of satire and boasts rough Broadway wit . . . The lyrics are good, the score characterful and original . . . Berkeley is a graduate of the old school that used to form the girls and boys into boats and steam engines and bring them on finally carrying a whole lot of little kitchen stoves . . ."

Walter Winchell—*New York Graphic*
". . . rollicking entertainment . . . brisk folderol . . . a smart, saucy and sophisticated song-and-stepping soirée . . . several singable songs, one of which will probably rock the city. It is called *Thou Swell,* a blazing foxtrot, which is enough to commend the production . . ."

John Anderson—*New York Post*
". . . The book is embarrassingly feeble and only the charming music, the radiant presence of Miss Constance Carpenter, and some expert foolishness by Mr. Gaxton save anything for amusement . . . Rodgers' score seemed to have all the capricious imagination that the book so woefully lacked, and Mr. Hart has fitted to the songs some rhymes of deft manipulation . . ."

E. W. Osborn—*New York Evening World*
"Those three precocious children, the young Fields, Rodgers and Hart, arrived last night, at the stage of the grand smash . . . Fields' book was snappy, Hart's lyrics, with their eccentric rhythms, were full of surprises, which Rodgers met blithely . . . His motif song, *My Heart Stood Still* is going to enjoy a wide vogue . . ."

Frank Vreeland—*New York Telegram*
". . . bouncing book and lyrics, and music that you could almost play on a typewriter . . . Let me urge you

GO THOU SLUGGARD
AND ENJOY
A CONNECTICUT YANKEE
AND TELL
YE COCKE-EYED WORLD
THOU HAST HAD
YE HELUVA TIME

. . . The songs had all the inescapable pulse of *Mountain Greenery* and all the other *Garrick Gaieties* hits, and were conducted by Rodgers himself, mostly with the spine and hips . . ."

Gilbert W. Gabriel—*New York Sun*
"They—and who else but that irrepressible young trinity, Fields, Rodgers and Hart?—have made a fresh and abundant lark of a musical comedy . . . music and lyrics which rival the best of several seasons past . . . a truly relishable and rememberable score with not a single dip into the rut . . ."

Sid Silverman—*Variety,* November 9, 1927
". . . neither a sequel nor an equal to *Peggy-Ann*. Its main fault is that the entire show is within the first hour . . . Weakness crops up in the spasmodic comedy undertowed by definitely slow spots in the book . . . moderate money at best . . ."

Charles Brackett—*The New Yorker,* November 12, 1927
". . . it is not *Peggy-Ann* by several damn sights . . . The lyrics by Lorenz Hart are, of course, far above average. They bubble with unexpected feminine rhymes very pleasing to ears used to blah masculine ones. But his songs, as entireties, seem curiously pointless when compared with the lyrics of Cole Porter, for instance—for lone contemporary instance, I must admit . . ."

Wells Root—*Time,* November 14, 1927
". . . Fields, Rodgers and Hart are emerging as dignitaries in the glossy world of musical comedy . . . moderate merry . . . The cast is capable and the dancing is violently good. And the music is so immensely better (in at least three songs) than is most music in most musical comedies, that all can be considered well—until, at any rate, the master song, *My Heart Stood Still,* becomes a nuisance."

Abbe Niles—*The New Republic,* November 23, 1927
". . . its best song, *Thou Swell,* is as cunning, capricious and infectious a tune as has reached New York since *Fascinating Rhythm* . . . does not sustain the level of Rodgers' score for *Peggy-Ann,* but any other now audible in Manhattan is, by comparison, hack-work, and it may well haul an otherwise so-so entertainment through a noble run. The contrast between the deftness and wit of Hart's lyrics and the beefy humor in the book is distressing . . ."

Robert Benchley—*Life,* November 24, 1927
". . . another in the noteworthy series of accomplishments to the credit of Fields, Rodgers and Hart . . . the loveliest musical comedy song in recent years is *My Heart Stood Still* . . . one of the showpieces of the year."

George Jean Nathan—*Judge,* November 26, 1927
". . . amusing . . . excellent tunes . . . This Rodgers is to be

congratulated for writing simple, spirited and lively music show tunes instead of posturing himself like certain of his colleagues who seem intent upon proving that they are expert musicians and composers and who write stuff that, whatever its merit, no more suits a gay girl and clown show than the Funeral March suits a hurdy-gurdy."

Tour

Shubert Majestic Theatre, Boston, October 29, 1928—Boulevard Theatre, Jackson Heights, New York, April 5, 1930 (49 cities).

Tour Reviews

Ashton Stevens—*Chicago Herald-Examiner*
". . . one of the best musicals I have ever seen. Its tunes are joyous, and so are its rhymes, and its story and dialog flatter, rather than insult, the so-called human intelligence . . ."

Claudia Cassidy—*Chicago Journal of Commerce*
". . . as insanely delightful a blend of song and dance idiocy as we have any right to expect . . ."

Selected Revivals

St. Louis Municipal Opera, August 3-9, 1936
Eddie Garr (MARTIN); Ruby Mercer (SANDY); Dorothy Vernon (FAY); Audrey Christie (EVELYN); Gil Lamb (GALAHAD); June Havoc (GUINEVERE); Harriet Hoctor (PREMIERE DANSEUSE).

St. Louis Municipal Opera, July 26-August 1, 1948
Wilbur Evans (MARTIN); Gale Sherwood (SANDY); Sue Ryan (FAY).

Goodspeed Opera House, East Haddam, Conn., July 16, 1964
Kenneth McMillan (MARTIN); Joan Hotchkiss (SANDY); Renata Vaselle (FAY).

Television Production

NBC Network, March 12, 1955
Produced and directed by Max Liebman; adaptation by William Friedberg, Neil Simon, Al Schwartz, and Will Glickman; book directed by William Hobin; choreography by Rod Alexander; music director, Charles Sanford; choral director, Clay Warnick; sponsored by Oldsmobile. *Cast:* Eddie Albert (MARTIN); Janet Blair (SANDY); Gale Sherwood (FAY); Boris Karloff (KING ARTHUR); John Conte (SIR KAY); Leonard Elliott (MERLIN); Bambi Linn and Rod Alexander (DANCERS).

A YANKEE AT THE COURT OF KING ARTHUR

(London Production of "A Connecticut Yankee"—1929)

Presented by British Amalgamated Theatres (Productions) Ltd.
Directed by David Miller
Choreography by Fred A. Leslie and Charles Brooks
Settings by F. L. Lyndhurst

Tryout

King's Theatre, Southsea, September 30-October 6, 1929

London Run

Daly's Theatre, October 10-November 16, 1929
43 performances

The Cast

SIR KAY, *the seneschal,* J. C. Aubrey
THE YANKEE, Harry Fox
THE DEMOISELLE ALISANDE LE CARTELOISE, Constance Carpenter
KING ARTHUR, Sam Livesey
SIR LAUNCELOT, William D. Fazan
SIR GALAHAD, *his son,* Billy Holland
MERLIN, *a mighty magician,* J. G. Taylor
MAID ANGELA, *lady-in-waiting to Queen Morgan Le Fay,* Dolly Summers
MISTRESS EVELYN LA BELLE-ANS, Gladys Cruickshank
QUEEN MORGAN LE FAY, Norah Robinson
QUEEN GUINEVERE, Victoria Sievers
NIBLO, Fred Hearne
SIR TRISTAM, Paul Stanton
SIR BORS, Cliff Jones
LAEMMLE, Clifford Kibbler

Musical Numbers

Same as New York production, with exception of *My Heart Stood Still,* which was replaced by *I Don't Know How* by Vivian Ellis and Desmond Carter. *I Never Thought of That* (sung by MERLIN) also written by Messrs. Ellis and Carter for this production.

Reviews

London Times

". . . the eclipse of the sun, to the credit of the electricians, was the brightest spot in the first act . . . In Act II the boisterous humours of plate armour gave place to a lighter and more cheerful scene . . . But it is a melancholy task to seek in memories of dullness for fragments that may be praised . . ."

London Daily Telegraph
". . . Harry Fox gives a sufficiently lively account of the part of the Yankee, but he has a somewhat uphill task . . ."

London Daily News
". . . the second act promises satire of our industrial age, but nothing comes of it . . . the music is bright and catchy, and the chorus is full of 'pep' . . ."

James Agate—*London Sunday Times,* October 13, 1929
". . . the authors cannot help one deeming the whole of the entertainment a little tame, and the consequent harking back to the time when nights were bolder. Yet there were compensations. There was the pleasure of listening to Mr. Harry Fox's agreeable Americanisms and the pleasant performance of Miss Constance Carpenter . . ."

Horace Horsnell—*London Observer,* October 13, 1929
". . . a musical comedy a long way after Mark Twain . . . contains some vigorous dancing, some loud prismatic scenery, a chummy young American comedian, and an abundance of back-chat humours such as invites the loud guffaw, but is depressing in its absence . . . it is only fair to add that my own rather sad reactions were by no means universal."

The Stage
"Poor Mark Twain! *Que diable allait-it faire dans cette galère?* . . ."

A CONNECTICUT YANKEE

(New York—1943)

Presented by Richard Rodgers
Directed by John C. Wilson
Choreography by William Holbrook and Al White, Jr.
Settings and costumes by Nat Karson
Music director, George Hirst
Orchestrations by Don Walker
Choral director, Clay Warnick

Tryout
Forrest Theatre, Philadelphia, October 28-November 14, 1943

New York Run
Martin Beck Theatre, November 17, 1943-March 11, 1944
135 performances

The Story
Basically the same as the original except that the non-dream sequences were updated and the part of Morgan LeFay was enlarged.

The Cast

IN HARTFORD
LT. (J. G.) KENNETH KAY, U.S.N., Robert Byrn
JUDGE THURSTON MERRILL, John Cherry
ADMIRAL ARTHUR K. ARTHUR, U.S.N., Robert Chisholm
ENSIGN GERALD LAKE, U.S.N., Chester Stratton
ENSIGN ALLAN GWYNN, U.S.N., Jere McMahon
LT. MARTIN BARRETT, U.S.N., Dick Foran
CAPT. LAWRENCE LAKE, U.S.N., Stuart Casey
LT. FAY MERRILL, W.A.V.E., Vivienne Segal
CORP. ALICE COURTLIEGH, W.A.C. (SANDY), Julie Warren

IN CAMELOT
SIR KAY, *the seneschal,* Robert Byrn
MARTIN, Dick Foran
THE DEMOISELLE ALISANDE LA COURTELLOISE (SANDY), Julie Warren
ARTHUR, KING OF BRITAIN, Robert Chisholm
MERLIN, John Cherry
QUEEN GUINEVERE, Katherine Anderson
SIR LAUNCELOT OF THE LAKE, Stuart Casey
SIR GALAHAD, *his son,* Chester Stratton
ANGELA, *hand-maiden to Queen Morgan LeFay,* Mimi Berry
QUEEN MORGAN LE FAY, Vivienne Segal
SIR GAWAIN, Jere McMahon
MISTRESS EVELYN LA RONDELLE, Vera-Ellen
DANCING GIRLS: Dorothy Blute, Carole Burke, Eleanor Eberle, Bea Farnum, Virginia Gorski, Janet Jay, Rose Marie Magrill, Frances Martone, May McDonnell, Beth Nichols, Murnai Pins, Dorothy Poplar, Joyce Ring, Rosemary Sankey, Helen Vent, Violette Weems, Doris York
DANCING BOYS: Tad Bruce, Buster Burnell, Pittman Corry, Frank deWinters, Bob Gari, William Hunter, Hal Loman, William Lundy, Jack Lyons
SINGING GIRLS: Marjorie Cowen, Toni Hart, Linda Mason, Martha Watson
SINGING BOYS: Lester Freedman, Vincent Henry, Craig Holden, Wayne McIntyre

Musical Numbers

PROLOGUE—BANQUET HALL OF A HOTEL IN HARTFORD, CONN., 1943
This Is My Night to Howl, FAY and ENSEMBLE
My Heart Stood Still, MARTIN and SANDY

ACT I
SCENE ONE—THE ROAD TO CAMELOT., 528 A.D.
Thou Swell, MARTIN and SANDY

SCENE TWO—COURTYARD OF KING ARTHUR'S CASTLE
At the Round Table, COMPANY
On a Desert Island With Thee, GALAHAD, EVELYN, GAWAIN and ENSEMBLE
To Keep My Love Alive, MORGAN LE FAY
Reprise, *My Heart Stood Still,* MARTIN and SANDY
Finale, COMPANY

ACT II
SCENE ONE—CORRIDOR OF A FACTORY
Ye Lunchtime Follies, GALAHAD and ENSEMBLE
Can't You Do a Friend a Favor?, MORGAN LE FAY and MARTIN
Reprise, *Thou Swell,* MARTIN and SANDY
I Feel at Home With You, GALAHAD, EVELYN, GAWAIN and ENSEMBLE

SCENE TWO—THE ROAD FROM CAMELOT
You Always Love the Same Girl, MARTIN and KING ARTHUR

SCENE THREE—PALACE OF QUEEN MORGAN LE FAY
The Camelot Samba, GAWAIN and ENSEMBLE

EPILOGUE—GARDENS OF THE HOTEL IN HARTFORD, 1943
Finale, COMPANY

Reviews

Lewis Nichols—*New York Times*
". . . colorful costumes and good settings . . . pretty to look at and agreeable to hear, and Mr. Rodgers has offered it with the same care with which he writes his songs."

Howard Barnes—*New York Herald Tribune*
"The team of Mark Twain and Richard Rodgers is still going strong . . . Since Rodgers has added half a dozen new tunes to the piece and Hart has equipped them with sly rhymes, the show lacks next to nothing in the music department . . . Take the original conceit and the songs in this latter day exhibit and you have the show—a good one."

John Chapman—*New York Daily News*
". . . a beautiful new production . . . lovely to see, lovely to listen

to, played by some very engaging people and almost funny enough to satisfy me . . ."

Robert Coleman—*New York Daily Mirror*
". . . smart and delightsome—a rousing hit, as big a hit as the Yankee made with the fair maid of Camelot."

Wilella Waldorf—*New York Post*
". . . Much of it struck us as a rather tony college musical got up by a bunch of the boys from the Dramatic and Musical Clubs . . . Mr. Rodgers' music is often very lovely . . . Now and then Mr. Hart sounds as if he were still an undergraduate . . . Go to hear Miss Segal sing *To Keep My Love Alive,* and watch Vera-Ellen and Jere McMahon dance . . ."

Burton Rascoe—*New York World-Telegram*
". . . a highly enjoyable entertainment, lavishly produced, full of pretty girls, and spiced here and there with fun . . ."

Ward Morehouse—*New York Sun*
". . . I found considerable tedium in the book . . . The production is a handsome one . . . I didn't feel that this new adaptation has the verve of the original production. The dance numbers, however, are splendid . . ."

Robert Garland—*New York Journal-American*
". . . a good deal skimpier in humor than we had remembered it to be . . . big, handsome and melodious . . ."

Louis Kronenberger—*PM*
". . . what was most fetching in the old production has been blended with some nice things in the new one. Whatever its shortcomings, it is in the tradition of sound and solid musical comedy . . . Mr. Rodgers' new music offers no topflight tunes, but one light number, *To Keep My Love Alive,* gives Lorenz Hart the chance to go to town with his wittiest and funniest lyric in years . . . a nice, clean, gay show, and something more than a straight revival."

Joe Schoenfeld—*Variety,* November 18, 1943
". . . not a very sprightly gentleman in 1943. There's a creakiness in its modernized book, a lack of humor in its dialog . . ."

George Jean Nathan—*New York Journal-American,* November 22, 1943
". . . The so-called modernization of the book does not noticeably improve it . . . I like Rodgers' old song *My Heart Stood Still.* I like

Hart's comical lyric for *To Keep My Love Alive,* and I like the way Vivienne Segal sings it. I like Vera-Ellen . . . What more could anyone ask for an allegedly impossible to please critic?"

Wolcott Gibbs—*The New Yorker,* November 27, 1943
". . . The old tunes are still fetching; the book, hauled up to date in a military and political sense, remains an ingenious idea; though a good deal more labored and elementary than I'd remembered . . . With the exception of one fine new song, *To Keep My Love Alive,* the new material is nothing much . . . Miss Segal is probably the greatest actress in musical comedy when it comes to suggesting a sort of genial carnality . . ."

Louis Kronenberger—*Time,* November 29, 1943
". . . despite a slow start and a rather trying book, it is a likable and lilting piece of Yankee-panky . . . Show-stopping new song, thanks to Hart's funny lyric and Vivienne Segal's brilliant delivery, is *To Keep My Love Alive* . . ."

Bibliography

Mr. Rodgers' Yankee —*New York Times,* November 21, 1943

Tour

Erlanger Theatre, Buffalo, March 13, 1944—Studebaker Theatre, Chicago, June 17, 1944 (8 cities).

SHE'S MY BABY

(1928)

A musical comedy with book by Guy Bolton, Bert Kalmar and Harry Ruby; music by Richard Rodgers; lyrics by Lorenz Hart.

Presented by Charles Dillingham
Directed by Edward Royce
John Tiller dances by Mary Read
Settings by Raymond Sovey
Costumes by Mr. Sovey and Francillon, Inc.
Music director, Gene Salzer

Tryout
National Theatre, Washington, December 12-17, 1927
Ford's Theatre, Baltimore, December 19-24, 1927
Shubert Theatre, Newark, December 26-31, 1927

New York Run
Globe Theatre, January 3-March 3, 1928
71 performances

The Story
Bob Martin needs money in order to put on a musical show which is to star his sweetheart, Polly. His wealthy uncle, Mr. Hemingway, must be convinced that Bob has a wife and child before he will advance him a loan. Tilly, the maid, serves as wife, and the janitor's infant as progeny. After complications, the ruse ends well for everybody.

The Cast
PEARL, Pearl Eaton
PHYLLIS, Phyllis Rae
THE DANCE DIRECTOR, Nick Long, Jr.
THE STAGE MANAGER, William McCarthy
JOAN, Joan Clement
MEADOWS, William Frawley
THE NIGHTINGALE QUARTETTE, Evelyn Sayers, Loretta Sayers, Jessie Payne, Doreen Glover
JOSIE, Ula Sharon
POLLY, Irene Dunne

BOB MARTIN, Jack Whiting
TILLY, Beatrice Lillie
CLYDE PARKER, Clifton Webb
MR. HEMINGWAY, *Martin's trustee,* Frank Doane
JOHN TILLER'S LILLIE COCKTAILS: Peggy Sowden, Lily Reilly, Grace Holt, Hilda Winstanley, Doris Waterworth, May Cornes, Iris Smith, Elsie Holt
LADIES OF THE ENSEMBLE: Cleo Cullen, Peggy Cunningham, Evelyn Dehkes, Teddy Denton, Evelyn Ellsmore, Geraldine Fitzgerald, Violet Hanbury, Muriel Hayman, Catherine NaVarro, Blanche O'Donahue, Charlotte Otis, Anna Riley, Georgia Sewell, Pearl Sodders, Florence Ware, Hazel Webb, Vivian Wilson, Dorothy Wyatt, Peti Reed, Topsy Humphries, Mary Louise

Musical Numbers

ACT I
SCENE ONE—THE STAGE
This Goes Up, DANCE DIRECTOR, PEARL, PHYLLIS, and ENSEMBLE
My Lucky Star, NIGHTINGALE QUARTETTE and ENSEMBLE
You're What I Need, POLLY, BOB, NIGHTINGALE QUARTETTE and ENSEMBLE
Here She Comes, ENSEMBLE
The Swallows, TILLY
When I Go on the Stage, TILLY and ENSEMBLE
Try Again Tomorrow, CLYDE and JOSIE
Reprise, *You're What I Need,* POLLY and BOB

SCENE TWO—BOB'S HOME IN GREENWICH
Dance, JOHN TILLER'S LILLIE COCKTAILS
Reprise, *You're What I Need,* POLLY and BOB
Camera Shoot, TILLY, CLYDE, BOB
Finale, COMPANY

ACT II
SCENE ONE—BOB'S HOME IN GREENWICH
Where Can the Baby Be? HEMINGWAY, PEARL, JOAN, PHYLLIS and ENSEMBLE
I Need Some Cooling Off, DANCE DIRECTOR, PEARL, PHYLLIS and ENSEMBLE
A Little House in Soho, CLYDE, JOSIE and ENSEMBLE
A Baby's Best Friend, TILLY
Reprise, *You're What I Need,* POLLY, BOB, PHYLLIS, NIGHTINGALE QUARTETTE
Whoopsie, TILLY, CLYDE and ENSEMBLE

SCENE TWO—ALLEY ADJOINING STAGE DOOR
Dance, JOHN TILLER'S LILLIE COCKTAILS

SCENE THREE—SUTTON PLACE
Trio, CLYDE, BOB, DANCE DIRECTOR
Dance, JOHN TILLER'S LILLIE COCKTAILS
Wasn't It Great?, BOB, DANCE DIRECTOR, STAGE MANAGER, JOAN, PEARL, PHYLLIS and ENSEMBLE
Finale, COMPANY

NOTE: *Morning Is Midnight, The Pipes of Pansy* and *How Was I to Know?* cut before New York opening. *If I Were You* also cut before opening, but put back shortly thereafter and sung by POLLY and BOB; danced by PHYLLIS. About the same time, *Whoopsie* and *Wasn't It Great?* were dropped, and *Smart People,* sung by ENSEMBLE; danced by CLYDE and PHYLLIS, was added. *March With Me* (by Ivor Novello and Douglas Furber) added in February and sung by TILLY. *A Little House in Soho* has same music as *A Tiny Flat Near Soho Square (Lido Lady); How Was I to Know?* same as *Why Do You Suppose? (Heads Up); A Baby's Best Friend* same as *Lullaby (Charlot's Masquerade).*

Reviews

J. Brooks Atkinson—*New York Times*
". . . Miss Lillie is good—hell, she's perfect . . . Hart still rhymes his lyrics ingeniously . . . several ingratiating tunes: *You're What I Need* and *My Lucky Star* are fresh and likable . . . it has its virtues. Strewn through an uninspiring book, they are maddeningly hard to appreciate."

Percy Hammond—*New York Herald Tribune*
". . . a wonderwork of inanity . . . Miss Lillie sails through her present doldrums with a merry ease . . . Rodgers' amorous music is often very pretty. The song selected by the composer as his favorite is named *You're What I Need,* a tricky ballad . . ."

Alexander Woollcott—*New York World*
". . . dreary rubbish . . . A farce so stale that it is musty, a few fetching tunes by Master Rodgers, a few lumbering songs by Master Hart, a fine and frantic dance by Nick Long, Jr.—these there are and Beatrice Lillie . . . Mr. Rodgers' most persuasive melody is entitled *You're What I Need,* harnessed to a fearful lyric . . . the whole entertainment leans so heavily on the comic from Canada that she will be black and blue by the end of the week."

Alan Dale—*New York American*
". . . one or two ditties had lilt and charm . . . The music was not Rodgers' best, or even his second best, but it was better than the 'first best' of many others . . ."

Burns Mantle—*New York Daily News*
". . . Hilarious it is . . . the music is lively . . . For those who like musical farces about borrowed babies, Beatrice Lillie will help them to think it worth at least half again as much as it is. I can't say more for it than that."

Robert Littell—*New York Post*
". . . Without Miss Lillie, it would have been a pleasantly flat and pretty show, but with her it seemed less ordinary than it actually was . . . The music was a nice, warm bath, but nothing particularly

worth remembering. The lyrics were genially pointless—which is pretty good, as lyrics go . . ."

E. W. Osborn—*New York Evening World*
". . . a ludicrous trifle . . . It was different with Rodgers' music which has so long and happily been wedded to Hart's rhythms . . . a faultless evening for the seeker of pleasure who wants no trouble thinking it out."

John Anderson—*New York Journal*
". . . a minor festival which, without Miss Lillie, would leave nothing much to write about . . . the songs are all pretty so-so, with one of them, *You're What I Need,* played to what should be wide popularity . . ."

Gilbert W. Gabriel—*New York Sun*
". . . Without the blessed mimicry of the English comedienne to give it occasional gas and guying, it would soon show signs of famine. This in spite of the collected help of Clifton Webb, some Tiller Girls, Rodgers' quite all right music, and other assorted assets . . . Some of the songs about Soho and so-forth have a decided London accent. Their Hart lyrics trip them nicely along . . ."

Sid Silverman—*Variety,* January 11, 1928
". . . a luke-warm show, and only that because of Miss Lillie . . . too many slow spots. It starts out briskly enough, but becomes well-nigh exhausted before the end of the first act . . . The piece is book-heavy . . . To help the Lillie name the best bets are the Tillers and *You're What I Need* . . . It won't greet May 1st on 46th Street."

Charles Brackett—*The New Yorker,* January 14, 1928
". . . Bolton, Kalmar and Ruby have given Miss Lillie about the break that a hostess hands to a guest when she whispers on his arrival, 'Now we're counting on you to make us laugh' . . . in one song, *A Baby's Best Friend,* she is at her gorgeous best . . . the score, for which Hart has tossed off some of his casual lyrics, is all pleasing . . ."

Robert Benchley—*Life,* January 19, 1928
". . . Simply to hear Beatrice Lillie sing *A Baby's Best Friend* is enough to salve the wounds caused by fifty previous rusty gags. In her singlehanded combat against the authors, she is forced to return to many of her old tricks, but to complain of her old tricks would be like complaining of the same old pay-envelope coming around every Saturday. The fortunately indefatigable team of Rodgers and Hart have written their customary satisfactory music . . ."

George Jean Nathan—*Judge,* January 28, 1928
"Beatrice Lillie, in very good comic trim, contrives to enliven an otherwise morose song-and-dance affair . . . By way of tunes, the usually fertile Rodgers has, save in the case of one melody, gone distinctly tin-pan . . . M. Hart has so strained himself to achieve original rhymes that the songs are as self-consciously recherché as so many Greenwich Village lampshades . . ."

Stark Young—*The New Republic,* February 29, 1928
". . . the book requires more memory than imagination . . . The score is by Rodgers and Hart, and for all that the latter rhymes 'Gigli' with 'sincerely,' he should have written the show . . ."

Tour

Ohio Theatre, Cleveland, March 5, 1928—Illinois Theatre, Chicago, May 5, 1928 (4 cities).

PRESENT ARMS

(1928)

A musical comedy with book by Herbert Fields; music by Richard Rodgers; lyrics by Lorenz Hart.

Presented by Lew Fields
Directed by Alexander Leftwich
Choreography by Busby Berkeley
Settings by Ward and Harvey
Costumes by Milgrim
Music director, Roy Webb

Tryout
Shubert Playhouse, Wilmington, April 9-14, 1928
Apollo Theatre, Atlantic City, April 18-21, 1928

New York Run
Lew Fields' Mansfield Theatre, April 26-September 1, 1928
155 performances

The Story
Chick Evans, a Marine from Brooklyn stationed at Pearl Harbor, woos and wins Lady Delphine Witherspoon, a titled English resident of the island. This is accomplished with the aid of his comrades in arms and a lively imagination, which all conspire to eliminate Herr Ludwig Von Richter as a rival for the lady's affections.

The Cast
MCKABE, a top sergeant, Jock McGraw
FRANK DERRYBERRY, *a buck private,* Franker Woods
CHICK EVANS, *another,* Charles King
MCKENNA, *another,* Fuller Melish, Jr.
GADGET, *another,* Robert Spencer
DOUGLAS ATWELL, *a sergeant,* Busby Berkeley
CAPTAIN WIGGINS, *Captain of the outfit,* Richard Lane
EDNA STEVENS, *a tourist,* Joyce Barbour
FAY, *another,* Rachel Chester
LADY DELPHINE WITHERSPOON, Flora Le Breton
LUANA, *a native girl,* Alma Ross

LORD OLIVER WITHERSPOON, *Lady Delphine's father,* Sydney Smith
HERR LUDWIG VON RICHTER, Anthony Knilling
MARIA, Florence Hunter
HORTENSE MOSSBACK, Gaile Beverley
DAISY, Demaris Doré
MINERVA, *a maid,* Aline Green
KARL, Alexander Lewis
ELSA, Frances Hess
MOULIKA, *a native fortune teller,* Alma Ross
LADIES OF THE ENSEMBLE: Dorothy Brown, Elva Adams, Wilda Barnum, Evelyn Crowell, Rachel Chester, Irene Evans, Aline Green, Sherry Gale, Kay Hunt, Geneva Jensen, Rita Jarson, Louise Joyce, Henrietta Kay, Gladys Kelley, Charlotte LeRose, Beth Meredith, Ann Mycue, Dorothy McKeon, Christine Nolan, Loraine Power, Polly Ray, Patricia Ross, Ruth Stickney, Genevieve Street, Greta Swanson, Helen Shepard, Gertrude Sheffield, Marion Stuart, Jean Sutro, Jessica Worth, Barbara Lee, Wanda Wood
GENTLEMEN OF THE ENSEMBLE: Thomas Arnold, Russell Bryant, Milton Brodus, James Beattie, William Burdee, Norman Clifton, William Cullo, Jack Douglas, Louis Delgado, Frank Gagen, Edward Gaillard, Albert Jordan, Frank Kimball, Frank Losee, Edwin Larkin, Dury Lane, Henry Ladd, Jerome Maxwell, David North, Bernard Mitchell, Julio Martell, Glenn McComas, Joe McCafferty, Ned McGurn, William Creston, Walter Pharr, Wilburn Riviere, Thomas Sternfield, Louis Talbott, Joe Vitale

NOTE: In June, Miss LeBreton succeeded by Doris Patston. On August 1, Miss Doré succeeded by Kitty O'Reilly; on August 2, Miss O'Reilly by Patricia Ross.

Musical Numbers.

ACT I

SCENE ONE—BARRACKS OF THE MARINE BASE, PEARL HARBOR, T.H.
Tell It to the Marines, CHICK, FRANK, MCKENNA, DOUGLAS and MARINES
You Took Advantage of Me, EDNA, DOUGLAS and ENSEMBLE
Do I Hear You Saying, "I Love You"?, DELPHINE and CHUCK

SCENE TWO—WITHIN THE QUARTERS
A Kiss for Cinderella, DOUGLAS, MCKENNA, FRANK, CHICK

SCENE THREE—SIR OLIVER'S HOME, HONOLULU
Is It the Uniform?, DELPHINE and ENSEMBLE
Reprise, *Do I Hear You Saying, "I Love You"?,* CHICK and DELPHINE
Crazy Elbows, DAISY and ENSEMBLE
Finale, COMPANY

ACT II

SCENE ONE—PROMENADE DECK OF ENDA'S YACHT
Down by the Sea, CHICK and COMPANY
I'm a Fool, Little One, EDNA, DOUGLAS, FRANK, HORTENSE

SCENE TWO—A RAFT AT SEA

SCENE THREE—A DESERTED ISLAND OFF MAUI
Reprise, EDNA and DOUGLAS
Finaletto, ENSEMBLE

SCENE FOUR—DELPHINE'S ROOM IN HONOLULU

SCENE FIVE—ABOARD THE TRANSPORT BOUND FOR KOHALA
Blue Ocean Blues, CHICK and MARINES

SCENE SIX—THE DOCK AT KOHALA
Hawaii, NATIVES
Kohala, Welcome, NATIVES and MARINES

NOTE: *Blue Ocean Blues* has same music as *Atlantic Blues (Lido Lady).*

Reviews

J. Brooks Atkinson, *New York Times*
". . . excellent music and lyrics . . . the show is what *Hit the Deck* and *Good News* might be if they were crossed. Rough, loud, compact and feverish . . . With his skill in melodies and transitions, Mr. Rodgers makes his score the most beautiful element in the production . . ."

Percy Hammond, *New York Herald Tribune*
". . . eye and ear filling . . . quite the most vehement opera that has aroused the sleepy playgoers in ten days to two weeks . . . a competent carbon copy of *Hit the Deck* . . . Rodgers' score was lit, now and then, with glowing tunes . . . All of them were rendered over and over again, since a cough could get an encore out of the generous musical director . . ."

Alison Smith, *New York World*
". . . underneath the familiar structure is the intermittent glimmer of mockery which emerges with every plot touched by this irreverent trio. It is a quality further enhanced by the persuasive melodies of Rodgers, which are rich enough in haunting, provocative phrases to create one of the distinctive scores of the season . . . genuinely entertaining . . ."

Alan Dale—*New York American*
". . . such pep, such vim, such ginger, such dash, such paprika, and such hip-hip-hoorah . . . Busby Berkeley achieved something quite phenomenal . . . adorable music. The 'toons' were quite as catchy as any from this particular factory. If you are not whistling *Do I Hear You* ere long, well, I don't hear you, and if you are not making a pest of yourself with *You Took Advantage of Me*—well, I'll eat my hat and I'm not hungry for chapeau food . . ."

Burns Mantle—*New York Daily News*
". . . amusing in the rough way, not too blarey, never silly, always lively with the high spirits of heel-cracking youth, and charmingly pictured. Its model is *Good News* . . . the music, with two or three song hits, is lilting and pleasant. The lyrics have wit and sanity to commend them . . . altogether, a highly satisfactory entertainment . . ."

E. W. Osborn—*New York Evening World*
". . . the tunefulest, the danciest, the fastest and the most colorful musical show of many a day . . ."

Katharine Zimmerman—*New York Telegram*
". . . a lusty, breezy, jubilant affair, with happy airs, snappy dances, and scores of pretty maids all in a row . . . the tunes will be leaping down your superheterodyne for many moons to come . . ."

Gilbert W. Gabriel—*New York Sun*
". . . no masterpiece, that's sure . . . some winning tunes, some fresh and cool Hawaiian stage effects, much vim, a not too careful romance, pretty girls pell-mell and other sure ingredients . . . Call it something of a combination of *Good News* and *Hit the Deck* . . . The Rodgers score serves happily. There is one darling of a tune to the sentiment *You Took Advantage of Me*—with not a single regretful note in it . . . good industrious dashes of lyrics . . ."

John Anderson—*New York Journal*
". . . large, handsome and tuneful . . . It's better, thank heaven, much better than *A Connecticut Yankee* . . . Of the three thirds which make up the show, Mr. Rodgers is easily seven-eights of the net result. His score is sprightly, graceful and often lovely. *Do I Hear You* promises to stand beside *Thou Swell* on the music racks . . ."

Sid Silverman—*Variety,* May 2, 1928
". . . doesn't indicate smash potentialities, but figures to get away to a fast start . . . Rodgers and Hart, the well known scribbling duo, have contributed their faithful share, although an attentive ear may discern more of interest in the lyrics than in the melodies. Of comedy, there is no abundance . . . *You Took Advantage of Me* and *Do I Hear You* impress as noteworthy assets . . ."

Charles Brackett—*The New Yorker,* May 5, 1928
". . . may be just a lump of paste, but to these sorely tried eyes it looked like the Kohinoor and the Hope diamond mounted together in ruby-studded platinum . . . The score is corking, and in *A Kiss for Cinderella,* Hart has written his most amusing lyric so far, which is saying a lot . . ."

George Jean Nathan—*Judge,* May 26, 1928
". . . hardly offers anything to get excited about . . . The book is as dolorous as these song and dance show books usually are, but we have stopped hoping for much in this direction, so we come to the theatre prepared . . ."

Stark Young—*The New Republic,* June 27, 1928
". . . excellent entertainment for occasional playgoers . . . follows hard on the heels of *Hit the Deck* . . . Rodgers' score is without any natural hits, but all of the half dozen or so printed songs are above standard, *You Took Advantage of Me* and *Do I Hear You* are the favorites, but less unusual than *Blue Ocean Blues* . . ."

Tour

Shubert's Detroit Theatre, Detroit, September 3, 1928—Erlanger Theatre, Philadelphia, October 6, 1928 (3 cities).

LEATHERNECKING

(Film Version of "Present Arms"—1930)

A Radio Picture
Produced by Louis Sarecky
Directed by Edward Cline
Screenplay by Jane Murfin
Adaptation by Alfred Jackson
Choreography by Mary Read
Music director, Victor Baravalle
Photographed by J. Roy Hunt

Release Date

September 12, 1930

The Cast

LADY DELPHINE WITHERSPOON, Irene Dunne
FRANK DERRYBERRY, Ken Murray
CHICK EVANS, Eddie Foy, Jr.
HORTENSE MOSSBACK, Louise Fazenda
NED SPARKS, Ned Sparks
EDNA STEVENS, Lilyan Tashman
STEIN, Benny Rubin
MOULIKA, Rita La Roy
DOUGLAS ATWELL, Fred Santley
BARON VON RICHTER, Baron William Brincken

JOHN TILLER'S "SUNSHINE" GIRLS: Mabel Hall, Doris Carter, Alice Wright, Cora Neary, Noreen Callow, Clara Gillett, Florence Stack, Freda Neary, Eileen Grady, Doris Yates, Dolly Mosely, Louise Gillett, Muriel Marlow, Bella Pilling, Queenie Jones, Marjorie Griffiths

Musical Numbers
Songs retained from original production: *You Took Advantage of Me* and *A Kiss for Cinderella.* Songs written specially for film by Harry Akst and Benny Davis: *All My Life, Shake It Off and Smile, Careless Kisses, Evening Star* and *Nice and So Particular.*

Reviews
New York Times
". . . the film's chief virtue is its failure to take itself seriously, and in so doing frolics along to a slapstick beat . . . the general lightness throughout makes it bearable and in spots most entertaining . . ."

Al Greason (Rush.)—*Variety,* September 17, 1930
". . . looks like a very moderate programmer . . . has funny lines and seasoned troupers but the basic comedy situations aren't supplied . . . What is the idea of casting charming, romantic Irene Dunne opposite comedian Eddie Foy Jr., masquerading as a romantic lead? . . ."

John Mosher—*The New Yorker,* September 20, 1930
". . . mediocre . . . doesn't presume to any great lengths, in spite of the urbane presence of Miss Tashman."

CHEE-CHEE

(1928)

A musical play with book by Herbert Fields, adapted from the novel "The Son of the Grand Eunuch" by Charles Petit; music by Richard Rodgers; lyrics by Lorenz Hart.

Presented by Lew Fields
Directed by Alexander Leftwich
Choreography by Jack Haskell
Settings by John Hawkins, Jr.
Costumes by John Booth
Music director, Roy Webb
Orchestrations by Mr. Webb

Tryout
Forrest Theatre, Philadelphia, August 27-September 15, 1928

New York Run
Lew Fields' Mansfield Theatre, September 25-October 20, 1928
31 performances

The Story
Chee-Chee and her husband, Li-Pi Tchou, the son of the Grand Eunuch, flee Peking to avoid his being his father's successor. On the road, they are beset by Tartars, monks and brigands who beat our hero and carry off his wife, but he rescues her. Finally, the Grand Eunuch catches up with his son, and brings him back to be prepared for his high office. However, Li-Li Wee, a friend of Chee-Chee, persuades her husband to kidnap and impersonate the surgeon, so that Li-Pi Tchou might escape.

The Cast
A EUNUCH, Ralph Glover
ANOTHER EUNUCH, Alan Lowe
PRINCE TAO-TEE, *son of His Majesty, the Holy Emperor, Son of Heaven,* Stark Patterson
LI-LI WEE, *daughter of His Excellency, the Grand Eunuch,* Betty Starbuck

LU-PI-SIAO, *the Most Noble and August Grand Eunuch,* George Hassell
MISS SMILE OF A ROSE AT THE DAWNING OF SPRING, Dorothy Roye
LI-PI TCHOU, *son of the Grand Eunuch,* William Williams
CHEE-CHEE, *his Dutiful Wife,* Helen Ford
SAN TOY, George Ali
A VERY NARROW-MINDED OWL, William Griffith
INNKEEPER, Philip Loeb
THE TARTAR CHIEF, George Houston
LEADER OF KHONGHOUSES, Marshall Bradford
RADIANCE AND FELICITY, *a Bronze,* William Griffith
PROFUNDITY AND MEDITATION, *The Grand Prior,* Philip Loeb
HOLY EMPEROR, Ralph Glover
DANCING IDOLS, Masa Sanami, Violetta Aoki
ENSEMBLE: Gloria Raymar, Biddy Boyde, Helen Mirtel, Jean Casewell, Catherine Huth, Ann Mycue, Velma Valentine, Engima Reno, Betty Glass, Betty Shirley, Grace Shipp, Marie Felday, Ruby Poe, Evelyn Hannons, Evelyn Kane, Bunny Moore, Urelda Smith, Pauline Hartman, Helen Sheppard, Gene Byrom, Charles Townsend, Frank White, Robert Davis, Al Birk, Ted White, Jay Lindsay, Paul Jensen, James Dale, Bob Matthews, Buddy Penny, R. P. Hall, Richardson Brown, George Lehrian, Ted Schultz, Eddie Larkin

Musical Numbers

ACT I

SCENE ONE—A CORRIDOR IN THE PALACE OF THE HOLY EMPEROR, SON OF HEAVEN, IN THE VIOLET TOWN OF PEKING
SCENE TWO—THE ROAD TO THE FUTURE
SCENE THREE—A WAYSIDE TAVERN

ACT II

SCENE ONE—A FOREST
SCENE TWO—VISITING DAY AT THE MONASTERY OF THE CELESTIAL CLOUDS
SCENE THREE—THE GALLERY OF TORMENTS
SCENE FOUR—THE PALACE

PROGRAM NOTE: The musical numbers, some of them very short, are so interwoven with the story that it would be confusing for the audience to peruse a complete list. Among the principal musical numbers are:

I Must Love You, CHEE-CHEE and LI-PI TCHOU
Dear, Oh Dear, CHEE-CHEE and LI-PI TCHOU
Moon of My Delight, LI-LI WEE and PRINCE TAO-TEE
Better Be Good to Me, LI-LI WEE and PRINCE TAO-TEE
The Tartar Song, TARTAR CHIEF and CHORUS
Singing a Love Song, TARTAR CHIEF and CHORUS

NOTE: *I Must Love You* has same music as *Send for Me,* and *Singing a Love Song* same as *I Still Believe in You* (both *Simple Simon*).

Reviews

J. Brooks Atkinson—*New York Times*
". . . a splendid surface of extravagant brocades . . . the triumvirate of Fields, Rodgers and Hart seem not to have preserved the animation and the originality of their *Dearest Enemy* and other musicals . . . their most pretentious production and the least entertaining."

Percy Hammond—*New York Herald Tribune*
". . . It seems that there is laughter in mutilation, and sentiment in the threatened demotion of a sturdy barytone into a falsetto tenor . . . as startling an opera as has been presented this season, and I commend it to those who love unprintable situations accompanied by tunes . . ."

St. John Ervine—*New York World*
"*Nasty! Nasty!* . . . there can rarely have been a play so ornately produced to so little effect . . . I did not believe that any act could possibly be duller than the first—until I saw the second . . ."

Pierre de Rohan—*New York American*
". . . a musical comedy without a single stenciled song or a solitary stereotyped situation . . . The lyrics are gems of wit and beauty, surpassing even those of *A Connecticut Yankee* . . ."

Burns Mantle—*New York Daily News*
". . . just the usual musical comedy-humor that emanates from the curbstones and is relished by the crowd for which it is written . . . the music is the most salable feature . . ."

Robert Coleman—*New York Daily Mirror*
". . . a revolutionary musical show . . . the spicy episodes of this amazing musical were rather dull . . . It is tragic, not comic . . . a lovely score, an excellent cast and gorgeous costumes . . . ultra sophisticated song-and-dance fare . . ."

E. W. Osborn—*New York Evening World*
"The most ambitious score in the whole series of Fields-Rodgers-Hart compositions; the most audacious libretto, the most sparkling lyrics . . . a thing of joy to the last of its melody . . . a rousing tale of stage adventure with a finale that was greeted by rousing cheers. And deserved them . . ."

Heywood Broun—*New York Telegram*
". . . Rodgers has never written a better score . . . You will dance many times to *Moon of My Delight* and *Dear, Oh Dear* . . . Before

another spring has ambled in at least a thousand couples will have to come to a decision for no better reason than the fact that somewhere an orchestra was playing *I Must Love You*. And it is haunting enough to cause divorces, too . . . Certainly the plot is novel and it is also brisk . . . All in all, it is excellent entertainment . . ."

Gilbert W. Gabriel—*New York Sun*
". . . Quality, novelty, a merrily made score, and an utterly charming mounting, all are there—and all have to give in at last to its book's own laziness and lack of interest . . . The music is truly ingratiating, often lovely. Much of it comes in short, seemingly extemporaneous spurts . . . But there are also definitely popular numbers, which they bring back often enough to convince you of their tunefulness and memorableness . . . I find Hart's lyrics going in for purposely simple and easier rhymes than he has used before. I like them . . ."

Abel Green—*Variety,* October 3, 1928
". . . For all of its cleverness, for all of its radical departure in operetta construction, for all of its tunefulness of score, it negates its economic opportunity by an unhappy theme . . . Its libretto is decidedly dull, and its unfolding is lethargic and well nigh boresome . . . Musically, it is to be regretted that Rodgers wasted the best score he has ever turned out . . . Hart seems to have been ultra class-conscious, and has striven hard for simplification . . ."

Charles Brackett—*The New Yorker,* October 6, 1928
". . . The music is good . . . The joke of the theme has become pretty tedious before the curtain is up ten minutes, and is practically intolerable before the evening is over . . . During the proceedings, innuendo is rolled to a black grit . . ."

Robert Benchley—*Life,* October 19, 1928
". . . Rodgers' score, to our trained ear, seems to contain some of the loveliest work he has done . . . Hart also is prodigal of delightful lyric ideas . . . Fields, it seems to us, has done his most legitimate piece of libretting . . . May we say that, although we became fairly accustomed to the theme joke, we were not offended by it? Make what you will out of that."

George Jean Nathan—*Judge,* October 20, 1928
". . . aches clumsily to be dirty and succeeds only in being tedious . . . if it were not for several pleasant melodies, the thing would be completely disastrous . . . I am sorry for Rodgers. His work deserves better settings and better human instruments than he is getting, poor fellow."

SPRING IS HERE

(1929)

A musical comedy with book by Owen Davis, adapted from his play, "Shotgun Wedding"; music by Richard Rodgers; lyrics by Lorenz Hart.

Presented by Alex A. Aarons and Vinton Freedley
Directed by Alexander Leftwich
Choreography by Bobby Connolly
Settings by John Wenger
Costumes by Kiviette
Music director, Alfred Newman
Pianists, Victor Arden and Phil Ohman

Tryout
Shubert Theatre, Philadelphia, February 25-March 8, 1929

New York Run
Alvin Theatre, March 11-June 8, 1929
104 performances

The Story
Terry's love for Betty is unrequited, for Betty thinks she loves Stacy. They are on the verge of an elopement, when Betty's father obstructs the way. On the advice of Betty's sister, Mary Jane, Terry sets off on a round of flirtations with other girls that soon makes Betty realize where her heart really lies.

The Cast
EMILY BRALEY, Maidel Turner
MAUDE OSGOOD, Thelma White
MARY JANE, Inez Courtney
STEVE ALDEN, Dick Keene
WILLIE SLADE, Gil Squires
PETER BRALEY, Charles Ruggles
BETTY BRALEY, Lillian Taiz
STACY HAYDON, John Hundley
TERRY CLAYTON, Glenn Hunter
RITA CONWAY, Joyce Barbour
EBEN, Cy Landry
JENNINGS, Lewis Parker

POLICEMAN, Frank Gagen
LADIES OF THE ENSEMBLE: Florence Allen, Louise Allen, Emily Burton, Dorothy Brown, Louise Blakeley, Margery Bailey, Mary Carlton, Billie Cortez, Marion Dixon, Ann Ecklund, Edith Martin, Madeleine Janis, Gladys Kelly, Beth Milton, Vida Manuel, Frances Markey, Lillian Michel, Elsie Neal, Ruby Nevins, Adeline Ogilvie, Wilma Roelof, Kay Stewart, Gladys Travers, Wanda Wood, Beryl Wallace
GENTLEMEN OF THE ENSEMBLE: Ward Arnold, William Cooper, Billy Carver, Frank Gagen, Edwin Gail, Bob Gebhardt, Fred May, Daniel O'Brien, Billy O'Rourke, Victor Pullman, Thomas Sternfeld, Jack Stevens

Musical Numbers

THE ACTION TAKES PLACE AT THE BRALEYS' HOME ON LONG ISLAND

ACT I
SCENE ONE—THE GARDEN
Opening, GUESTS
Spring Is Here, STEVE, MARY JANE and ENSEMBLE
Yours Sincerely, TERRY, BETTY and ENSEMBLE
Finaletto, TERRY, RITA, MARY JANE, SLADE, BETTY, MAUDE and ENSEMBLE

SCENE TWO—THE GARDEN WALL
You Never Say Yes, RITA, SLADE and ENSEMBLE
With a Song in My Heart, BETTY and STACY

SCENE THREE—THE GARDEN
Baby's Awake Now, MARY JANE, MAUDE and GIRLS
Finale, COMPANY

ACT II
SCENE ONE—MAUDE OSGOOD'S BARN DANCE
Opening, ENSEMBLE
Red Hot Trumpet, MAUDE, SLADE and GIRLS
What a Girl, TERRY
Rich Man! Poor Man!, MARY JANE, STEVE and ENSEMBLE
Specialty dance, EBEN

SCENE TWO—BETTY'S BEDROOM
Why Can't I?, BETTY and MARY JANE

SCENE THREE—MORNING ROOM
Reprise, *With a Song in My Heart,* STACY and BETTY
Finale, COMPANY

NOTE: *A Cup of Tea, A Word in Edgeways and The Color of Her Eyes* cut before New York opening.

Reviews

J. Brooks Atkinson—*New York Times*
". . . impudent and endlessly amusing . . . a book more solid than

the usual conventional plot of musical comedy . . . Rodgers' music seems very good, indeed . . . *With a Song in My Heart* is a lovely moonlight serenade."

Arthur Ruhl—*New York Herald Tribune*
". . . a routine musical comedy of the usual type . . . For the most part the book was dull . . . The song *Yours Sincerely* seemed possible to remember, and there was another somewhat more ingenious in its harmonies, *Why Can't I?*, which also caught on. The lyrics were of the usual Broadway pattern—'You need romance, Someone in pants' being characteristic . . ."

Gilbert W. Gabriel—*New York American*
". . . as fragrant and frothing as its name . . . a romp that is funny and lively and exultantly full of youth . . . What's its plot? You *would* ask . . . all very innocent, and a bit knee-pants, but it does serve. The Rodgers and Hart contributions are good musical-comedy currency . . . an impression of vivacity in pretty nearly all the tunes, nimbleness of rhyming . . . The title song and a *Yours Sincerely* and a rhythmic frenzy called *Baby's Awake Now* are probably the winners of the list . . ."

Louis Sobol—*New York Graphic*
". . . a haunting melody with a contagious lyric—*Yours Sincerely,* that should assail your ears from now until next spring. *With a Song in My Heart* is another, and *Rich Man! Poor Man!* still another . . ."

Robert Littell—*New York Post*
". . . something fresh and cheerful about this musical comedy that makes it unlike the others and better than most . . . Either the book or the lyrics and music would alone have made a very pleasant evening . . . Taken together, they give is much more fun, intelligence and melody than one has a right to expect . . . The score was excellent. *With a Song in My Heart, Yours Sincerely* and *Why Can't I?* were perhaps the best, but every bit of the music reminds you that there are only a handful of original talents in these parts and that Rodgers is always one of them . . ."

Bide Dudley—*New York Evening World*
". . . fast moving, youthful, tuneful, hokumish, harum-scarum, beautiful . . . so far as the story is concerned, the piece is lightweight. But do you care? Neither do I . . . Rodgers and Hart have done a good job . . ."

Stephen Rathbun—*New York Sun*
". . . It is a pleasure to report that the words and music seem to be

above even Rodgers and Hart's high average and that the occasional sentimental song was never 'mushy' . . . *Spring is Here* has everything one can require for a very pleasant evening's diversion."

Abel Green—*Variety,* March 13, 1929
". . . a moderate success, but as entertainment it is spotty. It's a summery musical, the first act of which is fair, with a second stanza starting slowly and accelerating to a bright finish . . . The songs will contribute not a little to what measure of moderate success this entry will achieve. They have a good ballad wow in *With a Song in My Heart* . . ."

Charles Brackett—*The New Yorker,* March 23, 1929
". . . contains just the right admixture of youth, horse-play, and lovemaking. The music isn't quite up to that of *Chee-Chee,* but it is far better than most Broadway music . . ."

Wilder Hobson—*Time,* March 25, 1929
". . . intelligent lyrics, and a book by Owen Davis who makes up with situations what amusement he fails to supply in the conversation."

George Jean Nathan—*Judge,* April 6, 1929
". . . in the way of book, music and dancing, the show is surely nothing to get excited about. Yet somehow it entertained this august professor while he was lending his handsome and distinguished presence to its first night performance . . . a leading girl, by name Taiz, rather fetches me . . . one fairly good tune by Rodgers, though his score is the poorest he has turned out in a long time . . ."

O. O. McIntyre—*Life,* April 12, 1929
". . . one of the best musicals of 1929 . . . This is Mr. Hunter's first time in musical comedy and he talks his songs, which is my idea of how most men should sing . . . The show would furnish an enjoyable evening without him, but candidly, for some reason or other, it is far better with him."

SPRING IS HERE

(Film Version—1930)

A First National-Vitaphone Picture
Directed by John Francis Dillon
Screenplay by James A. Starr
Photographed by Lee Garmes

Release Date
July 20, 1930

The Cast
TERRY CLAYTON, Alexander Gray
BETTY BRALEY, Bernice Claire
STEVE ALDEN, Lawrence Gray
MARY JANE, Inez Courtney
STACY HAYDON, Frank Albertson
PETER BRALEY, Ford Sterling
RITA CLAYTON, Natalie Moorhead
EMILY BRALEY, Louise Fazenda
MAUDE OSGOOD, Gretchen Thomas

Musical Numbers
Songs retained from original production: *Spring Is Here; Yours Sincerely* and *With a Song in My Heart.* Songs written for film by Harry Warren, Sam Lewis and Joe Young: *Crying for the Carolines* and *Have a Little Faith in Me.*

NOTE: In 1933, the Vitaphone Corp. released a 2-reel film version of *Spring Is Here* called *Yours Sincerely,* as part of its "Broadway Brevities" series. It was directed by Roy Mack and starred Lanny Ross. The above-listed songs were retained.

HEADS UP!

(1929)

A musical comedy with book by John McGowan and Paul Gerard Smith; music by Richard Rodgers; lyrics by Lorenz Hart.

Presented by Alex A. Aarons and Vinton Freedley
Directed and choreographed by George Hale
Settings by Donald Oenslager
Costumes by Kiviette
Music director, Alfred Newman
Orchestrations by Robert Russell Bennett
Pianist, Phil Ohman

Tryout
(known as "Me for You"; book by Owen Davis)
Shubert Theatre, Detroit, September 15-28, 1929
(known as "Heads Up!")
Shubert Theatre, Philadelphia, October 25-November 2, 1929

New York Run
Alvin Theatre, November 11, 1929-March 15, 1930
144 performances

The Story
Unknown to the Trumbells, their yacht is being used as a rum runner by Denny, the ship's captain. Jack Mason, a Coast Guard officer and Mary Trumbell's beloved, uncovers the smuggling venture, whereupon Denny sets the yacht afire and is finally apprehended.

The Cast
MARTHA TRUMBELL, Janet Velie
PEGGY PRATT, Alice Boulden
REX CUTTING, John Hundley
LARRY WHITE, John Hamilton
BETTY BOYD, Betty Starbuck
GEORGIE, Ray Bolger
"SKIPPY" DUGAN, Victor Moore
CAPTAIN DENNY, Robert Gleckler

MARY TRUMBELL, Barbara Newberry
JACK MASON, Jack Whiting
JAMES CLARKE, Lewis Parker
BOB and HARRY, Atlas and LaMarr
CARSON, Louis Delgado
DILLON, Richard Macaleese
HANSON, Chester Bree
GLADYS and HELEN, Reynolds Sisters
LADIES OF THE ENSEMBLE: Gene Brady, Margery Bailey, Margot Bazin, Helen Collins, Catherine Cathcart, Violet Carson, Alvina Carson, Chris Cane, Helen Doyle, Ann Echlund, Eleanor Etheridge, Fay Greene, Ruth Gordon, Gypsy Hollis, Eva Hart, Pat Hamill, Rita Jason, Clara Larinova, Muriel Lawler, Helen Lee, Jane Lane, Betty Morton, Elsie Neal, Clarita Nash, Lylie Olive, Helen Reinecke, Ruth Sato, Amy Weber, Wanda Wood, Paulette Winston, Grace Wright, Geraldine Pratt, Mary Kerr.
GENTLEMEN OF THE ENSEMBLE: Jerry Cushman, Hal Clyne, Louis Delgado, Bob Derden, Jack Fago, Harry Griffin, Bob Gebhardt, Tommy Jordan, Al Jordan, Lewis Parker, Jack Ross, George Rand, Bob Spencer, Edoard Gates, Charles McGrath, William Cooper, Fran Heyser, Chester Breen, Gordon Clark, Bud Tipton, Ben White, Richard Macaleese, LeRoy Kent, Paul Jensen, George Meyer

Musical Numbers

ACT I

SCENE ONE—THE GARDEN OF MRS. TRUMBELL'S HOME , NEW LONDON
You've Got to Surrender, ENSEMBLE
Play Boy, GEORGIE and ENSEMBLE

SCENE TWO—THE DOCK
Mother Grows Younger, MARTHA, MARY and CADETS
Why Do You Suppose?, MARY, JACK and GIRLS

SCENE THREE—"SKIPPY'S" GALLEY ABOARD THE "SILVER LADY"
Me for You, BETTY and GEORGIE
Reprise, *Why Do You Suppose?,* MARY and JACK

SCENE FOUR—THE YACHT CLUB
Ongsay and Anceday, GLADYS, HELENE and IRLSGAY
It Must Be Heaven, MARY and JACK
My Man Is on the Make, PEGGY and CHORUS; danced by BOB and HARRY

ACT II

SCENE ONE—THE WATERFRONT
The Lass Who Loved a Sailor, BETTY and SAILORS
A Ship Without a Sail, JACK and SAILORS

SCENE TWO—HEADQUARTERS OF UNITED STATES COAST GUARD, NEW LONDON

SCENE THREE—ABOARD THE "SILVER LADY"
Reprise, *Why Do You Suppose?*, MARY
Knees, PEGGY, GEORGIE and GIRLS
Reprise, *My Man Is on the Make,* PEGGY and GIRLS

SCENE FOUR—AN ISLAND

SCENE FIVE—MRS. TRUMBELL'S HOME
Specialty, BOB and HARRY; GLADYS and HELENE
Finale, COMPANY

NOTE: *Sky City, As Though You Were There* and *I Can Do Wonders With You* cut before New York opening. *Why Do You Suppose?* has same music as *How Was I to Know?* (cut from *She's My Baby*).

Reviews

New York Times
". . . a fairly lively diversion . . . the new tunes are worth a hearing . . . Mr. Hart's lyrics appear to be a concession to tin pan alley, neither so sophisticated nor tricky as they have been in the past . . . the whole production is quite tastefully turned out."

Arthur Ruhl—*New York Herald Tribune*
". . . a coherent and amusing book . . . plenty of real fun and a thoroughly capable cast . . . Rodgers' music was always pleasant, and in the frequently repeated *Why Do You Suppose?*, he and Mr. Hart achieved one of those rare things—a theme song which was as sophisticated in its biology as taking in its tune . . . a first-class entertainment . . ."

Finlay Peter Dunne, Jr.—*New York World*
". . . no departure from the common herd but, thanks above all to the charming score, a very pleasant evening may be had even by the world-weary . . ."

Gilbert W. Gabriel—*New York American*
". . . for speed and adroitness of choral work, for rollicking fun, and for imaginative direction, it will be hard to excel . . . Hart continues the monosyllabic course he set for himself a year ago when he escaped from complicated rhyming to make a more popular appeal. But he does not sacrifice cleverness for simplicity. On the other hand, the music of Rodgers aims more for unusual effects than for crowd appeal . . ."

John Chapman—*New York Daily News*
". . . In addition to Victor Moore at his funniest, it has some very distinguished musical-comedy material—a good-looking chorus, the tomboy monkeyshines of Betty Starbuck, Richard Rodgers

tunes, and Alice Boulden's pep . . . The tunes are lilting and melodious and two of them—*Why Do You Suppose?* and *A Ship Without a Sail*—are destined for repetition . . ."

William G. King—*New York Post*
". . . two and a half hours of such entertainment as Broadway rarely has a chance to enjoy . . . an almost perfect thing of its kind . . . gay, sophisticated, colorful and funny, and, above all, gorgeously tuneful . . . a half-dozen songs that are as good as Rodgers and Hart have ever done, and in *Why Do You Suppose?*, they have surpassed their own brilliant achievements of the past . . ."

Bide Dudley—*New York Evening World*
". . . a lively show . . . It's all fun, frolic, action, girls and tunes, and the mixture is one that should drive away a lot of blues by the time Little New Year has cut two or three teeth . . . catchy music . . ."

Robert Garland—*New York Telegram*
". . . enjoyed it tremendously . . . a melodious score and not too self-conscious lyrics . . . *Why Do You Suppose?* is easy to remember, but another song, *My Man Is on the Make,* is a better piece of music . . ."

Robert Benchley—*The New Yorker,* November 13, 1929
". . . the first real musical of the season in which the characters might not all be sisters and cousins of Chester Alan Arthur, and it certainly seems good to let out a good Broadway guffaw again . . . that justly busy team of Rodgers and Hart have furnished some very nice numbers . . ."

Jack Pulaski (Ibee.)—*Variety,* November 13, 1929
". . . pleasing musical entertainment. Perhaps it will not rate with the actual leaders in its field, but it is tastefully and colorfully presented . . . Easily the best song is *Why Do You Suppose?* Runner up is *My Man Is on the Make* . . ."

Frank Sullivan—*New York World,* November 14, 1929
". . . I am telling people frankly that I liked the show. I speak at some length on Rodgers' score, especially *A Ship Without a Sail,* which is the best song since *Ol' Man River* . . ."

Ralph Barton—*Life,* November 29, 1929
". . . a nice, stupid book, a batch of good hoofers, whistleable music, gaudy costumes, a chorus that can dance like everything, and the best gags of the season. The music is by Richard Rodgers, whose work is far more popular than such good work generally gets to be . . ."

George Jean Nathan—*Judge*, December 7, 1929
". . . some very amusing clowning by Victor Moore and a future popular phonograph record or two, but it follows a general plan too familiar to kick up much excitement . . ."

HEADS UP!

(London—1930)

Adaptation by Lauri Wylie
Directed by Harry Howell

Tryout
King's Theatre, Southsea, April 21-26, 1930

London Run
Palace Theatre, May 1-17, 1930
19 performances

The Cast
MARTHA TRUMBELL, Janet Velie
PEGGY DALE, Polly Ward
REX CUTTING, Jack Hobbs
LARRY WHITE, Cecil Humphreys
BETTY BOYD, Clarice Hardwicke
GEORGIE, Harland Dixon
"SKIPPY" DUGAN, Sydney Howard
CAPTAIN DENNY, Edmund Willard
MARY TRUMBELL, Louise Brown
JACK MASON, Arthur Margetson
JAMES CLARKE, Lennard Walker
TOM and STEVE, Atlas and LaMarr
SPECIALTY DANCER, Audrey Allan

Musical Numbers
Same as original production, except that *Mother Grows Younger* called *Daughter Grows Older.*

Reviews
London Times
". . . The music is often catchy, and the dancing is good, the performers being adept, and the choreography often ingenious . . ."

James Agate—*London Sunday Times,* May 4, 1930
". . . The hero asks the heroine why she supposes the robin has a red breast. Why, he asks, do pussies miaow? I take my oath, as Moses in the old comedy said, that this interrogatory actually happened. The tune which accompanies these imbecilities is weakly pretty, and it is good that it should be so for it is very nearly the only tune in the play. The plot is negligible, and I shall therefore neglect it . . . I would much rather not be asked for a critical opinion upon that which does not call for criticism. To say 'Thank you for a pleasant evening' is so much more gracious."

Ivor Brown—*London Observer,* May 4, 1930
". . . starts slowly and only with difficulty climbs to West End levels . . . The shore scenes are dull; the ozone does everybody good, and the chorus are in far better fettle when they find their sea-legs . . . The music, unlike the cast, does not profit by its sea-change . . ."

Bibliography

"Heads Up!" —*Illustrated Sporting and Dramatic News,* May 24, 1930

HEADS UP!

(Film Version—1930)

A Paramount Picture
Directed by Victor Schertzinger
Screenplay by John McGowan and Jack Kirkland
Choreography by George Hale
Photographed by William Steiner

Release Date

October 12, 1930

The Cast

JACK MASON, Charles "Buddy" Rogers
BETTY TRUMBELL, Helen Kane
"SKIPPY" DUGAN, Victor Moore
MARY TRUMBELL, Margaret Breen
REX CUTTING, Gene Gowing
MRS. TRUMBELL, Helen Carrington
GEORGIE MARTIN, Billy Taylor
CAPTAIN DENNY, Harry Shannon
LARRY WHITE, C. Anthony Hughes
CAPTAIN WHITNEY, John Hamilton

Musical Numbers
Songs retained from original production: *A Ship Without a Sail* and *My Man Is on the Make.*

Reviews
Mordaunt Hall—*New York Times*
". . . the thunder is stolen by Victor Moore . . . the film elicits a good deal of amusement, but the more serious numbers are rather out of place . . ."

Sid Silverman—*Variety,* October 15, 1930
". . . If this one gets above ordinary business anywhere it'll be a surprise and a break . . . rates as undistinguished with a tendency to become too dull too often."

Time, October 27, 1930
". . . has much glitter and is well put together; the main reason for its dullness is that the central role is serious . . ."

Pare Lorentz—*Judge,* November 1, 1930
". . . a dull movie simply because Messrs. Zukor, Lasky, Katz, Schulberg, et al., for some reason or other, think Charles 'Buddy' Rogers more important than a good comedian . . ."

SIMPLE SIMON

(1930)

A musical comedy with book by Ed Wynn and Guy Bolton; music by Richard Rodgers; lyrics by Lorenz Hart.

Presented by Florenz Ziegfeld
Directed by Zeke Colvan
Choreography by Seymour Felix
Settings by Joseph Urban
Artistic director, John Harkrider
Technical director, T. B. McDonald
Music director, Oscar Bradley

Tryout
Colonial Theatre, Boston, January 27-February 15, 1930

New York Run
Ziegfeld Theatre, February 18-June 14, 1930
135 performances

The Story
Although he is the proprietor of a newspaper shop in Coney Island, Simon prefers reading fairy tales to headlines. One night he dreams of Cinderella and her adventures in two kingdoms, Dullna ruled by Bluebeard, and Gayleria ruled by King Cole. The mean Bluebeard tries to capture Cinderella, but she is saved by Prince Charming who has come to her rescue with the aid of the Trojan Horse.

The Cast
BERT BLUE (BLUEBEARD), Paul Stanton
FINGY, *Bluebeard's henchman,* Alfred P. James
JACK HORNER } (JACK and JILL) { Will Ahearn
GILLY FLOWER } (JACK and JILL) { Bobbe Arnst
SIMON, *keeper of the Information and Newspaper Shop,* Ed Wynn
POLICEMAN, Anthony Hughes
ELAINE KING (CINDERELLA), Doree Leslie
OLEE KING (KING COLE), Lennox Pawle
OTTO PRINCE, Hugh Cameron
JONAH (GENII), Master George Offerman

POPPER, Gil White
TONY PRINCE (PRINCE CHARMING), Alan Edwards
SAL, Ruth Etting
JEWEL PEARCE, Helen Walsh
GLADYS DOVE, Hazel Forbes
CAPTAIN IN DULLNA ARMY, Douglas Stanbury
THE HORSE, Joseph Schrode, Pete La Della
THE GIANT HEAD, Frank DeWitt
THE FROG, William Ferry
PREMIERE DANSEUSE, Harriet Hoctor
LITTLE BOY BLUE, Dolores Grant
RED RIDING HOOD, Helen Walsh
THE WOLF, Clementine Rigeau, Elaine Mann
GOLDYLOCKS, Agnes Franey, Virginia McNaughton
PUSS IN BOOTS, Patsy O'Day
HANSEL, Elsie Behrens
GRETEL, Mable Baade
JAZZ, Bobbe Arnst
CAT AND THE FIDDLE, Marie Conway
THE COW, Gladys Pender
THE DOG, Dorothy Patterson
THE DISH, Lois Peck
THE SPOON, Neva Lynn
BO-PEEP, Dolores Grant
OLD LADY IN THE SHOE, Frieda Mierse
MISS MUFFETT, Georgia Payne, Caja Eric
FAIRY GODDESSES, Blanche Satchell, Marion Dodge
SNOW QUEEN, Pirkko Alquist
RAPUNZEL, Hazel Forbes
SNOW WHITE, Harriet Hoctor
LADIES OF THE ENSEMBLE: Caja Eric, Georgia Payne, Vili Milli, Marion Dodge, Helen Walsh, Pirkko Alquist, Frieda Mierse, Blanche Satchell, Neva Lynn, Mildred Ivory, Dolores Grant, Marie Conway, Mary Coyle, Elsie Behrens, Patsy O'Day, Elaine Mann, Mable Baade, Gladys Pender, Dorothy Patterson, Cleo Cullen, Clementine Rigeau, Agnes Franey, Virginia McNaughton, Lois Peck, Hazel Forbes
GENTLEMEN OF THE ENSEMBLE: Messrs. Roberts, Edwards, Fowler, Siegel, Uray, Sager, Doctoroff, Mandes, Butterworth, Lewis, Hervey, Costello, Simmons, Hall, Carswell, White, Barry

NOTE: During Boston tryout, SAL played by Lee Morse. For tour, Miss Etting succeeded by Wini Shaw.

Musical Numbers

ACT I

SCENE ONE—CONEY ISLAND
Coney Island, GIRLS, BOYS, BARKERS, DANCERS
Don't Tell Your Folks, JACK and JILL

SCENE TWO—FERRYMEN ALLEY
Magic Music, JILL and MAGIC GIRLS
I Still Believe in You, SAL
Send for Me, ELAINE, TONY and GIRLS

SCENE THREE—BOUNDARY LINE BETWEEN DULLNA AND GAYLERIA
Dull and Gay, CAPTAIN and VERA

SCENE FOUR—HUNTING ROOM IN KING COLE'S PALACE
Sweetenheart, JACK and JILL
Hunting the Fox, LEADER OF THE HUNT AND HUNTERS
Hunting Ballet, PREMIERE DANSEUSE, TOE DANCERS and SHOW GIRLS

SCENE FIVE—FOREST AT CHRISTMAS
Mocking Bird, SIMON
Finaletto, COMPANY

SCENE SIX—FAIRYLAND
I Love the Woods, GIRLS

SCENE SEVEN—IN THE CLOUDS

ACT II
SCENE ONE—CORNER DRUGSTORE IN DULLVILLE
On With the Dance, DRUGSTORE GIRLS

SCENE TWO—OUTSIDE THE WALLED CITY
I Can Do Wonders With You, CINDERELLA and PRINCE
Ten Cents a Dance, SAL
In Your Chapeau, SIMON
Roping, SIMON and JACK

SCENE THREE—THE KISSING FOREST
Kissing Forest Ballet, PREMIERE DANSEUSE and DANCERS

SCENE FOUR—INSIDE THE CITADEL OF KING OTTO'S PALACE
The Trojan Horse, KING OTTO'S SOLDIERS

SCENE FIVE—FERRYMEN ALLEY
Rags and Tatters, VAGABOND and BOYS

SCENE SIX—THE MAGIC HALL
Cottage in the Country, COMPANY

NOTE: *Dancing on the Ceiling* and *He Was Too Good to Me* cut before New York opening. *I Still Believe in You, I Can Do Wonders With You, In Your Chapeau* and *The Trojan Horse* dropped in April. *I Want That Man* (sung by JILL), *Happy Days and Lonely Nights* (music by Fred Fisher; lyric by Billy Rose) (sung by SAL), *Love Me or Leave Me* (music by Walter Donaldson; lyric by Gus Kahn) (sung by SAL) added in April. *I Want That Man* dropped in May. *Happy Days and Lonely Nights* dropped for tour, and replaced by *I'm Yours* (music by Johnny Green; lyric by E. Y. Harburg). *Bluebeard's Beard* and *Peter Pan* also added for tour. *I Still Believe in You* has same music as *Singing a Love Song,* and *Send for Me* same as *I Must Love You* (both *Chee-Chee*).

Reviews

J. Brooks Atkinson—*New York Times*

". . . vast, though unsteady . . . Ed Wynn has never seemed so indisputably great . . . Rodgers, who is a maker of dapple melodies, echoes his style without improving it, although Hart has written lyrics more sprightly than the tunes that carry them . . . a production lacking the stately flow of the best Ziegfeld shows . . ."

Arthur Ruhl—*New York Herald Tribune*

". . . a large, radiant and altogether attractive show, skillfully compounded of generous portions of what the public wants . . . Mr. Wynn is almost a whole show in himself."

Robert Littell—*New York World*

". . . except for a few bright spots and all moments when Ed Wynn is on the stage, it is by no means the best show that Ziegfeld has given us. It has Lorenz Hart lyrics, to be sure, and some nice tunes, but the book is often dull . . ."

Gilbert W. Gabriel—*New York American*

"*Superlatively Fanciful, Colorful and Innocent* . . . a Ziegfeld show up to the hilt—and to the first and last hurrah . . . that gracious song, *Send for Me,* is given you over and over again until you go home with it curled like silvery cigarette smoke through your memory . . ."

Burns Mantle—*New York Daily News*

". . . Ed Wynn is home and, so far as I'm concerned, all's right with the world . . . *Ten Cents a Dance* is particularly effective . . . The score is Rodgers and Hart in pleasant but not inspired form . . ."

Walter Winchell—*New York Daily Mirror*

". . . lyrics fall easily on the ears, and Rodgers revived some of his better melodies, particularly *Send for Me* . . . *Simple Simon* is another of the Ziegfeld delights, and is all the richer because of Ed Wynn, Harriet Hoctor and Ruth Etting . . ."

Gilbert Seldes—*New York Graphic*

". . . apart from *Send for Me,* the score seems rather ordinary . . . I regret the missed opportunity to make it also a beautiful production, but my regret is not particularly poignant. Given Ed Wynn I didn't much care about anything else."

John Mason Brown—*New York Post*

". . . a very grim fairy tale . . . negligible in its music and lyrics . . . Above everything, it is sadly in want of a book . . . a cumbersome and over intricate affair which is constantly getting in its own way . . . Mr. Wynn's presence will doubtless prove sufficiently persuasive to make audiences tolerant of the uncertain pleasures of the evening as a whole . . ."

Charles Darnton—*New York Evening World*
". . . gives the great clown his greatest extravaganza . . . something individual, something bearing the real Ziegfeld stamp . . . Received like a present!"

Richard Lockridge—*New York Sun*
"Ziegfeld has perhaps never produced a musical extravaganza which held more to delight the eye . . . Mr. Wynn, when given the slightest chance, is delightful . . . the purchase of a few good jokes and extensive cutting in the first act would leave it a show about which it would be easy to fall even further into superlatives . . . The music and lyrics are at no time particularly memorable . . ."

Jack Pulaski (Ibee.)—*Variety,* February 26, 1930
". . . good entertainment, and will pull down big money for a time. That it will measure up to some of the other shows in the length of run at this house is questionable . . . The hit number is *Send for Me* . . ."

Robert Benchley—*The New Yorker,* March 1, 1930
". . . a Mother Goose story of such banality as to affront even the children for which it is written, and a series of some of the highest-pensioned gags in the G.A.R. . . . And yet under the benign touch of Ed Wynn, the whole thing becomes a riot of rich comedy. It is positively legerdemain . . . Rodgers and Hart, by delving slightly into their files, have assembled a pot-pourri of pleasant tunes . . ."

Time, March 8, 1930
". . . Ruth Etting, a pensive blonde, sings one of the best tunes Rodgers and Hart ever wrote—*I Still Believe in You.* Children will enjoy *Simple Simon;* their elders may profitably join them."

George Jean Nathan—*Judge,* March 15, 1930
". . . Wynn is certainly a good clown . . . a beautiful show . . . for all the weakness of the music and periodic humorlessness of the book, it provides an evening worth every cent they charge you . . ."

Tour

Shubert Theatre, Newark, October 13, 1930—Shubert Theatre, Boston, April 18, 1931 (14 cities).

EVER GREEN

(London—1930)

A musical comedy with book by Benn W. Levy, based on an idea by Richard Rodgers and Lorenz Hart; music by Mr. Rodgers; lyrics by Mr. Hart.

Presented by Charles B. Cochran
Directed by Frank Collins
Choreography by Buddy Bradley and Billy Pierce
Settings mostly by Ernst Stern
Costumes mostly by Reville, Ltd.
Music director, Richard Crean
Orchestrations by Robert Russell Bennett

Tryout
King's Theatre, Glasgow, October 13-November 15, 1930

London Run
Adelphi Theatre, December 3, 1930-July 11, 1931
254 performances

The Story
To help further her stage career, Harriet Green, with the aid of her friend, Mary Tucket, passes herself off as a woman of sixty, preserved by her own special cosmetics. The ruse works (Harriet's mother is even accepted as her daughter), and she becomes a great success in Paris. Complications arise when Harriet and a young singer, Tommy Thompson, fall in love, though they break up because of his concern about the disparity in their ages. By revealing the truth from the stage, Harriet succeeds in winning over her public and winning back Tony.

The Cast
THE CHAIRMAN, Edward Irwin
MARY TUCKET, Joyce Barbour
HARRIET GREEN, Jessie Matthews
MISS LINDFIELD, Iris Browne
MISS CHELTENHAM, Madeline Gibson
MRS. PLATTER, Jean Cadell

MAJOR SACK, Aubrey Dexter
MR. OPENSHAW, W. E. C. Jenkins
MRS. OPENSHAW, Florence Wood
MRS. SACK, Christine Jensen
MR. TOLLEY, Claude Newman
A FLAPPER, Jean Bamberger
ERIC MERIVALE, Albert Burdon
TOMMY THOMPSON, Sonnie Hale
A CHAUFFEUR, Cyril Wells
SAINT-DIDIER, Leon Morton
ALBERT, Aubrey Dexter
DOLLY, Kay Hammond
ESME, W. E. C. Jenkins
NERO, George Child
GENTILLI, Aubrey Dexter
AN ENGLISHMAN, Val Gully
THE STRANGER, Edward Irwin
THE PIANIST, Jack Clark
MR. COCHRAN'S YOUNG LADIES: Margaret Braithwaite, Iris Browne, Hylda Burdon, Ann Barberova, Towyna Thomas, Eileen Clifton, Roma Darrell, Peggy de Reske, Gladys Godby, Mina Hillman, Kathleen Joyce, Florita Fey, Marie Masters, Bunty Pain, Pearl Rivers, Dorothie Willard
MR. COCHRAN'S YOUNG GENTLEMEN: George Bowler, Philip Clarke, Tom Carlisle, Peter Crawford, Jimmy Cameron, Warren Dalmayne, William Gleeson, Stephen Adeson, Cyril Wells, Claude Newman, Terry Rendle, Arthur Smeddles, William Rolston, D. A. Ellis
JOHN TILLER GIRLS: Hilda Partridge, Muriel McArthur, Olive Crane, Phyllis Nelson, Ivy Halstead, Kathleen Eaton, Enid Willshaw, Sylvia Thorne, Necia Belmore, Renee Brighton, Phyllis Hooper, Iris O'Sullivan, Rai Rhome, Olive Stevenson, Rita Cameron, Betty Birch

Musical Numbers

ACT I

SCENE ONE—THE ALBERT HALL, LONDON
Harlemania, MISS CHELTENHAM

SCENE TWO (Settings by G. E. Calthrop)
(a) AT THE SEASIDE
(b) MRS. PLATTER'S BOARDING ESTABLISHMENT
Doing a Little Clog Dance, ERIC and TOMMY
Dear, Dear, HARRIET and TOMMY

SCENE THREE (Settings by Marc Henri and Laverdet)
(a) EXTERIOR OF THE CASINO DES FOLIES, PARIS
(b) REHEARSAL AT THE CASINO DES FOLIES
Nobody Looks at the Man, TOMMY
Waiting for the Leaves to Fall, ERIC

SCENE FOUR—INTERIOR OF A TENT AT NEUILLY FAIR, PARIS
No Place but Home, TOMMY and HARRIET

SCENE FIVE—EXTERIOR OF THE TENT
The Lion King, TOMMY

SCENE SIX—NEUILLY FAIR

SCENE SEVEN (Settings by Marc Henri and Laverdet; costumes by Ada Peacock)
(a) EXTERIOR OF THE CASINO DES FOLIES
(b) PERFORMANCE OF A REVUE AT THE CASINO DES FOLIES (also c and d)
LA COMMÈRE, Mabel Couper
LE COMPÈRE, W. E. C. Jenkins
Quand Notre Vieux Monde Etait Tout Neuf (When the Old World Was New), LA COMMÈRE

(c) "THE NEW MASTER"
LE COMPÈRE, W. E. C. Jenkins
MR. SMITH, Albert Burdon
MME. ROBERT, *the Head Mistress,* Leon Morton
MUNDY, Kay Hammond
KATHLYN, Eileen Clifton
ALICE, Pearl Rivers
SCHOOL GIRLS, Mina Hillman, Kathleen Joyce, Decilla Mowbray, Madeline Gibson
MAID, Sara Sample

(d) FINALE—"LA SYTHÈSE DE LA BELLE DE SOIXANTE ANS"
DANCERS, Carlos, Chita and Company
L'INNOCENCE DU PREMIER AGE, Jay Loder
LA NAIVETÉ DE L'ENFANCE, Clarice Rudge
LE DEUX DEMOISELLES D'HONNEUR, Dilly Swinburne, Elizabeth
L'ÉCLAT DES VINGT ANS, Felicity Seddon
LA RESERVE DE LA FIANCÉE, Billy Schofield
LES DEUX DEMOISELLES D'HONNEUR, Dilly Swinburne, Elizabeth Corcoran
LA PASSION DE TRENTE ANS, Ena Burrell
LA VOLUPTÉ DES QUARANTE ANS, Sara Sample
LE SAGESSE DE LA MATURITÉ, Gladys Sammut
LES EXTRAVAGANCES, Molly Shannon
LES ESCORTES, Mr. Cochran's Young Gentlemen
LA BELLE DE SOIXANTE ANS, Jessie Matthews
SES VERTUS ET SES VICES, Mr. Cochran's Young Ladies
SES VANITIES, John Tiller Girls
La Femme a Toujours Vingt Ans! (Lovely Woman's Ever Young), LE COMPÈRE

ACT II
SCENE ONE—CATALONIA, SPAIN DURING THE FESTA MAJOR (music arranged by Pedro Morales; setting by Gustavo Bacarisis; costumes by Mr. Bacarisis, Doris Zinkeisen and Reville, Ltd.)

Sardana Dance, MR. COCHRAN'S YOUNG LADIES AND GENTLEMEN
The Colour of Her Eyes, ERIC and MRS. PLATTER
In the Cool of the Evening, MARY

SCENE TWO—HARRIET GREEN'S BEDROOM IN HER HOTEL IN PARIS (settings by G. E. Calthrop; costumes by Doris Zinkeisen and Reville, Ltd.)
Dancing on the Ceiling, HARRIET and TOMMY
Je M'en Fiche du Sex Appeal!, SAINT-DIDIER

SCENE THREE—AT THE CABARET DE L'ABBAYE
Hot Blues, danced by Jean Barry and Dave Fitzgibbon
Impromptu Song, TOMMY

SCENE FOUR—HARRIET GREEN'S DRESSING ROOM AT THE CASINO DES FOLIES
If I Give in to You, MARY and ERIC

SCENE FIVE (settings by Marc Henri and Laverdet; costumes by Ada Peacock)
(a) EXTERIOR OF THE CASINO DES FOLIES
(b) FINALE OF A REVUE AT THE CASINO DES FOLIES—"THE MOON AND THE STARS"
LA COMMÈRE, Mabel Couper
LE COMPÈRE, W. E. C. Jenkins
LA VOIE LACTÉE, Mr. Cochran's Young Ladies
LES ETOILES FILANTES, John Tiller Girls
VENUS, Clarice Rudge
LA COMÊTE, Dilly Swinburne
SATURNE, Billy Schofield
MARS, Molly Luck
URANUS, Molly Shannon
LA VIERGE, Elizabeth Corcoran
NEPTUNE, Sara Sample
CASTOR, Felicity Seddon
POLLUX, Gladys Sammut
L'ETOILE POLAIRE, Ena Burrell
JUPITER, Jay Loder
LA LUNE, Jessie Matthews
(c) BEHIND THE CURTAIN

Reviews
London Times
". . . really a revue with something like a narrative linking the different episodes . . . The story has a delicious impudence of its own . . . The spectacle is the chief charm of the entertainment . . ."

E. K.—*London Daily Telegraph*
". . . not lacking in surprises, colour and spectacle . . . Of Mr. Rodgers' entirely unpretentious score, I can only say that two or

three numbers struck me as neater and better-invented than the average, as also are some of Mr. Hart's lyrics . . ."

S. R. Littlewood—*London Morning Post*
"It is a splendid and indeed wonderful show, set round a nasty story and a witless 'book' and with one episode which the Censor should obviously and immediately suppress—if his office is to justify its existence . . . The music is agreeable without being very memorable . . ."

London News-Chronicle
". . . a great show and the music is bright and haunting . . ."

London Daily Mirror
". . . a clever blend of musical comedy and revue . . . several 'sure-fire' hit songs . . . Bravo, Mr. Cochran!"

Philip Page—*London Evening Standard*
". . . one of the loveliest entertainments I have ever seen . . . The music is tuneful (except that of a cacophonous stage band) and there are a couple of catchy duets. *Ever Green* is something new, something interesting, and something amazingly efficient."

James Agate—*London Sunday Times,* December 7, 1930
"To pretend that this lovely thing is a musical comedy is to evade truth, since Mr. Cochran's latest sophistication takes after its inept model about as little or as much as Man resembles his first progenitor . . . the whole show brilliantly captures the note and spirit of Paris . . . an entertainment so all-absorbing that I have no notion of what the new theatre looks like."

Ivor Brown—*London Observer,* December 7, 1930
"*Ever Green* was, as they say of race-horses, 'much expected.' There had been some trouble at the starting-post, but, once released for its run, it went off in the grand manner. To be present at the first night was to have the feeling that the new Adelphi is the Ascot of musical shows. The entertainment is a gorgeous spendthrift, proudly processional, and a notable grandee of its kind. It has a peacock's majesty of fine feathers, yet pirouettes with ease and grace upon the revolving stage . . . two or three tunes will captivate . . ."

Punch
"Mr. Cochran's Mixed Grill, by Musical Comedy out of Revue, should be a stayer. It is undoubtably a fast horse . . . The best of *Ever Green* is the best that Mr. Cochran has yet given us . . . Wherever the piece failed—it wasn't a piece, of course, but a mosaic of pieces—it was because the thread wore thin or broke . . ."

Henry Sherek—*The Sphere,* December 13, 1930
". . . the music and the lyrics are very good, for there are at least three numbers which will be heard everywhere. The best of these is *Dancing on the Ceiling* . . . Altogether, it is the most entertaining, amusing and thrilling musical show I have ever seen. . . ."

"Trunculo"—*The Tatler,* December 17, 1930
". . . a life-size marionette show for an audience of sophisticated giants. To mortals of normal stature, two eyes and as many senses are inadequate. It is a peep-show, a kaleidoscope, a merry-go-round, a miracle, all Hollywood and all Heaven . . . *Dear, Dear* is one of the three best ditties of the evening. The others are *No Place but Home,* ordinary but catchy, and *Dancing on the Ceiling,* original and insinuating . . ."

J.T. Grein—*The Sketch*
". . . the brain reels at the reminiscence of such splendours, such quivering humanity, such a whirligig of principals, chorus and producers, all set in motion by a magic wand. And then there is music, music mercifully discreet, far from the all-too-violent vagaries of jazz; here and there melodious, always joyous, English music too, with a little air of raciness . . ."

Theatre World, February, 1931
". . . Mr. Cochran's finest achievement to date, providing a feast of spectacle, wit, melody and dancing . . ."

Bibliography

"Ever Green" —*New York Times,* December 21, 1930

"Ever Green" (cover story) —*Play Pictorial,* January 1, 1931

EVERGREEN

(Film Version—1934)

A Gaumont British Picture
Produced by Michael Balcon
Directed by Victor Saville
Screenplay by Marjorie Gaffney and Emlyn Williams
Choreography by Buddy Bradley
Art director, Alfred Junge
Music director, Louis Levy
Photographed by Glen MacWilliams
Editor, Ian Dalrymple

British Release Date
June 7, 1934

U.S. Release Date
January 10, 1935

The Story
To help further her stage career and at the urging of boy friend-publicist Tommy Thompson, Harriet Green passes herself off as her own mother, an Edwardian star who had disappeared twenty-odd years before. The ruse works (even though Tommy is mistaken for her son), and she becomes a great success in London. However, Harriet's father threatens blackmail, which only spurs her to reveal the truth from the stage. She is jeered, then cheered—and even cleared in court.

The Cast
HARRIET GREEN }
HARRIET GREEN, JR. } Jessie Matthews
LESLIE BENN, Sonnie Hale
MAUDIE, LADY SHROPSHIRE, Betty Balfour
TOMMY THOMPSON, Barry MacKay
MARQUIS OF STAINES, Ivor MacLaren
GEORGE TREADWELL, Hartley Power
LORD SHROPSHIRE, Patrick Ludlow
MRS. HAWKES, Betty Shale

Musical Numbers
Songs retained from original production: *If I Give in to You, Dear, Dear* and *Dancing on the Ceiling.* Songs written for film by Harry M. Woods: *When You've Got a Little Springtime in Your Heart, Tinkle, Tinkle, Tinkle, Just By Your Example,* and *Over My Shoulder.* Other songs in film: *Daddy Wouldn't Buy Me a Bow-Wow* (by Joseph Tabrar), *I Wouldn't Leave My Little Wooden Hut for You.*

Reviews
London Times
". . . Without any ragged edges or abrupt changes of technique, it flows rather more smoothly than the majority of musical comedies on the stage . . ."

Andre Sennwald—*New York Times*
". . . the most pleasurable musical comedy yet offered us by the ambitious British screen industry. Both in its suave and expert technique and in its superb Rodgers and Hart songs, this film is a considerable joy . . . A joyous and captivating nymph, Jessie Matthews is the female counterpart of Fred Astaire . . ."

Richard Watts, Jr.—*New York Herald Tribune*
". . . the film displays Miss Matthews' talents in just about the best and liveliest of the London girl-and-music carnivals . . . The music is one of the brightest features of the sometimes stolid *Evergreen* . . ."

William Boehnel—*New York World-Telegram*
". . . The music, though pretty, is a trifle dull and the advance of the story is rather slow. But the settings are opulent and there is Miss Matthews. Thanks to her, it becomes tolerable enough song-and-dance entertainment."

Wolfe Kaufman—*Variety,* January 15, 1935
". . . not a strong musical, but it is good enough to get attention in spots and ought to do moderate business . . ."

John Mosher—*The New Yorker,* January 19, 1935
". . . would indicate that the English movie people have had an eye on our Hollywood musical productions . . . Their study has been, perhaps, a little too academic, for there is a lack of genuine sprightliness or freshness in the whole affair . . . manages to include some slightly droll *contretemps* and some fair tunes."

Penelope Gilliatt—*The New Yorker,* May 5, 1973
". . . an endearing musical . . . Jessie Matthews danced ravishingly . . . *Evergreen* has real charm, vivacity and gayness about it; not the biting wit of Lubitsch, but something silly and sweet."

AMERICA'S SWEETHEART

(1931)

A musical comedy with book by Herbert Fields; music by Richard Rodgers; lyrics by Lorenz Hart.

Presented by Laurence Schwab and Frank Mandel
Production supervision and choreography by Bobby Connolly
Book directed by Monty Woolley
Settings by Donald Oenslager
Costumes by Charles LeMaire
Music director, Alfred Newman
Orchestrations by Robert Russell Bennett

Tryout

Shubert Theatre, Pittsburgh, January 19-24, 1931
National Theatre, Washington, January 26-31, 1931
Shubert Theatre, Newark, February 2-7, 1931

New York Run

Broadhurst Theatre, February 10-June 6, 1931
135 performances

The Story

Michael and Geraldine come to Hollywood from St. Paul to become film stars, vowing never to separate. Geraldine soon becomes a success, while Michael is left struggling. This situation does not help their romance, but with the coming of talkies, Michael at last becomes a star. However, it is now Geraldine who must struggle, but love conquers all.

The Cast

S. A. DOLAN, *General Manager of Premier Pictures,* John Sheehan
LARRY PITMAN, *of the Comedy Films,* Gus Shy
MADGE FARRELL, *his partner,* Inez Courtney
MICHAEL PERRY, *from St. Paul,* Jack Whiting
GERALDINE MARCH, *also from St. Paul,* Harriette Lake (Ann Sothern)
DENISE TOREL, *an important star,* Jeanne Aubert
PAULA, *a movie actress,* Vera Marsh
DORITH, *a movie actress,* Dorothy Dare

LOTTIE, *a waitress,* Sue Moore
MISS MULLIGAN, *a secretary,* Virginia Bruce
TELEPHONE OPERATOR, Alice Burrage
DOLORES, Francetta Malloy
A STENOGRAPHER, Terry Carroll
MR. CORRIGAN, Jay Ford
MR. CLARK, Fred Shawhan
MR. GOULDING, *studio executive,* Herbert Hall
MR. BUTLER, Budd Clark
MR. MCCAREY, Charles Fowler
A BOOKING AGENT, Al Downing
GEORGIA, GEORGIANA, GEORGETTE, Hilda, Louise, and Maxine Forman
RADIO ANNOUNCER, Raoul DeTisne
A POLICEMAN, O.J. Vanasse
GIRLS: Mildred Webb, Jean Fursa, Flo Spink, Dorothy Day, Carola Taylor, Dorothy Van Hiest, Patti Hastings, Ann Hurdman, Wilma Novak, Billie Sallier, Jerry Downes, Sherry Pelham, Margaret Carolan, Frances Markey, Anita Pam, Evelyn Monte, Pamela Sweeney, Vida Manuel, Lorraine Webb, Virginia Webb, Adele Story, Rosalie Trego, Kay Stewart, Lucille Osborne, Sara Jane, Pam Bryant
BOYS: Jack Donohue, Frank Hulser, Jack Hubert, Don Lannon, William Cooper, Hy Mohan, Jack Ross, Gene Sherrin, Jack Ray, Al Bloom, Robert Penny, William Meader

Musical Numbers

ACT I

SCENE ONE—CAFETERIA ON THE LOT OF PREMIER PICTURES, HOLLYWOOD
Mr. Dolan Is Passing Through, MR. DOLAN, EXECUTIVES and ENSEMBLE
In Califor-n-i-a, DORITH, PAULA and MOVIE ACTRESSES

SCENE TWO—CORRIDOR OF THE MAIN EXECUTIVE BUILDING
My Sweet, MADGE and LARRY

SCENE THREE—A PRIVATE CONFERENCE ROOM
I've Got Five Dollars, GERALDINE and MICHAEL

SCENE FOUR—A CABIN IN THE TENNESSEE MOUNTAINS
Sweet Geraldine, GEORGIA, GEORGIANA, GEORGETTE

SCENE FIVE—BEFORE THE CASINO AT AGUA CALIENTE
There's So Much More, DENISE and LARRY
We'll Be the Same, GERALDINE, MICHAEL and ENSEMBLE
Reprise, MICHAEL and LARRY

SCENE SIX—BACK PORCH OF MADGE'S BUNGALOW
How About It?, MADGE and MICHAEL

SCENE SEVEN—RECEPTION ROOM AT THE BEVERLY WILSHIRE HOTEL
Innocent Chorus Girls of Yesterday, MOVIE STARS
A Lady Must Live, DENISE

ACT II

SCENE ONE—THE CASTING OFFICE AT PREMIERE PICTURES

Opening, MR. DOLAN and DIRECTORS

SCENE TWO—THE SILVER SCREEN, HOLLYWOOD THEATRE

SCENE THREE—ROOF GARDEN AT THE EMBASSY CLUB

You Ain't Got No Savoir Faire, MADGE and LARRY

Two Unfortunate Orphans, PAULA, DORITH and ENSEMBLE

I Want a Man, DENISE

SCENE FOUR—MADGE'S BUNGALOW

SCENE FIVE—GRAUMAN'S CHINESE THEATRE

Tennessee Dan, GEORGIA, GEORGIANA, GEORGETTE

Reprise, *How About It?,* DENISE, MICHAEL, LARRY and COMPANY

Finale, GERALDINE and MICHAEL

NOTE: *God Gave Me Eyes* cut before New York opening. *There's So Much More* has same music as *Someone Should Tell Them* (cut from *A Connecticut Yankee*).

Reviews

J. Brooks Atkinson—*New York Times*

". . . The wit is clumsy, much of the humor is foul, and the book goes to a great deal of trouble to make both ends meet . . . On the whole, Rodgers and Hart have acquitted themselves most creditably. There is a rush about the music and a mocking touch in the lyrics that makes the score more deftly satirical than the production. *Innocent Chorus Girls of Yesterday* has the true flair of opera-bouffe satire . . ."

Arthur Ruhl—*New York Herald Tribune*

". . . a good workmanlike job of its kind, without startling brilliance . . . a genuinely entertaining show . . ."

Robert Littell—*New York World*

". . . rough, tough, very funny and exuberantly performed . . . to be placed among the top layer of this season's song and dance shows . . . in the song *Sweet Geraldine* there are overtones of irony that one does not find often in musical comedy . . . far above the average were the performances of Harriette Lake, Inez Courtney, Jack Whiting, and, of course, the tunes and lyrics of Rodgers and Hart."

Gilbert W. Gabriel—*New York American*

". . . jovial, tuneful, lively . . . It is the songs that must be the standbys. Three or four excellent songs, happily phrased, insinuatingly clever and rememberable. They come close to being the pleasantest Rodgers and Hart have composed . . . I'm all for it."

Robert Coleman—*New York Daily Mirror*
". . . a home-run show. In fact, a long, long run show . . . Unlike most musical comedies, this piece has a book that stands out . . . some of the neatest tunes and lyrics heard hereabouts since Tom Thumb golf went into a decline. *I've Got Five Dollars* and *How About It?* will be driving you crazy for quite a spell . . . smart, sophisticated, sparkling entertainment . . . New York will clasp *America's Sweetheart* to its bosom until we get back our light wines and beer . . ."

John Mason Brown—*New York Post*
". . . fast-paced, decidedly unprudish, richly tuneful, and, on the whole, immensely entertaining . . . a gay, giddy and generally riotous affair that slows down only at rare intervals . . . A simple but decidedly serviceable book . . . Among its major blessings it must count many of the drolly rhymed lyrics of Mr. Hart, and, most expecially, such superior examples of Mr. Rodgers' music as *We'll Be the Same, How About It?* and *I've Got Five Dollars* . . ."

Charles Darnton—*New York Evening World*
". . . more dirt than humor . . . Smut leaves its mark on any book by Herbert Fields and the lyrics by Lorenz Hart. The music is necessarily clean, though never scoring a clean song hit . . . not too much in the way of originality, wit or melody. Of bad taste you may be sure . . . Fresh enough at times, it was pretty stale much of the time."

Richard Lockridge—*New York Sun*
". . . a musical of large proportions and abundant brightness . . . everything one might wish for in a musical comedy, with the possible exception of breathtaking inspiration . . ."

John Anderson—*New York Journal*
". . . fails to come up to the trade mark . . . sounds a good deal like a set of discarded cues from *Once in a Lifetime* . . . for all the ingratiating music and ingenious rhythms, it lacks a star and a major comic . . ."

Sid Silverman—*Variety,* February 18, 1931
". . . figures to enjoy a moderate Broadway stay . . . as sweet a group of topical lyrics as Hart has ever turned out. Maybe they're his best . . . two of Rodgers' tunes which listen as if they'll get beyond first base are *I've Got Five Dollars* and *We'll Be the Same* . . . Harriette Lake is a mild-mannered and pleasing morsel if void of any particular animation . . ."

Dorothy Parker—*The New Yorker,* February 21, 1931
". . . Mr. Fields has, apparently, compiled his libretto with a pair of

scissors and his poor thumb must be awfully sore after all that clipping of jokes . . . Mr. Hart has donated lyrics the rhymes of which are less internal than colonic; they have a peculiar, even for Broadway, nastiness of flavor . . . Mr. Rodgers has contributed a truly charming score, each number of which gets better each time you hear it . . ."

Time, February 23, 1931
". . . notable if only for its refreshing little plot, which consistently refuses to run the usual course of musicomedies . . . Another triumph for the peerless team of Fields, Rodgers and Hart . . . Miss Lake is a lovely synthesis, one part Ginger Rogers, one part Ethel Merman . . . Packed like honey in a hive are sweet, nostalgic tunes . . ."

George Jean Nathan—*Judge,* March 7, 1931
". . . has just two good points: a song number called *Sweet Geraldine,* and another called *Innocent Chorus Girls of Yesterday* . . . aside from this brace of tasties, the show is pretty dull stuff . . . some of the stalest wheezes heard in some time . . . Where the book isn't covered with cobwebs, it is, furthermore, dully dirty . . . a pleasant ingenue named Harriette Lake still has to learn how to dance . . ."

THE HOT HEIRESS

(Film—1931)

A musical film with screenplay by Herbert Fields; music by Richard Rodgers; lyrics by Lorenz Hart.

A First National Picture
Directed by Clarence Badger
Photographed by Sol Polito

Release Date
March 15, 1931

The Story
A young riveter follows a mistossed bolt into a rich girl's boudoir to prevent a fire. They fall in love and, despite class-conscious complications, all ends happily.

The Cast
HAP HARRIGAN, Ben Lyon
JULIETTE HUNTER, Ona Munson
CLAY, Walter Pidgeon
BILL DUGAN, Tom Dugan
MR. HUNTER, Holmes Herbert
MARGIE, Inez Courtney
LOLA, Thelma Todd
MRS. HUNTER, Nella Walker

Musical Numbers
Nobody Loves a Riveter, HAP and TOM
Like Ordinary People Do, HAP, MARGIE, JULIETTE
You're the Cats, HAP and JULIETTE

NOTE: *He Looks So Good to Me* cut before film was released.

Reviews
Andre Sennwald—*New York Times*
". . . The story is too fragile and stale even for the films, but the comedy is bright and the tunes are in the gay and lilting Rodgers and Hart manner . . ."

Marguerite Tazelaar—*New York Herald Tribune*
". . . Just when you have settled down for the simple little story which you have looked at countless times before, you find Mr. Lyon and Miss Munson lapse, without warning, into a song. Just as suddenly, they return to their previous uninspired conversation. The songs, it must be admitted, are catchy . . ."

William Boehnel—*New York World-Telegram*
". . . Three charming songs, but the book is commonplace . . . if there were more songs, the picture would fare better . . ."

Eileen Creelman—*New York Sun*
". . . pretty obvious stuff . . . suffers from a lack of musical nourishment . . ."

Joe Bigelow—*Variety,* March 16, 1931
". . . The songs are smart in their modern lyrical way and typical Hart-Rodgers fly stuff, but didn't sound like sock tunes. They needed the picture more than the picture needed them. But the combination increases the effectiveness of both . . ."

LOVE ME TONIGHT

(Film—1932)

A musical film with screenplay by Samuel Hoffenstein, Waldemar Young and George Marion, Jr., based on play, "Tailor in the Chateau," by Leopold Marchand and Paul Armont; music by Richard Rodgers; lyrics by Lorenz Hart.

A Paramount Picture
Produced and directed by Rouben Mamoulian
Art director, Hans Dreier
Costumes by Travis Banton
Music director, Nathaniel Finston
Photographed by Victor Milner
Editor, William Shea

Release Date
August 13, 1932

The Story
Maurice, a romantic Parisian tailor, falls in love with the lonely Princess Jeanette, and masquerades as a baron to win her affection. Eventually, the tailor's true identity is discovered by the servants in Jeanette's castle. Humiliated, Maurice leaves the Princess, but there is an inevitable reconciliation.

The Cast
MAURICE COURTELIN, Maurice Chevalier
PRINCESS JEANETTE, Jeanette MacDonald
VICOMTE DE VAREZE, Charlie Ruggles
COUNT DE SAVIGNAC, Charles Butterworth
COUNTESS VALENTINE, Myrna Loy
THE DUKE, C. Aubrey Smith
THREE AUNTS, Elizabeth Patterson, Ethel Griffies, Blanche Frederici
THE DOCTOR, Joseph Cawthorn
MAJOR-DOMO, Robert Greig
DRESSMAKER, Ethel Wales
BAKERY GIRL, Marion "Peanuts" Byron
MME. DUPONT, Mary Doran
EMILE, Bert Roach

LAUNDRESS, Cecil Cunningham
COMPOSER, Tyler Brook
VALET, Edgar Norton
GROOM, Herbert Mundin
GROCER, George "Gabby" Hayes
CHAMBERMAID, Rita Owin
SHIRTMAKER, Clarence Wilson
COLLECTOR, Gordon Westcott
PIERRE, George Davis
TAXI DRIVER, Rolfe Sedan
HAT MAKER, Tony Merlo
BOOT MAKER, William H. Turner
CHEF, George Humbert

Musical Numbers

That's the Song of Paree, MAURICE, with BAKERY GIRL, GROCER, PARISIANS
Isn't It Romantic?, MAURICE, EMILE, TAXI DRIVER, COMPOSER, SOLDIERS, GYPSY VIOLINIST, JEANETTE
Lover, JEANETTE
Mimi, MAURICE
A Woman Needs Something Like That, JEANETTE, DOCTOR
Reprise, *Mimi,* DUKE, GILBERT, AUNTS, COUNT
Deer Hunt Ballet, ORCHESTRA
The Poor Apache, MAURICE
Love Me Tonight, JEANETTE, MAURICE
The Son of a Gun Is Nothing but a Tailor, DUKE, AUNTS, VALENTINE, MAJOR DOMO, VALET, LAUNDRESS, CHAMBER MAID, CHEF
Reprise, *Love Me Tonight,* MAURICE, JEANETTE

NOTE: *The Man for Me (The Letter Song)* cut before film was released.

Reviews

Mordaunt Hall—*New York Times*
"Mamoulian gives to his scenes a charming poetic suggestion . . . With all its signs of precision straining for effect, it has moments when it is elastic, when it is nicely spontaneous. Mamoulian takes full advantage of the music and lyrics . . ."

Richard Watts, Jr.—*New York Herald Tribune*
". . . a lively score . . . Perhaps a bit more wit in the writing wouldn't have injured the photoplay, but at least it always maintains a mood of amiable gaiety."

William Boehnel—*New York World-Telegram*
". . . Fetchingly mounted, expertly directed and played, and possessing a lilting musical score, *Love Me Tonight* turns out to be a superior bit of make believe . . ."

Philip K. Scheuer—*Los Angeles Times*
". . . It has, for me, the sort of magic which makes the theatre, the screen, that rarest of places, a refuge from a troubled world . . . a picture I would like to take home with me . . . Excellently cast, kinetically photographed, flawlessly mounted, it rejoices additionally in a synchronic score which punctuates the flow of gay comedy and lends a final fillip to each camera sequence . . ."

Jerry Hoffman—*Los Angeles Examiner*
"It'll haunt you! I warn you—it will taunt you! *Love Me Tonight* does things to you. It delights, it makes one gurgle with glee. It's one of the best, if not the best, of the musical-comedy pictures—and not the least of the cause is the brilliant direction of Rouben Mamoulian . . . Rarely have lyrics and melodies been so intriguing in a picture. The explanation is simple. Rodgers and Hart wrote them . . ."

Al Greason (Rush.)—*Variety,* August 20, 1932
"A gem of a class production . . . takes on the color of a musical comedy frolic, whimsical in aim and deliciously carried out in its pattern, in its playing and in its direction . . . Musical numbers are as amusing for once in their lyrics as they are attractive in their melodies, and are blended in smoothly with the action . . ."

John Mosher—*The New Yorker,* August 20, 1932
". . . There is a gaiety here and there, always in the Rene Clair manner, and a kind of nice style to the whole effect, but it just isn't bright and it isn't witty . . . In fact, I think that the whole thing has a sort of Wagnerian quality. Wagner gone chichi!"

Time, August 29, 1932
". . . has that air of light poetry as well as farce that the French comedies of Rene Clair contributed to cinema technique. In a plot which seems scarcely more than an impromptu play on words and music, the only illogicality is Chevalier's preferring Jeanette MacDonald to Myrna Loy . . ."

Pare Lorentz—*Judge,* September, 1932
". . . an excellent picture, a picture distinguished by a demonstration of surprising skill by Mamoulian and made more than pleasant by a good musical score . . ."

London Times
". . . by some mysterious and recondite process, Mamoulian lifts the squalid yearnings and base humor which the musical comedy is intended to express into another and far more delicate world . . ."

Illustrated London News
". . . wholly enchanting, gay, witty, and exhilarating . . . Mamoulian has kept to an amiable spirit of make believe in which it is possible to skim lightly, elegantly and adroitly over thin ice . . . opens with a masterpiece of rhythm in the streets of Paris . . ."

THE PHANTOM PRESIDENT

(Film—1932)

A musical film with screenplay by Walter DeLeon and Harlan Thompson, based on the novel by George F. Worts; music by Richard Rodgers; lyrics by Lorenz Hart.

A Paramount Picture
Directed by Norman Taurog
Photographed by David Abel

Release Date
September 23, 1932

The Story
Party leaders feel that banker Theodore K. Blair would make a great President of the United States. However, his stuffy personality makes them decide to look elsewhere for a candidate. When they see "Doc" Varney, a medicine show man, they are struck with his resemblance to Blair and they prevail upon him to campaign as Blair. Varney then wins both the election and the affections of Felicia Hammond, Blair's sweetheart.

The Cast
THEODORE K. BLAIR
PETER "DOC" VARNEY } George M. Cohan
FELICIA HAMMOND, Claudette Colbert
CURLY COONEY, Jimmy Durante
JIM RONKTON, George Barbier
PROFESSOR AIKENHEAD, Sidney Toler
SEN. SARAH SCRANTON, Louise MacKintosh
JERRIDO, Jameson Thomas
SEN. MELROSE, Julius McVicker
GEORGE WASHINGTON, Alan Mowbray
ABRAHAM LINCOLN, Charles Middleton

Musical Numbers
The Country Needs a Man, DOC
Somebody Ought to Wave a Flag, DOC and CURLY
Give Her a Kiss, BIRDS and FROGS
The Convention, DOC, CURLY and ENSEMBLE

Reviews

Mordaunt Hall—*New York Times*
". . . a crackerjack show . . . Rodgers and Hart deserve high praise . . ."

Richard Watts, Jr.—*New York Herald Tribune*
". . . a delightful and uproarious burlesque that makes up in comic gusto for what it sometimes lacks in originality . . . sometimes brilliant, occasionally courageous and sometimes merely imitative, but it is so admirably acted that it is always superior fun."

William Boehnel—*New York World-Telegram*
". . . one of the year's most hilariously amusing and biting satirical comedies . . . For bright and astonishing novelty, nothing has come out of Hollywood all year to be compared with it . . ."

Edwin Schallert—*Los Angeles Times*
". . . as a whole it intrigues greatly, and the star's personality should be more than acceptable to picture-goers . . ."

Sid Silverman—*Variety*, October 4, 1932
". . . holds a full share of laughs without threatening to rate itself a smash . . . Cohan belongs to another generation . . ."

John Mosher—*The New Yorker*, October 8, 1932
"If most of the first half had been clipped and cut to nothing, this latest outgrowth from *Of Thee I Sing* might have been pretty good fun. Mr. Cohan is lively and agreeable . . . some of the music is bright, the general satire is in the line which seems to be generally relished . . ."

Time, October 10, 1932
". . . a strange combination of serious flagwaving, savage political comment, pure comedy, farce and romance, it owes much to *Of Thee I Sing* . . ."

Pare Lorentz—*Judge*, November, 1932
". . . runs all over the place and gets out of hand from time to time, but it is very funny . . . While Rodgers and Hart did a very mediocre job on the music and lyrics, the musical scenes make it loose-jointed and pleasant . . ."

London Times
". . . ruthless, fantastic and extremely entertaining . . . taken at great speed and as broad farce . . . the satire is sharper than might at first appear . . ."

HALLELUJAH, I'M A BUM

(Film—1933)

A musical film with screenplay by S. N. Behrman, adapted from a story by Ben Hecht; music by Richard Rodgers; lyrics and rhythmic dialogue by Lorenz Hart.

A United Artists Picture
Produced by Joseph M. Schenck
Directed by Lewis Milestone
Art director, Richard Day
Music director, Alfred Newman
Photographed by Lucien Andriot

Release Date

January 27, 1933

NOTE: In England title of film was *Hallelujah, I'm a Tramp.*

The Story

Bumper, the vagabond leader of a group of hoboes living in Central Park, is a close friend of Mayor Hastings. The mayor has a girl friend, June, of whom he is intensely jealous. One day he upsets her so that she wanders into the park and jumps into the lake, only to be rescued by Bumper. He falls in love with June, and she, suffering from amnesia, falls in love with him. But when Bumper finds out that she is his friend's girl, he brings them back together again.

The Cast

BUMPER, Al Jolson
JUNE MARCHER, Madge Evans
MAYOR HASTINGS, Frank Morgan
EGGHEAD, Harry Langdon
SUNDAY, Chester Conklin
MAYOR'S SECRETARY, Tyler Brooke
ORLANDO, Tammany Young
JOHN, Bert Roach
ACORN, Edgar Connor
APPLE MARY, Dorothea Wolbert

MA SUNDAY, Louise Carver
PHOTOGRAPHER, Richard Rodgers
BANK TELLER, Lorenz Hart

Musical Numbers

I Gotta Get Back to New York, BUMPER
My Pal Bumper, ACORN, BUMPER, EGGHEAD and BUMS
Hallelujah, I'm a Bum, BUMPER
Laying the Cornerstone, MAYOR and ENSEMBLE
Dear June, BUMPER
Bumper Found a Grand, ACORN, EGGHEAD, BUMPER and BUMS
What Do You Want With Money?, BUMPER
Hallelujah, I'm a Bum, BUMPER
Kangaroo Court, BUMPER, EGGHEAD, ACORN and BUMS
I'd Do It Again, BUMPER
You Are Too Beautiful, BUMPER

NOTE: *Hallelujah, I'm a Bum* was the title of two different songs. *Sleeping Beauty* was cut before film was released.

Reviews

Mordaunt Hall—*New York Times*
". . . Jolson's best film . . . a successful combination of fun, melody and romance, with a dash of satire . . . songs are tuneful . . ."

Richard Watts, Jr.—*New York Herald Tribune*
". . . the result of so much activity of so many masterminds is not a happy one . . . The Rodgers score is reasonably tuneful, but the lyrics are not worthy of the brilliant and miraculously resourceful Hart . . ."

Thornton Delehanty—*New York Post*
". . . Hecht must have gone berserk after seeing a preview of *A Nous la Liberte* . . . Though the story radiates a vague confusion, it is pulled together at sundry moments by the richly humorous performance of Frank Morgan . . ."

John S. Cohen, Jr.—*New York Sun*
". . . A good deal of the first part recalls forcibly the version of *The Beggar's Opera,* which was recently played in Berlin . . . For the direction, the aim, and certain admirable bits, I have nothing but praise. Yet these musical satirists should finish something as well as they start it."

Abel Green—*Variety,* February 14, 1933
". . . it's no wow but not half bad either, commanding attention because of its provocative nature and general treatment . . . Almost

Barrieish in its whimsy, the ethereal quality of the script foundation is its primary deficiency . . . *Bum* is a pip of a number . . ."

John Mosher—*The New Yorker,* February 18, 1933
". . . Jolson sang agreeably and I didn't mind the occasional rhymes which spurt out in the dialogue somewhat epileptically. But lightness is needed in this kind of thing, and lightness is sadly lacking . . ."

Time, February 20, 1933
". . . the score, loaded with rhythmic dialogue, turns out to be merely a superfluity of rhymes . . . Jolson's performance is notable for a great air of confidence, which is generally unjustified . . . The film is one more balloon tire with a blow-out . . ."

Pare Lorentz—*Vanity Fair,* April, 1933
". . . Mr. Jolson sings all songs as though they were entitled *Mammy* . . . The music, the story and the star were constantly warring with one another . . ."

Penelope Gilliatt—*The New Yorker,* June 23, 1973
". . . interesting spoken rhythms that are one of the American musical cinema's many beautiful and moving attempts to find an unimitative equivalent of operatic recitative . . . A film to welcome back, especially for what it tries to do for the progress of the American musical film in the direction that Gluck began for opera."

Bibliography

When the Music Tells the Story by Joseph O'Sullivan
—*Motion Picture Herald,* March 4, 1933

HOLLYWOOD PARTY

(Film—1934)

A musical film with screenplay by Howard Dietz and Arthur Kober; music by Richard Rodgers, Walter Donaldson and Nacio Herb Brown; lyrics by Lorenz Hart, Gus Kahn, Mr. Dietz and Arthur Freed.

A Metro-Goldwyn-Mayer Picture
Produced by Mr. Dietz and Harry Rapf
Directed by Edmund Goulding, Russell Mack, Richard Boleslawsky, Allan Dwan, Roy Rowland (none credited)
Choreography by Seymour Felix, George Hale, Dave Gould
Art director, Fredric Hope
Costumes by Adrian
Animated cartoon sequence by Walt Disney
Photographed by James Wong Howe
Editor, George Boemler
Color sequences by Technicolor

Release Date

May 25, 1934

The Story

Jimmy Durante dreams that he is Tarzan—or Schnarzan—and his detailed nightmare forms the incoherent story that culminates in the slapstick party of the title.

The Cast

LAUREL AND HARDY, Themselves
JIMMY, Jimmy Durante
HARVEY CLEMP, Charles Butterworth
HENRIETTA, Polly Moran
LUPE, Lupe Velez
FRANCES WILLIAMS, Herself
BARON MUNCHAUSEN, Jack Pearl
BOB, Eddie Quillan
LINDA, June Clyde
DUKE, George Givot
TED HEALY AND HIS STOOGES, Themselves
SHIRLEY ROSS, Herself
HARRY BARRIS, Himself

KNAPP, Richard Carle
BUTLER, Arthur Treacher
ROBERT YOUNG, Himself
BEAVERS, Tom Kennedy
CAB DRIVER, Leonid Kinskey
JIMMY'S WIFE, Jean Olsen Durante
MICKEY MOUSE, Himself (voice of Walt Disney)

Musical Numbers

Hollywood Party (Rodgers-Hart), FRANCES
I'm Feeling High (Donaldson-Dietz), SHIRLEY and HARRY
Hello (Rodgers-Hart), JIMMY and BARON, CHORUS
I've Had My Moments (Donaldson-Kahn), BOB and LINDA; JIMMY and HENRIETTA
Reincarnation (Rodgers-Hart, Durante), JIMMY and HENRIETTA
Hot Chocolate Soldiers (Brown-Freed), MICKEY MOUSE SYMPHONY

NOTE: Following songs by Rodgers and Hart, originally intended for film when it was known as *Hollywood Revue,* were cut before it was released: *Prayer* (sung by JEAN HARLOW), *Yes Me* (written with Durante), *Fly Away to Ioway, You've Got That, The Mahster's Coming, You Are, Black Diamond, I'm One of the Boys, The Pots, I'm a Queen in My Own Domain, Keep Away from the Moonlight, My Friend the Night, Give a Man a Job,* and *Burning.*

Reviews

Mordaunt Hall—*New York Times*
". . . may have been very funny while it was being made, but as it comes to the screen it is not a little disappointing . . . has several songs which are not particularly tuneful . . ."

Marguerite Tazelaar—*New York Herald Tribune*
". . . The trouble is that it has no director . . . For such an accumulation of talent it seems too bad that there couldn't have been a trace of continuity in the unfolding of the piece. However, almost anybody can get a laugh out of one thing or another . . ."

Thornton Delehanty—*New York Post*
". . . There are bad spots and dull spots, but the thing which endears it to us is that it is funny often enough to make it an exceptional venture in hilarity . . . bears the stamp of adult Broadway entertainment . . ."

Abel Green—*Variety,* May 25, 1934
". . . a succession of bits and numbers which are none too adroitly dovetailed but which will not bore. Averagely passable screen divertissement . . . Schnoz's reincarnation scene and his clowning are highlights . . ."

John Mosher—*The New Yorker,* June 2, 1934
"... an hilarious film. The whole thing has been put together somewhat casually, but among all the hit-or-miss moments there are some pretty funny ones ... I liked Durante's song concerning the substantial subject of reincarnation ..."

Time, June 4, 1934
"... should have been one of the funniest pictures of the season. That most of its antics turn out to be curiously dreary may be due to the fact that cinemusicomedy demands more continuity of plot than this film contains ..."

London Times, June 11, 1934
"... nothing more than a series of 'shorts' held together by a slight story and produced with the usual technical skill and polish ..."

MISSISSIPPI

(Film—1935)

A musical film with screenplay by Francis Martin and Jack Cunningham, adapted by Herbert Fields and Claude Binyon from the play "Magnolia" by Booth Tarkington; music by Richard Rodgers; lyrics by Lorenz Hart.

A Paramount Picture
Produced by Arthur Hornblow, Jr.
Directed by A. Edward Sutherland
Art directors, Hans Dreier, Bernard Herzbrun
Music director, Sigmund Krumgold
Photographed by Charles Lang
Editor, Chandler House

Release Date
April 2, 1935

The Story
At a party at the plantation of his fiancee, Lucy Rumford, Tom Grayson gets into an argument and is considered a coward because he refuses to fight a duel. Eventually he is made a "killing sensation"—at gambling—through the advice and counsel of a steamboat captain, Commodore Jackson.

The Cast
TOM GRAYSON, Bing Crosby
COMMODORE JACKSON, W. C. Fields
LUCY RUMFORD, Joan Bennett
ALABAM, Queenie Smith
ELVIRA RUMFORD, Gail Patrick
GERALD RUMFORD, Claude Gillingwater
MAJOR PATTERSON, John Miljan
JOE PATTERSON, Ed Pawley
CAPTAIN BLACKIE, Fred Kohler, Sr.
RUMBO, John Larkin
STAGE MANAGER, Harry Meyers
HEFTY, Paul Hurst
MISS MARKHAM, Theresa Maxwell Conover
FIRST GAMBLER, King Baggott
SECOND GAMBLER, Mahlon Hamilton
BIT PLAYER, Ann Sheridan

Musical Numbers

Roll Mississippi, ALABAM AND CABIN KIDS
Soon, TOM
Down by the River, TOM
Easy to Remember, TOM
Old Folks at Home (by Stephen Foster), TOM

NOTE: *The Steely Glint in My Eye, The Notorious Colonel Blake* and *Pablo, You Are My Heart* cut before film was released.

Reviews

Andre Sennwald—*New York Times*
". . . a tuneful and diverting show even when it isn't being particularly hilarious, and it is madly funny at sufficient length to satisfy us Fields idolators . . ."

Richard Watts, Jr.—*New York Herald Tribune*
". . . Fields is magnificent as usual . . . some pleasant songs but the tale isn't very deftly handled . . ."

Newsweek, April 6, 1935
". . . some fine Rodgers and Hart tunes . . . Fairly amusing in the Hollywood musical-comedy style."

Wolfe Kaufman—*Variety,* April 24, 1935
". . . a dull film, rambling and hokey . . . Three songs and all are good, although leaving something to be desired . . ."

John Mosher—*The New Yorker,* April 27, 1935
". . . Fields gives the piece what life it has. Not that there aren't some fairly agreeable moments . . . Crosby's new songs are not so bright, I thought, as his *Old Folks at Home.*"

London Times, April 22, 1935
". . . Fields and Crosby, although appearing to work together, are actually engaged in a tug of war, and the film is nearly wrecked in their struggle . . ."

JUMBO

(1935)

A musical comedy with book by Ben Hecht and Charles MacArthur; music by Richard Rodgers; lyrics by Lorenz Hart.

Presented by Billy Rose
Production directed by John Murray Anderson
Book directed by George Abbott
Equestrian, acrobatic and aerial dances by Allan K. Foster
Production and theatre designed by Albert Johnson
Costumes by Raoul Pene Du Bois
Additional costumes by Wynn and James Reynolds
Music director, Adolph Deutsch
Orchestrations by Mr. Deutsch, Murray Cutter, Joseph Nussbaum, Hans Spialek, Conrad Salinger
Choral director, Charles Henderson

New York Run
Hippodrome, November 16, 1935-April 18, 1936
233 performances

The Story
The son and daughter of two bitterly rival circus owners, John A. Considine and Matthew Mulligan, are mutually smitten. Amid all the big-top enchantments—from clowns to death-defying trapeze artists—they manage to save one circus from disaster, end the family feud, and unite themselves.

The Cast
MR. BALL, Bob Lawrence
MR. JELLICO, A. P. Kaye
ARTISTS, Tom Lomas and Fred Spear
"POODLES," Poodles Hanneford
JOHN A. CONSIDINE, Arthur Sinclair
FIRST RAZORBACK, Ray Miller
MICKEY CONSIDINE, Gloria Grafton
MATTHEW MULLIGAN, W. J. McCarthy
MATT MULLIGAN, JR., Donald Novis
SECOND RAZORBACK, Dave Adams
UNITED STATES MARSHAL, George Watts

CLAUDIUS B. BOWERS, Jimmy Durante
FLANAGAN, Henry LaMarr
AUCTIONEER, Willard Dashiell
LITTLE GIRL, Sybil Elaine
CHIEF OF POLICE, Donald Black
MR. PIPER, Philip Wood
SWEENEY, Gene Greenlaw
MCCARTHY, Walter Lewis
REILLY, John Keubler
JUMBO, "Big Rosie"
Paul Whiteman and his Orchestra
SHOW GIRLS: Anita Arden, Aina Constant, Madeline Ecklund, Maurine Holmes, Mildred Hughes, Carlotta Mann, Gayle Mellott, Julie Sterling, Ethel Summerville
DANCERS: Evelyn Bonefine, Dorothy Bradshaw, Violet Carson, Gloria Claire, Vyna Dale, Betty De Elmo, Margaret Donahue, Virginia Donahue, Joan Gray, Tilda Getze, Billie Joyce, Patricia Knight, Charlotte Lorraine, Lela Manor, Lila Manor, Edwina Steele
ALLAN K. FOSTER GIRLS: Nancy Antoine, Florence Belair, Mickey Elbert, Vivian Francis, Mona Gray, Betty Harris, Dorothy Keller, Gladys Lorraine, Josephine Martin, Kathryn McDonald, Virginia Moore, Lillian Sherry, Gwen Stader, Barbara Stuart, Dorothy Warren, Effie Winter, Mae Winter
HENDERSON'S SINGING RAZORBACKS: David Adams, Edward Angelery, Allen Bennett, Win Barker, Theodore Daniels, Daniel Dansby, Lipman Duckat, Lynn Eldredge, Phillip Eppens, William Freeman, Roger Gerry, Eugene Greenlaw, Julius Johnson, Robert Johnson, Joseph Kaplan, John Kuebler, Henry LaMarr, Jack Leslie, Walter Lewis, Rudolph Mattson, Ray Miller, J. H. Pendergast, Jack Phillips, Claude Ratliffe, Carol Tolle, Howard Urbach, Herbert Waldman, Merritt Wells, Solon West, Arnold Wilson, Clifford Whitcomb, Victor Young

NOTE: For Fort Worth engagement, Mr. Durante succeeded by Eddie Foy, Jr. However , shortly after that run began, role of CLAUDIUS eliminated, along with most of the plot.

Musical Numbers

ACT I

JOHN CONSIDINE'S WONDER SHOW
Over and Over Again, Bob Lawrence and HENDERSON'S SINGING RAZOR-BACKS
THE RINGMASTER, Poodles Hanneford
THE BAREBACK RIDER, Grace Elizabeth Hanneford
THE IRON-JAW MAN, Arthur LaFleur
THE JUGGLER, Takayama
THE CLOWN, A. Robins
THE CONTORTIONIST, William Ferry

THE WIREWALKER AND AERIALIST, Barbette
THE LOOP-THE-LOOP GIRL, Minnie LaPell
THE TRAPEZE GIRLS, Helen Harvey, Victoria Miller
THE GIRL IN THE CANNON, Helen Brooks
ALLAN K. FOSTER GIRLS

The Circus Is on Parade, HENDERSON'S SINGING RAZORBACKS
The Most Beautiful Girl in the World, MATT and MICKEY
Laugh, CLAUDIUS and A. Robins

THE GOLFER, Allen Bennett
THE KOO-KOO, Jack Barnes
THE HORSE, Albert Dewbery
THE WOODPECKER, William Selig
THE KANGAROO, Joseph Caplan, Margaret Donahue
THE SEE-SAW, Ray Miller
THE RUBE, Eugene Greenlaw
THE FOUR-ARMED MAN, William Ferry
THE COP, Robert Reano
THE MAN IN THE FISH BOWL, Sonny Lang
THE UPSIDE-DOWN MAN, William Brooks
THE ELEPHANT, Claude Ratliffe, William Freeman, Karl Kosicksy
ALLAN K. FOSTER GIRLS

My Romance, MATT and MICKEY
Little Girl Blue, MICKEY

THE CHILD, Sybil Elaine
THE COACHMAN, Karl Kosicksy
THE POSTILLIONS, Litri Wagner, Helen Brooks
THE MISTRESS OF THE RING, Frances Van Ritter
THE CLOWN, A. Robins
THE JUGGLER, Takayama
THE AERIALISTS, France and LaPell
THE IRON-JAW MAN, Arthur LaFleur
THE STILT MEN, The Lomas Troup
THE IRON-JAW GIRLS, Helene Brown, Helen Harvey, Edna Lee, Frances McMasters, Victoria Miller, Litri Wagner
HENDERSON'S SINGING RAZORBACKS

ACT II

SCENE ONE—CONSIDINE'S TENT

The Song of the Roustabouts, HENDERSON'S SINGING RAZORBACKS
Women, CLAUDIUS and Barbette
Memories of Madison Square Garden

P. T. BARNUM, Willard Dashiell
THE GIANT, Dave Ballard
GENERAL TOM THUMB, Karl Kosicksy
BAREBACK RIDER, Josie DeMotte
JUGGLER, Tom Breen
DOG TRAINER, Charles DeCamo

ACROBATS, Lenze Duo
FROG, William Ferry
FIRE-EATERS, The Nagyfys
IRON SKULL MAN, Jim Mandy
PUNCHING BAG ARTIST, Olivette
STRONG WOMAN, Tyana
MAN ON THE TABLES, Jack Pickford
ON THE REVOLVING LADDERS, Ed and Helen LaNole
THE AX THROWER, Harry Jackson, Sr.
THE TARGET, Mary Jackson
THE WHIPSNAPPER, Harry Jackson, Jr.
THE AERIALIST, Arthur Sherwood
THE SLIDE-FOR-LIFE GIRL, Tiny Kline

SCENE TWO—CONSIDINE AND MULLIGAN'S COMBINED CIRCUS
Diavalo, Bob Lawrence and HENDERSON'S SINGING RAZORBACKS
The Circus Wedding, COMPANY AND MENAGERIE

NOTE: *There's a Small Hotel* cut before opening.

Reviews

Brooks Atkinson—*New York Times*
". . . downright enjoyable . . . handsome, original and happily endearing . . . a calliope of good tunes . . . a gargantuan antic, a fool's paradise of bizarre and plain enjoyment . . ."

Percy Hammond—*New York Herald Tribune*
". . . It has been a long time since I heard as pretty a ballad as *Little Girl Blue* . . . a sane and exciting compound of opera, animal show, folk drama, harlequinade, carnival, circus, extravaganza and spectacle . . ."

Gilbert W. Gabriel—*New York American*
". . . as gay as all sorts of good songs and glittering scenes hung crowded on a giant pre-Christmas tree could make it . . . chockful of so many thrills, musical, scenic, gymnastic and humanitarian, it deserves endowment as an institution . . . happy, likeable songs, all of them . . . The charm and vitality that are in them echo the vitality and charm of the whole venture . . ."

Burns Mantle—*New York Daily News*
★★★+ . . . a story that MacArthur and Hecht must have spent all of half a day jotting down on scraps of paper . . . big and lively and full of attention-stabbing incidents . . . Several of the songs are good. *My Romance* for one. Durante's *Laugh* and *Women* for a couple of others . . ."

Walter Winchell—*New York Daily Mirror*
"*Hipp, Hipp, Hooray!* . . . gigantic spectacle, crowded with fun, amusement and talented Barnum and Bailey experts . . . a thread of a tale—but every bit of it agreeable . . . the town's outstanding entertainment."

John Mason Brown—*New York Post*
". . . a sort of super Bergdorf-Goodman circus . . . a colossal undertaking, produced with breath-taking virtuosity . . . a serviceable score . . . a good, brassy, bespangled, breath-taking and excellently displayed indoor tentshow . . . In short, it forces you to toss your hat in the air crying, 'The circus has come to town' . . ."

Robert Garland—*New World-Telegram*
". . . It's great, it's glamorous, it's gargantuan! . . . a happy, haphazard harlequinade . . . something different, something exciting that even a city slicker can enjoy . . . *Little Girl Blue* is ardently recommended along with *Memories of Madison Square Garden,* and the Rodgers-and-Hartian rest of the songs . . ."

Richard Lockridge—*New York Sun*
". . . great fun . . . it all adds up to a fairly superlative entertainment. This is largely due to what Albert Johnson has done in designing the show and, above all, the theatre . . . a delightful place to be in, and one rather hard to describe . . ."

John Anderson—*New York Journal*
". . . it is huge and it is magnificent . . . a plague take the plot. It is fool's fodder for dullwits . . . A. Robins is my favorite item . . . there are such pleasant tunes as *The Most Beautiful Girl in the World* and *My Romance* . . . a great show."

Jack Pulaski (Ibee.)—*Variety,* November 17, 1935
". . . may still have a bit too much book . . . *Little Girl Blue* looks like a cinch hit . . . *Jumbo* is indeed something different . . . Its name, its size, its varied diversions and its showmanship indicate certain success."

Robert Benchley—*The New Yorker,* November 23, 1935
". . . not just a circus, but it is enough of a circus deluxe to furnish thrills for those who like them. Me, I shut my eyes and always have. At a regular circus I sometimes shut my eyes and forget to open them, but you can't do that at *Jumbo,* or you will miss something that regular circuses don't have. (Beautiful girls for one thing.) But for circus-lovers, here is an ideal combination—lots of excellent acts, and only one ring to watch . . ."

Frank Norris—*Time,* November 25, 1935
". . . a megalomaniac medley of musicomedy and circus, with the circus gaining a shade the advantage . . . filled to the brim with good clean entertainment . . . Adults should enjoy Gloria Grafton singing a weird and hypnotic little song called *Little Girl Blue* . . ."

George Jean Nathan—*Life,* January, 1936
". . . gay, exciting and lovely . . . some comical jokes, a number of good songs, a ringful of girls that Ziegfeld might have found quite eligible, a staff of girl ushers that are even better looking . . . contains everything that the old-fashioned circus had but the bad smell . . . a salubrious show!"

Don Marquis—*Stage,* January, 1936
". . . The grand thing about it is that it makes you think of your first circus days, wherever they were spent, in Madison Square Garden or some dusty little midland village. You recapture that first, fine careless rapture. It is an evocation of the glamor and the light that never was on land or sea but only under the big top . . ."

Bibliography

Circus ("Jumbo") Parade —*New York Times,* August 12, 1935

Glorifying Barnum's Jumbo by Richard Maney —*New York Herald Tribune,* August 12, 1935

And Now It Can Be Told —*New York Times,* September 22, 1935

Mad Mahout —*Time,* October 28, 1935

Hippodrome, Rose, Rosie and a New Idea; Result—"Jumbo" (cover story) —*Newsweek,* November 23, 1935

The Mantles of Ziegfeld and Barnum —*Literary Digest,* November 30, 1935

Special Engagement

Texas Centennial, Fort Worth, July 18-September, 1936

JUMBO

(Film Version—1962)

A Metro-Goldwyn-Mayer Picture
Produced by Joe Pasternak and Martin Melcher
Associate Producer, Roger Edens
Directed by Charles Walters
Screenplay by Sidney Sheldon
2nd unit director, Busby Berkeley

Art directors, George W. Davis and Preston Ames
Costumes by Morton Haack
Music director, George Stoll
Photographed by William H. Daniels
Editor, Richard Farrell
Filmed in Panavision
Color by Metrocolor

Release Date
December 5, 1962

The Story
Because Pop Wonder, owner of the Wonder Circus, is constantly gambling away his money, the circus is having difficulty keeping its members from joining the rival Noble Circus. Sam Rawlins, a stranger, joins the circus and soon finds himself in love with Kitty, Pop's daughter. Sam, who is really the son of the owner of the Noble Circus, secretly pays off Pop's debts, and thereby gains control of the circus for his father. After losing the circus, Pop and Kitty try to set up a small side show, but when a repentant Sam finds them they all join in rebuilding the Wonder Circus.

The Cast
KITTY WONDER, Doris Day
SAM RAWLINS, Stephen Boyd (sung by James Joyce)
POP WONDER, Jimmy Durante
LULU, Martha Raye
JOHN NOBLE, Dean Jagger
HARRY, Joseph Waring
TINA, Lynn Wood
ELLIS, Charles Watts
PARSONS, James Chandler
MADISON, Robert Burton
HANK, Wilson Wood
EDDIE, Norman Leavitt
DRIVER, Grady Sutton
CIRCUS ACTS: Ron Henon, The Pedrolas, The Wazzans, Billy Barton, Corky Cristiani, Victor Julian, Richard Berg, Joe Monahan, Miss Lani, Adolph Dubsky, Pat Anthony, Janos Prohaska.

Musical Numbers
Songs retained from original production: *The Circus Is on Parade; Over and Over Again; The Most Beautiful Girl in the World; My Romance; Little Girl Blue.* Songs from other Rodgers and Hart musicals: *Why Can't I?; This Can't Be Love.* Songs written specially for film by Roger Edens: *Prologue; Sawdust, Spangles and Dreams.*

Reviews

Bosley Crowther—*New York Times*

"The only thing vastly wrong with *Jumbo* is that it is hitting the screen about 25 years late . . . blandly naive story . . . a great deal more novelty and character, more imagination and style are required . . . in the clowning of Jimmy Durante and Martha Raye may be found the few bright and solid nuggets of fun and frolic. Otherwise, it is simply unoriginal, solemn, sluggish, and slow . . . Miss Day, for all her pleasant singing, is a bore . . ."

Paul V. Beckley—*New York Herald Tribune*

". . . a glorious tribute to sawdust; it has sawdust in its veins but gold in its heart . . . the story is as familiar as the shape of a tent . . . But what really counts is the overwhelming good will that rises from every detail, overwhelming because it is not tinsel but is felt by the people who star in it . . . sentimentality isn't excessive, and it is for the most part beautifully balanced by really funny lines and some exciting camera studies of aerial acts . . . the music and lyrics stand up very well indeed . . ."

Archer Winsten—*New York Post*

". . . cornucopia quantities of circus entertainment, some of the best Rodgers and Hart songs, vast color spaces, workable comedy, and a couple of romances. The tests of time have been applied liberally to almost everyone involved, and they have all emerged triumphant . . . What's so enjoyable is the acrobatic color, the easy clowning, the fact that you're never asked to take the picture seriously, and the way it bounces along . . ."

Alton Cook—*New York World-Telegram & Sun*

". . . large, gaudy, jolly, and, above all, tuneful . . . a nice, shiny show, and do not expect one iota of anything else, certainly not the slightest crumb of good sense."

Robert Frederick—*Variety,* December 5, 1962

". . . great film entertainment with every prospect of big boxoffice . . . The music and lyrics are assets . . . among the all-time great screen musicals . . . Doris Day may never have sung better . . ."

Arthur Knight—*Saturday Review,* December 8, 1962

". . . wisely subordinates a completely predictable plot to a succession of production numbers that are lavish, colorful, and gay . . . the most engagingly abandoned camera work since the Busby Berkeley musicals of the Thirties . . . Charles Walters obviously is a man with a special affection for the tinsel, the humor, and the pathos of circus life . . ."

Brendan Gill—*The New Yorker,* December 15, 1962
"*Elephantiasis* . . . a doggedly jolly, relentlessly heartwarming treat 'for the whole family' . . . certainly contains goodies for all ages, provided none of the ages is very bright . . . preposterous screenplay . . . Even the Rodgers-and-Hart songs seem dated, at least in respect to their lyrics . . ."

David Slavitt—*Newsweek,* December 17, 1962
". . . not so much a picture for the whole family as hardly anything at all for anybody in particular."

Time, December 21, 1962
". . . a great big blubbery amiable polka-dotted elephant of a show, just the ticket for a holiday hoot with the wife and kiddies . . . Walters has the sense to let it seem exactly what it is: nonsense. He skillfully mingles cinemagic and circus-pocus, and he almost always gets the best out of his players . . . But the show belongs to Schnoz . . ."

Bibliography

Jumbo, Sydney and Rosie by Joseph Morgenstern
—*New York Herald Tribune,* December 2, 1962

ON YOUR TOES

(1936)

A musical comedy with book by Richard Rodgers, Lorenz Hart and George Abbott; music by Mr. Rodgers; lyrics by Mr. Hart.

Presented by Dwight Deere Wiman
Directed by Worthington Miner, George Abbott (uncredited)
Choreography by George Balanchine
Settings by Jo Mielziner
Costumes by Irene Sharaff
Music director, Gene Salzer
Orchestrations by Hans Spialek
Pianists, Edgar Fairchild and Adam Carroll

Tryout
Shubert Theatre, Boston, March 21-April 8, 1936

New York Run
Imperial Theatre, April 11-November 29, 1936
Majestic Theatre, November 30, 1936-January 23, 1937
315 performances

The Story
Junior Dolan, son of vaudevillians, forsakes the profession of his parents to become a music teacher. At school he meets co-ed Frankie Frayne, who is in love with him, and Sidney Cohn, a composer. Together they try to sell Sidney's jazz ballet to a Russian ballet company. Vera, the ballerina, is attracted to Junior, and with her help, it is produced with Dolan in the lead. He is mistaken by gangsters for another dancer who owes a gambling debt, but is saved by the police and returns to Frankie.

The Cast
PHIL DOLAN II, Dave Jones
LIL DOLAN, Ethel Hampton
PHIL DOLAN III, Tyrone Kearney
CALL BOY, Beau Tilden
LOLA, Betty Jane Smith
PHIL DOLAN III ("JUNIOR"), Ray Bolger
FRANKIE FRAYNE, Doris Carson

SIDNEY COHN, David Morris
VERA BARNOVA, Tamara Geva
ANUSHKA, Mae Noble
PEGGY PORTERFIELD, Luella Gear
SERGEI ALEXANDROVITCH, Monty Woolley
KONSTANTINE MORROSINE, Demetrios Vilan
SNOOPY, William Wadsworth
MISHKA, Valery Streshnev
VASSILLI, Robert Sidney
DIMITRI, Basil Galahoff
LEON, Harold Haskin
CALL BOY, Bob Long
A SINGER, Earle Mac Veigh
A WAITER, William Baker
STAGE MANAGER, Harry Peterson
A POLICEMAN, George Young
FIRST THUG, Nick Dennis
SECOND THUG, Louis Walsh
LADIES OF THE BALLET: May Block, Jill Christie, Dorothy Denton, Eleanor Fiata, Dorothy Hall, Joan Keena, Isabelle Kimpal, Gertrude Magee, Marie Monnig, Ursula Seiler, Betty Jane Smith, Alma Wertley
GENTLEMEN OF THE BALLET: William Baker, Edward Brinkman, Fred Danieli, Basil Galahoff, Harold Haskin, Julian Mitchell, Jack Quinn, Valery Streshnev
LADIES OF THE ENSEMBLE: Libby Bennett, Enes Earley, Peggy Thomas, Gloria Franklin, Grace Kaye, Betty Lee, Frances Nevins, Carol Renwick, Patsey Schenck, Drucilla Strain, Dorothy Thomas, Davenie Watson, Amy Weber
GENTLEMEN OF THE ENSEMBLE: Mortimer O'Brien, Henry Dick, Dave Jones, Robert Forsythe, Russ Milton, Harry Peterson, Beau Tilden, George Young

Musical Numbers

ACT I

SCENE ONE—A VAUDEVILLE STAGE, SIXTEEN YEARS AGO
Two-a-Day for Keith, PHIL II, LIL, PHIL III

SCENE TWO—THE VAUDEVILLE DRESSING ROOM

SCENE THREE—A CLASSROOM AT KNICKERBOCKER UNIVERSITY, W.P.A. EXTENSION
The Three B's, JUNIOR and ENSEMBLE
It's Got to Be Love, FRANKIE and JUNIOR

SCENE FOUR—VERA'S APARTMENT
Too Good for the Average Man, PEGGY and SERGEI

SCENE FIVE—CENTRAL PARK
There's a Small Hotel, FRANKIE and JUNIOR

SCENE SIX—GREEN ROOM, COSMOPOLITAN OPERA HOUSE
The Heart Is Quicker than the Eye, PEGGY and JUNIOR

SCENE SEVEN—A DRESSING ROOM, COSMOPOLITAN OPERA HOUSE

SCENE EIGHT—THE STAGE OF THE COSMOPOLITAN OPERA HOUSE
La Princesse Zenobia Ballet
LA PRINCESSE ZENOBIA, Tamara Geva
BEGGAR, Demetrios Vilan
OLD PRINCE, William Baker
YOUNG PRINCE, George Church

ACT II

SCENE ONE—THE PLANETARIUM ROOF GARDEN
Quiet Night, Earle MacVeigh and ENSEMBLE
Glad to Be Unhappy, FRANKIE and SIDNEY

SCENE TWO—THE STAGE OF THE COSMOPOLITAN OPERA HOUSE
On Your Toes, FRANKIE, JUNIOR, SIDNEY and ENSEMBLE

SCENE THREE—GREEN ROOM, COSMOPOLITAN OPERA HOUSE

SCENE FOUR—THE STAGE OF THE COSMOPOLITAN OPERA HOUSE
Slaughter on Tenth Avenue Ballet
HOOFER, Ray Bolger
STRIP TEASE GIRL, Tamara Geva
BIG BOSS, George Church

Reviews

Brooks Atkinson—*New York Times*
". . . the most remarkable thing about it is the uniformity of its viewpoint. If the word 'sophisticated' is not too unpalatable, let it serve as a description of the mocking book, the songs and the performances . . . Mr. Rodgers has written a jaunty score that entitles him to honors at the general final exam, and Mr. Hart has put words to it that are crisp, impish and gayly ingenious . . ."

Percy Hammond—*New York Herald Tribune*
". . . The episode which caused an uproar was called *Slaughter on Tenth Avenue* . . . a smartly sentimental exhibition, full of theatrical color, form and cadence . . . The songs are mildly hearable . . . I liked *On Your Toes* but moderately, while admiring its many superiorities . . . if you do not expect too much you will not be disappointed."

Gilbert W. Gabriel—*New York American*
". . . funny in large enough spurts, gaily dressed and prettily peopled, and full of some charming Summer-fare songs . . . a good hot weather satire . . . Rodgers' score is one of his neatest, most likable, most lilting . . ."

Burns Mantle—*New York Daily News*
"★★★ . . . a good show . . . *The Heart Is Quicker Than the Eye* and *Too Good for the Average Man* edge the periphery in suggestion but stay within the law . . . the singing isn't very good, nor the ballads, if any . . ."

Robert Coleman—*New York Daily Mirror*
". . . one of the seven wonders of 1936 . . . It's great! . . . some of the swingiest, most hummable and singable tunes and lyrics to soothe your play sampler's ears in many semesters . . . The libretto sets a new high in originality and smartness . . ."

John Mason Brown—*New York Post*
". . . a first-rate dancing show which is as witty as it is nimble . . . skilfully rhymed lyrics for Rodgers' pleasant melodies . . . an overlong book . . . real tension as well as genuine comedy abounds in the *Slaughter on Tenth Avenue* ballet . . . Mr. Bolger has scored a genuine triumph."

Robert Garland—*New York World-Telegram*
". . . a great big bountiful musical comedy . . . rich in color, costumes, and lovely ladies . . . words and music are dashing and daring . . . Even Hollywood hasn't dug chigger-like beneath Rodgers and Hart's skins . . . Mr. Bolger, a jazz Nijinski, an Astaire in mufti, is its savior and its star . . ."

John Anderson—*New York Journal*
". . . smart, amusing, debonair . . . a loose-jointed but amiable tale . . . an hilarious piece of foolishness called *Too Good for the Average Man* . . . The spirit of the show is informal and easy, gay, light-headed when it isn't light-hearted, and altogether genial . . ."

Jack Pulaski (Ibee.)—*Variety*, April 15, 1936
". . . second act is the strongest and the big moments of the performance are there . . . Show starts off brightly, and there are at least two likeable songs. Last half of the first act seems somewhat down . . . *There's a Small Hotel* is likely to be the show's best click tune . . . chances of clicking are strong."

Wolcott Gibbs—*The New Yorker,* April 18, 1936
". . . the only complaint I have about anything that goes on is that I am never sure when people are kidding the ballet because women always look funny to me when people start throwing them around . . . Hart's lyrics are bright without bringing in too many of the facts of life, which is a tougher trick than you'd imagine; Rodgers' music is cheerful, and simple enough to be pleasant even to the most elementary ear . . ."

Frank Norris—*Time,* April 20, 1936
". . . a definite milestone in the musical theatre . . . Further productions which fail to measure up to its stiff standards of achievement may be considered to have retrograded . . . Tunes in the best Rodgers manner: *Too Good for the Average Man* and *There's a Small Hotel.*"

Newsweek, April 25, 1936
". . . fandangoed with such skill that it hit the rarefied heights of perfection . . . Master hands assembled it . . . Inspiration cast Tamara Geva as the ballerina . . . Bolger's dancing defies description without superlatives . . ."

Joseph Wood Krutch—*The Nation,* April 29, 1936
". . . some pleasant Cole Porterish lyrics set to pleasant Cole Porterish tunes, and it rejoices in the presence of that solemnly agile dancer, Ray Bolger, as well as in the genially depreciatory comedienne, Luella Gear . . . meandering and casual to the last degree . . . the best song is a hesitant and plaintive melody called *There's a Small Hotel . . .*"

Ruth Woodbury Sedgwick—*Stage,* May, 1936
". . . giving the town a new lease of glitter, high stepping and bawdy laughter . . . a sprightly enough book . . . tunes and lyrics slip along pleasantly, too . . . *Slaughter on Tenth Avenue* is as skilfully executed as authentic ballet; and, of course, is much better because it isn't . . ."

George Jean Nathan—*Life,* June, 1936
". . . a honey. I haven't seen a more intelligently planned and more intelligently amusing thing of its kind in some seasons . . . a witty, humorous and riddling lampoon that simultaneously tickles the cerebrum and the diaphragm. Rodgers' tunes and Hart's lyrics are in happy key with the general lark . . . Nathan says *Yes!*"

Bibliography

"On Your Toes" —*Vogue,* May 15, 1936

Tour

Nixon Theatre, Pittsburgh, January 25, 1937—National Theatre, Washington, March 13, 1937 (5 cities).

Selected Revivals

St. Louis Municipal Opera, July 10-16, 1939
Lee Dixon (JUNIOR); Patricia Bowman (VERA); Doris Patston (FRANKIE); Gladys Baxter (PEGGY); Robert Chisholm (SERGEI).

Bucks County Playhouse, Pennsylvania, July 21-26, 1952
Bill Callahan (JUNIOR); Katharine Sergava (VERA); Joan Holloway (FRANKIE); Yvonne Adair (PEGGY); Arny Freeman (SERGEI).

ON YOUR TOES

(London—1937)

Presented by Lee Ephraim and Dwight Deere Wiman
Directed by Leslie Henson
Mr. Balanchine's choreography reproduced by Andy Anderson
Settings by Joseph and Phil Harker
Costumes by Betty Boor
Music director, Lew Stone
Pianists, Bruce Merryl and Harry Foster

London Run

Palace Theatre, February 5-March 20, 1937
(Hippodrome, Golders Green, March 29-April 3, 1937)
(Streatham Hill Theatre, Streatham Hill, April 5-17, 1937)
Coliseum, April 19-May 29, 1937
123 *performances*

The Cast

PHIL DOLAN II, Philip Morgan
LIL DOLAN, Irene North
PHIL DOLAN III, Barrie Manning
LOLA, Thelma Fabian
PHIL DOLAN III ("JUNIOR"), Jack Whiting
FRANKIE FRAYNE, Gina Malo
SYDNEY COHN, Eddie Pola
VERA BARNOVA, Vera Zorina
ANUSHKA, Vivien Chambers
PEGGY PORTERFIELD, Olive Blakeney
SERGEI ALEXANDROVITCH, Vernon Kelso
KONSTANTINE MORROSINE, Jack Donohue
SNOOPY, George Rydon
STAGE MANAGER, Pat McGrath
MISHKA, Dennis Rivers

VASSILLI, Dick Taylor
DIMITRI, Vladimir Meschkoff
LEON, Leo Lauer
SINGER, Stanley Hoban
WAITER, Ronnie Reed
GANGSTERS, Blake Dorne, Herbert Douglas
LADIES OF THE BALLET: Vivien Tandy, Thelma Fabian, Lena Martin, Anne Starling, Joan Acworth, Dorothy Hutchinson, Frances Mellor, Daphne Tietgen, Sylvia Nicholls, Diana Gardener, Ella Collis, Edna Leggit
GENTLEMEN OF THE BALLET: Dennis Rivers, Nicholas Podiofolsky, Tovarich, Bobby Blanc, Michel Geval, Leo Lauer, Sobischewsky, Vladimir Meschkoff
LADIES OF THE ENSEMBLE: Phyllis Neal, Hyacinth Hazell, Eileen Foster, Pamela DuCalion, Felicity Lawford, Mary Barton, Renee Guscott, Gladys Lincoln, Iris Tully, Brenda Catherall, Vivien Chambers, Joyce Harris, Patty Edgar
GENTLEMEN OF THE ENSEMBLE: Reg Taylor, Peter Crawford, Dick Taylor, Herbert Douglas, Max Carole, Pat McGrath, Ronnie Reed, Leslie Vallee, Leon Dove

Musical Numbers

Same as original production, except that *Two-a-Day for Keith* called *Twice-a-Night.*

Reviews

London Times
". . . Perhaps because of the plot, this tautly constructed production trips gaily along its path with a directness and certainty seldom found in English compositions of this kind. The hydra has just as many heads as usual; but they seem to have a single thought . . . The tunes are numerous, catchy and cheerful, though of a familiar pattern . . ."

Sydney W. Carroll—*London Daily Telegraph*
". . . something quite new, startlingly fresh . . . It is bewitching. It defies conventionality . . . Modern jazz is one of my principal abominations. Yet in this play, I found myself conquered by its rhythms, fooled into laughing with, as well as at, its hopeless inanity . . ."

Horace Horsnell—*London Observer*
". . . rises to a climax that gives it unusual distinction . . . music, lyrics and preliminary ensembles promise what the pièce de résistance performs . . . the show goes like clockwork, and strikes the hours with the authority of Big Ben."

James Agate—*London Sunday Times*
". . . an original and witty burlesque of Russian ballet by people who can dance . . . music catches the exact Rimsky-Korsakov note for the ballet . . . best light entertainment for years . . ."

David C. Fairweather—*Theatre World,* March, 1937
". . . a musical play that for sheer originality and novelty of treatment, allied to a witty libretto and an excellent musical score, has not been equalled for more years than I would care to mention . . . has lilt and gaiety that make it quite irresistible . . ."

Bibliography

"On Your Toes" a Musical That is Different by Sydney W. Carroll
—*Play Pictorial,* May, 1937

ON YOUR TOES

(Film Version—1939)

A Warner Brothers Picture
Produced by Hal B. Wallis
Directed by Ray Enright
Screenplay by Jerry Wald and Richard Macaulay
Choreography by George Balanchine
Art director, Robert Haas
Costumes by Orry-Kelly
Music director, Leo Forbstein
Orchestrations by Ray Heindorf
Photographed by James Wong Howe and Sol Polito
Editor, Robert Kolster

Release Date

October 21, 1939

The Story

Junior Dolan, son of vaudevillians, forsakes the profession of his parents to become a composer of serious music. He sells his jazz ballet to a Russian ballet company, and falls in love with Vera, a ballerina, whom he had known when they were both children in vaudeville. Peggy Porterfield, the ballet's angel, is attracted to Junior, and through her influence it is produced with Dolan in the lead. He is mistaken by White Russians for another dancer whom they suspect of being a traitor, but is saved by the police and returns to Vera.

The Cast

VERA BARNOVA, Vera Zorina
PHIL DOLAN, JR., Eddie Albert
SERGEI ALEXANDROVITCH, Alan Hale
PADDY REILLY, Frank McHugh
PHIL DOLAN, SR., James Gleason
IVAN BOULTONOFF, Leonid Kinskey
PEGGY PORTERFIELD, Gloria Dickson
MRS. DOLAN, Queenie Smith
KONSTANTINE MORROSINE, Erik Rhodes
DONALD HENDERSON, Berton Churchill
PHIL JUNIOR, *as a boy*, Donald O'Connor
VERA, *as a girl*, Sarita Wooten

Musical Numbers

Retained from original production: *La Princesse Zenobia* ballet and *Slaughter on Tenth Avenue* ballet, with *On Your Toes, Quiet Night,* and *There's a Small Hotel* used only as background.

Reviews

Frank S. Nugent—*New York Times*
". . . still an ingratiating show and never more so than in the ballet sequences . . . But off its toes, it has a habit of falling flat on its face . . . The farce has become too broad for comfort . . ."

Howard Barnes—*New York Herald Tribune*
"The lovely Zorina, the brilliant ballet parody, *Slaughter on Tenth Avenue,* and some superior bits of terpsichore are the sole virtues of a ragged and dull screen musical . . ."

William Boehnel—*New York World-Telegram*
". . . in spite of its faults and the grievous omission of the score, the screen version is reasonably good fun . . ."

Roy Chartier—*Variety,* October 25, 1939
"Fine performances, effective camera work and inspired direction make it very palatable entertainment in spite of the fact that here and there the picture droops a little . . ."

Time, November 6, 1939
". . . gets its leaden foot in its mouth at the outset, spends the rest of the time coyly failing to get it out again . . . Even *Slaughter on Tenth Avenue* has no more bang than the pop-pistol percussion with which the orchestra burlesques its pantomime killing . . ."

ON YOUR TOES

(New York—1954)

Presented by George Abbott
Directed by Mr. Abbott
Choreography by George Balanchine
Settings by Oliver Smith
Costumes by Irene Sharaff
Lighting by Peggy Clark
Music director, Salvatore Dell'Isola
Orchestrations by Don Walker

Tryout

Shubert Theatre, New Haven, September 25-October 2, 1954

New York Run

Forty-sixth Street Theatre, October 11-December 4, 1954
64 performances

The Cast

PHIL DOLAN II, Jack Williams
LIL DOLAN, Eleanor Williams
PHIL DOLAN III, David Winters
STAGE MANAGER, George Church
LOLA, Dorene Kilmer
PHIL DOLAN III ("JUNIOR"), Bobby Van
FRANKIE FRAYNE, Kay Coulter
SIDNEY COHN, Joshua Shelley
VERA BARNOVA, Vera Zorina
ANUSHKA, Patricia Wilkes
PEGGY PORTERFIELD, Elaine Stritch
SERGEI ALEXANDROVITCH, Ben Astar
KONSTANTINE MORROSINE, Nicholas Orloff
SNOOPY, John Robb
THUG, Nathaniel Frey
MISHKA, Patricia Welch
IVAN, John Nola
VASSILLI, Edward Pfeiffer
DIMITRI, Ted Adkins
LEO, Robert Lindgren
BALLET STAGE MANAGER, Bertram Wood
COP, Arthur Grahl

GIRLS: Phyllis Campbell, Lillian D'Honau, Patricia Drylie, Katia Geneznova, Carolyn George, Marilyn Hale, Dorene Kilmer, Helen Kramer, Sonja Lindgren, Paula Lloyd, Sigyn, Barbara Michaels, Lois Pratt, Nina Popova, Ruth Sobotka, Mary Stanton, Carol Stevens, Wendy Winn

BOYS: Ted Adkins, Marvin Arnold, Johnny Bowen, Timmy Everett, Arthur Grahl, Edward Kerrigan, Jack Leigh, Robert Lindgren, John Nola, Edward Pfeiffer

NOTE: Shortly after the New York opening, the roles of PHIL DOLAN II, LIL DOLAN and PHIL DOLAN III, as well as the first two scenes of the musical, were eliminated.

Musical Numbers

Same as original production, plus *You Took Advantage of Me,* sung by PEGGY in the third scene of the second act. *Two-a-Day for Keith* dropped shortly after New York opening.

Reviews

Brooks Atkinson—*New York Times*

". . . most of us had mercifully forgotten that it had a book . . . labored and mechanical and verbose. The mood of the day has passed beyond it . . . Not everything in the score may be worth reviving. But most of it is original and exhilirating, and most of Hart's easy, saucy rhymes are off the theatre's top shelf . . . a lot of excellent material in it, and the performance is flawless . . ."

Walter F. Kerr—*New York Herald Tribune*

". . . drifts across the stage like an autumn ghost, eerie and echoing and cut from the bough. That its once joyous revelry should be so completely stilled is something of a mystery . . . Vera Zorina moves with spidery grace through a raucous, still stimulating rendition of the historic *Slaughter* ballet . . . but the show springs into the air too rarely . . ."

John Chapman—*New York Daily News*

". . . the songs include some of the really good Rodgers-Hart numbers . . . *Slaughter on Tenth Avenue* still is a vigorous and colorful piece of work. Always the show is valiantly on its toes, but it gets off the ground only once in a while . . ."

Richard Watts, Jr.—*New York Post*

". . . still notable mainly for the ballet, *Slaughter on Tenth Avenue,* and for quite a number of songs in a characteristically delightful score . . . The weakness is in the book . . ."

William Hawkins—*New York World-Telegram*

"In its final half-hour, it suddenly cooks up the sort of hot, tingling excitement that is musical comedy at its best. Before that, it is a now-and-then evening . . . fond, lovely songs . . ."

John McClain—*New York Journal-American*
". . . it still has that memorable score, even improved with age . . . Yet I was disappointed . . . Maybe a dull book didn't matter so much in 1936, but last night it seemed whenever the music and hoofing stopped and the people got around to those old lines, the whole vehicle wheezed, coughed and quit . . ."

George Jean Nathan—*ibid.*
"I can't altogether sympathize with the general complaint that the book has greatly aged and is dated, since it was almost as aged and dated when we first engaged it back in 1936 . . . Some of Rodgers' songs are still pleasant and some of the lyrics are still fetching . . . I reviewed it fairly favorably when it was first produced. All I can say in extenuation is that I must have improved wonderfully in the intervening eighteen years."

Hobe Morrison—*Variety,* October 13, 1954
". . . What was a great show in 1936 seems tame in 1954, despite the surviving quality of the songs and the still electrifying *Slaughter on Tenth Avenue* . . . The book is transparently contrived and awkward now . . ."

Wolcott Gibbs—*The New Yorker,* October 23, 1954
"I took a junior member of my family and I'm afraid it was a rather discouraging evening for both of us . . . 'Did you and Mother really like these kind of things when you were young?' she whispered . . . It still sounds nice, the dancing is almost distinguished, but the book which was once at worst merely a nuisance, has turned into something close to a calamity . . ."

Louis Kronenberger—*Time,* October 25, 1954
"*On Your Toes* is a good deal oftener on its uppers . . . With its throbbing score, *Slaughter on Tenth Avenue* remains—when such ballets are no longer news—vibrant and exciting . . . But for notable stretches there is torpor on 46th Street. There are very nice songs like *There's a Small Hotel,* but Rodgers gave the show a ballet rather than top drawer show music, and Hart gave it lyrics that tend to shout their cleverness . . ."

Harold Clurman—*The Nation,* October 30, 1954
". . . some pleasant, by now nearly nostalgic, songs, a rather funny dance routine in which an American yokel busts up a Russian ballet, girls who show a pretty portion of thighs in Balanchine's disappoint-

ing choreography . . . The revival suffers from a lack of any central strength—originally supplied by Ray Bolger . . ."

Eric Bentley—*The New Republic,* November 1, 1954
". . . The breath of a less stuffy generation is in the piece . . . a cocky, satirical, devil-may-care philosophy that is certainly very attractive and possibly very useful. Anyhow, it makes for good light theatre . . . *On Your Toes* is true musical comedy . . ."

Bibliography

Vera Zorina Back in "On Your Toes" by Ward Morehouse
—*New York World-Telegram & Sun,* July 22, 1954

The Right to Revive by Richard Rodgers
—*New York Times,* October 10, 1954

"Times Have Caught Up"—Why Rodgers and Abbott Revived "On Your Toes"
by Irving Drutman —*New York Herald Tribune,* November 7, 1954

DANCING PIRATE

(Film—1936)

A musical film with screenplay by Ray Harris and Francis Faragoh, based on a story "Glorious Buccaneer," by Emma Lindsey-Squier; music by Richard Rodgers; lyrics by Lorenz Hart.

An RKO-Radio Release
A Pioneer Production
Directed by Lloyd Corrigan
Choreography by Russell Lewis
Color design by Robert Edmond Jones
Music director, Alfred Newman
Photographed by William Skall
Color by Technicolor

Release Date
June 17, 1936

The Story
A young dancing master, Jonathan Pride, shanghaied from Boston at the outset of the 19th century, is mistaken for a pirate chief by the people of a Spanish settlement in Southern California. Sentenced to hang, he is saved by Serafina, the Alcalde's daughter, when she discovers that he is an expert at the waltz.

The Cast
JONATHAN PRIDE, Charles Collins
THE ALCALDE, Frank Morgan
SERAFINA, Steffi Duna
PARFILO, Luis Alberni
DON BALTAZAR, Victor Varconi
CHAGO, Jack LaRue
BLANCA, Alma Real
TECOLOTE, William V. Mong
PIRATE CHIEF, Mitchell Lewis
PIRATE COOK, Cy Kendall
SHEPHERD, Julian Rivero
ORVILLE, Harold Waldridge
ORVILLE'S MOTHER, Vera Lewis

LANDLADY, Nora Cecil
MISS PONSONBY, Ellen Lowe
The Royal Cansinos

Musical Numbers

Are You My Love?, SERAFINA
When You're Dancing the Waltz, JONATHAN, SERAFINA and Royal Cansinos

Reviews

B. R. Crisler—*New York Times*
". . . Despite its technological importance as the very last word in color photography, it manages also to be a light and amusing trifle in song, dance and comedy . . ."

Marguerite Tazelaar—*New York Herald Tribune*
". . . it is skillful and professional in every aspect, from its score to its excellent performances, but it is in substance empty . . ."

Alton Cook—*New York World-Telegram*
". . . on the credit side, two tuneful songs. But taking it all in all, it is a rather monotonous mixture of romance, melodrama and music."

Time, June 1, 1936
". . . lively and colorful . . . Best of the songs: *Are You My Love?*"

Abel Green—*Variety*, June 24, 1936
". . . too comic operetta to qualify as 1936 film fare . . . songs are more or less incidental . . ."

London Times, October 19, 1936
". . . It starts a fantastic idea and by neglecting to take it seriously bumps along the ground what should flutter in the half light . . ."

Bibliography

Dancing in Colors for the Screen by H. H. Niemeyer
—*St. Louis Post-Dispatch*, May 31, 1936

BABES IN ARMS

(1937)

A musical comedy with book by Richard Rodgers and Lorenz Hart; music by Mr. Rodgers; lyrics by Mr. Hart.

Presented by Dwight Deere Wiman
Directed by Robert Sinclair
Choreography by George Balanchine
Settings by Raymond Sovey
Costumes by Helene Pons
Music director, Gene Salzer
Orchestrations by Hans Spialek
Pianists, Edgar Fairchild and Adam Carroll

Tryout
Shubert Theatre, Boston, March 31-April 12, 1937

New York Run
Shubert Theatre, April 14-October 23, 1937; Majestic Theatre, October 25-December 18, 1937
289 performances

The Story
To save themselves from being sent to a work farm, the babes in arms—children of old vaudeville troupers—produce a musical revue. Unfortunately, it is not very successful. Later, by staging an interview with a transatlantic French pilot, they attract enough publicity to put on a successful show and have their own youth center.

The Cast
MAIZIE LAMAR, Ethel Intropidi
DAN LAMAR, Jere Delaney
VAL LAMAR, Ray Heatherton
NAT BLACKSTONE, George E. Mackay
EMMA BLACKSTONE, Aileen Poe
MARSHALL BLACKSTONE, Alfred Drake
BILLIE SMITH, Mitzi Green
SHERIFF REYNOLDS, George Watts

GUS FIELDING, Rolly Pickert
BOOKER VANDERPOOL, Kenneth Wilkins
PINKIE, Bob Fishelson
LEE CALHOUN, Dana Hardwick
BEAUREGARD CALHOUN, Douglas Perry
SAM REYNOLDS, Ray McDonald
DOLORES REYNOLDS, Grace McDonald
LINCOLN VANDERPOOL, LeRoy James
PETER, Duke McHale
BABY ROSE, Wynn Murray
IVOR DE QUINCY, Harold Nicholas
IRVING DE QUINCY, Fayard Nicholas
RENE FLAMBEAU, Aljan de Loville
PHIL MCCABE, Alvin Kerr
DR. SNYDER, George E. Mack
MITZI, Mitzi Dahl
JEAN, Jean Owens
TED, Ted Gary
ALEX, Alex Courtney
CLIFF, Clifton Darling
JIMMY, James Gillis
BOB, Robert Rounseville
THE GANG: Bobby Lane, Elenore Tennis, Gloria Franklin, Don Liberto, Libby Bennett, Verna Ceders, Mickey Herson, Marjorie Jane, Betty Lee, Connie Leslie, Audrey Palmer, Claire Harvey, Davenie Watson, Stella Clausen, Tania Clell, Eleanore Fiata, Georgia Hiden, Gedda Petry, Ursula Seiler, Roy Adler, Buddy Allen, Mickey Alvarez, Jay Bee, Jack Stanton, Dan Dailey, Bronson Dudley

NOTE: For tour, Miss Green succeeded by Evelyn Wyckoff.

Musical Numbers

ACT I

SCENE ONE—THE KITCHEN OF THE LAMAR HOUSE, SEAPORT, L.I.
Where or When, BILLIE and VAL

SCENE TWO—A STREET
Babes in Arms, BILLIE, VAL, MARSHALL and THE GANG

SCENE THREE—THE OSCAR W. HEMMINGWAY POST OF THE AMERICAN LEGION
I Wish I Were in Love Again, DOLORES and GUS

SCENE FOUR—A DISCARDED RAILWAY BOXCAR
All Dark People, IVOR and IRVING

SCENE FIVE—THE CALHOUN LIVING ROOM
Way Out West, BABY ROSE, ALEX, CLIFF, JIMMY, BOB

SCENE SIX—THE BACK DOOR OF THE LAMAR HOUSE

SCENE SEVEN—STAGE OF THE OLD BARN THEATRE

SCENE EIGHT—WINGS OF THE OLD BARN THEATRE
My Funny Valentine, BILLIE

SCENE NINE—STAGE OF THE OLD BARN THEATRE DURING "LEE CALHOUN'S FOLLIES"
Johnny One Note
THE SINGER, Wynne Murray
THE CHILD, Douglas Perry
THE HIGH PRIEST, Alfred Drake
THE PRIESTESS, Elenore Tennis
THE NUBIANS, The Nicholas Brothers
THE ACROBAT, Bobby Lane
THE SPECIALTY DANCERS, Mitzi Green and Duke McHale

ACT II
SCENE ONE—THE STABLE ON THE WORK FARM
Imagine, BABY ROSE, ALEX, CLIFF, JIMMY, BOB
All at Once, BILLIE and VAL

SCENE TWO—"PETER'S JOURNEY" BALLET
Peter's Journey Ballet
THE PRINCE, Duke McHale
THE ATTENDANTS, Kenneth Wilkins and Leroy James
ROCKEFELLER, Rolly Pickert
THE MERMAID, Elenore Tennis
GRETA GARBO, Gedda Petry
MARLENE DIETRICH, Ursula Seiler
CLARK GABLE, Ted Gary

SCENE THREE—LAMAR'S FIELD
The Lady Is a Tramp, BILLIE

SCENE FOUR—BEDROOM IN THE LAMAR HOUSE

SCENE FIVE—SOLARIUM OF THE SEAPORT YOUTH CENTER
You Are So Fair, DOLORES, GUS, TED, MITZI, PETER, JEAN
Finale, COMPANY

Reviews
Brooks Atkinson—*New York Times*
". . . a good humored show . . . Not an inspired book, but one that is full of good feeling, and a score that is altogether superb . . . one of the most contagious Rodgers and Hart have written . . . Without condescending from the sublime heights of maturity, they have written a genial and buoyant show . . ."

Richard Watts, Jr.—*New York Herald Tribune*
". . . it isn't too condescending or ostentatious about its youthfulness . . . a surprisingly pleasant commodity, and, aided by another gay, tuneful and ingenious score, it is a fresh and likeable show . . . the airs are gay, resourceful and charming and again Mr. Hart proves that he is the slyest and most ingenious of lyric writers . . . a pleasant sign of spring."

Burns Mantle—*New York Daily News*
"★★★ . . . Robert Sinclair has done so good a job with the direction that he has been able to keep the entertainment nicely varied, and Rodgers and Hart have done the rest by a good selection of tunes and story incidents . . . The lyrics are in good taste. The tunes fall pleasantly upon the ear . . ."

Robert Coleman—*New York Daily Mirror*
". . . novelty, surprise and freshness . . . perfectly swell fun, clean, clever, tuneful and constantly amusing. Rodgers and Hart at their best . . . as free of blushes as an ingenue without makeup."

John Mason Brown—*New York Post*
". . . zestful, tuneful and brilliantly danced affair. It is a pleasant show, filled with talented striplings and bubbling over with the freshness and energy of youth . . . the book counts for little . . . a 'blessed event.' "

Douglas Gilbert—*New York World-Telegram*
". . . a musical of taste, smartness and delightful abandon . . . What it lacks in loud guffaws is compensated for by an original score, sprightly lines, some outstanding lyrics, spirited highjinks by rollicking kids, and a ballet—*Peter's Journey*—that is a wonderland fancy of the highest order . . . Mr. Rodgers is not as melodious as he usually is but he has piped some original ditties to clever lyrics . . ."

Richard Lockridge—*New York Sun*
". . . a gay and sprightly show, all done in a youthful and informal spirit . . . Rodgers and Hart have seldom turned out better tunes in more pleasing profusion . . . one fine one, *The Lady Is a Tramp* . . ."

John Anderson—*New York Journal*
". . . a bright new show . . . fresh, youthful and utterly captivating . . . pretty tunes and clever lyrics . . . Mr. Rodgers stirs himself to some of his gayest and most ingratiating music, and it is all sung and danced with disarming informality . . . I hope it lives long and never grows up."

Abel Green—*Variety,* April 21, 1937
". . . a fertile score and an engaging libretto . . . The book, where the breezy dialog affords the opportunities, is quite farcical . . ."

Time, April 24, 1937
". . . dewy and precocious . . . notable as a feat of theatrical cradle robbing; there is hardly a vote in the cast . . . Hart still maintains the lightest touch in the business. As usual, the Rodgers melodies are fresh as a May wind, artful and surprising as the flight of a barn swallow . . ."

Newsweek, April 24, 1937
". . . a joyous array of boys and girls who sing and dance and have a wonderful time without much of a story to hamper their frivolity . . . So gay and engaging that nobody cares much whether the show makes sense . . . good clean fun for everybody from first to second childhood. Catchy tunes, including *Babes in Arms, Johnny One Note* and *The Lady Is a Tramp,* tinkle through the evening."

Robert Benchley—*The New Yorker,* April 24, 1937
". . . a swell show . . . Rodgers and Hart have turned out one of their nicest scores. *Babes in Arms* has a crusading, evangelical quality about its rising surge which might well be used for a more sturdy Youth Movement than organizing a vaudeville show in a barn . . ."

Tour

Forrest Theatre, Philadelphia, December 24, 1937—Shubert Theatre, Newark, March 12, 1938 (3 cities).

Selected Revivals

St. Louis Municipal Opera, August 19-24, 1940
Audrey Christie (BILLIE); Harry Stockwell (VAL); Rolly Pickert (GUS); Wynn Murray (BABY ROSE); Bob Lawrence (RENE).

Royal Poinciana Playhouse, Palm Beach, March 30-April 4, 1959
Cocoanut Grove Playhouse, Miami Beach, April 6-18, 1959
Julie Wilson (BUNNY); Brian Davis (VAL); Joan Hovis (SUSIE); Barbara Sharma (TERRY). NOTE: This was revised version with book by George Oppenheimer.

Goodspeed Opera House, East Haddam, Conn., April 10-June 16, 1979
Marianne Challis (BILLIE); Ned Peterson (VAL); Andrea McArdle (BABY ROSE); Don Simeone (PETER); Barry Tarallo (GUS).

BABES IN ARMS

(Film Version—1939)

A Metro-Goldwyn-Mayer Picture
Produced by Arthur Freed
Directed by Busby Berkeley
Screenplay by Jack McGowan and Kay Van Riper
Art director, Merrill Pye
Costumes by Dolly Tree
Music director, George Stoll
Music adaptation by Roger Edens
Orchestrations by Leo Arnaud and George Bassman
Photographed by Ray June
Editor, Frank Sullivan

Release Date

September 19, 1939

The Cast

MICKEY MORAN, Mickey Rooney
PATSY BARTON, Judy Garland
JOE MORAN, Charles Winninger
JUDGE BLACK, Guy Kibbee
ROSALIE ESSEX, June Preisser
FLORRIE MORAN, Grace Hayes
MOLLY MORAN, Betty Jaynes
DON BRICE, Douglas McPhail
JEFF STEELE, Rand Brooks
DODY MARTINI, Leni Lynn
BOBS, John Sheffield
MADOX, Henry Hull
WILLIAM, Barnett Parker
MRS. BARTON, Ann Shoemaker
MARTHA STEELE, Margaret Hamilton
MR. ESSEX, Joseph Crehan

Musical Numbers

Songs retained from original production: *Babes in Arms* and *Where or When*. Songs written specially for film: *Good Morning* (music by Nacio Herb Brown; lyric by Arthur Freed), and *Daddy Was a Minstrel Man* (by Roger Edens). Other songs in film: *You Are My Lucky Star* and *Broadway Rhythm* (both by Brown and Freed); *I'm Just Wild About Harry* (by Eubie Blake and Noble Sissle); *Ida, Sweet as Apple Cider* (by Eddie Leonard); *I Cried for You* (music by Gus Arnheim and Abe Lyman; lyric by Arthur Freed); and *God's Country* (music by Harold Arlen; lyric by E. Y. Harburg).

Reviews

B. R. Crisler—*New York Times*

"*Babes in Arms*—to express it in two words—is Mickey Rooney . . . we definitely don't like the screenplay. If we must have hokum, let us at least disguise it gracefully, even when it's with music."

Robert W. Dana—*New York Herald Tribune*

". . . amiable, fresh and spirited . . . cleverer, far more entertaining on the screen . . ."

Irene Thirer—*New York Post*

". . . quite a show. It moves fast with guaranteed laughs and lots of sure-fire tunes."

Variety, September 20, 1939

". . . topflight filmusic entertainment. It will click mightily in the deluxers . . . rates with the best . . ."

John Mosher—*The New Yorker*, October 28, 1939

". . . the numbers are generally lively; it's the long, noisy, talky interludes that wear one down . . ."

Bibliography

"Babes in Arms" —*Life*, November 6, 1939

I'D RATHER BE RIGHT

(1937)

A musical comedy with book by George S. Kaufman and Moss Hart; music by Richard Rodgers; lyrics by Lorenz Hart.

Presented by Sam H. Harris
Book staged by Mr. Kaufman
Choreography by Charles Weidman, Ned McGurn
Settings by Donald Oenslager
Costumes by Irene Sharaff and John Hambleton
Music director, Harry Levant
Orchestrations by Hans Spialek

Tryout
Colonial Theatre, Boston, October 11-23, 1937
Ford's Theatre, Baltimore, October 24-29, 1937

New York Run
Alvin Theatre, November 2, 1937-May 21, 1938
Music Box Theatre, May 23-July 9, 1938
290 performances

The Story
Peggy and Phil want to marry, but must await Phil's raise, which will come when the national budget is balanced. They dream that they meet the President in Central Park, that he works mightily to balance the budget, but is hindered by various things, including the Supreme Court, Congress, and his own cabinet. The President never does quite work the budget out, but advises the young pair to have faith in their country and marry just the same. They do. Actual names are used in the satire.

The Cast
PEGGY JONES, Joy Hodges
PHIL BARKER, Austin Marshall
THE PRESIDENT OF THE UNITED STATES, George M. Cohan
HIS SECRETARY, Ralph Glover
THE POSTMASTER GENERAL, Paul Parks
THE SECRETARY OF THE TREASURY, Taylor Holmes

THE SECRETARY OF STATE, Marion Green
THE SECRETARY OF LABOR, Bijou Fernandez
THE SECRETARY OF THE NAVY, David Allman
THE SECRETARY OF COMMERCE, Al Atkins
THE SECRETARY OF AGRICULTURE, Robert Bleck
THE SECRETARY OF WAR, Jack Mills
THE SECRETARY OF THE INTERIOR, Charles McLoughlin
THE ATTORNEY-GENERAL, Robert Less
THE CHIEF JUSTICE, John Cherry
JAMES B. MAXWELL, Florenz Ames
FEDERAL THEATRE DIRECTOR, Joseph Macaulay
SOCIAL SECURITIES MESSENGER, Georgie Tapps
THE PRESIDENT'S MOTHER, Marie Louise Dana
A BUTLER, Joseph Allen
THE JUDGE'S GIRL, Mary Jane Walsh
SISTIE, Evelyn Mills
BUZZIE, Warren Mills
TONY, Joseph Macaulay
JOE, Joe Verdi
THE ACROBATS, Jack Reynolds and Sol Black
DANCE SPECIALTIES, Irene McBride, Margaret Sande, Jack Whitney
SINGING GIRLS: Virginia Berger, Cecil Carey, Ruth Clayton, Geraldine Hamilton, Linda Kellogg, Marie Nash, Erminie Randolph, Jane Richardson, Emily Stephenson
SINGING BOYS: Charles Bywater, Len Frank, John Fulco, Jack Leslie, Joe Granville, Jack Kearney, William Marel, John McWade, Bob Spencer, Norman Van Emburgh, Herbert Wood
DANCING GIRLS: Jeanette Bradley, Jeanette Lee, Kate Frederic, Ruth Gormley, Eleanor Dewitt, Georgette Lampsi, Velma Lord, Lili Mann, Austra Neiman, Tina Rigat, Patsey Schenk, Betty Schaeffer, Clarise Sitomer, Dorothy Waller
DANCING BOYS: Jack Barnes, Don Carter, Martin Fair, Jay Hunter, Beau Tilden, Edward Harrington, Robert Howard, Fred May

NOTE: For tour, Miss Hodges succeeded by Marie Nash. During last week of tour, Mr. Cohan succeeded by Mr. Holmes.

Musical Numbers

The action takes place in Central Park, New York, on July 4th.

ACT I

A Homogeneous Cabinet, CABINET MEMBERS
Have You Met Miss Jones?, PEGGY and PHIL
Take and Take and Take, THE JUDGE'S GIRL; danced by Irene McBride and ENSEMBLE
Spring in Vienna, FEDERAL THEATRE DIRECTOR; danced by Margaret Sande, Jack Whitney and ENSEMBLE

A Little Bit of Constitutional Fun, THE JUDGE'S GIRL and ENSEMBLE
Sweet Sixty-Five, PEGGY and PHIL; danced by SOCIAL SECURITIES MESSENGER and Jack Whitney
We're Going to Balance the Budget, THE PRESIDENT and COMPANY

ACT II
American Couple
THE GIRL, Margaret Sande
THE MOTHER, Irene McBride
THE BOY, Georgie Tapps
THE FATHER, Fred Nay
THE MINISTER, Jack Barnes
A FLOWER GIRL, Clarise Sitomer
A PHOTOGRAPHER, Jack Whitney
BEST MAN, Edward Harrington
THE NURSE, Jeanette Bradley
THE TEACHER, Lili Mann
THE SON, Warren Mills
RINGMASTER, Jack Whitney
CLOWN, Martin Fair
BAREBACK RIDER, Austra Neiman
A SEAL, Don Carter
ANOTHER MOTHER, Tina Rigat
ANOTHER FATHER, Joe Granville
THE SON *(grown up),* Georgie Tapps
HIS GIRL, Margaret Sande
Labor Is the Thing, MAXWELL and ENSEMBLE
I'd Rather Be Right, PEGGY, PHIL, THE JUDGE'S GIRL, THE PRESIDENT and ENSEMBLE
Off the Record, THE PRESIDENT
A Baby Bond, THE SECRETARY OF THE TREASURY

NOTE: The original title song, plus *The World Is My Oyster* and *Everybody Loves You* cut before New York opening. The *American Couple* sequence dropped shortly after opening, in favor of song *What It's All About* (sung and danced by SOCIAL SECURITIES MESSENGER and ENSEMBLE). *Spring in Vienna* changed to *Spring in Milwaukee* in May, 1938.

Reviews

Brooks Atkinson—*New York Times*

". . . Mr. Cohan has never been in better form . . . a pleasant-spoken musical comedy that leisurely ambles away the evening . . . There is some brisk stuff here and there but *Of Thee I Sing* was enormously more versatile and dynamic . . . All Rodgers and Hart's political ditties are keen . . . a clever and likeable musical comedy. But it is not the brilliant political satire most of us have been fondly expecting."

Richard Watts, Jr.—*New York Herald Tribune*
". . . by no means vicious in its attack, but there can be little doubt of its bias . . . So completely delightful is the Cohan portrayal that the whole show, despite its acid moments, takes on a winning charm . . . There is nothing brilliant or witty in the manner of *Of Thee I Sing* about it . . . Rodgers' score is delightful, and Hart's lyrics, while hardly among his best, are again ingenious . . ."

Burns Mantle—*New York Daily News*
★★★+ . . . one of the important musical plays of this generation and pretty consistently entertaining . . . But it just isn't the greatest musical comedy ever written or the greatest political satire ever staged . . . a good three star satire elevated to a three star plus rating by the presence of Mr. Cohan and a handsome production . . ."

Robert Coleman—*New York Daily Mirror*
". . . Mr. Cohan gives his greatest performance . . . catchy Rodgers and Hart songs . . . In sum, perfectly swell. An exhilarating cocktail, concocted of romance, hilarity, satire, swing music, tasteful color, and vivid personalities."

John Mason Brown—*New York Post*
". . . gay, witty, topical and audacious . . . an almost constant delight . . . if it is not (and nothing could be) as uproarious as it has been said to be, it is nonetheless an uncommonly good show. And a healthy, reassuring one . . . a series of slaps which for the most part are so good natured that their ultimate destination seems to be the back . . . To be sure, Mr. Kaufman and the *Zwei Herzen*—Moss and Lorenz—get many unsparing and uproarious things said . . . Mr. Rodgers' music seems more serviceable than catchy . . ."

Sidney B. Whipple—*New York World-Telegram*
". . . about on the level of a Gridiron Club performance and that is no shining mark to shoot at . . . the brighter moments are strung together so mechanically, and with such unamusing interludes, that the show drags . . . little in the music to bring the heart-thumping thrill you expect from Richard Rodgers, and certainly nothing to sweep the country . . ."

Richard Lockridge—*New York Sun* (page 1)
". . . a show without venom . . . An entertaining spoof, capitally acted and gayly sung; not always brilliant satire, but lively, home-grown stuff, produced with brilliance. It will not live after its authors by a long shot, but it will almost certainly make merriment for the winter."

John Anderson—*New York Journal-American*
". . . large and vastly amusing . . . The wonder is, not only that it is done, but that it is done so well, so good naturedly, so uproariously, and with such good taste. Even in its sharpest ribbing, it never seems offensive. Lorenz Hart's lyrics are deadly, but Richard Rodgers' music, witty and pertinently impertinent, soothes some of the wounds . . . My vote is Cohan for President . . ."

Heywood Broun—*New York World-Telegram,* November 5, 1937
". . . far more deft and also far less punishing than the average Gridiron show . . . if Roosevelt runs again both Moss Hart and George Kaufman might vote for him with practically clear consciences . . . Roosevelt is in a good spot to grin and bear it, for he can easily afford to let the orchestra go Maine and Vermont as long as he carries the gallery . . ."

Jack Pulaski (Ibee.)—*Variety,* November 10, 1937
". . . a good deal of fun . . . fine tunes . . . may arouse a difference of opinion, but it is fine theatre, and in many respects, the most unusual in modern times . . ."

Time, November 15, 1937
". . . Compared to *Of Thee I Sing,* it is a buttoned, if glistening, foil . . . The music, with no particular motif to follow, becomes largely a utilitarian accompaniment to fit the rhyme. Despite its genial aimlessness, it succeeds in venturing with impunity into an almost unprecedented form of satire . . ."

George Jean Nathan—*Newsweek,* November 15, 1937
". . . Why the idea of calling George M. Cohan Franklin D. Roosevelt should have engendered so intense an interest I can't figure out, unless it was because Franklin D. Roosevelt, on the other hand, has been called everything under the sun but George M. Cohan . . . The show proved itself a sprightly beanfest and one frequently rich in amiable monkeyshines . . . in the main it applies a droll and delightful slapstick to the seat of government and amounts to as happy a sport as the theatre has provided in some time . . ."

Stark Young—*The New Republic,* November 17, 1937
". . . though the second half falls off considerably, worst of all in the pantomimic inventions, the generous first half establishes such a happy delight, such good sense, caustic humor, carrying lyrics, effective costumes, and clever decor—not to mention Mr. Cohan's infallible performance—that the whole evening seems a banner one."

Edith J. R. Isaacs—*Theatre Arts Monthly*, December, 1937
". . . much closer to the French form of personal comment—with George M. Cohan speaking for the authors—than it is to the more frolicsome and less deeply satirical *Of Thee I Sing* . . . the whole first act is full of laughter . . . The second act is woefully thin . . . The music and lyrics are amiable and pleasant . . ."

Bibliography

NEWSPAPERS AND PERIODICALS

Cohan as Tap-Dancing Roosevelt —*New York Times*, October 12, 1937

Budget Balance Pledged Again by "President" by Bert Andrews
—*New York Herald Tribune*, October 12, 1937

Spoofing the Great (editorial) —*New York Times*, October 14, 1937

George M. Cohan Mimics Franklin D. Roosevelt in Play
—*Life*, October 25, 1937

Cohan & Friend —*Time*, October 25, 1937

The President on the Pan in a New Musical Comedy by Robert Sell
—*St. Louis Post-Dispatch Sunday Magazine*, October 31, 1937

Cohan Denies Attempting to Imitate Roosevelt by H. Allen Smith
—*New York World-Telegram*, November 6, 1937

Regarding Those Who Would Rather Be Right by John Peter Toohey
—*New York Times*, November 7, 1937

"I'd Rather Be Right" (editorial) —*New York Daily News*, November 9, 1937

Cohan's "Rather Be Right" Has 300G Advance Sale; May Gross $1,000,000
–*Variety*, November 10, 1937

Utopia '37 by Howard Brubaker —*Stage*, November, 1937

BOOKS

I'd Rather Be Right (Random House, New York; 1937)
Book and lyrics of the musical.

Tour

Forrest Theatre, Philadelphia, October 3, 1938—Playhouse, Wilmington, February 25, 1939 (27 cities).

FOOLS FOR SCANDAL

(Film—1938)

A musical film with screenplay by Herbert and Joseph Fields, based on the play "Food for Scandal" by Nancy Hamilton, James Shute and Rosemary Casey; music by Richard Rodgers; lyrics by Lorenz Hart.

A Warner Bros.-First National Picture
Produced and directed by Mervyn LeRoy
Art director, Anton Grot
Costumes by Milo Anderson, Travis Banton
Music director, Leo F. Forbstein
Orchestrations by Adolph Deutsch
Photographed by Ted Tetzlaff
Editor, William Holmes

Release Date
March 24, 1938

The Story
Kay Winters, an American screen actress in Paris on a holiday, is pursued by Rene, an impecunious marquis. His persistence leads him to become Kay's butler, when all other attempts to be near her have failed. Eventually she capitulates.

The Cast
KAY WINTERS, Carole Lombard
RENE, Fernand Gravet
PHILIP CHESTER, Ralph Bellamy
DEWEY GILSON, Allan Jenkins
LADY PAULA MALVERTON, Isabel Jeans
MYRTLE, Marie Wilson
JILL, Marcia Ralston
AGNES, Tola Nesmith
LADY POTTER-PORTER, Heather Thatcher
PAPA JOLI-COEUR, Jacques Lory
SINGER, Jeni LeGon
Les Hite and his Orchestra

Musical Numbers
There's a Boy in Harlem, Jeni LeGon
Food for Scandal, spoken by KAY and RENE with musical background
How Can You Forget?

Reviews
B. R. Crisler—*New York Times*
". . . this colossal, satin-upholstered whimsy is a painful and prolonged operation . . ."

William Boehnel—*New York World-Telegram*
". . . a trivial and not very lightfooted romance . . ."

Roy Chartier—*Variety*, March 30, 1938
". . . has many diverting moments and, on the whole, measures up well enough to deserve an average business or more . . . Rodgers and Hart's special music isn't prominently displayed . . ."

Time, April 4, 1938
". . . more fustian than fun . . . .Sawed-off, narrow-eyed, cigar-waving Producer LeRoy is best at purposeful melodrama . . . In drawing room comedy his approach is parvenu."

Newsweek, April 4, 1938
". . . the story is lacking in sprightliness and humor . . ."

Graham Greene—*The Spectator*, August 26, 1938
". . . a pity that Carole Lombard's directors should have given her so humourless, so hopeless a story (perhaps that's why she has to scream so loud) . . . Perhaps it is meant to be a crazy comedy, but the secret of the crazy comedy is that people do behave with the irrelevance of human beings and break out through the Hollywood frame into life . . ."

I MARRIED AN ANGEL

(1938)

A musical comedy with book by Richard Rodgers and Lorenz Hart, adapted from the play by Janos Vaszary; music by Mr. Rodgers; lyrics by Mr. Hart.

Presented by Dwight Deere Wiman
Directed by Joshua Logan
Choreography by George Balanchine
Settings by Jo Mielziner
Costumes by John Hambleton
Music director, Gene Salzer
Orchestrations by Hans Spialek
Harpist, Casper Reardon

Tryout
Shubert Theatre, New Haven, April 14-16, 1938
Shubert Theatre, Boston, April 19-30, 1938

New York Run
Shubert Theatre, May 11, 1938-February 25, 1939
338 performances

The Story
Disillusioned by his fiancee, Count Willy vows that he will only marry an angel. One does appear, he marries her, and she slowly and somewhat painfully becomes charmingly mortal—embarrassing Count Willy in the process. In the end all proves to have been for the best.

The Cast
MAJOR DOMO, David Jones
TWO GUESTS, The Dunham Brothers
OLGA MADAYN, Hene Damur
GENERAL LUCASH, Morton L. Stevens
GUEST, Arthur Kent
PETER MUELLER, Charles Walters
COUNT WILLY PALAFFI, Dennis King
COUNTESS PEGGY PALAFFI, Vivienne Segal
ANNA MURPHY, Audrey Christie
ANGEL, Vera Zorina

JUSTICE OF PEACE, Arthur Kent
VALET DE CHAMBRE, David Jones
FEMME DE CHAMBRE, Marie Louise Quevli
MODISTE, Ruth Urban
1ST VENDEUSE, Janis Dremann
2ND VENDEUSE, Marcella Howard
HARRY MISCHKA SZIGETTI, Walter Slezak
DUCHESS OF HOLSTEIN-KUHHOFF, Katherine Stewart
1ST CLERK, David Jones
2ND CLERK, Arthur Kent
1ST STENOGRAPHER, Barbara Towne
2ND STENOGRAPHER, Sylvia Stone
LUCINDA, Marie Louise Quevli
CLARINDA, Janis Dremann
PHILOMENA, Marcella Howard
ROSALINA, Barbara Towne
SERONELLA, Sylvia Stone
ARABELLA, Diana Gaylen
FLORABELLA, Althea Elder
PREMIER DANSEUR, Charles Laskey
LADIES OF THE BALLET: Genevieve Cook, Ronnie Cunningham, May Block, Marion Davison, Eleanor Fiata, Petra Gray, Ruth Haidt, Isabelle Kimpal, Nancy Knott, Evelyn Lafferty, Sonia Larina, Bobby Howell, Beatrice Lynn, Maria Monnig, Gedda Petry, Shirley F. Shaffer, Betty Jane Smith, Alma Wertley, Virginia Williams
GENTLEMEN OF THE BALLET: Milton Barnett, Edward Brinkman, Boris Butleroff, Harold Haskin, Michael Mann, John Marshall, Jack Quinn, Nicolai Popov, Harold Taub, Nikolas Vasilieff

NOTE: During tour, Miss Zorina succeeded by Karen Van Ryn; Mr. Walters by Dan Dailey; Mr. Slezak by Norman Roland; Miss Christie by Bobbe Arnst; Mr. Stevens by Burl Ives.

Musical Numbers

ACT I

SCENE ONE—WILLY'S SALON, BUDAPEST
Did You Ever Get Stung?, WILLY, PEGGY, PETER

SCENE TWO—WILLY'S STUDY

SCENE THREE—HOTEL BEDROOM, PARIS
I Married an Angel, WILLY
The Modiste, WILLY, ANGEL, MODISTE, 1ST and 2ND VENDEUSES

SCENE FOUR
Honeymoon Ballet, ANGEL, WILLY, PREMIER DANCER and CORPS DE BALLET

SCENE FIVE—WILLY'S STUDY
I'll Tell the Man in the Street, PEGGY and HARRY

SCENE SIX—WILLY'S SALON
How to Win Friends and Influence People, ANNA, PETER and ENSEMBLE
Finale, WILLY, PEGGY, ANGEL

ACT II
SCENE ONE—PALAFFI BROTHERS' BANK, BUDAPEST
Spring Is Here, WILLY and PEGGY

SCENE TWO—ANGEL'S BOUDOIR
Angel Without Wings, ANGEL, LUCINDA, CLARINDA, PHILOMENA, ROSALINA, SERONELLA, ARABELLA, FLORABELLA
A Twinkle in Your Eye, PEGGY

SCENE THREE—HARRY'S SALON
Reprise, *I'll Tell the Man in the Street,* HARRY
At the Roxy Music Hall, ANNA

SCENE FOUR—ROXY'S MUSIC HALL
Danced by COMPANY

SCENE FIVE—HARRY'S SALON
Finale, COMPANY

Reviews
Brooks Atkinson—*New York Times*
". . . one of the best musical comedies for many seasons . . . It perches on the top shelf of the Rodgers and Hart music cabinet. For this is no grinding of the Broadway hurdy-gurdy, but an imaginative improvisation with a fully orchestrated score and an extraordinarily beautiful production . . . Musical comedy has met its masters, and they have reared back and passed a Forty-fourth Street miracle."
Richard Watts, Jr.—*New York Herald Tribune*
". . . a pleasant and enlivening little fable, and thanks to a characteristically delightful score, imaginative settings, and the enchanting performance of Vera Zorina, it is a thoroughly charming musical comedy . . . I liked *Did You Ever Get Stung?, I Married an Angel* and *A Twinkle in Your Eye* the best of the songs, but all of the numbers are exceptionally attractive . . . an air of freshness and dexterity and even a bit of originality about the show . . ."

Burns Mantle—*New York Daily News*
"★★★ . . . Pretty dull as to story, but it brightened at the end with a hilarious travesty of a Roxy Music Hall stage show . . ."

Robert Coleman—*New York Daily Mirror*
". . . bright and bubbling . . . a grand score, intelligent lyrics, an excellent cast, and marked originality . . ."

John Mason Brown—*New York Post*
"... at all times a handsome show ... the most delightful score Mr. Rodgers has written in several seasons ... Mr. Hart's drollest lyrics ... Its first half is over-long and over-serious ... Once Mr. Rodgers abandons the book, the evening takes on a delightful turn for the better ... a parody of the Roxy Music Hall is side-splitting enough to make a visit to the Shubert imperative ... Altogether a very pleasant and most unusual evening."

Sidney B. Whipple—*New York World-Telegram*
"... satisfying and, to a mild degree, intoxicating. Good, cool and refreshing for hot weather audiences ... Many of the songs, particularly the title song, will be heard on the street and over the air throughout the summer ..."

Richard Lockridge—*New York Sun*
"... a gay and capricious delight, full of jauntiness and grace and happy songs. Its scenes shimmer and its comedy is pertinent ... pretty exactly, on the whole, what a musical comedy ought to be, and a bubbling oasis in a Springtime desert."

John Anderson—*New York Journal-American*
"... a winged wonderwork from the musical heavens of Rodgers and Hart ... It is the patrician successor to *On Your Toes* and *Babes in Arms,* cut with the same gaiety and imagination, out of the same smart pattern and better than either ... has everything it needs except a little trimming around the edges ... Mr. Rodgers' score is off his top music rack, and carries the whole thing admirably ..."

Abel Green—*Variety,* May 12, 1938
"... definitely boxoffice ... a fast-moving, episodic libretto which is by no means fragile ... an arresting book and a dandy score ..."

Wolcott Gibbs—*The New Yorker,* May 21, 1938
"... Once the preliminaries are out of the way, it settles down into as pretty and charming a comedy as you could want ... The story is no more simple-minded than the framework of most musicals, and it is hard to see how the rest could be better ... a parody of a Music Hall stage show seems to me as memorable in its eerie way as the *Slaughter on Tenth Avenue* ballet ..."

George Jean Nathan—*Newsweek,* May 23, 1938
"... Rodgers' score is one of his more recent best; the book, whatever its occasional lapses, is pointed with a lovely and delicate drollery ... Vera Zorina gratifies the vision not only with a real dance talent but a face and figure that do not demand the customary

volitional imaginative soft focus to help them out . . . The exhibit is maneuvered with capital taste, and, if your own taste is what it should be, will give you an evening of large delight."

Time, May 23, 1938
". . . plenty of Rodgers' silver tunes . . . For an act and a half, it pins all its hopes on being fluffy, fleecy, feathery swansdown . . . in the middle of Act II, Producer Wiman suddenly tosses Budapest into the Danube, lights out for Manhattan, hotchas up Broadway, and gives the signal for all kinds of people to rush in where angels fear to tread. The slightly incongruous result wakes up a drowsing show with the black coffee of a burlesque on a Radio City Music Hall routine . . ."

Bibliography

Newest Musical Hit Is About Angels —*Life,* May 30, 1938

The Inside Stuff Backstage at "I Married an Angel"
—*New York Herald Tribune,* August 7, 1938.

Tour

Nixon Theatre, Pittsburgh, February 28, 1939—Curran Theatre, San Francisco, January 28, 1940 (46 cities).

Selected Revivals

Dallas State Fair, July 23-August 5, 1951
Vera Zorina (ANGEL); John Brownlee (WILLY); Hiram Sherman (HARRY); Arlene Dahl (PEGGY); Jere MacMahon (PETER); Joan Holloway (ANNA).

Royal Poinciana Playhouse, Palm Beach, March 16-21, 1964
Cocoanut Grove Playhouse, Miami Beach, March 23-April 4, 1964
Westbury Music Fair, Long Island, July 7-12, 1964
Taina Elg (ANGEL); Clifford David (WILLY); Al Bernie (HARRY); Elaine Stritch (VALERIE); Jack Leigh (PETER); April Shawhan (ANNA). Note: This was a revised version with book by Lois Jacoby. In July, Mr. David was succeeded by Don Ameche, Miss Stritch by Margaret Whiting.

Productions Abroad

Theatre Royal, Sydney, Australia, May 12, 1939
Presented by Australian and New Zealand Theatres Ltd.; directed by Macklin Megley; choreography reproduced by Dan Eckley. *Cast:* Katrin Rosselle (ANGEL); Melton Moore (WILLY); Don Nicol (HARRY); Bernice Claire (PEGGY); George Dobbs (PETER); Kathryn Crawford (ANNA).

I MARRIED AN ANGEL

(Film Version—1942)

A Metro-Goldwyn-Mayer Picture
Produced by Hunt Stromberg
Directed by W. S. Van Dyke II
Screenplay by Anita Loos
Choreography by Ernest Matray
Art director, Cedric Gibbons
Costumes by Motley
Music director, Herbert Stothart
Photographed by Ray June
Editor, Conrad Nervig

Release Date

July 9, 1942

The Cast

ANNA (BRIGGITTA), Jeanette MacDonald
COUNT WILLY PALAFFI, Nelson Eddy
PETER, Edward Everett Horton
PEGGY, Binnie Barnes
"WHISKERS," Reginald Owen
BARON SZIGETHY, Douglass Dumbrille
MARIKA, Mona Maris
SUFI, Janis Carter
IRENE, Inez Cooper
ZINSKI, Leonid Kinskey
POLLY, Anne Jeffreys
DOLLY, Marion Rosamond

Musical Numbers

Songs retained from original production: *I Married an Angel, I'll Tell the Man in the Street* and *Spring Is Here.* New lyrics by Bob Wright and Chet Forrest written for *Did You Ever Get Stung?* and song then called *Little Work-a-day World.*

Reviews

Bosley Crowther—*New York Times*
". . . unless you are hardened to violence or are a doting Eddy-MacDonald fan steer clear. A more painful and clumsy desecration of a lovely fiction has not been perpetrated in years . . ."

Howard Barnes—*New York Herald Tribune*
". . . has a certain musical eloquence . . . a dull show, pretentious in the bargain . . ."

William Boehnel—*New York World-Telegram*
". . . The only thing I can recommend is Rodgers' original score. This is still lovely. I must add, too, that Miss MacDonald and Mr. Eddy sing it beautifully. But there praise ends. The narrative is hackneyed stuff . . ."

Newsweek, June 29, 1942
". . . brings the fantasy down to earth with a thud . . . a handsome production . . . a tuneful score . . . Yet heavy handed in writing, direction and acting . . ."

Whittaker Chambers—*Time,* July 6, 1942
". . . vigorously rubs the bloom from the wings of the brisk, fresh, imaginative Broadway musical . . . a fantastically mutilated plot."

Joe Schoenfeld—*Variety,* July 20, 1942
". . . a slow-moving, poorly acted, expensive production . . ."

THE BOYS FROM SYRACUSE

(1938)

A musical comedy with book by George Abbott, based on the play "The Comedy of Errors" by William Shakespeare, adapted from "Menaechmi" by Plautus; music by Richard Rodgers; lyrics by Lorenz Hart.

Presented by George Abbott
Directed by Mr. Abbott
Choreography by George Balanchine
Settings and lighting by Jo Mielziner
Costumes by Irene Sharaff
Music director, Harry Levant
Orchestrations by Hans Spialek

Tryout
Shubert Theatre, New Haven, November 3-5, 1938
Shubert Theatre, Boston, November 7-19, 1938

New York Run
Alvin Theatre, November 23, 1938-June 10, 1939
235 performances

The Story
Accompanied by his servant, Dromio, Antipholus of Syracuse visits Ephesus in search of his long lost twin brother, whose servant is Dromio's twin. Complications arise when Adrianna and Luce, wives of the Ephesian master and servant, mistake the boys from Syracuse for their husbands.

The Cast
THE MASKS, Robert Sidney and Harry Peterson
SINGING POLICEMAN, Bob Lawrence
ANOTHER POLICEMAN, James Wilkinson
ANTIPHOLUS OF EPHESUS, Ronald Graham
DROMIO OF EPHESUS, Teddy Hart
DANCING POLICEMAN, George Church
TAILOR, Clifford Dunstan
TAILOR'S APPRENTICE, Burl Ives
ANTIPHOLUS OF SYRACUSE, Eddie Albert

DROMIO OF SYRACUSE, Jimmy Savo
MERCHANT OF SYRACUSE, Byron Shores
DUKE OF EPHESUS, Carroll Ashburn
AEGEON, John O'Shaughnessy
LUCE, Wynn Murray
ADRIANA, Muriel Angelus
LUCIANA, Marcy Westcott
SORCERER, Owen Martin
COURTESAN, Betty Bruce
SECRETARY TO COURTESAN, Heidi Vosseler
ASSISTANT COURTESAN, Dolores Anderson
ANGELO, John Clarke
MAIDS, Florine Callahan, Claire Wolf, Alice Craig
MERCHANT OF EPHESUS, Clifford Dunstan
SEERESS, Florence Fair
SINGERS: Grace Albert, Laura Kellogg, Dolores Anderson, Armonce Wilkins, Marguerite Benton, Margaret Walsh, Herbert Wood, James Wilkinson, Joseph Scandor, Joe Granville
DANCERS: Libby Bennett, Ruth Brady, Renee Cettel, Stella Clausen, Alice Craig, Bee Farnum, Ruth Gormley, Claire Harvey, Lita Lede, Connie Leslie, Vivien Moore, Florine Callahan, Mildred Solly, Anna Mae Tesslo, Davenie Watson, Betty De Elmo, Claire Wolf; Micky Alvarez, Sidney Gordon, Dan Karry, Tommy Lynch, Jack Malis, Edwin Mills, Harry Peterson, Joe Harris, Lee Tannen, Beau Tilden, Robert Howard

NOTE: In May, Mr. Albert succeeded by Mr. Graham, and Mr. Graham by Mr. Lawrence.

Musical Numbers

Foreword, THE MASKS

ACT I

SCENE ONE—BEFORE THE TEMPLE OF JUSTICE, EPHESUS
I Had Twins, POLICEMEN and ENSEMBLE
Dear Old Syracuse, DROMIO and ANTIPHOLUS OF SYRACUSE; danced by ANTIPHOLUS OF SYRACUSE, MAIDS and DANCERS
What Can You Do With a Man?, LUCE and DROMIO OF EPHESUS

SCENE TWO—INSIDE THE HOUSE OF ANTIPHOLUS OF EPHESUS
Falling in Love With Love, ADRIANNA and LADIES

SCENE THREE—A SQUARE IN EPHESUS
The Shortest Day of the Year, ANTIPHOLUS OF EPHESUS, ASSISTANT COURTESAN and POLICEMEN; danced by COURTESAN, SECRETARY TO COURTESAN, DANCING POLICEMAN

SCENE FOUR—INSIDE THE HOUSE OF ANTIPHOLUS OF EPHESUS
This Can't Be Love, LUCIANA and ANTIPHOLUS OF SYRACUSE

SCENE FIVE—A STREET OUTSIDE ANTIPHOLUS' HOUSE
Let Antipholus In, COMPANY

ACT II

SCENE ONE—A STREET OUTSIDE ANTIPHOLUS' HOUSE
Ladies of the Evening, POLICEMEN and COURTESANS; danced by SECRETARY TO COURTESAN and DANCING POLICEMAN
He and She, LUCE and DROMIO OF SYRACUSE
You Have Cast Your Shadow on the Sea, LUCIANA and ANTIPHOLUS OF SYRACUSE

SCENE TWO—A SQUARE IN EPHESUS
Come With Me, SINGING POLICEMAN, ANTIPHOLUS OF EPHESUS, ANGELO, and POLICEMEN
Big Brother, DROMIO OF EPHESUS
Ballet, danced by DROMIO and ANTIPHOLUS OF SYRACUSE, SECRETARY TO COURTESAN, LUCE and DANCERS

SCENE THREE—INSIDE THE HOUSE OF ANTIPHOLUS OF EPHESUS
Sing for Your Supper, ADRIANA, LUCIANA, LUCE and LADIES; danced by COURTESAN and ENSEMBLE

SCENE FOUR—A SQUARE IN EPHESUS
Oh, Diogenes, LUCE; danced by DANCING POLICEMAN, COURTESAN and ENSEMBLE
Finale, COMPANY

Reviews

Brooks Atkinson—*New York Times*
". . . Nothing so gusty as this has come along for a week. Nothing so original has come along for a much longer period than that . . . Mr. Abbott has a knack of giving everything he touches freshness, spontaneity and spinning pace. Rodgers and Hart have written him a versatile score . . . some of their gayest songs . . . a beautiful feast of rollicking mummery . . ."

Richard Watts, Jr.—*New York Herald Tribune*
". . . the finest and most satisfying musical comedy that has reached New York in many a season of weary waiting. Its book is funny, its lyrics delightful, its score entrancing, its costumes and settings colorful and lovely and its cast perfect . . . If you have been wondering all these years just what was wrong with *The Comedy of Errors,* it is now possible to tell you. It has been waiting for a score by Rodgers and Hart and direction by George Abbott . . ."

Burns Mantle—*New York Daily News*
"★★★ . . . the liveliest and the most colorful of recent bids for

entertainment . . . lyrics that are coarse but cute, as the lady in the ermine reefer said going up the aisle, and tunes that have a popular lilt and occasionally a captivating military swing . . . I should not speak of the comedy as being actually riotous . . ."

Walter Winchell—*New York Daily Mirror*
". . . the composer has never provided a lovelier score . . . The book is so much Greek . . . breathlessly recommended."

John Mason Brown—*New York Post*
". . . given an uncommonly beautiful production . . . includes some of Mr. Hart's gayest lyrics and certainly some of the most beguiling music that has ever come from Mr. Rodgers' pen or that has floated upwards hereabouts in many a blue moon from an orchestra pit . . . something to see and hear—even if it proves far less convulsing than you had wanted, and far less shocking than you had anticipated . . ."

Sidney B. Whipple—*New York World-Telegram*
". . . I believe it will be regarded as the greatest musical comedy of its time . . . set to the most captivating, thrilling, humorous music and lyrics in the long and honorable history of the Messrs. Rodgers and Hart, and it has a modern, swiftly moving book, the brilliant handiwork of Mr. Abbott himself . . ."

Richard Lockridge—*New York Sun*
". . . one of the season's gayest . . . one of Mr. Rodgers' best scores and Mr. Hart offers many of his most accomplished lyrics . . . it all gets better as it goes along so that the plums are fattest in the second layer. Who could ask for anything more?"

John Anderson—*New York Journal-American*
". . . among the town's indispensable amusements . . . The assignment finds Mr. Rodgers at his musical best, and Mr. Hart at his daffiest lyrical inventions . . . the show stops for nothing but laughter . . . In fact, from where I'm sitting, I don't see anything the matter with it at all . . ."

Abel Green—*Variety,* November 30, 1938
". . . a musical smash . . . The score vies with an unusually canny casting job for the single outstanding highlight of the production . . . The book is punchy, pithy and replete with humor . . ."

Robert Benchley—*The New Yorker,* December 3, 1938
". . . the best score that Rodgers and Hart have given us for some time, in fact, for a longer time than that . . . its surroundings happen to be fairly reeking with class . . . but trying to make the tale into

even passable comedy (rollicking, yes—but not passable) was, from my seat, too tough an assignment . . . Without Mr. Savo's personality and Frère Hart's shadowing, my own personal laughter would have been confined to the lyrics . . ."

George Jean Nathan—*Newsweek,* December 5, 1938
". . . Rodgers has never written a better score, and Hart's lyrics are excellently witty. As for the book, this reviewer can't work up any particular glee over it . . . Nevertheless, in all other directions, it's a pretty lively and also a tastefully staged show."

Louis Kronenberger—*Time,* December 5, 1938
". . . hits the bull's eye, rings the bell. Far and away the best musical in many a year . . . brash, bawdy, witty lyrics . . . a gay, bright, lilting score, never better than it is in *This Can't Be Love, Sing for Your Supper* and *He and She* . . ."

Joseph Wood Krutch—*The Nation,* December 10, 1938
". . . neatly combines a certain contemporary flavor with an unimpeachable appropriateness . . . The score is rather fuller and more ambitious than that of the usual musical comedy of today, and in addition to some songs in the accepted manner of the moment, it includes several others which struck me as genuinely original—notable among the latter being the delightful lilting tune which accompanies the pantomime of the opening scene . . ."

Stark Young—*The New Republic,* December 14, 1938
". . . no doubt drags a little with, for example, the spun-out song about falling in love with love, with odd moments in the crowd action, and with the lack, I imagine, of a more genuine sense of suspense . . . In general, however, the whole production seemed to have gusto and a certain freshness along the ancient classic line . . . production is closer to the classic than the Elizabethan tradition could have been . . ."

Bibliography

Rodgers and Hart Do the Words and Music by Jack Gould
—*New York Times,* December 4, 1938

Old Shakespearean Comedy Comes to Broadway as a Ribald Musical
—*Life,* December 12, 1938

Hart and Savo and Their Pal, Bill Shakespeare by John H. Walker
—*New York Herald Tribune,* February 19, 1939

Selected Revivals

Pittsburgh Civic Light Opera, July 12-17, 1954

Royce Blackburn (ANTIPHOLUS OF SYRACUSE); Gloria Lind (ADRIANA); Joey Faye (DROMIO OF SYRACUSE); Herb Corey (DROMIO OF EPHESUS); Ramon Blackburn (ANTIPHOLUS OF EPHESUS); Evelyn Ward (LUCIANA); Mildred Cook (LUCE); Ronnie Cunningham (COURTESAN).

St. Louis Municipal Opera, August 3-9, 1964

Chet Sommers (ANTIPHOLUS OF SYRACUSE); Kelly Stephens (ADRIANA); Ralph McWilliams (DROMIO OF SYRACUSE); Martin Ross (DROMIO OF EPHESUS); John Smolko (ANTIPHOLUS OF EPHESUS); Judith McCauley (LUCIANA); Mary McCarty (LUCE); Cathryn Damon (COURTESAN).

Mineola Theatre, New York, June 22-July 9, 1966

Hal Linden (ANTIPHOLUS OF SYRACUSE); Ellen Hanley (ADRIANA); Rudy Tronto (DROMIO OF SYRACUSE); Gino Conforti (DROMIO OF EPHESUS); Seth Riggs (ANTIPHOLUS OF EPHESUS); Carole Woodruff (LUCIANA); Carol Arthur (LUCE); Cathryn Damon (COURTESAN).

Goodman Theatre, Chicago, 1972

Kenneth Cory (ANTIPHOLUS OF SYRACUSE); Gale Gill (ADRIANA); Danny Carroll (DROMIO OF SYRACUSE); Rudy Tronto (DROMIO OF EPHESUS); Bill Boss (ANTIPHOLUS OF EPHESUS); Jana Lapel (LUCIANA); Lu Leonard (LUCE); Carole (Kelly) Bishop (COURTESAN).

Productions Abroad

Theatre Royal, Drury Lane, London, November 7, 1963-February 1, 1964

(See page 198)

Theatre Royal, Sydney, Australia, February 5-April 13, 1966

Presented by J. C. Williamson Theatres Ltd.; directed by Christopher Hewett; choreography by Betty Pounder. *Cast:* Ted Hamilton (ANTIPHOLUS OF SYRACUSE); Hazel Phillips (ADRIANA); James Kenney (DROMIO OF SYRACUSE); Brian Hannan (DROMIO OF EPHESUS); David Williams (ANTIPHOLUS OF EPHESUS); Lynne Cantlon (LUCIANA); Nancye Hayes (LUCE); Darlene Johnson (COURTESAN). *Tour:* April 16-July 2, 1966.

THE BOYS FROM SYRACUSE

(Film Version—1940)

A Universal Picture
Produced by Jules Levey
Directed by A. Edward Sutherland
Screenplay by Leonard Spigelgass and Charles Grayson
Choreography by Dave Gould
Art director, Jack Otterson
Music director, Charles Previn

Photographed by Joe Valentine
Editor, Milton Carruth

Release Date
August 1, 1940

The Cast

ANTIPHOLUS OF EPHESUS / ANTIPHOLUS OF SYRACUSE } Allan Jones
LUCE, Martha Raye
DROMIO OF EPHESUS / DROMIO OF SYRACUSE } Joe Penner
PHYLLIS, Rosemary Lane
DUKE OF EPHESUS, Charles Butterworth
ADRIANNA, Irene Hervey
ANGELO, Alan Mowbray
PINCH, Eric Blore
AEGEON, Samuel S. Hinds

Musical Numbers

Songs retained from original production: *Sing for Your Supper, He and She, Falling in Love With Love,* and *This Can't Be Love.* Songs written specially for film:
The Greeks Have No Word for It, LUCE and ENSEMBLE
Who Are You?, ANTIPHOLUS OF SYRACUSE

Reviews

Bosley Crowther—*New York Times*
". . . the boys from Universal have watered down the raucous ribaldries of the story . . . relies in the main for its humor upon familiar low-comedy mugging and anachronistic gags . . . Disappointing too, is the casual fashion in which the producers have tossed away the lovely musical score of the original . . ."

William Boehnel—*New York World-Telegram*
". . . most of the gags are so corny that you marvel at the temerity of the scenarists . . . The film could have been helped a lot if some of the music, which is swell, had been used to greater advantage . . ."

Eileen Creelman—*New York Sun*
". . . depends for its merriment upon a superb score and upon a series of Hollywood gags . . ."

Herb Golden—*Variety,* July 17, 1940
". . . Sophisticated audiences will find the gags too unsubtle and

the action too obvious, but the greater part of the film audience will relish the out-and-out screwiness of the whole idea . . ."

Time, August 5, 1940
". . . prime Rodgers and Hart champagne, Broadway 1938, rebottled . . . The plot is the flattest part of the show. As bubbly as ever are the songs . . . a handsome, glittering cinemusical production . . ."

Sally Benson—*The New Yorker,* August 10, 1940
". . . When you are yearning to bundle off to the beach and relax under an umbrella, the sight of Martha Raye working like a beaver is oppressive . . . if you can stand seeing double, and don't mind hearing American slang in ancient Greece, you may be able to totter out of your nearest air-cooled theatre with a sultry sort of satisfaction . . ."

THE BOYS FROM SYRACUSE

(New York—1963)

Presented by Richard York
Directed by Christopher Hewett
Choreography by Bob Herget
Settings by Herbert Senn and Helen Pond
Costumes by Guy Kent
Music and choral director, Rene Wiegert
Orchestrations by Larry Wilcox
Ballet music by Peter Matz

New York Run (Off-Broadway)

Theatre Four, April 15, 1963-June 28, 1964
502 performances

The Cast

SERGEANT, Gary Oakes
DUKE, Fred Kimbrough
AEGEON, Matthew Tobin
ANTIPHOLUS OF EPHESUS, Clifford David
DROMIO OF EPHESUS, Rudy Tronto
TAILOR, Jim Pompeii
ANTIPHOLUS OF SYRACUSE, Stuart Damon
DROMIO OF SYRACUSE, Danny Carroll
MERCHANT OF SYRACUSE, Richard Colacino

APPRENTICE, Jeane Deeks
ANGELO, Richard Nieves
CORPORAL, Dom Salinaro
LUCE, Karen Morrow
ADRIANA, Ellen Hanley
LUCIANA, Julienne Marie
MAIDS, Jeane Deeks, Betsy Hepburn, Svetlana McLee
SORCERER, Matthew Tobin
COURTESAN, Cathryn Damon
FATIMA, Zebra Nevins
COURTESANS, Violetta Landek, Charlene Carter
MERCHANT OF EPHESUS, Jim Pompeii
GALATEA, Violetta Landek
PYGMALION, Richard Nieves
AMAZONS, Charlene Carter, Svetlana McLee, Jeane Deeks

NOTE: During run, Mr. Damon succeeded by Gary Oaks and Gene Bua; Mr. David by Jay Stuart; Mr. Carroll by Mr. Tronto; Mr. Tronto by Angelo Mango; Miss Hanley by Karen Shepard and Luce Ennis; Miss Marie by Marie Santell; Miss Morrow by Jane A. Johnston; Miss Damon by Dorothy Frank and Ann Hodges.

Reviews

Paul Gardner—*New York Times*
". . . sun-kissed production . . . the show is still remarkably alive and spirited . . . Rodgers and Hart were at their peak when they wrote the beguiling score, and this amazingly talented company plunges into each number as if it had been written yesterday—for them—by the legendary team . . . the perfect gin-and-tonic entertainment."

Judith Crist—*New York Herald Tribune*
"Oh joy, oh raptures—oh Rodgers and Hart! Let's not overlook lovely leggy girls, idiot plotting, creaky wisecracks and leers—but oh Rodgers and Hart! . . . Don't hum the word 'revival'; this is one musical whose music doesn't die between times, not even when the time between has been a quarter of a century . . . It's the music in this musical that counts—and it's been given not only the performers but a rich, colorful, clever series of sets to delight your eye as well as your ear. It's been worth the long wait."

James Davis—*New York Daily News*
". . . stylish, scintillating, and altogether charming . . . assembled with loving care and performed by genuine talents . . . gorgeous score . . ."

Jack Thompson—*New York Daily Mirror*
". . . magical songs . . . Seldom has any musical in history had so

many hits . . . Nearly every number is memorable . . . The book gets a bit soggy at times . . . You won't find a more agreeable and diverting evening anywhere off Broadway and too rarely, on Broadway, for that matter, this season."

Leonard Harris—*New York World-Telegram & Sun*
"*The Boys from Syracuse* was not revived last night; it was touched with a magic wand and sprang awake with hardly a sign that twenty-five years had passed since it played on Broadway . . . an evening of delight . . . all the numbers are charming. They catch the fresh tunefulness of Rodgers and the bright irreverence of Hart . . ."

Kenneth Leish—*Variety,* May 8, 1963
"The only problem is which of the dozen wonderful Rodgers and Hart songs to whistle leaving the theatre . . . a parade of lilting, memorable tunes and wry, sophisticated lyrics . . . a top-notch revival of an outstanding musical."

Time, May 12, 1963
"This can't be fluff because it unreels so well . . . Song and skin—but no sobs, no sorrows, no sighs."

Richard Watts, Jr.—*New York Post,* May 12, 1963
". . . every bit as enchanting as I had remembered it was . . . a delightful production, done with taste, freshness and imagination . . . How delicious the score still is! Rodgers was never in a more charmingly tuneful vein and Hart never wrote wittier or more gaily romantic lyrics . . . literally a feast of melody . . . one of the classics of American musical comedy . . ."

Henry Hewes—*Saturday Review,* August 10, 1963
". . . Its performers are merry, attractive and fun-loving. Its choreography is completely capricious. Its jokes are outrageously corny and naughty. Its songs are delicate and adventurously melodic. And perhaps most important of all, the 25-year old musical is a lovely reminder of how carefree both we and musical comedies were in 1938 . . ."

Walter Kerr—*New York Herald Tribune,* October 13, 1963
". . . I don't know that *anyone* has written more melodic surprise into what was meant to be a conventional musical comedy than Rodgers did, and to hear the still unexpected modulations of *The Shortest Day of the Year* or *You Have Cast Your Shadow on the Sea* is today, as twenty-five years ago, a shocker. Rodgers never did live along Tin Pan Alley; he was lost at sea as a boy and, when rescued,

kept hearing inappropriate sounds. They are still inappropriately perfect . . ."

Bibliography

A Night Out with the Boys by Richard Rodgers
—*New York Herald Tribune,* April 14, 1963

Everybody's Discovering "The Boys" by John Molleson
—*New York Herald Tribune,* July 28, 1963

The Golden Boys —*Newsweek,* September 16, 1963

Richard Rodgers Eyes Future with a Present of the Past by Norman Nadel
—*New York World-Telegram & Sun,* May 2, 1964

Awards

Vernon Rice Award, Outstanding Achievement in the Off-Broadway theatre 1962-63
Obie Award, Best Off-Broadway Musical 1962-63

THE BOYS FROM SYRACUSE

(London—1963)

Presented by Williamson Music, Ltd.
Directed by Christopher Hewett
Choreography by Bob Herget
Settings by Herbert Senn and Helen Pond
Costumes by Irene Sharaff
Music director, Robert Lowe
Orchestrations by Ralph Burns
Production supervised by Jerome Whyte

London Run

Theatre Royal, Drury Lane, November 7, 1963-February 1, 1964
100 performances

The Cast

TRAGEDY, John Heawood
COMEDY, Maurice Lane
CORPORAL, Robert Crane
SERGEANT, John Adams
FIRST CITIZEN, John Moore

DROMIO OF EPHESUS, Sonny Farrar
ANTIPHOLUS OF EPHESUS, Denis Quilley
TAILOR, Rod McLennon
APPRENTICE, Peter Ardron
AEGEON, Gavin Gordon
DUKE, Charles Fairbairn
ANTIPHOLUS OF SYRACUSE, Bob Monkhouse
DROMIO OF SYRACUSE, Ronnie Corbett
MERCHANT OF SYRACUSE, John Heawood
ANGELO, Adam Deane
LUCE, Maggie Fitzgibbon
ADRIANA, Lynn Kennington
LUCIANA, Paula Hendrix
LUCIANA'S ATTENDANTS, Carlotta Barrow, Kay Fraser
SORCERER, Edward Atienza
COURTESAN, Pat Turner
FATIMA, April Olrich
MIRROR COURTESAN, Jean Muir
JEWEL COURTESAN, Aimi Macdonald
POWDER PUFF COURTESAN, Jacqui Daryl
DANCING POLICEMAN, Ben Stevenson
DANCING POLICEMAN'S WIFE, Jeanette Minty
MAID, Jill Love
MERCHANT OF EPHESUS, Paul Hansard
SEERESS, Peggy Rowan
SINGERS: Wendy Bowman, Ann Brierly, Rita Cameron, Patricia Hall, Rosemary Lyford, Hilda Stewart, Sylvia Vale, Anna Vincent; Maurice Arthur, John Clifford, Vincent Charles, Robert Crane, John Moore, Thomas Walling
DANCERS: Carlotta Barrow, Jackie Dalton, Kay Fraser, Gigi Hauser, Vicki Karras, Julie Heydon, Jill Love, Jeanette Minty, Priscilla Pritchard, Willow Stockdale, Ruth Walters; Ivan Baptie, Peter Ardron, Hendrick Davel, Norman Furber, Ross Howard, Maurice Lane, Michael Meakin, Gordon Wales

Musical Numbers
Same as original production.

Reviews
London Times
". . . over a quarter of a century separates us from the show and its final arrival in London is less a revival than an exhumation . . . the music has a melodic freshness and theatricality . . ."

W. A. Darlington—*London Daily Telegraph*
". . . a show that drags horribly to its close . . ."

Milton Shulman—*London Evening Standard*
". . . thick lipped jokes . . . Rodgers' music casts a diverting smokescreen of sporadic delight . . ."

John Higgins—*London Financial Times*
". . . thoroughbred score . . . nothing better of its kind to be heard in London, nor likely to be for some time . . ."

Phillip Hope-Wallace—*Manchester Guardian*
". . . musically it was pretty enjoyable . . . the most obvious defect was the humor in the book . . . a middling success."

Harold Hobson—*London Sunday Times,* November 10, 1963
"Dionysus has got into the strong, sensual rhythms of the music Richard Rodgers composed . . . *Sing for Your Supper* is music to drive audiences beyond the simple point of rational pleasure into the primitive frenzy of aphrodisiac magic. *Falling in Love with Love* is rich, lush, entrail-stirring stuff. The sensuality to which Mr. Rodgers has given successful expression in his music can be reconciled with intelligence; the sensuality of the script the music decorates cannot . . . an interminable series of sexual jokes lamely and pathetically paraded . . ."

Bamber Gascoigne—*London Observer,* November 10, 1963
". . . an old Rodgers and Hart musical of quite sagging awfulness—mechanical clowning, raucous underlining of every joke, prosaically lavish sets, snatches of classical ballet . . . Two nice tunes are the only salvage from this ancient wreck."

TOO MANY GIRLS

(1939)

A musical comedy with book by George Marion, Jr.; music by Richard Rodgers; lyrics by Lorenz Hart.

Presented by George Abbott
Directed by Mr. Abbott
Choreography by Robert Alton
Settings and lighting by Jo Mielziner
Costumes by Raoul Pene Du Bois
Music director, Harry Levant
Orchestrations by Hans Spialek
Vocal arrangements by Hugh Martin

Tryout
Shubert Theatre, Boston, October 2-14, 1939

New York Run
Imperial Theatre, October 18, 1939-May 18, 1940
249 performances

The Story
In order to keep his daughter, Consuelo, out of trouble, Harvey Casey sends her to Pottawatomie College, protected by four former All-American football players. They all enroll, and Consuelo, not knowing who he is, falls in love with Clint Kelley, one of the bodyguards. When she finds out his identity, they separate, but fortunately, only temporarily.

The Cast
MRS. TEWKSBURY, Ivy Scott
MANUELITO, Desi Arnaz
CLINT KELLEY, Richard Kollmar
JOJO JORDAN, Eddie Bracken
AL TERWILLIGER, Hal LeRoy
HARVEY CASEY, Clyde Fillmore
MR. LISTER, Hans Robert
CONSUELO CASEY, Marcy Westcott
SHERIFF ANDALUZ, Byron Shores

EILEEN EILERS, Mary Jane Walsh
TALLULAH LOU, Leila Ernst
SUE, Mildred Law
STUDENT, Van Johnson
PEPE, Diosa Costello
BEVERLY WAVERLY, James MacColl
DEPUTY SHERIFF, Willis Duncan
COWBOY, Edison Rice
HAWKER, Harry Jackson
CO-EDS: Marjorie Baglin, Libby Bennett, Betty Boyce, Sondra Barrett, Florine Callahan, Renee Cettel, Marge Ellis, Betty De Elmo, Louise De Forrest, Lita Lede, Jeanette Lavis, Amarilla Morris, Charlene Harkins, Mildred Patterson, Dorothy Poplar, Mildred Solly, Olga Suarez, Anna Mae Tesslo, Davenie Watson, Claire Wolf
DANCERS: Alice Craig, Vera Fern, Mildred Law, La Verne Lupton, Leonor Sola, Diane Sinclair, Key Taylor
DANCING CO-EDS: Alice Craig, Vera Fern, Leonor Sola, Diane Sinclair, Key Taylor
STUDENT QUARTETTE: Robert Arnold, William Mende, Romolo di Spirito, James Wilkinson
STUDENTS: John Benton, Bob Howard, Randolph Hughes, Herb Lurie, Vernon Hammer, Clarence Yeager, Van Johnson, Harold Young, Russ Milton, Jack Riley, Harry Pedersen, Bob Shaw

NOTE: In April, 1940, Mr. Kollmar succeeded by Mr. Johnson.

Musical Numbers

ACT I

SCENE ONE—ROAD TO THE HUNTED STAG, A COLONIAL TAVERN, SKOWHEGAN, MAINE
Heroes in the Fall, James Wilkinson and SQUAD

SCENE TWO—THE HUNTED STAG
Tempt Me Not, MANUELITO, CLINT and CO-EDS; danced by AL and FIRST CO-ED.
My Prince, CONSUELO

SCENE THREE—GATE IN FRONT OF POTTAWATOMIE COLLEGE, STOP GAP, N. M.
Pottawatomie, MR. CASEY and MR. LISTER
'Cause We Got Cake, EILEEN; danced by DANCING CO-EDS and COMPANY

SCENE FOUR—THE CAMPUS
Love Never Went to College, CONSUELO and CLINT
Spic and Spanish, PEPE; danced by DANCING CO-EDS and COMPANY
I Like to Recognize the Tune, JOJO, CONSUELO, EILEEN, CLINT, AL
Look Out, EILEEN and COMPANY; danced by PEPE, MANUELITO and COMPANY

ACT II

SCENE ONE—A ROAD NEAR THE COLLEGE
The Sweethearts of the Team, EILEEN and CO-EDS

SCENE TWO—BELFRY OF POTTAWATOMIE CHAPEL
She Could Shake the Maracas, PEPE and MANUELITO

SCENE THREE—A ROCK IN THE DESERT
I Didn't Know What Time It Was, CONSUELO and CLINT

SCENE FOUR—THE CAMPUS
Reprise, *Spic and Spanish,* PEPE, CONSUELO, EILEEN, AL, CLINT, TALLULAH LOU; danced by DANCING CO-EDS and STUDENTS
Too Many Girls, MANUELITO; danced by CO-EDS

SCENE FIVE—THE CAMPUS
Give It Back to the Indians, EILEEN; danced by AL and STUDENTS

Reviews

Brooks Atkinson—*New York Times*
". . . a good knockabout score . . . a college rag for a story . . . fresh, humorous, exhilarating . . . Probably it would be impolite to suggest that some of the humor is too anatomical for quick enjoyment . . . thanks to Mr. Abbott for a cheerful evening."

Richard Watts, Jr.—*New York Herald Tribune*
". . . Gay, tuneful, attractively acted and generally enlivening, it is as pleasing a girl-and-music carnival as the theatrical season is likely to offer . . . The score is not exactly top-grade Rodgers, but he is better than almost anyone in sight . . . Hart reveals himself to be as acute in social criticism as he is brilliant and inventive in rhyming . . ."

Burns Mantle—*New York Daily News*
★★★+ . . . the freshest and most youthful of musical comedies to be brought to Broadway since *Good News* . . . Rodgers and Hart have studded this workable story with a collection of their best tunes and lyrics . . ."

Walter Winchell—*New York Daily Mirror*
"Superior, swifter and sweller than any surefire show Rodgers and Hart have ever scored before . . . The queen of musical comedies . . ."

John Mason Brown—*New York Post*
". . . speed, sparkle, high spirits and contagious youthfulness . . . sets you swaying to some of the most enchanting music the gifted

Mr. Rodgers has written . . . forces you to rock with laughter at some of Mr. Hart's most felicitous and audacious lyrics . . ."

Sidney B. Whipple—*New York World-Telegram*
". . . invariably cheerful and bright, flashing in its colors, dashing in its dances, smart in much of its dialogue . . . Mr. Hart's lyrics boast their usual facile rhyming . . . Mr. Rodgers' tunes are again captivating . . ."

Richard Lockridge—*New York Sun*
". . . Mr. Rodgers has done a little better now and then in the past, I think . . . But it's a lively and good-looking show and a lot of the time it is funny . . . Its spirit is always youthful and it wears its musical comedy sentiment with a gay and jaunty air . . ."

John Anderson—*New York Journal-American*
". . . bright, fresh and youthful, containing both zip and oomph, all accompanied by the impeccable felicities of the Rodgers and Hart songwork . . . The gaiety and grace, and exuberant spirits leave me in no mood to haggle over its story . . ."

Abel Green—*Variety,* October 25, 1939
". . . a hit musical. Its paprika, production and personality make it so primarily. The score is excellent; the libretto weak . . . light, sprightly and colorful . . ."

Wolcott Gibbs—*The New Yorker,* October 28, 1939
". . . a fine comedy . . . Rodgers and Hart have written one of their pleasantest scores . . . *I Like to Recognize the Tune* and *Give It Back to the Indians* seem so exceptional both in music and lyrics that I think they deserve special attention . . ."

Louis Kronenberger—*Time,* October 30, 1939
". . . Good as it is, the music is not Rodgers at quite his best or most individual. But where Rodgers has dropped the reins, Producer Abbott has seized them and gone to town like Yankee Doodle . . . one of those right-as-rain shows that don't stall at the start, break down in the middle, or run out of gas before the end."

George Jean Nathan—*Newsweek,* October 30, 1939
". . . has to thank the meritorious twain, Rodgers and Hart, and the decorative canary, Marcy Westcott, for its claim upon the attention . . . They atone liberally for what shortcomings the exhibit otherwise clearly has, including a book that Haldeman-Julius wouldn't publish even for his customary nickel."

Otis Ferguson—*The New Republic,* November 8, 1939
". . . the book is above average; Hart's lyrics are as bright as brass.

But the main reason for its modest but infectious air of gaiety seems to be George Abbott . . . It is the tune-deaf who suppose there are songs; outside of a steady-going arrangement, it's all in the words and who's behind them . . ."

Bibliography

Big Year for Musical Shows Begins on Broadway with "Too Many Girls"
—*Life*, October 23, 1939

Chicago Run

Opera House, August 31-September 21, 1940

Chicago Review

Ashton Stevens—*Chicago Herald-American*

". . . This merry and melodious show is a sometimes bawdy but never boring burlesque . . . Hart's lyrics were never gayer and seldom bluer; Rodgers' score contains more good music than hit-paraders . . ."

Selected Revivals

St. Louis Municipal Opera, June 23-29, 1941
Joan Edwards (EILEEN); Frankie Thomas (JOJO); Margaret Adams (CONSUELO); Jack Williams (AL); Betty Bruce (PEPE); Donald Burr (BEVERLY).

Dallas State Fair, August 7-13, 1941
Paula Stone (EILEEN); Jack Sheehan (JOJO); Joan Roberts (CONSUELO); Robert Chisholm (BEVERLY); Jack Goode (MANUELITO).

TOO MANY GIRLS

(Film Version—1940)

An RKO-Radio Picture
Produced and directed by George Abbott
Screenplay by John Twist
Choreography by LeRoy Prinz
Music director, George Bassman
Choral director, Hugh Martin
Photographed by Frank Redman

Release Date

November 22, 1940

The Cast

CONSUELO CASEY, Lucille Ball (sung by Trudy Erwin)
CLINT KELLEY, Richard Carlson

PEPE, Ann Miller
JOJO JORDAN, Eddie Bracken
EILEEN EILERS, Frances Langford
MANUELITO, Desi Arnaz
AL TERWILLIGER, Hal LeRoy
TALLULAH LOU, Libby Bennett
HARVEY CASEY, Harry Shannon
BEVERLY WAVERLY, Douglas Walton
MR. LISTER, Chester Clute
MIDGE MARTIN, Tiny Person
MRS. TEWKSBURY, Ivy Scott
SHERIFF ANDALUZ, Byron Shores
STUDENT, Van Johnson
COACH, Grady Sutton

Musical Numbers
Songs retained from original production: *Heroes in the Fall, Pottawatomie, 'Cause We Got Cake, Spic and Spanish, Love Never Went to College, Look Out,* and *I Didn't Know What Time It Was.*
Song written specially for film:
You're Nearer, CONSUELO, EILEEN, PEPE, TALLULAH LOU

Reviews
Bosley Crowther—*New York Times*
". . . pleasant, lighthearted and wholly ingenious . . . Abbott has permitted it to sag in the middle, at which point the thin spots badly show . . ."

Archer Winsten—*New York Post*
". . . Abbott doesn't think in terms of the screen, and the film abundantly shows it . . . But it has its moments of fun and satire, a lively story, and songs which are still pleasing."

Cecilia Ager—*PM*
"The lyrics are literate and have the contemporary point of view, the tunes are pleasant, the dialogue's amusing, the plot's fair enough for a musical . . . On the other hand, the movie lacks flow, the lighting's dreary, the production's cramped, and the direction wants for cinematic imagination and understanding . . ."

Walt Christie—*Variety,* October 9, 1940
". . . Despite its many obvious faults in filmusical form, it is sufficiently gay and giddy to get across for nominally profitable biz . . ."

Time, November 11, 1940
". . . faithful reconstruction . . . With the pace of a jackrabbit, it

bounds from song to dances to comedy to song, offers too short glimpses of some of Hollywood's abler and less familiar talent . . ."

John Mosher—*The New Yorker,* November 30, 1940
". . . lifted bag and baggage to the screen, with Eddie Bracken and the Rodgers and Hart songs all intact. It's nice for New Yorkers who don't care for musicals on the stage."

GHOST TOWN

(Ballet—1939)

An American Folk Ballet with libretto by Marc Platoff; music by Richard Rodgers.

Presented by S. Hurok
Produced by the Ballet Russe de Monte Carlo
Choreography by Mr. Platoff
Settings and costumes by Raoul Pene Du Bois
Historical research by Gerald Murphy
Music director, Mr. Rodgers
Orchestrations by Hans Spialek

New York Run

Metropolitan Opera House, November 12, 14, 15, 18, 19, 1939; March 29, 1940

The Story

The scene is the main street of a ghost town. Two young hikers talk to an old prospector who reminisces about the town's history. As he relates the tale, the scene changes to the time when the locale was a roaring mining town. Ralston, a young prospector in search of gold, is admired by Eilley Orrum, the town heiress. A fight ensues when the Bright Star miners tangle with the Comstock gang, but peace is finally restored by the fire brigade. Bonanza King Comstock sells Ralston a mine claim which, in his enthusiasm, he drops. Comstock takes it back, but Eilley in turn retrieves it from Comstock.

The stagecoach brings an assorted group including "The Mencken," an actress, "Benecia Boy" Heenan, Algernon Swinburne and Jenny Lind. Ralston strikes it rich, and celebrates by buying a red coat with gold buttons. Comstock accuses him of jumping the claim, and when Ralston cannot produce the papers, the Vigilantes try him in "Kangaroo court." He is saved from a lynching when Eilley produces the missing papers, and the crowd has a grand celebration. Suddenly the Assay Office indicator shows the ore yield petering out. Panic grips the town; everyone is ruined and they begin to flee. But despite Eilley's pleadings, Ralston remains, and she goes off with Comstock. After the town fades out, the ghost town reappears. As the hikers leave, they recognize the old prospector's tattered red coat with the gold buttons.

The Cast

EILLEY ORRUM, Mia Slavenska
RALSTON, Frederic Franklin
ORSON HYDE, *A Mormon apostle,* Roland Guerard
HIS FIVE WIVES, Rosella Hightower, Katia Geleznova, Virginia Rosson, Mugi Novikova, Nesta Williams
JENNY LIND, Nina Theilade
"BONANZA KING" COMSTOCK, Casimir Kokitch
BOY HIKER, Charles Dickson
GIRL HIKER, Milada Mladova
OLD PROSPECTOR, Simon Semenoff
ASSAY OFFICER, Paul Godkin
"BENECIA BOY" HEENAN, Robert Steele
ALGERNON SWINBURNE, James Starbuck
"THE MENCKEN", Marina Franca
A HOUSEWIFE, Tatiana Chanice
LADY SHOPPERS, Nathalie Kelepovska, Jeannette Lauret
BONANZA KINGS, Charles Dickson, Thomas Armour
STAGECOACH DRIVER, Michel Katcharoff
TOWN BOYS, Ian Gibson, Alexander Gaudovitch
BRIGHT STAR MINERS, Messrs. Starbuck, Milton, Irwin, Volkoff, Bochino
FIREMEN, Paul Godkin, Nicholas Beresoff, Michael Katcharoff
TOWN GIRLS, Mlles. Lacca, Pourmel
COMSTOCK MINERS, Messrs. Gibson, Gaudovitch, Belsky, Dickson, Armour
THE VIGILANTES, Messrs. Gibson, Gaudovitch, Belsky
DANCE HALL GIRLS, Mlles. Roudenko, Grantseva, Vallon, Korjinska, Flotat
CLOTHING STORE KEEPER, Nicholas Beresoff

Reviews

John Martin—*New York Times*
". . . not so much a ballet as a musical comedy without singing. As such, it is cute as Punch, but in certain ways a mite surprising to find at the Metropolitan. Rodgers' score might be tops a little further uptown, but as the musical setting for an American folk ballet, it is styleless anachronism . . ."

Walter Terry—*New York Herald Tribune*
"An applauding, cheering audience . . . As far as the audience as a whole was concerned, *Ghost Town* was a grand success and understandably so. The Rodgers score found the composer at his melodic and rhythmic best, with at least two hit tunes just waiting for

someone to write the words . . . could be condensed into a good musical-comedy number . . ."

Pitts Sanborn—*New York World-Telegram*
". . . The goings on were lively enough for a while . . . Obviously the action needed shortening and strengthening . . . The music, in the Broadway manner, is sometimes both appropriate and amusing. Elsewhere it is dull . . ."

Irving Kolodin—*New York Sun*
". . . has moments of vitality, but so many of the figures are derivative and their arrangements conventional that little suggestion of individuality emerges . . . Rodgers' score was a series of fragments, some of them promising, some of them less so, but the result can hardly be called a ballet score, even by Mr. Rodgers' own standards . . ."

Hobe Morrison—*Variety,* November 15, 1939
". . . doesn't rate an equal of several other ballets in the Monte Carlo repertory; its score is a trifle light, in the musical-comedy vein, and the choreography is still not completely developed. But its colorful theme should have wide appeal for U.S. audiences, the dancing is lively and at times humorous, and offers a vivid spectacle . . ."

Robert A. Simon—*The New Yorker,* November 18, 1939
". . . the whole layout is a useful basis for a ballet. Rodgers' music, well orchestrated by Hans Spialek, also is a useful basis for a ballet, for the melodies are, as usual, attractive . . . a pleasant show . . . what it seems to need is pointing and perhaps a fuller development . . ."

Edward Denby—*Modern Music,* January, 1940
". . . catchy and unpretentious and keeps going, and I enjoyed the clarity of it . . . It does say something of its own."

Tour
The Ballet Russe de Monte Carlo performed *Ghost Town* during its American tour following the engagement at the Metropolitan. It was also in the repertory during the spring engagement in New York, which opened late in March.

HIGHER AND HIGHER

(1940)

A musical comedy with book by Gladys Hurlbut and Joshua Logan, based on an idea by Irvin Pincus; music by Richard Rodgers; lyrics by Lorenz Hart.

Presented by Dwight Deere Wiman
Directed by Mr. Logan
Choreography by Robert Alton
Settings by Jo Mielziner
Costumes by Lucinda Ballard
Music director, Al Goodman
Orchestrations by Hans Spialek

Tryout

Shubert Theatre, New Haven, March 7-9, 1940
Shubert Theatre, Boston, March 12-30, 1940

New York Run

Shubert Theatre, April 4-June 15, 1940; August 5-24, 1940
108 performances

The Story

Led by Zachary Ash, the servants of a suddenly bankrupt millionaire decide to make their fortunes by passing off Minnie Sorenson, one of the maids, as a debutante. Their plan is to marry her to an affluent playboy. However, a trained seal from Minnie's native country, Iceland, helps foil the plot by biting Zachary in the pants at a party. All is set right before the final curtain.

The Cast

HILDA O'BRIEN, Eva Condon
BYNG, Robert Chisholm
DOTTIE, Billie Worth
MISS WHIFFEN, Hilda Spong
SANDY MOORE, Shirley Ross
ZACHARY ASH, Jack Haley
MIKE O'BRIEN, Lee Dixon
MINNIE SORENSON, Marta Eggert

SCULLERY MAID, Marie Louise Quevli
THREE NURSEMAIDS, Gloria Hope, Hollace Shaw, Jane Richardson
SODA JERKER, Robert Rounseville
LADIES' MAID, Marie Nash
FIRST COP, Robert Shanley
COPS, Joe Scandur, Richard Moore
FOOTMAN, Carl Trees
PATRICK O'TOOLE, Leif Erickson
ELLEN, Janet Fox
TRUCKMEN, Robert Rounseville, Joe Scandur
SNORRI, Fin Olsen
SHARKEY, *the seal,* Himself
THE HANDYMAN, Frederic Nay
THE CAT, Ted Adair
THE FROG, Lyda Sue
THE BAT, Sigrid Dagnie
THE COACHMAN, Frederic Nay
THE GORILLA, Joseph Granville
PURITY, Jane Ball
SINGING GIRLS: Kay Duncan, Gloria Hope, Marie Nash, Hollace Shaw, Marie Louise Quevli, Jane Richardson
SINGING BOYS: William Geery, Joseph Granville, Richard Moore, Robert Rounseville, Joe Scandur, Robert Shanley
SPECIALTY GIRLS: June Allyson, Irene Austin, Jane Ball, Ronnie Cunningham, Sigrid Dagnie, Eleanor Eberle, Vera Ellen, Miriam Franklin, Marguerite James, Kay Picture, Lyda Sue
SPECIALTY BOYS: Ted Adair, Cliff Ferre, Bunnie Hightower, Louis Hightower, Michael Moore, Frederic Nay, Burton Pierce, Harry Rogers, Jack Seymour, Billy Skipper Jr., Carl Trees

NOTE: In August, Miss Eggert succeeded by Marie Nash.

Musical Numbers

ACT I

SCENE ONE—SECTION OF A NEW YORK HOTEL BALLROOM
A Barking Baby Never Bites, ZACHARY and SANDY
From Another World, MINNIE, ZACHARY, SANDY, HILDA, BYNG, and COMPANY

SCENE TWO—KITCHEN OF THE DRAKE MANSION
Morning's at Seven, MIKE, DOTTIE, and ENSEMBLE
Nothing but You, MINNIE, PATRICK, and ENSEMBLE

SCENE THREE—DEBORAH DRAKE'S BEDROOM
Disgustingly Rich, ZACHARY, SANDY, MIKE, HILDA, BYNG, MISS WHIFFEN, DOTTIE, and ENSEMBLE

ACT II

SCENE ONE—KITCHEN OF THE DRAKE MANSION

Blue Monday, BYNG, NURSEMAID,SCULLERY MAID,LADIES' MAID, and ENSEMBLE

Ev'ry Sunday Afternoon, MINNIE and PATRICK

Lovely Day for a Murder, MIKE, DOTTIE, and ENSEMBLE

SCENE TWO—ZACHARY'S ROOM

How's Your Health?, ZACHARY, MINNIE, PATRICK

It Never Entered My Mind, SANDY

SCENE THREE—THE OLD CARRIAGE HOUSE

I'm Afraid, ZACHARY, SANDY and SPECIALTY BOYS and GIRLS; development, SANDY, ELLEN, MIKE, BYNG, HILDA, FIRST COP, and COMPANY

SCENE FOUR—SECTION OF A NEW YORK HOTEL BALLROOM

Finale, COMPANY

NOTE: *It's Pretty in the City* cut before New York opening.

Reviews

Brooks Atkinson—*New York Times*

". . . may fall a bit short of the highest ranking, but it deserves a comfortable passing grade . . . Not a brilliant score for purposes of gaiety or romance, it is imaginatively varied, and Mr. Hart's lyrics are idiomatically amusing . . ."

Richard Watts, Jr.—*New York Herald Tribune*

". . . the book does get so insistently in the way that it has a terrible time getting started, and then limps along between musical numbers. There are a lot of good songs and some pleasant entertainers, but I remain somewhat disappointed . . . the numbers are gay, attractive, and to say the most complimentary thing, characteristic of their authors . . ."

Burns Mantle—*New York Daily News*

"★★★ . . . Even without the seal, it is a salable musical show . . . the singing and dancing chorus, being one and the same, is an amazing collection of specialty talents . . ."

Walter Winchell—*New York Daily Mirror*

". . . what they call superior entertainment . . . Rodgers and Hart's score is crowded with good things . . . the town's newest number 1 musical show."

John Mason Brown—*New York Post*

". . . When Mr. Haley has to play stooge to a seal, however unconventionally trained, one thing is certain. Something is wrong with the musical comedy in which Mr. Haley is appearing . . . a dullish book that is downright soporific in its slow-moving first half . . . In several uninspired moments, the usually reliable Messrs. Rodgers and Hart appear to have dashed off some effortless lyrics and some energetic, though mediocre melodies . . ."

Sidney B. Whipple—*New York World-Telegram*
". . . chiefly for the new and bright personalities it brings to Broadway, it achieves a position well up on this department's preferred list . . . the tunes are gay and rollicking . . . a pleasant book . . ."

Richard Lockridge—*New York Sun*
". . . sweet and lively tunes; lyrics of suitable intricacy . . . Primarily it is a dancing show, and the dancers can do all the tricks . . . so vivacious and expert a show that the story doesn't matter . . ."

John Anderson—*New York Journal-American*
". . . a pedestrian and labored story . . . Though the Rodgers and Hart combination is not at top form, there are some pleasant numbers—*From Another World* and *Nothing but You*. The big dance numbers provide the most attractive moments . . . The show seems to stand violently still while moving nowhere in particular."

Abel Green—*Variety,* April 10, 1940
". . . an unqualified click. Show has everything necessary for boxoffice, from songs and bright comedy to cast values and production . . . ranks, like its title, in the top brackets as Broadway musical fare."

Wolcott Gibbs—*The New Yorker,* April 13, 1940
". . . There is a seal that I could look at with the greatest pleasure practically forever . . . Otherwise, the musical comedy is a rather confusing mixture of the very good, the fairly dull, and quite a lot of the kind of thing that proved so embarrassing to the Minsky brothers a couple of years ago. The good, of course, includes the score . . . The dull for the most part is concerned with the book . . ."

Oliver Claxton—*Cue,* April 13, 1940
". . . a fine addition to the musical list . . . has lilt and spirit that makes it most engaging . . . roundly recommended."

Louis Kronenberger—*Time,* April 15, 1940
". . . the book becomes as much of an outright menace as maggots in a cheese . . . it is really floored by The Servant Problem . . . Rodgers and Hart, who can usually save any show from taking a nose dive, aren't quite able to save this one. The score is agreeable

enough, with a few good swinging tunes like *Disgustingly Rich* and *How's Your Health?* But it's their slimmest job in a number of years . . ."

George Jean Nathan—*Newsweek,* April 15, 1940
". . . passes an evening lightly, gaily, and very satisfactorily . . ."

Bibliography

Debutantes Are Taught to Behave in New Musical "Higher and Higher"
—*Life,* April 15, 1940

HIGHER AND HIGHER

(Film Version—1943)

An RKO-Radio Picture
Directed by Tim Whelan
Screenplay by Jay Dratler and Ralph Spence
Additional dialogue by Howard Harris and William Bowers
Music director, C. Bakaleinikoff
Orchestrations by Axel Stordahl and Gene Rose
Photographed by Robert de Grasse
Editor, Gene Milford

Release Date

December 9, 1943

The Cast

MILLIE PICOT, Michele Morgan
MIKE O'BRIEN, Jack Haley
FRANK SINATRA, Himself
MR. DRAKE, Leon Errol
MICKEY, Marcy McGuire
KATHERINE KEATING, Barbara Hale
SIR VICTOR FITZROY VICTOR, Victor Borge
SANDY, Mary Wickes
MRS. KEATING, Elizabeth Risdon
MARTY, Mel Torme
BYNGHAM, Paul Hartman
HILDA, Grace Hartman
OSCAR, Dooley Wilson
MRS. WHIFFIN, Ivy Scott
MR. GREEN, Rex Evans

Musical Numbers

Song retained from original production: *Disgustingly Rich.* Songs written specially for film by Jimmy McHugh and Harold Adamson: *I Couldn't Sleep a*

Wink Last Night, A Lovely Way to Spend an Evening, The Music Stopped, Higher and Higher, It's a Most Important Affair, You're On Your Own, I Saw You First, Today I'm a Debutante, and *Minuet in Boogie.*

Reviews

Bosley Crowther—*New York Times*
"*Lower and Lower* . . . The best that the film offers is a multiplicity of songs. Frankie moans and disgorges five of them . . . the whole thing seemed but a slapdash setting for the incredibly unctuous renderings of the 'Voice.' "

Archer Winsten—*New York Post*
". . . so full of talent that it can afford to throw away the rare abilities of the Hartmans . . ."

Alton Cook—*New York World-Telegram*
". . . a pleasant and flimsy little musical, amusing most of the time, laborious some of the time in its overzealous eagerness to please . . ."

Roy Chartier—*Variety*, December 15, 1943
". . . first-rate entertainment. Light in vein but rich in comedy and song values, plus having very fine pace, it is destined to rank high at the boxoffice . . . Mr. Sinatra does not photograph very well . . ."

David Lardner—*The New Yorker*, January 29, 1944
". . . The main trouble lies in the book, which is just another unlikely and inconsistent movie-musical affair. Mr. Sinatra comes out fine. He has some acting to do and he does it."

James Agee—*Time*, January 31, 1944
". . . Sinatra's posture suggests St. Francis preaching to the birds, and the hysterical twittering of the audience sustained the illusion . . . the story is carefully simple-minded . . ."

PAL JOEY

(1940)

A musical comedy with book by John O'Hara, based on a series of short stories in "The New Yorker" by Mr. O'Hara; music by Richard Rodgers; lyrics by Lorenz Hart.

Presented by George Abbott
Directed by Mr. Abbott
Choreography by Robert Alton
Settings and lighting by Jo Mielziner
Costumes by John Koenig
Music director, Harry Levant
Orchestrations by Hans Spialek

Tryout

Forrest Theatre, Philadelphia, December 16-22, 1940

New York Run

Ethel Barrymore Theatre, December 25, 1940-August 16, 1941
Shubert Theatre, September 1-October 18, 1941
St. James Theatre, October 21-November 29, 1941
374 performances

The Story

Joey, a night club entertainer, makes his way by unscrupulous dealings. He drops the innocent Linda in favor of the older and very wealthy Vera, who builds a night club just for him. But she soon tires of him, and when last seen, Joey is on his way toward other conquests.

The Cast

JOEY EVANS, Gene Kelly
MIKE SPEARS, Robert J. Mulligan
THE KID, Sondra Barrett
GLADYS BUMPS, June Havoc
AGNES, Diane Sinclair
LINDA ENGLISH, Leila Ernst
VALERIE, Amarilla Morris
ALBERT DOANE, Stanley Donen

VERA SIMPSON, Vivienne Segal
ESCORT, Edison Rice
TERRY, Jane Fraser
VICTOR, Van Johnson
ERNEST, John Clarke
MAX, Averell Harris
STAGEHAND, Jerome Whyte
LOUIS, *the tenor,* Nelson Rae
MELBA SNYDER, Jean Casto
WAITER, Dummy Spelvin
LUDLOW LOWELL, Jack Durant
COMMISSIONER O'BRIEN, James Lane
ASSISTANT HOTEL MANAGER, Cliff Dunstan
SPECIALTY DANCER, Shirley Paige
DANCING GIRLS: Claire Anderson, Sondra Barrett, Alice Craig, Louise de Forrest, Enez Early, Tilda Getze, Charlene Harkins, Janet Davis, Mildred Law, Amarilla Morris, Olive Nicolson, Mildred Patterson, Dorothy Poplar, Diane Sinclair, Mildred Solly, Jeanne Trybom, Marie Vanneman
DANCING BOYS: Adrian Anthony, John Benton, Milton Chisholm, Stanley Donen, Richard Irving, Henning Irgens, Van Johnson, Michael Moore, Albert Ruiz

NOTE: In July, Miss Havoc succeeded by Vivienne Allen; in August, Mr. Durant by David Burns; in September, Mr. Kelly by George Tapps.

Musical Numbers

ACT I

SCENE ONE—MIKE'S NIGHT CLUB IN CHICAGO'S SOUTH SIDE
You Mustn't Kick It Around, JOEY, GLADYS, AGNES, KID, DANCING GIRLS and WAITERS

SCENE TWO—A PET SHOP
I Could Write a Book, JOEY and LINDA

SCENE THREE—THE NIGHT CLUB
Chicago, Michael Moore and GIRLS
That Terrific Rainbow, GLADYS, VICTOR, and GIRLS

SCENE FOUR—VERA'S AND JOEY'S ROOMS
Love Is My Friend, VERA

SCENE FIVE—THE NIGHT CLUB
Happy Hunting Horn, JOEY, TERRY, CHORUS GIRLS and BOY FRIENDS

SCENE SIX—A TAILOR SHOP
Bewitched, Bothered and Bewildered, VERA
Pal Joey, JOEY

SCENE SEVEN—BALLET
Joey Looks into the Future, JOEY, SPECIALTY DANCER and COMPANY

ACT II

SCENE ONE—CHEZ JOEY

The Flower Garden of My Heart, GLADYS, TENOR, SPECIALTY DANCER and ENSEMBLE

Zip, MELBA

Plant You Now, Dig You Later, LUDLOW, GLADYS and ENSEMBLE

SCENE TWO—JOEY'S APARTMENT

Den of Iniquity, VERA and JOEY

SCENE THREE—CHEZ JOEY

Do It the Hard Way, LUDLOW, GLADYS, Claire Anderson and ENSEMBLE

SCENE FOUR—JOEY'S APARTMENT

Take Him, VERA, LINDA and JOEY

Reprise, *Bewitched, Bothered and Bewildered,* VERA

SCENE FIVE—THE PET SHOP

Reprise, *I Could Write a Book,* JOEY

NOTE: *I'm Talking to My Pal* cut before New York opening. Lyric of *Love Is My Friend* changed shortly after opening and called *What Is a Man?*

Reviews

Brooks Atkinson—*New York Times*

"If it is possible to make an entertaining musical comedy out of an odious story, *Pal Joey* is it . . . Rodgers and Hart have written the score with wit and skill . . . offers everything but a good time . . . some scabrous lyrics to one of Rodgers' most haunting tunes—*Bewitched* . . . Although it is expertly done, can you draw sweet water from a foul well?"

Richard Watts, Jr.—*New York Herald Tribune*

". . . brilliant, sardonic and strikingly original . . . one of Rodgers' most winning scores, some of Hart's finest lyrics . . . an outstanding triumph . . . a bitter, satirical and yet strangely realistic account of the flora and fauna of the night clubs, done with such zest and scornful relish that it achieves genuine power . . . the spiritual kinship between Lorenz Hart and John O'Hara is something to be applauded . . ."

Burns Mantle—*New York Daily News*

"★★★ . . . a hit . . . O'Hara has been able to sustain some semblance of intelligence in his book . . . Rodgers and Hart have spattered the score with pleasant songs . . . isn't exactly on the clean side. It will never make the White List. But neither is it cheaply or slyly smutty . . . Kelly is likable as an individual and gifted as a dancer . . ."

Robert Coleman—*New York Daily Mirror*
". . . a hit if ever I saw one . . ."

John Mason Brown—*New York Post*
". . . had looked during its first half as if it were going to prove one of the season's brighter arrivals . . . sprightly music benefiting by some of Mr. Hart's glibbest rhymes . . . But from the moment the book gained in prominence, it began to slip. At first imperceptibly, then so noticeably that its slipping can only be described as a fall . . ."

Sidney B. Whipple—*New York World-Telegram*
". . . a bright, novel, gay and tuneful work, made interesting by the rich characterizations of its book . . . Gene Kelly is made for the part . . . The lyrics are brilliant in their reflection of night club life—smokey and blue . . ."

Richard Lockridge—*New York Sun*
". . . not really much plot . . . Mr. Rodgers has written gay tunes and Mr. Hart has written some of his brightest—and certainly some of his roughest—lyrics . . . it is always lively and almost always funny, and its humor has, at best, a sharp, distinctive flavor."

John Anderson—*New York Journal-American*
". . . the first half is nimble, clever and smartly amusing and the second half is not so nimble, clever, etc. . . . a somewhat unsteady and aimless tale . . . Mr. Hart's lyrics are urbane to the verge of smuttiness; but adroit as ever and immensely clever. Mr. Rodgers has written some pleasant tunes, especially *Bewitched* and *I Could Write a Book,* and he made hilarious mockery of night club floor shows in *The Flower Garden of My Heart* . . ."

Abel Green—*Variety,* January 1, 1941
". . . in some respects a quite unpleasant evening because of the complete lack of sympathy for our heel of a hero . . . holds lots of solid entertainment . . . extra values in Hart's devastating lyrics and O'Hara's realistic portraiture . . . Rodgers' equally fetching tune settings scintillate throughout . . . the blonde and very personable Van Johnson handles a few lines and manages to project himself quite vividly . . ."

Wolcott Gibbs—*The New Yorker,* January 4, 1941
"Musical comedy took a long step toward maturity . . . I am not optimistic by nature, but it seems to me just possible that the idea of equipping a song-and-dance production with a few living, three-dimensional figures, talking and behaving like human beings, may

no longer strike the boys in the business as merely fantastic . . . Mr. Rodgers and Mr. Hart have written some of their best songs . . ."

Time, January 6, 1941
". . . a bang-up musicomedy, a profane hymn to the gaudy goddess of metropolitan night life . . . gamy, funny, simple in outline . . . At least three more great Rodgers tunes: *I Could Write a Book* (sweet), *Love Is My Friend* (torchy), *Bewitched* (catchy). Cigar-chewing Hart, the pint-sized genius with a two-quart capacity, abets the spirit of the occasion . . ."

John Lardner—*Newsweek,* January 6, 1941
". . . the best musical comedy in a season of good musical comedies—the best in two or three seasons, for that matter . . . cool, sardonic and a little nasty. But the show has pace and point, most of the funny lines are funny, the cast is good, the dancing is expert . . . Rodgers' best score . . . Hart is in there punching too. I think he is running in a private sweepstakes with Cole Porter to see which can be the wickedest little rascal in the lyric-writing dodge."

Bibliography

NEWSPAPERS AND PERIODICALS

How a Musical is Made by Robert Rice
—*PM's Weekly,* December 22, 1940

John O'Hara and His Pal Joey by Benjamin Welles
—*New York Times,* January 26, 1941

"Pal Joey" —*Stage,* February, 1941

"Pal Joey" Continues Hits in Rodgers-Hart Career by Harold Eaton
—*Newark Star-Ledger* May 11, 1941

BOOKS

Pal Joey (Duel, Sloane and Pearce, New York, 1941)
Book and lyrics of the musical.

Tour

Shubert Theatre, Boston, December 1, 1941—Cass Theatre, Detroit, February 28, 1942 (5 cities).

Selected Revivals

Dallas State Fair, August 1-7, 1949
Vivienne Segal (VERA); Georgie Tapps (JOEY); Joan Mann (GLADYS); Jay Presson (MELBA); Dink Freeman (LUDLOW).

Westbury Music Fair, Long Island, July 2-7, 1956
Denise Darcel (VERA); Johnny Desmond (JOEY).

New York City Center Light Opera, May 31-June 24, 1961
Carol Bruce (VERA); Bob Fosse (JOEY); Sheila Bond (GLADYS); Harvey Stone (LUDLOW); Eileen Heckart (MELBA).

Oakdale Musical Theatre, Wallingford, Conn., July 16-21, 1962
Irene Manning (VERA); Steve Lawrence (JOEY); Mata Lynn (GLADYS); Al Bernie (LUDLOW); Renee Taylor (MELBA).

New York City Center Light Opera, May 29-June 9, 1963
Viveca Lindfors (VERA); Bob Fosse (JOEY); Elaine Dunn (GLADYS); Jack Durant (LUDLOW); Kay Medford (MELBA); Rita Gardner (LINDA).

Camden County Music Fair, New Jersey, 1963
Dorothy Lamour (VERA); Swen Swenson (JOEY); Wisa D'Orso (GLADYS); Georgie Kaye (LUDLOW); Annie Russell (MELBA).

Royal Alexandra Theatre, Toronto, March 6-19, 1966
Jane Russell (VERA); Joe Bennett (JOEY); Karen Jensen (GLADYS); Alan Zampese (LUDLOW).

Houston Music Theatre, February 27-March 10, 1968
Julie Wilson (VERA); Bobby Van (JOEY); Allen Jenkins (LUDLOW).

Circle in the Square, New York, June 27-August 29, 1976
Joan Copeland (VERA); Christopher Chadman (JOEY); Janie Sell (GLADYS); Joe Sirola (LUDLOW); Dixie Carter (MELBA); Boni Enten (LINDA). Note: Before the opening, VERA played by Eleanor Parker, JOEY by Edward Villella.

Ahmanson Theatre, Los Angeles, April 21-August 20, 1978
Orpheum Theatre, San Francisco, August 22-September 30, 1978
Lena Horne (VERA); Clifton Davis (JOEY); Louisa Flaningam (GLADYS); Norman Matlock (LUDLOW); Josephine Premice (MELBA). Note: Called *Pal Joey '78,* this was a revised version with book by Jerome Chodorov and Mark Bramble.

Productions Abroad

Det Nye Teater, Oslo, Norway, May 21-August 30, 1953
Translated by Nils Reinhardt Christensen; directed by Sven Age Larsen; choreography by Ivo Cramér. *Cast:* Synnøve Gleditsch (VERA); Toralv Maurstad (JOEY); Inga Brink (GLADYS); Henki Kolstad (LUDLOW); Eva Bergh (LINDA).

Princes Theatre, London, March 31-October 30, 1954
(See page 227)

Royal Lyceum Theatre, Edinburgh, Scotland, August 23-28, 1976
Oxford Playhouse Co. production for Edinburgh International Festival; directed by Philip Hedley; choreography by Eleanor Fazan. *Cast:* Pat Kirkwood (VERA); Bob Sherman (JOEY); Anna Quayle (GLADYS).

PAL JOEY

(New York—1952)

Presented by Jule Styne and Leonard Key
in association with Anthony B. Farrell
Production supervised by Robert Alton
Directed by David Alexander
Choreography by Mr. Alton
Settings by Oliver Smith
Costumes by Miles White
Lighting by Peggy Clark
Music director, Max Meth
Orchestrations by Don Walker and Hans Spialek
Dance arrangements by Oscar Kosarin

Tryout

Shubert Theatre, New Haven, December 25-29, 1951

New York Run

Broadhurst Theatre, January 3, 1952-April 18, 1953
542 performances

The Cast

JOEY EVANS, Harold Lang
MIKE SPEARS, Jack Waldron
THE KID, Helen Wood
GLADYS BUMPS, Helen Gallagher
AGNES, Janyce Ann Wagner
MICKEY, Phyllis Dorne
DIANE, Frances Krell
DOTTIE, Lynn Joelson
SANDRA, Eleanor Boleyn
ADELE, Rita Tanno
FRANCINE, Gloria O'Malley
LINDA ENGLISH, Patricia Northrop
VERA SIMPSON, Vivienne Segal
VALERIE, Barbara Nichols
WAITER, George Martin
AMARILLA, Thelma Tadlock
ERNEST, Gordon Peters
VICTOR, Robert Fortier
DELIVERY BOY, Barry Ryan
STAGE MANAGER, Reed Allyn
LOUIS, *the tenor,* Lewis Bolyard
MELBA SNYDER, Elaine Stritch

LUDLOW LOWELL, Lionel Stander
COMMISSIONER O'BRIEN, T. J. Halligan
DANCING GIRLS: Eleanor Boleyn, Bonnie Brae, Phyllis Dorne, Eleanor Fairchild, Jean Goodall, Patty Ann Jackson, Lynn Joelson, Helene Keller, Frances Krell, Ina Learner, Ethel Martin, June McCain, Gloria O'Malley, Thelma Tadlock, Rita Tanno, Norma Thornton, Janyce Ann Wagner
DANCING BOYS: Harry Asmus, Hank Brunjes, Peter Holmes, Ray Kyle, George Martin, Buzz Miller, David Neuman, Stanley Simmons, George Vosburgh

NOTE: Bob Fosse understudied role of JOEY. In December 1952, Miss Gallagher succeeded by Nancy Walker; in March 1953, by Beverley Bozeman. For tour, Miss Segal succeeded by Carol Bruce; Miss Stritch by Betty O'Neil. During tour, Miss Northrop succeeded by Pat Johnson; Mr. Stander by Harry Clark.

Musical Numbers
Same as original production.

Reviews
Brooks Atkinson—*New York Times*
". . . In 1940, there was a minority, including this column, that was not enchanted. But no one is likely now to be impervious to the tight organization of the production, the terseness of the writing, the liveliness and versatility of the score and the easy perfection of the lyrics . . . it is true that *Pal Joey* was a pioneer in the moving back of musical frontiers, for it tells an integrated story with a knowing point of view . . . Brimming over with good music and fast on its toes, it renews confidence in the professionalism of the theatre."

Walter F. Kerr—*New York Herald Tribune*
". . . one of the shrewdest, toughest, and in a way the most literate book ever written for a musical comedy. It has Rodgers' enchanting score, a perfect blending of witty inflection and honest melody. It has Hart's still gay, still effortlessly ingenious lyrics . . . It has, in fact, just about everything except a pal Joey . . . Harold Lang is a lamb in wolf's clothing . . . The defection does reduce it to a far more conventional musical than it once was. Taken conventionally, it has a lot of bright moments."

John Chapman—*New York Daily News*
". . . fast, funny, tough and tuneful, with a grand cast . . . There hasn't been a dancing chorus like this one around town in a long time—or dances like Alton's either . . ."

Robert Coleman—*New York Daily Mirror*
". . . this wonderful song-and-dancer has grown better with age . . . a masterpiece . . . The gorgeous music, the great lyrics and the sophisticated book are a perfect entertainment combination . . ."

Richard Watts, Jr.—*New York Post*
". . . handsome, vigorous and dynamic . . . the best and most exciting new musical play of the season . . . very definitely an authentic work of art. But it is also great fun, in its strangely savage and sardonic fashion . . . O'Hara's book is biting, real and filled with its author's celebrated gift for recognizable talk and characters. Rodgers' score is gayly delightful and Hart's lyrics are so sly, witty, inventive and sparkling that they are a constant joy . . ."

William Hawkins—*New York World-Telegram*
". . . as brisk, bright, cutting, funny and crisp as it was . . . the sort of evening where you hesitate to single individuals out for praise because everyone involved has done so admirably. If anyone is on a pinnacle it is Vivienne Segal . . ."

John McClain—*New York Journal-American*
". . . Judged on its own merits, with no backward glance at the original show or the memorable music, I found it fast, funny and feasible. I call it a hit—a homer inside the park . . . The great score is a tribute to the immortality of the late Lorenz Hart and the very current magic of Richard Rodgers . . ."

Hobe Morrison—*Variety,* January 9, 1952
". . . still suffers from the fact that not only its hero but all the characters are unsympathetic . . . the second act is a letdown . . . The paramount favorable element remains the great score, coupled with some of Hart's most skillful (and explicitly naughty) lyrics . . ."

Wolcott Gibbs—*The New Yorker,* January 12, 1952
". . . Standards apparently have changed, because up to now I have met nobody who found anything embarrassing in the goings on . . . The production is superlative. Vivienne Segal is even better now . . . in such numbers as *Bewitched, I Could Write a Book, The Flower Garden of My Heart* and *Den of Iniquity,* Hart contrived some of the most fascinating lyrics I have ever heard . . ."

Louis Kronenberger—*Time,* January 14, 1952
". . . a kind of musicomedy classic . . . O'Hara's book remains brilliantly alive; Rodgers' score is still delightfully fresh . . . his tunes were never suaver, wittier, more engaging . . . Seldom were Hart's lyrics brisker, brighter, more uninhibited . . . a twentieth century *Beggar's Opera* . . ."

Thomas H. Wenning—*Newsweek,* January 14, 1952
". . . as fresh as the daisy it was in 1940, *Pal Joey* is an exuberant new hit . . . tough, compact book . . . Vivienne Segal is still perfect . . .

such is the inspired mating of music and lyrics that the lesser known songs are recollected with delight: *Zip, Take Him* and *Happy Hunting Horn . . .*"

George Jean Nathan—*New York Journal-American,* January 21, 1952
". . . in many respects a much better job than the original production . . . an admirable company . . . a good, gay theatre evening, even if it's not the musical comedy masterwork it was hailed to be when first shown . . ."

Harold Clurman—*The New Republic,* January 21, 1952
"The first act is a musical comedy masterpiece. It is trim, sharp, tuneful, and, in its own hard little way, almost poignant. No one in our theatre was better able to combine Broadway wickedness with wistfulness than Hart . . . he was a sort of honky-tonk Heine. Rodgers understood him. Together they wrote such perfect songs as *Bewitched* . . . one of the most serious achievements of the present day New York stage."

John Mason Brown—*Saturday Review,* February 2, 1952
". . . a modern classic . . . the nearest Broadway has come to producing its own *Beggar's Opera* . . . one of the surest sources of its enchantment is the utterly disenchanted evening it provides . . . distinguished in its music, its lyrics, its choreography, its writing and in the manner in which it is acted, sung and danced . . ."

Bibliography

NEWSPAPERS AND PERIODICALS

Reflections on Musical Comedy by Clifton Fadiman
—*Holiday,* December, 1951

O'Hara Talks of Joey's Return by Ward Morehouse
—*New York World-Telegram & Sun,* December 14, 1951

"Pal Joey": History of a Heel by Richard Rodgers
—*New York Times,* December 30, 1951

The Heel as a Hero —*Life,* January 21, 1952

Balancing Joey's Budget by J. P. Shanley
—*New York Times,* February 17, 1952

BOOKS

Pal Joey (Random House, New York, 1952)
Book and lyrics of the 1952 production.

Awards

N. Y. Drama Critics Circle Award, Best Musical, 1951-52
Donaldson Award, Best Musical, 1951-52

Tour
Shubert Theatre, Washington, April 20, 1953—Nixon Theatre, Pittsburgh, November 28, 1953 (12 cities).

PAL JOEY

(London—1954)

Presented by Jack Hylton
Directed by Neil Hartley
Mr. Alton's choreography reproduced by George Martin
Settings by Oliver Smith
Costumes by Miles White
Music director, Cyril Ornadel

Tryout
New Theatre, Oxford, March 15-27, 1954

London Run
Princes Theatre, March 31-October 30, 1954
245 performances

The Cast
JOEY EVANS, Harold Lang
MIKE SPEARS, Arthur Lowe
THE KID, Maureen Creigh
GLADYS BUMPS, Jean Brampton
ADELE, Diana Daubeney
SANDRA, Babs Warden
GLORIA, Ann Lydekker
DOTTIE, Joanna Rigby
DOLORES, Leander Fedden
FRANCINE, Sylvia Russell
LINDA ENGLISH, Sally Bazely
VERA SIMPSON, Carol Bruce
VALERIE, Vera Day
ESCORT, Calvin Von Reinhald
AMARILLA, Carol Monk
AGNES, Jean Allison
ERNEST, Ernest Ulman
VICTOR, Malcolm Goddard
DELIVERY BOY, Lionel Blair
LOUIS, Frederick James

LUDLOW LOWELL, Lou Jacobi
MELBA SNYDER, Olga Lowe
O'BRIEN, George Street
DANCERS: Jean Allison, Maureen Creigh, Diana Daubeney, Patricia Ellis, Sheila Falconer, Leander Fedden, Gillian Low, Ann Lydekker, Sylvia Lynd, Carol Monk, Mary Reynolds, Joanna Rigby, Sylvia Russell, Babs Warden, Joan Wilshire; Bob Chandler, James Dark, Alexander Morrow, Billy Petch, Steven Shore

NOTE: In April, Mr. Lang succeeded by Richard France.

Musical Numbers
Same as original production.

Reviews
London Times
". . . something of a dramatic curio . . . a transition piece, its experimental quality is some excuse for its extreme ugliness . . . The sordid story is chiefly redeemed by Miss Carol Bruce, an actress of character . . . She has the best song, *Bewitched,* and she puts it across for a great deal more than its tasteless words are worth . . ."

London Daily Herald
". . . a musical comedy of real class. The show is clever, swift and smutty in an elegant way. I never heard such sexy lines sung before on a British stage, but never minded them less . . ."

Cecil Wilson—*London Daily Mail*
". . . this unsavory little tale is redeemed by wit of a slyness and sophistication rarely encountered in a musical comedy, by the punch of the production and the personal charm of Harold Lang."

Alan Dent—*London News-Chronicle*
". . . We are bothered by the ugly blackmailing scene in the last act. We are bewildered by the utter lack of sentiment. But we are bewitched, especially by the tunes, in the end."

London Daily Sketch
"The first musical play to wear long trousers . . . the first musical that deliberately explores the seamy facts of life . . ."

Harold Hobson—*London Sunday Times,* April 4, 1954
". . . stands up as a forerunner of 'black' art . . . In its way, *Pal Joey* is a fortifying moral exercise. But are moral exercises enjoyable? Its few sensuous satisfactions are strictly tuned to the mordant savagery of its main intention . . ."

Ivor Brown—*London Observer,* April 4, 1954
". . . an honest American musical which shoots the grubby glamour world of the night-club to pieces . . . a score which varies the smashing, the stunning and the tenderly mournful . . . In the nitery numbers the feminine form is displayed with the minimum of reservation and, although the body-line attack has its blue-line script, the whole effect is devastatingly ethical. Who wouldn't prefer unmitigated prayer and fasting to such a life of gaiety as *Pal Joey* presents?"

Eric Keown—*Punch,* April 7, 1954
". . . carefully calculated to have no charm whatever . . . Far from being a love-philtre, *Pal Joey* is an emetic . . . Good tunes would have helped, so would a good comedian, so would some singing voices . . ."

Harold Myers—*Variety,* April 7, 1954
". . . London, unlike Broadway, seems likely to take to it first time round . . . the integration of a positive story, music and ballet, is given a bold, imaginative treatment. Productionwise, it combines visual appeal with slickness of presentation and a score which was only slightly familiar to local audiences . . ."

Bibliography

"Pal Joey" Loses Accent in London —*New York Times,* April 1, 1954

Britain's "Pal Joey" Verdict: Sordid, Witty and Tuneful —*New York Herald Tribune,* April 4, 1954

PAL JOEY

(Film Version—1957)

A Columbia Picture
An Essex-George Sidney Production
Produced by Fred Kohlmar
Directed by Mr. Sidney
Screenplay by Dorothy Kingsley
Choreography by Hermes Pan
Art director, Walter Holscher
Costumes by Jean Louis
Music director, Morris Stoloff
Orchestrations by Nelson Riddle
Music adapted by Mr. Riddle and George Duning

Photographed by Harold Lipstein
Editors, Viola Lawrence, Jerome Thoms
Color by Technicolor

Release Date
September 9, 1957

The Story
Joey, a night club entertainer, makes his way by unscrupulous dealings. He drops the innocent Linda, a girl in a San Francisco night club chorus, in favor of the wealthy Vera, who promises to build a night club just for him. At the last minute, he has a change of heart and returns to Linda.

The Cast
VERA SIMPSON, Rita Hayworth (sung by Jo Ann Greer)
JOEY EVANS, Frank Sinatra
LINDA ENGLISH, Kim Novak (sung by Trudy Ewen)
GLADYS, Barbara Nichols
NED GALVIN, Bobby Sherwood
MIKE MIGGINS, Hank Henry
MRS. CASEY, Elizabeth Patterson
BARTENDER, Robin Morse
COL. LANGLEY, Frank Wilcox
MR. FORSYTHE, Pierre Watkin
ANDERSON, Berry Bernard
CAROL, Ellie Kent

Musical Numbers
Songs retained from original production: *Zip, Great Big Town (Chicago), That Terrific Rainbow, Pal Joey,* and *Bewitched, Bothered and Bewildered.* Songs by Rodgers and Hart from other musical shows added for film: *I Didn't Know What Time It Was, There's a Small Hotel, My Funny Valentine* and *The Lady Is a Tramp.*

Reviews
A. H. Weiler—*New York Times*
". . . this company is performing with admirable gusto in a swiftly-moving, cheerful and adult musical play that is one of the season's best . . . Although the lyrics have been bowlderized a mite, their general ideas come across charmingly. There is no doubt that this is largely Mr. Sinatra's show . . ."

William K. Zinsser—*New York Herald Tribune*
". . . only a distant cousin of the Broadway musical . . . If you're an

O'Hara and Hart man this version will be high heresy, almost as if the novels of Flaubert say, were adapted by Louisa May Alcott . . . On its own terms *Pal Joey* is a bright musical, designed for fun and not for satire, and it is no worse for having its mouth washed . . . Sinatra gives the movie its spark almost single-handed . . ."

Archer Winsten—*New York Post*
". . . a good musical, carrying a load of name performers, disappointing to admirers of the classic O'Hara musical but full of clever trinkets for the current Sinatra mob."

Gene Arneel—*Variety,* September 11, 1957
". . . a click. It can't miss being a blockbuster, the commercial values being so stacked up . . . strong, funny entertainment . . . Sinatra is potent . . . Standout in the score is *The Lady Is a Tramp* . . ."

Time, October 28, 1957
". . . a dandy piece of entertainment . . . some of the spunkiest and most graceful music Rodgers ever wrote, some wackily witty, leering lyrics . . . Almost everything that could be done wrong the moviemakers have done wrong in this production, and yet somehow the picture comes out remarkably right. The film oversanitizes *Pal Joey's* original fun-and-gaminess and, what's worse, imprisons the show's vitality in a plaster cast . . . Kim just trudges around in the well-known Novakuum . . . The show is saved by Frank Sinatra . . ."

Ted Robinson—*Newsweek,* October 28, 1957
". . . in song and dance, this slick, thoroughly professional entertainment is a rainbow of color; in dialogue and situation it is all blue . . ."

John McCarten—*The New Yorker,* November 2, 1957
". . . a poor, poor thing compared to the wonderful original . . . has lost much of its satiric bite, and while Frank Sinatra does his best to keep the film moving along, he just can't sustain the piece singlehanded . . . the score has been purified along with Joe's character . . ."

Bibliography

Hollywood "Joey" by Thomas M. Pryor —*New York Times,* April 28, 1957

Filming "Pal Joey" —*New York Times Magazine,* June 9, 1957

THEY MET IN ARGENTINA

(Film-1941)

A musical film with screenplay by Jerry Cady, from a story by Lou Brock and Harold Daniels; music by Richard Rodgers; lyrics by Lorenz Hart.

An RKO-Radio Picture
Produced by Mr. Brock
Directed by Leslie Goodwins and Jack Hively
Choreography by Frank Veloz
Music director, Lud Gluskin
Photographed by J. Roy Hunt
Editor, Desmond Marquette

Release Date
May 8, 1941

The Story
Tim, a Texas cowpuncher, tries to buy a famous Argentine race horse for his employer. However, Don Enrique, the horse's owner, doesn't want to sell. But the deal is aided when romance develops between Tim and Don Enrique's daughter, Lolita.

The Cast
LOLITA, Maureen O'Hara
TIM, James Ellison
ALBERTO, Alberto Vila
DUKE, Buddy Ebsen
DON ENRIQUE, Robert Barrat
SANTIAGO, Joseph Buloff
PANCHITA, Diosa Costello
NINA MARIA, Victoria Cordova
DON CARLOS, Antonio Moreno
GEORGE HASTINGS, Robert Middlemas
PETRO, Fortunio Bonanova
DON FRUTOS, Luis Alberni

Musical Numbers
North America Meets South America, PANCHITA and LOLITA
You've Got the Best of Me, DUKE and PANCHITA
Amarillo, TIM; ALBERTO

Lolita, ALBERTO
Cutting the Cane, PANCHITA and CHORUS
Never Go to Argentina, PANCHITA
Simpatica, ALBERTO

Reviews
Robert W. Dana—*New York Herald Tribune*
". . . Rodgers and Hart's tunes help some, and a new dance called the chaco is colorfully demonstrated . . . an American musical at its worst."

Irene Thirer—*New York Post*
". . . good willed, but certainly not important enough to have any effect on the good-will relations between the North and South Americas . . . gay song and dance numbers . . ."

Donald Kirkley—*Baltimore Sun*
". . . a lively and agreeable musical setting . . . moderate entertainment . . ."

F.S.—*Dallas Morning News*
". . . the story is just one of those things . . . choppy entertainment . . ."

Mike P. Wear—*Variety,* May 14, 1941
". . . it is extremely dubious if it will further the cause of hemispheric solidarity . . . doubtful if the film will cause much of a ripple with exhibitors, despite a sturdy score . . ."

Bibliography
Fumble in Film Good Will —*Newsweek,* June 16, 1941

BY JUPITER

(1942)

A musical comedy with book by Richard Rodgers and Lorenz Hart, based on the play "The Warrior's Husband" by Julian F. Thompson; music by Mr. Rodgers; lyrics by Mr. Hart.

Presented by Dwight Deere Wiman and Mr. Rodgers
in association with Richard Kollmar
Directed by Joshua Logan
Choreography by Robert Alton
Settings and lighting by Jo Mielziner
Costumes by Irene Sharaff
Music director, Johnny Green
Orchestrations by Don Walker
Vocal arrangements by Mr. Green and Clay Warnick

Tryout
(known as "All's Fair")
Shubert Theatre, Boston, May 11-30, 1942

New York Run
Shubert Theatre, June 3, 1942-June 12, 1943
427 performances

The Story
Led by their queen, Hippolyta, the Amazon women war with the men of Greece. After they are defeated, the women assume a role subordinate to both the invaders and the men of their own island.

The Cast
ACHILLES, Bob Douglas
A HERALD, Mark Dawson
AGAMEMNON, Robert Hightower
BURIA, Jayne Manners
SENTRIES, Rose Inghram, Martha Burnett, Kay Kimber
SERGEANT, Monica Moore
CAUSTICA, Maidel Turner
HEROICA, Margaret Bannerman
POMPOSIA, Bertha Belmore

BOYS, Don Liberto, Tony Matthews, William Vaux
HIPPOLYTA, Benay Venuta
SAPIENS, Ray Bolger
ANTIOPE, Constance Moore
A HUNTRESS, Helen Bennett
AN AMAZON DANCER, Flower Hujer
THESEUS, Ronald Graham
HOMER, Berni Gould
MINERVA, Vera-Ellen
SLAVES, Robert and Lewis Hightower
AMAZON RUNNER, Wana Wenerholm
HERCULES, Ralph Dumke
PENELOPE, Irene Corlett
FIRST CAMP FOLLOWER, Vera-Ellen
CAMP FOLLOWERS, Ruth Brady, Helen Bennett, Joyce Ring, Rosemary Sankey
GIRLS OF THE ENSEMBLE: Helen Bennett, Ruth Brady, Betty Jo Creager, June Graham, Babs Heath, Janet Lavis, Virginia Meyer, Marjorie Moore, Mary Virginia Morris, Beth Nichols, Dorothy Poplar, Bobby Priest, Joyce Ring, Rosemary Sankey, Toni Stuart, Olga Suarez, Wana Wenerholm
BOYS OF THE ENSEMBLE: Ray Koby, Don Liberto, Michael Mann, Tony Matthews, George Schwable, William Silvers, Ken Whelan, Robert Wilson, William Vaux

NOTE: During tryout, THESEUS originally played by Richard Ainley. Miss Moore succeeded by Nanette Fabray in January, 1943.

Musical Numbers

ACT I

SCENE ONE—A GREEK CAMP

For Jupiter and Greece, ACHILLES, HERALD and GREEK WARRIORS

SCENE TWO—A TERRACE OF HIPPOLYTA'S PALACE IN PONTUS

Jupiter Forbid, HIPPOLYTA, SENTRIES, SERGEANT; danced by SLAVES, AMAZON DANCER and ENSEMBLE
Life With Father, SAPIENS
Nobody's Heart, ANTIOPE
The Gateway of the Temple of Minerva, THESEUS and ENSEMBLE
Reprise, *Life With Father,* POMPOSIA and SAPIENS
Here's a Hand, THESEUS and ANTIOPE
No, Mother, No, SAPIENS and ENSEMBLE

ACT II

SCENE ONE—BEFORE HIPPOLYTA'S TENT

The Boy I Left Behind Me, BURIA and ENSEMBLE
Reprise, *Nobody's Heart,* SAPIENS
Ev'rything I've Got, SAPIENS and HIPPOLYTA

Bottoms Up, HERALD, HIPPOLYTA, ANTIOPE, HOMER, ACHILLES, MINERVA, AMAZON DANCER, SLAVES and ENSEMBLE
Careless Rhapsody, ANTIOPE and THESEUS
Finaletto, SAPIENS, HIPPOLYTA, POMPOSIA and ENSEMBLE

SCENE TWO—THE GREEK CAMP
Reprise, *Ev'rything I've Got,* HIPPOLYTA

SCENE THREE—INSIDE THESEUS'S TENT
Wait Till You See Her, THESEUS and ENSEMBLE
Now That I've Got My Strength, SAPIENS, PENELOPE, FIRST CAMP FOLLOWER and ENSEMBLE
Finale, COMPANY

NOTE: *Life Was Monotonous, Fool Meets Fool* and *Nothing to Do But Relax* cut before rehearsals. *Wait Till You See Her* dropped during run.

Reviews

Lewis Nichols—*New York Times*
". . . with a few of Rodgers' better tunes and a fistful of Hart's casually complicated lyrics, it is beautifully costumed, well directed, and played by everyone for all that is in it . . . Mr. Bolger is magnificent . . ."

Richard Watts, Jr.—*New York Herald Tribune*
". . . possesses a characteristically charming score, ingenious lyrics, beautiful settings and costumes, a first-rate comedian, brilliantly staged dances and a pleasant air of festivity . . ."

Burns Mantle—*New York Daily News*
"★★★ . . . all the earmarks of a rousing summer hit . . . the music is vigorous and soothing by turns . . ."

Walter Winchell—*New York Daily Mirror*
". . . a brisk dancing affair . . . not too much assistance from Rodgers and Hart . . . their familiar genius appeared arid . . ."

Wilella Waldorf—*New York Post*
". . . a handsome summer show distinguished by Ray Bolger's ingratiating performance. Without his antics to give it zip, we greatly fear it would prove fairly tame entertainment . . . several catchy songs but the score is not one of Mr. Rodgers' most tuneful efforts, and we thought Mr. Hart's lyrics sounded a little tired now and then . . ."

Barclay Hudson (Frank Farrell)—*New York World-Telegram*
". . . an artistic achievement in musical comedy and an overwhelming personal triumph for everyone even remotely connected with it

. . . gay, breezy, naughty, filled with spontaneous laughs, original dancing, catchy music, exquisite costumes and enchanting sets . . . If Rodgers and Hart haven't provided their usual average of hit tunes, the score they have delivered in this Tiffany-like package is more than adequate . . ."

Richard Lockridge—*New York Sun*
". . . has the fine gloss of the American musical theatre when expert and appreciative hands polish it. It moves with dash and that effortless enthusiasm which comes from the best kind of professionalism . . . Practically all the songs have the proper Rodgers and Hart flavor . . ."

John Anderson—*New York Journal-American*
". . . Its gender troubles are slyly naughty and amusing, Mr. Rodgers' music is beguiling, the production superbly pictorial, and Ray Bolger superb. Altogether it is, I suspect, the gayest and prettiest show of what passes for the season . . ."

Louis Kronenberger—*PM*
". . . professional and lavish and large-scale . . . one charming tune *Nobody's Heart,* and several perfectly all right ones; but the score as a whole lacks distinction. It has some clever lyrics, but a good many of them merely seemed strained . . . a good farce idea for a book, but it begins after a while to wear a little thin . . ."

Abel Green—*Variety,* June 10, 1942
". . . a lush and lavish musical comedy which will enjoy a moderate run . . . The monotone of masculine femmes and effeminate men makes for not too inspired comedy. The first act is strong; the second act lets down considerably . . . much clever—sometimes too much so—lyrical wordage . . . The score is a bit too ultra for popular consumption . . ."

Wolcott Gibbs—*The New Yorker,* June 13, 1942
". . . With minor reservations—I am never quite sure, for instance, just how funny effeminacy really is on the stage—I think it is a very fine show . . . it isn't subtle, or especially delicate, but a lot of it seemed very funny to me . . . it may be that Rodgers and Hart's songs weren't as inventive as some they have produced in the past, but they still have a comfortable lead over the field . . ."

Time, June 15, 1942
". . . its large-scale lavishness is one of its two real assets. The other is Ray Bolger . . . makes smirking and off-color copy—which soon

palls and sometimes offends . . . Rodgers and Hart have done a fair enough job, but nothing to show that they are the top team in the business. The lyrics, sometimes gay, are often gamy. The score, except for one charming tune, *Nobody's Heart,* is mildly pleasant . . ."

Thomas H. Wenning—*Newsweek,* June 15, 1942
"*A Hit, by Jove* . . . Bolger swooned, smirked and smashed his way into being a star instead of merely a co-star. Without Bolger, *By Jupiter* would be just a slick, smartly paced, professional musical—handsome to watch, pleasant to hear, but hardly in the top-drawer class . . . the score has at least two or three hits in the offing—including probably *Nobody's Heart, Ev'rything I've Got* or *Careless Rhapsody* . . ."

Bibliography

"*By Jupiter*" by Robert Rice —*PM Magazine,* May 31, 1942

"*By Jupiter*" *May Be Last Broadway Musical in Grand Pre-War Style* —*Life,* June 1, 1942

Selected Revivals

Goodspeed Opera House, East Haddam, Conn., Summer, 1967
Leonard Frey (SAPIENS); Fern Sloan (ANTIOPE); Barbara Cason (HIPPOLYTA); Fred Kimbrough (THESEUS).

BY JUPITER

(New York—1967)

Presented by Robert Cherin
in association with Christopher Hewett
Directed by Mr. Hewett
Additional material by Fred Ebb
Choreography by Ellen Ray
Settings by Herbert Senn and Helen Pond
Costumes by Winn Morton
Lighting by Robert L. Steele
Music director, Milton Selzer
Orchestrations by Abba Bogin
Dance arrangements by Lee Holdridge

New York Run (Off-Broadway)

Theatre Four, January 19-April 30, 1967
118 performances

The Cast

THESEUS, Robert R. Kaye
HOMER, Emory Bass
HERCULES, Charles Rydell
HERALD, Richard Marshall
ACHILLES, Ben Gerard
BURIA, Rosemarie Heyer
SERGEANT, Renata Vaselle
FIRST SENTRY, Fayn Le Veille
SECOND SENTRY, Alice Glenn
THIRD SENTRY, Joyce Maret
CAUSTICA, Ronnie Cunningham
HEROICA, Norma Doggett
POMPOSIA, Irene Byatt
TRUMPETERS: Joyce Maret, Debra Lyman
HIPPOLYTA, Jackie Alloway
SAPIENS, Bob Dishy
MESSENGER, Alice Glenn
ANTIOPE, Sheila Sullivan
HUNTRESS, Alice Glenn
RUNNER, Debra Lyman
PENELOPE, Renata Vaselle

Musical Numbers

Same as original production.

Reviews

Walter Kerr— *New York Times*

". . . this particular score—which always was a second best in the Rodgers-Hart canon—is full of tunes that are little more than titles . . . Though the Hart lyrics are most noticeably uneven, the sustained anticipation makes the nice ones seem nicer . . . So *By Jupiter,* in its neat-as-a-pin, black, gold and white revival, was worth it to me . . ."

James Davis—*New York Daily News*

"*A Fun Musical*. . . . Pretty girls, attractive men, a soupcon of bawdy men, and, most important, a Rodgers-Hart score . . . an appetizing dish indeed . . . a spanking-new, expensive-looking production . . . Everyone can take a bow for this one . . ."

Richard Watts, Jr.—*New York Post*

". . . a thoroughgoing delight . . . its melodiousness, humor, high spirits and charm, together with the skill and freshness of its presentation made it one of the joys of the season . . . the attractiveness of the girls is notable among its blessings . . . the distinguished team of Rodgers and Hart had been in glorious and spendidly characteristic form . . ."

Norman Nadel—*New York World Journal Tribune,* February 5, 1967
"*Bright Revival* . . . doesn't represent the fullest flowering of the Rodgers-Hart collaboration, but even after 25 years of changing styles in musical comedies, it makes for a mildly pleasant evening . . . The production is sprightly and joyful, tastefully staged and peopled with likeable, enthusiastic players. Some of it is too broad and more than a trifle corny, but the musical is worth bringing back to life . . ."

Tom Morse—*Variety,* January 25, 1967
". . . spiffy revival . . . still a melodious laughrouser, and major league talent is evident on every crucial front . . . *Wait Till You See Her* is the musical highlight of the show . . . brilliant orchestrations . . ."

Edith Oliver—*The New Yorker,* January 28, 1967
"One's chief impression amid the joy and merriment is of quality—the quality of the music and words and the quality of the comedy and singing and dancing and settings and costumes and orchestrations . . . It is minor Rodgers and Hart, but it is a lovely show all the same. There is one beautiful song, *Wait Till You See Her;* one charming song, *Nobody's Heart* . . . I cannot imagine a pleasanter place to be any evening of the week except Monday."

Henry Hewes—*Saturday Review,* February 11, 1967
". . . Bob Dishy is scoring an off-Broadway triumph . . . the musical is a neat if slight spoofing . . . all the numbers have the special tender, funny grace at which Rodgers and Hart were supreme . . . Hewett has staged the fable crisply . . . emerges as a sophisticated excursion that recalls a more lighthearted and naive era."

Bibliography

Rodgers and Hart: The Test of Time by Fred Ebb
—*New York World Journal Tribune,* January 15, 1967

WORDS AND MUSIC

(Film—1948)

A musical film with screenplay by Fred Finklehoffe, adapted by Ben Feiner, Jr., from a story by Guy Bolton and Jean Holloway; music by Richard Rodgers; lyrics by Lorenz Hart.

A Metro-Goldwyn-Mayer Picture
Produced by Arthur Freed
Directed by Norman Taurog
Choreography by Robert Alton, Gene Kelly
Art director, Cedric Gibbons
Costumes by Helen Rose and Valles
Music director, Lennie Hayton
Orchestrations by Conrad Salinger
Vocal arrangements by Robert Tucker
Photographed by Charles Rosher and Harry Stradling
Editors, Albert Akst, Ferris Webster
Color by Technicolor

Release Date

December 9, 1948

The Story

A fictionalized biography of Rodgers and Hart, from their first meeting in 1919 to Hart's death in 1943.

The Cast

LORENZ "LARRY" HART, Mickey Rooney
RICHARD "DICK" RODGERS, Tom Drake
HERBERT FIELDS, Marshall Thompson
EDDIE LORRISON ANDERS, Perry Como
JOYCE HARMON, Ann Sothern
PEGGY LORGAN MCNEIL, Betty Garrett
DOROTHY FEINER, Janet Leigh
MRS. HART, Jeanette Nolan
BEN FEINER, JR., Richard Quine
SHOE CLERK, Clinton Sundberg
DR. RODGERS, Harry Antrim
MR. FEINER, Emory Parnell
MRS. FEINER, Helen Spring
JAMES FERNBY KELLY, Edward Earle

Guest Appearances
June Allyson
Judy Garland
Lena Horne
Gene Kelly
Cyd Charisse (sung by Eileen Wilson)
Mel Torme
Vera-Ellen
Dee Turnell
Allyn Ann McLerie
Blackburn Twins

Musical Numbers
Manhattan, DICK, LARRY and HERBERT
There's a Small Hotel, PEGGY
Way Out West, PEGGY
With a Song in My Heart, DICK
Spring Is Here, unidentified voice; lyric spoken by LARRY

CAPITOL THEATRE SEQUENCE
On Your Toes, Cyd Charisse and Dee Turnell
This Can't Be Love, Cyd Charisse and Dee Turnell
The Girl Friend, Cyd Charisse and Dee Turnell

"THE GIRL FRIEND" (LONDON) SEQUENCE
Blue Room, EDDIE; danced by Cyd Charisse

"THE GARRICK GAIETIES II" SEQUENCE
Mountain Greenery, EDDIE; danced by Allyn Ann McLerie and ENSEMBLE

"PEGGY-ANN" SEQUENCE
A Tree in the Park, JOYCE
Where's that Rainbow?, JOYCE and Blackburn Twins
A Little Birdie Told Me So, danced by Blackburn Twins

"A CONNECTICUT YANKEE" SEQUENCE
Thou Swell, June Allyson and Blackburn Twins
Someone Should Tell Them, June Allyson and Blackburn Twins

RITZ PLAZA HOTEL SEQUENCE
Where or When?, Lena Horne
The Lady Is a Tramp, Lena Horne

HOLLYWOOD PARTY SEQUENCE
I Wish I Were in Love Again, Judy Garland and LARRY
Johnny One Note, Judy Garland
Blue Moon, Mel Torme

"ON YOUR TOES" SEQUENCE
Slaughter on Tenth Avenue, Gene Kelly and Vera-Ellen

TRIBUTE TO LARRY HART SEQUENCE
With a Song in My Heart, EDDIE
My Heart Stood Still, CHORUS

Reviews
Bosley Crowther—*New York Times*
"Fortunately, the wonderful music is treated with passable justice . . . the film is as far from the facts in its reporting as it is standard in its sentimental plot . . ."

Howard Barnes—*New York Herald Tribune*
". . . the story rarely succeeds in giving one a persuasive, panoramic picture of a theatrical period. The songs are all important . . ."

Alton Cook—*New York World-Telegram*
". . . full of huge sets, crowded with all the Metro stars who could be reached by 'phone . . ."

Herb Golden—*Variety,* December 8, 1948
". . . The tunes have an irrepressible froth and pleasantness, even more listenable than when they were written. Biog sticks to truth about as closely as can be presented on the screen . . . a strong boxoffice entry . . ."

Thomas H. Wenning—*Newsweek,* December 13, 1948
". . . the desultory story is frankly a device for stringing together (with blissful disregard of chronology) a series of handsome production numbers and an exciting, nostalgic album of songs . . ."

John McCarten—*The New Yorker,* December 18, 1948
". . . includes many of the grand melodies and lyrics . . . It also, unfortunately, includes Mickey Rooney, who is still chewing up all the scenery in sight with an appetite cultivated recklessly over the years . . ."

Lester Bernstein—*Time,* December 27, 1948
". . . has just the right proportion of garlicky bad taste and more than oriental splendor which add up to a Hollywood dream of heaven—an M-G-M supermusical . . . a version of the careers of Rodgers and Hart preserved from too much resemblance to reality throughout . . . But the Rodgers and Hart wizardry gets the ultimate, if unconscious, tribute. Against all the odds that money could buy, the tunes are still mighty pretty and the words are still mighty cute."

OSCAR HAMMERSTEIN II

Charles Winninger in Scene 6, Act I, of "Show Boat" (1927).

BIOGRAPHICAL FACT SHEET

OSCAR HAMMERSTEIN II

BORN: New York, N.Y., July 12, 1895.

PARENTS: William and Alice (Nimmo) Hammerstein.

FATHER'S OCCUPATION: Manager, Victoria Theatre.

OTHER THEATRICAL LINEAGE: Oscar Hammerstein (grandfather), theatre builder and impresario of the Manhattan Opera House; Arthur Hammerstein (uncle), Broadway producer.

EDUCATION: Hamilton Institute (1908-12); Columbia University (1912-16); Columbia Law School (1915-17).

MARRIED: Myra Finn, August 22, 1917 (divorced); Dorothy Blanchard Jacobson, May 14, 1929.

CHILDREN: William, Alice (first marriage); James (second marriage); Susan, Henry (step-children).

DIED: Doylestown, Pa., August 23, 1960.

FIRST SCORE: *Home, James* (amateur, 1917), music by Robert Lippmann, lyric with Herman Axelrod.

FIRST SONGS WITH MR. RODGERS: *Weaknesses, Can It* and *There's Always Room for One More,* all in *Up Stage and Down* (amateur, 1919).

FIRST PROFESSIONAL SONG: *Make Yourself at Home,* music by Silvio Hein, in *Furs and Frills* (1917).

FIRST PROFESSIONAL SCORE: *Always You,* music by Herbert Stothart.

FIRST PROFESSIONAL SONG WITH MR. RODGERS: *Oh, What a Beautiful Mornin'* in *Oklahoma!* (1943).

FIRST PROFESSIONAL SCORE WITH MR. RODGERS: *Oklahoma!*

LAST SONG: *Edelweiss,* music by Mr. Rodgers, in *The Sound of Music* (1959).

COMPOSER COLLABORATORS BESIDES MR. RODGERS:

Herbert Stothart (1895-1949), 9 stage scores
Lewis Gensler (1896-1978), 1 stage score
Dudley Wilkinson (born 1897), 1 stage score
Vincent Youmans (1898-1946), 3 stage scores
Rudolf Friml (1879-1972), 2 stage scores
Jerome Kern (1885-1946), 7 stage scores, 1 film score
George Gershwin (1898-1937), 1 stage score
Sigmund Romberg (1887-1951), 5 stage scores, 3 film scores
Emmerich Kalman (1882-1953), 1 stage score
Richard A. Whiting (1891-1938), 1 stage score

Paul Abraham (1893-1960), 1 stage score
Erich Wolfgang Korngold (1897-1957), 1 film score
Ben Oakland (born 1907), 1 film score
Johann Strauss, Jr. (1825-1899), 1 film score
Arthur Schwartz (born 1900), 1 stage score
Georges Bizet (1838-1875), 1 stage score

LYRICIST COLLABORATORS:
Otto Harbach (1873-1963), 11 stage scores
William Cary Duncan (1874-1945), 1 stage score

TOTAL STAGE AND FILM WORKS:
31 Broadway musicals, lyrics and librettos (23 with various composers; 8 with Rodgers)
2 Broadway musicals, lyrics only (1 with Romberg; 1 with Rodgers)
2 Broadway musicals, librettos only
2 Broadway plays (both with Milton Gropper)
2 Non-Broadway musicals, librettos and lyrics (1 with Kern; 1 with Schwartz)
2 plays that closed before Broadway (1 alone; 1 with Frank Mandel)
2 London musicals, lyrics and librettos (1 with Abraham; 1 with Kern)
4 film musicals, lyrics and screenplays (2 with Romberg; 1 with Kern; 1 with Rodgers)
5 film musicals, lyrics only (with various composers)
2 film musicals, screenplays only
1 television musical, lyrics and libretto (with Rodgers)

PERFORMANCE STATISTICS
The number of performances achieved to date by all of Mr. Hammerstein's Broadway stage works—including revivals—totals 16,453. On the basis of eight performances per week, this is equivalent to almost 2,057 weeks—or an unbroken run of about 39½ years.

PROFESSIONAL POSITIONS: Partner, Rodgers and Hammerstein productions; partner, Williamson Music, Inc.

PROFESSIONAL ASSOCIATIONS: American Society of Composers, Authors and Publishers (ASCAP) (director, 1939-60); Authors League of America; Dramatists Guild (president, 1950); Screen Writers Guild; American Guild of Authors and Composers.

BOARD MEMBERSHIP: United World Federalists (vice president, 1947-60).

ENDOWMENTS: Max Dreyfus Annual Scholarship, Juilliard (endowed with Mr. Rodgers) (1954); 2 scholarships, American Theatre Wing (Rodgers and Hammerstein Foundation) (1955); Rodgers and Hammerstein annual award to individual who has done the most for the theatre in the Boston area (1959); Rodgers and Hammerstein annual award to individual who has done the most for the theatre in the Southwest (1960); Rodgers and Hammerstein Archives of Recorded Sound, Lincoln Center (Rodgers and Hammerstein Foundation).

PERSONAL HONORS AND AWARDS (awards for specific works found under stage and film productions)

1949 Columbia University Medal for Excellence
Drury College honorary LL.D.
1950 100 Year Association Gold Medal
1951 Connecticut State Bar Assn. Distinguished Public Service Award
1952 Dartmouth College honorary DHL
Columbia College Outstanding Achievement Award
1954 Columbia University honorary LL.D.
University of Massachusetts honorary DHL
1955 Elected to membership National Institute of Arts and Letters
1956 Columbia College Alexander Hamilton Medal
Knox College honorary LL.D.
1958 Dutch Treat Club Distinguished Achievement Award
1959 National Conference of Christians and Jews Human Relations Award
1971 Elected to Songwriters Hall of Fame
1972 Elected to Theatre Hall of Fame

AMATEUR PRODUCTIONS

1915

On Your Way

A musical comedy with book and lyrics by Kenneth S. Webb; music by Roy S. Webb. Presented by the Columbia University Players as the Varsity Show of 1915; directed by Kenneth Webb; music director, Roy Webb. Cast included Mr. Hammerstein as CLARENCE MONTAGUE, a poet.

1916
The Peace Pirates
A musical comedy with book and lyrics by Herman J. Mankiewicz; music by Ray Perkins; interpolated scene by Oscar Hammerstein II. Presented by the Columbia University Players as the Variety Show of 1916; directed by Kenneth S. Webb. Cast included Mr. Hammerstein as WASHINGTON SNOW; Lorenz M. Hart as MRS. ROCKYFORD.

1917
Home, James
A musical comedy with book and lyrics by Herman A. Axelrod and Oscar Hammerstein II; music by Robert Lippmann; additional music and lyrics by Kenneth S. Webb, Roy S. Webb, M. S. Wolff, Robert A. Simon. Presented by the Columbia University Players as the Varsity Show of 1917; directed by Kenneth Webb. Cast included Mr. Hammerstein as ARMAND DUBONNET, head waiter at Roget's. MUSICAL NUMBERS: included *Annie McGinnis Pavlova* by Messrs. Axelrod, Hammerstein and Lippmann. NEW YORK RUN: Astor Hotel Grand Ballroom, March 28, 1917.

1918
Ten For Five
A musical comedy with book and lyrics by Oscar Hammerstein II; music by Robert K. Lippmann; additional music and lyrics by Henry William Hanemann. Presented by the Columbia University War Show Committee as the War Show of 1918; directed by Mr. Hammerstein; music director, Roy S. Webb.

1919
Up Stage and Down
A musical comedy with music by Richard C. Rodgers.
MUSICAL NUMBERS: included *Weaknesses, There's Always Room for One More,* and *Can It,* all with lyrics by Oscar Hammerstein II.

1920
You'd Be Surprised
A musical comedy with music by Richard C. Rodgers.
MUSICAL NUMBERS: included *That Boy of Mine* with lyric by Oscar Hammerstein II.

Fly With Me
A musical comedy with music by Richard C. Rodgers.
MUSICAL NUMBERS: included *There's Always Room for One More* and *Weaknesses,* both with lyrics by Oscar Hammerstein II.

1921
You'll Never Know
A musical comedy with music by Richard C. Rodgers. Directed by Oscar Hammerstein II.

Say It With Jazz
"A Coq-d'Orian Fantasy" with music by Richard C. Rodgers.
MUSICAL NUMBERS: included *Weaknesses* with lyric by Oscar Hammerstein II.

1922
Jazz a la Carte
A musical comedy with music by Richard C. Rodgers.
MUSICAL NUMBERS: included *There's Always Room for One More,* with lyric by Oscar Hammerstein II.

THE LIGHT

(1919)

A play by Oscar Hammerstein II.

Presented by Arthur Hammerstein
Directed by Walter Wilson

Tryout

Shubert Theatre, New Haven, May 21, 1919
4 performances

New York Run

None

The Story

To escape from her unpleasant homelife, Nancy agrees to marry a young man other than the one she loves and with whom she has had an affair. When her fiancé is killed, she runs away from home to avoid another arranged marriage. While working in a gambling resort, Nancy is eventually reunited with her first love.

The Cast

BEN HARDING, David Higgins
EMMA PORTER, Lois Frances Clarke
MARY WALKER, Sadie Radcliffe
NANCY, Vivienne Osborne
CHARLES HARRISON, Brandon Peters
ALLAN PORTER, J. Frank McGlynn
JOHN TROWBRIDGE, Saxon Kling
"BLACKIE" SMITH, Florence Huntington
"BABE," Charlotte Carter
MAID, Gertrude Gustin
GEORGE DENT, John Flood
MR. BURNHAM, George Westlake

ACT I—Home of Allan Porter. Three years ago.
ACT II—Same. The next morning.
ACT III—Apartment of "Blackie" Smith. Time, Present.
ACT IV—Nancy's Boudoir in "Blackie's" apartment.

Reviews

New Haven Journal-Courier

"Old fashioned drama . . . If you are fond of this sort of a performance you will find the play mildly interesting, well done in spots and average for the best. The author, however, has accomplished one thing exceedingly well; he has pictured some types that are alarmingly true to life . . ."

The New Haven

"Its christening robe may well suffice as shroud for a deadly dull play. Its serious moments are absurd, and of comedy there is none except such as results from scenes and incidents which the author did not intend to be comic . . . incredible and impossible . . ."

Bibliography

Play by Oscar Hammerstein II —*New York Telegraph,* May 16, 1919

ALWAYS YOU

(1920)

A musical comedy with book and lyrics by Oscar Hammerstein II; music by Herbert Stothart.

Presented and directed by Arthur Hammerstein
Choreography by Robert Marks
Settings by Julius Dove
Costumes by Paul Arlington, Inc.
Music director, Mr. Stothart

Tryout

(known as "Joan of Arkansaw" and "Toinette")
Poli's Theatre, Washington, December 29, 1919-January 3, 1920

New York Run

Central Theatre, January 5-March 1, 1920
66 performances

The Story

Bruce Nash of the A.E.F. fell in love with Toinette Fontaine while in France during the war. Back in the United States he becomes engaged to his former sweetheart, Joan Summers. He returns to France where he has a change of heart, and after complications have been adjusted, persuades Toinette to marry him.

The Cast

TOINETTE FONTAINE, Helen Ford
BRUCE NASH, Walter Scanlon
EAST INDIAN PEDDLER, Edouard Ciannelli
JULIE FONTAINE, Julia Kelety
CHARLIE LANGFORD, Russell Mack
MONTMORENCY JONES, Ralph Herz
A MYSTERIOUS CONSPIRATOR, Bernard Gorcey
JOAN SUMMERS, Anna Seymour
THOMAS, Joseph Barton
A WAITRESS, Emily Russ
DANCERS, Cortez and Peggy
PIANIST, Burton Green
GIRLS OF THE ENSEMBLE: Marietta O'Brien, Alicia Smith, Virginia Clark, Irma

Marwick, Emily Russ, Memphis Russell, Mildred Rowland, Helen Neff, Rose Cardiff, Jose Carmen, Marvee Snow, Rheba Stewart, Elinore Cullen, Gene Morrison

NOTE: For tour, Miss Ford succeeded by Elizabeth Gergely; Miss Seymour by Irene Franklin. During tour, Miss Gergely succeeded by Maggie Touhey; Mr. Scanlon by Harold Murray.

Musical Numbers

PROLOGUE—TROUVILLE, FRANCE—AUGUST, 1918
Always You, TOINETTE and BRUCE

ACT I—GROUNDS OF A HOTEL IN TROUVILLE—AUGUST, 1919
The Voice of Bagdad, INDIAN PEDDLER
A Wonderful War, JULIE and CHORUS
Reprise, *Always You,* TOINETTE
I Never Miss, CHARLIE and GIRLS
Syncopated Heart, TOINETTE and CHARLIE
Same Old Places, TOINETTE and BRUCE
Some Big Something, JOAN
Hayward's Harlem Hellions, JOAN
My Pousse-Café, JULIE and MONTMORENCY

ACT II—LOUNGE OF THE TROUVILLE CASINO
Dance divertissement, Cortez and Peggy
Woman, MONTMORENCY
I'll Say So, CHARLIE and JOAN
Reprise, *Always You,* BRUCE
Passing Through, JOAN and PIANIST
Drifting On, BRUCE
The Tired Business Man, JOAN and CHARLIE
Finale, COMPANY

NOTE: *A String of Girls, Don't You Remember?,* and *Misterioso* cut before New York opening. *Let's Marry* added during run in place of *I'll Say So.*

Reviews

New York Times
". . . full of melody, jazz, girls and comedy, all of the right kind, if the delight of the audience goes for anything . . . The music is catchy and a pretty chorus helps to put 'pep' into it . . . Also the lyrics are more clever than those of the average musical comedy."

New York Tribune
". . . adheres, for the most part, to the traditional and conventional models . . . Mr. Stothart is the only one deserving of any congratulations, for one or two of his songs are tuneful, notably the one from which the show takes its name . . ."

New York World
". . . a musical comedy for tired business men, with the prettiest chorus in town . . . The play got off to such a fast start it looked like a sure winner. This excellence continued through most of the first act . . . In the second act, the author burlesqued the story which he had been carefully building up . . . Mr. Hammerstein couldn't forget the dear old college days . . . the lyrics are good as a whole, and some of them are keen . . . generally tuneful music . . . The show is free of suggestiveness and there is only the suggestion of a shimmy dance . . ."

New York Sun
". . . fairly musical and moderately comic . . . The jokes, for the most part, should go on Broadway. They always have. The music is quite catchy, but it has a very strong familiar resemblance to other musical comedy tunes."

New York Journal
". . . a show for tired business men—and just that . . . Unlike most musical comedies, it has a plot that lifts its head more than once or twice during a performance . . . an entrancing musical score . . ."

New York Evening Mail
". . . a happy combination of book, music, settings and singers . . ."

New York Globe
". . . Both Hammerstein and Stothart have done far above the ordinary . . . has the unusual appeal of improvising as it progresses . . . delightfully staged, the music is tuneful, the book above par . . ."

Weed Dickinson—*New York Morning Telegraph*
". . . The plot—but why speak of the plot of a musical comedy? Suffice it to say that it is fairly typical, and banal in theme, although a little 'jazz' has been worked into it in spots . . . several tuneful melodies . . . *Woman* can hardly be called tuneful, but it is highly amusing because of the quality of the lyric. Hammerstein, who wrote both book and lyrics, has handled the latter better than the former . . ."

Fred Schader—*Variety*, January 9, 1920
". . . some tuneful melodies, some reminiscent, but none that will set the world afire . . . The first act contains some good comedy and some fast dancing. The second act slows down, and up to the finish

there is little or nothing stirring until the closing number . . . *My Pousse-Café* was a corking comedy number . . . a show that will please . . ."

Tidden—*New York Dramatic Mirror,* January 15, 1920
". . . Hammerstein appears to be a far better lyricist than librettist. His lyrics have a distinct quality, while his wheezes are rather antiquated. The plot is inconsequential but it is sturdy enough not to be lost, ever. The music is frequently very catchy and pleasing . . ."

James S. Metcalfe—*Life,* January 22, 1920
". . . better than the average of its kind and strikes a few new combinations in music and humor . . ."

Arthur Hornblow—*Theatre Magazine,* March, 1920
". . . compounded according to the most approved formula . . . an unlimited number of jokes like great-grandmother used to make . . . The song part is rather the most successful . . . several pleasing jingly and jazzy tunes. They, too, are almost meticulously unoriginal . . ."

Tour

Globe Theatre, Atlantic City, March 3-8, 1920
Orpheum Theatre, Harrisburg, August 31, 1920—Hanna Theatre, Cleveland, October 16, 1920 (10 cities).

TICKLE ME

(1920)

A musical comedy with book by Otto Harbach, Oscar Hammerstein II and Frank Mandel; music by Herbert Stothart; lyrics by Messrs. Harbach and Hammerstein.

Presented by Arthur Hammerstein
Directed by William Collier
Choreography by Bert French
Settings by Joseph Physioc
Costumes by Charles LeMaire
Music director, Mr. Stothart

Tryout
Stamford Theatre, Stamford, Conn., August 2-3, 1920
Auditorium, Long Branch, N.J., August 4-7, 1920
Apollo Theatre, Atlantic City, August 9-14, 1920

New York
Selwyn Theatre, August 17, 1920-February 12, 1921
207 performances

The Story
Frank Tinney—as himself—wins a role in a film being made in California and Tibet. He plays several parts before the camera and several more before the footlights while the scenery is being changed backstage.

The Cast
MARY FAIRBANKS, Louise Allen
JACK BARTON, Allen Kearns
MARCEL POISSON, Vic Casmore
FRANK TINNEY, Himself
ALICE WEST, Marguerite Zender
CUSTOMS INSPECTOR, Benjamin Mulvey
A NATIVE BOATMAN, William Dorriani
OLGA and MISHKA, Frances Grant and Ted Wing
A SLAVE, Jack Heisler
THE TONGRA, Marcel Rousseau

BLAH BLAH, Harry Pearce
KEEPER OF THE SACRED HORSE, Tex Cooper
GIRLS OF THE ENSEMBLE: Betty Nevins, Ruby Nevins, Marietta O'Brien, Sunshine Heyerdahl, Rose Cardiff, Memphis Russell, Emma Pesh, Alys Roby, Josie Carmen, Constance Reed, Laura Maverick, Mildred Mason, Ruth Andrews, Rheba Stewart, Muriel Graham, Florence Dixon, Muriel Reed
BOYS OF THE ENSEMBLE: George Griffin, Bobbie Culbertson, Jerome Kirkland, Jack O'Brien, Arnold Gluck, Harry Pearce, Gerard Gardner, Arthur Conway

Musical Numbers

ACT I

SCENE ONE—STUDIO OF POISSON PICTURES, HOLLYWOOD
Safe in the Arms of Bill Hart, MARCEL and CHORUS
You're the Type, MARCEL and CHORUS
A Perfect Lover, JACK and CHORUS
Finaletto, MARY, ALICE, JACK and CHORUS

SCENE TWO—CUSTOMS HOUSE, CALCUTTA
I Don't Laugh at Love Any More, JACK and ALICE

SCENE THREE—GARDEN OF PARADISE, TIBET
The Sun Is Nigh, NATIVE BOATMAN
Adagio, OLGA and MISHKA
Then Love Again, JACK and MARY
Little Hindoo Man, JACK, MARY and CHORUS

SCENE FOUR—THE VEIL OF MYSTERY

SCENE FIVE—CEREMONY OF THE SACRED BATH
The Ceremony, WHITE LAMA, OLGA and MISHKA, and CHORUS

ACT II

SCENE ONE—THE BOWER OF TEMPTATION
Until You Say Goodbye, JACK and ALICE
Temptation, JACK and CHORUS

SCENE TWO—ANYWHERE

SCENE THREE—CUSTOMS HOUSE, CALCUTTA
Reprise, *Until You Say Goodbye,* ALICE

SCENE FOUR—ABOARD THE "SS TICKLE-ME"
Valse du Salon, danced by OLGA and MISHKA
We've Got Something, Marietta O'Brien and CHORUS
Bagpipe Specialty, FRANK
Tickle Me, MARY and CHORUS
If a Wish Could Make It So, ALICE, JACK and CHORUS
Broadway Swell and Bowery Bum, FRANK and MARY

NOTE: *Come Across, Famous You and Simple Me, The Log of the Ship, India Rubber, Tears of Love, Bones, You Never Know What a Kiss Can Mean, Tragedy and Comedy* and *Didja Ever See the Like?* cut before New York opening.

Reviews

New York World
". . . has little to distinguish it . . . suffers through lack of more comedians . . ."

New York Telegram
". . . a riot of fun . . . more than lives up to its title. From first to last, it was a round of surprises and pleasure . . . a plot more cohesive than the average, and it holds the laughs together nicely . . ."

New York Sun
". . . lavish and pleasing . . . strikingly well done and well worth doing . . ."

New York Journal
". . . remarkable for its novelties and richness of scenic effects, to say nothing of a chorus which is pretty nearly the last word in pulchritudinous perfection . . . a collection of tunes that all seem 'whistleable' . . . Frank Tinney, always good, is at his best . . ."

Burns Mantle—*New York Evening Mail*
". . . no dull stretches and much good entertainment. The book is rather better than the lyrics for a change, and the music reaches a high musical comedy level with at least two of the songs—*Until You Say Goodbye* and *If a Wish Could Make It So* . . ."

New York Globe
". . . a joyous, romping absurdity . . . Frank Tinney has never been so entertaining. The score is uniformly excellent and has several particularly tuneful numbers . . ."

Joshua Lowe—*Variety,* August 17, 1920
". . . Frank Tinney is not the all important thing in it. The most impressive things are the gowns and hats and the startling scenery . . . Some of the lyrics are excellent. The most successful number is *If a Wish Could Make It So,* in which the girls utter a bunch of clever chorus girl slang . . . may turn out to be a hit . . ."

Edward Allen—*New York Dramatic Mirror,* August 21, 1920
". . . a hodge-podge of this and that, with timely odds and ends that are given adequate scenic embellishment and has a girly background as well as a capable contingent of feminine principals . . . several catchy tunes, one of the outstanding being *If a Wish Could Make It So* . . ."

Robert Benchley—*Life,* September 9, 1920
". . . The music is much the easiest to remember of anything played so far this season . . . Mr. Tinney remarked that he had never dared to have more than three children because statistics show that every fourth child is a Chinaman. Frankly, after that I don't remember much that happened, except that an usher was bathing my head and asking me if I knew my name."

Arthur Hornblow—*Theatre Magazine,* October, 1920
". . . The music, some of it with attempts at oriental color which only succeed in being jazzy, offered nothing of distinction. Of plot there was none, it being a musigirl comedy, but there was, and let us be thankful—Frank Tinney."

Tour

Shubert Theatre, Philadelphia, February 21, 1921—Illinois Theatre, Chicago, May 21, 1921 (5 cities).
Shubert Theatre, Boston, September 5, 1921—Shubert Theatre, Cincinnati, January 14, 1922 (12 cities).

JIMMIE

(1920)

A musical comedy with book by Otto Harbach, Oscar Hammerstein II and Frank Mandel; music by Herbert Stothart; lyrics by Messrs. Harbach and Hammerstein.

Presented by Arthur Hammerstein
Directed by Oscar Eagle
Choreography by Bert French
Settings by Joseph Physioc
Costumes by Henri Bendel
Music director, Mr. Stothart

Tryout

Playhouse, Wilmington, October 8-9, 1920
Park Square Theatre, Boston, October 11-November 13, 1920

New York Run

Apollo Theatre, November 17, 1920-January 15, 1921
71 performances

The Story

Though Jimmie is the long-lost daughter of wealthy Jacob Blum, her guardian, restaurateur Vincenzo Carlotti, keeps her identity a secret and even tries passing off his own daughter as the missing heiress. But the deception is revealed, and Jimmie—who has now become a successful cabaret star—is eventually reunited with her father.

The Cast

VINCENZO CARLOTTI, Paul Porcasi
MADAME GAMBETTI, Dee Loretta
BEATRICE, Hattie Burks
JIMMIE, Frances White
TOM O'BRIEN, Don Burroughs
MILTON BLUM, Harry Delf
JERRY O'BRIEN, Howard Truesdale
JACOB BLUM, Ben Welch
WATKINS, Tom O'Hare
A DANCER, Rita Owin

A VIOLINIST, Irwin Rossa
PETERS, Peter Mott
HENRI, Raymond Oswald
GIUSEPPI, Jack Heisler
ANTONIO, George Clifford
WANDA HOLMES, Betty Marshall
ROSE, Mary Jane
HENRIETTA, Helen Neff
BLANCHE, Tess Mayer
GIRLS OF THE ENSEMBLE: Jessie Lorraine, Edna Fenton, Geraldine Bernhardt, Laura Maverick, Mary Jane, Helen Neff, Tess Mayer, Lottie Graham, Evelyn Palmer, Adelaide Starr, Dorothy Gilbert, Frances Lawrence, Marjorie Flynn

Musical Numbers

ACT I

SCENE ONE—PRIVATE DINING ROOM ABOVE CARLOTTI'S RESTAURANT
An Aria, BEATRICE, GAMBETTI, CARLOTTI
Baby Dreams, JIMMIE

SCENE TWO—CARLOTTI'S RESTAURANT
Below the Macy-Gimbel Line, ROSE, DANCER, and GIRLS
Cute Little Two by Four, JIMMIE and TOM
All That I Want, MILTON and GIRLS
Carlotti's, CARLOTTI, BLUM, DANCER, and GIRLS
Jimmie, JIMMIE
She Alone Could Understand, BEATRICE
Finale, COMPANY

ACT II—JACOB BLUM'S HOME
Don' Yo' Want to See de Moon?, BEATRICE, VIOLINIST and GIRLS
It Isn't Hard to Do, MILTON, HENRIETTA and GIRLS
Reprise, *Jimmie,* TOM and GIRLS
Just a Smile, TOM and GIRLS
Do, Re, Mi, JIMMIE
Some People Make Me Sick, JIMMIE
I Wish I Was a Queen, JIMMIE

ACT III—APARTMENT OF "THE LITTLE BLUE KITTEN"
Toodle Oodle Um, JIMMIE and GIRLS
A Little Plate of Soup, MILTON
Fantasie, JIMMIE
Finale, COMPANY

NOTE: *Try Me, That's As Far As I Can Go, Cabaret Girl, Tum-Tiddly-Tum-Tum, Tu Carrisimo, Ming Poo, Up Is a Long, Long Climb, Dig, Sister, Dig,* and *Clothes* cut before New York opening. *Rickety Crickety* also cut before opening, but put back in January.

Reviews

New York Times

". . . a lavishly gowned and splashy piece with a nearly humorless book, but brought up to standard of good entertainment by the presence of the pert Miss White . . . production as a whole is spirited . . ."

New York Herald

"The Selwyns have built a new theatre and Arthur Hammerstein has organized a company to surround Miss White that she may be a star . . . But it never used to be necessary to build playhouses for this sort of thing . . ."

New York Tribune

". . . really an olio affording Miss White and Mr. Welch and half a dozen adept in dance and mimicry the opportunity to put on the thing they do best . . . a tuneful score with several melodies that purse the lips to whistle . . ."

New York World

"Amusement loving New York is happy enough when it peeks into a splendid new theatre, but it rejoices in being presented on the same night to a musical production like this . . . To Stothart all hats must be off . . . His ballads *Jimmie* and *Baby Dreams* will linger long . . . a rather ordinary little story . . ."

Alan Dale—*New York American*

". . . a very curious affair—a sort of crazy patchwork of sentiment, very cheap comedy and songs . . ."

New York Sun

". . . One could wish that the Apollo had opened with a higher class attraction . . ."

Burns Mantle—*New York Evening Mail*

". . . bears all the surface indications of a hit . . . Stothart's score is unusually melodious, and the book is equal to such strain as is put upon it . . ."

Jack Pulaski (Ibee.)—*Variety*, November 26, 1920

". . . certainly has too much story, and the plot is naturally transparent . . . the two best numbers were *Baby Dreams* and *Jimmie* . . ."

Louis R. Reid—*New York Dramatic Mirror*, November 27, 1920

". . . conventional . . . The piece merely provides song cues for the star and conversational cues for Ben Welch . . . Both are at their best . . . The music is tinkly."

Robert Benchley—*Life,* December 9, 1920
". . . some very pleasing and old fashioned music . . . Ben Welch, without his accustomed gefülte fish make-up, is genial and amusing when left to his own resources. The comedy lines and sentimental touches are simply terrible."

Arthur Hornblow—*Theatre Magazine,* January, 1921
". . . a bit better than average, in that being tailor made it succeeds in fitting very well the individual talents and abilities of Miss White . . ."

Tour

Auditorium, Baltimore, January 24, 1921—Alvin Theatre, Pittsburgh, May 7, 1921 (5 cities).

POP

(1921)

A comedy by Frank Mandel and Oscar Hammerstein II.

Presented by Arthur Hammerstein and A. H. Woods
Directed by Lester Lonergan

Tryout
Globe Theatre, Atlantic City, November 8-19, 1921

New York Run
None

The Story
A comedy involving an elderly, incompetent husband, his thrifty wife, and two additional couples who quarrel and make up in the course of the evening.

The Cast
O. P. Heggie
Joe Allen
Edgar Nelson
Harold Vermilye
Raymond Hackett
Harry Boller
Leah Winslow
Ruth Rose
Rose Ludwig
Lucille Webster
Henry Duggan

Reviews
Scheuer—*Variety,* November 11, 1921
"There is little to be said for this play save that it is an imitation of *Lightnin'*. Undoubtably the authors wrote a comedy of pathos and humor about their chief actor, but Mr. Allen has squeezed the last laugh out of the authors' intended pathos with his unnecessary additions—hence the near funeral of *Pop* last evening . . ."

DAFFY DILL

(1922)

A musical comedy with book by Guy Bolton and Oscar Hammerstein II; music by Herbert Stothart; lyrics by Mr. Hammerstein.

Presented by Arthur Hammerstein
Directed by Julian Mitchell
Settings by Clifford Pember
Costumes by Charles LeMaire
Music director, Mr. Stothart

Tryout

Apollo Theatre, Atlantic City, August 14-19, 1922

New York Run

Apollo Theatre, August 22-October 21, 1922
71 performances

The Story

An updated Cinderella tale about Lucy Brown, who is poor and old-fashioned, and Kenneth Hobson, who is determined to free himself from the bondage of his millions.

The Cast

ESTELLE, Marion Sunshine
TEACHER, Genevieve Markam
LUCY BROWN, Irene Olsen
SCHOOL INSPECTOR, Ben Mulvey
FRANK TINNEY, Himself
DAN BROWN, *Lucy's father,* Harry Mayo
KENNETH HOBSON, Guy Robertson
LUCY'S GRANDMOTHER IN 1867, Jacquelyn Hunter
LUCY'S GRANDFATHER IN 1867, Lynne Berry
LUCY'S MOTHER IN 1899, Imogene Wilson
HARRY JONES, Rollin Grimes
GERTIE, Georgia O'Ramey
SPECIALTY DANCERS: Frances Grant and Ted Wing; Mary Haun and Galdino Sedano; Margaret and Elizabeth Keene; Frederick Renoff

LADIES OF THE ENSEMBLE: Jacqueline Hunter, Bernice Ackerman, Peggy Stohl, Grace LaRue, Fern Oakley, Violet Lobel, Imogene Wilson, Irene Anderson, Violet Andrews, Jessie Howe, Marjorie Clements, Grace Culbert, Marion Philips, Genevieve Markham, Yvette DuBoise, Beatrice O'Connor, Ethel Kinley, Joane Warner, Carolyn Maywood, Eleanor Dell

GENTLEMEN OF THE ENSEMBLE: Lynne Berry, Charles Townsend, Harry Rocca, Harry Miller, Alfred Milano, Victor Kenfield, Marius Rogate, Samuel Vean

Musical Numbers

ACT I

SCENE ONE—THE OLD SWIMMIN' HOLE
Let's Play Hookey, ESTELLE and GIRLS
Kindergarten Blues, ESTELLE and GIRLS
Prince Charming, LUCY
Fantasy, *Cinderella Meets the Prince,* LUCY and KEENE TWINS

SCENE TWO—THE FRONT STOOP OF LUCY'S HOUSE
Two Little Ruby Rings, LUCY, KENNETH, DAN

SCENE THREE—DAN BROWN'S STORE, DOWN TOWN, N.Y.
My Boy Friend, ESTELLE and CHORUS; danced by Grant and Wing
I'm Fresh from the Country, GERTIE and CHORUS
I'll Build a Bungalow, FRANK, GERTIE, KENNETH, LUCY

SCENE FOUR—THE BUNGALOW

SCENE FIVE—INSIDE THE BUNGALOW

SCENE SIX—A REHEARSAL OF "THE COACHMAN'S HEART"
A Coachman's Heart, FRANK and ESTELLE

SCENE SEVEN—KENNETH HOBSON'S CALIFORNIA GARDEN
Adagio, danced by Mary Haun and Galdino Sedano
Fair Enough, KENNETH, HARRY, DAN, Keene Twins and CHORUS

ACT II

SCENE ONE—SPANISH COURTYARD NEAR THE BURLINGAME HORSESHOW, CALIFORNIA
My Little Redskin, Keene Twins, Frances Grant and GIRLS

SCENE TWO—A CHINESE PARTY
Chinky Chink, ESTELLE, Mary Haun, Keene Twins, Bernice Ackerman, Grace Culbert, Yvette DuBoise

SCENE THREE—SCREEN GARDEN, KENNETH'S ESTATE
Doctor (lyric by Kenneth Keith), GERTIE and CHORUS
Fantasy, *At the stroke of twelve, Cinderella runs away, leaving only a glass slipper,* LUCY, Keene Twins, Violet Lobel

SCENE FOUR—A MUSICALE

Pianologue, FRANK and Jacqueline Hunter, Imogene Wilson, Fern Oakley, Bernice Ackerman, Peggy Stohl

SCENE FIVE—THE JOLLY ROGER, A FASHIONABLE INN

Pantomime, *Pirate's Gold,* danced by Grant and Wing with Frederick Renoff

Captain Kidd's Kids, DAN, ESTELLE, Keene Twins and CHORUS

Finale

NOTE: *One Flower That Blooms for You, Tartar* and *You Can't Lose Me* cut before New York opening.

Reviews

New York Times

". . . a somewhat hybrid entertainment . . . the plot itself is something terrible, but by paying a minimum of attention to it, Arthur Hammerstein has managed to put together a pretty good entertainment. The mystery, of course, is why anyone who had Frank Tinney at his command should strive so desperately to achieve continuity in a musical comedy . . . Stothart's music is pleasant enough . . ."

New York Herald

"*Frank Tinney at His Amusing Best* . . . just enough plot not to get in anybody's way . . . *A Coachman's Heart* was a new touch, a clever skit, in which the comedian and Miss Marion Sunshine succeeded in getting entirely away from the prevalent lyrics of one syllable words and gave the intellect a chance . . . Stothart's music is gay and catchy, and moderately original. The lyrics are amusing . . ."

New York Tribune

". . . pleasing enough, indeed, except for a passing sense of disappointment with Tinney . . ."

Quinn Martin—*New York World*

"Everything about Frank Tinney's new girl-and-music show seems to be pretty good with the exception of the chorus. Unlike the jokes and the music and the scenery, the score or more of young ones who scamper through it are much better than that. They are delightful . . ."

Alan Dale—*New York American*

". . . It is down to the lowest intelligence and it has all the 'popularities' of the average musical . . . a summer show designed for people with warm weather intellects . . . some lively moments, and when in doubt, choruses bleated and nice young women did stunts . . ."

Charles Pike Sawyer—*New York Post*
". . . Stothart has not only provided charming melodies that have a delightful lilt, but has set them well, the orchestrations being far better than is usual. Bolton and Hammerstein have also aided materially in the book, which has a plot and a lot of clever lines, and holds its own very well . . . fun and frolic were fast and furious . . . Frank Tinney was never more amusing . . ."

New York Telegram
". . . pure joy . . . Not since the *Chauve-Souris* burst on the astonished gaze of New York has a piece with women, song and dancing gone with such spirit as this one . . ."

New York Sun
". . . full of fun, frolic and pretty girls . . . a pleasant entertainment for an idle evening."

Harry Ennis (Bell.)—*Variety,* August 25, 1922
". . . isn't fast enough in a comedy way and can stand a lot more laughs . . . Several of the songs have a likably lyrical jingle, especially a jazzy nursery rhymed number, *My Boy Friend, Chinky Chink* and *My Little Redskin* . . ."

Arthur Hornblow—*Theatre Magazine,* October 1922
"Comedy! Actual fact! . . . Not only comedy but humor, which is something else again and an even rarer commodity . . . Frank Tinney and the writers of a trite but fun-filled book are responsible for the innovation . . ."

Tour

Shubert Theatre, Philadelphia, November 6, 1922—Shubert-Majestic Theatre, Providence, December 2, 1922 (2 cities).

QUEEN O' HEARTS

(1922)

A musical comedy with book by Frank Mandel and Oscar Hammerstein II; music by Lewis Gensler and Dudley Wilkinson; lyrics by Mr. Hammerstein; additional lyrics by Sidney Mitchell.

Presented by Max Spiegel
Directed by Ira Hards
Choreography by David Bennett
Settings by Herbert Ward
Costumes by Cora Macgeachy
Music director, Gene Salzer

Tryout
Wieting Opera House, Syracuse, September 27, 1922
Toledo, September 29-30, 1922
Lafayette Theatre, Detroit, October 2-7, 1922

New York Run
George M. Cohan Theatre, October 10-November 11, 1922
39 performances

The Story
The Armstrong brothers, seeking wives, call upon a matrimonial agency, run by Elizabeth Bennett, known as the "Queen O' Hearts." She visits them at their home, and manages to straighten out everyone's matrimonial problems, including her own.

The Cast
TOM, Max Hoffman, Jr.
GRACE, Norma Terriss
ISABELLA BUDD, Florence Morrison
FERDINAND BUDD, Franker Woods
MISS SWANSON, Gladys Dore
ALABAMA (AL) SMITH, Georgie Brown
ELIZABETH BENNETT, Nora Bayes
HENRY RIVERS, Harry Richman
MYRA (MIKE), Edna Hibbard
DUDLEY, Dudley Wilkinson

ALFRED ARMSTRONG, Lorin Raker
WILLIAM ARMSTRONG, Arthur Uttry
POLICEMAN, Sidney Brook
AUNT ABIGAIL, Laura Alberta
GEORGIA, Eva Taylor
BUTLER, Thomas Bradley
LADIES OF THE ENSEMBLE: Janet Megrew, Consuelo Flowerton, Elza Peterson, Cecille Ann Stevens, Lillian McKenie, Muriel Harrison, Betty Hill, Loretta Morgan, Gladys Dore, Irene Enright

Musical Numbers

ACT I—FIFTH FLOOR OF A BUILDING NEAR TRINITY CHURCH, NEW YORK
Sizing Up the Girls, GRACE, TOM and APPLICANTS
Dreaming Alone (Wilkinson), WILLIAM
My Busy Day, ELIZABETH and OFFICE FORCE
Marriage C.O.D., ALFRED and MYRA
You Need Someone (Gensler), ELIZABETH and WILLIAM
Topics of the Day (by Cliff Friend and Harry Richman), HENRY and GIRLS
System, ELIZABETH, PRINCIPALS and OFFICE FORCE
Finale, ELIZABETH and WILLIAM

ACT II—HOME OF THE ARMSTRONGS, FAIRFIELD, N.J.
Reprise, *Dreaming Alone,* WILLIAM and GUESTS
A Long Time Ago (lyric by Morrie Ryskind), MYRA, ALFRED, TOM and GRACE
That's That (Wilkinson-lyric by Nora Bayes and Harry Richman), ELIZABETH, MYRA, WILLIAM, ALFRED
Tom-Tom (Gensler), HENRY and COMPANY
Dear Little Girlie (Wilkinson-lyric by Nora Bayes), ELIZABETH, MYRA and GIRLS
My Highbrow Fling, GEORGIA and ALABAMA
Specialty, Nora Bayes
Finale, company

NOTE: *Some Fine Day, When You're Only Seventeen, Ding Dong Ding* (Gensler), *Just a Touch, Why Do You Keep Us Guessing?, Every Silver Lining* and *Stop, Look and Kiss 'Em* cut before New York opening.

Reviews

New York Times

"The pleasing ingredients are Nora Bayes, Edna Hibbard, and unusually attractive chorus, and some good tunes . . . Otherwise it is a thoroughly conventional musical comedy, equipped with a story whose complications manage to be even sillier than these things usually are, which is no faint praise. Not infrequently it becomes terribly dull . . ."

New York Herald
". . . sparkling, jingling . . . ever welcomed Bayes school of fun . . ."

New York World
". . . Miss Bayes is her normally amusing self, and she sings one or two fairly good songs with her usual vigor . . ."

Charles Pike Sawyer—*New York Post*
". . . capitally done . . . the queen of musical play comediennes was at her best . . . some charming music . . . great entertainment . . ."

New York Telegram
". . . measures up to the very best that Nora Bayes has offered. It is strictly a Norabayes, tuneful, harmonious entertainment of exceeding promise and wholesome lines . . . Harry Richman fills in with some jazz specialties that promise to be the hit of the show . . ."

New York Journal
". . . goes with a bang . . . several numbers that are a delight to the ear . . . Miss Bayes is the queen o' the show."

Tracy Hammond Lewis—*New York Morning Telegraph*
". . . good music, a set of good-looking chorus girls who seem to enjoy their work immensely and lines a good deal above the average . . ."

Jack Conway—*Variety,* October 13, 1922
". . . should enjoy prosperity mainly through the drawing ability of the star and the tuneful, whistly melodies . . . A conventional story . . . Harry Richman clicked loudly . . . The song hit was *You Need Someone* . . . a pleasing night's entertainment . . ."

Robert Benchley—*Life,* November 9, 1922
". . . The chief thing to note is the chorus . . . They are the first chorus girls we ever saw who looked as if they would be any fun at all on a party; and now it's too late. Oh yes it is, girls."

Arthur Hornblow—*Theatre Magazine,* December 1922
"A miserably poor show in all departments . . . no deft ditties in it, nor anything deft of any kind . . ."

WILDFLOWER

(1923)

A musical play with book and lyrics by Otto Harbach and Oscar Hammerstein II; music by Vincent Youmans and Herbert Stothart.

Presented by Arthur Hammerstein
Directed by Oscar Eagle
Choreography by David Bennett
Settings by Frank E. Gates and E. A. Morange
Costumes by Charles LeMaire
Music director, Mr. Stothart
Orchestrations by Russell Bennett

Tryout
Grand Theatre, Wilkes-Barre, January 26-27, 1923
Auditorium, Baltimore, January 29-February 3, 1923

New York Run
Casino Theatre, February 7, 1923-March 29, 1924
477 performances

The Story
In Italy, the willful and capricious Nina Benedetto will inherit her grandfather's millions only if she can keep her temper under control for six months. Not only does she manage to do this in spite of many provocations, but she also manages to win the hand of the handsome Guido.

The Cast
LUIGI, Jerome Daley
GABRIELLE, Olin Howland
GASTON LA ROCHE, Charles Judels
BIANCA BENEDETTO, Evelyn Cavanaugh
ALBERTO, James Doyle
GUIDO, Guy Robertson
NINA BENEDETTO, Edith Day
LUCREZIA LA ROCHE, Esther Howard
SPECIALTY DANCERS, Marion and Martinez Randall

LADIES OF THE ENSEMBLE: Helen Lews, Emmy Tettersall, Genevieve Markham, Marie Otto, Agnes Horter, Florence Ashton, Margarete Morris, Myrtle Miller, Ursula Mack, Elizabeth Coyle, Peggy Stohl, Viola Clarens, Sybil Steward, Verona Oakley, Marion Phillips, Marjorie Wood, Beverly Maude, Adele Hart, Muriel Harrison

GENTLEMEN OF THE ENSEMBLE: Robert Hurst, Al Kinley, Paul Porter, Charles Froom, Louis Laub, Frank Grinnel, William McGurn, Kenneth Smith

Musical Numbers

ACT I—LUIGI'S FARMYARD NEAR CASIMO, LOMBARDY, ITALY
I Love You, I Love You, I Love You! (Youmans), GABRIELLE and GIRLS
Some Like to Hunt (Stothart), LAROCHE and GIRLS
Wild-Flower (Youmans), GUIDO
Bambalina (Youmans), NINA and ENSEMBLE
I'll Collaborate with You (Stothart), LUCREZIA and GABRIELLE
April Blossoms (Stothart), NINA and GUIDO
Finale, ENSEMBLE

ACT II—THE BENEDETTO VILLA ON LAKE COMO
The Best Dance I've Had Tonight, BIANCA and ENSEMBLE
Course I Will (Youmans), NINA, ALBERTO, GABRIELLE
Girl from Casimo (Stothart), GUIDO and ENSEMBLE; danced by Marion and Martinez Randall
If I Told You (Youmans), NINA and BOYS
Good Bye Little Rose-Bud (Stothart), GUIDO and ENSEMBLE
Finale, ENSEMBLE

ACT III—LUIGI'S FARMYARD
Reprise, *Bambalina,* NINA, ALBERTO and ENSEMBLE
The World's Worst Woman (Stothart), LUCREZIA and GABRIELLE
I Can Always Find Another Partner (Youmans), NINA and ENSEMBLE
Finale, COMPANY

NOTE: *True Love Will Never Grow Cold, Friends Who Understand* and *Everything Is All Right* cut before New York opening. *You Never Can Blame a Girl for Dreaming* (Youmans) added in March in place of *If I Told You.*

Reviews

New York Times

". . . contains the most tuneful score that Rudolf Friml [sic] has written in a number of seasons . . . A melody called *Bambalina* is destined to be heard all over town for a long time to come . . . an adroit and workmanlike example of the genus musical comedy . . . To be sure, it is practically never funny, and now and then even a little dull . . . the songs are worked into the piece with not a little cleverness . . ."

Alexander Woollcott—*New York Herald*
"It is difficult to make a communicative report about so uneventful an enterprise . . . an entirely unobjectionable mixture of songs and dances which we are going to have a mighty hard time remembering when someone asks us next September what show followed *Sally, Irene and Mary* at the Casino . . . It is brightened considerably by the presence of Edith Day and by a recurrent song called *Bambalina* . . ."

Percy Hammond—*New York Tribune*
". . . When Spring shall press on Summer's confines, as the slim-shanked Pans of Broadway say, the sweet of the year may yield nothing more dulcet than the crimson-mouthed traffic now wafting from the stage of the Casino . . ."

Quinn Martin—*New York World*
". . . delightful manner and really gorgeous melodies. Wait for *Bambalina* and *Apple Blossoms.* These song numbers not only are prepared with taste and understanding, they seem a most essential part in the makeup of the whole . . . it's a real musical comedy . . ."

Alan Dale—*New York American*
". . . a real prima donna, some real music, and some real effects . . . the book and lyrics seem a trifle less banal than usual . . . Altogether, a neat occasion . . ."

Burns Mantle—*New York Daily News*
"There is one thing you can say for Arthur Hammerstein. He certainly does pick good looking peasants. In *Wildflower*—the same being one of those 'here-come-the-girls-and-boys-now' operettas—the peasants are the flower of the Times Square district. And when they get all dressed up in their holiday silks they look a picture . . ."

M.M.—*New York Post*
". . . one of the prettiest musicals of the season . . . The melodies are tuneful . . . a fresh and blooming flower . . ."

Charles Darnton—*New York Evening World*
". . . at first the music seemed too good to last, but this fear proved groundless as the score offered one gay, youthful, charming melody after another. Edith Day was equally charming in the best role that has fallen her eventful lot since *Irene* . . . *Bambalina* was the outstanding novelty . . ."

Kenneth MacGowan—*New York Globe*
". . . the plot is none too staggering . . . Originality and Ingenuity

run neck and neck in the attempt to develop the plot and lose to Banality by three furlongs . . ."

James Craig—*New York Evening Mail*
"Plenty of catchy and tuneful music, much pep, some good dancing, attractive and colorful costumes, a book that is so-so—and Edith Day . . . Several of the numbers are of the kind that everybody will be whistling as soon as they get into the talking machine records . . ."

Jack Pulaski (Ibee.)—*Variety,* February 15, 1923
". . . looks like a hit . . . The book is quite adequate . . . three or four hits and all the tunes have been expertly handled . . ."

Robert Benchley—*Life,* March 1, 1923
". . . one of the best musicals of the season . . . True, the book isn't much, but if you're going in for books you might as well stay home and tell stories every evening . . ."

Arthur Hornblow—*Theatre Magazine,* August, 1923
". . . with an intelligent book, music that is more than ordinarily fresh and original, and a cast of capable performers, it seems destined to continue at its present stand until the next coal bill comes due . . ."

Tour

Alvin Theatre, Pittsburgh, March 31, 1924—Garrick Theatre, Chicago, July 26, 1924 (4 cities).
Shubert Theatre, Philadelphia, September 6, 1924—Shubert-Detroit Theatre, Detroit, February 14, 1925 (12 cities).

WILDFLOWER

(London—1926)

Presented by Joseph Benson, George Grossmith and J.A.E. Malone
Directed by Fred J. Blackman
Choreography by Mr. Blackman and Max Rivers
Settings by Marc Henri
Costumes by Irene Segalla
Music director, Philip Braham

Tryout

Alhambra Theatre, Bradford, February 1-13, 1926

London Run

Shaftesbury Theatre, February 17-March 27, 1926
Adelphi Theatre, April 3-May 15, 1926
His Majesty's Theatre, May 17-June 12, 1926
(Hippodrome, Golders Green, June 14-19, 1926)
114 performances

The Cast

LUIGI, Leonard Shepherd
GABRIELLE, Mark Daly
GASTON LAROTTA, Thomas Weguelin
BIANCA BENEDETTO, Evelyn Drewe
ALBERTO, Peter Gawthorne
GUIDO, Howett Worster
NINA BENEDETTO, Kitty Reidy
LUCREZIA LAROTTA, Julia Hartley-Milburn
NICOLINA, Jane Ayr
CORTEZ, Wesley Pierce
LOLITA, Hazel Harris
LADIES OF THE ENSEMBLE: Phyllis Cartwright, Dorothy Rundle, Phyllis Dawn, Iris May, Shelagh Harley, Mary Martin, Teddie Gamble, Dorothy Dolman, Ruby King, Angela Reid, Ena Craigie, Eileen McCarthy, Laura Towers, N. Davies, F. Davies, Eileen Winckworth, Ina Carleton, Freda Paton, Peggy Staples, Peggy Bradford
GENTLEMEN OF THE ENSEMBLE: Leslie Dawson, Pat Worsley, Ben Norman, Sanders Warren, Harold Dickinson, Frank Prebble, William Abbott, D. Percival, Cecil Curtis, W. Rolson, A. Bronard, N. Ablet, B. Digby, T. Barrett, H. Pringle

NOTE: In April, Miss Hartley-Milburn succeeded by Maisie Gay, Mr. Weguelin by Mark Daly, later by Eddie Morris.

Musical Numbers

Same as original production except for following changes: *I'll Collaborate With You*, *If I Told You* and *The World's Worst Women* replaced by, respectively, *If Your Name Had Been LaRotta*, *The Como Camel Corps* and *Spring Is Here*.

Reviews

London Times

"The success of *Wildflower* is largely due to Miss Kitty Reidy . . . The framework is good enough although one could wish for a little more light relief. One could not, however, wish for more catchy music. The ditties are remarkably tuneful and there are half dozen of them that set the feet tapping . . ."

James Agate—*London Sunday Times,* February 21, 1926
". . . Is *Wildflower* born to blush unseen? was on everybody's lips. The answer is in the negative. This musical play is too exactly like every other musical play not to have the same kind of success. The *Bambalina* song and dance have a certain gaiety of tune and rhythm, but the piece, alas!, has too many deserts unbesprinkled with oases . . ."

St. John Ervine—*London Observer,* February 21, 1926
". . . It may be that English authors and composers are tired or simply no good, but I cannot help thinking that even the least capable of them could have concocted a play as good as this. It has some lively music but none of it is especially notable . . . The story of the play cannot have caused its authors any brain-fog, and what there is of it was badly told . . ."

Variety, March 13, 1926
". . . old-fashioned in design and poor in execution . . . unlikely to receive more than the overflow of its neighbor, *No, No, Nanette* . . ."

Theatre World, April, 1926
". . . without being outstandingly brilliant, a pleasant enough musical play . . . The music is pleasantly, though not unusually, melodious—we are given rather too much opportunity to appreciate the tunefulness of *Bambalina* . . ."

MARY JANE MCKANE

(1923)

A musical comedy with book and lyrics by William Cary Duncan and Oscar Hammerstein II; music by Vincent Youmans and Herbert Stothart.

Presented by Arthur Hammerstein
Directed by Alonzo Price
Choreography by Sammy Lee
Settings by Frank E. Gates and E. A. Morange
Costumes by Charles LeMaire
Music director, Mr. Stothart

Tryout

Irving Theatre, Wilkes-Barre, October 25-27, 1923
Auditorium, Baltimore, October 31-November 3, 1923
Shubert Theatre, Boston, November 5-24, 1923

New York Run

Imperial Theatre, December 25, 1923-May 3, 1924
151 performances

The Story

Mary Jane McKane comes from the country to work in the offices of Andrew Dunn, Sr., but she is turned down because Dunn feels she would prove to be too distracting for his son, Andy Jr. So Mary Jane returns wearing glasses and plain clothes and gets the job. When Andy still finds her attractive, papa fires them both—which gives the couple the chance to go into business for themselves and become successful on their own.

The Cast

JOE MCGILLICUDY, Hal Skelly
MAGGIE MURPHY, Kitty Kelly
MARY JANE MCKANE, Mary Hay
CASH and CARRIE, Margaret and Elizabeth Keene
MARTIN FROST, Dallas Welford
ANDREW DUNN, JR. (ANDY), Stanley Ridges
DORIS DUNN, Laura DeCardi
LOUISE DRYER, Eva Clark

GEORGE SHERWIN, Louis Morrell
ANDREW DUNN, SR., James Heenan
LADIES OF THE ENSEMBLE: Muriel Harrison, Frances Lindell, Dorothy June, May Sullivan, Grace LaRue, Lillian Mitchell, Edna Miller, Dorothy Hollis, Ann Buckley, Bobby Pierce, Sunny Saunders, Peggy Quinn, May Fox, Theresa Carroll, Marietta Adams, Grace Culbert
GENTLEMEN OF THE ENSEMBLE: Bert Crane, Lester New, Lionel Maclyn, Allen Grey, Eldred Murray, John Wainman, Joe Carey, Harry Howell

Musical Numbers

ACT I

SCENE ONE—IN A SUBWAY
The Rumble of the Subway, ENSEMBLE

SCENE TWO—PRIVATE OFFICE OF ANDREW DUNN, JR.
Speed, JOE, CASH and CARRIE
Not in Business Hours, ANDY, LOUISE and CHORUS

SCENE THREE—MARY JANE'S ROOM
Stick to Your Knitting (Stothart), MARY JANE, JOE and CHORUS

SCENE FOUR—PRIVATE OFFICE OF ANDREW DUNN, JR.
My Boy and I (Youmans), LOUISE and CHORUS
Toodle-oo (Youmans), MARY JANE and ANDY
Down Where the Mortgage Grow, JOE, MAGGIE and CHORUS

ACT II—OFFICE AND RECREATION ROOM OF THE DANDY DOBBIN NOVELTY COMPANY
Time-Clock Slaves, CASH and CARRIE and CHORUS
Laugh It Off, MARY JANE, ANDY, MAGGIE
Reprise, *Stick to Your Knitting,* MARY JANE, ANDY and CHORUS
The Flannel Petticoat Gal (Youmans), JOE, MAGGIE and CHORUS

ACT III

SCENE ONE—GARDEN OF ANDREW DUNN'S HOME
Thistledown (Stothart), LOUISE and CHORUS
Reprise, *Toodle-oo,* ANDY, CASH and CARRIE

SCENE TWO—MARY JANE'S ROOM
Mary Jane McKane, MARY JANE and BOYS

SCENE THREE—CENTRAL PARK
Reprise, *Mary Jane McKane,* COMPANY

NOTE: *Come On and Pet Me* (Youmans) and *All For Charity* cut before New York opening. Former with new lyric by Irving Caesar and Clifford Grey and called *Sometimes I'm Happy,* was in score of *A Night Out* (1925) and also *Hit the Deck* (1927). *You're Never Too Old* (sung by LOUISE, FROST and CHORUS) and *Just Look Around* (sung by MARY JANE, ANDY and CHORUS) added in February. *My Boy and I* with new lyric by Otto Harbach and called *No, No, Nanette* was in musical of same name (1925).

Reviews

New York Times
"... a happy combination of popular merriment and popular folk songs ... The plot is unimportant as long as Mary Hay is on the stage ... The whole production is splendidly mounted and directed."

New York Herald
"... capsizes many of the current notions of musical comedy with such winning grace that you are glad to be shocked by such unorthodoxy ... The book takes a theme that is not unusual ... Yet the authors and producer have invested this almost with the meaning of a new revelation ..."

Percy Hammond—*New York Tribune*
"... There is a lot of fun in the show; the girls are pretty and good at dancing, and the songs, ranging from sprightly to mellow, are as you wish them in an entertainment of the kind ... I liked it as well as anything of its kind in years."

Laurence Stallings—*New York World*
"Few musical comedies have broken so many rules and few this season have been as entertaining ... someone at last has staged a production number that doesn't present girls as soft drinks or popular race horses ... Almost anyone should be pleased with it. Especially those who do not care who writes our country's songs, just so long as they may laugh at its comedy."

Burns Mantle—*New York Daily News*
"... a clean and pleasing entertainment ... the girls score the greatest hit in a *Flannel Petticoat Gal* song ..."

New York Evening World
"... royal entertainment ... one chic scene after another, but the novelties have an air of having slipped in naturally instead of being crammed into place ... Even a joke about Brooklyn seems witty ... Among the swinging musical numbers, *Toodle-oo* seems already branded as a hit ... a very merry Jane indeed."

Variety, January 3, 1924
"... doesn't look like a knockout ... Its book isn't much ... The music is well scored, but it falls flat in providing an outstanding number ..."

Time, January 7, 1924
"... unquestionably the best musical comedy currently exhibiting on Broadway. And Miss Hay is unquestionably the best of the play

. . . Music, color and dancing are supplied in wholesale lots of excellent quality . . ."

George Jean Nathan—*Judge,* January 19, 1924
". . . an attractive chorus, a couple of engaging steppers in the Keene twins, a good tune or two by Youmans, and a fairly attractive get-up, but a completely stereotyped libretto, stereotyped lyrics and humor of the usual Broadway cut . . ."

Robert Benchley—*Life,* January 24, 1924
". . . much duo-dancing, some stepping tunes, and the pleasing presence of the two featured players . . ."

Arthur Hornblow—*Theatre Magazine,* March, 1924
". . . a number of clever lines, quite a few catchy songs (particularly the one with the idiotic title *Toodle-oo*); a bountiful crop of good-looking bobbed-hair girls, and plenty of zestful dancing . . ."

Tour

Shubert-Detroit Theatre, Detroit, August 18, 1924—Garrick Theatre, Chicago, September 27, 1924 (2 cities).

GYPSY JIM

(1924)

A drama by Oscar Hammerstein II and Milton Herbert Gropper; incidental music by Herbert Stothart.

Presented by Arthur Hammerstein
Directed by Clifford Brooke
Settings by Clifford Pember
Costumes by Charles LeMaire

Tryout
Fulton Theatre, Oakland, California, August 12, 1923

New York Run
Forty-Ninth Street Theatre, January 14-February 25, 1924
41 performances

The Story
Harry Blake is a broken attorney; his wife, Mary, is a hypochondriac; their daughter, Lucy, is unhappy at home and plans to elope; their son, Tom, is a discouraged inventor who is thinking of suicide. Then Gypsy Jim, an eccentric millionaire in disguise, knocks on their door, convinces them he possesses almost supernatural powers, restores their faith in themselves, and leaves them happy.

The Cast
HARRY BLAKE, George Farren
MARY BLAKE, Elizabeth Patterson
CRAIG, George Anderson
LUCY BLAKE, Martha Bryan Allen
TOM BLAKE, Wallace Ford
GYPSY JIM, Leo Carrillo
WORTHING, Harry Mestayer
DAN, Fleming Ward
ESTELLE, Ethel Wilson
KENT, Averell Harris
GRACE, Virginia Wilson
BUTLER, Joseph Spence

ACTS I and II—HOME OF THE BLAKES IN A SMALL MID-WESTERN TOWN

ACT III—HOME OF MR. PRENTISS

Reviews

John Corbin—*New York Times*
". . . the play is one of the *Pollyanna* order . . . The prime question is not whether it is socially justified but whether it is persuasive, convincing—imaginatively and emotionally stimulating . . . Upon most of the audience, including the most critical, it exerted its true spell . . ."

Alexander Woollcott—*New York Herald*
". . . there are plays which seem to have been written without an atom of thought or skill, and yet which somehow do not bore you at all. The new piece belongs to the latter class . . . The lyric speech became so contagious that the authors were in grave danger of seeing the newspapers break out in a rash of notices such as this:

Oscar Hammerstein II and Milton Gropper
Wrote a comedy that came an awful cropper.

Percy Hammond—*New York Tribune*
". . . its naive prattle and its cunning ways are but a baby's step from the kindergarten . . . Much of its language is the serious elegance of the tender ages, and there are other distracting evidences of leading strings . . ."

Heywood Broun—*New York World*
". . . sticky and tricky, but there is some honest writing in it, and quite a good deal of excellent playing. The mixture results in a fair-to-middling entertainment . . ."

Charles Pike Sawyer—*New York Post*
"Capital entertainment is *Gypsy Jim*. As a play it is not worth considering . . . a series of pleasing scenes and incidents . . . In less competent hands the piece might have come a cropper, but the people in the cast were all good . . . It's clean, wholesome and enjoyable, and should have a prosperous career."

E.W. Osborn—*New York Evening World*
". . . brought surprise, interest and a good deal of genuine pleasure to its first-night hearers . . ."

Jack Lait—*Variety*, January 27, 1924
". . . clean and entertaining . . . should go through the summer in prosperity . . ."

Wells Root—*Time,* January 28, 1924
". . . Utterly banal in theme and rather juvenile in treatment, the play succeeds moderately as amusement, largely due to the persuasive personality of the star . . ."

Robert Benchley—*Life,* January 31, 1924
". . . behind the determined whimsicality of Mr. Carrillo's smile brings the message that Faith will move any reasonable-sized mountain with, of course, a little tug now and then from the playwright . . ."

NEW TOYS

(1924)

A comedy by Oscar Hammerstein II and Milton Herbert Gropper.

Presented by Sam. H. Harris
Directed by Sam Forrest
Settings by Raymond Sovey

Tryout
Ford's Theatre, Baltimore, January 14-26, 1924

New York Run
Fulton Theatre, February 18-March 8, 1924
24 performances

The Story
In their second year of marriage, Ruth and Will Webb have a baby—which still isn't enough to distract Ruth from the boredom of housekeeping. After a brief fling trying her luck on the stage, she returns to Will who, in the meanwhile, has bravely defended himself against the advances of an old flame.

The Cast
RUTH WEBB, Vivienne Osborne
WILL WEBB, Ernest Truex
GEORGE CLARK, Robert McWade
MRS. WARNER, Louise Closser Hale
KATE WILKES, Frances Neilson
SAM WILKES, Robert E. O'Connor
NATALIE WOOD, Mary Duncan
TOM LAWRENCE, James Spottswood

ACTS I, II and III—THE LIVING ROOM OF THE WEBBS' HOME

Reviews
John Corbin—*New York Times*
". . . In the opening scenes there seemed to be a fair prospect of success. The lines are laconically amusing and the stage business apt . . . perhaps the real fault is that with all its surface pretense of realism, it is plain buncombe through and through . . ."

Alexander Woollcott—*New York Herald*
". . . might have slipped into town with no further note than that it was cheerfully ordinary entertainment, were it not full of gropings to be something better than that . . . the truth of the humor does not go very deep and though a good deal of mild merriment is provided, it is festooned on a pretty pedestrian and laboriously contrived play . . ."

Percy Hammond—*New York Tribune*
". . . Mr. Truex was very amusing even if the play was not . . . its principal faults are those of immaturity, technical inexperience and general unintelligence . . ."

Heywood Broun—*New York World*
". . . moments of engaging truth and humor, but it is well behind too many plays which have done the same thing . . . no evidence whatsoever that the authors have any sincere convictions concerning the problems which they discuss . . ."

J. Ranken Towse—*New York Post*
". . . mildly amusing in its conventional way but utterly stagy and much too long . . . has the merit of being entirely harmless . . ."

E. W. Osborn—*New York Evening World*
". . . Speaking as one who laughed, we should say that this merriment is bound to hold the Fulton for its own for a long time to come."

Jack Lait—*Variety*, February 21, 1924
". . . an economic affair, palpably a vehicle. A Ford is a vehicle, too . . . There must be support and there must be sympathy and story as well as the entertaining personality of one artist . . . looks good for a few weeks . . ."

Time, March 3, 1924
"Though the authors had no hand in *The First Year*, it might be called *The Second Year*. Like most sequels, it is comparatively weak . . ."

Robert Benchley—*Life*, March 6, 1924
". . . unfortunately, hasn't much to distinguish it, so far as the text goes, from the eighteen or nineteen like it which jumped into the boat after *The First Year*. But it has Ernest Truex and that is a great deal for any play to have . . ."

George Jean Nathan—*Judge*, March 8, 1924
". . . tries as hard to be popular as a ward politician . . . The authors have worked like longshoremen to capture 'the tear that lurks

behind the smile,' but the chief moisture that they achieve is their own copious perspiration . . ."

Tour

Playhouse, Chicago, March 23, 1924—St. James Theatre, Boston, October 28, 1924 (3 cities).

NEW TOYS

(Film Version—1925)

A First National Picture
An Inspiration Production
Directed by John Robertson
Screenplay by Joseph Lovett
Photographed by Roy Overbaugh

Release Date

February 15, 1925

The Cast

WILL WEBB, Richard Barthelmess
WILL WEBB, JR., Baby Pat O'Connor
MARY LANE, Mary Hay
THOMAS LAWRENCE, Clifton Webb
NATALIE WOOD, Catherine Wilson
MRS. LANE, Bijou Fernandez
GEORGE CLARK, Francis Conlon
STAGE DOORMAN, Tammany Young

Reviews

Mordaunt Hall—*New York Times*
". . . rather thin . . . mildly diverting, but it is healthy and wholesome . . ."

Harriette Underhill—*New York Herald Tribune*
". . . far more entertaining on the screen . . . a perfect cinema comedy . . ."

Louella O. Parsons—*New York American*
". . . holds an appeal for many persons for the reason that it not only contains real comedy but a love story and a wholesome domestic story . . ."

New York Sun
". . . Barthelmess proved himself a likeable comedian . . . The film is amusing. Its only fault is that it doesn't know when to stop."

Jack Lait—*Variety,* February 18, 1925
". . . an excellent example of how a bad play can make a good film. And still leave much to be desired . . . the scenario is more than perfect. It is constructive, salutary . . . just misses being a great money picture . . ."

Robert E. Sherwood—*Life,* March 5, 1925
"There is probably no actor in the entire movie business who is more completely unfunny than Richard Barthelmess; it is therefore painful to watch him attempting a part which was written for Ernest Truex. He does this with woeful results . . ."

ROSE-MARIE

(1924)

A musical play with book and lyrics by Otto Harbach and Oscar Hammerstein II; music by Rudolf Friml and Herbert Stothart.

Presented by Arthur Hammerstein
Directed by Paul Dickey
Choreography by David Bennett
Settings by Frank E. Gates and E. A. Morange
Costumes by Charles LeMaire
Music director, Mr. Stothart
Orchestrations by Robert Russell Bennett

Tryout

Apollo Theatre, Atlantic City, August 18-23, 1924
Auditorium, Long Branch

New York Run

Imperial Theatre, September 2, 1924-January 16, 1926
557 performances

The Story

Rose-Marie, the featured singer at Lady Jane's Hotel in Saskatchewan, is a great favorite with the Mounties and fur trappers, though her heart belongs only to trapper Jim Kenyon. Wealthy Edward Hawley, who also loves Rose-Marie, witnesses a murder and puts the blame on Jim, but promises to save him if Rose-Marie agrees to become Mrs. Hawley. Though she agrees to the proposal, she and her true love are reunited when the real murderer is discovered.

The Cast

SGT. MALONE, Arthur Deagon
LADY JANE, Dorothy Mackaye
BLACK EAGLE, Arthur Ludwig
EDWARD HAWLEY, Frank Greene
EMILE LA FLAMNE, Edward Ciannelli
WANDA, Pearl Regay
HARD-BOILED HERMAN, William Kent
JIM KENYON, Dennis King

ROSE-MARIE LA FLAMME, Mary Ellis
ETHEL BRANDER, Lela Bliss
LADIES OF THE ENSEMBLE: Almerita Voudray, Carol Joyce, Ann Wood, Mabel Martin, Peggy Sletner, Ruby Poe, Lee Byrne, Eve Wendt, Beatrice Bickel, Violet McKinley, Lillian Burke, Nerene Swinton, Sylvia Stoll, Peggy Bolton, Peggy Driscoll, Gladys LaResche, Lucille Morrison, Rosalee King, Dorothy Kane, Billy Fish, Marjorie Talcott, Mary Morrison, Connie Best, Ellen Rose, Alice Hanley, Lucille Constant, Helen Bell, Ivia Perrini, Gloria Frank, Allyn Loring, Dolly Donnelly, Marion Alta, Ivy Palmer, Glada Gray, Emily Armstrong, Gwen Gordon, Betty Carlstadt, Genevieve Tierney, Clarie Rossi, Lillian White, Cynthia Whyte, Mary Walsh, Lenore Cornwall, Grace Carlisle, Nadya Miller, Ripples Covert
GENTLEMEN OF THE ENSEMBLE: Edward Gargon, John Lambie, George Jimos, Jerome Robertson, Ellis Doyle, Joseph Ames, Morris Tepper, Norman Johnstone, L. Nash, Jack Lerner, Leslie Ostrander, Irvin Arnold, Bert Bowlen, Richard Neeley

NOTE: Miss Ellis succeeded by Desiree Ellinger (June 1925) and Madeleine Massey (January 1926). Mr. King by Sam Ash (June 1925) and Allan Rogers (October 1925). Miss Mackaye by Judith Fairfield (November 1925) and Beatrice Kay (December 1925).

Musical Numbers

ACT I

SCENE ONE—LADY JANE'S HOTEL, FOND DU LAC, SASKATCHEWAN, CANADA
Vive la Canadienne (Stothart), MALONE and CHORUS
Hard-Boiled Herman (Stothart), HERMAN and CHORUS
Rose-Marie (Friml), JIM and MALONE
The Mounties (Friml-Stothart), MALONE and CHORUS
Lak Jeem (Friml), ROSE-MARIE and CHORUS
Reprise, *Rose-Marie,* ROSE-MARIE, MALONE, HAWLEY, EMILE and CHORUS
Indian Love Call (Friml), ROSE-MARIE and JIM

SCENE TWO—A CAMPFIRE

SCENE THREE—BLACK EAGLE'S CABIN

SCENE FOUR—CAMPFIRE

SCENE FIVE—TOTEM POLE LODGE, NEAR KOOTENAY PASS, CANADIAN ROCKIES
Pretty Things (Friml), ROSE-MARIE and CHORUS
Eccentric dance (Stothart), HERMAN, LADY JANE and CHORUS
Why Shouldn't We? (Stothart), LADY JANE and HERMAN
Totem Tom-Tom (Friml-Stothart), WANDA and CHORUS
Finale (Friml-Stothart), EMILE, ROSE-MARIE, HAWLEY, HERMAN, MALONE and CHORUS

ACT II

SCENE ONE—NOVELTY SHOP, QUEBEC
Reprise, *Pretty Things,* ETHEL and GIRLS

Only a Kiss (Stothart), HERMAN, LADY JANE, MALONE
Finaletto, *I Love Him* (Friml), ROSE-MARIE, JIM, HAWLEY, EMILE, ETHEL, WANDA

SCENE TWO—GRAND BALLROOM, CHATEAU FRONTENAC
The Minuet of the Minute (Stothart), ROSE-MARIE and HERMAN
One Man Woman (Stothart), LADY JANE, HERMAN and CHORUS
Door of Her Dreams (Bridal Procession) (Friml), CHORUS
Bridal Finale (Stothart), EMILE, WANDA, ROSE-MARIE and CHORUS

SCENE THREE—CELLAR OF HOTEL ON THE RIVER FRONT, QUEBEC

SCENE FOUR—HILL NEAR KOOTENAY PASS

SCENE FIVE—"THE CASTLE"
Finale Ultimo (Friml), ROSE-MARIE and JIM

NOTE: Instead of listing the musical numbers as above, the original program contained the following information: "The musical numbers of this play are such an integral part of the action that we do not think we should list them as separate episodes. The songs which stand out, independent of their dramatic associations are *Rose-Marie, Indian Love Call, Totem Tom-Tom,* and *Why Shouldn't We?* in the first act, and *Door of Her Dreams* in the second act."

Reviews

New York Times
". . . one of the big musical successes of the new season . . . a plot slightly less banally put forward than has been customary . . . The score, in part made up of music above the average standard of musical plays, contained several numbers that will probably become nuisances before long . . ."

Charles Belmont Davis—*New York Herald Tribune*
". . . the bon-voyage basket of musical shows. It contains a little of everything, some of the offerings are superlative, others good, and the gay ribbons with which the basket itself is decorated are worthy of the fairest lady's corsage . . . A beautiful and highly colored composite photograph of a three-ring circus and shown to the accompaniment of the most entrancing music it has long been our privilege to hear . . . not only unusual but an unusual success."

Wells Root—*New York World*
". . . looked like one of the best mixtures of music and drama that has yet cracked its shell in the early season incubating . . . The music interrupts the action only now and then—always to excellent effect . . . a thoroughly diverting evening."

Alan Dale—*New York American*
". . . a most elaborate affair, and if you want novelty, why surely

Saskatchewan will supply it. I can't remember finding that clime set to toons before. There was one mighty good one, too—*Totem Tom-Tom* . . ."

New York Daily News
". . . another *Wildflower* without a *Bambalina*. The score contains such good numbers as the title song and *Indian Love Call*, but nothing that would set a universe afire. Mary Ellis scored a decisive hit . . . the *Totem Tom-Tom* number brought down the house, or almost."

New York Post
". . . the tom-tom dance, with two score totem poles led by Pearl Regay, was almost overwhelmed by the shouts that arose from a discriminating audience . . . Mary Ellis was bewitching . . . The book was well written and interesting, and the music was of a higher average than is usual in pieces of this sort . . . Thoroughly enjoyable from start to finish."

Bide Dudley—*New York Evening World*
"Quite the most substantial musical play New York has seen since *Blossom Time* . . . music of a higher order than the casual stroller along Broadway usually is apt to discover; it has a story interest-impelled enough to stand alone if it had to, and it has Mary Ellis . . . The fertile brain of Oscar Hammerstein has lent valuable aid to the more experienced Harbach and the collaboration has spelled Efficiency with a capital E . . . We recommend *Rose-Marie* to all who like genuine musical comedy. Try it—you can't go wrong."

New York Telegram
". . . all that a hot weather musical should be . . . Its songs soothe, but never reach rapid, vibration propensities . . . Its plot clings together sufficiently to sustain interest . . . sends the intelligence and emotions on a blithe vacation . . ."

New York Sun
". . . should be seen by every Diogenes who has been searching for an honest-to-goodness musical play. It is worth every minute of the time of anyone from bank clerk to member of the Reparations Commission . . . Mary Ellis sings like the proverbial nightingale . . . jokes and lyrics unknown to the razor, in contrast to the usual bearded jests . . . the sort of show to which you can take your mother and sister. If you don't, you can be sure they'll go anyway."

Jack Pulaski (Ibee.)—*Variety*, September 10, 1924
". . . the first of the unusual number of high-scale musicals being

topped at $4.40 . . . exceptionally bright and colorful . . . melodious score . . . Indications are strongly in favor of a run . . ."

Wells Root—*Time,* September 15, 1924
". . . deserted the beaten path of musical entertainment and emerged from the woods of the opening night equipped with just about everything that lurks in the thicket of novelty . . . one of the best musical shows that has settled itself upon Broadway in months."

Robert Benchley—*Life,* October 2, 1924
". . . As customary with musical comedies in which the score is superior, the book is a little too much in evidence, but to hear Mary Ellis and Dennis King sing the music is an experience so far unequalled in the new season . . . The Totem Pole dance is one of the most effective chorus numbers we have ever seen . . ."

George Jean Nathan—*Judge,* October 4, 1924
". . . an expensively produced musical comedy containing a well trained chorus, some nimble concerted dancing, a leading woman with a good voice, and a libretto that is pretty sad. The comedy is anything but comic . . . Friml's melodies are now and again engaging . . ."

Deems Taylor—*New York World,* October 30, 1924
". . . we decline to rate the score more than moderately high, either as regards inventiveness or workmanship. But that stern verdict does not alter the fact that it is very tuneful music, easy to hear and very, very difficult to avoid humming, unless you are careful . . ."

Arthur Hornblow—*Theatre Magazine,* November, 1924
". . . genuinely magnificent . . . intelligent, tuneful, beautiful and decent . . . Friml has done especially well . . . a book that is head, shoulders and waist above the customary dribble about Prohibition and Brooklyn . . . Mary Ellis establishes herself as the peer of any musical-show star in the country . . ."

ROSE-MARIE

(Touring Company—1925)

Music director, Charles Ruddy

The Cast

SGT. MALONE, Charles Meakins
LADY JANE, Beatrice Kay
BLACK EAGLE, William C. Skavlan
EMILE LA FLAMME, Milton Nobles
WANDA, Phebe Brune
HARD-BOILED HERMAN, Charles Silber
JIM KENYON, Guy Robertson
ROSE-MARIE LA FLAMME, Irene Pavloska
ETHEL BENDER, Cora Frye
LADIES OF THE ENSEMBLE: Olive Bond, Ann Ju Rika, Lillian Lyndon, Carol Andrews, Ellen DeVany, Lillian Arnold, Dorothy Sipley, Irene Mayo, Beatrice Fox, Ruth Schofield, Gertrude Waldron, Betty Weber, Lovey Silver, Rose Grady, Sophia Ross, Ursula Murray, Laurie Green, Rita Miles, Beth Meakins, Thea Thompson, Phoebe Hughes, Peggy McCarthy, Maud Neul, Sylvia Seville, Dolores Suarez, Viora Fay, Dorothy Forbes, Rose Mills, Winnie Dunn, Trilby Greener
GENTLEMEN OF THE ENSEMBLE: Tom Chadwicke, Charles Angle, Russell Griswold, John Duncan, Homer Wallen, Frank Dobert, Clinton Corwin, Ernest Ehler, Edward Williams, Stanley Johnson, Thomas Rider, Thomas Brady

NOTE: Miss Pavloska succeeded by Desiree Ellinger (April 1925) and Madeleine Massey (June 1925). In April 1925, Mr. Robertson succeeded by Paul Donah; Mr. Silber by Houston Richards. By the fall of 1925, there was more than one touring company, and members occasionally left one company to join another. Others who played ROSE-MARIE were Dorothy Seegar (1925), Beulah Berson (1926/28), Ethel Louise Wright (1926/27), Bonnie Emerie (1928) and Virginia Fox (1928/29); JIM KENYON, Sam Ash (1925) and Paul Gregory (1927); HERMAN, Harry Koler (1925); LADY JANE, Peggy Pates (1926).

Tours

Poli's Theatre, Washington, February 9, 1925—Reade's Theatre, Trenton, May 8, 1926 (31 cities).
Shubert Theatre, Philadelphia, September 14, 1925—Shubert Theatre, Boston, May 29, 1926 (19 cities).
Opera House, Providence, September 13, 1926—Auditorium, Scranton, December 11, 1926 (20 cities).
Auditorium, Henderson, North Carolina, September 29, 1926—Shubert Alvin Theatre, Pittsburgh, March 12, 1927 (24 cities).
Opera House, Detroit, November 8, 1926—Teller's Shubert Theatre, Brooklyn, April 23, 1927 (22 cities).

Hanna Theatre, Cleveland, September 4, 1927—Shubert-Detroit Theatre, Detroit, March 17, 1928 (29 cities).
Princess Theatre, Montreal, September 3, 1928—Denham Theatre, Denver, April 6, 1929 (21 cities).

Selected Revivals

St. Louis Municipal Opera, June 2-11, 1939
Nancy McCord (ROSE-MARIE); Lansing Hatfield (JIM); Lester Allen (HERMAN).

Chicago Civic Light Opera, June 9-17, 1944
Marguerite Piazza (ROSE-MARIE); Arthur Maxwell (JIM); William Kent (HERMAN).

Los Angeles Civic Light Opera, July 2-28, 1945
San Francisco Civic Light Opera, July 30-August 18, 1945
Irene Manning (ROSE-MARIE); Walter Cassel (JIM); Eddie Foy Jr. (HERMAN); Collette Lyons (LADY JANE); Clarissa (WANDA).

Detroit Civic Light Opera, Summer, 1948
Andzia Kuzak (ROSE-MARIE); Allan Jones (JIM); Pinky Lee (HERMAN); Sue Ryan (LADY JANE); Clarissa (WANDA).

San Francisco Civic Light Opera, July 3-29, 1950
Los Angeles Civic Light Opera, July 31-August 26, 1950
Patrice Munsel (ROSE-MARIE); Walter Cassel (JIM); Jack Goode (HERMAN); Clarissa (WANDA); George Britton (MALONE).

Dallas State Fair, August 19-September 1, 1957
Anna Maria Alberghetti (ROSE-MARIE); John Reardon (JIM); Reuben Noel (HERMAN); Alice Ghostley (LADY JANE); Joe Layton (BLACK EAGLE).

Productions Abroad

Theatre Royal, Drury Lane, London, March 20, 1925-March 26, 1927
(See page 298)

Théatre Mogador, Paris, April 9, 1927
Presented by Les Frères Isola; translated by Roger Ferreol and Saint-Granier; directed by J. Kathryn Scott. *Cast* Rose Carday (ROSE-MARIE); André Pierrel (JIM); Maurice Porterat (HERMANN); Monette Dinay (LADY JANE); Felix Oudart (MALONE); Wanda de Muth (WANDA).

Admirals Palast Theater, Berlin, March 30, 1928
Translated by Rideamus; music director, Herbert Stothart. *Cast* Margaret Pfahl Wallerstein (ROSE-MARIE); Aagard Oestvig (JIM); Paul Heidemann (HERMANN); Myra Nirska (WANDA).

Theatre Royal, Drury Lane, London, September 12, 1929; *100 performances*
Edith Day (ROSE-MARIE); Roy Russell (JIM); Gene Gerrard (HERMAN); Clarice Hardwicke (LADY JANE); Charles Meakins (MALONE).

Stoll Theatre, London, July 16, 1942; *149 performances*
Marjorie Brown (ROSE-MARIE); Raymond Newell (JIM); George Lacy (HERMAN); Phyllis Monkman (LADY JANE).

Harringay Arena, London, July 13, 1950
Performed on ice. Barbara Scott (ROSE-MARIE).

Victoria Palace, London, August 22-December 17, 1960; *135 performances*
Presented by Tom Arnold and Leslie Macdonnell; directed by Freddie Carpenter. *Cast* Stephanie Voss (ROSE-MARIE); David Whitfield (JIM); Ronnie Stevens (HERMAN); Maggie Fitzgibbon (LADY JANE); Andy Cole (MALONE); Gillian Lynne (WANDA).

Théatre Mogador, Paris, 1963
Presented by Henri Varna; translated by Roger Ferreol and Saint-Granier; choreography by Evelyn Gray; music director, Jacques Pastory. *Cast* Paulette Merval (ROSE-MARIE); Marcel Merkès (JIM); Robert Roibin (HERMANN); Ginette Baudin (LADY JANE); Pierre Plessis (MALONE); Cecile Tchernova (WANDA).

ROSE-MARIE

(London—1925)

Presented by Sir Alfred Butt
Directed by Felix Edwardes
Choreography by J. Kathryn Scott
Settings by Joseph and Phil Harker
Costumes by Comelli
Music director, Herman Finck
Opening-night conductor, Mr. Stothart

London Run

Theatre Royal, Drury Lane, March 20, 1925-March 26, 1927
851 performances

The Cast

SERGEANT MALONE, John Dunsmure
LADY JANE, Clarice Hardwicke
BLACK EAGLE, Percy Parsons
EDWARD HAWLEY, Brian Gilmour
EMILE LA FLAMME, Michael Cole
WANDA, Ruby Morriss
HARD-BOILED HERMAN, Billy Merson
JIM KENYON, Derek Oldham
ROSE-MARIE, Edith Day

ETHEL BRANDER, Marjorie Chard

LADIES OF THE CHORUS: Phyllis Bellonini, Mary Morris, Signe Ekman, Irene Page, Norah Wilson, Madeleine Bailey, Nan Forster, Doris Treverne, Betty Bailey, Norah Edwards, Benita Benham, Gladys Kelsey, Lola Waring, Phyllis Neale, Phyllis Beadon, Maisie Barry, Joyce Beadon, Heather Featherstone, Paula Reid, Frances Day, Violet Timms, Stephanie Insall, Myrette Morven, Roma Forster, Veda Wardman, Kathleen Fitchie, Sybil Rhoda, Anne Crecy, Lena Fitchie, Inez O'Connor, Marjorie Poncia, Joan Layton, Pauline Gilmer, Pauline Collins, Anne Layton, Antoinette Gilsenan, Rosamund Gardner, Margaret Watson, Doris Merritte, Connie Deedes, Vera Roebuck, Patience Miller, Nance Miriam, Madeleine Bray, Maureen Moore, Eileen Scott, Vera Anderson, Dorothy Hardy, Eileen Murphy, Mildred Nicoll, Audrey Tiffen, Babette Moore, Joan Carr, Helen Stephens, Marie Brooke, Dorothy Eyre, Helene Francois, Gaby Garay, Pat Andrew, Linda Lindose

GENTLEMEN OF THE CHORUS: Hugh Foster, Roberto Wood, Selwyn Morgan, Felix Hill, Wilfrid Ward, Hal Hatswell, Victor Hamal, Frank Nolan, Arturo Gomez, Sinclair Cole, Gordon Crocker, George Hayes, George Sylvester, Harold Farrar, Edward Ward, Louis Garnett, Richard Bodley, Alfred Atkins, Edgar Pierce Arthur Rees

Reviews

London Times

". . . the music is distinctly above the average and the singing throughout is admirable . . . the humour is a trifle slender . . . Last night the first part was inclined to drag a little . . . the *Totem Tom-Tom* chorus roused the audience to unusual enthusiasm . . ."

James Agate—*London Sunday Times,* March 22, 1925

"Pretty, derivative music, Mr. Derek Oldham's enchanting voice, Mr. Billy Merson at grips with the feeblest part ever written for a principal comedian—what else is there? Well, there is Miss Day . . . And, of course, there is the spectacle . . . At any other theatre—fine! But is there not melancholy in the thought that this whoppingest of monuments to inanity should have been raised on these boards? . . . The applause was cataclysmic and, in my view, the piece will run one hundred and eleven years and fifteen days . . ."

Hubert Griffith—*London Observer,* March 22, 1925

". . . gave us the spectacle of an ordinary and very typical musical comedy put to the difficult task of holding the vast stage, succeeding where it was good and failing where it was bad. The story was half-hearted and there was a prompt and spontaneous tendency to coughing whenever it was dwelt upon for more than a minute or two. The music was so-so, best in its dance numbers . . . The dancing was good enough really to 'get' the whole house and to hold it . . . The Lane has seen worse in its time. But the point is that lately it has seen better . . ."

The Stage
". . . at times ambitious, generally expressive and tuneful, refined even when ragtimey, and never, at any rate hardly ever, jazzish music . . ."

The Era
". . . a very good entertainment; a carefully contrived compromise between a melodrama and a musical comedy, and a splendid vehicle for a number of bright spectacular effects and some fine ensembles. If the production has a weakness it is that the piece is lacking in humour . . . the music is tuneful and vigourous . . ."

ROSE MARIE

(Film Version—1928)

A Metro-Goldwyn-Mayer Picture
Directed and adapted by Lucien Hubbard
Photographed by John Arnold
Editor, Carl F. Pierson

Release Date
February 11, 1928

The Cast
ROSE MARIE, Joan Crawford
JIM KENYON, James Murray
SGT. MALONE, House Peters
ETIENNE DORAY, Creighton Hale
LADY JANE, Polly Moran
BLACK BASTIEN, Gibson Gowland
HENRI, Lionel Belmore
WANDA, Gertrude Astor
GRAY, Harry Gribbon
EMILE, William Orlamond

Musical Numbers
Accompanying this silent film was a score (available for piano, organ or full orchestra) featuring *Rose-Marie* and *Indian Love Call.* In the larger presentation houses, an off-stage singer accompanied the *Indian Love Call* sequence.

Reviews

Mordaunt Hall—*New York Times*
"... The praiseworthy passages of this effort are more than offset by the muddled story, the ridiculous suspicions and the tedious and frequently absurd incidents . . ."

Harriette Underhill—*New York Herald Tribune*
". . . just another story of the Northwest Mounted. All along Broadway at midnight men who could whistle were whistling the *Indian Love Call.* This is the song from the original production which made whistling famous . . ."

Sid Silverman—*Variety,* February 15, 1928
". . . isn't as bad as the advance reports rated it . . . The heavy dramatic incidents and the slow-motion miniature ice break climax figure to hold enough interest to make it passable with the average audience . . ."

Pare Lorentz—*Judge,* March 3, 1928
". . . a tinted souvenir post card of the musical comedy bearing that name, with orchestral accompaniment."

ROSE MARIE

(Film Version—1936)

A Metro Goldwyn-Mayer Picture
Produced by Hunt Stromberg
Directed by W. S. Van Dyke
Screenplay by Frances Goodrich, Albert Hackett and Alice Duer Miller
Choreography by Chester Hale
Operatic staging by William von Wymetal
Art director, Cedric Gibbons
Costumes by Adrian
Music director, Mr. Stothart
Photographed by William Daniels
Editor, Blanche Sewell

Release Date
January 13, 1936

The Story
Marie de Flor, an opera star, travels through the Canadian Northwest in search of her brother, John Flower, who is wanted for

murder. Also on the trail is Sgt. Bruce of the Northwest Mounted Police. Complications arise when Bruce discovers the relationship, but in the end the Mountie gets both his man and his prima donna.

The Cast

MARIE DE FLOR, Jeanette MacDonald
SGT. BRUCE, Nelson Eddy
JOHN FLOWER, James Stewart
MYERSON, Reginald Owen
OPERA SINGER, Allan Jones
BONIFACE, George Regas
HOTEL MANAGER, Robert Greig
ANNA, Una O'Connor
STOREKEEPER, Lucien Littlefield
PREMIER, Alan Mowbray
TEDDY, David Niven
MR. DANIELS, Herman Bing
BELLE, Gilda Gray
JOE, James Conlin
EDITH, Dorothy Gray
CORN QUEEN, Mary Anita Loos
GORDON, Halliwell Hobbs
EMIL, Paul Porcasi
COMMANDANT, Russell Hicks
DANCERS: David Robel, Rinaldo Alacorp

Musical Numbers

Songs retained from original production: *Rose-Marie, The Mounties, Indian Love Call, Totem Tom-Tom.* Songs written specially for film by Herbert Stothart and Gus Kahn: *Just for You* (music written with Friml) and *Pardon Me, Madame.* Other musical numbers: *Dinah* (Harry Akst-Joe Young, Sam Lewis), *Some of These Days* (Shelton Brooks), waltz from Gounod's *Roméo et Juliette,* aria from Puccini's *Tosca.*

Reviews

Frank S. Nugent—*New York Times*
"As blithely melodious and rich in scenic beauty as any picture that has come from Hollywood . . . If the script writers have dealt less respectfully with the original's book, they may be pardoned on the ground that here the song—and its singers—are the thing . . ."

Richard Watts, Jr.—*New York Herald Tribune*
". . . stands high among the cinema's romantic musical successes . . . a trifle long-winded on occasion, but invariably an exceptionally successful example of its school . . ."

William Boehnel—*New York World-Telegram*
". . . has both charm and vigor . . . as pleasant as this form of cinema entertainment is ever likely to be. Handsome, lavishly staged, imaginative, it is a gayly romantic and rhapsodically tuneful piece of work . . ."

Abel Green—*Variety,* February 5, 1936
". . . like the Northwest Mounted Police this M-G b.o. entry will get the money . . . wholly satisfying . . ."

John Mosher—*The New Yorker,* February 8, 1936
". . . some tuneful items of the popular variety, a snack or two from grand opera, one or two musical renderings of Indian love calls, or mating calls, and a tendency to humor, a quality I am inclined to look for in musical shows and don't always find . . ."

Don Herold—*Life,* April, 1936
"A trifle buckeye as to dialogue, but great stuff when Jeanette MacDonald and Nelson Eddy are singing the tunes . . ."

London Daily Telegraph, March 30, 1936
". . . a generous and entertaining film . . . Whenever it moves out of doors it makes itself impressive, and it is not difficult to understand why . . . once Miss MacDonald and Mr. Eddy have started singing the *Indian Love Call,* they find it so hard to stop . . ."

ROSE MARIE

(Film Version—1954)

A Metro-Goldwyn-Mayer Picture
Produced and directed by Mervyn LeRoy
Screenplay by Ronald Millar and George Froeschel
Choreography by Busby Berkeley
Art directors, Cedric Gibbons, Merrill Pye
Music director, George Stoll
Photographed by Paul Vogel
Editor, Harold Kress
Color by Ansco Color
Filmed in CinemaScope

Release Date
April 1, 1954

The Cast
ROSE MARIE LEMAITRE, Ann Blyth
SGT. MIKE MALONE, Howard Keel

JAMES SEVERN DUVAL, Fernando Lamas
BARNEY MCCORKLE, Bert Lahr
LADY JANE DUNSTOCK, Marjorie Main
WANDA, Joan Taylor
INSPECTOR APPLEBY, Ray Collins
BLACK EAGLE, Chief Yowlachie

Musical Numbers

Songs retained from original production: *The Mounties, Indian Love Call, Rose Marie* and *Totem Tom-Tom.* Songs written specially for film by Mr. Friml and Paul Francis Webster: *The Right Place, Free to Be Free, Love and Kisses,* and *I Have the Love. The Mountie That Never Got His Man* (by George Stoll and Herbert Baker) also written for film.

Reviews

Bosley Crowther—*New York Times*
". . . The scenery and its songs are its salvation, for the story is an antique and mannered contemplation. It slowly develops with a fearfully fixed deliberation . . ."

Otis L. Guernsey, Jr.—*New York Herald Tribune*
". . . The melodies are still sweet . . . The real production is its scenic backgrounds, the setting for a little bit of sentiment and quite a lot of song . . ."

Hy Hollinger—*Variety,* March 3, 1954
". . . Unfortunately, typical operetta plot of yesteryear is sweet and occasionally sad, but with little substance . . . Old score fares better than the plot . . ."

Henry Bradford Darrach, Jr.—*Time,* March 15, 1954
". . . manages to combine almost all the worst features of the preceding productions with a few especially thought up for the occasion . . ."

John McCarten—*The New Yorker,* April 17, 1954
". . . has no way improved with age and CinemaScope . . ."

Arthur Knight—*Saturday Review,* April 17, 1954
". . . the old score still has its charm . . . a tedious and ill-advised venture, another of M-G-M's beautiful bores. It will probably make millions."

Bibliography

Rose Marie, They Still Love You —*Life,* February 22, 1954

SUNNY

(1925)

A musical comedy with book and lyrics by Otto Harbach and Oscar Hammerstein II; music by Jerome Kern.

Presented by Charles Dillingham
Directed by Hassard Short
Choreography by Julian Mitchell and David Bennett
Hunt Dance by Alexis Kosloff
Eight Marilyn Miller Cocktails dances by John Tiller
Marilyn Miller's dances with boys by Fred Astaire
Settings and costumes by James Reynolds
Music director, Gus Salzer
Orchestions by Robert Russell Bennett

Tryout

Forrest Theatre, Philadelphia, September 9-19, 1925

New York Run

New Amsterdam Theatre, September 22, 1925-December 11, 1926
517 performances

The Story

Sunny Peters, a circus performer in Southampton, England, meets Tom Warren again after a long absence. Though the flame is rekindled, Tom must embark soon for the United States. Sunny stows on board to escape the advances of the circus owner, Harold Harcourt Wendell-Wendell, and agrees to marry Jim Deming, one of Tom's friends, in order to be allowed to land. Once in America, Sunny and Jim no sooner get their agreed-to divorce than they discover that they love each other.

The Cast

MLLE. SADIE, Helene Gardner
BALLY HOO, Charles Angelo
TOM WARREN, Paul Frawley
SIEGFRIED PETERS, Joseph Cawthorn
HAROLD HARCOURT WENDELL-WENDELL, Clifton Webb
SUE WARREN, Esther Howard

SAM, Cliff Edwards
SUNNY PETERS, Marilyn Miller
JIM DEMING, Jack Donahue
WEENIE WINTERS, Mary Hay
MARCIA MANNERS, Dorothy Francis
MAGNOLIA, Pert Kelton
FIRST MATE, Louis Harrison
SHIP'S OFFICERS: Elmer Brown, Abner Barnhart
SHIP'S CAPTAIN, James Wilson
DIANA MILES, Jeanne Fonda
MILLICENT SMYTHE, Joan Clement
GROOM, Don Rowan
SPECIALTY DANCERS: Linda; Marjorie Moss and Georges Fontana
George Olsen and his Orchestra
EIGHT MARILYN MILLER COCKTAILS: Peggy Soden, Lelia Riley, Grace Holt, Hilda Stanley, Doris Waterworth, May Cornes, Iris Smith, Nellie Douglas
SHOW GIRLS: Dorothy Durland, Trude Marr, Claire Hopper, Maida Palmer, Helene Gardner, Rita Glynde, Alice Brady, Pauline Hall, Anna May Dennehey, Tatiana
DANCERS: Virginia Clark, Victoria Webster, Helen Shepard, Miriam Miller, Phyllis Reynolds, Helen MacDonald, Zelletta Johnson, Collette Francey, Jet Stanley, Betty McLaughlin, Beatrice de Shaw, Christine Conniff, Marie Maxwell, Betty Darling, Pearl Bennett, Rita Royce, Marion Swords, Adelaide Robinson, Louise Stark, Katherine Frey, Elva Pomfret, Julia Lane, Lorna Sommerville, Margaret Kolloch, Vera Coburn, Laverne Lindsay, Lorraine Eason
BOYS: Ward Tallman, Marshall Sullivan, William Sholar Jr., Robert Williams, Maurice Lupue, Albert Birk, Marcos de Abreau, Minard Roosa, Irving Carter, Donald Oltrash, Bill O'Donnell, Walter Fairmont, Wensley Johnston, Ray Justus, Richard Renaud, Louis Yaeckel, Gordon Clark, Roy Moore, Lee Moore, Russell Ash, Albert Royal, Bob Leroy, Eddie Graham, Don Rowen, Joe Billings, George Comtois, Fred Comtois, Ted Wenning

NOTE: From November 1925 to August 1926, Mr. Edwards replaced by Borrah Minevitch. For Philadelphia engagement during tour, Miss Miller replaced by Mary Eaton.

Musical Numbers

ACT I

SCENE ONE—OUTSIDE A CIRCUS TENT, SOUTHAMPTON, ENGLAND
Opening, *Here We Are Together Again,* ENSEMBLE
Dance, MARILYN MILLER COCKTAILS

SCENE TWO—IN BACK OF THE CIRCUS TENT
Sunny, TOM and BOYS
Who?, SUNNY and TOM

INTERLUDE—A STREET IN SOUTHAMPTON
So's Your Old Man, WENDELL-WENDELL and COCKTAILS

SCENE THREE—IN FRONT OF WEENIE'S HOUSE
Let's Say Goodnight 'Til It's Morning, JIM and WEENIE

INTERLUDE—THE GANGPLANK

SCENE FOUR—S.S. TRIUMPHANT
D'Ye Love Me?, SUNNY; danced by JIM
The Wedding Knell, SUNNY and BOYS

SCENE FIVE—S.S. TRIUMPHANT

SCENE SIX—A PARK IN SOUTHAMPTON
Two Little Bluebirds, WENDELL-WENDELL and WEENIE

INTERLUDE—JIM'S CABIN ON THE S.S. TRIUMPHANT

SCENE SEVEN—GRAND SALON OF THE S. S. TRIUMPHANT
Finale, COMPANY

ACT II
SCENE ONE—JIM'S GYM AT A FASHIONABLE RESORT
Opening, *We're Gymnastic,* ENSEMBLE
When We Get Our Divorce, SUNNY and JIM
Sunshine, MARCIA and BOYS; danced by Linda
Reprise, *Who?,* SUNNY and TOM; danced by SUNNY, JIM, WENDELL-WENDELL, WEENIE and ENSEMBLE

SCENE TWO—A GROVE
Paddlin' Madelin' Home (by Harry Woods), SAM
Just a Little Thing Called Rhythm (Eddie Ward-Chick Endor), SAM

SCENE THREE—A POPPY FIELD
The Chase, ENSEMBLE
Strolling, or What Have You?, WENDELL-WENDELL and WEENIE

SCENE FOUR—THE WOODS
Magnolia in the Woods (by Pert Kelton), MAGNOLIA

SCENE FIVE—HOTEL BALLROOM
The Hunt Dance, SUNNY
Dance, Marjorie Moss and Georges Fontana
Finale, COMPANY

NOTE: *Dream a Dream* cut before New York opening.

Reviews
New York Times
". . . when it was not 'glorifying' the particularly luminous beauty of Miss Miller, it was 'glorifying' a certain standard of finesse and

virtuosity in the composition of musical entertainment. For although this expansive entertainment sets no new limits to show humor, music or beauty, the performance has been skillfully pulled together, produced with a touch of glamour, and it never runs bare or dry . . . the music blends well with the general scheme . . ."

Percy Hammond—*New York Herald Tribune*
". . . for sumptuousness and beauty it outdressed all the shows within the eye's memory . . . The book was clean, the score was comparatively aristocratic and the principal members of the company were the best of their kind. One song, entitled *Who?*, was attractive enough to indicate that ere the snow falls it will be a pest . . . the wheezes, however obvious, are more sanitary than those of the routine Times Square amusements . . . decent, gorgeous, sophisticated and amusing."

New York World
". . . a swollen and handsome extravaganza fashioned from a pattern left lying around the theatre. It was the pattern from which *Sally* had been made . . . Dillingham packed everything into his gay and good-looking show with the possible exception of novelty . . . some lovely tunes and we shall all be sick to death of the one called *Who?* before the town is done with it . . ."

Alan Dale—*New York American*
". . . At first you were inclined to think that *Sunny* was slow. You looked for pep; you searched for vim—and then they danced and all was well . . . Miss Miller danced way from that stupid book, way from everything, into the realms of lissomeness and charm and airiness that good dancing always conjures up . . . The music was not remarkable. It had some effective harmonies, however, and it was at least scholarly, and it wasn't treacle . . . *Sunny* whilst it did not shed a tropical heat at least managed to diffuse a gentle warmth and a sense of comfort."

Burns Mantle--*New York Daily News*
". . . Dillingham has put everything into it but the Hippodrome elephants . . . one of those big music shows that cost so much it just has to be good. It is a little like *Sally* in size and also in quality . . . Past Kern's excellent score, which contains at least three hits in *Sunny, Who?* and *D'Ye Love Me?*, and past the beauty of the decorations, the personnel is the big note . . . a lively show, a tuneful show, an entertaining show. In addition it has Marilyn in person. You might ask for more, but would you deserve it? . . ."

John Anderson—*New York Post*
". . . nearly everybody except Mrs. Fiske and E. H. Sothern seems to be in it . . . People who like musical comedy will find it indispensable. People who don't may be converted by it, for *Sunny* is a deluxe panorama and great entertainment . . . two lingering pieces, *D'Ye Love Me?* and *Who?* . . ."

E. W. Osborn—*New York Evening World*
". . . Miss Miller is back to the tricks of the trade which made *Sally* a blooming 'go.' Only now she is even more so . . . a night which kept getting better right up to the finish . . . most of the music was joyous, all of it melodious and some of it exquisite . . ."

Frank Vreeland—*New York Telegram*
". . . Miss Miller's resplendent charm has taken on an added lustre . . . a sumptuous offering, produced on a scale of unsurpassed magnificence . . . The chief appeal, aside from the lavishness of mounting, lay in the incessant trickle of bright principals . . . Kern's music was pleasantly fluid when it wasn't infectious, as in the *Sunny* song . . ."

Gilbert W. Gabriel—*New York Sun*
". . . a lavish and hippodromatic vaudeville . . . a perfectly usable and usual musical-comedy plot . . . The chief ingredient is, of course, Jack Donahue . . . Kern's music is spread rather thin . . . The lyrics are at least workable . . ."

Sid Silverman (Skig.)—*Variety*, September 30, 1925
". . . shouldn't miss and it doesn't . . . Kern's music is not up to many of his former compositions . . . it's as much entertainment as has ever been crammed into one piece as far as 'names' are concerned . . ."

Herman J. Mankiewicz—*The New Yorker*, October 3, 1925
". . . one of the most gorgeous and luxurious musicals the town has seen in recent years . . ."

Wells Root—*Time*, October 5, 1925
". . . unquestionably the most lavish musical ever assembled and seems to suffer only through an excess of talent . . . lacks unity and a focal interest. As a five-dollar vaudeville show, it is the very best . . ."

Robert Benchley—*Life*, October 15, 1925
". . . good substantial entertainment from beginning to end . . . it isn't so much that it is consistently good, but that it has practically no bad spots . . ."

Arthur Hornblow—*Theatre Magazine*, December, 1925
". . . the combination of brilliant shuffling feet, graceful dancing, beauty and lilting songs and amusing comedy brought about a verdict that it's a darned good show . . ."

Tour
Forrest Theatre, Philadelphia, December 20, 1926—Illinois Theatre, Chicago, June 4, 1927 (4 cities).

Selected Revivals
St. Louis Municipal Opera, July 15-21, 1935
Marjorie Peterson (SUNNY); Gil Lamb (JIM); Earle MacVeigh (BOB); Audrey Christie (WEENIE); Gertrude Niesen (MARCIA).

St. Louis Municipal Opera, June 14-20, 1943
Evelyn Wyckoff (SUNNY); Gordon Dilworth (BOB); Leonard Elliott (WENDELL).

St. Louis Municipal Opera, August 2-8, 1948
Laurel Hurley (SUNNY); Hal LeRoy (JIM); John Elliott (TOM); Gale Sherwood (SUE); Patricia Bowman (PREMIERE DANSEUSE).

Goodspeed Opera House, East Haddam, Conn., Summer, 1972
Leland Palmer (SUNNY); John Remme (JIM); David Christmas (TOM).

SUNNY

(London—1926)

Presented by Moss' Empires, Ltd.
in conjunction with Lee Ephraim and Jack Buchanan
Directed by Charles Mast
Settings by Joseph and Phil Harker
Costumes by Idare et Cie.
Music director, Philip Braham

Tryout
Palace Theatre, Manchester, September 20-October 3, 1926

London Run
Hippodrome, October 7, 1926-July 16, 1927
363 performances

The Cast
BALLY HOO, Dennis Wyndham
TOM WARREN, Jack Hobbs

SIEGFRIED PETERS, Nicholas Adams
HAROLD HARCOURT WENDELL-WENDELL, Claude Hulbert
SUE WARREN, Maidie Hope
SAM, Sam Macrae
SUNNY PETERS, Binnie Hale
JIM DEMING, Jack Buchanan
WEENIE WINTERS, Elsie Randolph
MARCIA MANNERS, Nancie Lovat
FIRST MATE, Gus Oxley
FIRST SHIP'S OFFICER, Harry Clemens
SHIP'S CAPTAIN, Robert Gordon
PREMIERE DANSEUSE, Ula Sharon
Alfredo and his Princes' Band
EIGHT "SUNNY" GIRLS: Dorothy Marlow, Vera Owen, Esme Westhead, Roma Darrell, Betty Birch, Rene Force, Edith Lamb, Gladys Holt
LADIES OF THE CHORUS: Elsie Barton, Ella Atherton, Mollie Crafter, Dorothy Fenwick, Vera Fothergill, Eileen McCarthy, Dorothea Stone, Zoe Andrews, Esme Brown, Nancy Beard, Ivy Donnelly, Peggy Eccles, Vivian Farnham, Peggy Kendall, Olive Kilgom, Marie Masters, Audrey Milner, Jill Mureen, Monti Ryan, Margot St. Leger, Rita Shield, Marjorie Hall, May Baker, Kathleen Clifford, Joan Reddrop, Stella Garrard
GENTLEMEN OF THE CHORUS: Herbert Brett, Ian Lennox, Douglas Percival, Louis Roslyn, Jack Stewart, Frank Townsend, Fred Wallace, Eric Wardroper, Claude Watts, Harry Werndley, Billy Reynolds, Paul Barrie, Noel Fisher, W. H. Kearton, Joe Roncoroni, Eric Lambert, Morriss Sennett, Fred Maxwell, John Barker

Musical Numbers

Same as original production except that Cliff Edwards and Pert Kelton specialties dropped, and following songs added:
It Won't Mean a Thing, SUNNY, TOM and JIM
I've Looked for Trouble (lyric by Desmond Carter), JIM
I Might Grow Fond of You, WENDELL-WENDELL and WEENIE
The Fox Has Left His Lair, QUARTETTE (including JIM)

Reviews

London Times

". . . Precisely what the plot is we know, of course, at once when song and dance combine to tell us who is betrothed to whom and who would prefer to be betrothed to somebody else. Comic business in a circus, elaborate business on a liner, and quite impossible business at a meet help the characters in the untangling of the least complex of puzzles . . . this frolicsome affair is the very thing for frolicsome people . . . The audience loved it dearly."

Horace Horsnell—*London Observer,* October 10, 1926
". . . starts with a bang. Then, one by one, in as strict an order of precedence as governs a royal conclave, the stars come out, take their meed of welcoming applause and their place in a plot that is hard put to it to absorb its riot of ingredients . . . No order of precedence could obscure Mr. Jack Buchanan's right to the zenith . . . I noticed as we came out that even the programme sellers were singing and dancing. Can you imagine a happier augury?"

James Agate—*London Sunday Times,* October 17, 1926
". . . To be present while the talents of incredibly perfect revue artists like Miss Binnie Hale, Mr. Claude Hulbert and Mr. Jack Buchanan are frittered away on perfectly incredible banalities first dispirits me and then fires me with a blaze of economic fury. Surely this is unforgiveable waste! . . ."

The Stage
". . . The melodious and catchy music is distinctive in tune and daintiness. Some witty and well-turned lyrics . . . a very agreeable entertainment . . ."

The Era
". . . a great success because of the exceedingly clever people in the company. Binnie Hale radiates 'sunniness' . . . Kern's music is as uninspired as the plot, except for one tune—*Who?*—which sets one humming and moving one's feet uneasily . . ."

S.T.H.—*Theatre World,* November, 1926
". . . Kern's music is, on the whole, tuneful and pleasant. He refuses to pander to the modern demand for syncopation at all costs, and contents himself with simple, well-scored melody . . . In many ways a delightful show, but it might have been very much better."

SUNNY

(Film Version—1930)

A First National Picture
Directed by William A. Seiter
Screenplay by Humphrey Pearson and Henry McCarthy
Choreography by Theodore Kosloff
Music director, Erno Rapee
Photographed by Ernest Haller

Release Date
December 26, 1930

The Cast
SUNNY PETERS, Marilyn Miller
TOM WARREN, Lawrence Gray
JIM DEMING, Joe Donahue
HAROLD HARCOURT WENDELL-WENDELL, Mackenzie Ward
SIEGFRIED PETERS, O. P. Heggie
WEENIE WINTERS, Inez Courtney
MARCIA MANNERS, Barbara Bedford
SUE WARREN, Judith Vosselli
SAM, Clyde Cook
THE BARKER, Harry Allen
SHIP'S OFFICERS, William Davidson, Ben Hendricks

Musical Numbers
Songs retained from original production: *Sunny, Who?, D'Ye Love Me?* and *Two Little Bluebirds.* First song by Messrs. Kern and Hammerstein written specially for a film: *I Was Alone.*

Reviews
Mordaunt Hall—*New York Times*
". . . an ably directed film, with pleasing light touches and effective backgrounds . . ."

Al Greason (Rush.)—*Variety,* December 31, 1930
". . . furnishes testimony that the straight filming of a musical comedy is a hazard. In this case it is particularly weak because of an especially inane book . . . Addressing polite musical-comedy fun to a mob that is addicted to Sennett horseplay is thankless business all around . . ."

John Mosher—*The New Yorker,* January 3, 1931
". . . too much old libretto conversation to give Miss Miller many opportunities."

Time, January 5, 1931
". . . old and dull . . . When Miss Miller is dancing, the picture is bearable but not when Joe Donahue is trying to be funny . . ."

Harry Evans—*Life,* January 16, 1931
". . . considerably more entertaining than most of these All-Singing, All-Dancing, All-Wet and All-Washed-Up talkies . . . The one important thing is the appearance of Joe Donahue in the role that his brother Jack played on the stage . . ."

SUNNY

(Film Version—1941)

An RKO-Radio Picture
Produced and directed by Herbert Wilcox
Screenplay by Sig Herzig
Music director, Anthony Collins
Orchestrations by Mr. Collins and Gene Rose
Photographed by Russell Metty

Release Date

June 12, 1941

The Cast

SUNNY SULLIVAN, Anna Neagle
BUNNY BILLINGS, Ray Bolger
LARRY WARREN, John Carroll
HENRY BATES, Edward Everett Horton
JULIET RUNNYMEDE, Grace Hartman
EGGHEAD, Paul Hartman
ELIZABETH WARREN, Frieda Inescort
AUNT BARBARA, Helen Westley
MAJOR MONTGOMERY SLOAN, Benny Rubin
MUGGINS, Muggins Davies
REPORTER, Richard Lane
HEAD WAITER, Torben Meyer
QUEEN OF HEARTS, Martha Tilton

Musical Numbers

Songs retained from original production: *Sunny, Who?, D'Ye Love Me?*

Reviews

Bosley Crowther—*New York Times*
". . . they have twisted it into a routine Cinderella story . . . as bright as a new penny and pretty nearly as flat."

Howard Barnes—*New York Herald Tribune*
". . . a dull translation and a ponderous entertainment . . . the action is so slow paced that sequence after sequence dies of its own inertia . . . it never should have been made."

William Boehnel—*New York World-Telegram*
". . . a rollicking, thoroughly amiable and streamlined version . . ."

Walt Christie—*Variety,* May 21, 1941
". . . still a typical operetta Cinderella tale . . . a mild attraction . . ."

John Mosher—*The New Yorker,* June 7, 1941
". . . Plot trouble adds considerable tonnage to an item which should be as light as a feather . . . The melodies survive it all, and in them we find the charm and delicacy which we want and which the treatment of the film can't obscure."

Time, June 16, 1941
". . . No masterpiece, it is pleasant entertainment."

SONG OF THE FLAME

(1925)

A musical play with book and lyrics by Otto Harbach and Oscar Hammerstein II; music by George Gershwin and Herbert Stothart.

Presented by Arthur Hammerstein
Directed by Frank Reicher
Choreography by Jack Haskell
Settings by Joseph Urban
Costumes by Mark Mooring
Music director, Mr. Stothart
Orchestrations by Robert Russell Bennett

Tryout
Playhouse, Wilmington, Dec. 10-12, 1925
Academy of Music, Baltimore, December 14-19, 1925
Shubert Theatre, Philadelphia, December 21-26, 1925

New York Run
Fourty-fourth Street Theatre, December 30, 1925-June 19, 1926
219 performances

The Story
During the Russian Revolution, Prince Volodya falls in love with Aniuta, a young girl whom he later discovers to be a revolutionary leader known as "The Flame." After hostilities cease, they meet again in Paris, and discover that their love is stronger than their political differences.

The Cast
KONSTANTIN, Greek Evans
ANIUTA ("THE FLAME"), Tessa Kosta
GRUSHA, Dorothy Mackaye
NICHOLAS, Hugh Cameron
COUNT BORIS, Bernard Gorcey
NADYA, Ula Sharon
NATASHA, Phebe Brune
PRINCE VOLODYA, Guy Robertson
FEATURED DANCER, Leonard St. Leo

OLGA, Blanche Collins
ALEXIS, Paul Wilson
AN AVENGER, Louise Dalberg
RUSSIAN ART SINGERS (directed by Alexander U. Fine): Konstantin Buketoff, Zina Ivanova, Anna Petrenko, Vasily Andrewsky (soloists)
AMERICAN BALLET: Verdi, Milli, Lucille Osborne, Alice Ankers, Lotta Fanning, Louise Hersey, Marion Booth, Mary Green, Dorothy Booth, Eileen Wenzel, Frances Thress, Georgia Gwynne, Ann Constance, Miriam Avendale, Christine Moray, Audrey Sturges, Dorothy Thattell, Gene Hylan, Emily Sherman, Adelaide Permin, Terry Carroll, Elvinne Hall, Ruby Poe, Ruth Sato, Sylvia Pagano, Laurie Phillips, Elsie Marcus, Dorothy Lee, Carolyn Johnson, Margie Horton, Buddie Haines, Betty Credito, Helen Bowers, L. Ojala, Ima Berline, Adelaide Candee, Edith Higgens, Beth Hill, Lillyan Lyndon, Frances Nevins, Elsa Roelofsma, Jeannie St. John
GENTLEMEN OF THE ENSEMBLE: Chester Bennett, Hal Bird, William Cooper, Paul Florence, James Herold, Bob LeRoy, Harry Long, Troupe Reynolds, Willard Tyson, Philip Titman, Donald Wells

NOTE: Miss Kosta replaced temporarily by Desiree Ellinger from June to November, 1926.

Musical Numbers

PRELUDE
Protest

PROLOGUE—A STREET IN MOSCOW, MARCH, 1917
Far Away (Gershwin-Stothart) (refrain based on folk song theme—the peasants' lament on a late spring), KONSTANTIN and RUSSIAN ART SINGERS
Song of the Flame (Gershwin-Stothart), ANIUTA, KONSTANTIN and RUSSIAN ART SINGERS

ACT I

SCENE ONE—NEAR A CANAL TRIBUTARY OF THE VOLGA—OCTOBER, 1917
Woman's Work Is Never Done (Gershwin), GRUSHA and ENSEMBLE
Great Big Bear (Stothart), GRUSHA, NICHOLAS and ENSEMBLE

SCENE TWO—THE WESTERN GATE OF THE KAZANOV PALACE
The Signal (Gershwin), ANIUTA, VOLODYA and OCTETTE
The Cossack Love Song (Gershwin-Stothart), ANIUTA, VOLODYA and ENSEMBLE
Tartar (Stothart), KONSTANTIN and RUSSIAN ART SINGERS; danced by Emily Sherman and AMERICAN BALLET

SCENE THREE—OUTSIDE ANIUTA'S LODGINGS
Wander Away (Stothart), ANIUTA and VOLODYA
Finaletto (Gershwin-Stothart), ANIUTA, VOLODYA and ENSEMBLE

SCENE FOUR—ART SALON OF THE KAZANOV PALACE
Vodka (Gershwin-Stothart), GRUSHA and ENSEMBLE DANCE, NADYA and FEATURED DANCER
Finale, COMPANY

ACT II

SCENE ONE—A ROOM IN A LATIN QUARTER PENSION, PARIS, TWO YEARS LATER
I Want Two Husbands (Stothart), GRUSHA, BORIS, NICHOLAS
Midnight Bells (Gershwin), ANIUTA
Reprise, *The Cossack Love Song*, VOLODYA

SCENE TWO—OUTSIDE THE CAFE DES CAUCASIENS, MONTMARTRE

SCENE THREE—SAMOVAR ROOM OF THE CAFE DES CAUCASIENS
The First Blossom Ballet, danced by NADYA, FEATURED DANCER and AMERICAN BALLET

(NOTE: This ballet is symbolic of Russia's long winter of adversity and the arrival of the first blossom of victorious ideals. At first, the blossom is repulsed and chilled by the snows of bitterness, but the sunlight she brings with her melts the snows.)

A Capella, RUSSIAN ART SINGERS
Finaletto, COMPANY

SCENE FOUR—OUTSIDE THE CAFE DES CAUCASIENS

SCENE FIVE—KAZANOV ESTATE IN THE CHATEAU DISTRICT, FRANCE
Going Home on New Year's Morning, RUSSIAN ART SINGERS

EPILOGUE—SONG OF THE FLAME
Finale Ultimo, COMPANY

NOTE: *You Are You* (Gershwin-Stothart) and *You and You and Me* (Stothart) cut before New York opening. *I Want Two Husbands* and *Midnight Bells* dropped in January in favor of reprise of *Wander Away* sung by KONSTANTIN.

Reviews

J. Brooks Atkinson—*New York Times*
". . . perhaps most distinguished for the gay-colored, variegated settings and the frequent ensemble groups . . . although all the music is not so distinguished as the two opening numbers, and some of it merely fulfills the conventions of musical comedy, the composers frequently express the fullness and superstitious wealth of their subject matter. *The Cossack Love Song*, for instance, is a rich number . . . the size of the production makes the opera generally heavy . . ."

Percy Hammond—*New York Herald Tribune*
". . . a large, beautiful and serious feast . . . Yet, with all its assets, the play, I fear, lacked what used to be known as 'that something.'

Its personality, if I may be permitted to suspect so, was not exhilarating . . . What I liked best was the sprite-like dancing of Miss Ula Sharon . . ."

Wells Root—*New York World*
". . . appeared to be the most gorgeous entertainment in New York . . . the book was pretty hopeless . . . The story did not burn very fiercely with life nor did it crackle crisply with humor . . . a score of richness and variety . . ."

Alan Dale—*New York American*
". . . a handsome and rather lavish production, quite beautifully done, and colored majestically enough . . . The book is a trifle soggy at times—that is to say it is neither poetic nor amusing . . . very good music . . ."

Burns Mantle—*New York Daily News*
". . . grand and heavy in the Russian manner, high-colored and barbaric. There is a thrill in the pictures alone that few productions get . . . a perfect thing. Or as near perfect as we are likely to see staged . . ."

Walter Winchell—*New York Graphic*
". . . Resplendent mountings and costumes, added to the magic of Stothart's and Gershwin's rich musical score, swept the new production to the top of the current and imposing list of operettas. Its only sour note (or shall we say handicap?) is its ineffectual humorous passages . . ."

John Anderson—*New York Post*
". . . while its impoverished humors are regrettable they are only cotton patches upon the velvet pants of its splendor . . . *Song of the Flame* is a cajoling, insinuating tune . . . a sumptuous and lovely entertainment, executed with taste and prodigality . . ."

E. W. Osborn—*New York Evening World*
". . . a superfine concert, to which has been added the attractions of a superb costume ball . . . The score is by turns inspiring, charming, gay, agitating, stirring and an almost irresistible invitation to the dance . . ."

Frank Vreeland—*New York Telegram*
". . . a cloudburst of melodies, a rainbow of settings, a symphony of costumes, a cascade of liquid sounds pouring from the fountain called Miss Kosta's throat, and a flaunting, challenging banner of choral harmonies flung to the breeze by the Russian Art Singers . . .

the score is so sweeping and vibrant that it would blow out a whole row of gas jets . . . towering shafts of melody in *Song of the Flame* and *Midnight Bells* . . ."

Gilbert W. Gabriel—*New York Sun*
". . . a glittering, jubilating business . . . If the opulence of it all could not induce the Messrs. Harbach and Hammerstein to supply a brighter book and a lighter lot of lyrics, they have at any rate compounded something stanch and serviceable . . . resplendent, romantic opera . . ."

Jack Pulaski (Ibee.)—*Variety*, January 6, 1926
". . . the first act is dazzling . . . The second act tapered off . . . But even then there was fine entertainment . . . though without the popular elements of *Rose-Marie*, it is one of the finest operettas produced."

Herman J. Mankiewicz—*The New Yorker*, January 9, 1926
". . . huge, beautiful, melodious, unfunny and generally dull . . . It is not for us. If Mr. Hammerstein wants to answer that he didn't produce it for us, he's probably right."

George Jean Nathan—*Judge*, January 16, 1926
". . . the libretto is so poor that the virtues of the entertainment have a tough time battling against it . . . the leading role, that of a fiery Russian Joan of Arc, has been entrusted to a nice, quiet little American girl who has about as much Russian fire as an English foot-warmer . . ."

Wells Root—*Time*, January 18, 1926
". . . a moderately tasty plot, but lacking romance's true savor . . . an earnest and expensive effort at light opera. It is rich, vivid, entertaining. But another such as *Rose-Marie*? Not quite."

Arthur Hornblow—*Theatre Magazine*, March, 1926
". . . If the libretto had been as exciting in its execution as it is in its intent, the result would have been much more dramatic . . . very little sustained interest in the play, and the music does not quite make up with its vast quantity for its sparse melodiousness . . ."

Tour

Hanna Theatre, Cleveland, October 11, 1926—Shubert Theatre, Boston, January 1, 1927 (5 cities).

Selected Revivals

St. Louis Municipal Opera, August 14-20, 1939
Nancy McCord (ANIUTA); Lansing Hatfield (VOLODYA); Robert Chisholm (KONSTANTIN); Lester Allen (BORIS); Valya Valentinoff (PREMIER DANCER).

St. Louis Municipal Opera, June 22-28, 1942
Marthe Errolle (ANIUTA); Wilbur Evans (VOLODYA); Bob Lawrence (KONSTANTIN); Teddy Hart (BORIS); Patricia Bowman (NADYA).

SONG OF THE FLAME

(Film Version—1930)

A First National Picture
Directed by Alan Crosland
Screenplay by Gordon Rigby
Choreography by Jack Haskell
Music director, Leo Forbstein
Photographed by Lee Garmes
Color by Technicolor

Release Date

May 6, 1930

The Cast

PRINCE VOLODYA, Alexander Gray
ANIUTA ("THE FLAME"), Bernice Claire
NATASHA, Alice Gentle
KONSTANTIN, Noah Beery
NADYA, Bernice Gray
COUNT BORIS, Bert Roach
GRUSHA, Inez Courtney
ALEXIS, Shep Camp
OLGA, Janina Smolinska

Musical Numbers

Songs retained from original production: *Song of the Flame* and *The Cossack Love Song*. Songs written specially for film by Harry Akst and Grant Clarke: *Liberty Song, One Little Drink, Petrograd, Passing Fancy,* and *The Goose Hangs High*.

Reviews

Mordaunt Hall—*New York Times*
"Melody saves the day . . . so far as the story is concerned, it is, with all its implausible romanticism, no worse than the tales of most musical offerings. In fact, it is less exasperating, for the songs come often and one can smile at the melodramatic action . . ."

Sime Silverman—*Variety*, May 14, 1930
". . . a very well produced romantic programmer that should hold up to average grosses in the deluxers and elsewhere . . ."

Time, May 19, 1930
". . . elaborate staging, good tunes and five thousand voices . . . extravagantly unreal, entirely out of the tradition of natural cinema . . ."

Richard Dana Skinner—*Commonweal*, May 28, 1930
". . . runs a close second to *The Vagabond King* in general excellence . . . a stirring picture . . . a purely romantic but thoroughly acceptable tale in which the musical numbers are introduced logically enough to keep the unities . . ."

Harry Evans—*Life*, June 6, 1930
". . . in transferring it to the screen the charm of the piece has been lost . . ."

Pare Lorentz—*Judge*, June 7, 1930
". . . one of those frozen operettas in which six or seven thousand people, all but obscured by a smear of color, stand around and sing until a hero and heroine fall into a last embrace . . ."

THE WILD ROSE

(1926)

A musical play with book and lyrics by Otto Harbach and Oscar Hammerstein II; music by Rudolf Friml.

Presented by Arthur Hammerstein
Directed by William J. Wilson
Choreography by Busby Berkeley
Settings by Joseph Urban
Costumes by Mark Mooring
Music director, Herbert Stothart

Tryout
Playhouse, Wilmington. September 16-18, 1926
Forrest Theatre, Philadelphia, September 20-October 9, 1926

New York Run
Martin Beck Theatre, October 20-December 11, 1926
61 performances

The Story
Monty Travers, an American traveler in Europe, falls in love with Princess Elise of Borovina, just as her father, King Augustus III, is overthrown. Monty is imprisoned by the usurpers but the princess wins his release by promising to marry the leader of the rebellion. After the army is brought back into the services of the king, the kingdom is restored and the lovers reunited.

The Cast
BARON FREDERICK, Joseph Macaulay
GEN. HODENBERG, Len Mence
MONTY TRAVERS, Joseph Santley
BUDDY HAINES, Gus Shy
LUELLA HOLTZ, Inez Courtney
GIDEON HOLTZ, William Collier
COUNTESS NITA, Nana Bryant
KING AUGUSTUS III, Fuller Mellish
PRINCESS ELISE, Desiree Ellinger
CARL, Jerome Daley

PETER, Neil Stone
ZEPPO, Dink Trout
FLOWER VENDOR, George Djimos
DANCERS, The Randalls
STREET ENTERTAINERS, Pasquali Brothers
LADIES OF THE ENSEMBLE: Jeanne LaMont, Marguerite Wyatt, Rachel Chester, Natalie Manning, Katherine Sacker, Anne Austin, Ann Constance, Lotta Faning, Mary Paige, Lydia Shields, Mary Carney, Mary Harrison, Doris May, Elinore Heinemann, Mildred Brower, Polly Ray, Bobby Campbell, Sylvia Pagano, Ruth Sato, Helene McGlynn, May Boyle, Cora Andrews, Bella Graf, Eve Sinclair, Josephine Paretto, Bettye Holmes, Ethel Allen, Gene Hitch, Claire Davis, Frances Grace, Dorothy Forbes, Mabel Martin, Madeleine Montelin, Patricia Ross, Mae Burke, Guerida Crawford
GENTLEMEN OF THE ENSEMBLE: Frank Chapman, John Fredericks, Boris Milman, Arthur Milens, Zachary Marr, Benn Carswell, Michael Afanasief, James Esipoff, Michael Miroshnik, John Krivokosenke, Leon Kartavy, Josef Zitrinik, George Fisher, Anatole Safanov, Eugene Gnotow, Morris Tepper, George Magis, Joseph Gary, Waevolod Anisimo, Jack Danziger, David Kladkoff, Philemon Zivaly, Orlando DeSalas, Dan Harris, Donald Robert, Clifford Stone, Charles Frye, Lawrence Arcuri, Richard Neely, Joseph Rogers

NOTE: Mr. Collier assumed role of GIDEON HOLTZ within 24 hours, after Lew Fields, who had played the part during tryout, was taken ill.

Musical Numbers

ACT I

SCENE ONE—OUTSIDE THE CASINO AT MONTE CARLO
Riviera, FREDERICK and ENSEMBLE; danced by the Randalls
Lovely Lady, MONTY and CHORUS

SCENE TWO—OUTSIDE A TAVERN IN BOROVINA

SCENE THREE—A CORNER OF THE TAVERN
Brown Eyes, MONTY, LUELLA, BUDDY and CHORUS
Love Me, Don't You?, NITA, HOLTZ and GIRLS

SCENE FOUR—OUTSIDE THE TAVERN
It Was Fate, ELISE and CHORUS
Wild Rose, ELISE, FREDERICK and MALE CHORUS
Lady of the Rose, ELISE, FREDERICK and MALE CHORUS

SCENE FIVE—A GARDEN WALL
L'heure d'or (One Golden Hour) (French lyric by J. B. Kantor), ELISE and MONTY
Finaletto, *One Golden Hour,* NITA, FREDERICK, MONTY and ENSEMBLE

SCENE SIX—GARDEN OF THE KING'S PALACE
Reprise, *Lady of the Rose,* MALE CHORUS
Finale, COMPANY

ACT II
SCENE ONE—THE STUDY IN KING AUGUSTUS' PALACE
Opening, AUGUSTUS, CARL and MALE CHORUS
We'll Have a Kingdom, ELISE and MONTY

SCENE TWO—COURTYARD OF THE PALACE
Revolution Festival, STREET ENTERTAINERS

SCENE THREE—THE FRONTIER
Dramatico—Musical scene

SCENE FOUR—THRONE ROOM OF THE KING'S PALACE
Won't You Come Across?, BUDDY and LUELLA
The Coronation, ELISE, FREDERICK and ENSEMBLE
Finale, COMPANY

NOTE: *I'm the Extra Man, How Can You Keep Your Mind on Business?, Rumble, Rumble, Rumble* and *That's Why I Love You* cut before New York opening.

Reviews

J. Brooks Atkinson—*New York Times*
". . . spirited and charming, produced with the glamorous beauty of a work of art . . . The key song, *Wild Rose,* lovely and imaginative, summons the best qualities of Miss Ellinger's voice . . . Like many excellent musical plays, it does not pack its book with humor . . ."

Ward Morehouse—*New York Herald Tribune*
". . . a well sung, handsomely mounted specimen of the prince-and-princess school of musical comedy, or even operetta. It has moments of rare quality . . . Some of the music is singularly rich . . . *Lady of the Rose,* for instance. The book can be described as 'pretty good,' though reminiscent . . ."

Jeffrey Holmesdale, Earl of Amherst—*New York World*
". . . a stately affair on a large scale . . . Also on a large scale is the complicated story . . . The plot bobs up so often it threatens to smother all else . . . A score that lacks any big tune but is graceful and musicianly at all times and never once resorts to a blue jazz note . . ."

Burns Mantle—*New York Daily News*
". . . has spirit, romance and color . . . in all ways typical of the good taste and opulent decoration that are Arthur Hammerstein's trademarks . . . Neither score nor book has the novelty of *Rose-Marie,* but they are well above the average . . ."

Alan Dale—*New York American*
". . . Friml has not achieved any of those twinkling gems that he used to perpetrate . . . a nice, warm and opulent production. There are no superfluities, and although very long, it is never draggy . . . On the whole, a creditable entertainment, unsensational but cheerful."

E. W. Osborn—*New York Evening World*
". . . rose to, and at some of its moments, even above our fondest expectations. And if we lay a large portion of the credit to Friml, it is not to be supposed for an instant that we are slighting or forgetting the principals, the chorus, the almost overwhelming scenic effects or the colorful splendor of the costumes . . ."

Richard Lockridge—*New York Sun*
". . . very pleasant music . . . it is not a production filled particularly with surprise . . . But if it fails altogether short of distinction, it has its happy moments . . . safe, sane and amiable . . ."

Abel Green—*Variety,* October 27, 1926
". . . no *Rose-Marie, Wildflower* or *Vagabond King* . . . The music in toto shapes up as a let-down . . . will linger for a few months . . . The libretto is shy . . . Friml's score seems barren of any real hit material . . . *Brown Eyes* and *L'Heure d'Or* are possibilities . . ."

Charles Brackett—*The New Yorker,* October 30, 1926
". . . Its book isn't particularly objectionable, or maybe, I've just grown so callous to royal musical comedies that things don't hurt me anymore and the only arrestingly bad part of the whole thing is the words of its songs . . . I'm admitting, in a grumpy way, that I rather liked it."

Wells Root—*Time,* November 8, 1926
". . . floats along on Friml's melodies to merited success. *Wild Rose* and *We'll Have a Kingdom* especially, belong at the top of the day's popular music . . . Thin comedy . . ."

George Jean Nathan—*Judge,* November 20, 1926
"The Friml tunes are the best things in it . . . The libretto is the conventional one in which Douglas Fairbanks invades the Kingdom of Eswarnicht, pulls the whiskers of the Prime Minister, swings up a ropevine to the fair Princess' balcony and bestows a smack upon the proud beauty's lip rouge, swings down again and kicks the chief revolutionist in the rear, and winds up leading the regal flapper to the altar . . ."

Arthur Hornblow—*Theatre Magazine,* January, 1927
". . . The book . . . even though the theme be old—is romantic with an element of humor that is really fresh and funny. Its score has a fine succession of melodies interspersed with numbers almost grand operatic in composition. It has a cast that can both act and sing, and the production for the richness of appeal, would be difficult to excel . . ."

THE DESERT SONG

(1926)

A musical play with book by Otto Harbach, Oscar Hammerstein II and Frank Mandel; music by Sigmund Romberg; lyrics by Messrs. Harbach and Hammerstein.

Presented by Laurence Schwab and Frank Mandel
Directed by Arthur Hurley
Choreography by Bobby Connolly
Settings by Woodman Thompson
Costumes by Vyvyan Donner and Mark Mooring
Music director, Oscar Bradley

Tryout

(known as "Lady Fair")
Playhouse, Wilmington, October 21-23, 1926
Poli's Theatre, Washington, October 25-30, 1926
Shubert Theatre, New Haven, November 1-6, 1926
Shubert Theatre, Boston, November 8-27, 1926

New York Run

Casino Theatre, November 30, 1926-October 8, 1927
Century Theatre, October 10-31, 1927
Imperial Theatre, November 2, 1927-January 7, 1928
471 performances

The Story

Unknown to anyone, Pierre Birabeau, son of the French governor of a Moroccan province, is also the "Red Shadow," leader of the native Riff tribes. When Margot Bonvalet arrives from Paris, Pierre, in disguise, makes love to her and abducts her to the retreat of Ali Ben Ali. After the French forces are captured by the Riffs, Pierre refuses to fight a duel with his father and is banished by his men for this seemingly cowardly behavior. Carrying the clothes and mask of the "Red Shadow," he returns to French headquarters where he is hailed as a hero for having killed the outlaw.

The Cast

SID EL KAR, *The Red Shadow's lieutenant,* William O'Neal
MINDAR, O. J. Vanesse
HASSI, Earle Mitchell
BENNIE KIDD, *society correspondent for the Paris Herald,* Eddie Buzzell
CAPT. PAUL FONTAINE, Glen Dale
AZURI, Pearl Regay
SGT. LA VERGNE, Charles Davis
SGT. DUBASSAC, Albert Baron
MARGOT BONVALET, Vivienne Segal
GEN. BIRABEAU, *Governor of a French Moroccan Province,* Edmund Elton
PIERRE BIRABEAU, *his son,* Robert Halliday
SUSAN, *his ward,* Nellie Breen
ETHEL, Elmira Lane
ALI BEN ALI, *Caid of a Riff tribe,* Lyle Evans
CLEMENTINA, *a Spanish "Lady,"* Margaret Irving
NERI, Rachel May Clark
HADJI, Charles Morgan
SERVANTS OF GEN. BIRABEAU, Victor Rosales, B. Flack
FRENCH GIRLS; SPANISH CABARET GIRLS: Maude Lydiate, Marion Case, Audree Van Lieu, Grace Fleming, Bobbe Decker, Winifred Seale, Blanche Granby, June Lovewell, Betty Lomax, Valeri Petrie, Bernice Walder, Gertrude Napp, Betty De Fest, Mildred Mann, Helen Shepard, Ethel Lorraine, Beatrice Fox, Gladys Lake, Edna Coates
SOLDIERS' WIVES; LADIES OF THE BRASS KEY: Helen Bourne, Gertrude McKinley, Eileen Hargraves, Kathlyn Huss, Elmira Lane, Tatiana, Rowena Scott, Patricia O'Connell, Clementine Rigeau, Almajane Wilday, Florence Baker, Miriam Stockton, Hilda Steiner, Robey Lyle, Betty Holmes, Dorothy Lee
SOLDIERS OF THE FRENCH LEGION; MEMBERS OF THE RED SHADOW'S BAND: Alan Green, Jack Kiernan, John Lister, B. Flack, Nathan Goodman, E. A. Harker, Peter Flomp, Raymond Winfield, John Stanley, Jack Edwards, Armond King, John Daly, Jack Spiegel, William D. Galpen, Charles Davis, John Hammond, William Ehlers, C. Pichler, Morton Croswell, Vance Elliott, Charles Mantia, Talbott Vaughn, George St. John, Z. Norman, Harold Westcott, Victor Rosales, Morris Siegel, Albert Coiner, Elmer Pichler, Nat Broffman, Phil Snyder
NATIVE DANCERS: Grace Fleming, Bobbe Decker, Winifred Seale, Blanche Granby, June Lovewell, Gertrude Napp, Mildred Mann
SOLDIERS OF ALI: Jack Kierman, E. A. Harker, John Daly, Jack Spiegel, Charles Mantia, Phil Snyder

NOTE: During tryout, MARGOT played by Mildred Parisette. Miss Segal succeeded by Charlotte Lansing (June 1927) and Ethel Louise Wright (August 1927). From June to August 1927, Mr. Halliday temporarily replaced by Alexander Gray, and in November 1927, Mr. Halliday succeeded by Leonard Ceeley. From June to September 1927, Mr. Buzzell temporarily replaced by Bobby Jarvis. In August 1927, Miss Lane succeeded by Katherine Carrington, Mr. O'Neal by Harold Stanton.

Musical Numbers

The action takes place in North Africa.

ACT I

SCENE ONE—RETREAT OF THE RED SHADOW IN THE RIFF MOUNTAINS
Opening, *High On a Hill,* SID and RIFFS
Ho! (The Riff Song), RED SHADOW, SID and RIFFS
Margot, PAUL and SOLDIERS

SCENE TWO—GARDEN OF GENERAL BIRABEAU'S HOME
I'll Be a Buoyant Girl, SUSAN

SCENE THREE—DRAWING ROOM OF GENERAL BIRABEAU'S HOME
Why Did We Marry Soldiers?, SOLDIERS' WIVES
French Military Marching Song, MARGOT and ENSEMBLE
Romance, MARGOT and SOLDIERS' WIVES
Then You Will Know, PIERRE and MARGOT
I Want a Kiss, PAUL, MARGOT, PIERRE and ENSEMBLE
It, BENNIE, SUSAN and GIRLS
The Desert Song, RED SHADOW and MARGOT
Finale, COMPANY

ACT II

SCENE ONE—THE GREAT HALL IN ALI BEN ALI'S RETREAT
Opening, *My Little Castagnette,* CLEMENTINA and GIRLS
Song of the Brass Key, CLEMENTINA and GIRLS
One Good Man Gone Wrong, BENNIE and CLEMENTINA
Eastern and Western Love
  Let Love Go, ALI and MEN
  One Flower Grows Alone in Your Garden, SID and MEN
  One Alone, RED SHADOW and MEN

SCENE TWO—A CORRIDOR

SCENE THREE—ROOM OF THE SILKEN COUCH
The Sabre Song, MARGOT
Finaletto, PIERRE, MARGOT and GENERAL BIRABEAU

SCENE FOUR—EDGE OF THE DESERT
Farewell, RED SHADOW and RIFFS

SCENE FIVE—COURTYARD OF GENERAL BIRABEAU'S HOME
Opening, *All Hail to the General,* MARGOT, PAUL, GENERAL BIRABEAU and GIRLS
Let's Have a Love Affair, BENNIE, SUSAN and GIRLS
Dance, AZURI
Finale, COMPANY

NOTE: *Love's Dear Yearning* (also called *Dreaming in Paradise), Not for Him, Ali-Up* and *Love Is a Two-Edged Sword* cut before New York opening. *Let's Have a Love Affair* dropped in January, 1927, in favor of a reprise of *It.*

Reviews

New York Times

". . . floridly contrived and executed in the grand, unstinting manner of the more affluent impresarios, but by sheer weight possibly, it seems to be a little more important than the books of several kindred entertainments . . . Two of the outstanding features were the excellent and sometimes rather imposing score, and the stirring and resonant male chorus . . . a large, slightly topheavy entertainment, providing full value for your money . . ."

Richard Watts, Jr.—*New York Herald Tribune*

"The question of how simple-minded the book of a musical comedy can be was debated last night, and the verdict arrived at was 'no end' . . . lavish, ornate, colorful and costly . . . a score that, though never violently original nor strikingly distinguished, yet manages to be generally tuneful and attractive—in fact it always has been . . . I am perhaps ungrateful in regretting that, with the exception of one song called *It,* the lyrics gave indication that W.S. Gilbert lived and died in vain."

Jeffrey Holmesdale, Earl of Amherst—*New York World*

"Full scale operetta done as it should be done . . . equals if not surpasses *The Vagabond King* . . . the main factor was the score. Nearly all the numbers were good . . . *Ho!* was the best in the show . . . The comedy was very much on the weak side . . ."

New York American

". . . the 'book' is its weakest point, and even that may 'draw,' for it appeals to those who like silly, sheikish stories, with a dashing He pursuing a shrinking She . . . music of a 'superior' quality. Although some of it sounds like 'left-overs' from *The Student Prince* there are one or two numbers that are delightful . . ."

Burns Mantle—*New York Daily News*

". . . handsomely staged, a generously and wisely cast operetta that has all the virtues of the best of its kind . . ."

Walter Winchell—*New York Graphic*

". . . one of the treats of the town. A tuneful, gay and lavishly upholstered entertainment . . ."

Bide Dudley—*New York Evening World*

". . . much vitality, both in its romantic story and in its music. In addition, it is cast excellently . . . there are melodies stirring and others sweetly haunting . . . The book teems with heroics, carefully handled however . . . a big, red-blooded musical treat . . ."

Frank Vreeland—*New York Telegram*
". . . color, swing, glamor . . . I can't remember to have seen a better trained nor more capable chorus . . . Romberg has never composed anything better . . ."

New York Sun
". . . The credit goes to the composer and librettists and their worthy assistants working together to produce color, rhythm, good dramatic values, and true singing choruses . . . The songs gave little promise of general appeal as played in free or ballad rhythm, but *One Alone* and *I Want a Kiss* may yet become time-worn . . . Pageantry, romance, ringing music, vitality and humor—that's *The Desert Song*. What more do you want?"

Sid Silverman (Skig.)—*Variety,* December 8, 1926
". . . the strength of the show is in its battery of male voices, not the music, production or cast . . . a pretty fair yarn . . . Romberg's music sounds as being too involved to ever be whistled by the populace at large . . . It is picturesque and has something beside the usual hokus-pokus story to tell. It may catch that all important word-of-mouth heralding and should run."

Charles Brackett—*The New Yorker,* December 11, 1926
". . . a great, roaring, splendid musical show . . . The music is Romberg's best, and in the book it seemed to me that the sheik plot has found at last its really happy medium . . ."

Wells Root—*Time,* December 13, 1926
". . . a huge cast, gorgeous settings, some good singing and Vivienne Segal make it alluring, but the sands of Broadway do not burn."

Robert Benchley—*Life,* December 16, 1926
". . . Miss Segal sings some nice songs very prettily and a fine, strong male chorus booms out occasionally, with the result that the audience gets a very good evening for its money."

George Jean Nathan—*Judge,* December 25, 1926
". . . no less than three good melodies . . . it is well sung by Vivienne Segal and Robert Halliday; it has some good low humor; and it is nicely put on. Its libretto is a dud. But there is enough in it otherwise to give you a pleasant theatrical evening."

Arthur Hornblow—*Theatre Magazine,* February, 1927
". . . a success both as to artistic and popular appeal . . . the music is nearly always stirring. The story, more or less romantic, is perhaps a little too complicated in its sheikish incidents . . ."

Tour
Teck Theatre, Buffalo, January 9, 1928—Shubert Theatre, Philadelphia, May 19, 1928 (9 cities).

THE DESERT SONG

(Touring Company—1927)

Music director, Sig Saunders

The Cast
BENJAMIN KIDD (BENNIE), Bernard Granville
AZURI, Lucille Middleton
MARGOT BONVALET, Charlotte Lansing
PIERRE BIRABEAU, John Ehry
SUSAN, Betty Gallagher

NOTE: During tour, Mr. Ehry succeeded by Alexander Gray, Miss Lansing by Bernice Claire. A second company began its tour in 1928.

Tours
Hanna Theatre, Cleveland, August 21, 1927—English Theatre, Indianapolis, December 29, 1928 (14 cities).
Majestic Theatre, Chicago, December 17, 1928—Maryland Theatre, Baltimore, May 11, 1929 (20 cities).

Selected Revivals
St. Louis Municipal Opera, August 9-14, 1933
Leonard Ceeley (PIERRE); Marion Claire (MARGOT); Jack Sheehan (BENNIE); Allan Jones (SID); Nancy McCord (AZURI).

St. Louis Municipal Opera, August 5-11, 1935
Robert Halliday (PIERRE); Ruby Mercer (MARGOT); Bobby Jarvis (BENNIE); Audrey Christie (SUSAN); Odette Myrtil (CLEMENTINA).

Los Angeles Civic Light Opera, May 15-20, 1939
San Francisco Civic Light Opera, May 22-27, 1939
Allan Jones (PIERRE); Margaret Carlisle (MARGOT); Sterling Holloway (BENNIE).

Dallas State Fair, July 31-August 5, 1941
Alexander Gray (PIERRE); Bernice Claire (MARGOT); Jack Goode (BENNIE).

Los Angeles Civic Light Opera, April 30-May 19, 1945
San Francisco Civic Light Opera, May 21-June 9, 1945
Walter Cassel (PIERRE); Dorothy Sarnoff (MARGOT); Sterling Holloway (BENNIE); Clarissa (AZURI); George Burnson (George London) (ALI).

Tour: September 17, 1945 (San Diego)-May 11, 1946 (New Orleans). NOTE: During tour, Miss Sarnoff was succeeded by Dorothy Sandlin, Mr. Cassel by Harry Stockwell, Mr. Holloway by Jack Goode.

Greek Theatre, Los Angeles, Summer, 1947
Brian Sullivan (PIERRE); Andzia Kuzak (MARGOT); Pinky Lee (BENNIE).

Dallas State Fair, August 7-19, 1950
Wilbur Evans (PIERRE); Doretta Morrow (MARGOT); Billy Gilbert (BENNIE).

Iroquois Amphitheatre, Louisville, August 1, 1955
Edward Roecker (PIERRE); Jean Fenn (MARGOT); Benny Baker (BENNIE); Michael Kermoyan (ALI).

St. Louis Municipal Opera, July 4-10, 1960
Stephen Douglass (PIERRE); Elaine Malbin (MARGOT); Will B. Able (BENNIE).

Academy of Music, Philadelphia, June 12-17, 1973
David Cryer (PIERRE); Chris Callan (MARGOT); Jerry Dodge (BENNIE); Michael Kermoyan (ALI); Britt Swanson (SUSAN); Stanley Grover (PAUL); Shepperd Strudwick (BIRABEAU). NOTE: This company also played Baltimore, Chicago, Washington (Kennedy Center), and New York (Uris Theatre), where it ended its tour September 16, 1973.

Television Production

NBC Network, May 7, 1955
Produced and directed by Max Liebman; adaptation by William Friedberg, Neil Simon, Will Glickman; book directed by Milton Lyon; choreography by Rod Alexander; music director, Charles Sanford; sponsored by Oldsmobile. *Cast:* Nelson Eddy (PIERRE); Gale Sherwood (MARGOT); Otto Kruger (BIRABEAU); John Conte (PAUL); Bambi Linn and Rod Alexander (FEATURED DANCERS); Salvatore Baccaloni (ALI); Viola Essen (AZURI).

Productions Abroad

Theatre Royal, Drury Lane, London, April 7, 1927-April 14, 1928
(See page 335)

Alhambra Theatre, London, June 8, 1931
Directed by Harry Winton. *Cast:* Alec Fraser (PIERRE); Sylvia Welling (MARGOT); John E. Coyle (BENNIE); Sidney Pointer (SID); Barry Mackay (PAUL); Elsa Palmer (SUSAN); Ruby Morriss (AZURI); Dennis Hoey (ALI).

Coliseum, London, September 24-December 12, 1936; *146 performances*
Presented and directed by Lee Ephraim. *Cast:* Harry Welchman (PIERRE); Edith Day (MARGOT); Frederic Bentley (BENNIE); Sidney Pointer (SID); Walter Bird (PAUL); Clarice Hardwicke (SUSAN).

His Majesty's Theatre, Sydney, Australia, December 5, 1937
Robert Halliday (PIERRE); Margaret Adams (MARGOT); Don Nicol (BENNIE); Marjorie Gordon (SUSAN).

Garrick Theatre, London, June 29, 1939
Directed by Frederick G. Lloyd. *Cast:* Bruce Carfax (PIERRE); Doris Francis (MARGOT); Alexander Cameron (BENNIE); Warwick Ashton (PAUL); Phyllis Bourke (SUSAN).

Prince of Wales Theatre, London, January 16, 1943
Harry Welchman (PIERRE); Eleanor Fayre (MARGOT); Frederic Bentley (BENNIE); Sidney Pointer (SID); Victor Standing (PAUL); Helen Barnes (SUSAN); Arthur Wontner (BIRABEAU).

Her Majesty's Theatre, Sydney, Australia, April 21, 1962
Presented by J.C. Williamson Theatres Ltd.; directed by Cid Ellwood; choreography by William Carse. *Cast:* John Larsen (PIERRE); Deidree Thurlow (MARGOT); Ernie Bourne (BENNIE); John Sanger (PAUL); Eileen Hattam (SUSAN); Chin Yu (AZURI).

Palace Theatre, London, May 13, 1967; *383 performances*
Presented by John Hanson; directed by Joan Davis; choreography by Virginia Courtney. *Cast:* John Hanson (PIERRE); Patricia Michael (MARGOT); Tony Hughes (BENNIE); Doreen Kay (SUSAN); Lita Scott (AZURI).

THE DESERT SONG

(London—1927)

Presented by Sir Alfred Butt
in conjunction with Lee Ephraim
Directed by Laurence Schwab
Choreography by Bobby Connolly
Settings by Joseph and Phil Harker
Costumes by Robert E. Groves
Music director, Herman Finck
Opening night conductor, Mr. Romberg

London Run

Theatre Royal, Drury Lane, April 7, 1927-April 14, 1928
432 performances

The Cast

SID EL KAR, Sidney Pointer
MINDAR, Edgar Pierce
HASSI, Clifford Heatherley
BENNIE KIDD, Gene Gerrard
CAPT. PAUL FONTAINE, Barry Mackaye
AZURI, Phebe Brune
LT. LAVERGNE, Alfred Atkins

SGT. DUBASSAC, Gordon Crocker
MARGOT BONVALET, Edith Day
GEN. BIRABEAU, Leonard Mackaye
PIERRE BIRABEAU, Harry Welchman
SUSAN, Clarice Hardwicke
ALI BEN ALI, Dennis Hoey
CLEMENTINA, Maria Minetti
NERI, Ruby Morriss
HADJI, Caton Woodville
FRENCH GIRLS; SPANISH CABARET GIRLS; SOLDIERS' WIVES: Aybil Allnatt, Pat Andrews, Betty Bailey, Jean Barnes, Margaret Boyle, Madeline Bray, Millicent Cane, April Clare, Anne Crecy, Tina Dakyn, Norah Edwards, Nancy Eshelby, Dorothy Eyre, Heather Featherstone, Kathleen Fitchie, Lena Fitchie, Nan Forster, Roma Forster, Helene Francois, Pauline Gilmer, Stephanie Insull, Mavis Kalmar, Elsie Lawrence, Joan Layton, Linda Lindose, Nance Miriam, Maureen Moore, Mynette Morven, Phyllis Neal, Inez O'Connor, Esme Oxley, Marjorie Poncia, Paula Reed, Sybil Rhoda, Marjorie Robertson (Anna Neagle), Noranne Rose, Eileen Scott, Eunice Vickridge, Rosalind Wade, Veda Wardman, Lola Waring, Margaret Watson
NATIVE DANCERS: April Clare, Kathleen Fitchie, Lena Fitchie, Esme Oxley, Marjorie Robertson (Anna Neagle), Noranne Rose, Eunice Vickridge, Anne Crecy
SOLDIERS OF THE FRENCH LEGION; MEMBERS OF THE RED SHADOW'S BAND: Jack Allen, Reginald Austen, Edward Barrie, Richard Bodley, Hayden Campbell, Richard Crawford, Geoffrey Davies, Cecil Dereham, Walter Farrance, Reginald Gibson, Frank Grant, Victor Hamel, Alvon Hawke, Hal Hatswell, William Herbert, Felix Hill, Eric Hidges, Evan John, Cliff Jones, Donald Kingston, Ernest Ludlow, Grant Maclean, Fred Maguire, Berand Marais, Selwyn Morgan, Fred Rickett, Joseph Robinson, Kilmore Scott, Geoffrey Startin, Harry Stevenson, Scott Thompson, Edgar Villiers, Wilfred Ward
SOLDIERS OF ALI: Richard Bodley, Reginald Gibson, Victor Hamel, Hal Hatswell, Selwyn Morgan, Harry Stevenson, Edgar Villiers, Wilfred Ward

NOTE: During run, Mr. Welchman succeeded by Howett Worster.

Musical Numbers

Same as original production

Reviews

London Times

". . . It is, for a musical play, a lively story and it is not poor in opportunities for romantic colour. But when all is said and done, it is the massed dancing that remains the chief pleasure of this delightful evening . . ."

London Daily Mail
". . . at least as good as *Rose-Marie* in every way . . ."

London Daily News
". . . the music is certainly above the average of musical comedy . . . a preposterous story . . ."

James Agate—*London Sunday Times,* April 10, 1927
"It would be stupid to say that *The Desert Song* is not a good show. It is a very good show which caters with genius and the single mind with everything that the big public is known to demand and, on receiving, to applaud to the echo . . . If anyone suggests that all this is nonsense, there is only one answer. Of course, it's nonsense, like any voluntary abdication of the mind. Nonsense is the virtue here . . . the masculine members of the chorus put on a soldierly parade worthy of Wellington Barracks and sing in a manner to entrap the birds of Birdcage Walk."

Horace Horsnell—*London Observer,* April 10, 1927
". . . Everything set the audience cheering. The only thing I am sure they didn't applaud is myself. Throughout the evening, despite the loin-stirring rhythms and the full-throated choruses, it was a toss-up whether more cheerful noise was made on our side of the footlight or the other . . . The production was an expert display of familiar talents rather than a knockdown work of art . . . The music—a melodic tide that swept everything before it and swamped even the entracte gossip in the corridors—was tireless without being tiresome . . ."

The Stage
". . . built largely on the same lines as *Rose-Marie* . . . The music is generally flowing and melodious, and in it one may forgive reminiscent tendencies on account of the absence of jazz . . ."

The Era
". . . In most respects it is better than *Rose-Marie.* It has a book that holds the play together more satisfactorily, the comedy is more amusing . . . exceedingly melodious and graceful . . ."

S.T.H.—*Theatre World,* May, 1927
". . . magnificent spectacular entertainment which calls more for the warmest whole-hearted praise than for criticism. Romberg's music is of unusually high quality, if one judges by the ordinary musical-play standards. Apart from such obviously melodious tunes as *Ho!, It,* and *The Desert Song,* the whole of the score is distinguished . . ."

Bibliography

"The Desert Song" —*The Sketch,* April 27, 1927

"The Desert Song" (cover story) —*The Play Pictorial,* July, 1927

THE DESERT SONG

(Film Version—1929)

A Warner Brothers-Vitaphone Picture
Directed by Roy Del Ruth
Screenplay by Harvey H. Gates
Music director, Ernest G. Grooney
Photographed by Bernard McGill

Release Date
May 1, 1929

The Cast
PIERRE BIRABEAU, John Boles
MARGOT BONVALET, Carlotta King
SUSAN, Louise Fazenda
BENJAMIN KIDD, Johnny Arthur
CAPT. PAUL FONTAINE, John Miljan
AZURI, Myrna Loy
GEN. BIRABEAU, Edward Martindel

Musical Numbers
Songs retained from original production: *Ho! (The Riff Song), French Military Marching Song, Romance, Then You Will Know, It, The Desert Song, One Flower Grows Alone In Your Garden, One Alone, The Sabre Song,* and *Farewell.*

Reviews
Mordaunt Hall—*New York Times*
". . . an interesting experiment, but one wherein the story even allowing for the peculiar license necessary for such offerings, lays itself open to chuckles rather than sympathy or concern . . ."

Thornton Delehanty—*New York Post*
"Under the merciless eye and ear of the listening camera, the pretty little conventions—the infantile plot, the stilted acting and the chartless continuity which we have tacitly come to expect in the American musical comedy—were revealed and magnified to painful proportions on the screen . . . some very pleasant songs and some well-sung male choruses."

Arthur Unger—*Variety,* April 10, 1929
". . . another boxoffice winner . . . the music may be more entrancing and seductive from the boxoffice angle than the acting . . . a number of gorgeous scenes in which chanting was the principal ingredient . . ."

John Mosher—*The New Yorker,* May 11, 1929
". . . the first musical comedy moved in toto—or thereabouts—to the screen, and does not indicate that the idea is especially successful. The songs are pleasant enough, but the libretto seems to obtrude itself more aggressively than it does on the stage . . ."

Harry Evans—*Life,* May 24, 1929
". . . excellent photography . . . Myrna Loy deserves commendation for her work in a difficult part . . . not consistently entertaining, but it is certainly a commendable maiden effort in a new field . . ."

THE DESERT SONG

(Film Version—1943)

A Warner Brothers Picture
Produced by Robert Buckner
Directed by Robert Florey
Screenplay by Mr. Buckner
Choreography by LeRoy Prinz
Art director, Charles Novi
Music director, Leo Forbstein
Orchestrations by Ray Heindorf
Musical adaptation by H. Roemheld
Photographed by Bert Glennon
Color by Technicolor

Release Date
December 17, 1943

The Story
The Nazis are trying to build a railroad from Dakar to the coast of North Africa, using Riff laborers impressed by the local French authorities. Led by El Khobar (really Paul Hudson, an American café singer-pianist), the natives rebel and foil the plans.

The Cast
PAUL HUDSON (EL KHOBAR), Dennis Morgan
MARGOT, Irene Manning

CAPTAIN FONTAINE, Bruce Cabot
CAID YOUSSEFF, Victor Francen
JOHNNY WALSH, Lynne Overman
BENOIT, Gene Lockhart
HAJY, Faye Emerson
TARBOUGH, Marcel Dalio
HEINTZELMAN, Felix Basch
HAASAN, Gerald Mohr
ABDEL RAHMAN, Noble Jonson
FRANCOIS, Curt Bois
MUHAMMED, Albert Morin
LIEUTENANT BERTIN, Jack LaRue
DANCER, Sylvia Operte

Musical Numbers
Songs retained from original production: *Ho! (The Riff Song), Romance, One Flower Grows Alone in Your Garden, One Alone, The Desert Song, French Military Marching Song*. Songs written for film: *Fifi's Song* (Sigmund Romberg-Jack Scholl); *Long Live the Night* (Romberg-Scholl-Mario Silva); *Gay Parisienne* (Serge Walter-Jack Scholl).

Reviews
Bosley Crowther—*New York Times*
". . . utterly fantastic . . . Somehow you feel a strange hiatus between the Nazi and a rousing chorus of *The Riff Song*. But otherwise this brash and gaudy picture is relaxing entertainment and spirited fun . . ."

Howard Barnes—*New York Herald Tribune*
". . . Warners has been content to shoot a desert horse opera and toss in musical interludes almost at random . . . The color is the best feature . . ."

Alton Cook—*New York World-Telegram*
". . . All in all, this is a much better version than you ever came across before . . ."

Walt Christie—*Variety*, December 15, 1943
". . . a combo of tuneful escapist entertainment that will catch strong box office reactions in all runs . . ."

David Lardner—*The New Yorker*, December 18, 1943
". . . pretty views of a great deal of sand. Mr. Overman as an American war correspondent, doesn't behave at all like Vincent Sheean."

James Agee—*Time,* January 10, 1944
". . . an amusingly archaic story . . . The one bit which heartily recommends it to a world at war is a sizzling dancer by name Sylvia Operte, who really hits the ouled-nail on the head."

THE DESERT SONG

(Film Version—1953)

A Warner Brothers Picture
Produced by Rudi Fehr
Directed by Bruch Humberstone
Screenplay by Roland Kibbee
Choreography by LeRoy Prinz
Art director, Stanley Fleischer
Costumes by Leah Rhodes, Marjorie Best
Music director, Ray Heindorf
Musical adaptation by Max Steiner
Photographed by Robert Burks
Editor, William Ziegler
Color by Technicolor

Release Date

May 20, 1953

The Cast

MARGOT, Kathryn Grayson
PAUL BONNARD, Gordon MacRae
CAPT. FONTAINE, Steven Cochran
YOUSSEFF, Raymond Massey
BENJY, Dick Wesson
AZURI, Allyn McLerie
GENERAL BIRABEAU, Ray Collins
HASSAN, Paul Picerni
MINDAR, Frank DeKova
LACHMED, William Conrad
NERI, Trevor Bardette
LT. DUVALLE, Mark Dana

Musical Numbers

Same as 1943 film version, with exception of *Fifi's Song,* which was dropped.

Reviews

Howard Thompson—*New York Times*
". . . a handsome, burnished Technicolor background to sandy rhapsodies which never sounded better . . . a wealth of slipshod absurdities. At this point, *The Desert Song* may be considered dying of thirst."

Paul V. Beckley—*New York Herald Tribune*
". . . bright and spirited . . . a pleasant package of romance and adventure for the warm weather."

Bill Brogdon—*Variety*, April 29, 1953
". . . has just about run out of entertainment vitamins . . . nothing to indicate a more than spotty boxoffice pace . . ."

Henry Bradford Darrach, Jr.—*Time*, May 25, 1953
". . . seems unable to make up its mind whether to play it straight or kid the whole thing. Even in this arid adaptation, however, its famed score keeps its melodic bloom."

Bibliography

With Dromedaries and Ditties on the Dunes by Carl Combes
—*New York Times*, June 8, 1952

GOLDEN DAWN

(1927)

A musical play with book and lyrics by Otto Harbach and Oscar Hammerstein II; music by Emmerich Kalman and Herbert Stothart.

Presented by Arthur Hammerstein
Directed by Reginald Hammerstein
Choreography by David Bennett
Settings by Joseph Urban
Costumes by Mark Mooring
Music director, Mr. Stothart

Tryout
Shubert Playhouse, Wilmington, September 22-24, 1927
Shubert Alvin Theatre, Pittsburgh, September 26-October 8, 1927
Detroit Opera House, October 10-22, 1927
Hanna Theatre, Cleveland, October 24-29, 1927
Shubert Theatre, Philadephia, November 14-26, 1927

New York Run
Hammerstein's Theatre, November 30, 1927-May 5, 1928
184 performances

The Story
Dawn, an English girl captured by an African tribe when she was a child, has been brought up by her native nurse, Mooda, to believe that she is the destined princess of the tribe. Thoughts of royal destiny, however, are interrupted by the appearance of Steve Allen, an escaped war prisoner of the Germans, who falls in love with Dawn. Despite efforts of Shep Keyes to keep Dawn in the tribe, she and Steven eventually escape.

The Cast
ANZAC, Archie Leach (Cary Grant)
DAGO, Carlo Benetti
PIGEON, Len Mence
MOODA, Marguerita Silva
HASMALI, Kurnar Ghoshal
CAPTAIN ERIC, Reginald Pasch

SISTER HEDWIG, Paula Ayers
SHEP KEYES, Robert Chisholm
STEVE ALLEN, Paul Gregory
BLINK JONES, Gil Squires
SIR ALFRED HAMMERSLEY, Olin Howland
DAWN, Louise Hunter
JOHANNA, Nydia d'Arnell
COLONEL JUDSON, W. Messenger Bellis
ANN MILFORD, Barbara Newberry
DR. MILFORD, Henry Pemberton
AN OLD MAN, Robert Paton Gibbs
A WITCH DANCER, Jacques Cartier
A DANCING GIRL, Princess Kohana
MOMBASSA MOLL, Hazel Drury
AN ENSEMBLE OF FRENCH, ENGLISH and ITALIAN PRISONERS, ASKARI GUARDS, GERMAN SOLDIERS, NATIVE MEN and WOMEN, WOMEN OF MOMBASSA, NURSES and SISTERS
LADIES OF THE ENSEMBLE: Wilma Roelof, Lucy Lawler, Irene Carroll, Peggy Messinger, Vivian Russell, Barbara Carrington, Hellene Counihan, Norine Bogen, Mimi Jordan, Bunny Schumm, Sorena Mumma, Frances Denny, Frances Dumas, Janet Hale, Leona Riggs, Jean Hitch, Leola Buelow, Grace LaRue, Mabel Olsen, LeVergne Evans, Alice Busee, Maud Carlton, Alva McGill, Norma France, Karol Kayne, Ann Anderson, Louise Baer, Marie Foster, Geraldine Gooding, Rosena Weston, Inez Clough, Geneva Grant, Julia F. Mitchell, Alma Reynolds, Maud White, Christine David, Mary Mason, Beneveneta Washington, Ruth Matson, Louise Turner, Elizabeth Holloway, Zina Ivanova, Klara Grosheva, Magda Trauberg, All Kisselava, Saloma Barton, Dora Grebenetsky, Maria Grushko, Valia Valentinova, Lida Ordynsky, Ann Ouzoroff, Helene Chaudaroff, Emilia Andrievska, Xenia Dalsky
GENTLEMEN OF THE ENSEMBLE: Tom Chadwick, Joseph Vitale, Milton Rae, Arnold Basil, Frank Dobert, Raymond Otto, Edward Watkins, Tom Rider, Irving Andrievsky, Vladimir Danieloff, Mikl Dalsky, Joseph Davidenko, Konstantine Smith, Alexander Ouzoroff, Leonard Gorlenko, Peter Ordunsky, Vsevolad Andrenoff, Peter Kosloff, Vladimir Chavdaroff, George Brant, Toni Klimovitch, F. J. Accoll, James Earl, William Walker, Harold DesVerney, Adolph Henderson, McKinley Reeves, William McFarland, H. Webster Elkins, W. Service Beel, Amos Guerrant, Earl Wilson, James Grey, Robert Jackson, Henry Brown
RUSSIAN ART CHOIR, directed by Alexander U. Fine

NOTE: Miss Hunter succeeded by Lucy Lord in February, 1928, and by Bonnie Emerie in April.

Musical Numbers

ACT I

SCENE ONE—MOODA'S CANTEEN NEAR A PRISON CAMP, GERMAN EAST AFRICA, 1917

SCENE TWO—TEMPLE CAVE
SCENE THREE—THE JUNGLE
SCENE FOUR—THE GERMAN PRISON STOCKADE
SCENE FIVE—THE TREE OF MULUNGHU

ACT II
SCENE ONE—MOODA'S CANTEEN, 1919
SCENE TWO—THE OLD STOCKADE
SCENE THREE—GENG LEE'S JOINT IN MOMBASSA
SCENE FOUR—TEMPLE CAVE
SCENE FIVE—GATE TO THE MISSION
SCENE SIX—GOLDEN DAWN

NOTE: The original program contained following information: "The musical numbers are an integral part of the story as it evolves; and therefore are not listed as independent songs." The titles of the principal themes are:
When I Crack My Whip, SHEP
We Two, JOHANNA and SIR ALFRED
Here in the Dark, DAWN, STEVE and SHEP
My Bwana, DAWN and CHORUS
Consolation, BLINK and ANN
Africa, ERIC and ENSEMBLE
Dawn (music by Robert Stolz and Herbert Stothart), DAWN and STEVE
Jungle Shadows, MOMBASSA MOLL
Mulunghu Thabu, HASMALI and CHORUS

Reviews

J. Brooks Atkinson—*New York Times*
". . . The singers alchemize *Golden Dawn* into a musical delight . . . If the drama seems artificial and rather more prolonged than necessary, the score and the singers make complete amends. The libretto deserts the hard-trodden paths of romance for a grim march . . . From the point of view of drama, it seems ponderous and mannered. From the point of view of music, it is uncommonly substantial . . ."

Percy Hammond—*New York Herald Tribune*
". . . a stately opera, swimming in luscious tunes, depicting unusual dramatic circumstances, and sung and acted by a superior group of artists . . . one of the best of its kind . . ."

Alison Smith—*New York World*
". . . has all the steady, reliable ingredients which made *Rose-Marie* a satisfactory financial venture . . . a conventional Broadway series of song hits . . . the most vivid memory is visual—the fateful, ominous Voodoo dance of Jacques Cartier . . ."

Burns Mantle—*New York Daily News*
". . . frequently striking . . . fairly pretentious . . . The score is full-bodied and melodious and the story commands some novelty of situation . . ."

Walter Winchell—*New York Graphic*
"*The Golden Yawn* . . . the most stupendous operatta ever attempted. It contains an abundance of gripping and tense entertainment and a fine cast . . . A rich show with fine music and good singing. But a second rate comedian would have been a welcome addition to this diversion seeker."

Alan Dale—*New York American*
". . . It was worthy; it was dignified, and—well, I'll have to say it—it was heavy and at times ponderous, as most good things are. Oh, it isn't so good to be bright and frisky and happy. Not at all . . . its music is lovely . . . not too frolicsome, not jazz-like and not cheap. Yet it has lilt and charm and great appeal . . . *When I Crack My Whip* was excellent in its vigor and pep."

John Anderson—*New York Post*
". . . near midnight, indeed, some restless first nighters seemed to fear that the title might be altogether too literal, and took it at best for its silver lining of music and movement. It has that in luscious plenty . . . The music is sinewy, at least . . ."

E. W. Osborn—*New York Evening World*
". . . It is casting no slur upon the accomplishments of the librettists to write that the music was the crowning triumph of the occasion. It was of real grand opera type, introducing many novelties of orchestration . . ."

Gilbert W. Gabriel—*New York Sun*
". . . solid, plotful, melodic, dramatic . . . a great big bouncing libretto which threshes resoundingly from Verdi-gurdy to *The Shanghai Gesture,* with a couple of bass notes from *Trader Horn* thrown in . . . Precious little humor . . . The music is industriously high class. Which means that it manages to recur at the right descriptive times, and to serve the action with as much pomp and color, if with no special distinction . . ."

Abel Green—*Variety,* December 7, 1927
". . . a boxoffice winner . . . a wealth of intriguing musical settings, rich in commercial song possibilities . . . the most consistently tuneful and captivating score heard in many a season . . . a show that merits support and boosting . . ."

Charles Brackett—*The New Yorker,* December 10, 1927
". . . Frivolity enters but slightly into its composition. Not that it isn't good operetta. Quite the contrary . . . The score is excellent for this type of entertainment . . . quite apt to prove another *Rose-Marie*."

Wells Root—*Time,* December 12, 1927
". . . Lacking only briskness, it is the early winter's most eminent sample of its type."

George Jean Nathan—*Judge,* December 24, 1927
". . . the best singing troupe heard hereabouts in a long time . . . some tasty scenic backgrounds, some engaging melodies . . . But it also offers some of the most pathetic comedy I have seen in months and a libretto that is a curious omelet of Rider Haggard, Robert Hichens, Harry B. Smith, Pola Negri and E. F. Albee . . ."

The New Republic, January 18, 1928
". . . billed as the successor to *Rose-Marie,* it has more pride of ancestry than hope of posterity . . . the humor is largely the accidental by-product of a dreadful book . . . the finest choruses and soloists cannot vivify the score . . ."

Bibliography

New Hammerstein Theatre Dedicated —*New York Times,* December 1, 1927

Tour

Shubert Theatre, Boston, September 3, 1928—Shubert Theatre, Cincinnati, January 12, 1929 (7 cities).

GOLDEN DAWN

(Film Version—1930)

A Warner Brothers—Vitaphone Picture
Directed by Ray Enright
Screenplay by Walter Anthony
Photographed by Dev Jennings
Color by Technicolor

Release Date

July 29, 1930

The Cast

TOM ALLEN, Walter Woolf
DAWN, Vivienne Segal

SHEP KEYES, Noah Beery
MOODA, Alice Gentle
PIGEON, Lupino Lane
JOHANNA, Marion Byron
BLINK, Lee Moran
HASMALI, Nigel de Brulier
CAPT. ERIC, Otto Mettieson
DUKE, Dick Henderson
MAID-IN-WAITING, Nina Quartaro
COL. JUDSON, Edward Martindel

Musical Numbers
Songs retained from original production: *When I Crack My Whip, My Bwana, Dawn* and *We Two.* Song written for film by Harry Akst and Grant Clarke: *Africa Smiles No More.*

Reviews
New York Times
". . . while it is acceptable in flesh and blood portrayal, it is less effective on the screen, being a hybrid of pasteboard realism and a romantic musical background that do not seem to dovetail . . ."

Lucius Beebe—*New York Herald Tribune*
"Reason totters at the thought that anyone could have conceived in seriousness such a definite catalogue of vulgarity, witlessness, and utterly pathetic and preposterous nonsense . . ."

Sime Silverman—*Variety,* July 30, 1930
". . . At best it has but some names, mostly from the legit stage. They will not help . . . Story is trite or tripe . . . too many songs with none outstanding . . ."

SHOW BOAT
(1927)

A musical play with book and lyrics by Oscar Hammerstein II, based on the novel by Edna Ferber; music by Jerome Kern.

Presented by Florenz Ziegfeld
Directed by Zeke Colvan and Mr. Hammerstein (uncredited)
Choreography by Sammy Lee
Settings by Joseph Urban
Costumes by John Harkrider
Music director, Victor Baravalle
Orchestrations by Robert Russell Bennett
Choral director, William Vodery

Tryout
National Theatre, Washington, November 15-19, 1927
Nixon Theatre, Pittsburgh, November 21-November 26, 1927
Ohio Theatre, Cleveland, November 28-December 3, 1927
Erlanger Theatre, Philadelphia, December 5-24, 1927

New York Run
Ziegfeld Theatre, December 27, 1927-May 4, 1929
572 performances

The Story
Cap'n Andy and his wife, Parthy, bring up their daughter, Magnolia, on the Mississippi showboat, *Cotton Blossom.* She falls in love with a dashing gambler, Gaylord Ravenal, who joins the troupe as an actor. After the couple marry, they settle in Chicago where they are soon beset by misfortune. Ravenal deserts Magnolia and their child, but mother and daughter win fame in the theatre. Years later, Magnolia is reunited with her husband on the showboat.

The Cast
WINDY MCLAIN, Allan Campbell
STEVE BAKER, Charles Ellis
PETE GAVIN, Bert Chapman
QUEENIE, Tess Gardella (Aunt Jemima)
PARTHY ANN HAWKS, Edna May Oliver

CAP'N ANDY HAWKS, Charles Winninger
ELLIE MAY CHIPLEY, Eva Puck
FRANK SCHULTZ, Sammy White
RUBBER FACE, Francis X. Mahoney
JULIE LAVERNE, Helen Morgan
GAYLORD RAVENAL, Howard Marsh
SHERIFF IKE VALLON, Thomas Gunn
MAGNOLIA HAWKS RAVENAL, Norma Terris
JOE, Jules Bledsoe
FARO DEALER, Jack Wynn
GAMBLER, Phil Sheridan
BACKWOODSMAN, Jack Daley
JEB, Jack Wynn
LA BELLE FATIMA, Dorothy Denese
OLD SPORT, Bert Chapman
LANDLADY, Annie Hart
ETHEL, Estelle Floyd
SISTER, Annette Harding
MOTHER SUPERIOR, Mildred Schwenke
KIM, *as a child,* Eleanor Shaw
KIM, *as a young woman,* Norma Terris
JAKE, *a piano player,* Robert Faricy
JIM, Jack Daley
MAN WITH GUITAR, Ted Daniels
CHARLIE, *doorman at the Trocadero,* J. Lewis Johnson
LOTTIE, Tana Kemp
DOLLY, Dagmar Oakland
HAZEL, Maurine Holmes
OLD LADY ON LEVEE, Laura Clairon

JUBILEE SINGERS: George Nixon, Lames Lillard, J. Mardo Brown, Willis Bradley, John Warner, L. Pinard, William Waithe, J. Lewis Johnson, E. D. Killingsworth, George Myrick, Richard Cooper, J. W. Moberly, H. George Iuano, Edgar Hall, Llewellyn Ransom, Blanche Thompson, Henrietta Lovelace, Estelle Floyd, Bertha Wright, Mamie Cartier, Josephine Gray, Lolo Waters, Maine Briggs, Gertrude Harris, Bertha Des Verney, Gladys Greenwood, R. Jamison, Maude Simmons, Angeline Lawson, Charlotte Junius, Julienne Barbour

DAHOMEY DANCERS: Elida Webb, Jessie Crawford, Alma Smith, Billie Caine, Ethel Sheppard, Lulu Williams, Rose Gillard, Theresa Jentry, Catherine Pearce, Dorothy Bellis, Betty Allison, Selma Myrick

GIRLS: Constance McKenzie, Mary Farrell, Sophie Howard, Nancy Kaye, Adrienne Armand, Lillian Clark, Betty Collette, Betty Junod, Una Val, Pansy Maness, Nellie Mayer, Essie Moore, Clementine Rigeau, Kathryn Ringquist, Rosalyn Smith, Eleanor Tierney, Frances Hope, Maurine Holmes, Dinorah Castillo, Peggy Green, Peggy Udell, Ethel Allen, Rose Gallagher, Hazel Jennings, Helen Chandler, Martha Marr, Tana Kemp,

Ethel O'Dell, Annette Harding, Modette Hunt, Dorothy Foster, Mildred Schwenke

BOYS: John Daly, Ted Daniels, William Ehlers, Dell Fradenburg, William Galpen, Ed Hale, Rees Jenkins, Ralph Knight, Ray Mace, Pat Mann, William Bailey, Joseph Minitello, Earl Sanborn, Phil Sheridan, Jack Wynn, William Lawless

NOTE: During January 1929, Miss Puck temporarily replaced by Barbara Newberry. For tour, Miss Terris succeeded by Irene Dunne; Miss Morgan by Kathryn Manners; Miss Oliver by Maude Ream Stover. During tour, Miss Manners succeeded by Margaret Carlisle.

Musical Numbers

ACT I

SCENE ONE—THE LEVEE AT NATCHEZ ON THE MISSISSIPPI, IN THE 1880'S

Opening

Cotton Blossom, STEVEDORES and TOWNSPEOPLE

Parade and Ballyhoo, ANDY, SHOW BOAT TROUPE, TOWNSPEOPLE

Where's the Mate for Me?, RAVENAL

Make Believe, RAVENAL and MAGNOLIA

Ol' Man River, JOE and JUBILEE SINGERS

SCENE TWO—KITCHEN PANTRY OF THE "COTTON BLOSSOM"

Can't Help Lovin' Dat Man, JULIE, QUEENIE, MAGNOLIA, JOE and WINDY

SCENE THREE—OUTSIDE A WATERFRONT SALOON

Life Upon the Wicked Stage, ELLIE and GIRLS

Till Good Luck Comes My Way, RAVENAL and MEN

SCENE FOUR—AUDITORIUM AND STAGE OF THE "COTTON BLOSSOM"

Misery theme, JUBILEE SINGERS

SCENE FIVE—BOX-OFFICE ON THE FOREDECK

I Might Fall Back on You, ELLIE, FRANK and GIRLS

C'mon Folks (Ballyhoo), QUEENIE and JUBILEE SINGERS

SCENE SIX—AUDITORIUM AND STAGE OF THE "COTTON BLOSSOM" DURING THIRD ACT OF "THE PARSON'S BRIDE"

SCENE SEVEN—UPPER DECK OF THE "COTTON BLOSSOM"

You Are Love, RAVENAL and MAGNOLIA

SCENE EIGHT—THE LEVEE

Finale, ENSEMBLE

ACT II

SCENE ONE—THE MIDWAY PLAISANCE AT THE CHICAGO WORLD'S FAIR, 1893

Opening

At the Fair, SIGHTSEERS, BARKERS, DANDIES

Adagio dance, Sidell Sisters

Dandies on Parade, SIGHTSEERS, BARKERS, DANDIES

Why Do I Love You?, MAGNOLIA, RAVENAL, ANDY, PARTHY and CHORUS
In Dahomey, JUBILEE SINGERS and DAHOMEY DANCERS

SCENE TWO—A ROOM IN ONTARIO STREET IN CHICAGO, 1904

SCENE THREE—REHEARSAL ROOM OF THE TROCADERO MUSIC HALL
Bill (lyric by P. G. Wodehouse and Mr. Hammerstein), JULIE
Reprise, *Can't Help Lovin' Dat Man*, MAGNOLIA

SCENE FOUR—ST. AGATHA'S CONVENT
Service and Scene music

SCENE FIVE—CORNER OF THE LOBBY OF THE SHERMAN HOTEL

SCENE SIX—TROCADERO MUSIC HALL, NEW YEAR'S EVE
Apache dance, Sidell Sisters
Goodbye, My Lady Love (by Joe Howard), FRANK and ELLIE
After the Ball, (by Charles K. Harris), MAGNOLIA

SCENE SEVEN—IN FRONT OF THE OFFICE OF THE "NATCHEZ EVENING DEMOCRAT," 1927
Reprise, *Ol' Man River*, JOE
Hey, Feller, QUEENIE and JUBILEE SINGERS

SCENE EIGHT—TOP DECK OF THE NEW "COTTON BLOSSOM"
Reprise, *You Are Love*, RAVENAL

SCENE NINE—THE LEVEE AT NATCHEZ
Reprise, *Why Do I Love You?*, KIM and FLAPPERS
Eccentric dance, Constance MacKenzie
Imitation of her mother and stars of the 1920's, KIM
Tap dance, Una Val
Finale, COMPANY

NOTE: *Mis'ry's Comin' 'Round, I Would Like to Play a Lover's Part, My Girl, Coal Black Lady, Bully Song, Hello, Ma Baby* (by Joe Howard) and *It's Getting Hotter in the North* cut before New York opening.

Reviews

John Byram—*New York Times*

". . . with a few reservations in favor of the earlier *Follies* and possibly *Sally*, it is just about the best musical piece ever to arrive under Mr. Ziegfeld's silken gonfalon . . . has about every ingredient that the perfect song and dance concoction should have . . . better than average lyrics . . . an exceptionally tuneful score—the most lilting and satisfactory that the wily Jerome Kern has evolved in several seasons . . ."

Richard Watts, Jr.—*New York Herald Tribune*

". . . a beautiful, colorful and tasteful production, so full of gorgeously pictorial atmosphere and so assisted by an excellent score that it seems bound to be one of the outstanding triumphs of the season . . . though librettist, lyric writer, scenic designer, and dance director did their work with a fine competence, it was Mr. Kern who came out of the proceedings with the highest credit . . ."

Alison Smith—*New York World*
". . . the most colorful and melodious production that has filled a Ziegfeld stage for many seasons past . . . a complete demonstration of the composer's and lyric writer's dependence on their basic idea . . . *Ol' Man River* has the lazy warmth of the Mississippi in its cadences and there is a casual crooning of an impromptu Negro lament in *Can't Help Lovin' Dat Man* . . . The plot has preserved several scenes from the original with a fidelity unrecognized by most musical comedy bookmakers . . ."

Alan Dale—*New York American*
"Here at last we have a story that was not submerged in the trough of musical molasses; here we had a 'book' the humor of which emerged naturally and the unusual quality of which struck one as something peculiarly different . . . *Show Boat* is going to have a wonderful sail—no storms—no adverse winds—nothing to keep it from making port—goodness knows when. I don't."

Burns Mantle—*New York Daily News*
". . . What Ziegfeld has done to the Ferber story is plenty. He has scrubbed it from river to deck, prettied it with silks and satins, and glorified it with shining young faces . . . It seems rather a pity that this modern story classic must be treated thusly. But so long as its guardians decided that Ziegfeld money was what they wanted, it is fortunate that he took over the job . . ."

Robert Coleman—*New York Daily Mirror*
". . . a new note in musical production . . . It is daring in its originality and shows that managers have not until now realized the tremendous possibilities of the musical comedy as an art form. It is a work of genius . . ."

Walter Winchell—*New York Graphic*
"What probably will prove to be New York's greatest smash hit . . . startling and glorious . . . a masterpiece and the most artistically entertaining show thing with us now . . . the music is most always pleasant . . ."

Wilella Waldorf—*New York Post*
". . . Every little while somebody in the cast dipped into Edna Ferber's novel and came up clutching a bit of plot, whereupon

everybody who happened to be on stage at the time sang it, danced it, turned it into witty repartee, or played it on a musical instrument . . . Another one of those Ziegfeld successes, perhaps even more deserving than some of its predecessors."

Robert Garland—*New York Telegram*
". . . a wonder and a wow . . . An American masterpiece which is never too precious for dancing, never too elegant for fun . . . the piece moves steadily forward, faltering, like many another offering, only when it approaches the end . . ."

Stephen Rathbun—*New York Sun*
". . . has more story than is usually displayed in musical comedies, and there is a happy mingling throughout of humor and pathos . . . From any angle, costumes, score, story, singing or acting, it deserves the highest praise . . ."

Abel Green—*Variety,* January 4, 1928
". . . Meaty and gripping, rich with plot and character, it's almost a pity that the novel wasn't dramatized 'straight,' sans the musical setting. But, musicalized and Ziegfeldized, it's a worthy, sturdy entertainment. It has everything and tops everything ever done before by Ziegfeld . . . Miss Morgan could have made her impression a wow click, instead of passably fair, with a song specialty in lieu of the mild *Bill* number . . . music is typically Kernian, titillating, infectious, refreshing and never tiring . . ."

Charles Brackett—*The New Yorker,* January 7, 1928
". . . even though so heralded by Philadelphia, I found thoroughly satisfying . . . A triple A score, beautiful Ziegfeld settings, a beautiful Ziegfeld chorus, and a spirited Negro one . . . I can't imagine anyone's being disappointed except the out-of-town buyer who demands that a Ziegfeld show be a fashion parade, or the pathological wise-crack addict . . ."

J. Brooks Atkinson—*New York Times,* January 8, 1928
". . . one of those epochal works about which garrulous old men gabble for twenty-five years after the scenery has rattled off to the storehouse . . . Somehow, by shrewd casting and commanding direction, the producers have kept everything in tune, subordinating wit to humor and cleverness to entertainment . . . a full complement of 'song hits' . . ."

Percy Hammond—*New York Herald Tribune,* January 8, 1928
". . . the most distinguished light opera of its generation . . . it does as much as the Theatre can do to be tuneful, dramatic, funny and

picturesque. Its libretto is a comparatively reverent approximation of the novel, and its songs are pretty and atmospheric . . ."

Wells Root—*Time,* January 9, 1928
". . . established itself magnificently as the best of its kind in town . . . tunes were by Jerome Kern, written at his best . . . superbly competent principals added full value."

Robert Benchley—*Life,* January 12, 1928
". . . The news previous to its New York opening was that it was the most remarkable show in the world. It is not quite that, especially during the second act, but it is pretty swell entertainment just the same . . ."

Alexander Woollcott—*New York World,* January 15, 1928
"I share in full the general festivity at *Show Boat,* a charming and eventful evening, thanks chiefly, I think, to the potent, hypnotic spell which Edna Ferber's glamorous story cast upon Jerome Kern. Until the last scene, when it all goes gaudy and empty and routine, it is a fine and distinguished achievement, worthy of the lovely music which brought it into being . . ."

The New Republic, January 18, 1928
". . . for all-round distinction it can hardly be surpassed by any musical show whatever . . . The book is good theatre; rich in incident and by-play . . . Kern's score is one of his strongest, and *Ol' Man River,* for its tune as well as Hammerstein's lyric, is among the few finest twentieth century American songs . . ."

George Jean Nathan—*Judge,* January 21, 1928
". . . with the best score Kern has written in several seasons, with a libretto that gives the critics a welcome holiday from the usual grumbling and with some colored wenches so talented in the art of hoofing that it is rumored Pavlowa is thinking of entering a convent, the dish proves to be just about as satisfactory a pastime as even the chronic belly-acher, the M. George Jean Nathan, could wish for . . ."

Stark Young—*McCall's,* June, 1928
". . . far more interesting than most musical comedies; its plot keeps going at least enough to maintain the suspense and interest; its music is sufficiently related to the story and situation so as not to break up the dramatic action too hopelessly . . . some of its best numbers are so successful in their combination of the theatrical elements, music, acting, scene, as to suggest openings for the development not of mere musical comedy, but of popular opera."

Bibliography

NEWSPAPERS AND PERIODICALS

"Show Boat" (painting by Doris Lee) —*Life,* November 27, 1939

Memories of First "Show Boat" Launching by Oscar Hammerstein II —*New York Times,* June 23, 1957

My Son, the Show Boat by Edna Ferber —*New York Times,* July 16, 1966

BOOKS

Show Boat: The Story of a Classic American Musical by Miles Kreuger (Oxford, New York 1977)

Tour

Colonial Theatre, Boston, May 6-June 15, 1929
Shubert Theatre, Newark, September 23, 1929—Ford's Theatre, Baltimore, March 8, 1930 (9 cities).

Tour Reviews

H.T. Parker—*Boston Transcript,* May 21, 1929
". . . By common consent, less a few envious rivals, *Show Boat* is the paragon, thus far, of American musical plays. Perhaps it also has a bowing acquaintance, several times renewed, with what the high-browed and the middle-browed friends to the theatrical cause call 'art' . . ."

SHOW BOAT

(Return Engagement—1932)

Music director, Oscar Bradley

New York Run

Casino Theatre, May 19-October 22, 1932
180 performances

The Cast

Same as original production, except for following changes:
PETE, James Swift
GAYLORD RAVENAL, Dennis King
JOE, Paul Robeson
FARO DEALER, Gladstone Waldrup
SISTER, V. Ann Kaye
KIM, *as a child,* Evelyn Eaton
MAN WITH GUITAR, Pat Mann
LOTTIE, Gertrude Walker

DOLLY, Tana Kemp
ECCENTRIC DANCER, Betty Colette

NOTE: In June, Miss Oliver succeeded by Bertha Belmore; in October, Mr. Winninger succeeded by William Kent. For tour, Mr. Robeson succeeded by Mr. Bledsoe. During tour, Mr. Kent succeeded by Sam Hearn; Mr. King by Paul Keast; Miss Terris by Margaret Adams; Mr. White by Harland Dixon.

Reviews

J. Brooks Atkinson—*New York Times*
". . . After four and one-half years it is still a thoroughbred; still the most beautifully blended musical show we have had in this country . . . Having developed logically out of a fragment of folklore, it is a work of art and a classic."

Percy Hammond—*New York Herald Tribune*
". . . seems determined to become a classic . . . Paul Robeson and Dennis King excelled their talented predecessors . . ."

Gilbert W. Gabriel—*New York American*
". . . remains the colorful, panoramic, sweeping treat it was before—and the music does something better than just remain the same. Familiarity with the score has bred nothing but a conviction that *Ol' Man River* is worthy of Stephen Foster on the Volga, a veritable folksong via the footlights . . . Its finely fashioned story holds fast to its dramatic liveliness and hearty loveliness, to its gratification of all the senses . . . all as fond as just yesterday and all as fresh as tomorrow . . ."

John Mason Brown—*New York Post*
". . . returns in better shape, and with even more to offer . . . it was by all odds the most engaging musical romance known to our stage . . . it still is something to be seen again—and again."

Robert Garland—*New York World-Telegram*
". . . the best of American-made operettas . . . scored all over again."

Richard Lockridge—*New York Sun*
". . . long may it roll . . . one of the best of the old school . . . seems even better now than when it was first produced . . ."

Abel Green—*Variety*, May 24, 1932
". . . still packs charm and a heart-wallop, and boasts perhaps the best balanced score of all times . . . almost an embarrassment of riches . . ."

Robert Benchley—*The New Yorker*, May 28, 1932
". . . the best all-around musical comedy of modern times . . . once

again, let us call attention to young Mr. Hammerstein's not-enough-recognized claim to distinction as a lyricist and librettist . . . he has fashioned words in such a manner as not only to bear analysis but also to dig pretty deeply into the heart-strings for a succession of good ripe chords . . ."

Henry Hazlitt—*The Nation,* June 8, 1932
". . . Robeson brings a rich sonority and even a sort of racial significance to the singing of *Ol' Man River.* But what is most remarkable is that neither its humor nor its sentiment has dated."

George Jean Nathan—*Judge,* June 11, 1932
". . . still far above the general run, both in respect to its book and its score . . . Yet even a good musical comedy, save it be written by Gilbert and Sullivan, is no more susceptible of highly prosperous revival than an old love affair."

Bibliography

"Show Boat" —*Time,* May 30, 1932

"Show Boat" (cover story) —*The Stage,* July, 1932

Tour

Shubert Theatre, Boston, October 24, 1932—Loew's Metropolitan Theatre, Brooklyn, March 9, 1933 (13 cities).

Selected Revivals

St. Louis Municipal Opera; August 11-24, 1930
W.C. Fields (ANDY); Charlotte Lansing (MAGNOLIA); Guy Robertson (RAVENAL); Margaret Carlisle (JULIE); Lois B. Deppe (JOE); Sammy White (FRANK); Eva Puck (ELLIE); Maude Ream Stover (PARTHY).

St. Louis Municipal Opera, August 13-26, 1934
William Kent (ANDY); Charlotte Lansing (MAGNOLIA); Allan Jones (RAVENAL); Gladys Baxter (JULIE); Lois B. Deppe (JOE); Sammy White (FRANK); Doris Patston (ELLIE); Maude Ream Stover (PARTHY).

San Carlo Opera, Randall's Island, New York, June 29-August 6, 1938
William Kent (ANDY); Bettina Hall (MAGNOLIA); Guy Robertson (RAVENAL); Natalie Hall (JULIE); Lansing Hatfield (JOE); Harry K. Morton (FRANK); Nina Olivette (ELLIE); Zella Russell (PARTHY).

St. Louis Municipal Opera, August 15-28, 1938
George Rasely (ANDY); Norma Terris (MAGNOLIA); Ronald Graham (RAVENAL); Margaret Carlisle (JULIE); Kenneth Spencer (JOE); Jack Sheehan (FRANK); Vicki Cummings (ELLIE); Helen Raymond (PARTHY); Annamary Dickey (SISTER).

Los Angeles Civic Light Opera, May 13-18, 1940
San Francisco Civic Light Opera, May 20-25, 1940
Guy Kibbee (ANDY); Norma Terris (MAGNOLIA); John Boles (RAVENAL); Helen Morgan (JULIE); Paul Robeson (JOE); Sammy White (FRANK); Helen Lynd (ELLIE); Winifred Harris (PARTHY); Gwen Verdon (CHORUS).

Los Angeles Civic Light Opera, May 8-20, 1944
San Francisco Civic Light Opera, May 22-June 3, 1944
Gene Lockhart (ANDY); Marthe Errolle (MAGNOLIA); Lansing Hatfield (RAVENAL); Carol Bruce (JULIE); Todd Duncan (JOE); Sammy White (FRANK); Collette Lyons (ELLIE); Bertha Belmore (PARTHY).

Greek Theatre, Los Angeles, July 4, 1949
Charles Winninger (ANDY); Evelyn Wyckoff (MAGNOLIA); Charles Fredericks (RAVENAL); Terry Saunders (JULIE); Caleb Peterson (JOE); Sammy White (FRANK); Collette Lyons (ELLIE).

Dallas State Fair, August 15-27, 1949
Ralph Dumke (ANDY); Beverly Tyler (MAGNOLIA); Lawrence Brooks (RAVENAL); Carol Bruce (JULIE); William C. Smith (JOE); Hal LeRoy (FRANK); Bertha Belmore (PARTHY); Helen Dowdy (QUEENIE).

New York City Center Opera, April 8, 17, May 2, October 28, 31, 1954
New York City Center Light Opera, May 5-16, 1954
Stanley Carlson (ANDY); Laurel Hurley (MAGNOLIA); Robert Rounseville (RAVENAL); Helena Bliss (JULIE); William C. Smith (JOE); Jack Albertson (FRANK); Diana Drake (ELLIE); Marjorie Gateson (PARTHY). NOTE: On May 5, Mr. Carlson succeeded by Burl Ives, Mr. Smith by Lawrence Winters, Mr. Albertson by Donn Driver. Produced & directed by William Hammerstein.

Jones Beach Marine Theatre, Long Island, June 21-September 3, 1956
Jones Beach Marine Theatre, Long Island, June 27-September 7, 1957
Paul Hartman (ANDY); Gloria Hamilton (MAGNOLIA); David Atkinson (RAVENAL); Helena Bliss (JULIE); William C. Smith (JOE); Hal LeRoy (FRANK); Marie Foster (ELLIE); Helen Raymond (PARTHY); Helen Dowdy (QUEENIE); Geoffrey Holder (DAHOMEY KING). NOTE: For 1957 season, Mr. Hartman was succeeded by Andy Devine, Mr. LeRoy by Lou Wills, Jr.

Dallas State Fair, August 13-September 2, 1956
Stanley Carlson (ANDY); Shirley Jones (MAGNOLIA); William Tabbert (RAVENAL); Betty Colby (JULIE); Lawrence Winters (JOE); Margaret Hamilton (PARTHY).

Los Angeles Civic Light Opera, August 15-September 24, 1960
San Francisco Civic Light Opera, September 26, 1960
Joe E. Brown (ANDY); Jacqueline McKeever (MAGNOLIA); Richard Banke (RAVENAL); Julie Wilson (JULIE); Lawrence Winters (JOE); Eddie Foy, Jr. (FRANK); Ruta Lee (ELLIE); Helen Raymond (PARTHY); Virginia Capers (QUEENIE).

New York City Center Light Opera, April 12-23, 1961
Joe E. Brown (ANDY); Jo Sullivan (MAGNOLIA); Robert Rounseville (RAVENAL); Anita Darian (JULIE); Andrew Frierson (JOE); Richard France (FRANK); Jane Kean (ELLIE); Carol Brice (QUEENIE).

Dallas State Fair, August 19,-September 1, 1963
Charlie Ruggles (ANDY); Jacqueline McKeever (MAGNOLIA); Richard Fredricks (RAVENAL); Rosalind Elias (JULIE); Brock Peters (JOE); Rosetta LeNoire (QUEENIE); Sandy Duncan (KIM).

Music Theater of Lincoln Center, New York, July 19-September 10, 1966
David Wayne (ANDY); Barbara Cook (MAGNOLIA); Stephen Douglass (RAVENAL); Constance Towers (JULIE); William Warfield (JOE); Eddie Phillips (FRANK); Allyn Ann McLerie (ELLIE); Margaret Hamilton (PARTHY); Rosetta LeNoire (QUEENIE). *Tour:* September 12-November 5, 1966.

Los Angeles Civic Light Opera, September 19-November 4, 1967
San Francisco Civic Light Opera, November 7, 1967
Pat O'Brien (ANDY); Eileen Christy (MAGNOLIA); John Tyers (RAVENAL); Gale Sherwood (JULIE); Robert Mosley (JOE); Eddie Foy, Jr. (FRANK); Sandra O'Neill (ELLIE); Audrey Christie (PARTHY); Virginia Capers (QUEENIE).

St. Louis Municipal Opera, August 5-11, 1968
Arthur Godfrey (ANDY); Judith McCauley (MAGNOLIA); Frank Porretta (RAVENAL); Jean Sanders (JULIE); Edward Pierson (JOE); Mary Wickes (PARTHY).

Jones Beach Marine Theatre, Long Island, July 1-September 5, 1976
Max Showalter (ANDY); Barbara Meister (MAGNOLIA); Robert Peterson (RAVENAL); Beth Fowler (JULIE); Lee Roy Reams (FRANK).

St. Louis Municipal Opera, July 26,-August 1, 1976
Gale Gordon (ANDY); Shirley Jones (MAGNOLIA); Ron Husmann (RAVENAL); Kelly Garrett (JULIE); Bruce Hubbard (JOE); Betty Ann Grove (ELLIE).

Productions Abroad

Theatre Royal, Drury Lane, London, May 3, 1928-March 2, 1929
(See page 361)

Stoll Theatre, London, April 17, 1943; *264 performances*
Presented by Prince Littler. *Cast:* Mark Daly (ANDY); Gwyneth Lascelles (MAGNOLIA); Bruce Carfax (RAVENAL); Pat Taylor (JULIE); Mr. Jetsam (JOE); Hester Paton Bronson (PARTHY).

Adelphi Theatre, London, July 29, 1971-Sept. 29, 1973; *910 performances*
Presented by Harold Fielding; directed and choreographed by Wendy Toye. *Cast:* Derek Royle (ANDY); Lorna Dallas (MAGNOLIA); Andre Jobin

(RAVENAL); Cleo Laine (JULIE); Thomas Carey (JOE); Kenneth Nelson (FRANK); Jan Hunt (ELLIE); Pearl Hackney (PARTHY); Ena Cabayo (QUEENIE). NOTE: During run, Mr. Carey succeeded by Valentine Pringle, Miss Laine by Wilma Reading, Miss Hackney by Margo Cunningham.

SHOW BOAT

(London—1928)

Presented by Sir Alfred Butt
Directed by Felix Edwardes
Choreography by Max Scheck
Settings by Joseph and Phil Harker
Costumes by Irene Segalla
Music director, Herman Finck
Choral director, John Payne

London Run

Theatre Royal, Drury Lane, May 3, 1928-March 2, 1929
350 performances

The Cast

WINDY MCLAIN, Jack Martin
STEVE BAKER, Colin Clive
PETE, Fred Hearne
QUEENIE, Alberta Hunter
PARTHY ANN HAWKS, Viola Compton
CAP'N ANDY HAWKS, Cedric Hardwicke
ELLIE MAY CHIPLEY, Dorothy Lena
FRANK SCHULTZ, Leslie Sarony
RUBBER FACE, Henry Thomas
JULIE LAVERNE, Marie Burke
GAYLORD RAVENAL, Howett Worster
SHERIFF IKE VALLON, Percy Parsons
MAGNOLIA HAWKS RAVENAL, Edith Day
JOE, Paul Robeson
FARO DEALER, William Wallace
GAMBLER, Alec J. Willard
LOUNGER, Felix Hill
BACKWOODSMAN, Roy Emerton
JEB, Gordon Crocker
LA BELLE FATIMA, Lenore Gadsden
OLD SPORT, Cecil Dereham
LANDLADY, Largaret Yarde

ETHEL, Kathleen Thomas
KIM, *as a young woman,* Edith Day
JAKE, *a piano player,* Michael Cole
MAX, Will Stuart
MAN WITH GUITAR, Walter Webster
CHARLIE, *doorman at the Trocadero,* Norris Smith
LOTTIE, Nancy Brown
DOLLY, Peggy Lovat
HAZEL, Anne Barbour
LADIES OF THE CHORUS: Sybil Allnott, Patricia Andrew, Babette Archer, Cynthia Arthurs, Anne Barbour, Margaret Boyle, Nancy Brown, Zita Da Costa, Nancy Eshelby, Kathleen Fitchie, Lena Fitchie, Roma Forster, Nan Forster, Esther Gill, Stephanie Insall, Mavice Kalmar, Elsie Lawrence, Linda Lindose, Irene Lister, Peggy Lovat, Yetta Luberti, Nance Miriam, Mary Morris, Mynette Morven, Phyllis Neal, Esme Oxley, Eileen Penberthy, Heather Price, Noranna Rose, Joanna Sands, Eileen Scott, Frances Seymour, Ruby Simpson, Rosalind Snow, Christine Symons, Eunice Vickridge
GENTLEMEN OF THE CHORUS: Jack Allen, Hadyn Campbell, Richard Crawford, Cecil Dereham, Walter Farrance, Henry Ferguson, Victor Hamel, William Herbert, Felix Hill, Donald Kingston, Alfred Lawton, Ernest Ludlow, Selwyn Morgan, Frank Ogg, Kilmore Scott, Reginald Smith, William Wallace, Walter Webster, Alec J. Willard
MISSISSIPPI CHORUS AND DANCERS: Louise Alexander, Kathleen Blay, Alma Chester, May Downs, Violet Downs, Vera Gomez, Eva Hudson, Marie Lawrence, Lavinia Lewis, Ella Minto, Connie Smith, Kathleen Thomas, Dorothy St. Elmo, Margaret Wyng, Irene Zulia, Kummiane Alexander, William Banks, J. N. Caldwell, Ardash Dorian, H. N. Downes, Frank Essien, Arthur Gibson, Amos Howard, Bud Hudson, Nicholas Kofie, Alexander Lofton, Oscar Paul, James Solomon, Morris Smith, George Williams
DANCERS; Rosa Austin, Rachel Berch, Glennie Chessman, Doris Colbert, Viola Colston, Nonia Davis, Evelyn Dickerson, Lenore Gadsden, Rosalind Jackson, Corinne Meaux, Lois Parker, Ethel Taylor

NOTE: In January 1929, Miss Day succeeded by Margery Hicklin.

Musical Numbers

Same as original production except that *How'd You Like to Spoon with Me* (lyric by Edward Kosta) replaced *Goodbye, My Lady Love; Hey, Feller* was dropped; *Dance Away the Night* added in place of Kim's imitations. The scene at St. Agatha's Convent was eliminated. A new song, *Me an' My Boss,* written for Mr. Robeson, was added during tryout but dropped before London opening.

Reviews

London Times

". . . one has always an impression that Magnolia's own life had more in it of genuine emotion than can be conveniently expressed in limelit duets under the continuous threat of choral interruption . . . the subject does not fit the medium, and the uses of the medium have been, in consequence, rather uncomfortably strained . . . the songs are asked to carry rather more than they can bear . . . a rather heavy-weight entertainment."

London Daily Express
". . . wants only more humour—and more of Paul Robeson . . ."

London Daily News
". . . Drury Lane has never staged a more brilliant production, though the end is rather sudden and falls a bit flat . . ."

James Agate—*London Sunday Times,* May 6, 1928
". . . a stupendous thing . . . one had the feeling of being exhaustively entertained without ever quite getting to the heart of the entertainment . . . Mr. Hammerstein contrived to say nothing whatever, and I doubt whether a whole dynasty of Hammersteins could have said less. As a piece of story-telling, it is as inept and clumsy as anything I have ever seen on any stage . . . my impression remains that this inane play has been carved out of something which in itself was not inane . . ."

St. John Ervine—*London Observer,* May 6, 1928
". . . we are appalled to find so much effort and ingenuity and expense incurred on the mere fripperies of the play when so little effort and ingenuity were expended on the play itself. The dialogue meanders without meaning to impotent conclusions, and is skillful only in avoiding distinction and character . . . Mr. Robeson roused the only enthusiasm that was manifested at the end of the play . . . Mr. Kern has done his job exceedingly well . . . Miss Ferber put the Mississippi into her novel; Oscar Hammerstein the Second has put a squirt in its place."

G. W. Bishop—*The Era*
". . . There will be those to complain that the story is thin and ill-connected, but as a stirring, moving review of American life it is first-rate entertainment . . . More humour could have been introduced with advantage . . . *Ol' Man River* is the choicest memory of the evening . . ."

Horace Shipp—*The English Review,* June, 1928
"In certain respects the trouble is that it has more story and consequence than is usual in these big musical shows . . . the audience, having once allowed its attention to wander from the

devices of the story, lives for the tune, the dance or the fun of the moment . . ."

Bibliography

"Show Boat" (cover story) —*The Play Pictorial,* July, 1928

SHOW BOAT

(Film Version—1929)

A Universal Picture
Produced by Carl Laemmle
Directed by Harry Pollard
Screenplay by Charles Kenyon
Dialogue by Tom Reed and Harry Pollard
Prologue directed by Arch B. Heath
Art director, Charles D. Hall
Costumes by Johanna Mathieson
Music director, Joseph Cherniavski
Photographed by Gilbert Warrenton

Release Date
May 5, 1929

The Cast
MAGNOLIA HAWKS RAVENAL, Laura La Plante (sung by Eva Olivotti)
GAYLORD RAVENAL, Joseph Schildkraut
CAP'N ANDY HAWKS, Otis Harlan
PARTHY ANN HAWKS, Emily Fitzroy
JULIE LA VERNE, Alma Rubens
MAGNOLIA, *as a child* }
KIM, *as a child* } Jane LaVerne
WINDY MCLAIN, Jack MacDonald
SCHULTZY, Neely Edwards
ELLIE MAY CHIPLEY, Elise Bartlett
JOE, Stepin Fetchit
QUEENIE, Gertrude Howard

Prologue
Helen Morgan
Jules Bledsoe
Tess Gardella (Aunt Jemima)
Plantation Singers
Carl Laemmle
Florenz Ziegfeld

Musical Numbers
This was a part-talking picture, with a synchronized score. Songs included in the 18-minute Prologue: *Bill, Can't Help Lovin' Dat Man, Ol' Man River, Hey, Feller, C'mon Folks.* Songs in main part of film retained from original production: *Ol' Man River* and *Can't Help Lovin' Dat Man.* Songs written specially for film: *The Lonesome Road* (Nat Shilkret-Gene Austin), *Here Comes the Show Boat* (Maceo Pinkard-Billy Rose), *Love Sings a Song in My Heart* (Joseph Cherniavski-Clarence Marks), *Down South* (Sigmund Spaeth-William Myddleton).

Reviews
Mordaunt Hall—*New York Times*
". . . splendidly recorded songs sung by some of Ziegfeld's luminaries . . . The melodies in this well staged lachrymose tale are so fine they atone for some of the prolonged melodramatic stretches . . ."

Sime Silverman—*Variety,* April 24, 1929
". . . There can be no alibi for the cutting for Universal's best effort on the screen . . . merely a matter of recutting to develop the full strength of this splendidly made picture . . ."

John Mosher—*The New Yorker,* April 27, 1929
"*Old Man River Takes His Time* . . . It is enormous, twice as long as the ordinary picture, elaborate and ponderous, sometimes agreeable to the eye, but more often depressing the spirit with a sense of intolerable sluggishness . . ."

Time, May 17, 1929
". . . a picturesque, old-fashioned, tedious melodrama, full of conventional photography and exaggerated acting . . ."

A. M. Sherwood, Jr.—*Outlook,* May 22, 1929
". . . You might like it if you could see it in an unwired theatre, with an orchestra—or even a good piano . . . a truly fine performance by Laura La Plante—the only good thing in the picture."

Bibliography
"Show Boat" as an Audible Picture —*New York Times,* April 14, 1929

SHOW BOAT

(Film Version—1936)

A Universal Picture
Produced by Carl Laemmle, Jr.
Directed by James Whale

Screenplay by Oscar Hammerstein II
Choreography by LeRoy Prinz
Art director, Charles D. Hall
Costumes by Doris Zinkeisen
Technical director, Leighton K. Brill
Music director, Victor Baravalle
Orchestrations by Robert Russell Bennett
Photographed by John J. Mescall and John P. Fulton
Editors, Ted Kent and Bernard Burton

Release Date
April 30, 1936

The Cast
MAGNOLIA HAWKS RAVENAL, Irene Dunne
GAYLORD RAVENAL, Allan Jones
CAP'N ANDY HAWKS, Charles Winninger
JOE, Paul Robeson
JULIE LAVERNE, Helen Morgan
PARTHY ANN HAWKS, Helen Westley
STEVE, *Julie's husband,* Donald Cook
FRANK SCHULTZ, Sammy White
ELLIE SCHULTZ, *Frank's wife,* Queenie Smith
QUEENIE, *Joe's wife,* Hattie McDaniel
RUBBERFACE, Francis X. Mahoney
SHERIFF VALLON, Charles Middleton
PETE, Arthur Hohl
WINDY, J. Farrell MacDonald
JIM GREEN, *Trocadero owner,* Charles Wilson
KIM, *as a baby,* Patricia Barry
KIM, *as a child,* Marilyn Knowlden
KIM, *at 16,* Sunnie O'Dea
LANDLADY, May Beatty
SAM, *Trocadero janitor,* Clarence Muse
JEB, *backwoodsman,* Stanley Fields
CHORUS GIRL, Barbara Pepper
JAKE, *pianist,* Harry Barris
TINY, *backwoodsman,* Stanley Sandford
LOST CHILD, Bobby Watson
ENGLISH MANAGER, E. E. Clive
REPORTER, Helen Jerome Eddy
DANCE DIRECTOR, LeRoy Prinz
DEAF WOMAN, Flora Finch
YOUNG NEGRO, Eddie "Rochester" Anderson
RACE FAN, Jack Mulhall
HOTEL CLERK, Selmer Jackson
THEATRE MANAGER, Forrest Stanley

Musical Numbers

Songs retained from original production: *Cotton Blossom, Where's the Mate for Me?, Make Believe, Ol' Man River, Can't Help Lovin' dat Man, You Are Love, Bill, After the Ball,* and *Goodbye, My Lady Love.*

Following songs written specially for film by Kern and Hammerstein:
Gallavantin' Around, MAGNOLIA
Ah Still Suits Me, JOE and QUEENIE
I Have the Room Above Her, RAVENAL and MAGNOLIA

NOTE: *Got My Eye on You* written for film but not used.

Reviews

Frank S. Nugent—*New York Times*
". . . Universal's excellent screen transcription is the pleasantest kind of proof that it was not merely one of the best musical shows of the century but that it contained the gossamer stuff for one of the finest musical films we have seen . . ."

Howard Barnes—*New York Herald Tribune*
"One of the sturdiest and most captivating shows of our time has been shaped into an opulent, spectacular and generally enchanting screen musical . . . It still has the power to move and divert one and offers exciting possibilities for color and atmosphere . . ."

Winston Burdett—*Brooklyn Daily Eagle*
". . . handsome, tuneful and generally enjoyable . . . The main point is that the operetta is still its quaintly agreeable self, that the music is remarkably fresh, that the libretto is reasonably serviceable, and that the whole thing has been brought to the screen with technical skill . . ."

Abel Green—*Variety,* May 20, 1936
". . . a smash film musical. A cinch for big grosses, from the deluxers down . . ."

John Mosher—*The New Yorker,* May 23, 1936
". . . Never have I seen a musical show so satisfactorily and intelligently adapted. And, I assume, the credit goes chiefly to its director . . . From story to song and back again, the film passes with sure ease . . ."

Katherine Best—*Stage,* June, 1936
". . . The *Ol' Man River* sequence is musically and photographically as excellent as anything yet accomplished on the sound screen. It is woven majestically into a film which intermittently exalts and moves and amuses."

Mark Van Doren—*The Nation,* June 10, 1936
". . . Paul Robeson sings *Ol' Man River* even a little better than he ever sang it before. The setting is frankly artificial and I am not sure that this is right. But neither am I sure that a genuine Mississippi River would have consorted with what we have to look at and listen to. The documentary might very well have dampened what otherwise remains after several years as crisp and bright as ever."

Sydney W. Carroll—*London Times,* June 14, 1936
". . . of its kind it is as good a film as anyone has made . . . Its very familiarity has charm. Its world-famous haunting melodies thrill us on repetition. Its characters for the most part are novel, picturesque, well-drawn, human and nicely sentimentalised . . ."

Graham Greene—*The Spectator,* June 26, 1936
". . . because there are times, particularly after several drinks, when one can watch money being squandered without a pang, *Show Boat* for three-quarters of its length provides good entertainment, sentimental, literary, but oddly appealing."

Don Herald—*Life,* July, 1936
"This sedate department would like to throw up its hat and yell yippee. An embarrassing hot flood of superlatives rushes to our lips. I mean I loved *Show Boat.* Somebody did something to keep it almost perfect every foot of the way. I suspect Director James Whale . . . I know this all sounds a little high-school papery, but let me be; it isn't often that I want to rave on the praise side . . ."

Bibliography

"Show Boat" Must Go On by Edward Eustace
—*New York Times,* May 10, 1936

SHOW BOAT

(New York—1946)

Presented by Messrs. Kern and Hammerstein
Production directed by Hassard Short
Book directed by Mr. Hammerstein
Choreography by Helen Tamiris
Settings by Howard Bay
Costumes by Lucinda Ballard
Music director, Edwin McArthur
Orchestrations by Robert Russell Bennett

Choral director, Pembroke Davenport
Associate, William Vodery

New York Run

Ziegfeld Theatre, January 5, 1946-January 4, 1947
418 performances

The Cast

WINDY MCLAIN, Scott Moore
STEVE BAKER, Robert Allen
PETE GAVIN, Seldon Bennett
QUEENIE, Helen Dowdy
PARTHY ANN HAWKS, Ethel Owen
CAP'N ANDY HAWKS, Ralph Dumke
ELLIE MAY CHIPLEY, Collette Lyons
FRANK SCHULTZ, Buddy Ebsen
RUBBER FACE, Francis X. Mahoney
JULIE LAVERNE, Carol Bruce
GAYLORD RAVENAL, Charles Fredericks
SHERIFF IKE VALLON, Ralph Chambers
MAGNOLIA HAWKS RAVENAL, Jan Clayton
JOE, Kenneth Spencer
BACKWOODSMAN, Howard Frank
JEB, Duncan Scott
SAL, Pearl Primus
SAM, LaVerne French
BARKER, Hayes Gordon
FATIMA, Jeanne Reeves
OLD SPORT, Willie Torpey
STRONG WOMAN, Paula Kaye

SPANISH		Andrea Downing
ITALIAN		Vivian Cherry
FRENCH		Janice Bodenhoff
SCOTCH		Elana Keller
GREEK	*Congress of Beauties*	Audrey Keane
ENGLISH		Marta Becket
RUSSIAN		Olga Lunick
INDIAN		Eleanor Boleyn

DAHOMEY QUEEN, Pearl Primus
ATA, Alma Sutton
MALA, Claude Marchant
BORA, Talley Beatty
LANDLADY, Sara Floyd
ETHEL, Assota Marshall
SISTER, Sheila Hogan
MOTHER SUPERIOR, Iris Manley
KIM, *as a child,* Alice Mace

JAKE, *a piano player,* Max Showalter
JIM, Jack Daley
MAN WITH GUITAR, Tom Bowman
CHARLIE, *doorman at the Trocadero,* William C. Smith
DRUNK, Paul Shiers
LOTTIE, Nancy Kenyon
DOLLY, Lydia Fredericks
SALLY, Bettina Thayer
KIM, *as a young woman,* Jan Clayton
OLD LADY ON LEVEE, Frederica Slemons
JIMMY CRAIG, Charles Tate
GIRL SINGERS: Carmine Alexandria, Grace Benton, Clarise Crawford, Lydia Fredericks, Adah Friley, Marion Hairston, Katie Hall, Marion Holvas, Jean Jones, Frances Joslyn, Charlotte Junius, Assota Marshall, Linda Mason, Eulabel Riley, Agnes Sundgren, Bettina Thayer, Fannie Turner, Ethel Brown White, Evelyn Wick
BOY SINGERS: Jerome Addison, Gilbert Adkins, William Bender, Thomas Bowman, Robert Bulger, Glenn Burris, Edward Chappel, William Cole, Erno Czako, Richard DiSilvera, John Garth III, Hayes Gordon, George Hall, Thomas Jordan, Robert Kimberly, James Lapsley, Albert McCary, William McDaniel, Bowling Mansfield, Walter Mosby, Clarence Redd, Paul Shiers, William C. Smith, William Sol, Rodester Timmons, David Trimble
GIRL DANCERS: Marta Becket, Elmira Jones Bey, Janice Bodenhoff, Eleanor Boleyn, Vivian Cherry, Andrea Downing, Betty Jane Geiskopf, Carol Harriton, Vickie Henderson, Audrey Keane, Elana Keller, Orak Leak, Olga Lunick, Lean Reeves, Alma Sutton, Viola Taylor, Yvonne Tibor, Paula Kaye
BOY DANCERS: Talley Beatty, Terry Dawson, LaVerne French, Eddie Howland, Gerard Leavitt, Claude Marchant, William Miller, Nick Nadeau, Joseph Nash, Stanley Simmons, William Weber, Henry Wessell, Francisco Xavier
CHILDREN: Betty Barker, Dolores Gamble, Carol Lewis, Miriam Quinn, Sybil Stocking; Billy DeForest, Roland Gamble, Edward Hayes, Bobby O'Connor, Eugene Steiner

NOTE: In April, Miss Clayton succeeded by Nancy Kenyon; in November, Mr. Fredericks by Joe (Brian) Sullivan.

Musical Numbers

Same as original production, with following changes: *Till Good Luck Comes My Way, I Might Fall Back On You* and *Hey, Feller* dropped; *Nobody Else But Me* added in place of Kim's imitations. Scene outside waterfront saloon and scene in Sherman Hotel lobby eliminated.

Reviews

Lewis Nichols—*New York Times*
". . . still one of the real musicals of the modern American stage . . .

its music was unstaled by repetition, its familiar lyrics seemed new . . . sentimental and gay, colorful, gaudy, nostalgic affair . . . the present sponsors have given the American near-classic an excellent production. The arrival of the Cotton Blossom is welcome news . . ."

Howard Barnes—*New York Herald Tribune*
"The greatest of American musical comedies has been revived, and it is a joy to hear and to behold. After almost twenty years, it has lost none of its melodic magnificence, dramatic excitement and abiding humor . . . a privilege as well as a great treat to attend the celebrated classic . . . an inspired job in 1927, it is still full of inspiration and delight . . ."

John Chapman—*New York Daily News*
". . . a musical play in the grand manner . . . it is what every musical should be—and no other has ever been . . . deserves about every superlative that can be found on a typewriter keyboard . . ."

Wilella Waldorf—*New York Post*
". . . a tremendously elaborate, colorful, densely populated affair . . . a decorative, somewhat overdone extravaganza, distinguished by a really superior score. The story had the virtue of being somewhat less hackneyed twenty years ago than it is now, and so had the music . . ."

Burton Rascoe—*New York World-Telegram*
". . . every bit as lavish as the one Ziegfeld gave us, if not more so . . . Jules Bledsoe has a magnificent successor in Kenneth Spencer . . . Carol Bruce carries the torch with splendor . . ."

Ward Morehouse—*New York Sun*
". . . the finest evening that the current season has brought along to date. It is still magnificent . . . has beauty, pathos, nostalgia, panoramic pattern and a score that will endure for as long as the theatre exists . . . The production is stunning . . . a timeless memorial to the genius of Jerome Kern . . ."

Robert Garland—*New York Journal-American*
". . . continues to suffer from its old last act trouble . . . After eighteen years and nine days it still starts a story it never really finishes . . . the immortal score maintains its magical appeal. It was, it is, it always will be *Show Boat*'s crowning glory."

Louis Kronenberger—*PM*
". . . As musicals go, it is full-bodied and full-flavored . . . its glory always was and always will be its music, quite possibly the best ever written for a musical comedy; it certainly is the best wearing . . . Even the songs I'd forgotten are pleasant ones . . . Miss Tamiris' dances seem to me, after the music, the best thing in the show . . ."

Arthur Bronson—*Variety,* January 9, 1946
". . . a sumptuous production, a treat to see and hear . . . as striking, appealing and eye-filling as before. It is amazing how well the songs stand up over the years; they sound as fresh and verdant as ever . . ."

Wolcott Gibbs—*The New Yorker,* January 12, 1946
". . . not only equal to the old ones in almost every respect but also in some ways rather superior . . . with the assistance of that enchanting music, it is easy to accept the outrageous devices of the plot, easy to identify yourself with the terrible sorrow of unfaithful love, and even easy to laugh at jokes that might be considered primitive in a comic strip . . ."

George Jean Nathan—*New York Journal-American,* January 14, 1946
". . . a cause for rejoicing because it shows up all the new musicals like sunlight shows up complexions and moonlight idiots. Its story and its melodies remain among our musical stage's treasures . . . a lovely, insinuating, honestly romantic and uncommonly tuneful show, and its virtue is that it not only brings back delicate and desirable memories to us oldsters but induces delicate and desirable expectations in those younger ones who now are seeing it for the first time . . ."

Louis Kronenberger—*Time,* January 14, 1946
". . . Still one of the most satisfying of all musicals. Few shows can boast a more delightful score. Instead of seeming dated, it is merely very nostalgic . . . Only toward the end when the plot runs down, does the revival lose its lure . . ."

Richard Watts, Jr.—*Saturday Review of Literature,* January 26, 1946
". . . just as enchanting as memory had made it; in fact, if anything, it is even a more sturdy dramatic structure than I had remembered. As for the new production, it is in most ways as brilliant as the original and in some it is better . . . The triumph belongs very completely to Carol Bruce . . ."

Rosamond Gilder—*Theatre Arts,* March, 1946
". . . The stars of this new production are not so much the perform-

ers as the creators of the show itself . . . the production is as lavish as though it were new-born into a world that had never seen it before . . . stands up magnificently against the years. Its songs seem as fresh as ever . . ."

Bibliography

"Show Boat" (cover story) —*Life,* January 28, 1946

"Show Boat" (paintings by Edna Eicke) —*Vogue,* July 1, 1946

SHOW BOAT

(Touring Company—1947)

Presented by Messrs. Rodgers and Hammerstein
Directed by William Hammerstein
Music director, Frederick Dvonch

The Cast

WINDY, Arthur R. Edwards
STEVE, Fred Brookins
PETE, Gerald Prosk
QUEENIE, Helen Dowdy
PARTHY ANN HAWKS, Bertha Belmore
CAP'N ANDY, Billy House
ELLIE, Clare Alden
FRANK, Sammy White
RUBBER FACE, George Cassidy
JULIE, Martha King
GAYLORD RAVENAL, Norwood Smith
VALLON, Fred Ardath
MAGNOLIA, Pamela Caveness
JOE, William C. Smith
BACKWOODSMAN, Howard Frank
JEB, Gerald Prosk
SAM, LaVerne French
SAL, Lawaune Ingram
BARKER, Walter Russell
FATIMA, Jeanne Reeves
SPORT, Alan Wisser
DAHOMEY KING, LaVerne French
LANDLADY, Sara Floyd
ETHEL, Assota Marshall
MOTHER SUPERIOR, Rae Abruzzo
KIM, *as a child,* Alyce Mace

JAKE, Harry Holton
JIM, Jack Daley
MAN WITH GUITAR, George Cassidy
CHARLIE, *doorman at the Trocadero,* Walter Mosby
DRUNK, Walter Russell
LOTTIE, Sara Dillon
DOLLY, Elaine Hume
SALLY, Janet VanDerveer
OLD LADY ON LEVEE, Sara Floyd
SINGERS, GIRLS: Rae Abruzzo, Sybol Cain, Clarice Crawford, Sara Dillon, Betty Graeber, Marion Hairston, Kate Hall, Elaine Hume, Charlotte Junius, Assota Marshall, Nancy Randal, Eulabel Riley, Janet Vanderveer, Grace Varik, Lorraine Waldman, Mae Williams
SINGERS, BOYS: Jerome Addison, Gilbert Adkins, Gordon Alexander, Ivory Bass, Victor Bender, James Gordon, Oliver Busch, William Cole, Elijah Hodges, Delbert Starrett, Clarence Jones, Abie Levi, Albert McCary, Walter Mosby, Walter Russell, William Sol, Charles Welch, Alan Wisser
DANCERS: Joyce Arbuckle, Donna Beaumont, Rita Christian, Mable Hart, Lawrence Ingram, Gladys Justsen, Elana Keller, Margaret Scott, Jacqueline Maddox, Evelyn Pilcher, Jeanne Reeves, Gloria Smith, Jean Thomas, Louise Fitzpatrick; Isaiah Clark, Norman Dejoie, James Hunt, Reginald Ridgely, George Thomas, James Fields

NOTE: After summer layoff, Miss Belmore succeeded by Ruth Gates; Miss King by Carol Bruce, who was succeeded by Terry Saunders in October.

Tour

Bushnell Auditorium, Hartford, October 20, 1947—Shubert Theatre, Chicago, June 26, 1948 (14 cities).
New York City Center, September 7, 1948—Hartman Theatre, Columbus, April 30, 1949 (45 cities).

Tour Reviews

Brooks Atkinson—*New York Times*
". . . one of the immortal works of the musical stage . . . *Show Boat* and *Oklahoma!*—those are the great musical stage works of the century. Since the century has produced little else to be proud of, let us congratulate ourselves on being contemporaries of two illustrious musical dramas . . . your correspondent is not disposed to quibble about any part of this admirable revival . . ."

Otis L. Guernsey, Jr.—*New York Herald Tribune*
". . . joyous music and open-handed sentiment which has made it a theatrical classic . . . some of the spirit seems to have left the show with the original revival cast. This *Show Boat* is, as always, good to

hear, but it settles for a rather mechanical repetition instead of a gay rebirth . . ."

Robert Coleman—*New York Daily Mirror*
". . . has heart and melody. What the heck—it has everything. It is one of those rare shows that must be seen again and again and again . . ."

Richard Watts, Jr.—*New York Post*
". . . not the ideal performance that such a work deserves, but it has the high virtue of keeping the qualities of a masterpiece intact and presenting them in a fashion that makes it clear why it gives every sign of theatrical immortality . . ."

William Hawkins—*New York World-Telegram*
". . . confirms again that it is inspired corn, which is the best kind of theatre there is. What keeps the production so stirring is that its unabashed heart tugs remain deep pure sentiment and never lose their dignity . . ."

Ward Morehouse—*New York Sun*
". . . a bargain buy . . . retains its magic; it still holds you in its spell . . . The score is magnificent—yes, the music and the lyrics will live as long as the theatre does . . . its story is solid, and it is a musical play of great tenderness and emotion . . ."

Robert Garland—*New York Journal-American*
". . . seldom looked lovelier. Or sounded more melodious . . . How well these melodies have worn! How fresh, and yet familiar they sound, with Hammerstein's literate lyrics as goodly companion pieces to Kern's mellifluous melodies . . ."

Arthur Bronson—*Variety*, September 7, 1948
". . . The show is too big for the small City Center stage and gives a sense of being crowded. Otherwise, it's just right. Rodgers and Hammerstein treat the revival with care and respect, and the result is a worthy production, fresh and melodious as ever . . ."

Harold Clurman—*The New Republic*, September 27, 1948
". . . It is not too much to say that it is a classic. Seeing this musical, therefore, is not like seeing any other show. It is like recapturing a mood . . . I loved the original; I have enjoyed it every time I have seen it since . . . a story that perpetuates for twentieth century Americans the dream of a kindly nineteenth century past. It was born nostalgic . . ."

Elliot Norton—*Boston Post*
". . . the boat is beginning to list pretty badly and is not so seaworthy as she once was; but the melodies linger on, of course . . ."

SHOW BOAT

(Film Version—1951)

A Metro-Goldwyn-Mayer Picture
Produced by Arthur Freed
Associate producers, Ben Feiner Jr. and Roger Edens
Directed by George Sidney
Screenplay by John Lee Mahin
Choreography by Robert Alton
Art directors, Cedric Gibbons and Jack Martin Smith
Costumes by Walter Plunkett
Music director, Adolph Deutsch
Orchestrations by Conrad Salinger
Vocal arranger, Robert Tucker
Photographed by Charles Rosher
Editor, John Dunning
Color by Technicolor

Release Date
July 3, 1951

The Cast
MAGNOLIA HAWKS RAVENAL, Kathryn Grayson
JULIE LA VERNE, Ava Gardner (sung by Annette Warren)
GAYLORD RAVENAL, Howard Keel
CAP'N ANDY HAWKS, Joe E. Brown
ELLIE MAY CHIPLEY, Marge Champion
FRANK SCHULTZ, Gower Champion
STEVE BAKER, Robert Sterling
PARTHY ANN HAWKS, Agnes Moorehead
JOE, William Warfield
CAMEO MCQUEEN, Adele Jergens
PETE, Leif Erickson
QUEENIE, Frances Williams
WINDY MCCLAIN, Owen McGiveney
SHERIFF IKE VALLON, Regis Toomey
KIM RAVENAL, Sheila Clark
HERMAN, Chick Chandler
TROCADERO PIANO PLAYER, Fuzzy Knight

SEAMSTRESS, Anna Q. Nilsson
DRUNK, Bert Roach
JAKE GREEN, Emory Parnell
MARK HALLSON, Frank Wilcox

Musical Numbers

Songs retained from original production: *Cotton Blossom, Where's the Mate for Me?, Make Believe, Can't Help Lovin' dat Man, I Might Fall Back on You, Ol' Man River, You are Love, Why Do I Love You?, Bill, Life Upon the Wicked Stage, After the Ball.*

Reviews

Bosley Crowther—*New York Times*
". . . it is doubtful if even the first performance on the stage surpassed, except in novelty and freshness, this faithful translation . . ."

Otis Guernsey, Jr.—*New York Herald Tribune*
". . . the melodies and lyrics shine with an independent brilliance in the red plush and gold paint costume settings of a massive Hollywood period recreation . . ."

Bill Brogdon—*Variety*, June 6, 1951
". . . Boxoffice indications are the best . . ."

Lester Bernstein—*Time*, July 2, 1951
". . . has steamed across the screen twice before but never with such a lavish hand . . . The memorable score is as dependable a mainstay as ever. But never has *Show Boat* seemed so filled to the scuppers with corn . . ."

Thomas H. Wenning—*Newsweek*, July 2, 1951
". . . Neither radio nor repetition have blurred the melodic clarity of the score and, if anything, the passing years make it easier for the sentimental libretto to act its age as a plush romantic period piece . . . Warfield surpasses Bledsoe and Robeson . . . Miss Gardner makes a stunning Julie . . ."

John Rosenfield—*Dallas Morning News*, July 12, 1951
". . . For all the effort it seems tired. It clicks only when the Champions are singing and dancing . . ."

John McCarten—*The New Yorker*, July 28, 1951
". . . the only person who comes up to the standards of the very first company is William Warfield . . . Howard Keel, as the gambler, didn't impress me as the kind of man who could know the secrets of manipulating three walnut shells and a pea . . . in the improbable

circumstance that you've never laid eyes on *Show Boat* before, you'll probably love the thing."

Bibliography

The Director Points His Candid Camera at "Show Boat"
—*Look,* May 22, 1951

"Show Boats" in Review by Charles J. Lazarus
—*New York Times,* July 8, 1951

GOOD BOY

(1928)

A musical comedy with book by Otto Harbach, Oscar Hammerstein II, and Henry Myers; music by Herbert Stothart and Harry Ruby; lyrics by Bert Kalmar.

Presented by Arthur Hammerstein
Book staged by Reginald Hammerstein
Dances by Busby Berkeley
Settings by John Wenger
Costumes by Mark Mooring
Technical director, Leighton K. Brill
Mechanical effects by Peter Clark, Inc. and Edward Dolan
Music director, Mr. Stothart

Tryout
Nixon's Apollo Theatre, Atlantic City, August 13-18, 1928
Shubert Theatre, Philadelphia, August 20-September 1, 1928

New York Run
Hammerstein's Theatre, September 5, 1928-April 13, 1929
253 performances

The Story
Walter Meakin comes from Arkansas to New York to seek his fortune as an actor. He meets and marries Betty Summers, an actress, loses her, makes his fortune, and wins her back again.

The Cast
PA MEAKIN, Sam Hearn
MA MEAKIN, Effie Shannon
ELVIRA HOBBS, Evelyn Bennett
CICERO MEAKIN, Charles Butterworth
WALTER MEAKIN, Eddie Buzzell
PANSY MCMANUS, Helen Kane
A.A. STONE, Lester Bernard
"NEW YORK," Ariel Millars
"MANHATTAN," Milton Douglass
BETTY SUMMERS, Barbara Newberry
BOBBY DARNELL, Dan Healy

JIMMIE, Borrah Minevitch
POLICEMAN, Dick Neely
BRAKEMAN, Stan Rock
TICKET SPECULATOR, Joseph Ames
PAWN BROKER, Maurice Tepper
MOVIE THEATRE DOORMAN, Neil Vtone
OLD LADY, Elsie Percival
A GRAFTER, Gus Quinlan
MISS BADGER, Virginia Chase
HOTEL CLERK, Jack O'Hare
BELLBOYS: Tom Martin, Arthur Sullivan
ELEVATOR BOY, Gordon Merrit
TREVOR, Austin Clark
JUSTICE OF THE PEACE, Joseph Ames
LICENSE CLERK, Bob Abbott
LANDLADY, Muriel Greel
THEATRE DOORMAN, Neil Stone
THEATREGOER, Phil Daly
THEATRE TREASURER, William Meek
GIRL, Louise Blakeley
STREET CLEANER, Howard Raymond
GOB, Henry Corsell
A FRAIL, Jean Unger
DAGO, Will Withe
MEMBERS OF THE CHORUS: Louise Allen, Alice Akers, Mary Bay, Lillian Burke, Margaret Callan, Irene Carroll, Virginia Case, Georgette Caryl, Billie Cortez, Sylvia Collinson, Betty Croke, Ruth Cunliffe, Peggy Driscoll, Alice Raisen, Helen McGlyn, Boo Phelps, Bunny Schumm, Betty Wright, Flo Whyte, Kay Wolf, Dorothy Ward; Austin Clark, Arthur Craig, Edwin Gaillard, Jack Irwin, Ned Lynn, Gordon Merrick, Tom Martin, Gus Quinlan; Madeleine Eubanks, Jeanne Fayal, Rosemary Farmer, Loretta Flushing, Beryl Golden, Bobby Gorman, Muriel Griswold, Buddie Haines, Dorothy Jocelyn, Aida Conkey, Olive Kenyon, Grace LaRue, Mildred Lorain, Ruth Mason, Lucille Mercier, Delores Nito, Mabel Olsen

NOTE: During tryout, CICERO played by Hal Sherman. In November, Mr. Buzzell succeeded by Elliott Nugent, Miss Newberry by Vivian Hart.

Musical Numbers

ACT I

SCENE ONE—OUTSIDE MEAKIN'S FARMHOUSE, BUTLERSVILLE, ARKANSAS
Opening, *Down in Arkansas,* PA and GIRLS
What Makes You So Wonderful?, ELVIRY and CICERO
Good Boy, MA and WALLY
Finaletto, ENSEMBLE

SCENE TWO—SECTION 10 OF THE ARKANSAS FLYER

SCENE THREE—BOW OF THE NEW JERSEY-NEW YORK FERRY
SCENE FOUR—SKYLINE OF NEW YORK
SCENE FIVE—BROADWAY
Voice of the City, NEW YORK, MANHATTAN, GYPS THAT PASS IN THE NIGHT
SCENE SIX—UPPER BROADWAY
Manhattan Walk, BOBBY and BETTY
SCENE SEVEN—OUTSIDE A BOARDING HOUSE
SCENE EIGHT—A KITCHEN
Some Sweet Someone, WALLY and BETTY
SCENE NINE—ON THE STREET
SCENE TEN—INTERIOR OF MEAKIN'S FARMHOUSE IN BUTLERSVILLE
I Have My Moments, PA, ELVIRY, CICERO
SCENE ELEVEN—STAGE OF A THEATRE
I Wanna Be Loved by You, PANSY and BOBBY
SCENE TWELVE—A TAXICAB
SCENE THIRTEEN—A HOTEL ENTRANCE
Reprise, *Some Sweet Someone,* WALLY and BETTY
SCENE FOURTEEN—CORRIDOR OF A HOTEL
The Three Bears, PANSY and JIMMIE
SCENE FIFTEEN—HOTEL SUITE
Oh, What a Man, BOBBY
SCENE SIXTEEN—A BALCONY
Finale, WALLY and BETTY

ACT II
SCENE ONE—INTERIOR OF MEAKIN'S FARMHOUSE
Reprise, *Voice of the City,* MANHATTAN
SCENE TWO—WALLY'S WEDDING AS MA IMAGINES IT
Good Boy Wedding March, ENSEMBLE
SCENE THREE—A COUNTRY ROAD
SCENE FOUR—A PAWN SHOP
SCENE FIVE—THE LICENSE BUREAU
SCENE SIX—A JUSTICE OF THE PEACE
SCENE SEVEN—BETTY'S ROOM
Nina, BETTY and GIRLS
SCENE EIGHT—TELEPHONE PAY STATION
SCENE NINE—A STREET
SCENE TEN—A THEATRE LOBBY
SCENE ELEVEN—THE STAGE
SCENE TWELVE—CELLAR OF THE BOYS' CLUB
JIMMIE AND HIS GANG
SCENE THIRTEEN—PEACOCK ALLEY
SCENE FOURTEEN—A HOTEL LOBBY
Reprise, *I Wanna Be Loved by You,* PANSY and BOBBY, PA and MA, CICERO and ELVIRY
SCENE FIFTEEN—A HOTEL BEDROOM
SCENE SIXTEEN—FANTASIA
Fantasia, WALLY, BETTY and ENSEMBLE

NOTE: *Papa Get Hot, When I Hit Broadway, Something to Call Our Own, Disappointed Suitors, This Little Doll, Peacock Alley, Twinkle Little Stars,* and *You're the One* (Arthur Schwartz-Otto Harbach) cut before New York opening. In November, *Don't Be Like That* added in place of *The Three Bears,* and *Let's Give a Cheer* (sung by "MANHATTAN") added in place of *Oh, What a Man.*

Reviews

New York Times

". . . a show whose book is not one of the innovations . . . even moving scenery begins to pall in time, and then the spectator becomes acutely conscious that he is witnessing just another version of the story of the farm boy who makes good in the city . . . sufficiently snappy tunes . . ."

Richard Watts, Jr.—*New York Herald Tribune*

". . . The story is commonplace; the music, with the exception of *I Wanna Be Loved By You* and one other piece, is hardly exceptional, and there are frequent spots that are less than stimulating. In fact, it might not be a very good show if it weren't for the Misses Newberry and Kane and Mr. Butterworth . . ."

Jeffrey Holmesdale, Earl of Amherst—*New York World*

". . . one of those large, full-blooded musical comedies that border on the territory of operetta. It is built around a familiar type of plot, but given a slightly different twist, and it is staged with thoroughness and novelty that make it sparkle and stand out . . . Although it is short on the music side, the score being mostly dull and uninspired, it is a darned good show . . ."

Robert Coleman—*New York Daily Mirror*

". . . darn good entertainment. Swift, unique, lovely, amusing, tuneful and youthfully gay . . ."

Walter Winchell—*New York Graphic*

". . . fashioned from salable material . . . when the treadmill goes into operation, the show takes on pace and you find it quite pleasant . . ."

Wilella Waldorf—*New York Post*

". . . When the numerous stage technicians read the plot outline, they must have wept. Somebody, however, recovered in due time and recalled, possibly, an old production of *Ben-Hur,* proceeded to mount the creaky old plot on an infinite series of treadmills . . . several good tunes. Chiefly memorable, however, are Helen Kane, Charles Butterworth and the treadmills."

William O. Trapp—*New York Evening World*

". . . has more plot than usually falls to the musical comedy type of entertainment . . . *I Wanna Be Loved By You* is the most popular song, though another tuneful one called *Voice of the City* is probably technically better . . . lively and fascinating throughout . . . delightful . . ."

Stephen Rathbun—*New York Sun*
". . . The originality lies in the production itself, which was impressionistic and almost expressionistic . . . a good show . . ."

Abel Green—*Variety,* September 12, 1928
"Treadmill mechanical effects are the saving grace . . . the book weakens after the first act . . . Should enjoy a healthy run . . . three song hit possibilities . . ."

Charles Brackett—*The New Yorker,* September 15, 1928
". . . fair . . . Right in the middle, there came over me the realization that I was watching a Morality Play tricked out with a few tunes and two treadmills. That brought on a bad attack of what physicians know as Morality Play lumbago. There's nothing to do for it except get right up and take a long walk . . ."

Time, September 17, 1928
". . . the actors, trotting briskly along to keep pace with the changing scenery, had a little bit the look of squirrels in a cage or the race horses in the last act of *The Girl From Kentucky* . . . Aside from the mechanical innovations, the most noteworthy ingredient was Charles Butterworth . . ."

Tour
Shubert Theatre, Boston, April 16—May 18, 1929

Tour Reviews
H. T. Parker—*Boston Transcript*
". . . a new sort of musical play—the musical play panoramic. It holds the eye and catches the fancy . . . The machinery is workable, noiseless and unobtrusive . . . And the music? Neatly enough, in the middle way between mere noise and mere jingle, overworking no one manner . . . And 'the story'? Years ago Horatio Alger invented it. It is just as simple now."

THE NEW MOON

(1928)

A musical play with book by Oscar Hammerstein II, Frank Mandel and Laurence Schwab; music by Sigmund Romberg; lyrics by Mr. Hammerstein.

Presented by Messrs. Schwab and Mandel
Directed by Messers. Hammerstein, Schwab and Mandel (all uncredited)
Choreography by Bobby Connolly
Settings by Donald Oenslager
Costumes by Charles LeMaire
Music director, Alfred Goodman
Orchestrations by Emil Gerstenberger and Mr. Goodman

Tryout

Chestnut St. Opera House, Philadelphia, December 26, 1927-January 7, 1928 *(closed for revisions)*
Hanna Theatre, Cleveland, August 27-September 8, 1928
Shubert Alvin Theatre, Pittsburgh, September 10-15, 1928

New York Run

Imperial Theatre, September 19, 1928-November 16, 1929
Casino Theatre, November 18, 1929-December 14, 1929
509 performances

The Story

Robert, a bondservant to Monsieur Beaunoir in New Orleans in 1788, is really a French nobleman wanted for murder. He is captured and sent back to France on *The New Moon,* whose passenger list also includes his beloved, Marianne Beaunoir. During the trip Robert is rescued by his followers and, along with Marianne, establishes a colony of freemen on the Isle of Pines. After the French Revolution a year later, Robert is named governor of the island.

The Cast

JULIE, *Marianne's maid,* Marie Callahan
MONSIEUR BEAUNOIR, *a ship owner of New Orleans,* Pacie Ripple
CAPT. PAUL DUVAL, *Commander of "The New Moon",* Edward Nell Jr.
VICOMTE RIBAUD, Max Figman

ROBERT MISSON, *a bondservant to M. Beaunoir,* Robert Halliday
ALEXANDER, *another bondservant,* Gus Shy
BESAC, *boatswain of "The New Moon",* Lyle Evans
JACQUES, *a ship carpenter,* Earle Mitchell
MARIANNE, *Beaunoir's daughter,* Evelyn Herbert
PHILIPPE, *a friend of Robert,* William O'Neal
CLOTILDE LOMBASTE, *of the bride ship,* Esther Howard
PROPRIETOR OF THE TAVERN, Daniel Barnes
FLOWER GIRL, Olga Albani
A SPANIARD, Herman Belmonte
A DANCER, Edith Sheldon
FOUCHETTE, Thomas Dale
THE DANCERS, Rosita and Ramon
THE MUSICIANS, Hernandez Brothers Trio
CAPTAIN DEJEAN, Lester Dorr
LADIES: Elizabeth Taylor, Sylvia LaMard, Marion Frances, Phyllis Marren, Dulcie Bond, Elmira Lane, Dorothy Verlaine, Barbara Dare, Kay Burnell, Dorothy Christie, Dean Wheeler, Rita Marks, Marjorie Sneller, Sylvia Roberts, Beulah Baker, Doddy Donnelly, Constance King, Frances Mildren, Olga Grannis, Rosalie Brumm, Ida Berry, Ruth Grady, Rae Powell, Rosalie Trego, Novella Fromm, Tina Jensen, Helen Casey, Dorothy Higgins, Carola Taylor, Gloria Lee, Dorothy Grady, Ruth Jennings, Marnie Sawyer, Cecilia Caskey, Christine Morey, Dorice Covert, Gloria Glennon
GENTLEMEN: R. E. Garcia, Edward Smythe, Frank Dowling, Herman Belmonte, Charles Muhs, Lazlo Aliga, Sol Leimas, David DeGrave, Lean Sabater, A. Keller, Basil Prock, Cornell Pilcher, Irving Weinstein, Frank Dobert, Al Monty, Zellig Norman, Bart Schilling, Arthur Verbowvans, Joe Rogers, Vance Campbell, John Cardini, James Davis, Wallace McLeod, W. M. Rytter, John Gutcher, Ernest McChesney, Sigmund Glukoff, Tome Coppe, William Prevost, Patrick Henry, George Kirk, Jack Murray, Charles Maynard, Frank Grimmel, T. W. Kendall, Carl Linke, Sverre Rasmussen, Ned Byers, Carl Streib, Frank Vaughn

NOTE: During 1927 tryout, MARIANNE played by Desiree Tabor, ALEXANDER by William Wayne. Miss Herbert temporarily replaced by Charlotte Lansing (June-August 1929) and Margaret Carlisle (August-September 1929). In August 1929, Mr. Halliday temporarily replaced by George Houston. For tour, Mr. Shy succeeded by William Sully.

Musical Numbers

ACT I

SCENE ONE—GRAND SALON OF M. BEAUNOIR'S MANSION, NEW ORLEANS, 1788

Opening, *Dainty Wisp of Thistledown,* ENSEMBLE
Marianne, ROBERT
The Girl On the Prow, MARIANNE and ENSEMBLE

Gorgeous Alexander, JULIE, ALEXANDER and GIRLS
An Interrupted Love Song, DUVAL, MARIANNE, ROBERT

SCENE TWO—ENTRANCE TO CHEZ CREOLE

SCENE THREE—INTERIOR OF CHEZ CREOLE
Tavern Song (Red Wine), FLOWER GIRL, DANCER and ENSEMBLE
Softly, As In a Morning Sunrise, PHILIPPE and ENSEMBLE
Stouthearted Men (Liberty Song), ROBERT, PHILIPPE and MEN

SCENE FOUR—ENTRANCE TO CHEZ CREOLE

SCENE FIVE—GRAND SALON OF M. BEAUNOIR'S MANSION
Fair Rosita, GIRLS; danced by Rosita and Ramon
One Kiss, MARIANNE and ENSEMBLE
The Trial (Ladies of the Jury), ALEXANDER, JULIE, LOMBASTE and GIRLS
Wanting You, MARIANNE and ROBERT
Finale, ENSEMBLE

ACT II
SCENE ONE—DECK OF "THE NEW MOON"
Opening, *A Chanty,* BESAC and MEN
Funny Little Sailor Men, LOMBASTE, BESAC and ENSEMBLE
Lover, Come Back to Me, MARIANNE
Finaletto, MARIANNE, ROBERT, PHILIPPE and MEN

SCENE TWO—A ROAD FROM THE BEACH
Love Is Quite a Simple Thing, LOMBASTE, BESAC, ALEXANDER, JULIE

SCENE THREE—THE STOCKADE, ONE YEAR LATER
Try Her Out at Dances, ALEXANDER, JULIE and GIRLS

SCENE FOUR—A ROAD FROM THE BEACH
Reprise, *Softly, as in a Morning Sunrise,* PHILIPPE and MEN

SCENE FIVE—MARIANNE'S CABIN
Never for You, MARIANNE
Reprise, *Lover, Come Back to Me,* ROBERT and MEN

SCENE SIX—A ROAD FROM THE BEACH

SCENE SEVEN—THE STOCKADE
Finale, COMPANY

NOTE: *Paree, La-La-La-La, A Voice in the Dark, One Day, When I Close My Eyes, 'Neath a New Moon, Women, Women, Women, The Call of Home,* and *I Love You* cut after 1927 tryout. *Hot and Cold, The First Man I Kiss, A Love that Lasts, One Kiss Is Waiting for One Man, Liar,* and *I'm Just a Sentimental Fool* cut before New York opening.

Reviews

J. Brooks Atkinson—*New York Times*
". . . unusually pleasing . . . full-bodied score . . . It is not merely a good book; it is almost too good and begins to weigh a little on the

entertainment in the first act. Painstaking as the authors have been, Mr. Romberg has caught the spirit rather more intelligibly in his strong and virtuoso score. Deep, rushing, stirring, it is one of the best scores written for many months . . ."

Percy Hammond—*New York Herald Tribune*
". . . a distinguished song service performed by many soulful musicians . . . Too dignified to be very funny, it makes up for absent clowning by the beauty of its tailoring, the seductiveness of its score, the spryness of its dancers, and the solemnity of its plot . . . Melting songs are numerous—*One Kiss, Wanting You,* and also a hot torch psalm entitled *Lover, Come Back to Me* . . ."

St. John Ervine—*New York World*
". . . the most charming and fragrant entertainment of its sort that I have seen for a long time. It is beautifully produced and beautifully acted and beautifully sung. It has taste and distinction . . . very fine and tuneful, if occasionally reminiscent, music . . . an intelligent story. It is not a piece of immortal literature, but neither is it, as a majority of stories in musical pieces are, a piece of pure imbecility . . ."

Burns Mantle—*New York Daily News*
". . . a score studded with hits . . . silly things, these operetta plots, but they are heaps better than the average musical comedy plots . . . grand entertainment for the matinee crowds."

Robert Littell—*New York Post*
". . . a silky leisurely thing with nice music and some of the handsomest costumes ever seen . . . even if it was long and many of the solo songs were pretty dull, there was something full-measured and gay and brightly colored about it, which was satisfying and a welcome relief from the usual cheap stuff . . . the music, which without giving you anything to take home, filled the air with something for which there is only one word—tuneful . . ."

E. W. Osborn—*New York Evening World*
"A great glory descended upon West 45th Street last night. A glory of fine voices; a glory of costumes and scenery and living people; a glory of romance shaded in not too many places by comedy of the cleanest and happiest. A glory, take it for all in all of light opera at its best, as far from the plain musical play as the sun is from the stars . . . stirring music . . . *The Girl on the Prow* and *Lover, Come Back to Me* were numbers sweetly alluring; *Marianne* and *Wanting You* were love songs in very truth . . ."

Courtenay Terrett—*New York Telegram*
". . . very beautiful and very costly, at once elegant and voluptuous, comic and almost operatic, and as excellent a show of this kind as this season is likely to bring forth . . . a score better than Romberg has written for a number of seasons . . ."

Gilbert W. Gabriel—*New York Sun*
". . . certainly and superlatively as good as they come . . . great scenic pomp and grandiose sentiments . . . the brightest dancing numbers I've seen this year, and the loveliest costumes I've seen since many years before that . . ."

John Anderson—*New York Journal*
". . . a lavish and tuneful operetta which comforts the eye and ear without offending the most offensive intelligence . . ."

Jack Pulaski (Ibee.)—*Variety,* September 26, 1928
". . . another musical success . . . intelligently written, smartly produced and gifted with plenty of melody . . . Maybe the Hammerstein kid needs a press agent. He has contributed to many a musical success and his work is now accepted as a matter of course . . ."

Charles Brackett—*The New Yorker,* September 29, 1928
". . . the best of the musical shows I've seen so far this year. (Check up on that. It doesn't rate very high as a trade last.) . . . Grave operatic doings . . . The score, I must admit, is the sort which sends an ammonia-gas chill through my veins . . . It turns the performers into vocalists, who do a great deal of gesturing, palms up and fingers brought to the clench on certain notes . . . Robert Halliday dashes and dashes as the hero."

Time, October 1, 1928
". . . While this long and shiny fable professes no Marxian solemnity, it is less silly than most operetta plots . . . Dressed in the magnificent rags of theatrical insurgence, surrounded by beautiful girls and elaborate scenery, yodeling a plea for stout-hearted men made tuneful by Sigmund Romberg, Robert organizes his golden expedition . . ."

Robert Benchley—*Life,* October 5, 1928
". . . an elaborate production with an old fashioned score . . . We haven't seen such refayned acting since the days when the Mysterious Stranger with the white plume turned out to be Prince Boris in disguise. And *then* what merry-making at the inn there was! A toast, a toast to Prince Boris!"

George Jean Nathan—*Judge,* October 13, 1928
". . . As for the score, it isn't merely familiar; one might say that it is presumptuous. It not only pats Victor Herbert and, occasionally, George Gershwin on the back, it goes right up to them and puts its arms around them. The *One Kiss* number persuades us to believe that Herbert is not dead, but merely very sick, and *Lover, Come Back to Me* owes at least a share of its royalties to Gershwin's *The Man I Love.* But the show is so greatly superior to the other new musical exhibitions, that I commend it to your notice . . ."

Bibliography

Fixing Up "The New Moon" —*New York Times,* September 20, 1928

Tour

Forrest Theatre, Philadelphia, December 23, 1929—Shubert Theatre, Newark, May 17, 1930 (5 cities).

Selected Revivals

St. Louis Municipal Opera, August 6-12, 1934
Allan Jones (ROBERT); Charlotte Lansing (MARIANNE); Jack Sheehan (ALEXANDER); Paul Haakon (FEATURED DANCER).

Carnegie Hall, New York, August 18-September 6, 1942
Wilbur Evans (ROBERT); Ruby Mercer (MARIANNE); Teddy Hart (ALEXANDER); Viola Essen, Peter Birch (FEATURED DANCERS).

San Francisco Civic Light Opera, May 1-20, 1944
Los Angeles Civic Light Opera, May 22-June 10, 1944
Walter Cassel (ROBERT); Helena Bliss (MARIANNE); Kenny Bowers (ALEXANDER); Eric Mattson (PHILIPPE); John Miljan (RIBAUD).

Belmont Operetta, City Center, New York, May 17-June 24, 1944
Earl Wrightson (ROBERT); Dorothy Kirsten (MARIANNE); Johnny Morgan (ALEXANDER).

St. Louis Municipal Opera, June 9-19, 1949
Edward Roecker (ROBERT); Dorothy Sarnoff (MARIANNE); Buster West (ALEXANDER); Sidney Blackmer (RIBAUD); Mary Wickes (CLOTILDE).

Greek Theatre, Los Angeles, Summer, 1949
John Raitt (ROBERT); Lucille Norman (MARIANNE); Sterling Holloway (ALEXANDER); Collette Lyons (JULIE).

St. Louis Municipal Opera, July 10-16, 1967
Bruce Yarnell (ROBERT); Margot Moser (MARIANNE); R. G. Brown (ALEXANDER); William Lewis (PHILIPPE); Travis Hudson (CLOTILDE).

Productions Abroad
Theatre Royal, Drury Lane, London, April 4-August 10, 1929
(See below)

Chatelet Théatre, Paris, December, 1929
Cast: Jane Flynn, Danielle Bergis, Boucot, André Bauge, Sancie Duncan, Gont Charova. (retitled *Robert Casse-Cou.*)

THE NEW MOON

(London—1929)

Presented by Sir Alfred Butt
Directed by Felix Edwardes
Choreography by Bobby Connolly
Settings by Prince Galitzine and Joseph and Phil Harker
Costumes by Irene Segalla
Music director, Herman Finck
Opening night conductor, Mr. Romberg

London Run
Theatre Royal, Drury Lane, April 4-August 10, 1929
147 performances

The Cast
JULIE, Dolores Farris
MONSIEUR BEAUNOIR, Vincent Clive
CAPT. PAUL DUVAL, Jack Livesey
VICOMTE RIBAUD, Edmund Willard
FOUCHETTE, Barrie Livesey
ROBERT MISSON, Howett Worster
ALEXANDER, Gene Gerrard
BESAC, Roy Emerton
JACQUES, John MacMahon
MARIANNE BEAUNOIR, Evelyn Laye
PHILIPPE, Ben Williams
EMILE, Walter Donahue
CLOTILDE LOMBASTE, Vera Pearce
WAITER, A. J. Willard
LANDLORD, Selwyn Morgan
BRUNET, Ernest Ludlow
FLOWER GIRL, Margery Hicklin
SPANIARD, William Wallace
DANCER, Kathleen Gerrard
CAPT. DEJEAN, Hubert Ennor

LADIES OF THE CHORUS: Hero Allen, Sybil Allnatt, Cynthia Arthurs, Margaret Boyle, Corinne Brandon, Nancy Brown, Dorothy Cooper, Dorothy Crofts, Muriel Cronshaw, Zita DaCosta, Eileen Dubarry, Constance Edwards, Molly Egbert, Nancy Eshelby, Kathleen Fitchie, Lena Fitchie, Winnie Ford, Nan Forster, Doreen Gabelle, Kathleen Gerrard, Grace Garrod, Hazel Carnegie, Joyce Holloway, Maureen Julian, Mavice Kalmar, Elsie Lawrence, Alma Lee, Linda Lindose, Peggy Lovat, Nance Miriam, Mary Morris, Myrette Morven, Phyllis Neal, Esme Oxley, Eileen Pemberthy, Constance Perrin, Sylvia Phipps, Audrey Robbins, Marjorie Rose, Rosalind Snow, Christine Symons, Winifred Talbott, Billie Webb

GENTLEMEN OF THE CHORUS: Bernard Adams, Reginald Allen, C. Britten-Eldred, Kennedy Brooker, Eric Boster, Hadyn Campbell, William Colvin, Richard Crawford, Herbert Court, Gordon Crocker, Walter Cutler, Vincent Davis, John Delaney, Edward Del Foss, Thomas Drew, Alfred Fairhurst, Walter Farrance, Egbert Paul, Harry Fergussen, Reginald Gibson, Walter Gummow, Alvon Hawke, Ivan Hawkes, George Hawarth, William Herbert, Evan Jones, Donald Kingstone, Harry Lacey, Leonard Lowe, Ernest Ludlow, Guy Lyngan, T. G. MacBenn, Trevor Mansell, Philip Merrit, David Morgan, Selwyn Morgan, Basil Neale, Roy Neilson, G. Pennington, H. E. Richards, J. W. Robinson, John Scott, Ronald Stear, Eric Sutherland, William Wallace, Wilfred Ward, Walter Webster, G. C. Whitehead, A. J. Willard

NOTE: During run, Mr. Worster succeeded by Harry Welchman.

Musical Numbers

Same as original production.

Reviews

London Times

". . . Such is the nature of these entertainments that the story matters a great deal less than the songs and dances in which it is told . . . In the first phase there is little to distinguish the entertainment from a musical comedy of average merit . . . But the second phase provides rich opportunities for a lavish use of the equipment at Drury Lane . . ."

London Daily Telegraph

". . . marvellously drilled crowds, picturesque (and intricate) mass movements, splendour of decoration and so forth . . . musically, the chief feature of the performance was the superb singing of the male chorus . . ."

London Morning Post

". . . never has Evelyn Laye sung better than in her *One Kiss*, a song which bears repetition better than any other in the piece . . . the way even the girls sent *Stouthearted Men* over the footlights did one's heart good . . . "

James Agate—*London Sunday Times,* April 7, 1929
". . . the verb 'to balfe' harkens back to the fourth member of the group of statues in the foyer of Drury Lane. The other three are Shakespeare, Garrick and Kean . . . To balfe, then, means to elevate something to a position which it is not entitled to hold . . . To pay that respect to a semi-serious, semi-comic, and demi-semi-musical entertainment which the musical foreigner pays to an opera by Strauss, to raise the show to the rank of a social event, to discuss it, and, in fine, do anything but dismiss it as a high-spirited lark is also balfing . . ."

Ivor Brown—*London Observer,* April 7, 1929
". . . The hero has all a nobleman's passion for abstract democracy . . . he founds his Land of the Free on a site which the realtors will now have turned into a second Palm Beach, and there rules over a community with a strange passion for such borgeois institutions as matrimony and fine linen . . . the plugged song is a kind of dithyramb of the stout *fellahin* . . . The first night was a very long sitting, and something will have to go overboard; at the same time room might be found for some low comedy on the high seas . . ."

G. W. Bishop—*The Era*
". . . about as silly as anything that America has sent to this country . . . part of the second act is not only stupid but dull . . . nevertheless, a fine spectacle . . . Romberg's music, if nearly always reminiscent, goes with a splendid swing . . . the best part of the entertainment is the chorus singing."

Bibliography

"The New Moon" —*The Play Pictorial,* June, 1929

NEW MOON

(Film Version—1930)

A Metro-Goldwyn-Mayer Picture
Directed by Jack Conway
Screenplay by Sylvia Thalberg and Frank Butler
Dialogue by Cyril Hume
Photographed by Oliver T. Marsh

Release Date
December 28, 1930

The Story
In Russia during the time of the Czar, Lieutenant Petroff falls in love with Tanya, who is betrothed to Governor Brusiloff. He is sent to the border to command hitherto unmanageable troops, and is later joined by Tanya and her father, Count Strogoff. They become surrounded by Turkoman troops, which are routed by Petroff's men. He marries Tanya and is honored by the Czar.

The Cast
LIEUTENANT MICHAEL PETROFF, Lawrence Tibbett
PRINCESS TANYA STROGOFF, Grace Moore
GOVERNOR BORIS BRUSILOFF, Adolphe Menjou
COUNT STROGOFF, Roland Young
POTKIN, Gus Shy
COUNTESS ANASTASIA STROGOFF, Emily Fitzroy

Musical Numbers
Songs retained from original production: *Softly, as in a Morning Sunrise, Stouthearted Men, One Kiss, Wanting You, and Lover, Come Back to Me.* Songs written for film: *Once There Was a Farmer's Daughter* and *Women.*

Reviews
Mordaunt Hall—*New York Times*
". . . quite a good story . . . One never has enough of the singing despite the interesting narrative . . . An excellent combination of fine singing, romance and adventure . . ."

Joe Bigelow—*Variety,* December 31, 1930
". . . As it is 100% romantic, the shortcomings in performances are hard on the picture . . . will entertain the minority who relish that which is more at home in concert. For the rest, there's not enough along with the singing, either in the players or the play . . ."

John Mosher—*The New Yorker,* January 3, 1931
. . . I don't happen to be one of those people addicted to movie operettas. If you belong to that party of art-lovers, you will get your proper pleasure . . ."

Time, January 5, 1931
". . . a plotty affair . . . *Lover, Come Back to Me* is sung probably better than it has ever been sung before . . ."

Pare Lorentz—*Judge,* January 17, 1931
"The more pretentious singing becomes in the movies, the duller the show, and if you don't believe me go see *New Moon* . . . If the producers wanted to make their two opera singers work, I do not see why they compromised on an operetta that was neither important nor entertaining . . ."

NEW MOON

(Film Version—1940)

A Metro-Goldwyn-Mayer Picture
Produced and directed by Robert Z. Leonard
Screenplay by Jacques Deval and Robert Arthur
Choreography by Val Raset
Art director, Cedric Gibbons
Costumes by Adrian, Giles Steel
Music director, Herbert Stothart
Photographed by William Daniels
Editor, Harold Kress

Release Date

June 18, 1940

The Cast

MARIANNE DE BEAUMANOIR, Jeanette MacDonald
CHARLES MICHON (né CHARLES-HENRI, DUC DE VILLIERS), Nelson Eddy
VALERIE DEROSSAC, Mary Boland
VICOMTE RIBAUD, George Zucco
FATHER MICHAEL, H.B. Warner
GOVERNOR OF NEW ORLEANS, Grant Mitchell
TAMBOUR, Stanley Fields
ALEXANDER, Richard Purcell
PIERRE, William Tannen
BRUGNON, John Miljan
GUIZOT, Ivan Simpson
JULIE, Bunty Cutler
DUBOIS, Claude King
GOVERNOR'S WIFE, Cecil Cunningham
MAURICE, Joe Yule
SHIP'S CAPTAIN, George Irving
CAPT. DEJEAN, Edwin Maxwell
PRISONER, Buster Keaton
COCO, Raymond Walker

Musical Numbers

Songs retained from original production: *Paree* (in tryout), *Softly, as in a Morning Sunrise, Wanting You, Lover, Come Back to Me, Stouthearted Men,* and *Marianne.* Other musical pieces in film: *Rondolet, Shoe Shine Song, Bayou Trouble Tree* (by Herbert Stothart), and Handel's *Largo.*

All songs sung by Miss MacDonald and Mr. Eddy.

Reviews

Bosley Crowther—*New York Times*
". . . Somehow the familiar lilt of the old MacDonald-Eddy extravaganzas is missing . . . never quite comes alive . . . we rather sadly suspect that this sort of sugar-coated musical fiction has seen its better days."

Howard Barnes—*New York Herald Tribune*
"As handsome and as dated as you might suspect . . . not being partial to the form, I found it too long and tiresome, but there is no denying its entertainment potentialities . . . a dull and lavish formula . . ."

Archer Winsten—*New York Post*
". . . not a surprise in the entire carload of celluloid . . . Verdict: this picture is best for loyal Eddy and MacDonald fans, operetta addicts, and kids who started their movie going careers within the past two years."

Walt Christie—*Variety,* June 19, 1940
". . . pretentious and elaborately mounted . . . the general lightness and the excellence of the musical numbers provide relief from the gloomy atmosphere of current events . . "

Time, July 15, 1940
". . . Between *One Kiss* and another, there is too much palling palaver, too much time to observe that the Eddy figure is becoming almost as operatic as the Eddy acting . . ."

Russell Maloney—*The New Yorker,* July 27, 1940
". . . The total effect on the average moviegoer will, I believe, be a dull persistent feeling of irritation. After much pondering, I have concluded that the trouble with the MacDonald-Eddy cycle is that these two are given songs too negligible for their old-fashioned concert-hall technique, and acting assignments beyond their abilities . . ."

RAINBOW

(1928)

A musical play with book by Laurence Stallings and Oscar Hammerstein II; music by Vincent Youmans; lyrics by Mr. Hammerstein.

Presented by Philip Goodman
Directed by Mr. Hammerstein
Choreography by Busby Berkeley
Settings by Frank E. Gates and E.A. Morange
Costumes by Charles LeMaire
Technical director, Leighton K. Brill
Music director, Max Steiner

Tryout

Chestnut Street Opera House, Philadelphia, October 29-November 10, 1928
Maryland Theatre, Baltimore, November 12-17, 1928

New York Run

Gallo Theatre, November 21-December 15, 1928
29 performances

The Story

Harry Stanton, a young scout at Ft. Independence, Missouri, kills Major Davolo in self-defense. He is imprisoned, escapes, follows a wagon trail to California, and eventually woos and wins the hand of Virginia Brown.

The Cast

MAJOR DAVOLO, Rupert Lucas
LOTTA, Libby Holman
MESS SERGEANT, Ned McGurn
SERGEANT MAJOR, Harland Dixon
PENNY, Helen Lynd
COL. BROWN, Henry Pemberton
NASTY HOWELL, Charlie Ruggles
CAPT. ROBERT SINGLETON, Brian Donlevy
VIRGINIA BROWN, Louise Brown
FANNY, Herself

HARRY STANTON, Allan Prior
CORPORAL, Leo Mack
PRIVATES: Stewart Edwards, Leo Dugan, Ward Arnold
ROOKIE, Randall Fryer
BARTENDER, Frank King
SENORA MENDOZA, Mary Carney
PEON, Leo Nash
SERVANT, Charles Ralph
SPANISH GIRL, Valia Valentinova
SNOW BALL, May Barnes
FRENCHIE, George Magis
MR. JACKSON, Chester Bree
EGG, Edward Nemo
TOUGH, Ralph Walker
KITTY, Kitty Coleman
SHOW GIRLS: Ann Austin, Harriette Brinton, Mary Carney, Kitty Coleman, Ann Constance, Christine Gallagher, Margaret Grove, Dorothy Pensel, Rowena Scott, Valia Valentinova, Emily Wentz, Elinor Witmar
DANCING GIRLS: Margaret Alexander, Phyllis Buck, Virla Buley, Lee Byrne, Bobbe Campbell, Christine Crane, Dorothy Dodd, Irene Evans, LaVergne Evans, Gracea Fleming, Evelyn Kermin, Helen Madigan, Edith Martin, Ruth Martin, Pauline Maxwell, Betty McNulty, Mildred Morgan, Beth Meredith, Ruby Nevins, Margaret Pidgin, Helen Rauth, Betty Sherman, Maragret Todd, Jean Watson, Betty Waxston, Claire White
DANCING BOYS: Ward Arnold, Milton Brodus, Frank Gagen, Frank Kimball, Harry Lake, Larry Larkin, Glenn McComas, Clinton McLeer, Ned McGurn, Lewis Parker, John Perkins, Thomas Sternfeld, Paul Taft
SINGING BOYS: James Beattie, Vladimir Chavdaroff, Vincent Curran, Thomas Dendy, Vincent Funaro, Christopher Gerard, Don Heebner, Ludovic Huot, Cyril Joyce, Charles Mack, George Magis, Leo Nash, Ray Otto, Efin Vitis, Victor Young, Randall Fryer, Lu Talbott

Musical Numbers

ACT I

SCENE ONE—FORT INDEPENDENCE, MISSOURI, 1849
Opening, *On the Golden Trail,* ENSEMBLE
My Mother Told Me Not to Trust a Soldier, SERGEANT-MAJOR and PENNY
Virginia, VIRGINIA, SINGLETON and BOYS
I Want a Man, LOTTA

SCENE TWO—GUARD ROOM OF THE FORT
Soliloquy, STANTON

SCENE THREE—A WAGON TRAIN ON THE PLAINS
I Like You as You Are, STANTON and VIRGINIA
Finaletto, LOTTA

SCENE FOUR—IN THE MOUNTAINS
Dance, VIRGINIA
The One Girl, STANTON and MEN
Finaletto, *Let Me Give All My Love to Thee* (hymn), VIRGINIA, LOTTA, STANTON and ENSEMBLE

SCENE FIVE—RED DOG, CALIFORNIA, A MINING TOWN
Diamond in the Rough, NASTY and PENNY
Who Wants to Love Spanish Ladies?, ENSEMBLE
Dance, SERGEANT-MAJOR
Reprise, *I Like You as You Are,* STANTON and VIRGINIA
Finale, COMPANY

ACT II
SCENE ONE—GAMBLING ROOM OF THE SILVER DOLLAR SALOON, SACRAMENTO
Opening, ENSEMBLE
Hay! Straw!, VIRGINIA and SERGEANT-MAJOR
Reprise, *I Like You as You Are,* LOTTA
Finaletto, STANTON, VIRGINIA, LOTTA, SINGLETON and MEN

SCENE TWO—OUTSIDE OF SALOON
The Bride Was Dressed in White, NASTY and PENNY

SCENE THREE—THE PRESIDIO OF SAN FRANCISCO
Reprise, *On the Golden Trail,* ENSEMBLE
Finale, COMPANY

NOTE: *Get a Horse, Get a Mule, I Look for Love, How to Win a Man, Who Am I?* (lyric by Gus Kahn), *Coming Through the Rye, Forty-Niner and His Clementine, A Faded Rose* and *Sunrise* cut before New York opening.

Reviews

J. Brooks Atkinson—*New York Times*
". . . although it is long to the point of tedium, it yields robust entertainment that never succumbs to the general musical comedy fol-de-rol. Not to be unduly secretive, it is lively fun . . . No musical play of recent season has boasted such a roistering book . . . If Mr. Youmans has not realized his opportunity completely, he has written in a harmonious key and occasionally with genuine distinction. The contralto blues, *I Want a Man* is sung splendidly by the scowling, menacing Libby Holman . . ."

Howard Barnes—*New York Herald Tribune*
". . . a prodigal, bright-hued entertainment, with absorbing melodramatic undertones which burst through the thin veil of a graceful score and pretty dances . . . the conventional musical comedy pattern was ever in peril of being rudely shattered . . . Youmans maintains his place as one of our first jazz composers in the piece,

which boasts not so much a nosegay of song hits as a coordinated score . . ."

St. John Ervine—*New York World*
". . . I suggest Stallings and Hammerstein persuade Mr. Goodman to go to Italy for a month and fill himself with food so that he may fall into a torpor from which he may not easily be roused. In that time they can revise and recast their play, quickening the pace and adding at least one lady who can act and who possesses personality . . . Its notable merits will then be plainly apparent to everybody . . . a plausible story, and in this sort of play a story at all is something of a novelty . . ."

Burns Mantle—*New York Daily News*
". . . can boast a story that holds together almost as well as did that of *Rose-Marie* . . . a good steady business for numerous weeks is assured."

Robert Coleman—*New York Daily Mirror*
"At the end of his *Rainbow,* Mr. Goodman should find a pot of gold . . . a thrilling show . . . should glitter gloriously across the theatrical skies for many months . . ."

Gilbert W. Gabriel—*New York American*
". . . too hearty for quibbling, too big to be trifled with . . . a lusty, happy, often handsome show, picturesque—but never too much so to cease being lively too—and somehow full of that simple and effective fervor which seems to inform almost every project in which Stallings has a hand . . . Things are modeled pretty flatteringly after *Show Boat.* Which means that the story is pellmell with incident and action, with colorful scene upon scene, with all varieties of glee of song and dance threaded firmly into the main excitement . . ."

Robert Littell—*New York Post*
"The best is wonderfully good enough and also brand new, and for that Stallings must be credited with one of the most refreshingly original musicals on record . . . one wishes that it didn't sink into the groove of regular musical comedy here and there—but it's a brave show just the same, one that often makes one want to stand up and cheer . . . *I Like You As You Are* was one of the neatest and most original lyrics I have ever heard . . . so gorgeously different in its high spots that the weaker spots didn't matter very much."

E. W. Osborn—*New York Evening World*
". . . Libby Holman's voice was peculiar and popular . . . Concerning the book, there was a general verdict that perhaps they did

things a bit more roughly in '49. Also that there was room for considerable trimming . . ."

Robert Garland—*New York Telegram*
". . . costly and pretentious . . . not nearly as worth while as it should have been . . . *I Like You As You Are* is a lilting number . . ."

Richard Lockridge—*New York Sun*
"This *Rainbow*—however it may have dragged through its almost endless first act—has pots of gold hung gayly both at the ends and between them . . . has lines the actors can speak without hiding their heads and lyrics which actually make sense . . . It is almost exciting to find a musical with some faint notion that there is a palpable difference between romance and lugged-in sentimentality . . . the music is at all times very good; it carries always the spirit of the words Hammerstein has written with so much vigor and gayety . . ."

John Anderson—*New York Journal*
". . . beautiful and tuneful . . . a score that sings and twirls itself into every whistling cranny of the memory . . ."

Jack Pulaski (Ibee.)—*Variety,* November 28, 1928
". . . *I Like You as You Are* is the best of Youmans' very good score . . . *Rainbow* has enough stuff in it to draw people . . . should register moderately well . . ."

Charles Brackett—*The New Yorker,* December 1, 1928
". . . There is strength and virility in many of its anecdotes very welcome after the diluted insipidity of most musical comedies . . . The music is not up to Youmans' best, however, and on opening night the story seemed both too long and badly cut up . . ."

George Jean Nathan—*Judge,* December 22, 1928
". . . If ever a good musical show was ruined by careless production on its initial performance, this is the show. Of all the musical comedies disclosed hereabouts in several years, excepting only *Show Boat* and *The Three Musketeers,* it enjoys by far the best book . . . Youmans' melodies are extremely agreeable . . . with competent showmanship, it might have been a first-rate thing of its kind . . ."

SONG OF THE WEST

(Film Version of "Rainbow"—1930)

A Warner Brothers Picture
Directed by Ray Enright
Screenplay by Harvey Thew
Photographed by Dev Jennings
Color by Technicolor

Release Date

February 27, 1930

The Cast

HARRY STANTON, John Boles
VIRGINIA BROWN, Vivienne Segal
LOTTA, Marie Wells
"HASTY" HOWELL, Joe E. Brown
MAJOR DAVOLO, Sam Hardy
PENNY, Marion Byron

Musical Numbers

Songs retained from original production: *The One Girl, I Like You As You Are, Hay! Straw!, Let Me Give All My Love to Thee* and *The Bride Was Dressed In White.* Songs written for film: *West Wind* (by Mr. Youmans and J. Russel Robinson) and *Come Back to Me* (by Harry Akst and Grant Clarke).

Reviews

Mordaunt Hall—*New York Times*
". . . Compelling prismatic scenes of the covered wagon days and good comedy are the chief attributes . . . the story calls for so many odd doings that even in its more serious sequences it is apt to arouse undue mirth . . ."

Richard Watts, Jr.—*New York Herald Tribune*
". . . as cruel a desecration of a superior stage work as the cinema has yet devised . . . had the advantage of combining a serviceable story, a brilliant score and the scope and pictorial range of a sort of 'Covered Wagon' background. Yet the result is a slovenly, ugly, clumsy and generally dull motion picture . . ."

Harry Evans—*Life,* February 27, 1930
". . . some beautiful technicolor photography . . . a fine performance by Joe E. Brown who sings an amusing song *The Bride Was Dressed In White.* Other than these two items there is nothing of particular interest . . . The music is not distinctive . . ."

Laird.—*Variety,* March 5, 1930
". . . less than completely satisfying . . . just a nice looking program feature—no more, no less. Falters in the story department. It's a chronicle rather than a plot . . . stretches of snail-like slowness . . . a couple of lilting tunes . . ."

John Mosher—*The New Yorker,* March 8, 1930
". . . the whole thing is somewhat routine and a bit on the dull side, except for an absurd song: *The Bride Was Dressed in White.*"

Pare Lorentz—*Judge,* March 22, 1930
". . . nothing but a very dull routine plot about frustrated love and several people who sing and dance and cry at you. It is very bad."

SWEET ADELINE

(1929)

A musical play with book and lyrics by Oscar Hammerstein II; music by Jerome Kern.

Presented by Arthur Hammerstein
Directed by Reginald Hammerstein
Choreography by Danny Dare
Settings by Frank E. Gates and E. A. Morange
Costumes by Charles LeMaire
Technical director, Leighton K. Brill
Music director, Gus Salzer
Orchestrations by Robert Russell Bennett

Tryout

Apollo Theatre, Atlantic City, August 19-24, 1929
Shubert Theatre, Newark, August 26-31, 1929

New York Run

Hammerstein's Theatre, September 3, 1929-March 22, 1930
234 performances

The Story

Addie, daughter of Emil Schmidt, a beer garden proprietor, sings at her father's establishment. She loves Tom Martin, but he goes off to the Spanish-American war. Addie subsequently wins fame on the stage, stars in a Broadway show, and discovers that she really loves James Day, the show's backer. However, his socially prominent family disapproves, and Addie runs away. But Sid Barnett, the composer of the score for the show, finds her and persuades her to return to the show and to him.

The Cast

SGT. MALONE, Thomas Chadwick
AUGUST, *a student,* George Raymond
LENA, Pauline Gorim
DOT, *a piccolo player,* Violet Carson
EMIL SCHMIDT, Robert C. Fischer
ADDIE SCHMIDT, *his older daughter,* Helen Morgan

NELLIE SCHMIDT, *his younger daughter,* Caryl Bergman
LULU WARD, *an actress,* Irene Franklin
DAN WARD, *a press agent,* Robert Emmett Keane
TOM MARTIN, *first mate of the S.S. St. Paul,* Max Hoffman Jr.
RUPPERT DAY, Charles Butterworth
DOCTOR, Jack Gray
ORDERLY, Tom Thompson
COLONEL, Martin Shepard
JAMES DAY, Robert Chisholm
GUS AND WILL, Themselves
SAM HERZIG, *a theatrical manager,* Len Mence
EDDIE, *man-of-all-work around theatre,* Wally Crisham
SID BARNETT, *a composer and orchestra leader,* John D. Seymour
THE SULTAN, Thomas Chadwick
THE JESTER, George Djimos
MAIZIE O'ROURKE, Helen Ault
HEAD CARPENTER, Willie Sheppard
PROPS, Joe Reilly
GUS, *first violinist,* Gus Salzer
GEORGE, Borrah Levinson
YOUNG BLOOD, Jackson Fairchild
GABE CASE, *proprietor McGowan's Pass Tavern,* Ben Wells
A CABBY, Tom Rider
OLD SPORT, Harry Esmond
DOC, George Magis
JIM THORNTON, Jim Thornton
MR. GILHOOLEY, Jerry Jarnagin
HESTER VAN DOREN DAY, Sally Bates
WILLIE DAY, Peter Bender
ORCHESTRA, George Smith's Girl Band (Frances Flanigan, Polly Fisher, Josephine Ricci, Mabel Thibault, Gertrude Clave, Laura Mutch)
GIRLS: Helen Ault, Louise Bernhardt, Harriett Britton, Mary Carney, Dorothy Brown, Lillian Burke, Kaye Carroll, Louise Chowning, Nora Clift, Aida Conkley, Myrtle Cox, Betty Croke, Nonie Dale, Fanilla Davies, Christine Gallagher, LaVergne Evans, Helene Gardner, Mildred Getkins, Pauline Gorin, Evelyn Hammons, Muriel Harrison, Dorothy Hiller, Cyrilla Juitt, Helen Kelly, Grace La Rue, Evelyn Laurie, Madge MacAnally, Helen McDonald, Marion Martin, Peggy Messinger, Gladys Nelson, Ruby Nevins, Ruth Penery, Robertina Robert, Madgio Schmylee, Bertha Mae Swan, Elenore Tierney, Emily Van Hoven, Genevieve Van Hoven, Marion Young, Lorena Walcott, Gloria LeBow, Baum Sturz
GENTLEMEN OF THE ENSEMBLE: John Campbell, Don Carter, Joseph Davidenko, Frank Dobert, Lynn Eldridge, Jackson Fairchild, Andy Lieb, George Magis, Paul Moran, George Raymond, Tom Rider, Len Sasion, Martin Shepard, Bob Shutta, Alexis Sokoloff, Morris Tepper, Tom Tompson, Efim Vitis, Robert Vernon

NOTE: For tour, Violet Carson succeeded by Beatrice Kay.

Musical Numbers

Fin de Siecle (based on melodies of the period by Mr. Kern)

ACT I

SCENE ONE—SCHMIDT'S BEER GARDEN, HOBOKEN, N.J., 1898
Play Us a Polka Dot, DOT and ENSEMBLE
'Twas Not So Long Ago, ADDIE and ENSEMBLE
My Husband's First Wife (lyric by Miss Franklin), LULU

SCENE TWO—HOSPITAL TENT NEAR SAN JUAN HILL, CUBA

SCENE THREE—KITCHEN ENTRANCE TO THE SCHMIDT HOME
Here Am I, ADDIE and DOT
First Mate Martin, TOM, RUPPERT and ENSEMBLE
Spring Is Here, DOT, RUPPERT and GIRLS

SCENE FOUR—UNDER THE STAGE OF THE OLYMPIC BURLESQUE THEATRE, THE BOWERY
Out of the Blue, JIM, TOM and BOYS; DOT, NELLIE and GIRLS; GUS and WILL
Naughty Boy, LULU, RUPPERT and GIRLS

SCENE FIVE—STAGE AND AUDITORIUM, OLYMPIC BURLESQUE THEATRE
Oriental Moon, SULTAN, JESTER and ENSEMBLE
Mollie O'Donahue, MAIZIE and GIRLS
Why Was I Born?, ADDIE
Finale, COMPANY

ACT II

SCENE ONE—CORRIDOR OF A BROADWAY THEATRE
Reprise, *'Twas Not So Long Ago,* SCHMIDT

SCENE TWO—MCGOWAN'S PASS TAVERN
Winter in Central Park, ENSEMBLE
The Sun About to Rise, SID, ADDIE, JIM and ENSEMBLE

SCENE THREE
(a) A HORSE CAR GOING DOWN AVENUE A
(b) A HANSOM GOING UP BROADWAY

SCENE FOUR—HOFFMAN HOUSE BAR
Some Girl Is on Your Mind, JIM, TOM, SID, THORNTON and ENSEMBLE

SCENE FIVE—JIM'S SLOOP
Don't Ever Leave Me, ADDIE and JIM
Reprise, *Here Am I,* ADDIE and DOT
Finaletto, ADDIE

SCENE SIX—MADISON SQUARE GARDEN

SCENE SEVEN—STAGE OF THE MADISON SQUARE GARDEN ROOF
Indestructible Kate (music by Jerry Jarnagin; lyric by Miss Franklin), LULU

SCENE EIGHT—ON FORT GEORGE HILL
Take Me for a Honeymoon Ride, DOT, RUPPERT, GUS and WILL, and GIRLS

SCENE NINE—ALONGSIDE THE "CITY OF PARIS"
Scene, ADDIE, SID, JIM

SCENE TEN—A BROADWAY THEATRE
Reprise, *'Twas Not So Long Ago,* CHORUS
Finale, COMPANY

Reviews

J. Brooks Atkinson—*New York Times*
". . . captivating music . . . downright enjoyable all the while . . . a generous brocade of many delights . . . But the joy is Mr. Kern's abiding score, the broad range of personalities and the skill with which the lines and staging employ them . . ."

Percy Hammond—*New York Herald Tribune*
". . . a gentle opera with appropriate music . . . It was all semi-serious and smartly old-fashioned . . . an enticing score . . . one of the politest frolics of the new year."

Robert Littell—*New York World*
". . . a grand and gorgeous show; I don't see how it could possibly be better . . . not only hits all the high spots, but it has no low spots whatever. It is 100%, usually 200 or 300% in every department. And, rarest thing of all in a musical show, it all hangs together—it seems to be made out of one piece . . . melting, romantic music . . . one of the rarest treats you are likely to find on Broadway . . ."

John Mason Brown—*New York Post*
". . . a pleasant, sprawling, overgenerous evening . . . It was when the plot had been tossed off into the wings as so much super cargo that it rose to its moments of most complete enjoyment . . . Then it was straightforward in its humor and engaging . . ."

Charles Darnton—*New York Evening World*
"Old Broadway has been brought to the new Broadway of noisy rush and garish signs, and there is cause for rejoicing. Never was the Gay Nineties gayer than it was last night . . . it has glamour, charm, beauty, variety, and what's more, it swings along with loads of fun. Better entertainment seldom comes our way. The last rose of Summer may well go into the buttonhole of Jerome Kern for the fragrant music he has written, and Hammerstein deserves at least a hearty slap on the back for the laughs his book and lyrics have given the grateful natives . . ."

Robert Garland—*New York Telegram*
"... a tuneful, rowdy and romantic parody, as up-and-doing an evening as Broadway has on display. You'll enjoy it ... In Helen Morgan's hands Adeline is tearful without being tiresome ... *Here Am I, Why Was I Born?,* and *Don't Ever Leave Me* are songs to be remembered ... If the 1890's were as gay as this, what price Prohibition?"

Richard Lockridge—*New York Sun*
"... rich in sentiment and melody, in color and heroics. And it is rich, too, in laughter, so that anyone will find in its lavishness much that is satisfying ... a very pretty and lilting show ..."

John Anderson—*New York Journal*
"... an elaborate and captivating operetta, which is likely to linger longer hereabouts than any quartette has ever been able to make it ... a pretty, handsome and enjoyable sightseeing tour through the Gay Nineties ... *Why Was I Born?* was a velvety woe-song, *The Sun About to Rise* a gorgeous dawn waltz. The other outstanding piece was a German folk song, *'Twas Not So Long Ago* ..."

Sime Silverman—*Variety,* September 11, 1929
"... a hit ... Kern has hung onto his reputation ... a very attractive book ... If other musicals are worth $6.60, then *Sweet Adeline* at that price is a bargain entertainment."

Robert Benchley—*The New Yorker,* September 14, 1929
"... something different and, at the same time, pretty consistently amusing ... not without its dull stretches and when they are dull they are *good* and dull ... Kern's score is somehow disappointing in that there isn't much in it to tuck away and take home, but a Kern score is a Kern score and there is no way of getting around that ..."

Joseph Wood Krutch—*The Nation,* September 18, 1929
"... very pleasantly beguiling ... both lively and entertaining ... The librettist exhibits some signs of that intelligence and wit which seem generally denied those who compose librettos; and several of the performers are possessed of talents first-rate in their kind ... mawkishly doleful ballads ..."

Gilbert Seldes—*The New Republic,* September 20, 1929
"... disappointed only those who, like myself, had extravagant hopes ... the music is more of a concentration of the spirit of the 1890's than a reminiscence of its tunes. Kern is a master of many styles and handled the charm and rather awkward grace of the time perfectly ..."

O. O. McIntyre—*Life,* September 27, 1929
". . . a tuneful score . . . The theme of the piece does not sparkle with any too much originality, but it will be a success and deservedly so, because of the vogue of Miss Morgan and the hilarity of Mr. Butterworth . . ."

George Jean Nathan—*Judge,* September 28, 1929
". . . a book above the average; Kern in excellent melodic trim; and Helen Morgan, Charles Butterworth and a tasty cast do the whole thing up brown. No less than four of Kern's songs are as charming as anything he has previously written . . . if you are sick of the usual stuff and seek a nostrum for your aural malaise, gallop to this performance. It has originality, tunefulness, movement and lots of fresh humor."

Bibliography

Concerning That Hit Up 53rd Street Way
—*New York Times,* September 15, 1929

Tour

Colonial Theatre, Boston, September 8, 1930—Erlanger Theatre, Philadelphia, January 24, 1931 (5 cities).

Selected Revivals

St. Louis Municipal Opera, June 4-10, 1934
Gladys Baxter (ADDIE); Leonard Ceeley (JIM); Frank Gaby (RUPPERT); Edith King (LULU).

Goodspeed Opera House, East Haddam, Conn., May 7, 1976
Cynthia Wells (ADDIE); Doyle Newberry (SID); John Remme (RUPERT); Travis Hudson (LULU); Jay Garner (DAN).

SWEET ADELINE

(Film Version—1935)

A Warner Brothers Picture
Directed by Mervyn LeRoy
Adapted by Erwin S. Gelsey
Choreography by Bobby Connolly
Art director, Robert Haas
Music director, Leo Forbstein
Photographed by Sol Polito
Editor, Harold McLernon

Release Date
January 5, 1935

The Cast
ADDIE SCHMIDT, Irene Dunne
SID BARNETT, Donald Woods
RUPERT ROCKINGHAM, Hugh Herbert
DAN HERZIG, Ned Sparks
OSCAR SCHMIDT, Joseph Cawthorn
MAJOR DAY, Louis Calhern
ELYSIA, Winifred Shaw
NELLIE, Nydia Westman
DOT, Dorothy Dare
SINGER, Phil Regan
RENALDO, Don Alvarado
BOB, Jack Mulhall
SULTAN, Noah Beery

Musical Numbers
Songs retained from original production: *'Twas Not So Long Ago, Here Am I, Mollie O'Donahue, Why Was I Born?, Don't Ever Leave Me.* Song added to film: *Down Where the Wurzberger Flows* (Harry Von Tilzer-Vincent Bryan). Song written for film by Messrs. Kern and Hammerstein:
Lonely Feet, ADDIE
We Were So Young, ADDIE

Reviews
Andre Sennwald—*New York Times*
". . . sentimental, naive and a little dull . . . except for the lovely music and one or two of the blazing production numbers, it appears to snore in dulcet measures . . ."

Richard Watts, Jr.—*New York Herald Tribune*
". . . it is during the presentation of the Kern melodies that the film is, naturally, at its best. It is engaging too, in its humorous and sprightly recreation of the atmosphere of New York and Hoboken during the Spanish-American War . . . If the plot doesn't annoy you too much, you should find quiet amusement . . ."

Eileen Creelman—*New York Sun*
". . . As drama it is just an old operetta fixed up for the movies, but it serves well enough to bring in the atmospheric background which, with the score, is the real point of the production . . ."

John Mosher—*The New Yorker,* December 22, 1934
"Libretto trouble rather overwhelms it, and Irene Dunne doesn't sing *Why Was I Born?* in a way to make you forget Helen Morgan forever . . ."

Time, December 31, 1934
". . . the melodies *(Why Was I Born?, Don't Ever Leave Me)* are its chief charm . . . attractive and colorful if somewhat languorous . . ."

Joe Bigelow—*Variety,* January 8, 1935
". . . As production it is in the big-time musical class, but strictly on merit it rates no better than fair . . ."

VIENNESE NIGHTS

(Film-1930)

A musical film with screenplay and lyrics by Oscar Hammerstein II; music by Sigmund Romberg.

A Warner Brothers-Vitaphone Picture
Directed by Alan Crosland
Art director, Max Parker
Music director, Louis Silvers
Photographed by James Van Trees and Frank Good
Color by Technicolor

Release Date
November 11, 1930

The Story
Otto, son of a poor man, falls in love with Elsa, daughter of a court bootmaker, who forces her to marry the wealthy Baron Franz. Dejected, Otto goes to America, where he becomes a violinist in an orchestra, marries and has a son. Years later, Elsa also goes to America, but they must again part after seeing each other. Many years after, Otto's grandson, a famous young composer, meets Elsa's granddaughter in Vienna, and their romance indicates a happy ending for the third generation.

The Cast
ELSA HOFNER, Vivienne Segal
OTTO STIRNER, Alexander Gray
BARON FRANZ VON RENNER, Walter Pidgeon
HERR HOFNER, Jean Hersholt
GUS SACHER, Bert Roach
GRETL KRUGER, Louise Fazenda
BARBARA, Alice Day
"MARY", June Purcell
"BILL JONES", Milton Douglas
OTTO STIRNER, JR., Freddie Burke Frederick
BARON, Lothar Mayring
EMMA, Virginia Sales

Musical Numbers

PART ONE—VIENNA, 1879
Opening, *Wake Up,* ENSEMBLE
Oli, Oli, Oli, ENSEMBLE
You Will Remember Vienna, OTTO, FRANZ, GUS
Brass Band March, ORCHESTRA
Regimental March, FRANZ and ENSEMBLE
Goodbye, My Love, ELSA, OTTO, GUS and ENSEMBLE
Here We Are, FRANZ, ELSA and ENSEMBLE
When You Have No Man to Love, GRETL, ELSA and GIRLS
I Bring a Love Song, ELSA and OTTO
Ja, Ja, Ja!, ENSEMBLE
Finale, *Pretty Gypsy,* ENSEMBLE

PART TWO—NEW YORK, 1890
Opening, *Waiting,* ENSEMBLE
I'm Lonely, "BILL" "MARY" and ENSEMBLE

PART THREE—VIENNA, 1930
Poem Symphonic (based on *I Bring a Love Song*), LOS ANGELES SYMPHONY ORCHESTRA

Reviews

Mordaunt Hall—*New York Times*
"Appealing musical compositions, agreeably sung and well played, compensate for imperfections in the dialogue and story . . . A few sequences may be a trifle slow, but nevertheless, its virtues decidedly counter-balance its shortcomings."

Richard Watts, Jr.—*New York Herald-Tribune*
". . . carefully produced, well sung and entirely successful in the creation of a rueful, quietly moist-eyed, gently nostalgic mood . . . the music, if usually less than striking, is invariably pleasant, and, in the presentation of the symphony, it is particularly admirable . . ."

Sime Silverman—*Variety,* December 3, 1930
". . . pretty and clean . . . The picture should go over, it deserves to for the screen story runs along smoothly and pleasantly . . . nothing striking in the story, except its complete abstinence from any sexy angle . . ."

John Mosher—*The New Yorker,* December 6, 1930
". . . a rather fair-to-middling picture with a few good songs, that goes to pieces clumsily toward the end . . ."

Time, December 8, 1930
". . . succeeds principally because of its music . . . Audiences will hum *You Will Remember* and *Here We Are* . . ."

Pare Lorentz—*Judge,* December 27, 1930
". . . Why anybody pays money for such tasteless hash is beyond my comprehension or worry."

Theatre Magazine, April, 1931
"Though it just falls short of being a great picture, it has the advantage of being written expressly for the screen by two experts in their art . . . a complete and exquisite romance . . ."

THE GANG'S ALL HERE

(1931)

A musical comedy with book by Russel Crouse, with Oscar Hammerstein II and Morrie Ryskind; music by Lewis E. Gensler; lyrics by Owen Murphy and Robert A. Simon.

Presented by Morris Green and Mr. Gensler
Directed by Mr. Hammerstein and Frank McCoy
Choreography by Dave Gould, Tilly Losch
Settings by Henry Dreyfuss
Costumes by Russell Patterson
Music director, Gene Salzer
Orchestrations by Hans Spialek

Tryout
Shubert Theatre, Philadelphia, January 26-February 7, 1931
Shubert Theatre, Newark, February 9-14, 1931

New York Run
Imperial Theatre, February 18-March 9, 1931
23 performances

The Story
Baby Face Martini and his gang try to put millionaire Horace Winterbottom on the spot. He is saved, however, by Indian Ike Kelly, a fake doctor, who cures him of his ills through psychoanalysis.

The Cast
HORACE WINTERBOTTOM, Tom Howard
JULIE WINTERBOTTOM, Gina Malo
A MAN, Jack Bruns
A WOMAN, Anita Avila
A GIRL, Phyllis Cameron
A YOUNG MAN, Hal Morton
ANOTHER WOMAN, Elsie Duffy
ANOTHER MAN, Harry Anderson
HIS WIFE, Ethel Britton
BABY FACE MARTINI, Jack McCauley
ANDY LENNOX, Jack Barker

HAL LE ROY, Himself
PROF. CAVANAUGH, Eddie Moran
DR. INDIAN IKE KELLY, Ted Healy
STOOGES: Paul Garner, Jack Walls, Dick Hackins
BIG CASINO, Ben Wise
LITTLE CASINO, Joe McKeon
LE JONGLEUR DE NOTRE DAME, Monsieur DuPont
SWISS BELLRINGER, Dr. Faust
TWO ON THE ISLE, Johnnie Dale and Rheta Stone
DR. T. SLOCUM SWINK, Thomas F. Tracy
LONGFELLOW / WHITTIER } Shaw and Lee
PEGGY KELLY, Ruth Tester
HOTEL MANAGER, Jack Bruns
WILLY WILSON, Zelma O'Neal
HECTOR WINTERBOTTOM, John Gallaudet
DANCERS, Gomez and Winona
CHIEF OF POLICE, Earl Gilbert
STREET VENDOR, Joe Verdi
SAILOR, Bert Fay
HOTEL PROPRIETOR, Albert F. Hawthorne
BALLET SOLOIST, Gertrude Stanton
LYRIC QUARTET: Robert Duenweg, Jack Bruns, Harry Anderson, Joseph Vitale
TILLY LOSCH BALLET: Joan English, Senta Stephany, Marie Grimaldi, Catherine Laughlin, Jeanie Lavra, Katherine Gallimore, Anita Avila, Alice Kellerman
DANCERS: Lois Maye, Phyllis Saule, Gertrude McPherson, Arline Ingram, Bunny Moore, Evelyn Hannon, Dorothy Foster, Bonnie Alvin, Estelle Phillips, Ruth Raidt, Ruth Martin, Dorothy Waller, Julia Gorman, Carrol Renwick, Mary Alice Rice, Agnes Reilly, Gene Carpenter, Elsie Lauritsen
LADIES OF THE ENSEMBLE: Wynn Terry, Irma Philbin, Helen Edwards, Irene King, Madgio Smylie, Ethel Britton, Elsie Duffy, Louise Joyce, Loretta Goss, Jeanne Adams, Phyllis Cameron, Margaret Dixon, Rheta Stone, Beth Holt, Gloray Pierre
GENTLEMEN OF THE ENSEMBLE: Joseph Lennon, Hal Morton, Frank Reynolds, Jack Montgomery, Beau Tilden, Tom Jordan, Jack Kay, Jack Voeth, Kenneth Williams, Frank Edmonds, Gus Hyland, Jack Raymond, Russel Duncan, Henry King, Jimmy Ryan, George Weeden

NOTE: During tryout, Miss Malo replaced Ruby Keeler Jolson and Mr. Howard replaced Dallas Welford. In March, Miss Malo succeeded by Caryl Bergman.

Musical Numbers

ACT I

SCENE ONE—ON THE BOARDWALK, ATLANTIC CITY

Opening, ENSEMBLE

What Have You Done to Me?, JULIE, ANDY and ENSEMBLE
Dance, HAL
The Gang's All Here, BABY FACE, LYRIC QUARTET, RACKETEERS and ENSEMBLE

SCENE TWO—PEACOCK ALLEY, RITZ CARLTON HOTEL, ATLANTIC CITY
Dumb Girl, PEGGY and BABY FACE

SCENE THREE—WINTERBOTTOM'S SUITE, RITZ CARLTON HOTEL
Dance, BUTLERS and MAIDS
Gypsy Rose, HECTOR
Baby Wanna Go Bye-Bye With You, WILLY and HECTOR

SCENE FOUR—DR. KELLY'S OFFICE
Adorable Julie, KELLY, JULIE and ENSEMBLE

SCENE FIVE—THE APPROACH TO A PRIVATE BOATHOUSE
Husband, Lover and Wife, WILLY, LONGFELLOW and WHITTIER

SCENE SIX—THE BOATHOUSE
Speaking of You, ANDY, JULIE, Gomez and Winona, and ENSEMBLE
By Special Permission of the Copyright Owners, I Love You, PEGGY and BABY FACE
Finale, COMPANY

ACT II

SCENE ONE—A STREET IN NANTUCKET
The Moon, the Wind and the Sea, ANDY, JULIE, LYRIC QUARTET, Tilly Losch Ballet and ENSEMBLE
Reprise, *By Special Permission of the Copyright Owners, I Love You*, PEGGY, BABY FACE and ENSEMBLE
Dance, HAL

SCENE TWO—A SQUARE IN NANTUCKET

SCENE THREE—THE LOBBY OF THE WILSON HOTEL
It Always Takes Two, WILLY and HECTOR

SCENE FOUR—A WING OF THE HOTEL

SCENE FIVE—A DOCK
How Can I Get Rid of Those Blues?, ANDY and Tilly Losch Ballet

SCENE SIX—THE DECK OF A REVENUE CUTTER

SCENE SEVEN—A STREET
Reprise, *What Have You Done to Me?*, ENSEMBLE

SCENE EIGHT—A NIGHT CLUB
Speak Easy, Frank Swanee and ENSEMBLE
Dance, Gomez and Winona
Finale, COMPANY

NOTE: *More than Ever, Do It Right, Doo-Daddle-Doo, Yes, Sir, Very Good, Sir, You're Looking Very Good, Marie,* and *In the Pink* were cut before New York opening.

Reviews

J. Brooks Atkinson—*New York Times*
"... a thumping hurdy-gurdy with several excellent tunes, a good deal of spasmodic merriment and a high population of musical-comedy talent ..."

Arthur Ruhl—*New York Herald Tribune*
"... a large, elaborately mounted, routine musical comedy, which was excessively long-winded and, for the most part, labored and dull ..."

Robert Littell—*New York World*
"... Gensler's music is one of its very, very few bright spots ... plenty of material here for lots of burlesque fun. Yet hardly any of it comes off as intended ..."

Gilbert W. Gabriel—*New York American*
"*The Gang's All Here* is not quite all there ... probably the most unsparing effort the city has seen for many seasons. And that is why I weep sincerely for it ..."

John Chapman—*New York Daily News*
"... big and handsome ... though it dragged through several uneasy moments, the audience liked what it liked extravagantly ..."

John Mason Brown—*New York Post*
"... the production proved as painful as it was long. Certainly it offered as wasteful and oppressive an evening as the season has known ..."

Richard Lockridge—*New York Sun*
"... a collection of sideshows under one top; it lacks both the integration and the pace which would have made of it the superlative show the excellent material which has been tossed into it should have produced ..."

Jack Pulaski (Ibee.)—*Variety,* February 25, 1931
"... too much show. Properly spliced and rearranged, it should land ..."

Dorothy Parker—*The New Yorker,* February 28, 1931
"... a fantastically confused and preposterously elongated entertainment—and that's a big word ... young ladies who render songs in the Boop-a-Doop-Your-Overcoat manner are no longer novelties ... Above all, Zelma O'Neal should never wear sailor pants ..."

Time, March 2, 1931
". . . seldom has wealth been more hopelessly, tastelessly squandered . . ."

George Jean Nathan—*Judge,* March 14, 1931
". . . if the MM. Green and Gensler had laid in a carload of blue pencils they might have had a good show. They have enough material to give *Strange Interlude* and *Back to Methuselah* a head start of several hours and still outrun them by a couple of days, and, when the time came to raise their curtain, hadn't done anything about it . . ."

CHILDREN OF DREAMS

(Film—1931)

A musical film with screenplay and lyrics by Oscar Hammerstein II; music by Sigmund Romberg.

A Warner Brothers-Vitaphone Picture
Directed by Alan Crosland
Art director, Max Parker
Music director, Louis Silvers
Photographed by James Van Trees

Release Date

July 19, 1931

The Story

Molly and Tommy fall in love while working in the apple orchard of Molly's parents, Hubert and Sara Standing. Her singing voice attracts the attention of a wealthy socialite, who sends her to Italy to study. After becoming a success in Rome, she returns to America to sing at the Metropolitan Opera House. Tommy hears her there, but leaves the theatre when he realizes the barriers now between them. However, a reconciliation is brought about through the intervention of Dr. Joe, the family physician.

The Cast

MOLLY STANDING, Margaret Schilling
TOMMY MELVILLE, Paul Gregory
GUS ANGELO, Tom Patricola
DR. JOE THOMPSON, Charles Winninger
GERTIE MCNULTY, Marion Byron
HUBERT STANDING, Bruce Winston
SARA STANDING, Alison Skipworth
SIGNOR BOCCABADOTTI, Louis Alberni
SQUIZZY MURPHY, Ivan Simpson
BOYO, Milton Douglas
MARIE, May Boley
RICHARD JARMAN, John Litel
ERCOLE BENONI, Paul Porcasi

Musical Numbers

PART ONE—AN APPLE ORCHARD IN CALIFORNIA, NEAR WATSONVILLE
Fruit Pickers' Song, ENSEMBLE
Oh, Couldn't I Love That Girl, TOMMY, BEPPO, GUS, MOLLY, GERTIE and ENSEMBLE
Children of Dreams, MOLLY, SQUIZZY and ENSEMBLE
Sleeping Beauty, TOMMY, MOLLY and ENSEMBLE
If I Had a Girl, MOLLY and TOMMY
That Rare Romance, MOLLY and ENSEMBLE
Yes, Sir, GERTIE and GUS
Finale, TOMMY, MOLLY and ENSEMBLE

PART TWO—ROME, ITALY

PART THREE—NEW YORK
Aria from *Antonia,* a new opera at the Metropolitan, MOLLY
Tango D'Amour, MOLLY

PART FOUR—THE APPLE ORCHARD
Finale Ultimo, TOMMY, MOLLY and ENSEMBLE

Reviews
Lewis Nichols—*New York Times*
". . . The assets of the romance lie entirely along musical lines. The story is a simple one and there is little or no effort at characterization or motivation. But running through the picture are a number of excellent songs, which are pretty and well put on . . ."

Sime Silverman—*Variety,* July 21, 1931
". . . no special boxoffice here . . . Best thing to be said about it is that it's clean, and adding it's too clean . . . not a bit of comedy worth while . . . nothing popular in the compositions . . . just blah."

FREE FOR ALL

(1931)

A musical comedy with book by Oscar Hammerstein II and Laurence Schwab; music by Richard A. Whiting; lyrics by Mr. Hammerstein.

Presented by Laurence Schwab and Frank Mandel
Directed by Mr. Hammerstein
Choreography by Bobby Connolly
Settings by Donald Oenslager
Costumes by Kiviette
Music director, John McManus
conducting Ben Goodman's Orchestra

Tryout
Colonial Theatre, Boston, August 10-22, 1931
Garrick Theatre, Philadelphia, August 24-September 5, 1931

New York Run
Manhattan Theatre, September 8-19, 1931
15 performances

The Story
A group of Socialist-minded Leland Stanford students are given a mining camp in which to test some of their theories. The donor is Stephen Potter, Sr., the wealthy father of one of the undergraduates. The nearby Nevada townfolks misinterpret the idealistic companionate living, and force the students into marriages.

The Cast
TOM, *a butler at Mr. Potter's house,* Peter Lang
STEPHEN POTTER, SR., *a captain of industry,* Edward Emery
JOE BUTLER, *perpetual student at Leland Stanford,* David Hutcheson
GRACIE MAYNARD, Thelma Tipson
ANITA ALLEN, Vera Marsh
MICHAEL BYRNE, *a radical poet,* Peter Higgins
MARISHKA TARASOV, Tamara
ANDY BRADFORD, Don Tomkins
JOAN SUMMER, *youngest of the gang,* Dorris Groday
STEPHEN POTTER, JR., Jack Haley
MARIE SINNOT, *editor of "Free for All,"* Lilian Bond
MISS GIBBS, *Dr. Allen's secretary,* Dorothy Knapp

DR. RAYMOND ALLEN, *a psychoanalyst and Anita's father,* Philip Lord
VERGIL MURGATROYD, *a patient,* Charles Althoff
IDA JONES, *another,* Jeanette Loff
PETER WEBER, *a Navada sheriff,* Seth Arnold
MINERS, Gus Howard, Clair Kramer, John Donahue
TERENCE CANAVAN, *a mine foreman,* G. Pat Collins
JIM ALLISON, *a metallurgist,* Harry Shannon
SILVER DOLLAR KATE, Grace Johnston
DIVORCEES, Olive Bayes, Dorothea James, Julia Chandler
DIGGER WATKINS, Al Downing
A REPORTER, Robert Randell
A NURSE, Rae Powell
PRESTON, E. Saulpaugh
A JUDGE, Edward Walters

Musical Numbers

ACT I

SCENE ONE—DINING ROOM OF STEPHEN POTTER'S HOME, PALO ALTO, CALIFORNIA
I Love Him, the Rat, ANITA and JOE
Free for All, MICHAEL and the GANG

SCENE TWO—OFFICE OF DR. RAYMOND ALLEN, IN SACRAMENTO
The Girl Next Door, ANITA and STEVE

SCENE THREE—TOP OF THE SHAFT OF THE RAMBLER COPPER MINE, NEVADA
Living in Sin, GRACIE, JOAN, JOE, ANDY

SCENE FOUR—FREE FOR ALL COMMUNITY HOUSES
Just Eighteen, JOAN and ANDY
Not That I Care, ANITA and STEVE
Slumber Song (Goodnight), MARISHKA and MICHAEL
Finale, PRINCIPALS

ACT II

SCENE ONE—SILVER DOLLAR KATE'S, A SPEAKEASY NEAR NEW LEAF CORNERS, NEVADA
Dance, JOAN and ANDY
Reprise, MICHAEL, DIVORCEES, MARISHKA

SCENE TWO—TOP OF THE SHAFT OF THE RAMBLER COPPER MINE
When Your Boy Becomes a Man, KATE and ANITA

SCENE THREE—DOWN IN THE MINE
Tonight, MARISHKA and MICHAEL

SCENE FOUR—A SQUARE IN NEW LEAF CORNERS
Nevada Moonlight, JOE, GRACIE and ENSEMBLE
Finale, COMPANY

NOTE: *Open Your Eyes, How I React to You, Ain't Everything Grand!, The Carefree Miner, Russian Song, Men and Women Are Awful, Psychoanalyse Me* cut before New York opening.

Reviews

John Byram—*New York Times*
". . . Although much of it is funny, and although it is handsomely and expertly produced, it has not found effective substitutes for the conventions, trite though they be, which it so blithely disregards . . . In extenuation, let it be said that it is a show of promise not completely realized . . ."

Percy Hammond—*New York Herald Tribune*
"There were evidences last night that musical comedies are more enjoyable with chorus girls than without . . . many faults which might have been hidden behind the women were exposed . . . But the show is by way of being an innovation, and deserves perhaps to be encouraged . . ."

Gilbert W. Gabriel—*New York American*
". . . My inability to enjoy almost anything in the show grew almost nightmarish. I thought it had the most unsuitable and lugubrious of stories, the clumsiest sort of humor, and little else around Mr. Whiting's pleasant songs . . ."

John Mason Brown—*New York Post*
". . . Though it has occasional outbursts of comedy, and is enlivened here and there by a good tune, it is for the most part a slow and labored affair that never succeeds in throwing off the shackles of the complicated and silly plot which imprisons it . . ."

Ben Washer—*New York World-Telegram*
". . . an effort in the direction of a comedy which heightens its believability by discarding a chorus and depending upon a first rate cast dealing with a sophisticated story interspersed with songs . . . But it is a musical comedy which gives up in the end."

Stephen Rathbun—*New York Sun*
". . . the alleged humor is sophomoric and seldom funny . . . The music is far better than the book, and includes one song, *Not That I Care,* that will be heard soon around town . . . pretty fair entertainment . . ."

John Anderson—*New York Journal*
". . . quiet, innocent entertainment which goes in one ear and out the other . . . The mainspring, the pivot, the sine qua non, of a musical comedy is lacking—the structure which is fondly supposed to hold the music, if any, and the comedy, when bought . . ."

Jack Pulaski (Ibee.)—*Variety,* September 15, 1931
". . . its chances are dubious, indeed. Show isn't that bad. First act

amusing and diverting, with the second shading off, due to book trouble and minus the tunefulness of the earlier chapter . . ."

Robert Benchley—*The New Yorker,* September 19, 1931
". . . the score was charming, and quite out of the ordinary run of current thefts . . . the book was both intelligent and funny. At any rate, it had the only burlesque on psychoanalysis which did not indicate that psychoanalysis had something to do with the kidneys . . . any number of civilized comedy lines so foreign to the average of musical comedy as to sound almost affected. In short, although I may be wrong for the eight thousandth time, I think it is a swell show, and am completely mystified by my colleagues' decision to the contrary."

Time, September 21, 1931
". . . the uninterrupted libretto may pall if you think about it too much, but there is good music, a little lively dancing and a dozen pleasant faces . . . Tunes to tintinnabulate through early autumn tea dancing: *I Love Him, the Rat, The Girl Next Door, Not That I Care.*"

George Jean Nathan—*Judge,* October 3, 1931
". . . leaves something to be desired, but it is a pleasant relief to be rid of the routine ensemble dancing numbers, with their stereotyped stomping, leg-liftings, arm-wrigglings, torso-shakings and concluding ejaculations of *hooray* . . . Although the book strains itself so hard to be satirical that it quickly ruptures itself, the tunes are better than most such things, no less than eight or ten passages in the dialogue are really humorous, and several of the feminine principals aren't too ocularly painful . . ."

EAST WIND

(1931)

A musical play with book by Oscar Hammerstein II and Frank Mandel; music by Sigmund Romberg; lyrics by Mr. Hammerstein.

Presented by Laurence Schwab and Frank Mandel
Directed by Mr. Hammerstein
Choreography by Bobby Connolly
Settings by Donald Oenslager
Costumes by Charles LeMaire
Music director, Oscar Bradley
Orchestrations by Hans Spialek

Tryout

Nixon Theatre, Pittsburgh, October 5-10, 1931
Cleveland, October 13-17, 1931
Baltimore, October 19-25, 1931

New York Run

Manhattan Theatre, October 27-November 14, 1931
23 performances

The Story

Claudette is loved by two brothers. She marries Rene, and returns with him to his home in Indo-China. Rene proves unfaithful, and the disillusioned Claudette is finally reunited with Paul, when he saves her life in a waterfront saloon.

The Cast

MONSIEUR GRANIER, Greek Evans
JACQUES, Vance Elliot
GABRIELLE, Betty Junod
JULIE, Frances Markey
CLAUDETTE FORTIER, Charlotte Lansing
RENE BEAUVAIS, William Williams
CLAIRE, Rose Mullen
MIMI, Sherry Pelham
LORRAINE FORTIER, Dennie Moore
MARIE MARTEL, Vera Marsh

CAPT. PAUL BEAUVAIS, J. Harold Murray
CAPT. DEJAN, Thomas Chadwick
TAXI DRIVER, I. Anchong
A TOURIST, Gus Howard
PIERRE FORTIER, Jules Espailly
VICTOR CLIQUOT, Joe Penner
TSOI TSING, Ahi
KING OF LUANG-PRABANG, Ivan Izmailov
INTERPRETER, Y. Y. Hsu
KING OF CAMBODIA, Frank Dobert
INTERPRETER, S. Wong
HOP SING, J. L. Donsu
CAPT. GERVAIS, Gladstone Waldrip
PAPA GOULI, Raymond Bramley
PIANIST, Bobby Dolan
A MAID, Marjorie Dille
STAGE MANAGER, C. J. Vanasse
COMPERE, Emile Ladoux
MCNULTY SISTERS, Lorraine and Leatrice Pearl
KING IN BALLET, Alex Yakovleff
PRINCE IN BALLET, Aron Tomaroff
DR. DUVAL, George Chapell
SINGERS: Anna May Colburn, Sylvia Nelson, Mildred Gethins, Olga Leigh, Sylvia Roberts, Norma Nash, Helen Haynes, Peggy Strickland, Marie DeJardin, Jackson Stuart, Harry Pickering, James Renard, Bert LeRoy, Edward Martin, Alfonso Inglasia, Eugene King, Alfred Russ, John Fredericks, Walter Leven, Herman Belmonte, Paul Ayres, Andrew Keller, William Warren, Frank Vaughn, Bart Schilling, Cornelius Pichler, Basil Prock, Nat Broffman, Tom Chadwick, Charles Glazer, Gladstone Waldrip, Ivan Sokoloff, Ivan Ismailov, Vance Elliott, Frank Dobert
DANCERS: Sherry Pelham, Kay Stewart, Carola Taylor, Anita Pam, Ruth Green, Katherine Cameron, Amy Weber, Frances Markey, Clara Blackath, Dorothy Van Hest, Rita Marks, Rosalie Trego, Ruth Gordon, Betty Junod, Gypsy Hollis, Jocelyn Lyle, Adrienne Lampel
INTERNATIONAL GYPSIES: Alado Sio, Fred Orbowski, Harry Sacher, Benny Ladner, Milton Steckler

Musical Numbers

ACT I

SCENE ONE—A COUNTRY FAIR NEAR MARSEILLES
Opening, ENSEMBLE
It's a Wonderful World, CLAUDETTE, GRANIER, and ENSEMBLE
Musical interlude, CLAUDETTE, RENE, MARIE, LORRAINE

SCENE TWO—ON BOARD SHIP
East Wind, PAUL and ENSEMBLE
I Saw Your Eyes, CLAUDETTE, PAUL, RENE and OFFICERS

SCENE THREE—PIERRE FORTIER'S CASINO, SAIGON, INDO-CHINA
These Tropics, MARIE, VICTOR and DANCERS
Congai, TSOI TSING, RENE and ENSEMBLE

SCENE FOUR—VICTOR'S ELEPHANT ENCLOSURE

SCENE FIVE—PIERRE FORTIER'S HOME
Wedding scene, CLAUDETTE, RENE, PAUL and ENSEMBLE
Are You Love?, CLAUDETTE, RENE, PAUL
You Are My Woman, PAUL

SCENE SIX—VICTOR'S ELEPHANT ENCLOSURE
Minnie, VICTOR

SCENE SEVEN—ALONG THE RIVER FRONT, SAIGON
Embrace Me, RENE and Mullen Sisters

ACT II
SCENE ONE—RESTAURANT "AUX BELLES POULES" IN PARIS
The Americans Are Coming, MARIE and ENSEMBLE
I'd Be a Fool, CLAUDETTE
Finaletto, PAUL and GRANIER

SCENE TWO—PAPA GOULI'S APARTMENT

SCENE THREE—STAGE OF A PARIS MUSIC HALL
Regardez-moi, MCNULTY SISTERS
Indo-Chinese Ballet, TSOI TSING, KING, PRINCE and DANCERS

SCENE FOUR—MONSIEUR GRANIER'S STUDY
When You Are Young, PAUL and GRANIER

SCENE FIVE—LORRAINE'S WINE SHOP, MARSEILLES
Finale, COMPANY

NOTE: *Young Man in Love* cut before New York opening.

Reviews

J. Brooks Atkinson—*New York Times*
". . . Mr. Romberg's scores are gratifyingly loud. His serenades and love babblings have a fine basic metabolism . . . a dull book . . ."

Percy Hammond—*New York Herald Tribune*
"To some of Romberg's softest and stormiest songs, the authors have affixed as dreary a libretto as ever dejected a musical play . . . The girls, the scenery and the dress are capital, and the story is a pretty tale . . . Its too bad there isn't more fun in it . . ."

Burns Mantle—*New York Daily News*
". . . not a bad romance, but it furnishes nothing much on which to

hang a Romberg score. There is no inspiration in it, and not much sense. Only the background is interesting and colorful . . ."

Ed Sullivan—*New York Graphic*
"The grandest romantic story ever compressed into the pages of a musical comedy book, It guarantees a delightful evening . . ."

Gilbert W. Gabriel—*New York American*
". . . a standard operetta of the good old stock sort, and it simply can't be as dumb and duddy and devoid of the seven cardinal virtues of musical comedy as I thought it last night . . ."

John Mason Brown—*New York Post*
". . . about as unexciting as an operetta can be . . . it is all strangely dull and negative. Yes, and stupid, too . . . the ramifications of an overly busy plot blight whatever romance and amusement it offers . . ."

Robert Garland—*New York World-Telegram*
". . . it won't come off. Even if it were good, it would be too old-fashioned."

Richard Lockridge—*New York Sun*
". . . the plot is everywhere. Hardly a song can be turned over without revealing a large piece of it; the most sinuous dance has its place in the story . . . the play is by no means expert. Its lines are flat, its entrances and exits entirely arbitrary, its complications faintly exhausting . . ."

John Anderson—*New York Journal*
". . . pretty tedious stuff, superbly spendthrift in its settings and costumes and miserly in its amusement . . . even for a musical comedy, the cumbersome tale is a good deal too thick."

Jack Pulaski (Ibee.)—*Variety*, November 3, 1931
"If the second act was as good as the first, it would have a much better chance. As it is, it may not survive the struggle . . . the score has much excellent melody. The music more than counterbalances what book weaknesses there are. First half of the second act rather sags, but quickens to good going for the finale. The number impressing as the top melody is *I'd Be a Fool* . . . Penner scored with a comic lyric *Minnie* . . ."

Time, November 9, 1931
". . . Romberg's melodies, usually boomed by a great big band, come out thick as fudge. For *East Wind*, he has done his fudgiest. Pleasing result: *East Wind, You Are My Woman* and *I'd Be a Fool* . . .

East Wind's velocity is extremely low except for the sporadic appearance of a funny man named Joe Penner . . ."

Robert Benchley—*The New Yorker,* November 14, 1931
". . . evidently Schwab and Mandel's revenge on the people who panned them for trying to be different in *Free for All.* They have avoided being different in *East Wind* with a tenacity which, had it been converted into foot-pounds of energy, would have lifted the Empire State Building three inches off its base . . . Of course the musical comedies of an elder day weren't so bad, but we do remember how they went and *East Wind* goes that way . . ."

George Jean Nathan—*Judge,* November 21, 1931
". . . the musical play that we have been seeing at least once or twice every year for the past decade or more . . . Despite the fact that Romberg has written several pleasing melodic paraphrases, it is too bad that the whole thing was ever brought up again."

Selected Revivals

St. Louis Municipal Opera, July 2-8, 1934
Charlotte Lansing (CLAUDETTE); Allan Jones (PAUL); Leonard Ceeley (RENE); Frank Gaby (VICTOR); Barnett Parker (GOULI).

St. Louis Municipal Opera, August 5-11, 1940
Nancy McCord (CLAUDETTE); Walter Cassel (PAUL); Bob Lawrence (RENE); Sterling Holloway (VICTOR).

St. Louis Municipal Opera, June 26-July 2, 1950
Marguerite Piazza (CLAUDETTE); Brian Sullivan (PAUL); John Elliott (RENE); Buster West (VICTOR).

MUSIC IN THE AIR

(1932)

A musical play with book and lyrics by Oscar Hammerstein II; music by Jerome Kern.

Presented by Peggy Fears and A. C. Blumenthal (uncredited)
Directed by Messrs. Kern and Hammerstein
Assistant to Mr. Hammerstein, Leighton K. Brill
Settings by Joseph Urban
Costumes by Joseph Harkrider, Howard Shoup
Music director, Victor Baravalle
Orchestrations by Robert Russell Bennett

Tryout
Garrick Theatre, Philadelphia, October 17-November 5, 1932

New York Run
Alvin Theatre, November 8, 1932-March 30, 1933
Forty-fourth Street Theatre, March 31-September 16, 1933
342 performances

The Story
From their home in Edendorf, Karl Reder, his sweetheart Sieglinde, and her father, Dr. Lessing, travel to Munich to sell Karl's song to music publisher Ernst Weber. There Sieglinde has a brief flirtation with librettist Bruno Mahler, while his mistress, Frieda Hatzfeld, casts roving eyes at Karl. When Frieda, an operetta prima donna, becomes jealous and refuses to appear in Bruno's new work, Sieglinde gets the chance to take over the role. But her lack of stage experience soon becomes obvious, Frieda returns to Bruno, and the Edendorf trio return home.

The Cast
DR. WALTHER LESSING, *the music teacher,* Al Shean
HERMAN, Charles Belin
TILA, Mary McQuade
SIEGLINDE LESSING, *Dr. Lessing's daughter,* Katherine Carrington
KARL REDER, *the schoolmaster,* Walter Slezak
BURGOMASTER, Marty Semon
PFLUGFELDER, *the hotel proprietor,* Robert Williamson
FRAU PFLUGFELDER, Gabrielle Guelpi

TOWN CRIER, Robert Rhodes
HEINRICH, *the postman,* Cliff Heckinger
THE APOTHECARY, George Bell
WIDOW SCHREIMANN, Lydia Van Gilder
FATHER JOCH, *the priest,* Paul Donah
HANS, *the goatherd,* Edward Hayes
CORNELIUS, *a bird breeder,* Reinald Werrenrath
ERNST WEBER, *the music publisher,* Nicholas Joy
UPPMANN, *the musical director,* Harry Mestayer
MARTHE, *secretary to Weber,* Dorothy Johnson
FRIEDA HATZFELD, *the star,* Natalie Hall
BRUNO MAHLER, *a librettist,* Tullio Carminati
HULDE, *a bubble dancer,* Desha
STOUT MOTHER, Carrie Weller
STOUT FATHER, Carl Edem
THEIR SON, George Dieter
WAITER, George Ludwig
ZOO ATTENDANT, Alfred Russ
THE BEAR, Laura
BEAR TRAINER, H. Pallenberg
HERR DIREKTOR KIRSCHNER, Alexis Obolensky
FRAU DIREKTOR LILLI KIRSCHNER, Ivy Scott
SOPHIE, *Sieglinde's dresser,* Kathleen Edwards
ASSISTANT STAGE MANAGER, Frank Dobert
ANNA, *Frieda's maid,* Marjorie Main
BAUM, *the lawyer,* Carl Spiegel
GUSTERL, *his clerk,* William Torpey
THE TOBACCONIST, George Gerhardi
THE DOCTOR, Paul Janvert
MEMBERS OF THE EDENDORF CHORAL SOCIETY: Leone Newman, Kathleen Edwards, Finette Walker, Claire Cole, Marion Stuart, Sally Hadley, Gertrude Houk, June Elkins, Vivian Vance, Rose Collins, Frances Marion; Eugene King, Alfred Russ, George Gerhardi, Alexander McKee, Robert Rhodes, Norman Gray, Paul Donah, Paul Janvert, Anton Lieb, Frank Dobert, John Brook
MEMBERS OF THE EDENDORF WALKING CLUB: Rita Marks, Beatrice Berenson, Marie Cartwright, Leone Newman, Anne Moss, Theo Bayles, Finette Walker, Grace Panvini, Kathleen Edwards, Carol Gay, Kathleen Spector, Nomy Bencid, Marguerite Morano, Peggy Burgess, Helen Taylor, Virginia Ray, Marion Stuart, Peggy Frazier, Elise Joyce, Rosalind Shaw, Mary Alice Rice, Georgina Dieter, Betty Howson, Beatrice Hannen, Tamara Zoya, Vivian Vance, Frances Marion; Alexander McKee, Robert Rhodes, Norman Gray, John Brook
EDENDORF GIRLS: Joan Kent, Marcelle Miller, Rene McAfee, Noel Gordon, Diana Walker, Frances Kruger, Mary Lange, Stella Bailey, Jane Manners

NOTE: In March, 1933, Miss Carrington succeeded by Ann Barrie; in July, Mr. Carminati succeeded by Donald Brian, Miss Hall by Desiree Tabor.

Musical Numbers

ACT I

SCENE ONE—DR. LESSING'S HOME, EDENDORF, BAVARIA

SCENE TWO—KARL REDER'S CLASSROOM

Melodies of May (based on the second movement of Beethoven's Piano Sonata No. 3 in C, opus 2; vocal arrangement by Mr. Kern), EDENDORF CHORAL SOCIETY
I've Told Ev'ry Little Star, KARL
Prayer, KARL, SIEGLINDE, and ENSEMBLE
There's a Hill Beyond a Hill, EDENDORF WALKING CLUB

SCENE THREE—AT STONY BROOK, ON THE ROAD TO MUNICH

And Love Was Born, CORNELIUS

SCENE FOUR—ERNST WEBER'S OFFICE, MUNICH

Bubble Dance, HULDE
Reprise, *I've Told Ev'ry Little Star,* KARL and SIEGLINDE
Excerpts from Bruno's new play *Tingle-Tangle:*
I'm Coming Home (Letter Song), BRUNO
I'm Alone, FRIEDA
I Am So Eager, BRUNO, FRIEDA and ENSEMBLE
Finaletto, MARTHE, ERNST, WALTHER

ACT II

SCENE ONE—THE ZOO IN MUNICH

One More Dance, BRUNO
Night Flies By, FRIEDA
Reprise, *I've Told Ev'ry Little Star,* SIEGLINDE

SCENE TWO—FRIEDA'S APARTMENT, FOUR SEASONS HOTEL, MUNICH

Reprise, *I'm Alone,* FRIEDA

SCENE THREE—SIEGLINDE'S ROOM IN HER HOTEL, MUNICH

When the Spring Is in the Air, SIEGLINDE and ENSEMBLE
In Egern on the Tegern See, LILLI

SCENE FOUR—FRIEDA'S DRESSING ROOM

The Song Is You, BRUNO

SCENE FIVE—THE STAGE AND ORCHESTRA PIT

Excerpts from *Tingle-Tangle,* orchestra

SCENE SIX—FRIEDA'S DRESSING ROOM

Reprise, *I'm Alone,* FRIEDA
Reprise, *The Song Is You,* FRIEDA and BRUNO

SCENE SEVEN—EDENDORF

We Belong Together, KARL, SIEGLINDE, CORNELIUS, and COMPANY

NOTE: *One More Dance* has same music as *Night Flies By.*

Reviews

J. Brooks Atkinson—*New York Times*
"At last the musical drama has been emancipated . . . Without falling back into the cliches of the trade, Hammerstein has written sentiment and comedy that are tender and touching. It is an amusing story and an effortless piece of craftsmanship, and it provides a perfect setting for Mr. Kern's score . . ."

Percy Hammond—*New York Herald Tribune*
". . . a honeypot of romance and melody whose only fault, perhaps, is that it is overbountiful . . . it is aptly titled, for almost every minute of it is full of Mr. Kern's mesmeric airs . . ."

Gilbert W. Gabriel—*New York American*
". . . elected quite by acclimation to long tenancy in all local hearts . . . something to be seen, heard and treasured . . . some of Mr. Kern's most delicious songs . . . I dearly loved it all . . ."

Burns Mantle—*New York Daily News*
"★★★★ . . . Speaking of landslides, that scored last night by the new musical piece, *Words and Music* [sic], is not to be overlooked . . . a typical Kern success—a romantic operetta erected on a solid melodic base, and such a simple story that any amateur Broadway cynic can knock the props from under with a single sneer . . . The charm is in the simple honesty of its authors and the professional skill with which they have cast and staged it . . ."

John Mason Brown—*New York Post*
". . . abounds in the sort of soft, insinuating melodies which rarely are heard along Broadway and of which Mr. Kern is a past master. It is subtle, captivating music . . . a book which, though not so good as the one contributed to *Show Boat,* is nonetheless far more acceptable than most . . . combines a nice sense of humor with all the more usual conventions of a musical romance . . . something to be thankful for . . ."

Robert Garland—*New York World-Telegram*
". . . So smooth is its unfolding, so unforced is its humor, so absolutely in keeping with the time, the place and the romantic narrative is its music . . . an illustrious cast . . . a beautiful, pulsating score without a boop-boop-a-doop, a hot-cha-cha, or a torch song in it . . ."

Richard Lockridge—*New York Sun*
". . . an ample and happy show . . . it lilts with the music Mr. Kern has written. It is graceful and sweet music, and will be in the air . . .

its story is stanch enough to build a play on—a deft freshening up of the old story, with interludes of prankishness which have nothing to do with physical misfortunes of comedians, and always an affair of sound romantic swing . . ."

John Anderson—*New York Journal*
". . . I am shouting that it is a grand show, that it has quality all through it and an engaging charm that gives it special distinction. Kern's music is lovelier, to my notion, than even *The Cat and the Fiddle* and Hammerstein has provided an excellent book . . . The show's most ingratiating quality is a sort of casual method which avoids all the outworn stuff of blueprint musicals . . . a nicely sentimental, richly colorful tale, about which Kern's music eddies in the most rapturous beguilements . . ."

Jack Pulaski (Ibee.)—*Variety,* November 15, 1932
". . . so beautifully tuned, so well enacted, so lively in story and so well presented that it will be a favorite Broadway diversion for the balance of the season and probably next season . . ."

Robert Benchley—*The New Yorker,* November 19, 1932
". . . It seems to me to be one of Mr. Kern's loveliest scores, which is saying a great deal . . . As for Mr. Hammerstein's book, I was swept into its sentimental mood by the music . . . what with laughing and crying and crying and laughing I had an elegant time . . ."

Time, November 21, 1932
". . . an exquisite frieze of melody against the background of Bavaria . . . With much sympathy and good humor, Messrs Hammerstein and Kern send their audiences home with a sense of benign gratification. Best tunes: *I've Told Ev'ry Little Star, Night Flies By, In Egern on the Tegern See.*"

The Stage, December, 1932
". . . Here one breathes an air cooled by the mountain breeze and warmed, when occasion required, not by hot rhythm, but by the benign Bavarian sun . . . a book which tells a story and a story which has a beginning, a middle and an end, with an abundance of lyric moments in between . . . the score is reticent, delicate, nicely rhythmed to the more restrained movements of the dance . . ."

Alexander Woollcott—*The New Yorker,* March 11, 1933
". . . that endearing refuge, that gracious shelter from a troubled world, the piece called *Music in the Air*—the engaging romance which our Mr. Kern has so drenched with melody that it is an unfailing delight . . . enchanting work in the smallest parts, notably

the small part played to perfection by Marjorie Main. But of them all, the contributors who rejoice me most are Al Shean and Kern himself . . . Once again, as so often before, Jerome Kern has deserved well of the Republic."

Bibliography

The Oldest Musical in Town Nearly Mislaid in 1932 Shuffle by Charles Washburn —*New York Herald Tribune*, June 2, 1933

Tour

Colonial Theatre, Boston, September 11, 1933—Auditorium, Chicago, December 2, 1933 (6 cities).

Selected Revivals

St. Louis Municipal Opera, July 16-22, 1934
Gladys Baxter (FRIEDA); Leonard Ceeley (BRUNO); Charlotte Lansing (SIEGLINDE); Allan Jones (KARL); Jules Epailly (LESSING); Reinald Werrenrath (CORNELIUS).

San Francisco Civic Light Opera, June 8-20, 1942
Los Angeles Civic Light Opera, June 22-July 4, 1942
Irra Petina (FRIEDA); John Charles Thomas (BRUNO); Jan Clayton (SIEGLINDE); Francis Lederer (KARL); Al Shean (LESSING); G.P. Huntley (WEBER); Fritz Leiber (UPPMANN).

Greek Theatre, Los Angeles, Summer, 1948
Polyna Stoska (FRIEDA); Charles Fredericks (BRUNO); Jan Clayton (SIEGLINDE); Ralph Magelssen (KARL); Walter Kingsford (LESSING).

St. Louis Municipal Opera, June 25-July 1, 1951
Marina Koshetz (FRIEDA); Gilbert Russell (BRUNO); Gail Manners (SIEGLINDE); Joe E. Marks (LESSING).

MUSIC IN THE AIR

(London—1933)

Presented by Charles B. Cochran
Directed by Messrs. Kern and Hammerstein
Settings and costumes supervised by G.E. Calthrop
Music director, Hyam Greenbaum
Orchestrations by Robert Russell Bennett

London Run

His Majesty's Theatre, May 19, 1933-January 13, 1934
275 performances

The Cast

DR. WALTHER LESSING, Horace Hodges
HERMAN, Ryall Cordrey
TILA, Lydia Craddock
SIEGLINDE LESSING, Eve Lister
KARL REDER, Bruce Carfax
BURGOMASTER, S. Major Jones
PFLUGFELDER, Robert Ashby
FRAU PFLUGFELDER, Marie Minto
WIDOW SCHREIMANN, Molly Hamley-Clifford
FATHER JOCH, Jo Monkhouse
HANS, John Gould
CORNELIUS, Lance Fairfax
ERNST WEBER, Herbert Ross
MARTHE, Betty Elburn
FRIEDA HATZFELD, Mary Ellis
UPPMANN, Herbert Ross
BRUNO MAHLER, Arthur Margetson
HULDE, Jean Gillie
WAITER, Francis Lindon
THE BEAR, Bobby
BEAR TRAINER, Syd Howes
ZOO ATTENDANT, Stuart Harding
HERR DIREKTOR KIRSCHNER, Claude Fleming
FRAU DIREKTOR LILLI KIRSCHNER, Muriel George
SOPHIE, Donalda Warne
ASSISTANT STAGE MANAGER, George Hancock
ANNA, Phyllis Morris
BAUM, Gordon Crocker
HEINRICH, Ernest Freeman
MEMBERS OF THE EDENDORF CHORAL SOCIETY: Mavis Andrews, Jean Beckworth, Winifred Campbell, Freda Pettit, June Spencer, Jane Villiers, Grace Gorrod, Muriel Heath, Beth Alys, Jane Grey, Joyce May, Winifred Talbott; Gordon Crocker, Claud Britten, E.G. Freeman, J. Farleigh Price, Stuart Harding, G. Hancock, William Jones, Francis Lindon, John McDonald
MEMBERS OF THE EDENDORF WALKING CLUB: Moira Malone, Dorothy Morgan, Barbara Thomson, Donalda Warne, Molly McColl, Renee Veronica, Ann Angelo, Peggy Barton, Helen Callaghan, Hazel Cox, Rita Deane, Stephanie Insall, Sylvia Robin, Madge Taylor, Marjorie Yorke, Peggy Dunbar, Peggy Hale, Dodo Nevern
EDENDORF GIRLS: Angela Litolff, Margaret Neeson
EDENDORF CHILDREN: Doris Davies, Betty Parker, Marjorie Pilking, Kathryn Todd, Henry Bryce, John Jacques, Arthur Payne

Musical Numbers

Same as original production.

Reviews

London Times
"The charm of this piece is proportionate to its simplicity . . . The drag becomes evident whenever the dramatist's device of using an operetta within an operetta overburdens the simplicity of the tale . . . abundant good humour and prettiness that outweighs its minor defects."

London Daily Telegraph
". . . Mary Ellis is almost as good a singer as she is an actress . . . Kern's music is much above the average for this kind of show . . ."

London Daily Mail
". . . Another successful attempt by Mr. Kern to dominate a libretto by his score. Paradoxically, the story is so respected that every 'number' is fitted into it naturally . . . Miss Ellis is a thrilling joy . . . full of exquisite humour and romance . . ."

London Morning Post
". . . a triumph of fragrance, melody and charm . . . Never surely has an operetta so perfectly fulfilled a happy title . . ."

London News Chronicle
". . . Hammerstein has fortunately treated his subject with welcome satire . . . much charm in Kern's suave and pretty music . . . it made me thirsty for cool beer and the longing for the dreamy twilight among the mountains . . ."

James Agate—*London Sunday Times,* May 21, 1933
"For three-quarters of the journey this well-mannered musical comedy 'pursues the even tenours of its ways'—a poor quotation but a good description. But then theatre-pieces are like show horses; they cannot all be sensational. There is your nice level mover with correct and beautifully balanced action, though not quite enough of it to head the class. So it is with this musical comedy . . . Miss Ellis's singing is no soundless pipe but a full-throated blackbird fluting . . . The music was delightful."

Ivor Brown—*London Observer,* May 21, 1933
". . . Is it merely habituation to lustier methods that makes one feel something lacking in this lavish outlay of decorative and musical taste? . . . It moves to music of a very pleasant, chasy kind and it moves at a moderate tempo . . . Eye and ear need never go in want, but there are times, as the story wends its way, when it is tempting to withdraw the mind. By all means let the musical piece learn manners, but when was wit ruled out of mannerly behavior? . . ."

Bibliography
"Music in the Air" (cover story) —*The Play Pictorial*, July, 1933

MUSIC IN THE AIR

(Film Version—1934)

A Fox Film
Produced by Erich Pommer
Directed by Joe May
Screenplay by Howard I. Young and Billy Wilder
Continuity by Robert Liebmann
Choreography by Jack Donahue
Music director, Louis De Francesco
Orchestrations by Franz Waxman
Photographed by Ernest Palmer

Release Date
December 13, 1934

The Cast
FRIEDA HATZFELD, Gloria Swanson
BRUNO MAHLER, John Boles
KARL REDER, Douglass Montgomery (sung by James O'Brien)
ERNST WEBER, Reginald Owen
DR. WALTHER LESSING, Al Shean
SIEGLINDE LESSING, June Lang (sung by Betty Hiestand)
UPPMANN, Joseph Cawthorn
CORNELIUS, Hobart Bosworth
MARTHE, Sara Haden
HERR DIREKTOR KIRSCHNER, Jed Prouty
NICK, Fuzzy Knight

Musical Numbers
Songs retained from original production: *One More Dance, The Song Is You, We Belong Together, There's a Hill Beyond a Hill, I've Told Ev'ry Little Star* and *I Am So Eager.*

Reviews
Andre Sennwald—*New York Times*
". . . a skillfully photographed work which includes among its ballads, songs and snatches some of the most distinguished melodies of this cinema season . . . gay, tender and superbly romantic lyrics . . . Kern's matchless songs are enough to insure it a position among the superior musical pictures . . ."

William Boehnel—*New York World-Telegram*
". . . a pleasurable job . . . Although it is tuneful—grandly tuneful—gay and reasonably humorous, it has moments when it gets a little bit windy about what it has to say . . . likable, melodious and entertaining . . ."

Time, December 10, 1934
". . . the music is a sort of operetta through which continuously looms the grave, offended shade of Victor Herbert . . . Miss Swanson sings through her teeth in a sprightly way . . ."

Abel Green—*Variety,* December 18, 1934
". . . a poor flicker . . . it's never believable . . . appealing beauty of the music is almost totally lost . . ."

John Mosher—*The New Yorker,* December 22, 1934
". . . That there is too much plot is almost a routine complaint of mine about the movies of stage musical shows, yet *Music in the Air* is not conspicuously victimized by its libretto. Altogether, the thing moves along brightly, with a shimmer of honor and acceptable good nature."

Don Herold—*Judge,* February, 1935
". . . a lot of the comedy is on the same level as that of Uncle Elmer when he gets a few drinks and puts on a lampshade and a piano shawl. In fact, someone does put on a lampshade and a piano shawl . . . Kern's music still gets in your veins, of course . . ."

London Times, April 7, 1935
". . . Almost the entire value of the lilting tunes is destroyed by the jumble and confusion of the story . . ."

MUSIC IN THE AIR

(New York—1951)

Presented by Reginald Hammerstein
Directed by Oscar Hammerstein II
Settings and costumes by Lemuel Ayers
Lighting by Charles Elson
Music director, Maurice Levine
Orchestrations by Robert Russell Bennett

Tryout
Olney Theatre, Olney, Maryland, September 25-29, 1951

New York Run
Ziegfeld Theatre, October 8-November 24, 1951
56 performances

The Cast
FRAU PFLUGFELDER, Julie Kelety
TILA, Marybeth Fitzpatrick
HERMAN, Richard Case
KARL REDER, Mitchell Gregg
BURGOMASTER, Hal Frye
SIEGLINDE LESSING, Lillian Murphy
DR. WALTER LESSING, Charles Winninger
SCHMIDT, Carlo Corelli
PRIEST, Milton Watson
PFLUGFELDER, Walter Born
ERNST WEBER, Conrad Nagel
UPPMANN, Guy Spaull
MARTHE, Terry Saunders
FRIEDA HATZFELD, Jane Pickens
BRUNO MAHLER, Dennis King
WAITER, John M. King
ZOO ATTENDANT, Waldorf
ANNA, Norah Howard
PORTER, James Beni
HERR DIREKTOR KIRSCHNER, Richard Bishop
FRAU DIREKTOR LILLI KIRSCHNER, Muriel O'Malley
SOPHIE, Julie Kelety
ASSISTANT STAGE MANAGER, John M. King
BAUM, Gordon Alexander
BARMAID, Biruta Ramoska
WILLI, James Beni
FRAU SCHREIMANN, Jean Ellsperman
FRAU MOELLER, Susan Steell
WOMEN: Madeleine Chambers, Jean Ellsperman, Joan Keenan, Julie Kelety, Rosemary Kuhlmann, Sheila Matthews, Grace Olsen, Biruta Ramoska, Marjorie Samsel, Helen Stanton, Susan Steell
MEN: Gordon Alexander, Robert Baird, James Beni, Walter Born, Robert Busch, Carlo Corelli, Charles Dunn, Warren Galjour, Robert Gilson, John M. King, William Krach, Frederick Olsson, Fred Rivetti, Donald Thrall
CHILDREN: Richard Case, Marybeth Fitzpatrick, Georgianna Catal, May Hover, Charles Lee Saari

NOTE: During rehearsals, ERNST WEBER played by Henry Stephenson who left cast because of illness. During tryout, role of CORNELIUS (played by William Wilderman) was eliminated.

Musical Numbers
Same as original production, except for following changes: *All The Things*

You Are, which had been added during tryout, and *And Love Was Born* were both cut before New York opening. Locale changed from Munich to Zurich, Switzerland.

Reviews

Brooks Atkinson—*New York Times*
". . . it is a shock to discover that half of the first act is wasted on some silly mumbo-jumbo about wicked city people . . . the plot has a lot of hackneyed playwriting in it. Hammerstein writes with much greater simplicity now . . . But the immortal songs still flow through it like enchanted improvisations. They are part of the theatre's richest treasury."

Bert McCord—*New York Herald Tribune*
"An abundance of silver threads and a few golden tunes . . . the action still lags and the material is dated. And as agreeable as they are, Kern's melodies just are not capable of lifting the book off the stage . . . One of the ironies is that Hammerstein is perhaps more responsible than anyone else for the fact that the show can't finish in the running today. By his work with Rodgers, he has been instrumental in educating audiences to more developed musical theatre . . ."

John Chapman—*New York Daily News*
". . . a captivating, heartwarming play performed by a company of experts. It is better than it was in 1932. The tunes are Kern at his most melodious and soft-hearted mood . . . The book is smarter and tighter than I'd remembered it . . . Hammerstein has staged it with his notable skill . . ."

Robert Coleman—*New York Daily Mirror*
". . . boasts the finest score Kern ever composed, aside from his immortal *Show Boat* . . . Every number is sheer delight . . . The libretto seems a little sparse and dated in spots, though it still offers many rewarding moments . . ."

Richard Watts, Jr.—*New York Post*
". . . a little wan and pallid. The score is still rich and delightful, and some of the old romantic gaiety clings to its story-telling, but it no longer possesses the sparkle and excitement that made it so notable a contribution to its field of dramatic art. It is quite a blow to us sentimental old-timers . . . the haunting *In Egern on the Tegern See* is certainly one of the most exquisite songs ever composed . . ."

William Hawkins—*New York World-Telegram & Sun*
". . . A lacy, fragile conversation piece that interrupts, and is

interrupted by, the lovely songs . . . If Hammerstein's book seems dated, he certainly can only blame himself, who, more than anyone else in the theatre, has advanced the fashions in musicals since *Music in the Air.*"

Robert Garland—*New York Journal-American*
". . . the music is as good as ever. But the book limps more than it ought to. It is older than its age . . . As long as it lives up to its title, it is as it should be. But the libretto does need priming. Words age faster than notes. Especially words which were not flawless in the beginning . . . It's awkward, it's long-drawn, it's not too interesting . . . it seldom comes alive save when it lifts its voice in song. Then it soars . . ."

Whitney Bolton—*New York Morning Telegraph*
". . . a pleasant, leisurely, gemütlich item which accomplishes two major aims: it establishes anew that Kern was a music maker for your buttons, and that the currently Olympian Oscar Hammerstein II was a shrewd phrasemaker and word painter far back there when . . . Reginald Hammerstein was completely right in deciding to bring this back to us."

Arthur Bronson—*Variety,* October 10, 1951
"This was a mistake . . . Changing times, and above all, changing tastes in theatrical musicals, makes this seem like incredible corn, and the wonder of it is that the Hammersteins couldn't see it. But see it they didn't . . ."

George Jean Nathan—*New York Journal-American,* October 15, 1951
". . . still provides the theatre with an engaging evening in spite of spotty casting and some changes in the book that are not for the better . . . even so, the exhibit imparts much of its original appeal to that share of gentle starlight that is in the heart of even the drabbest of us . . . a score embracing some soothing melodies and a book that, while it has aged some and while it doesn't weather close critical scrutiny, gets no more in the way of the score than the book of *Fledermaus* . . ."

Wolcott Gibbs—*The New Yorker,* October 20, 1951
". . . In spite of a prevailing atmosphere of leisurely and dated innocence, it remains an engaging show . . . Kern's score is among the most charming ever written . . . Hammerstein's book in this case is rather discouraging but his lyrics combine sorrow and gaiety in almost exactly the right proportions . . ."

Louis Kronenberger—*Time,* October 22, 1951
". . . still has an extremely engaging score. It no longer has very much else . . . the show as badly lacks bouquet as the production lacks style . . . it plods as both story and satire . . ."

Harold Clurman—*The New Republic,* November 12, 1951
". . . with its charming score, it seems to me as original today as it must have been 19 years ago . . . The show, thank heaven, has no oomph, bang, zip, or zowie. It is friendly, old fashioned, jolly, serene . . ."

Bibliography

Jerome Kern: A Tribute by Richard Rodgers
—*New York Times,* October 7, 1951

An Old Favorite Returns by Oscar Hammerstein II
—*New York Herald Tribune,* October 7, 1951

BALL AT THE SAVOY

(London—1933)

A musical play with book by Alfred Grunwald and Fritz Lohner-Beda, adapted into English by Oscar Hammerstein II; music by Paul Abraham; lyrics by Mr. Hammerstein.

Directed by Oscar Hammerstein II
Book staged by Reginald Hammerstein
Choreography by Jack Donohue
Settings by Joseph and Phil Harker
Music director, Charles Prentice

London Run

Theatre Royal, Drury Lane, September 8, 1933-January 13, 1934
148 performances

The Story

The newly married Marquis and Marquise Faublas are quite happy until the Marquis decides to have a secret meeting with an old love at a ball at the Savoy. The Marquise learns of this, and determines to practice a similar deception, although quite innocently. Complications and misunderstandings arise at the ball, but all ends satisfactorily.

The Cast

ARISTIDE, LE MARQUIS DE FAUBLAS, Maurice Evans
MADELEINE, *his wife,* Natalie Hall
ARCHIBALD, *his butler,* Dick Francis
BEBE, *Madeleine's maid,* Rita Nugent
LILY, Brenda Clether
PAULETTE, MAURICE, RENE, *guests at the de Faubias house,* Shelagh Patrick, Bruce Seton, John Huson
MUSTAPHA BEI, *Attaché at the Turkish Embassy,* Oskar Denes
KATHI MIHAZY, *Madeleine's cousin,* Rosy Barsony
ALBERT, *a dressmaker,* Basil Neale
NINA, *a dancer,* Joan Marion
CELESTIN FROMANT, *a young lawyer,* Barry Mackay
ERNEST BENUET, *his friend,* Leo Britt

POMEROL, *head waiter at the Savoy,* Tom Scott
GARDNER, Barry Sherwood

LENA, *of Berlin*	*divorced wives of Mustapha Bei*	Pamela Dawn
ANGELA, *of Paris*		Kate Cavil
LUCIA, *of Rome*		Eileen Clifton
LOLA, *of Rio de Janeiro*		Valerie Tuck
BESS, *of London*		Bobby Huby
GRACIE, *of Manchester*		Valerie Hobson

Musical Numbers

PROLOGUE

Wherein the Marquis and Marquise de Faublas, under the spell of the Venetian Moon, decide to make their honeymoon last forever.

The Moon Will Ride Away, ARISTIDE and MADELEINE
This Lovely Night, ARISTIDE and MADELEINE

ACT I

SALON IN THE HOUSE OF THE MARQUIS DE FAUBLAS, NICE

Opening, ENSEMBLE
Le Marquis de Faublas, ARCHIBALD and ENSEMBLE
I Think I'm in Love with My Wife, MADELEINE and ARISTIDE
On the Bosphorus, MUSTAPHA BEI and GIRLS
Up and Down, KATHI and BOYS
Baby, Wait Till It Happens to You, MADELEINE and KATHI
Soliloquy, MADELEINE
I'll Show You Off, KATHI, MUSTAPHA BEI and ENSEMBLE
Finale, *The Night Is Young,* COMPANY

ACT II

SCENE ONE—FOYER AND BAR AT THE SAVOY HOTEL, NICE (THAT NIGHT)

There Is a Ball at the Savoy, ENSEMBLE
A Girl Like Nina, NINA and ENSEMBLE

SCENE TWO—TWO PRIVATE DINING ROOMS

SCENE THREE—BALL ROOM OF THE SAVOY HOTEL

All I Want Is a Home, MUSTAPHA BEI and GIRLS
I Live for Love, MADELEINE, ARISTIDE, MUSTAPHA BET and MEN
I Always Keep My Girl Out Late, KATHI, MUSTAPHA BEI and ENSEMBLE
Reprise, *I Live for Love,* MADELEINE
Finale, *Oh Why, Oh Why, Oh Why,* COMPANY

ACT III

SCENE ONE—TWO BEDROOMS IN THE DE FAUBLAS HOME (NEXT MORNING)

SCENE TWO—TERRACE OUTSIDE THE DE FAUBLAS HOME (THAT EVENING)

If It's Good Enough for Gentlemen, ENSEMBLE

SCENE THREE—TWO BEDROOMS

SCENE FOUR—TERRACE
Reprise, *Oh Why, Oh Why, Oh Why,* ENSEMBLE
Finale Ultimo, COMPANY

Reviews
London Times
". . . Mr. Maurice Evans is the best *jeune premier* that there has been in musical comedy for some time . . . the scenery is elaborately gorgeous . . . the dances and those mysterious delights called *ensembles* are extremely good in their kind; the chorus has a genuine air of joy and vitality . . ."

London Daily Telegraph
". . . luxurious and gay . . ."

London Morning Post
". . . The outstanding feature was the superlative dancing ensembles . . ."

London News Chronicle
". . . What interested me as a critic was the masterly manner in which Oscar Hammerstein and his lieutenants had built such an elaborate production on this material . . . The spectacle of the piece is amazing . . . some charming music . . ."

James Agate—*London Sunday Times,* September 10, 1933
". . . A jaundiced view would be that the scenery was pre-anybody with any kind of taste. That the music, except for the patter numbers, was exactly what we have been hearing for years in scores of other musical comedies. That the plot bored to tears even our grandmothers. That the dialogue had not a line of wit from beginning to end . . . the audience gave the impression of liking the show."

Horace Horsnell—*London Observer,* September 10, 1933
". . . an untiring score . . . The eye rather than the ear is catered for with a generosity that presupposes either a good dinner or a good heart in the onlooker . . . entertainment whose subtleties will not escape the most distant spectator . . ."

Illustrated Sporting and Dramatic News
". . . hardly worthy of Drury Lane . . . one of those old-fashioned musical plays . . . But it provides an adequate vehicle for the brilliant fooling of Oskar Denes and the delightful dancing of Rosy Barsony . . ."

David C. Fairweather—*Theatre World,* October, 1933
". . . nothing yet seen at Drury Lane can compare with the scene depicting the ballroom at the Savoy . . . It is as a lavish spectacle that this operetta is chiefly memorable . . . the score contains several numbers destined to achieve wide popularity . . ."

Bibliography

"Ball at the Savoy" (cover story) —*The Play Pictorial,* October, 1933

"Ball at the Savoy" —*Theatre World,* October, 1933

THREE SISTERS

(London-1934)

A musical play with book and lyrics by Oscar Hammerstein II; music by Jerome Kern.

Presented by H. M. Tennent
Directed by Messrs. Hammerstein and Kern
Assistant to Mr. Hammerstein, Leighton K. Brill
Choreography by Ralph Reader
Settings and costumes by G. E. Calthrop
Music director, Charles Prentice
Orchestrations by Robert Russell Bennett

London Run
Theatre Royal, Drury Lane, April 9-June 9, 1934
45 performances

The Story
Traveling photographer Will Barbour and his three daughters are at Epsom Downs for the Derby. Daughter Tiny has her eye on Constable Eustace Titherley; daughter Dorrie is after any young man of aristocratic blood; daughter Mary sets her cap for a busker named Gypsy Hood. In spite of difficulties, the three sisters move unflaggingly toward their goals.

The Cast
WILL BARBOUR, *a photographer,* Eliot Makeham
TINY, *his eldest daughter,* Charlotte Greenwood
DORRIE, *his second daughter,* Adele Dixon
MARY, *his youngest daughter,* Victoria Hopper
ALF, *his brother,* Dick Francis
GEORGE PURVIS, *a busker,* Albert Burdon
GYPSY HOOD, *George's partner,* Esmond Knight
EUSTACE TITHERLEY, *A Constable,* Stanley Holloway
PHILIP, *a delivery boy at Alf's shop,* Leonard Thorn
DAVID GLAINLEY, Anthony Hankey
SIR JOHN MARSDEN, *David's friend,* Richard Dolman
MRS. TITCHMARSH, *proprietress of The White Hart,* Gladys Henson
LADY MARSDEN, *Sir John's Mother,* Clare Lindsay
HUGH WILLOUGHBY, Bruce Seton

ZENIDA, Eileen Clifton

LADIES OF THE CHORUS: Jane Box, Betty Bucknelle, Kate Cavil, Eileen Clifton, Rosalind Daniel, Guinevere Fellows, Dorothy Fox, Kathleen Francis, Ruby Gilchrist, Joan Grundy, Bobby Hubby, Mary Hargreaves, Marjorie Ingram, Edith Juster, Ruth Lieder, Lillian Logan, Molly MacColl, Eileen Penberthy, Freda Pettitt, Leonta Proctor, Pam Randall, Pegi Rhys, Sylvia Robin, Barbara Silverins, Alberta Yates

GENTLEMEN OF THE CHORUS: Bruce Clark, Robert Coomber, Winter Coppin, Gordon Crocker, Harry Foster, Herbert Garry, Leonard Granville, Thomas Hancock, Harry Lacey, Archibald Levers, Ernest Ludlow, Henry Millidge, David Morgan, Basil Neale, Max Oldacre, Victor Peduzzi, Andrew Reid, James Robertson, Richard Rogers, Warren Saunders, Bruce Seton, Barry Sherwood, Reginald Smith, Frederick Warren

DANCERS: Margaret Ann, Betty Bevan, Daphne Blake, Ann Coventry, Elsie Fuller, Alethea Jermaine, Vera Laine, Patricia Lovegrove, Esme Oxley, Freda Reeve, Bubbly Rogers, Trixie Seales, June Seymour, Rosalind Snow, Marjorie Streeter-Paine, Mary Taylor, Iris Tully, Renee Veronica; Adrian Beaumont, Jack Carden, Peter Crawford, Hugh Fraser, Thomas Gillis, Stanley Haig-Brown, Ivan Hawkes, Pat Hulley, Tony Hulley, Edward King, Frederick Nye, Neil O'Brien, William Rolston, Ronald Urquhart.

Musical Numbers

ACT I—THE NIGHT BEFORE THE EPSOM MEETING, EPSOM DOWNS, MAY, 1914

Roll On Rolling Road, GYPSY, GEORGE and ENSEMBLE
Now That I Have Springtime, GYPSY, GEORGE, MARY and ENSEMBLE
My Beautiful Circus Girl, GYPSY, GEORGE, TINY, MARY, WILL and ENSEMBLE
What's In the Air Tonight?, ENSEMBLE
There's a Joy That Steals Upon You, MARY, TINY, GYPSY, GEORGE
Hand In Hand, EUSTACE
Somebody Wants to Go to Sleep, TINY; danced by MARY, GYPSY and DANCERS

ACT II

SCENE ONE—TATTENHAM CORNER, FIVE MINUTES BEFORE THE RUNNING OF THE DERBY

An Impression of the Derby, COMPANY

SCENE TWO—A DESERTED MERRY-GO-ROUND ON THE DOWNS

You Are Doing Very Well, TINY and EUSTACE

SCENE THREE—THE MARSDEN ESTATE

Lonely Feet, DORRIE and ENSEMBLE
Finaletto, *What Good Are Words?,* MARY and GYPSY

SCENE FOUR—(a) A ROOM IN ALF'S HOUSE
(b) THE STREET BETWEEN
(c) A PRIVATE ROOM IN THE WHITE HART

Funny Old House, EUSTACE, MARY, GYPSY, MALE SEXTETTE

SCENE FIVE—(a) THE VILLAGE COMMON
Welcome to the Bride, EUSTACE and ENSEMBLE
(b) AT THE ALTAR OF THE CHURCH
(c) THE VILLAGE COMMON
Finale, COMPANY

ACT III
SCENE ONE—MARY'S ROOM, SUMMER, 1915
Reprise, *Funny Old House,* MARY

SCENE TWO—TERRACE OF THE MARSDEN ESTATE
Keep Smiling, EUSTACE

SCENE THREE—OUTSIDE AN ESTAMINET IN FRANCE, 1917
I Won't Dance, DORRIE, JOHN and CHORUS

SCENE FOUR—INSIDE A Y.M.C.A. HUT IN FRANCE DURING A REHEARSAL
The Gaiety Chorus Girls, GYPSY, GEORGE, EUSTACE, PONY BALLET and MALE ENSEMBLE

SCENE FIVE—MARY'S ROOM

SCENE SIX—THE RIVER DURING THE AUGUST BANK HOLIDAY, 1924
Reprise, MARY, GYPSY, TINY, WILL
Finale, COMPANY

NOTE: *Here It Comes* cut before London opening. In 1935, revised version of *I Won't Dance* given new lyric by Dorothy Fields and sung by Fred Astaire and Ginger Rogers in *Roberta.*

Reviews
London Times
". . . Whenever the play is cheerfully using its crowds, it is full of high-spirited confidence . . . But the entertainment gives the impression of a team of lively and willing horses that go splendidly when they are given their heads but are too often held back . . . a harmlessly romantic and more than usefully coherent story. What is needed is a firm blue pencil . . ."

W. A. Darlington—*London Daily Telegraph*
". . . lamentably short of comic material. But there is attractive material in it, and when it has been pulled together and certain dull patches have been brightened or eliminated, it may do well . . . The music is cleverly handled and pleasant, but not original . . ."

James Agate—*London Sunday Times,* April 9, 1934
". . . how long is Drury Lane to be the asylum for American inanity? The answer is: Forever, dear heart! . . . both Mr. Kern's music and Mrs. Calthrop's settings are exquisite. Probably there is no other

country in the world in which visual and aural embroidery of such delicacy is tacked on to calico so coarse . . . Mr. Hammerstein is no Shakespeare, and that is why he reigns in our national theatre."

The Sphere, April 14, 1934
". . . sweet and not very fizzy lemonade . . . The story is long, rambling, and over-sentimental, the gallery on the first night showing their disapproval in the usual mannerless manner. But, on the whole, it is a good show . . . Mr. Jerry Kern's music is an enormous asset . . ."

Ivor Brown—*London Observer,* April 16, 1934
". . . at least one tune that will be drowsily hummed and two that will set all feet moving . . . as much of an invitation to use the eye as temptation to withdraw the mind. As encouragement to the latter process there is a deal of sentimental dithering; as excitement to attention there are the energy and elasticity of Miss Charlotte Greenwood . . ."

Joshua Lowe—*Variety,* April 24, 1934
". . . of the romantic type calculated to appeal to the majority of theatregoers. As such it was almost boring to the large theatrical contingent and sophisticated first nighters . . . a magnificently spectacular production about nothing much . . . gives promise of a healthy run . . ."

Bibliography

Kern's "Three Sisters" Makes Hit in London by Robert Garland
—*New York World-Telegram,* April 26, 1934

"Three Sisters" (cover story) —*Theatre World,* May, 1934

THE NIGHT IS YOUNG

(Film—1935)

Screenplay by Edgar Allen Woolf and Franz Schulz, based on a story by Vicki Baum; music by Sigmund Romberg; lyrics by Oscar Hammerstein II.

A Metro-Goldwyn-Mayer Picture
Produced by Harry Rapf
Directed by Dudley Murphy
Art director, Cedric Gibbons
Costumes by Dolly Tree
Dances by Chester Hale
Photographed by James Wong Howe
Editor, Conrad Nervig

Release Date
January 11, 1935

The Story
Archduke Paul Gustave, nephew of Emperor Franz Josef, falls in love with Lisl, a ballerina. Their romance is gay and spirited, but as it is the archduke's duty to marry a princess, the girl must eventually give him up.

The Cast
ARCHDUKE PAUL GUSTAVE, Ramon Novarro
LISL, Evelyn Laye
WILLY, Charles Butterworth
FANNI, Una Merkel
SZERENY, Edward Everett Horton
TONI, Donald Cook
EMPEROR FRANZ JOSEF, Henry Stephenson
COUNTESS RAFAY, Rosalind Russell
NEPOMUK, Herman Bing
RICCARDI, Charles Judels

Musical Numbers
The Night Is Young, PAUL and LISL
When I Grow Too Old to Dream, PAUL and LISL
My Old Mare, WILLY and FANNI
Lena, I Love You

There's a Riot in Havana
The Noble Duchess
Vienna Will Sing
Wiener Schnitzel

Reviews

Andre Sennwald—*New York Times*
". . . The able music masters have written a variety of numbers which are nostalgic and humorous, and also neatly undistinguished . . . the film is without any distinguishing virtue except for its appalling competence in every department . . ."

Marguerite Tazelaar—*New York Herald Tribune*
". . . a vacuous little romance . . . despite its trite plot and its frothy substance, the sentimentality in its later scenes moves one to a sweet, dewy-eyed melancholy . . . Miss Laye's songs are not to be ignored . . ."

Eileen Creelman—*New York Sun*
". . . lushly romantic, heavily fragrant, laden with sighs and smiles and sweet remembrances. The acting is as theatrical as the plot. The music is grand, soft and sad and pleasant to hum . . ."

Roy Chartier—*Variety,* January 15, 1935
". . . a disappointment . . . Feeble in plot, film also seems to lack a single strong musical number . . ."

John Mosher—*The New Yorker,* January 19, 1935
". . . considerably duller and heavier all around than I was prepared for, being always the optimist . . ."

Time, January 21, 1935
". . . pallid . . . pleasant but unremarkable songs . . . would probably be less dull if Edward Everett Horton and Charles Butterworth were given more elbow room for their buffooneries . . ."

Don Herold—*Life,* March, 1935
". . . a preposteroperetta with a couple of good tunes and a plot that is as stale as they come."

MAY WINE

(1935)

A musical play with book by Frank Mandel, based on novel, "The Happy Alienist" by Wallace Smith, suggested by story related by Erich Von Stroheim; music by Sigmund Romberg; lyrics by Oscar Hammerstein II.

Presented by Laurence Schwab
Directed by José Ruben
Settings by Raymond Sovey
Costumes by Kay Morrison
Music director, Robert Emmett Dolan
Orchestrations by Don Walker, Robert Russell Bennett

Tryout
Playhouse, Wilmington, November 22-24, 1935
Ford's Theatre, Baltimore, November 25-30, 1935

New York Run
St. James Theatre, December 5, 1935-June 6, 1936
213 performances

The Story
Professor Johann Volk, a Viennese psychiatrist, loves Marie, the impoverished Baroness Von Schlewitz, who, in turn, loves Baron Kuno Adelhorst. Johann marries Marie, and she learns to love him. But an evil-minded assistant turns him against his wife by insisting that Johann is being made a cuckold. After drinking heavily, Volk shoots what he thinks is his wife. The "victim" turns out to be a dummy, and husband and wife declare their mutual love and relief.

The Cast
PROFESSOR JOHANN VOLK, Walter Slezak
INSPECTOR SCHNORRHEIM, Roy Gordon
SERGEANT, Tomes Chapman
POLICEMEN, Edward Galloway, Leonard Berry, Chester Herman
WILLI ZIMMERKOPF, Robert Sloane
BARON KUNO ADELHORST, Walter Woolf King
HERR SCHMIDT, *a barber,* Carlo Conte
HANS, *his assistant,* Victor Casmore

GYPSY, Marie Louise Quevli
MUSICIANS, Bela Loblov, Charles Palloy
HERR SCHRAMMEL, Mitchell Harris
FRAU SCHRAMMEL, Igna Hill
THEIR SON, Radley Collins
THEIR DAUGHTER, Marian Huntley
WAITER, Maury Tuckerman
THE LOVERS, Earle MacVeigh, Betty Kerr
MARIE, BARONESS VON SCHLEWITZ, Nancy McCord
PAGE BOY, Radley Collins
BOX HOLDERS, Tomes Chapman, Devona Doxie, Lee Childs
VERA HUBER, *Volk's assistant,* Patricia Calvert
STROLLERS, Flora Laney, Leonard Berry, Clifford Menz
JOSEF, *a clarinet player,* Robert C. Fischer
UNCLE PISHKA, Leo G. Carroll
MR. RUNTSCHLI, *of "Die Wochende,"* Earle MacVeigh
OLD COUPLE, Jessie Graham, Leonard Berry
DANCERS, Jack Cole, Alice Dudley
KATHI, *maid at the Hotel Schildersturn,* Inga Hill
FRIEDL, *Willi's model,* Vera Van
PAWNBROKER, Victor Casmore
DR. VON SCHLAGER, Mitchell Harris
DR. HERBST, Leonard Berry
DR. KARPIS, Carlo Conte
NEWSBOY, Radley Collins

Musical Numbers

ACT I

SCENE ONE—PROFESSOR VOLK'S LIVING ROOM
Something in the Air of May, VOLK

SCENE TWO—A BARBER SHOP
Interlude in a Barber Shop, VOLK and KUNO

SCENE THREE—A PRATER CAFE
A Chanson on the Prater, VOLK, MARIE, SCHRAMMELS

SCENE FOUR—THE BENEFIT PERFORMANCE
A Doll Fantasy, MARIE

SCENE FIVE—MARIE'S ROOM
You Wait and Wait and Wait, MARIE and KUNO

SCENE SIX—PROFESSOR VOLK'S LIVING ROOM
I Built a Dream One Day, VOLK, KUNO, JOSEF

SCENE SEVEN—A RAILROAD STATION
Dance, My Darlings, MARIE and ENSEMBLE
Dance, Jack Cole and Alice Dudley

SCENE EIGHT—BRIDAL SUITE OF HOTEL SCHILDERSTURN
Finale, MARIE and KUNO

ACT II
SCENE ONE—BRIDAL SUITE, HOTEL SHILDERSTURN
Always Be a Gentleman, MARIE and KUNO

SCENE TWO—WILLI'S STUDIO
Reprise, *I Built a Dream One Day,* JOSEF

SCENE THREE—PROFESSOR VOLK'S LIVING ROOM

SCENE FOUR—THE CLUB FLORIDA
Somebody Ought to Be Told, FRIEDL

SCENE FIVE—PROFESSOR VOLK'S STUDY
Something New Is in My Heart, MARIE
Dance, Jack Cole and Alice Dudley

SCENE SIX—A PAWN SHOP

SCENE SEVEN—A CONFERENCE ROOM

SCENE EIGHT—A STREET
Just Once Around the Clock, FRIEDL, KUNO, PISHKA

SCENE NINE—PROFESSOR VOLK'S LIVING ROOM
Reprise, *Something New Is in My Heart,* MARIE

Reviews

Brooks Atkinson—*New York Times*
". . . 'good in kind' . . . a sheaf of well bred tunes that have pleasant melodies and manners . . . Everyone has made a conscientious attempt to produce a popular operetta shorn of the excrescences and stock appurtenances. To some extent, they have succeeded . . . But operetta has certain plodding mannerisms that dull the fine edge of appreciation unless they are ground in brilliance. *May Wine* is not a brilliant improvisation, wrapt in soft Lydian airs . . ."

Percy Hammond—*New York Herald Tribune*
". . . a dignified little grand opera . . . some of Romberg's most luscious tinkles and melodies, it may be emphasized that *May Wine* is quite an animated concert . . . I have pleasant memories of a solo called *Something New Is in My Heart*—a song full of sway and melody . . . first rate in its settings, dress, cast, composer and librettists. There is no chorus and none seems necessary."

Burns Mantle—*New York Daily News*
"★★★ . . . happily the good old excuse that even if the book is heavy, the music is light and engaging still holds . . . Pains have deen taken

to tie songs and story together, as was done so successfully with *Music in the Air*. The result is not a perfect joining, but it is better than it would be if the effort had not been made . . ."

Robert Coleman—*New York Daily Mirror*
". . . has a little of everything and not quite enough of any one thing. It lacks a dominant quality, a sustained mood. Romberg has done exceptionally well . . . And Hammerstein has equipped the music with lyrics that become an integral part of the play . . . a commendable endeavor to improve upon our conventional musical comedy formula . . ."

Gilbert W. Gabriel—*New York American*
". . . highly melodious and briskly sentimental . . . often charming music . . . one of those fragrant and tasty concoctions which, poured in one ear, warms the affections and tickles the humors considerably before it flies out the other. Take it—and drink heartily."

John Mason Brown—*New York Post*
". . . its good points are numerous enough to make the evening a pleasant one—as musical comedy evenings go—although they at no time make it distinguished or even exciting . . . Some mention must be made of Hammerstein's uncomfortably obvious rhymes . . ."

Robert Garland—*New York World-Telegram*
". . . a curious concoction . . . Some of it is revue and some of it is musical comedy; some of it is operetta and some of it is melodrama . . . With no little to recommend it—a good deal, if you press your correspondent—it doesn't seem to jell. The outstanding contributor is Romberg . . ."

Richard Lockridge—*New York Sun*
". . . manages to be, at one and the same time, slightly clotted with plot and rather vapory . . . The songs are agreeable . . . One could, with a fairly deep breath, blow the whole business away—and it would be hard, if one did, to notice much difference."

John Anderson—*New York Journal*
". . . I found it somewhat dry, with too much body, as the vintners say, and not enough alcoholic content—nothing, in fact, to get intoxicated over or on. Though some of Prof. Romberg's tunes are gracefully stimulating, and it is all sung, said and dressed up in Mr. Schwab's accustomed lavish manner, *May Wine* crushes more than the grape . . . Hammerstein's lyrics are deft and clever . . . whenever the story reared its ugly head the music had to stand on its own two feet. The plot was standing all evening on mine."

Jack Pulaski (Ibee.)—*Variety,* December 11, 1935
". . . set in good taste, but the book is strung out too long in the second act . . . enchanting score . . . Show is a novelty and should develop into a favorite."

Robert Benchley—*The New Yorker,* December 14, 1935
". . . while it is very pleasant, it can hardly be called red meat for us lions to toss about in the cage. As a matter of fact, its very charm lies in the fact that one can go to it and sit back and listen to Romberg's music with no more mental effort than is involved in murmering *'Wien, Wien, nur du allein'* and sobbing softly into one's *Schnurrbart* . . ."

Time, December 16, 1935
". . . somehow fails to click . . . Lyricist Hammerstein sets no record for originality . . . Romberg manages to do well without a singing chorus, has written a charming waltz, *Something in the Air of May,* and an appealing fox trot, *Just Once Around the Clock* . . ."

Ruth Woodbury Sedgwick—*Stage,* January, 1936
"Virginia Dare wine would perhaps be a more accurate name for this innocuous and far from heady show . . . some pleasant, if uneventful, songs which frisk in and out of the plot; and, in its lighter moments, it is wanly reminiscent of *Music in the Air* . . ."

George Jean Nathan—*Life,* February, 1936
". . . went back to musical play file 36-J and dug out again the Alt Wien hoke. It offered us considerably more of the Alt, however, than the Wien . . . a musical mothball laid scenically in Vienna and critically in Cain's."

Bibliography

Mr. Romberg, Mr. Schwab and a Play With Music (Rommy's) Called "May Wine" by Ward Morehouse —*New York Sun,* December 14, 1935

GIVE US THIS NIGHT

(Film—1936)

A musical film with screenplay by Edwin Justus Mayer and Lynn Starling, based on a story by Jacques Bachrach; music by Erich Wolfgang Korngold; lyrics by Oscar Hammerstein II.

A Paramount Picture
Produced by William LeBaron
Directed by Alexander Hall
Art directors, Hans Dreier, Roland Anderson
Music director, Mr. Korngold
Photographed by Victor Milner
Editor, Ellsworth Hoagland

Release Date
April 4, 1936

The Story
Sorrento fisherman Antonio loves to sing and prima donna Maria loves to hear him. She is about to appear in an opera written by her teacher, Marcello Bonetti, when the temperamental tenor who is to sing opposite her quits during rehearsals. Antonio takes over the part and, after some problems, wins over Maria.

The Cast
ANTONIO, Jan Kiepura
MARIA, Gladys Swarthout
TOMASSO, Benny Baker
MARCELLO BONETTI, Philip Merivale
FRANCESCA, Michelette Burani
FORCELLINI, Alan Mowbray
CARABINIERE, Sidney Toler
PRIEST, William Collier, Sr.
VINCENTI, John Miltern

Musical Numbers

Sweet Melody of Night
I Mean to Say I Love You
My Love and I

Music in the Night
Was There Ever a Voice?
Luigi (music by Richard A. Whiting)

All songs sung by Mr. Kiepura and Miss Swarthout.

NOTE: *Give Us This Night* was cut before film was released. Another song with same title, written by Vee Lawnhurst and Tot Seymour, was used as film theme song.

Reviews

Frank S. Nugent—*New York Times*
". . . The especially written operatic score is melodious, if scarcely more enduring than the sound track on which it has been recorded . . . On the whole, however, the film does not solve the problem of opera on the screen; neither is it particularly noteworthy as a contribution to the operatic cycle . . ."

Thornton Delehanty—*New York Post*
". . . a routine plot which is relieved only occasionally by humorous incidents and situations . . . The music seems undistinguished . . ."

Eileen Creelman—*New York Sun*
". . . In spite of its cast, in spite of the first-rate singing, in spite of the flashes of comedy, it is only fair entertainment."

Roy Chartier—*Variety,* April 8, 1936
". . . stilted and slow . . . The music listens well . . ."

John Mosher—*The New Yorker,* April 11, 1936
". . . flat stuff, aside from the music. And the music, if not flat, isn't of any great charm . . . There is a splash of humor, such as the spectacle of a fat tenor in a corset."

Don Herold—*Life,* June, 1936
"As sappy as these singer shows know how to be, but you can't miss the elegant warbling of Jan Kiepura and Gladys Swarthout . . ."

SWING HIGH, SWING LOW

(Film—1937)

A musical film with screenplay by Virginia Van Upp and Oscar Hammerstein II, based on the play "Burlesque" by George M. Watters and Arthur Hopkins.

A Paramount Picture
Produced by Arthur Hornblow, Jr.
Directed by Mitchell Leisen
Art directors, Hans Dreier and Ernst Fegte
Costumes by Travis Banton
Music director, Boris Morros
Orchestrations by Victor Young and Phil Boutelje
Vocal arrangements by Al Siegel
Photographed by Ted Tetzlaff
Editor, Eda Warren

Release Date
March 15, 1937

The Story
Skid Johnson, an ex-soldier down on his luck in the Canal Zone, meets Maggie King, who encourages him in his career as a trumpeter. They marry, and Skid gets the chance to play at a fashionable night club in New York. He becomes a success, ignores Maggie, and hits the bottle after she leaves him. Eventually they are reunited and Skid reforms.

The Cast
MAGGIE KING, Carole Lombard
SKID JOHNSON, Fred MacMurray
HARRY, Charles Butterworth
ELLA, Jean Dixon
ANITA ALVAREZ, Dorothy Lamour
HARVEY DEXTER, Harvey Stephens
TONY, Charles Judels
MURPHY, Cecil Cunningham
GEORGIE, Charles Arnt

HENRI, Franklin Pangborn
PANAMANIAN DAN, Anthony Quinn
CHIEF OF POLICE, Harry Semels
INTERPRETER, Richardo Mandia
JUDGE, Enrique De Rosas
THE PURSER, Bud Flanagan (Dennis O'Keefe)
SERVANT, Chris-Pin Martin
MEN IN NIGHT CLUB: Nick Lukats, Lee Bowman
CUSTOMER, Esther Howard

Musical Numbers

Swing High, Swing Low (Burton Lane-Ralph Freed); *I Hear a Call to Arms* (Al Siegel-Sam Coslow); *Panamania* (Siegel-Coslow); *Then It Isn't Love* (Ralph Rainger-Leo Robin); *Spring Is in the Air* (Charles Kisco-Freed).

Reviews

Frank S. Nugent—*New York Times*
"Carole Lombard and Fred MacMurray skip through the familiar devices with their usual ease, raising a routine story to a routine picture. The plus is extremely small, sometimes being almost invisible . . ."

Howard Barnes—*New York Herald Tribune*
"The sentimental saga has been remade with a shrewd display of showmanship . . . the dialogue is pungent and racy . . . it has pace, excitement and a fine motion picture flair."

Katharine Best—*Stage*, April, 1937
". . . gay and slow by turns, much of the fun being too hysterical for complete effectiveness. Its swings low oftener than it swings high."

Abel Green—*Variety*, April 21, 1937
". . . no reason to believe that it will not jam 'em at the gate . . ."

Time, March 22, 1937
". . . Vastly over-ballyhooed by Paramount, this picture's chief virtue is providing pretty Carole Lombard with a few comedy lines almost up to the standard of the ones she had in *My Man Godfrey* . . ."

Newsweek, March 27, 1937
". . . As long as the story stays in the Canal Zone it is flip, bright comedy . . . Unfortunately plot and protagonists move to New York at the half-way mark."

London Times, April 5, 1937
". . . Miss Lombard and Mr. MacMurray deserve a better story as

the relationship they build up between themselves has at moments the stamp and feeling of authenticity. The pity was the film could not keep to the standards it set in the first half hour."

Pare Lorentz—*Judge,* May, 1937
". . . the typical Lombard-MacMurray young-love stuff, but with just enough crackpottery in it to be worth seeing."

HIGH, WIDE AND HANDSOME

(Film—1937)

A musical film with screenplay and lyrics by Oscar Hammerstein II; additional dialogue by George O'Neill; music by Jerome Kern.

A Paramount Picture
Produced by Arthur Hornblow Jr.
Directed by Rouben Mamoulian
Dances by LeRoy Prinz
Art directors, Hans Dreier, John Goodman
Costumes by Travis Banton
Music director, Boris Morros
Orchestrations by Robert Russell Bennett
Photographed by Victor Milner and Theodore Sparkuhl
Editor, Archie Marshek

Release Date
July 22, 1937

The Story
Peter Cortlandt, a Pennsylvania farmer in the mid 1800s, befriends Sally Watterson, an entertainer with a medicine show. They fall in love and are happily drenched on their wedding day by oil spouting on their land. Oil wells soon spring up all over and when the railroad boosts freight rates to force the farmers to sell out their oil lands, Peter and his friends start a pipeline to the refinery. Despite armed efforts to stop them, the men eventually finish the task.

The Cast
SALLY WATTERSON, Irene Dunne
PETER CORTLANDT, Randolph Scott
MOLLY, Dorothy Lamour
DOC WATTERSON, Raymond Walburn
JOE VARESI, Akim Tamiroff
RED SCANLON, Charles Bickford
SAMUEL, Ben Blue
GRANDMA CORTLANDT, Elizabeth Patterson
MAURICE, William Frawley
WALTER BREMMAN, Alan Hale
STARK, Irving Pichel

DR. LIPPINCOTT, Lucien Littlefield
MRS. LIPPINCOTT, Helen Lowell
ROY, Tommy Bupp
JOHN THOMPSON, Russell Hopton
SHORTY, Billy Bletcher
LEM MOULTON, Stanley Andrews
GABBY JOHNSON, Frank Sully
WASH MILLER, Jack Clifford
STACKPOLE, James Burke
SEAMSTRESS, Claire MacDowell
BOWERS, Roger Imhoff
COL. BLAKE, Purnell Pratt
FOREMAN, Ed Gargan
PHINEAS T. BARNUM, Raymond Brown
PHOTOGRAPHER, Rolfe Sedan

Musical Numbers

High, Wide and Handsome, SALLY
Can I Forget You?, SALLY
Will You Marry Me Tomorrow, Maria?, MAURICE and WEDDING GUESTS
The Folks who Live on the Hill, SALLY
The Things I Want, MOLLY
Allegheny Al, MOLLY and SALLY

Reviews

Frank S. Nugent—*New York Times*
". . . Against it, *Show Boat* was an effeminate piece, nostalgic and sentimental . . . it is picturesque, folksy, brimful to Americana. The songs have that quality too; they almost seem to be plucked from the minstrelsy of the pre-Civil War years than coined this season . . ."

Howard Barnes—*New York Herald Tribune*
". . . a substantial book and fetching tunes . . . Mamoulian's staging is shrewdly effective and the characterizations solid . . . it has a splendid capacity for being ornamentally entertaining and can best be described by the adjectives of its title."

William Boehnel—*New York World-Telegram*
". . . magnificent entertainment . . . a musical score that is not only gay and tuneful but that is also definite of the period in which the story is set . . . a film of uncommon quality, a superb piece of picture telling . . ."

Abel Green—*Variety,* July 28, 1937
". . . a $1,900,000 western . . . Something went wrong in scripting and production from what was, undoubtably, an intriguing script on paper . . . after teeing off vigorously, it flounders as it progresses

. . . Among the major disappointments are the songs. Score is sturdy but not socko . . ."

Russell Maloney—*The New Yorker,* July 31, 1937
". . . Rouben Mamoulian's handling of the story leaves something to be desired (he's pretty preoccupied with apple blossoms and hillsides) but the general effect of the picture is pleasant."

Newsweek, July 31, 1937
". . . colorful and ingratiating . . . story owes its greatest debt to the shrewd and lively direction of Mamoulian . . . pleasant score . . . one of the most spectacular finishes ever supplied to a musical romance."

London Times, August 23, 1937
". . . a story which gives the authentic impression and atmosphere of the pioneer days . . . the songs are typical and evocative of the period . . . delightfully refreshing . . ."

Graham Greene—*Night and Day,* August 26, 1937
". . . long, dumb and dreary . . . masses of irrelevant Mamoulian blooms flowering at the right, the sentimental, time; nature panting to keep abreast with studio passions, flowering for first love and falling for separation."

Katharine Best—*Stage,* September 1937
". . . It's generous, fanciful melodrama—handsome hero, beautiful heroine, ugly villain, a chase—buoyed by the spontaneity of acting and directing. The lively moments come often."

GENTLEMEN UNAFRAID

(1938)

A musical play with book and lyrics by Oscar Hammerstein II and Otto Harbach, adapted from a story by Edward Boykin; music by Jerome Kern.

Presented by the Municipal Theatre Association of St. Louis
under the direction of Richard Berger
Directed by Zeke Colvan
Choreography by Theodor Adolphus and Al White, Jr.
Settings by Raymond Sovey
Costumes by Billi Livingston
Assistant to the authors, Leighton K. Brill
Music director, George Hirst
Associate music director, Jacob Schwartzdorf (Jay S. Blackton)

Tryout
Municipal Open Air Theatre, St. Louis, June 3-12, 1938

New York Run
None

The Story
At the outbreak of the Civil War, a group of West Point cadets from the South are faced with the problem of fighting against their native states, or rebelling against the government which has trained them. One of them, Bob Vance, asks Lincoln's advice, which is impartial. However, he decides to join the Northern side, thus estranging Linda Mason, his fiancée who lives in Virginia. Later, he captures her brother, Don, whom he finds engaged in espionage. After the end of the war and the assassination of Lincoln, Bob and Linda are reunited.

The Cast
PIGNATELLI, Ralph Riggs
MISS MURDOCK, Marcella Uhl
POLLY EVANS, Kay Picture
BOB VANCE, Ronald Graham
JIM ALLEN, Barry Sullivan
LINDA MASON, Hope Manning
BUD HUTCHINS, Richard (Red) Skelton

DON MASON, Kirk Alyn
BETSY HAVENS, Vicki Cummings
JOHN CARTER, Roland Drew
BENNY HAVENS, Fred Persson
COMMANDANT REYNOLDS, Carroll Ashburn
JOE, Avon Long
LIZA, Minto Cato
MRS. MASON, Annamary Dickey
MR. MASON, George E. Mack
SENATOR VANCE, Al Downing
ABRAHAM LINCOLN, Victor Thorley
JOHN WILKES BOOTH, Jerry Sloane
MAIZIE LATOUR, Lori Trivers
DANCERS: Marjorie Ammon, Lalla Bauman, Catherine Burke, Janet Bradford, Mary Louise Crowe, Aurelia Dehkoff, Kay Eibert, Jane Finnegan, Jane Fox. Georgiann Grant, Betty Herbert, Jane Hooker, Virginia Jones, Ruth Katt, Patricia Moorman, G. Evelyn Moser, Doris Padgett, Rosemary Powell, Marifrances Rosenstein, Sally Styles, Willadean Sparks, Jane Stribling, Melba Stephens, Dorothy Steidemann, Frances Winklemeier; Herman Desmond, Ken Hornbeck, Robert Josias, William Keegan, Mortimer O'Brien, John Parlow, Clarence Reed, Bob Riley, Vincent Vernon, Eddie Wells, Wynn Wendell, Willis Wylie
SINGERS: Barbara Addicks, Jeanne Archibald, Geraldine Botkin, Vivian Chandler, Aline Daly, Mary Donahue, Helen Dolley, Ruth Finke, Lucille Floetman, Katherine Ganley, Jeanette Gorman, Jeanne Gustavison, Marjorie Johnson, Jacqueline Jones, Melba Milde, Dorothy Newlund, Rochelle Payntar, Lauramae Pippin, Marie Ryan, Virginia Speaks, Virginia Stanford, Helen Stephens, Vilan Tully, Edith Wood; Millard Allen, Jay Amiss, Ben Basone, Michael Bilgere, Dryden Carver, R. Leon Cordell, Alan Easterling, Gordon Felts, Anthony Ferrara, Roy Greene, Dudley Harder, Ken Hartung, Charles Kanter, Lowry Koehler, Douglas Lloyd, Garvin Martini
CELESTIAL CHORISTERS, directed by C. Spencer Tocus
R.O.T.C. BOYS, from Christian Brothers College

Musical Numbers

ACT I

SCENE ONE—BALLROOM OF THE OLD WEST POINT HOTEL, May 16, 1860
Opening, ENSEMBLE
Virginia Hoe Down, POLLY, DON, ENSEMBLE and DANCERS
Our Last Dance, LINDA and ENSEMBLE

SCENE TWO—BENNY HAVENS' TAVERN
Gentlemen Unafraid, DON, BOB, LINDA and MALE ENSEMBLE
What Kind of Soldier Are You?, BETSY, BUD and MALE ENSEMBLE

SCENE THREE—KOSCIUSKO'S GARDEN, WEST POINT
Your Dream, LINDA and BOB

SCENE FOUR (A)—EXTERIOR OF MASON HOME, PINECREST, OUTSIDE RICHMOND, VA.
Reprise, *Virginia Hoe Down,* JOE and ENSEMBLE
(B)—SMALL LIBRARY IN MASON HOME
(C)—EXTERIOR OF MASON HOME
De Land o'Good Times, LIZA, LINDA, BOB, POLLY and ENSEMBLE
Finaletto, LINDA, BOB and ENSEMBLE

SCENE FIVE—LINCOLN'S STUDY IN THE WHITE HOUSE
Abe Lincoln Has Just One Country, MALE ENSEMBLE

SCENE SIX—TROPHY POINT, NORTH END OF PARADE GROUNDS, WEST POINT
Reprise, *What Kind of Soldier Are You?,* ENSEMBLE
Fantasie
VOICE, Rochelle Payntar
BETSY, Lalla Bauman
CARTER, Rosemary Powell
BUD, Richard (Red) Skelton
PIGNATELLI, Ralph Riggs
FEMALE ENSEMBLE and DANCERS
Finale, COMPANY

ACT II
SCENE ONE—LAWN IN FRONT OF BENNY HAVENS'S TAVERN
Opening, MALE ENSEMBLE
When You Hear That Humming (Harbach), BETSY, BUD and ENSEMBLE
It's Gayer Whistling as You Go (Harbach), BETSY, BUD, BOB and MALE ENSEMBLE

SCENE TWO—A ROOM IN THE OLD WEST POINT HOTEL

SCENE THREE—BACK GATE TO THE MASON HOME (MONTAGE: 4 YEARS OF WAR)
Mister Man, LINDA
How Would I Know? (Hammerstein), LIZA and NEGRO ENSEMBLE; MALE ENSEMBLE; LINDA and FEMALE ENSEMBLE

ACT III
SCENE ONE—GEARY'S RESTAURANT, WASHINGTON, D.C. APRIL 14, 1865
Reprise, *What Kind of Soldier Are You?,* BOB, JIM and MALE ENSEMBLE
Little Zouave, BETSY, BUD, PIGNATELLI and MALE ENSEMBLE
Zouave Drill, DANCING GIRLS

SCENE TWO—KOSCIUSKO'S GARDEN, WEST POINT
Finale, COMPANY

NOTE: *Sweet as a Rose* and *Many a Lofty Mountain* (Hammerstein) cut before opening.

Reviews

New York Times

". . . Among those most concerned the impression left is simply music swell, book not so swell."

Christian Science Monitor
". . . Not one page of impressive music-drama declamation in the entire score. Is it not inept to set passages of tragic history to shallow music? Only in the lighter episodes is the music commensurate with the character of the text . . . judicious cutting and tightening would doubtless give strength and symmetry to the whole."

Sam Hurst—*Variety,* June 8, 1938
". . . Kern's music is up to his usually fine standard . . . the dramatic tension at times reaches startling heights . . . it moves at a nice pace . . . looks to have a good chance in the big city."

Time, June 13, 1938
". . . maintained the best swashbuckling, love & war traditions of the Victor Herbert era."

NOTE: In 1942, the musical was released by the National Theatre Conference under the title *Hayfoot, Strawfoot.*

THE LADY OBJECTS

(Film—1938)

A musical film with screenplay by Gladys Lehman and Charles Kenyon; music by Ben Oakland; lyrics by Oscar Hammerstein II and Milton Drake.

A Columbia Picture
Produced by William Perlberg
Directed by Erle C. Kenton
Art director, Stephen Goosson
Music director, Morris Stoloff
Photographed by Allen G. Siegler

Release Date

October 12, 1938

The Story

After marrying college sweetheart Ann Adams, former star halfback Bill Hayward plods along as an architect while his wife becomes a successful lawyer. Bill's frustration leads to a separation and a new career as a nightclub singer. When June Lane, another singer at the club, is murdered Bill is accused of the crime. At the ensuing trial he is acquitted after being defended by his estranged wife. This prompts both a reconciliation and a radio contract.

The Cast

WILLIAM HAYWARD, Lanny Ross
ANN ADAMS, Gloria Stuart
JUNE LANE, Joan Marsh
KEN HARPER, Robert Paige
GEORGE MARTIN, Roy Benson
MR. HARPER, Pierre Watkins
CHARLES CLARKE, Arthur Loft
BAKER, Stanley Andrews
MRS. HARPER, Bess Flowers

Musical Numbers

Following with lyrics by Mr. Hammerstein:
That Week in Paris
A Mist Is Over the Moon
Home in Your Arms
When You're in the Room

Following with lyrics by Mr. Drake:
Victory Song
Naughty Naughty
Sky High

All of above songs sung by Mr. Ross

Reviews
New York Journal-American
". . . satisfactory . . . Lanny's tenor notes warrant your money's worth."

Variety, October 12, 1938
". . . a fair cast but its stereo story is a challenge to the film's success . . . *A Mist Is Over the Moon* is the only one of the songs to show possibilities . . ."

THE GREAT WALTZ

(Film—1938)

A musical film with screenplay by Samuel Hoffenstein and Walter Reisch, based on a story by Gottfried Reinhardt; music by Johann Strauss II; lyrics by Oscar Hammerstein II.

A Metro-Goldwyn-Mayer Picture
Produced by Bernard Hyman
Directed by Julien Duvivier,
Victor Fleming (uncredited), Josef Von Sternberg (uncredited)
Choreography by Albertina Rasch
Art director, Cedric Gibbons
Costumes by Adrian
Music director, Arthur Gutmann
Music adapted and orchestrated by Dimitri Tiomkin
Photographed by Joseph Ruttenberg

Release Date
November 4, 1938

The Story
Johann Strauss, a bank teller in Vienna, is fired for paying more attention to music than to his work. He becomes a pianist at Dommayer's Café where he meets opera star Carla Dormer, is smitten with her but marries his fiancée, Poldi. During a revolution, he saves Carla's life and writes *Die Fledermaus* for her. Though it is Carla he loves, Strauss, in the end, returns to his wife.

The Cast
POLDI VOGELHUBER STRAUSS, Luise Rainer
JOHANN STRAUSS II, Fernand Gravet
CARLA DORMER, Miliza Korjus
HOFHAUER, Hugh Herbert
COUNT HOHENFRIED, Lionel Atwill
KIENZL, Curt Bois
DUDELMAN, Leonid Kinskey
CELLIST, Al Shean
MRS. HOFHAUER, Minna Gombell
SCHILLER, George Houston
VOGELHUBER, Herman Bing

MRS. VOGELHUBER, Greta Meyer
MRS. STRAUSS, Alma Kruger
EMPEROR FRANZ JOSEF, Henry Hull
WERTHEIMER, Sig Rumann
COACHMAN, Christian Rub

Musical Numbers

I'm in Love with Vienna, KIENZL, DUDELMAN, CELLIST, SCHILLER, CHORUS
There'll Come a Time, CARLA
Revolutionary March, CHORUS
Tales from the Vienna Woods, CARLA, JOHANN, COACHMAN
One Day When We Were Young, JOHANN; reprised by CARLA
Only You, CARLA, SCHILLER, CHORUS
The Blue Danube, ORCHESTRA

Reviews

Frank S. Nugent—*New York Times*
". . . Metro makes the most beautiful bores in the world . . . No other studio could make so big a picture out of so small a script . . . a confectioner's delight among extravaganzas—ornamental and artificial . . ."

Robert W. Dana—*New York Herald Tribune*
". . . a sumptuous musical as far as the music and ensemble scenes are concerned, but it is much too pretentious . . . the story is weighty and the cast an admixture of actors who are fine in their own right but make Vienna seem like a seat of the League of Nations . . ."

Archer Winsten—*New York Post*
". . . Perhaps Duvivier has shown more ingenuity than the material deserves, but at any rate, the waltzes are always fresh and beautiful . . ."

Mike P. Wear—*Variety,* November 2, 1938
". . . a field day for music lovers plus elegant entertainment . . . should click nicely . . ."

Newsweek, November 14, 1938
". . . loose framework, padded with little in the way of human drama . . . Duvivier manages to construct a generally gay and always handsome screen spectacle . . . a treat for music lovers."

John Mosher—*The New Yorker,* November 26, 1938
". . . in the treatment of *Tales From the Vienna Woods* and *The Blue Danube,* the director lightly and airily combines his music and his

story, and the combination is winning and a pleasure . . . A Madame Miliza Korjus turns out to be very, very coloratura . . ."

London Times
". . . The scenes of dancing are almost all both elaborate and delightful . . . long wastes of purely American sentimentality expressed in heavily inarticulate dialogue . . ."

Awards
Motion Picture Academy Awards, 1938
Best cinematography, Joseph Ruttenberg

THE STORY OF VERNON AND IRENE CASTLE

(Film—1939)

A musical film with screenplay by Richard Sherman, adapted by Oscar Hammerstein II and Dorothy Yost from the book "My Husband" by Irene Castle.

An RKO-Radio Picture
Produced by George Haight
Directed by H. C. Potter
Choreography by Hermes Pan
Art director, Van Nest Polglase
Costumes, Walter Plunkett
Technical advisor, Mrs. Castle
Music director, Victor Baravalle
Orchestrations by Roy Webb and Robert Russell Bennett
Photographed by Robert DeGrasse
Editor, William Hamilton

Release Date
March 31, 1939

The Story
The life of the famed dancing team from their first meeting in New Rochelle in 1910, through their early struggles, international success, and death of Vernon Castle in an airplane crash in 1918.

The Cast
VERNON CASTLE, Fred Astaire
IRENE CASTLE, Ginger Rogers
MAGGIE SUTTON, Edna May Oliver
WALTER, Walter Brennan
LEW FIELDS, Himself
AUBEL, Etienne Girardot
ANNIE FOOTE, Janet Beecher
EMILE AUBEL, Rolfe Sedan
ARTIST, Leonid Kinskey
DR. HUBERT FOOTE, Robert Strange

PETERS, *student pilot,* Douglas Walton
LOUIS BARRAYA, Clarence Derwent
CHARLIE, Sonny Lamont
CLAIRE FORD, Frances Mercer
GRAND DUKE, Victor Varconi
HOTEL MANAGER, Donald MacBride
ACTOR IN "PATRIA," Roy D'Arcy
TRAIN CONDUCTOR, Dick Elliott
IRENE'S FRIEND, Marjorie Bell (Marge Champion)

Musical Numbers
Oh, You Beautiful Doll, Glow-Worm, By the Beautiful Sea, Row, Row, Row, Yama Yama Man, Come Josephine in My Flying Machine, By the Light of the Silvery Moon, Cuddle Up a Little Closer, Lovey Mine, Waiting for the Robert E. Lee, The Darktown Strutters' Ball, Too Much Mustard, Rose Room, Très jolie, When They Were Dancing Around, Little Brown Jug, Dengozo, You're Here and I'm Here, Chicago, Hello, Frisco, Hello, Way Down Yonder in New Orleans, Take Me Back to New York Town, It's a Long Way to Tipperary, Hello, Hello, Who's Your Lady Friend?, Keep the Home Fires Burning, Smiles, Destiny Waltz, Night of Gladness, Missouri Waltz, Over There. Song written for film: *Only When You're in My Arms* (Con Conrad-Bert Kalmar-Harry Ruby).

Reviews
Frank S. Nugent—*New York Times*
". . . no two persons more perfectly qualified to celebrate the history of the famous dancing team than Astaire and Rogers . . . they have managed the narrative equally well . . . a beautifully told story, with sincere and vigorous performances."

Howard Barnes—*New York Herald Tribune*
". . . a history of the modern dance as well as a romantic tragedy. Rich in terpsichorean spectacle . . . the fault of the script is the determined effort to make the film a factual record of a great dancing team's private lives as well as their professional history."

Archer Winsten—*New York Post*
". . . possesses virtues not always found together, high entertainment quality, historical reproductions of the most painstaking sort, and sentimental values . . ."

Abel Green—*Variety,* March 31, 1939
". . . sure-fire box office . . . top-flight cinematic entertainment . . . holds a wealth of nostalgic appeal for the show-wise as well as general film audiences . . ."

Newsweek, April 3, 1939
". . . has dramatized the dancers' amazing career with a minimum

of distortion . . . Rogers and Astaire brilliantly recreate the famous couple's inspired contributions . . . not only a refreshing musical but a haunting screen biography . . ."

John Mosher—*The New Yorker,* April 8, 1939
". . . One does not expect a Rogers-Astaire movie to be what is called a documentary, and one would have been content to have had the story presented as something all music and dancing and pretty clothes. Until tragedy has the impertinence to intrude upon this gay musical-comedy stage, everything is graceful, just as it should be . . ."

C.A. Lejeune—*London Observer*
". . . one of the most graceful biographies ever set out on celluloid. It is true clear through; true to fact, and what is even better, true to mood and memory . . ."

Graham Greene—*The Spectator,* June 9, 1939
". . . it is all champagne, young love and tears . . . It must have been an odd experience for Mrs. Castle to watch her own life lifted out of reality altogether . . . (but) it's an admirable film, perhaps the best the marvellous couple have made since *The Gay Divorcee.* We can accept the sentimental convention because it is never broken: no other world than the film world of eternal fidelity, picturesque starvation and meteoric success is ever held up to it for comparison. The whole affair takes wings, and what do we care if it is through the inane? . . ."

Bibliography

Building Castles in Hollywood by Douglas W. Churchill —*New York Times,* January 22, 1939

Astaire and Rogers Revive the Castles —*Life,* March 27, 1939

Castles in Pictures by Bosley Crowther —*New York Times,* April 2, 1939

VERY WARM FOR MAY

(1939)

A musical comedy with book and lyrics by Oscar Hammerstein II; music by Jerome Kern.

Presented by Max Gordon
Production directed and designed by Vincente Minnelli
Book directed by Mr. Hammerstein
Assistant to Mr. Hammerstein, Leighton K. Brill
Choreography by Albertina Rasch and Harry Losee
Music director, Robert Emmett Dolan
Orchestrations by Robert Russell Bennett

Tryout

Playhouse, Wilmington, October 20-21, 1939
National Theatre, Washington, October 23-28, 1939
Forrest Theatre, Philadelphia, October 30-November 4, 1939
Shubert Theatre, Boston, November 6-11, 1939

New York Run

Alvin Theatre, November 17, 1939-January 6, 1940
59 performances

The Story

Over the opposition of her father, veteran actor William Graham, and her brother, playwright Johnny Graham, May Graham runs away from home to join a barn theatre run by an arty impressario named Ogden Quiler. By the time her family discovers where she is, May and her friends have taken over the theatre and turned it into a popular success.

The Cast

WILLIAM GRAHAM, Donald Brian
JACKSON, Avon Long
MAY GRAHAM, Grace McDonald
JOHNNY GRAHAM, Jack Whiting
KENNY, Ray Mayer
RAYMOND SIBLEY, Robert Shackleton
SONNY SPOFFORD, Richard Quine

LIZ SPOFFORD, Frances Mercer
LOWELL PENNYFEATHER, Max Showalter
OGDEN QUILER, Hiram Sherman
JETHRO HANCOCK, William Torpey
WINNIE SPOFFORD, Eve Arden
BEAMISH, Len Mence
SCHLESINGER, Seldon Bennett
ELECTRICIAN, Bruce Evans
MEMBERS OF THE OGDON QUILER PROGRESSIVE WORKSHOP:
SUSAN, Vera Ellen
SMOOTHY WATSON, Don Loper
HONEY, Maxine Barrat
MR. PRATT, Frank Egan
JANE, Evelyn Thawl
SYLVIA, Kate Friedlich
MR. MAGEE, Peter Chambers
MISS WASSERMAN, Virginia Card
MISS HYDE, Kay Picture
CARROLL, Hollace Shaw
CHARLES, Ralph Stuart
ALICE, Marie Louise Quevli
HELEN, Helena Bliss
WALTER, Walter Long
ANDRE, Andre Charise
SALLY, Sally Craven
OTHER MEMBERS: Pamela Randell, Dolores Anderson, Beulah Blake, Louis Hightower, Jack Seymour, Webb Tilton, Jack Wilson, William Collins, Eleanor Eberle, Helen Donovan, Rudy Miller, Ethel Lynn, June Allyson, Claire Harvey, Billie Worth, Miriam Franklyn
ALVIN'S ORCHESTRA, Matty Malneck's Orchestra
ALVIN, *violin,* Matty Malneck
O'CEDAR, *accordion,* Milton Delugg
HOMER, *trumpet,* Charles Marlowe
OTHER MEMBERS: Marshal Fisher, Ralph Hansell, Joseph Quintile, Jean Plummer, Russ Morhoff

NOTE: In January, Mr. Whiting succeeded by Guy Robertson.

Musical Numbers

ACT I

SCENE ONE—THE GRAHAM HOME, GREAT NECK, LONG ISLAND
In Other Words, Seventeen, MAY and WILLIAM
Stop dance, JACKSON

SCENE TWO—WINNIE'S BARN
Characterization, OGDON; babbling brook dance by MISS HYDE
All the Things You Are, OGDON, LIZ, CARROLL, CHARLES

Audition, WINNIE; accordionist, O'CEDAR
May Tells All, MAY
Heaven in My Arms, JOHNNY, LIZ, CARROLL; danced by JANE, SALLY, SYLVIA
Reprise, *In Other Words, Seventeen,* WINNIE

ACT II

SCENE ONE—TERRACE OF WINNIE'S HOUSE
That Lucky Fellow, RAYMOND
L'Histoire de Madame de la Tour, CARROLL; danced by MISS WASSERMAN, JANE, ANDRE
That Lucky Lady, MAY
The Strange Case of Adam Standish, OGDON
In the Heart of the Dark, CARROLL
Ballet Peculiaire, WALTER and HONEY

SCENE TWO—A CORNER OF WINNIE'S BARN THEATRE
Audition, ALVIN'S ORCHESTRA
Dance, MAY
Reprise, *In the Heart of the Dark,* LIZ

SCENE THREE—STAGE OF WINNIE'S BARN THEATRE DURING DRESS REHEARSAL
The Deer and the Park Avenue Lady, danced by ANDRE and MISS HYDE
All in Fun, LIZ and JOHNNY
Schottische Scena, JOHNNY and MAY

SCENE FOUR—A CORNER OF WINNIE'S BARN THEATRE
Reprise, *All the Things You Are,* KENNY

SCENE FIVE—STAGE OF WINNIE'S BARN THEATRE DURING PERFORMANCE
Dance Da Da
LADY IN RED, Kate Friedlich
THE BLACKBIRD, Don Loper
LADY IN WHITE, Maxine Barrat
Reprise, *All in Fun,* LIZ and JOHNNY
Interlude, MAY and SONNY
Finale, COMPANY

NOTE: *Me and the Role and You* and *High Up in Harlem* cut before New York opening.

Reviews

Brooks Atkinson—*New York Times*

". . . the book is a singularly haphazard invention that throws the whole show out of focus and makes an appreciation of Mr. Kern's music almost a challenge. They have mounted it lavishly; they have populated it with some beguiling people. But there has seldom been a book that fought entertainment as successfully as has this . . . The score is rich in variety and feeling and a testament to honest composing . . . the return of Kern and Hammerstein is not so hot in November with *Very Warm for May*."

Richard Watts, Jr.—*New York Herald Tribune*
"*Not Too Warm* . . . handsome, lavish, attractively played and curiously unexhilarating. The trouble is that the score seems surprisingly undistinguished and the book is excessively tedious and humorless . . . the music is naturally tasteful and intelligent, but somehow the songs never manage to be as effective and as memorable as they are always on the verge of being . . . There is a pleasant air of grace, charm and pictorial attractiveness about the work, but it seems to miss fire most of the way . . ."

Burns Mantle—*New York Daily News*
"★★★. . . a very nice sentimental score . . . The book is an attempt to dove-tail story, song cues, and incidental solo items into one consistently compact entertainment . . . the joining is somewhat labored and often pulled out at the seams . . ."

Robert Coleman—*New York Daily Mirror*
"Kern and Hammerstein were in fine fettle when they wrote the songs but Mr. Hammerstein was in a bit of a slump when he got around to penning a libretto on which to string them . . ."

Wilella Waldrof—*New York Post*
". . . a very dull show, enlivened at rare intervals by a smile or two, decorated by a great deal of scenery and many luscious costumes, and supplied with a musical score that provides several pleasant enough songs, but never manages to make them seem anything but routine . . ."

Sidney B. Whipple—*New York World-Telegram*
". . . gay and delightful . . . Given an entire set of Kern songs, with Hammerstein's lyrics to complement them, and you can fling away the book as not worth bothering about . . . the flimsy plot is never permitted to intrude and halt the joyful abandon of the musical numbers . . . as gorgeous a spectacle as Broadway has seen in years . . . the most charming song is *All the Things You Are,* and I have no hesitation in predicting that it will take the country by storm . . ."

Richard Lockridge—*New York Sun*
". . . never, I think, have elements so promising been tangled more hopelessly in the barbed wire of a thoroughly exasperating plot . . . There are fine songs—*In the Heart of the Dark, Heaven in My Arms, All the Things You Are, All in Fun.* These are plums in the dough . . ."

John Anderson—*New York Journal-American*
". . . I found it delightful . . . its behavior is civilized, its humor sanitary and its manners good. Its jokes assume that the taste of the

audience is higher than the municipal incinerator . . . the plot keeps the stage going without getting into everybody's way . . . a score carrying the inevitable imprint of Kern's style, and grace and mellow humor . . . a show that should prove pretty glowing in any month on a street where, as shows go, it isn't the heat so much as the stupidity."

Abel Green—*Variety,* November 22, 1939
". . . Particularly on its plot structure, the new musical is confusing, involved and, coupled with an uncertain score, a dubious question whether it is such a hot Broadway entry . . . Kern's score is graceful and fraught with many potentialities which, as time usually does, should assert themselves . . ."

Robert Benchley—*The New Yorker,* November 25, 1939
". . . lovely to the ear and complimentary to the intelligence . . . although it retains its adolescent charm throughout, it manages to achieve a certain maturity in its comedy and, unlike most musicals, actually gets better and funnier as it goes on . . . The Kern score is delightful, with no one number, except possibly *All the Things You Are,* written especially for the Hit Parade . . ."

Louis Kronenberger—*Time,* November 27, 1939
". . . Kern's tunes were bright and strummy enough, but a raucous, epileptic plot made the show a bird that could sing but not fly . . . The atmosphere, at its thickest, is very warm for mayhem . . ."

BROADWAY RHYTHM

(Film Version of "Very Warm for May"—1944)

A Metro-Goldwyn-Mayer Picture
Produced by Jack Cummings
Directed by Roy Del Ruth
Screenplay by Dorothy Kingsley and Harry Clark
Story by Jack MacGowan
Choreography by Charles Walters, Jack Donohue, Robert Alton, Don Loper
Art directors, Cedric Gibbons, Jack Martin Smith
Costumes by Irene Sharaff
Music director, Johnny Green
Orchestrations by Ted Duncan, Sy Oliver, Lewis Raymond, Phil Moore
Photographed by Leonard Smith
Editor, Albert Akst
Color by Technicolor

Release Date
January 19, 1944

The Story
Jonnie Demming, a Broadway producer, has troubles involving Helen Hoyt, a temperamental Hollywood actress, his sister, Patsy, who wants to go on the stage, and his father, Sam, who plans to put on a rival production. Jonnie ends up with two shows that he combines into one. And, of course, Helen.

The Cast
JONNIE DEMMING, George Murphy
HELEN HOYT, Ginny Simms
SAM DEMMING, Charles Winninger
PATSY DEMMING, Gloria De Haven
TRIXIE SIMPSON, Nancy Walker
FELIX GROSS, Ben Blue
FERNWAY DE LA FER, Lena Horne
EDDIE, Eddie "Rochester" Anderson
HAZEL SCOTT, Herself
RAY KENT, Kenny Bowers
MAGGIE, AGGIE, ELMIRA } The Ross Sisters
HIRED MAN, Dean Murphy
FARMER, Louis Mason
BUNNY, Bunny Waters
DOUG KELLY, Walter B. Long
Tommy Dorsey and His Orchestra

Musical Numbers
Song retained from original production: *All the Things You Are,* sung by Miss Simms. Songs written for film by Gene DePaul and Don Raye: *Solid Potatoe Salad, Milkman, Keep Those Bottles Quiet, I Love Corny Music, Who's Who* and *Irresistible You.* Other songs in film: *Brazilian Boogie* (by Hugh Martin and Ralph Blane), *Pretty Baby* (by Egbert Van Alstyne and Gus Kahn) and *Amor* (by Gabriel Ruiz and Sunny Skylar).

Reviews
Bosley Crowther—*New York Times*
". . . A studio less extravagant could have made two or three pictures out of it. As a matter of fact, *Very Warm for May* has been compressed so insouciantly within it that you'd hardly know it was there . . ."

Howard Barnes—*New York Herald Tribune*
". . . There is a profusion of entertainment, dished out in gaudy technicolor . . . A higgledy-piggledy assortment of song and dance antics."

Archer Winsten—*New York Post*
". . . presents the world of M-G-M through rose-colored magnifying glasses . . . looking for the plot is like trying to inspect the trunk of a department store Christmas tree. It's there, but what's the use of thinking about it when there are so many pretties to watch."

Walt Christie—*Variety,* April 19, 1944
". . . a typical backstage filmusical wheeled out in the usual Metro elaborate and colorful style . . . a fragile and hodge-podge yarn . . . diverting entertainment . . ."

David Lardner—*The New Yorker,* April 22, 1944
". . . occasional specialties that are good and dozens of absurdities and inanities that are murder . . ."

James Agee—*Time,* May 8, 1944
". . . a Technicolored, tune-stirred summer salad . . . plenty of time to doze between the best moments . . . a great many tunes, of which the best remains *All the Things You Are* . . ."

AMERICAN JUBILEE

(1940)

A musical pageant with book and lyrics by Oscar Hammerstein II; music by Arthur Schwartz.

Presented by the New York World's Fair Corporation
Produced and designed by Albert Johnson
Directed by Leon Leonidoff
Choreography by Catherine Littlefield
Assistant to Mr. Johnson, Lester Polakov
Costumes by Lucinda Ballard
Music director, Don Voorhees
Orchestrations by Hans Spialek
Choral director, Ken Christie

New York Run
New York World's Fair Grounds, May 12-October 2, 1940

The Story
Important occasions in American history—the times of Washington, Lincoln, Jenny Lind, Barnum, Diamond Jim Brady—as told by a school teacher to her class. Ends with a projection to a future presidential inauguration.

The Cast
Lucy Monroe
Ray Middleton
Wynn Murray
Paul Haakon
Margaret Adams
George L. Spaulding
Jack Howard
Lee Frederick
Harry Meehan
Tony Blair
Gene Marvey
Fred Ardath
Irene Christie
Joe Jackson
Lime Trio

CHILDREN: Lloyd Warren, Walter Kelly, Jeri Anne Raphael, Joan Flicker, Carol Renee, Gerry McMillan

LADIES OF THE ENSEMBLE: May Muth, Evelyn Mills, Vicki Michak, Erminie Randolph, Eleanor Brownell, Jane O'Gorman, Xenia Bank, Joyce Doncaster, Dorothy Calvert, Marjorie Nielson, Marie Fox, Dolores Flanders, Elinore Rutherford, Mildred Talbott, Frances Williams, Alice George, Byrtie Ladd, Geraldine Hamilton, Anne Courtney, Lucille Werner, Sally Billings, Wilma Simonson, Erika Zaranova, Gloria Hart, Elise Eckert, Diana Corday, Jill Townsend, Alice Talton, Carol Ann Brown, Nadine Cassel, Nea Francyss, Evonne Kummer, Leslie Bryan, Nedra Harrison, Frances King, Mary Joan Punch, Janice Parmenter, Bliss Farren, Juanita Bredt, Marian Marvis, Eleanor Moore, Linda Faghn, Charlotte Lorraine, Marion Bailey, Evelyn Eckhardt, Dale Preston, Marguerite Adams, Edith Vincent, Jean Stanton, Vera Divine, Julia Sully, Anna Minot, Dorothy Wygal, Viola Layton, Helen Price, Janet Palmer, Genevieve Frizzell, Betty Hull

GENTLEMEN OF THE ENSEMBLE: Harold Crane, Charles Burrows, Allan Lee, Ben Roberts, Paul Wilson, Gerald Lysley, Eugene Keith, Francis Carpenter, Ward Tallman, Donald Campbell, Ralph Glover, Milton Feher, Tony Albert, William Lane, Jesse Saunders, Philip Gordon, Carl Clayton, Andre Renald, Charles Pinckney, Thomas Cannon, Jerome Andrews, Parker Wilson, Robert Hauser, Harry Grissin, Charles Duncan, J. B. Laster, John Russel, Bruce Hamilton, James Burrell, Max Benson, Walter John, Sam Adams, Norman Van Emburgh, Larry Siegle, Edward Heisler, Frank Taylor, Philip Crosbie, Carter Farriss, Eric Brotherson, Richard Reeves, Richard Browning, Bob Wayne, Roy Johnston, Wally Berg, Tony Caridi, Norman Farrow, Joseph Kendrick, Jack Leslie, James Allison, Max Edwards, Finley Walker, Leon Frank, William Raible, Oscar Catoire, John Fulco, Roy Williams, Frank Chamberlin, Randolph Symmonette, James Carroll, Ernest McLean, Murvyn Vye, Bob Evans, Norman McKay, Harold Gordon, Jack Wright, Bert Hillner, Walter Searle, Roger Hill, Henry Williamson, Rudy Williams, Paul Kirk Giles, Kendall Crawford, John Barry, Tony Mongiello, William Lee, Frank Godek, Tony Orlando, Dwight Bull, Shelden Tapp, Joe Brennan, Don Pierce, Jim Ferguson, Martin McKail, Buck Woodward, Howard Brenard, Edgar Stone, Bill Kelly, Buddy Baldwin, Tom Early, John Ryan, Babe Courveisier, Tony McKail, Philip Coleman, Tom La Russo, Vincent Burrell, Frank Basarab, Frank Czyz, Vincent Ferguson, Tony Madden

DANCERS: Virginia Rand, Maude Carroll, Luba Matiuk, Kathryn Lozell, Hortense Kahrklin, Barbara Bernard, Eleanor Fairchild, Jessie Fullum, Mary Heater, Jane Johnstone, Dolores Goodman, Chula Morrow, Norma Gentner, Helen Kramer, Rita Charise, Joan Patschke, June Graham, June McLaren, Doris Call, Barbara Steele, Constance Love, Ruth Neslie, Georgette Lampsi, Doris Guignet, Mary Woods, Lucille Bremer, Jeanette Lea, Josephine McCann, Kathleen McLean, Stephanie Cekan, Louise Girard, Julie Steward, Eleanor Bolyn, Betty Gour, Bobbie Howell, Evelyn Foster, Selma Hoffman, Patricia Deering, Alma Wertley, Dorothie Littlefield, Bernice Dollarton, Tina Rigat, Joan Hope Lee, Audrey Beggs, Dorothy Swain, Paula Kaye, Blanche Fields, Betty Clary, Marion Warnes, Pamela Clifford, Janna Perlova, George Hecht, William Lang, Michael Kidd, Joseph Johnson, Egor Meller, Leo Senweska, George Kiddon, Bill Howell, Stephen Comfort, Edward Harrington, Teddy James, Joseph Bastian, Zachary Zolov, William Hecht

Musical Numbers

PROLOGUE
SCENE—THE SCHOOL ROOM
Another New Day, TEACHER (Miss Adams) and CHILDREN

I—WE LIKE IT OVER HERE
SCENE—FEDERAL HALL, NEW YORK CITY, APRIL 30, 1789

CAPTAIN, Ray Middleton
GEORGE WASHINGTON, George L. Spaulding
WASHINGTON'S AIDES, Harry Meehan, Tony Blair

We Like It Over Here, CAPTAIN, TRADESMEN, WASHINGTON'S FOOT GUARD, WASHINGTON'S HORSE GUARD, GUESTS ON THE BALCONY
Flag Drill, LITTLEFIELD BALLET

II—UNION FOREVER
(a) BARNUM AND JENNY LIND
SCENE—BROADWAY DURING THE 1860's

PHINEAS T. BARNUM, Jack Howard
BARKER, Lee Frederick
FIRE CHIEF, Harry Meehan
JENNY LIND, Lucy Monroe

Specialty, Lime Trio
Jenny Lind, FIRE CHIEF and MEN
How Can I Ever Be Alone?, JENNY LIND and Gene Marvey
Waltz, danced by Paul Haakon and LITTLEFIELD BALLET

(b) LINCOLN
ABRAHAM LINCOLN, Ray Middleton

SCENE ONE—GETTYSBURG, NOVEMBER 19, 1863
Of the People, ABRAHAM LINCOLN

SCENE TWO—TORCHLIGHT PARADE
By the People, MALE ENSEMBLE

SCENE THREE—FORD'S THEATRE, WASHINGTON, APRIL 14, 1865
For the People, ENSEMBLE

III—THE DAY BEFORE YESTERDAY
SCENE—OUTSIDE RECTOR'S, NEW YORK CITY, AT THE TURN OF THE CENTURY

TEDDY ROOSEVELT, Fred Ardath
DIAMOND JIM BRADY, Tony Blair

LILLIAN RUSSELL, Irene Christie
MAY IRWIN, Wynn Murray

My Bicycle Girl, Gene Marvey
Bicycle routine, LITTLEFIELD BALLET
Specialty, Joe Jackson
Old Time Automobile Parade
Tennessee Fish Fry, MAY IRWIN and ENSEMBLE
Cakewalk, danced by Paul Haakon and LITTLEFIELD BALLET
Equestrian Drill, TEDDY ROOSEVELT and his ROUGH RIDERS

IV—TOMORROW
SCENE—WASHINGTON, 1941

THE PRESIDENT, Ray Middleton

One in a Million, Wynn Murray, Harry Meehan and LITTLEFIELD BALLET
Finale, COMPANY
The Star Spangled Banner (music origin unknown; lyric by Francis Scott Key), Lucy Monroe

Reviews

Brooks Atkinson—*New York Times*
". . . handsome and enjoyable . . . As a lithographic sketchbook of American history it is sincerely affectionate. As a spectacle it is exuberant—with a good book and rousing score . . . It is done in good taste; it is beautiful, and some of it is patriotically stirring . . ."

Richard Watts, Jr.—*New York Herald Tribune*
". . . a lively and colorful show, with pleasant music, fine sets and some good dancing by Paul Haakon."

John Chapman—*New York Daily News*
". . . stunning . . . for gorgeous color and sweeping size is something this reporter has never seen approached . . . But it needs tightening . . . The songs should be popular . . ."

Robert Coleman—*New York Daily Mirror*
". . . one of the great spectacles of all time. And probably the largest ever to stun your reviewer's eyes . . . vastly entertaining and often moving . . . a titanic thriller . . ."

John Mason Brown—*New York Post*
". . . a lightening bug's view of our history . . . staged on a huge scale, the ballet of the cyclists is excellent, the costumes are pretty, Mr. Schwartz's tunes are agreeable . . ."

Sidney B. Whipple—*New York World-Telegram*
". . . a fretful rain could not conceal the undeniable fact that the

World's Fair has been lavish in providing its costuming and setting, generous in staffiing it with an acre of smart looking actors and dancers, and open-handed in the mechanical contrivances that make it run smoothly and brightly . . ."

Richard Lockridge—*New York Sun*
". . . even in the rain, it is an enormous and also handsome show . . . like most big things, it is a little naive, but it is broad and sweeping, and more fun to look at than to listen to . . ."

John Anderson—*New York Journal-American*
". . . the incidents have not been put together with much emotional effect . . . Not all the deficiences could be blamed on the weather. The show plainly needs much more rehearsing . . ."

Jack Pulaski (ibee.)—*Variety,* May 15, 1940
". . . That a show of such magnitude could be assembled within a fortnight period is an accomplishment. For the 40¢ admission it is certainly worthwhile . . . adds punch to the amusement area . . ."

Wolcott Gibbs—*The New Yorker,* May 25, 1940
"I couldn't, I'm afraid, make a great deal out of it . . . In spite of the rendering of pretty songs, I am obliged to say that it struck me as a stately imbecile."

Bibliography

"American Jubilee" by Sidney M. Shalett —*New York Times,* May 19, 1940

SUNNY RIVER

(1941)

A musical play with book and lyrics by Oscar Hammerstein II; music by Sigmund Romberg.

Presented by Max Gordon
Production supervised by John Murray Anderson
Book directed by Mr. Hammerstein
Choreography by Carl Randall
Settings by Stewart Chaney
Costumes by Irene Sharaff
Music director, Jacob Schwartzdorf (Jay S. Blackton)
Orchestrations by Don Walker

Tryout

(known as "New Orleans")
Municipal Open Air Theatre, St. Louis, June 5-10, 1941
Shubert Theatre, New Haven, November 27-29, 1941

New York Run

St. James Theatre, December 4, 1941-January 3, 1942
36 performances

The Story

Marie Sauvinet, a singer at the Cafe des Oleandres, and Cecilie Marshall, of New Orleans society, are both in love with the socially prominent Jean Gervais. Cecilie tricks Jean into marrying her, and Marie goes to Europe to become a famous opera singer. When she returns to New Orleans, she still tries to win Jean back, but abandons the idea when she realizes how much Cecilie loves him. Jean is killed fighting with Andrew Jackson in the War of 1812, and both women mourn his loss.

The Cast

CHILDREN, Carol Renee, Joan Shepherd, Edwin Bruce Moldow
OLD HENRY, Richard Huey
ARISTIDE, Oscar Polk
GABRIEL GERVAIS, Ainsworth Arnold

MOTHER GERVAIS, Ivy Scott
JEAN GERVAIS, Bob Lawrence
JIM, Donald Clark
HARRY, George Holmes
EMIL, Gordon Dilworth
EMMA, Vicki Charles (Cummings)
LOLITA, Ethel Levey
GEORGE MARSHALL, Dudley Clements
JUDGE PEPE MARTINEAU, Frederic Persson
MARIE SAUVINET, Muriel Angelus
DANIEL MARSHALL, Tom Ewell
CECILIE MARSHALL, Helen Claire
WATCHMAN, Byron Milligan
MADELEINE CARESSE, Joan Roberts
MARTHA, Peggy Alexander
HARLEQUIN, Jack Riano
COLUMBINE, Miriam La Velle
ACHILLE CARESSE, William O'Neal
DRUNK, Howard Freeman
DOCTOR, Kenneth Tobey
LADIES OF THE ENSEMBLE: Barbara Barton, Henni Brooks, Betty Gilpatrick, Lodema Legg, Gwenn Mann, Ann Marlowe, Helen Marshall, Mariquita Moll, May Muth, Ethel Taylor, Stephanie Turash, Helen Wagner
GENTLEMEN OF THE ENSEMBLE: James Allison, Jay Amiss, Russ Anderson, Alfredo Costello, Edward Dunbar, William Hearne, Philip Jones, William Hogue, John Marshall, Byron Milligan, Robert Ormiston, Fred Peronne, Michael Sigel, Roy Williams, Buddy Worth

Musical Numbers

PICTORIAL OVERTURE—LEVEE STREET, NEW ORLEANS, 1806
Symphonic Pantomime, ENSEMBLE
My Girl and I, JEAN

ACT I

SCENE ONE—PATIO OF THE CAFE DES OLEANDRES
Call It a Dream, MARIE and ENSEMBLE
It Can Happen to Anyone, MARIE and ENSEMBLE
The Butterflies and the Bees, DANIEL, EMMA, LOLITA, MARSHALL, JUDGE
Along the Winding Road, MARIE and MEAN
Finaletto, MARIE, LOLITA, DANIEL, EMMA and ENSEMBLE

SCENE TWO—UPSTAIRS SITTING ROOM IN THE HOME OF M. AND MME. GERVAIS, 1811
Bundling, DANIEL
Reprise, *Along the Winding Road,* MARIE and JEAN

SCENE THREE—JEAN'S DRESSING ROOM

SCENE FOUR—RECEPTION HALL IN THE GERVAIS HOME
Can You Sing?, MARIE and ENSEMBLE
Making Conversation, MARIE, CECILIE and ENSEMBLE
Reprise, *The Butterflies and the Bees*, DANIEL and MADELEINE
Let Me Live Today, MARIE, JEAN and ENSEMBLE

ACT II
SCENE ONE—PATIO OF THE CAFE DES OLEANDRES
Bow-Legged Sal, ENSEMBLE
Sunny River, LOLITA and ENSEMBLE
Reprise, *Call It a Dream*, MARIE and ENSEMBLE
The Duello, ACHILLE and DANIEL
She Got Him, MADELEINE, EMMA, ACHILLE, DANIEL and ENSEMBLE

SCENE TWO—LEVEE STREET
Reprise, *My Girl and I*, JEAN
Time Is Standing Still, MARIE and JEAN
Reprise, *Let Me Live Today*, JEAN, MARIE and MALE ENSEMBLE
Finaletto, JEAN and THE DRUNK

SCENE THREE—PATIO OF THE CAFE DES OLEANDRES, 1815
Finale Ultimo, MARIE, CECILIE, LOLITA

NOTE: *Lordy* and *Eleven Levee Street* cut before New York opening.

Reviews

Brooks Atkinson—*New York Times*
". . . a workmanlike item . . . Every element of romance is put in its proper place in the book and the score goes through a polite sequence of heavily orchestrated numbers . . . Its deportment is correct but it is not really interesting."

Richard Watts, Jr.—*New York Herald Tribune*
". . . a dull and commonplace musical show that is bowed down under the weight of its stencils . . . When the plot isn't going on and the comedy lags, the new Romberg score is prettily sung . . . as a whole, the music struck me as being both conventional and synthetic . . ."

Burns Mantle—*New York Daily News*
"★★+ . . . If you can overlook one of the worst books with which musical comedy has been burdened in recent years, you will find the music fairly rewarding, and the production practically smothered in color and attractive scenery . . ."

Wilella Waldorf—*New York Post*
". . . if this is the best new operetta Max Gordon could discover, it is not surprising that few producers these days are inclined to give much attention to this form of entertainment . . ."

John Mason Brown—*New York World-Telegram*
". . . To say the evening depressed me would be to indulge in a form of understatement not habitual with this department . . . the operetta which tries to be Puccini on a piccolo is no favorite form of mine . . . lovers who are always being separated bore me so unconsciously that the only fate worse than death which I can dream of for them is that they should be brought together again . . . *Sunny River* happens to contain every one of the ingredients which I most deplore . . ."

Richard Lockridge—*New York Sun*
". . . a reasonably coherent and pleasantly written book, with numerous nice speeches and intervals of pathos . . . But neither the composer nor the librettist often wanders from the straight and narrow path of sweet romance. Personally, I like a little joking around and, on occasion, even a little nonsense . . . very handsome, very good of its kind and not very lively . . "

John Anderson—*New York Journal-American*
". . . large, lavish, colorful and handsomely sung. Thus far I can agree with its enthusiastic first audience before my own pulse taps out a sour 'No.' For these assets seem heavily over-weighed by the show's insistent dullness . . . The total effect is that of a journeyman job, synthetic and uninspired . . ."

Louis Kronenberger—*PM*
". . . as full-blown and high-romanced as anything produced in the old days, but it turns out to be something less than an unalloyed delight . . . a terribly long-winded plot isn't the only thing we're in for. There is the dialogue, some of it stilted, some of it fancy, some of it arch . . . warm and sometimes winning melodies . . ."

Jack Pulaski (Ibee.)—*Variety,* December 10, 1941
". . . should do fairly well. It possesses the best warbling of any musical in years. It has a lively second act that nearly equalizes the drag of the first portion. Seems to have a fair content of scoring comedy, too . . . Ewell's work puts him in the limelight . . ."

Wolcott Gibbs—*The New Yorker,* December 13, 1941
"The persistent rumor that what New York really needs in these trying times is a nice old-fashioned operetta exploded vehemently the night that *Sunny River* made its appearance . . . a majestic bore . . . In a word that I have found very useful on similar occasions, the music and scenery are characteristic."

Wilder Hobson—*Time,* December 15, 1941
". . . attempts to revive big-scale, full-throated operetta without knowing how. It seizes on the cobwebs of the oldtime musical instead of the charm. Its lush, long-winded plot, its stilted dialogue, its leering humor have everybody's nostalgia in full retreat before the evening is half over . . . The music, sometimes warm and romantic, is often florid and stale."

John O'Hara—*Newsweek,* December 15, 1941
". . . the book is one of those things you are tempted to dismiss by saying the less said about it the better . . . It has some of the loudest four-part harmony I've ever heard, and if you're in the mood for being blasted by a chord, this surely is your show . . ."

Bibliography

Max Gordon Tells an Interviewer How He Does It by Lucius Beebe
—*New York Herald Tribune,* November 30, 1941

SUNNY RIVER

(English Production—1943)

Presented by Emile Littler
Directed by Maxwell Wray
Choreography by Cleo Nordi
Settings and costumes by Doris Zinkeisen
Music director, Michael Collins
Orchestrations by Alfred Reynolds

Tryout

Hippodrome, Coventry, July 26-31, 1943
Opera House, Manchester, August 2-7, 1943

London Run

Piccadilly Theatre, August 18-October 23, 1943
86 performances

The Cast

GOSSIPS, Marcelle Turner, Meta Murray
LADIES OF THE TOWN, Sylvia Saxton, Mildred Letts
A REFUGEE, Patricia Thomas
A LOUISIANIAN, Michael Fletcher
GABRIEL GERVAIS, Bernard Ansell
MME. GERVAIS, Marjorie Wilson
JEAN GERVAIS, Dennis Noble
STREET SINGER, Lionel Trim

EMMA, LUCILLE, ELAINE, STELLA, MILLIE, JOY, JEANNE } *girls at the cafe* { Marion Wilson, Marilyn Day, Eugenie Castle, Gladys Cowper, Sonia Peters, Marjorie Williett, Bernice Lamont

LOLITA, Edith Day
ARISTEDE, James Rich
GEORGE MARSHALL, Bertram Wallis
JUDGE PEPE MARTINEAU, Kenneth Blain
JACQUES, Dewey Gibson
EMIL, Frank Wignall
GEORGES, Desmond Campbell
HARRY, Bert Harding
MARIE SAUVINET, Evelyn Laye
DANIEL MARSHALL, Don Avory
CECELIE MARSHALL, Ena Burrill
WATCHMEN, Edwin Saxton, Frank Grant
MADELEINE, Edna Proud
HELEN, Gabrielle Rees
MARTHA, Bunty Barnett
THERESE, Jean O'Neill
WILLIAM, *the butler,* Basil Austin
PROSPEROUS LADY, Helen Lawrence
ACHILLE, George Gower
BARTENDER, Gordon Whelan

Musical Numbers
Same as original production.

Reviews
A.V. Cookman—*London Times*
"The show is unusually rich in good songs. Miss Edith Day brings the story to a standstill with the title song, which catches the strong movement and cheerfulness of a great river flowing in sunlight to the sea . . . In virtue of these songs the piece is likely enough to prosper . . . The story is curiously uneven. It appears to suffer from a craving after originality which Mr. Hammerstein can neither wholly repress nor indulge . . ."

James Agate—*London Sunday Times,* August 22, 1943
"Does this play hold water? No. But is water-tightness the criterion? . . . Romberg reminds us of *Tristan, Meistersinger, Til Eulenspiegel* and even the *Londonderry Air* . . . Be this as it may, the score is extraordinarily tuneful throughout . . . I rate this piece as the best

since *Bitter Sweet* . . . the plot is not more nonsensical than any other . . . the piece keeps to its period, and there is no low comedian to make gags about 'utility' trousers . . . brilliantly acted . . ."

Horace Horsnell—*London Observer,* August 22, 1943
". . . a somewhat solemn and congested story . . . The characters are capitally led by Evelyn Laye and Dennis Noble in brilliant command of the tunefully royal forces . . ."

James Redfern—*The Spectator,* August 27, 1943
". . . it certainly derives from the great success of *Show Boat* and should also prove successful . . . abundant and mellifluous music . . ."

The New Statesman and Nation, August 28, 1943
". . . has much to recommend it . . . There are charming costumes and scenery, several good tunes, and, happily, no rows of frantically smiling, hectically kicking ladies . . ."

Beverley Baxter, M.P.—*London Evening Standard* (follow-up)
". . . a piece of such charm and musicianship that it was worth two or three visits. Unfortunately, the public not only failed to turn up twice or thrice but did not put in a sufficiently strong initial appearance to make it a success."

CARMEN JONES

(1943)

A musical play with book and lyrics by Oscar Hammerstein II, based on libretto by Henri Meilhac and Ludovic Halevy, adapted from story, "Carmen," by Prosper Merimée; music by Georges Bizet.

Presented by Billy Rose
Production directed by Hassard Short
Book directed by Charles Friedman
Choreography by Eugene Loring
Settings by Howard Bay
Costumes by Raoul Pène duBois
Lighting and color schemes by Mr. Short
Music director, Joseph Littau
Orchestrations by Robert Russell Bennett
Choral director, Robert Shaw

Tryout
Erlanger Theatre, Philadelphia, October 19-November 7, 1943
Opera House, Boston, November 9-28, 1943

New York Run
Broadway Theatre, December 2, 1943-February 10, 1945
502 performances

The Story
Joe, an army corporal, is stationed near a parachute factory in a Southern town, where Carmen Jones is employed. She wins Joe away from his fiancee, Cindy Lou, and they run off together to Chicago. But Carmen loses interest in Joe and she becomes enamored of a boxer named Husky Miller. Mad with jealousy, Joe kills Carmen outside the arena the night of Miller's big fight.

The Cast
CORPORAL MORRELL, Napoleon Reed or Robert Clarke
FOREMAN, Robert Clarke or George Willis
CINDY LOU, Carlotta Franzell or Elton J. Warren
SERGEANT BROWN, Jack Carr
JOE, Luther Saxon or Napoleon Reed
CARMEN JONES, Muriel Smith or Muriel Rahn

SALLY, Sibol Cain
T-BONE, Edward Roche
TOUGH KID, William Jones
DRUMMER, Cosy Cole
BARTENDER, Melvin Howard
WAITER, Edward Christopher
FRANKIE, June Hawkins
MYRT, Jessica Russell
RUM, Edward Lee Tyler
DINK, Dick Montgomery
HUSKY MILLER, Glenn Bryant
SOLDIERS, Robert Clarke, George Willis, Elijah Hodges
MR. HIGGINS, P. Jay Sidney
MISS HIGGINS, Fredye Marshall
PHOTOGRAPHER, Alford Pierre
CARD PLAYERS, Urylee Leonardos, Ethel White, Sibol Cain
DANCING GIRL, Ruth Crumpton
PONCHO, William Dillard
DANCING BOXERS, Sheldon B. Hoskins, Randolph Sawyer
BULLET HEAD, Melvin Howard
REFEREE, Tony Fleming Jr.
SOLDIERS, FACTORY WORKERS, SOCIALITES: Viola Anderson, Lee Allen, Carmine Brown, William Archer, Miriam Burton, Sibol Cain, Clarice Crawford, Ruth Crumpton, Robert Clarke, Anne Dixon, Marguerite Duncan, Edwina Divers, Richard DeVaultier, George Dosher, William Davis, Awilda Frasier, Elijah Hodges, Melvin Howard, Clarence Jones, Elsie Kennedy, Fredye Marshall, Theresa Merritte, Vivienne Mussenden, Maithe Marshall, Bertha Powell, Alford Pierre, Fred Randell, Chauncey Reynolds, Edward Roche, Randolph Steplight, Andrew Taylor, Harold Taylor, Audrey Vanterpool, Ethel White, George Willis, Robert Woodland, William Woolfolk, Howard Carter, Urylee Leonardos, Inez Matthews
DANCERS: Valerie Black, Al Bledger, Posie Flowers, Tony Fleming, Jr., Audrey Graham, J. Prioreau Gray, Frank Green, Erona Harris, Mabel Hart, Sheldon Hoskins, Rhoda Johnson, Richard James, Dorothy McNichols, Vera McNichols, Betty Nichols, Frank Neal, Joseph Noble, Bill O'Neil, Evelyn Pilcher, Edith Ross, J. Flashe Riley, Randolph Sawyer, Randolph Scott, Royce Wallace, Dorothy Williams, Edward Christopher
CHILDREN: Albert Bailey, Robert Bailey, Raymond Brooks, William Jones, Joe Green, Gilbert Irvis, Richard Granaday, Oliver Hamilton, Arthur Rames, Robert Smith, LeRoy Westfall, Carlos VanPutten, Delano Vanterpool, James Holman

NOTE: In September, 1944, Miss Rahn succeeded by Inez Matthews. For tour, Mr. Saxon succeeded by LeVern Hutcherson, Miss Russell by Theresa Merritte, Mr. Tyler by John Bubbles, Mr. Montgomery by Ford Buck. During tour, Miss Matthews succeeded by Urylee Leonardos, Miss Franzell by Coreania Hayman, Miss Hawkins by Ruth Crumpton.

Musical Numbers

Prelude

ACT I

SCENE ONE—OUTSIDE A PARACHUTE FACTORY NEAR A SOUTHERN TOWN
Opening scene, MORRELL, CINDY LOU, WORKMEN
Lift 'Em Up and Put 'Em Down, STREET BOYS
Honey Gal o' Mine, WORKMEN
Good Luck, Mr. Flyin' Man, ENSEMBLE and DANCERS
Dat's Love, CARMEN and ENSEMBLE
Scene, JOE and CINDY LOU
You Talk Just Like My Maw, JOE and CINDY LOU
Finale, CARMEN, JOE, BROWN, SALLY and ENSEMBLE
Entr'scene, *Carmen Jones Is Goin' to Jail,* ENSEMBLE

SCENE TWO—A NEARBY ROADSIDE
Dere's a Cafe on de Corner, CARMEN and JOE
Finaletto, CARMEN and JOE

SCENE THREE—BILLY PASTOR'S CAFE
Beat Out Dat Rhythm on a Drum, MYRT, DRUMMER, DANCERS and ENSEMBLE
Stan' Up and Fight, MILLER and ENSEMBLE
Whizzin' Away Along de Track, RUM, DINK, MYRT, FRANKIE, CARMEN
Scene, CARMEN and JOE
Dis Flower, JOE
If You Would Only Come Away, CARMEN and JOE
Finale, COMPANY

ENTR'ACTE (based on Entr'acte music between Acts III and IV of "Carmen")

ACT II

SCENE ONE—TERRACE OF THE MEADOWLAWN COUNTRY CLUB, SOUTHSIDE OF CHICAGO
De Cards Don't Lie, FRANKIE, MYRT and CARD PLAYERS
Dat Ol' Boy, CARMEN
Poncho de Panther From Brazil, FRANKIE, MYRT, MILLER, RUM and ENSEMBLE
Ballet Divertisement, DANCING BOXERS and DANCERS
My Joe, CINDY LOU
Finale, CARMEN, JOE, CINDY LOU, MILLER, RUM, DINK, FRANKIE, MYRT

SCENE TWO—OUTSIDE A SPORT STADIUM
Get Your Program for de Big Fight, ENSEMBLE
Dat's Our Man, ENSEMBLE
Scene, JOE and CARMEN
Finale, COMPANY

PROGRAM NOTE: "Believing *Carmen* to be a perfect wedding of story and music, we have adhered as closely as possible to its original form. All the melodies—with a few very minor exceptions—are sung in their accustomed order. The small deviations we have made were only those which seemed honestly demanded by a transference of *Carmen* to a modern American background.

"In our elimination of the recitatif passages, we are not taking as great a liberty as may be supposed. Bizet and his collaborators originally wrote *Carmen* with spoken dialogue scenes between the airs that were sung. The work was intended for theatres of average size, like the Opera Comique in Paris (where it is played today as a dialogue opera).

"*Carmen* was not converted to a 'grand opera' until after Bizet's death. The music set to the dialogue is not his music. It was written by Ernest Guiraud.

Oscar Hammerstein II"

Reviews

Lewis Nichols—*New York Times*

". . . beautifully done in every way, with gay colors and gay ballets, and singers who can sing as if they meant it . . . just call it wonderful, quite wonderful . . . Hammerstein has not written a parody in any sense, but simply a parallel. Many of his lyrics are light, but there are no Broadway gags . . . It is quite a libretto he has turned out . . ."

Howard Barnes—*New York Herald Tribune*

"*Bravo!* The theatre and music have had a memorable wedding . . . as wonderful and exciting as it is audacious . . . The libretto has been brilliantly translated . . . something more than a major theatrical event. It opens infinite and challenging horizons for the fusing of two art forms . . . Hammerstein has retained every mood and movement of a tortured romance, giving it immediate meaning and dramatic force. He has written lusty and intelligent lyrics, which are superbly suited to the new Negro idiom . . ."

John Chapman—*New York Daily News*

". . . rates all the adjectives that hurried fingers can find on a midnight keyboard. It is superb; it is enchantingly beautiful; it is musically exciting and visually stirring . . . Hammerstein, the best lyric writer in the business, has done a poet's and a musician's job with the libretto. His incandescent imagination sets your own afire . . . Billy Rose, my hat is off to you and I bow low."

Robert Coleman—*New York Daily Mirror*

". . . a terrific job . . . Hammerstein has worked wonders with the fable . . . It's ever so much more wonderful and exciting than mere words can make it sound . . . magnificent . . ."

Wilella Waldorf—*New York Post*
". . . a half-and-half affair. The opera was pretty bad . . . none of the leading singers is more than passable, vocally or dramatically . . . the less grand operatic moments were thoroughly enjoyable . . . Its lyrics are so neatly done that we wish Hammerstein would take the trouble sometime to do a 'straight' English version of grand opera . . ."

Alton Cook—*New York World-Telegram*
". . . opera with the addition of a wild, primitive charm . . . A restrengthened poignance and an altogether new humorous undertone has been written into the story . . . such a startling and unexpected departure from anything you ever saw before, the whole thing has the air of a dream production—a mighty nice dream, too."

Herrick Brown—*New York Sun*
". . . Hammerstein has done a splendid job . . . He has succeeded admirably in making the gayety and the tragedy truly that of the Negro race while preserving the essential spirit of the opera . . . a brilliant idea brilliantly carried out."

Robert Garland—*New York Journal-American*
". . . fresh, stalwart and exciting . . . a memorable milestone in the upward and onward course of the great American showshop. In theatrical history, it will go down as something fresh, imaginative, and, for the most part, hitherto unattempted in the theatre of today . . . thrilling, human and altogether three-dimensional . . . a great operetta, a great show, and a great theatrical achievement on the part of Billy Rose!"

Louis Kronenberger—*PM*
"All in all, it is a delight . . . an exciting and richly colored show . . . Its lyrics are fresh and clean-cut—at times humorous, at times poignant in their simplicity—as in Cindy Lou's big aria . . . Much of the virtue of the show lies in the staging . . . By comparison with what follows, the first scene is self-conscious and unanimated; but all the rest is swift and alive without being boisterous, and bright without being lurid."

Jack Pulaski (Ibee.)—*Variety*, December 8, 1943
". . . hypoed Bizet into big biz . . . terrific b.o. appeal. It's the top colored show to hit the big street to date, and rates superlatives in all departments . . . Hammerstein is now at the peak of his career . . ."

Wolcott Gibbs—*The New Yorker*, December 11, 1943
". . . It is hard to see why the application of rowdy or simply colloquial words to highly respectable music should always seem so comic, but it does. Hammerstein is dealing in basic humor but he manages it superbly . . . If *Carmen Jones* had to be taken seriously as tragedy, along with all its other wonders, it might be too much of an experience to crowd into one night."

Louis Kronenberger—*Time*, December 13, 1943
". . . the most brilliant show on Broadway . . . Carmen has been refired in a kiln, not warmed over in an oven . . . Respectfulness everywhere chaperones audacity . . . Hammerstein's lyrics are as right and renovating as his book . . . as a production it is drenched with light and smeared with color, yet lean and swift-moving . . ."

Thomas H. Wenning—*Newsweek*, December 13, 1943
". . . should put Bizet on the hit parade with *Dere's a Café on de Corner* and *My Joe* . . . *Carmen Jones* is the greatest proof the theatre has had thus far that opera can be a living art and not a museum of memories . . . most of the credit goes to two men: Oscar Hammerstein and Hassard Short . . ."

Olin Downes—*New York Times*, December 19, 1943
". . . brilliant entertainment . . . the audacious and original way in which the story is presented amounts, for at least three-quarters of the time, to excellent theatre and a good show . . . all we are waiting for is our own music-drama . . ."

Stark Young—*The New Republic*, December 20, 1943
". . . The first half of the event is the encouraging part. It is full of life and go . . . The second half slumps considerably and becomes at length fairly tedious. The novelty has worn off somewhat . . ."

Bibliography

Billy Rose and "Carmen Jones" by Richard Maney
—*New York Times*, November 28, 1943

"Carmen Jones" —*Life*, December 20, 1943

"Carmen Jones" by Kyle Crichton —*Collier's*, January 15, 1944

"Carmen" to "Carmen Jones": 1875-1944 —*Life*, May 8, 1944

Hassard Short—The Palette Mixer by Karl Schriftgiesser
—*New York Times*, June 18, 1944

Tour

New York City Center, May 2, 1945—New York City Center, May 4, 1946 (26 cities).

Auditorium, Atlantic City, August 27, 1946—Music Hall, Kansas City, December 28, 1946 (35 cities).

Tour Reviews

Lewis Funke—*New York Times*
". . . remains one of Rose's great inspirations . . . superb lyrics . . . one of the pleasant items of our theatre . . ."

Robert Garland—*New York Journal-American*
". . . an even better show than before . . ."

Claudia Cassidy—*Chicago Tribune*
". . . the best *Carmen* I have ever laid eyes or ears on . . ."

Elliot Norton—*Boston Post*
". . . one of the great shows on the stage today; a rare and exhilarating combination of antic comedy and high tragedy, magnificent music and exuberant dancing . . ."

Lewis Nichols—*New York Times*
". . . should be brought back every year or so, by main force if need be."

Harriett Johnson—*New York Post*
". . . As a sour critic, I'm forced to admit that I admire *Carmen* but I love *Carmen Jones*."

Burton Rascoe—*New York World-Telegram*
". . . immeasurably better in many ways than when it was first shown . . ."

Tour Bibliography

"Carmen Jones" Popular Show by Oscar Hammerstein II
—*Boston Post*, February 23, 1946

Selected Revivals

Greek Theatre, Los Angeles, Summer, 1949
Urylee Leonardos (CARMEN); LeVern Hutcheron (JOE); Carlotta Franzell (CINDY LOU); Zutty Singleton (DRUMMER).

Boston Summer Theatre, June 23, 1952
Muriel Rahn (CARMEN); Luther Saxon (JOE); Elton J. Warren (CINDY LOU); William Dillard (HUSKY); Eric Henry (DRUMMER).

New York City Center Light Opera, May 31-June 17, 1956
Muriel Smith (CARMEN); William DuPree (JOE); Reri Grist (CINDY LOU); James Randolph (HUSKY); Buck and Bubbles (RUM, DINK); Cosy Cole (DRUMMER). Produced and directed by William Hammerstein.

New York Hudson Celebration, Central Park, August 17-23, 1959
Ethel Ayler (CARMEN); William DuPree (JOE); Christine Spencer (CINDY LOU); James Randolph (HUSKY); Sticks Evans (DRUMMER).

CARMEN JONES

(Film Version—1954)

A Twentieth Century-Fox Picture
Produced and directed by Otto Preminger
Screenplay by Harry Kleiner
Choreography by Herbert Ross
Art director, Edward L. Ilou
Costumes by Mary Ann Nyberg
Music director, Herschel Burke Gilbert
Orchestrations by Leon Birnbaum and George Brand
Photographed by Sam Leavitt
Editor, Louis Loeffler
Color by Deluxe, Filmed in CinemaScope

Release Date

October 5, 1954

The Cast

CARMEN JONES, Dorothy Dandridge (sung by Marilyn Horne)
JOE, Harry Belafonte (sung by LeVern Hutcherson)
CINDY LOU, Olga James
FRANKIE, Pearl Bailey
MYRT, Diahann Carroll (sung by Bernice Peterson)
RUM, Roy Glenn (sung by Brock Peters)
DINK, Nick Stewart (sung by Joe Crawford)
HUSKY MILLER, Joe Adams (sung by Marvin Hayes)
SGT. BROWN, Brock Peters
T-BONE, Sandy Lewis
SALLY, Mauri Lynn
TRAINER, DeForest Covan
DANCERS: Carmen DeLavillade, Archie Savage

Musical Numbers

Same as original production.

Reviews

Bosley Crowther—*New York Times*
". . . a big musical shenanigan and theatrical tour-de-force. Do not

expect to hear a fully integrated opera sung or see a particularly sensitive or intelligent Negro drama performed. The product betrays from every angle its jerry-built incongruities. It is not so much poignant as it is lurid and lightly farcical . . . The music does not fit the people or the words. The consequences is a crazy mixed-up film."

Otis L. Guernsey, Jr.—*New York Herald Tribune*
". . . Carmen could not be better acted without setting the theatre on fire. The screenplay takes the story seriously, tells it well . . . Preminger preserves the mood of earthiness and extroverted passion without over-exploiting it . . ."

Archer Winsten—*New York Post*
". . . comes close to the edge of greatness . . . doesn't quite jell as an experience that takes you inside itself . . . a production of considerable beauty and excitement, proving nothing . . ."

Mike Kaplan—*Variety*, October 6, 1954
". . . a healthy boxoffice outlook . . . perhaps the first picture in both Cinemascope and Sensuoscope . . . the standout songs—as a result of Hammerstein's lyricizing—are *Stan' Up and Fight, Beat Out Dat Rhythm On a Drum* and *Dat's Love* . . ."

Henry Bradford Darrach, Jr.—*Time*, November 1, 1954
". . . a pretty obvious device for converting color into coin . . . With back-country U.S. Negroes, the music goes about as well as pink champagne at a hoe down . . . On top of this, Hammerstein dipped his big toe in the Mississippi mud and wrote some lyrics that should be thrown back to the catfish. Fortunately, he also supplied a book that is considerably better than the original . . . Energy is the essence of this picture; the audience is not merely stimulated, it is all but electrocuted . . ."

John McCarten—*The New Yorker*, November 6, 1954
". . . As an anthropological treatise, it is highly suspect, but as a piece of entertainment, it is pretty diverting . . . there may be some debate over whether Bizet's tunes are quite adaptable to the jive idiom in which they are clothed; I can only report that the results struck me as somewhat spotty . . ."

Robert Hatch—*The Nation*, November 13, 1954
". . . rousing entertainment . . . No artistic end is served by this bizarre restyling of the opera; it is a work of shrewd commercial packaging . . ."

John Appleton (Mr. Harper)—*Harper's Magazine*, January, 1955
". . . the best that Hollywood can do—a fast, colorful film, superb

acting and singing, with more impact and drama than any but the finest stage performances of the opera can have . . . what I liked best was the fact that Hollywood didn't underestimate the taste of their audience . . ."

Bibliography

Miss Carmen Jones —*New York Times Magazine,* October 17, 1954

A New Beauty for Bizet (cover story) —*Life,* November 1, 1954

RODGERS AND HAMMERSTEIN

Alfred Drake and Joan Roberts in the "Surrey with the Fringe on Top" in "Oklahoma!" (1943). Lee Dixon, Celeste Holm and Joseph Buloff are in front.

OKLAHOMA!

(1943)

A musical play with book and lyrics by Oscar Hammerstein II, based on the play "Green Grow the Lilacs" by Lynn Riggs; music by Richard Rodgers.

Presented by the Theatre Guild
Directed by Rouben Mamoulian
Choreography by Agnes de Mille
Settings by Lemuel Ayers
Costumes by Miles White
Music director, Jacob Schwartzdorf (Jay S. Blackton)
Orchestrations by Robert Russell Bennett
Production supervised by Theresa Helburn and Lawrence Langner

Tryout

(known as "Away We Go!")
Shubert Theatre, New Haven, March 11-13, 1943
Colonial Theatre, Boston, March 15-27, 1943

New York Run

St. James Theatre, March 31, 1943-May 29, 1948 (five years, nine weeks)
2,212 performances (including 44 special matinees for the armed forces)

NOTE: For fifteen years—from July 1, 1946 through July 11, 1961—*Oklahoma!* held the record as the longest-running musical in Broadway history.

The Story

In the days of the Oklahoma land rush, both Jud Fry and Curly, ranch hands, are in love with Laurey. Although it is really Curly whom she loves, Laurey spites him by going to a dance with Jud. There, Curly proves his love by bidding all he owns for Laurey's food basket. They marry, and after the ceremony, Jud picks a fight with Curly and is killed by his own knife. Curly is acquitted on the spot.

The Cast

AUNT ELLER MURPHY, Betty Garde
CURLY MCLAIN, Alfred Drake
LAUREY WILLIAMS, Joan Roberts
IKE SKIDMORE, Barry Kelley
FRED, Edwin Clay

SLIM, Herbert Rissman
WILL PARKER, Lee Dixon
JUD FRY, Howard da Silva
ADO ANNIE CARNES, Celeste Holm
ALI HAKIM, Joseph Buloff
GERTIE CUMMINGS, Jane Lawrence
ELLEN, Katharine Sergava
KATE, Ellen Love
SYLVIE, Joan McCracken
ARMINA, Kate Friedlich
AGGIE, Bambi Linn
ANDREW CARNES, Ralph Riggs
CORD ELAM, Owen Martin
JESS, George Church
CHALMERS, Marc Platt
MIKE, Paul Shiers
JOE, George S. Irving
SAM, Hayes Gordon
SINGERS: Elsie Arnold, Harvey Brown, Suzanne Lloyd, Ellen Love, Dorothea MacFarland, Virginia Oswald, Faye Smith, Vivienne Simon; John Baum, Edwin Clay, Hayes Gordon, George S. Irving, Arthur Ulisse, Herbert Rissman, Paul Shiers, Robert Penn
DANCERS: Diana Adams, Margit DeKova, Bobby Barrentine, Nona Feid, Rhoda Hoffman, Maria Harriton, Kate Friedlich, Bambi Linn, Joan McCracken, Vivian Smith, Billie Zay; Kenneth Buffet, Jack Dunphy, Gary Fleming, Eddie Howland, Ray Harrison, Erik Kristen, Kenneth LeRoy

NOTE: Miss Garde succeeded by Ruth Weston (Dec. 1944), Edith Gresham (Jan. 1948). Mr. Drake by Harry Stockwell (June 1944), Bob Kennedy (June 1945), Harold (Howard) Keel (Sept. 1945), Jack Kilty (June 1946), Mr. Keel (Sept. 1946), Mr. Kilty (April 1947), Wilton Clary (July 1947). Miss Roberts by Evelyn Wyckoff (July 1944), Iva Withers (Sept. 1945), Betty Jane Watson (Oct. 1945), Ann Crowley (Feb. 1946), Miss Watson (March 1946), Mary Hatcher (Dec. 1946), Gloria Hamilton (Aug. 1947), Carolyn Tanner (Jan. 1948). Mr. Dixon by Paul Crabtree (Jan. 1945), Tom Avera (July 1945), James Parnell (Oct. 1945). Mr. da Silva by Murvyn Vye (June 1944), Richard Rober (Nov. 1944), Bruce Hamilton (May 1946), Mr. Rober (Aug. 1946), Mr. Hamilton (Sept. 1946). Miss Holm by Edna Skinner (June 1944), Bonita Primrose (Oct. 1945), Dorothea MacFarland (Dec. 1946), Vivienne Allen (April 1947), Shelley Winters (Sept. 1947), Miss Allen (Jan. 1948). In December 1947, Miss Holm returned to cast for three weeks. In July 1944, Mr. Buloff replaced by Herbert Berghof for three weeks. Mr. Buloff succeeded by David Burns (Aug. 1946), Max Willenz (July 1947), Owen Martin (Sept. 1947), Guy Rennie (Nov. 1947), Marek Windheim (Feb. 1948), Hy Anzell (July 1948). Miss Lawrence by Pamela Britton (Aug. 1943), Betty Jane Watson (Nov. 1943), Dorothea MacFarland (July 1944), Vivienne Allen (Aug. 1945), Patricia Englund (July 1946), Margot Moser (Feb. 1948), Bonita Atkins (April 1948). Miss Sergava by Dania Krupska (Sept. 1945), Gemze de Lappe (July 1946), Alicia Krug (April 1947). Mr. Church by Vladimir Kostenko (May 1943). Mr. Platt by Erick Hawkins (May 1944), David Tihmar (June 1944), Scott Merrill (Nov. 1944), John Butler (Oct. 1945), Erik Kristen (Sept. 1946), Boris Runanin (April 1947).

Musical Numbers

The action takes place in Indian territory (now Oklahoma), just after the turn of the century.

ACT I

SCENE ONE—THE FRONT OF LAUREY'S FARMHOUSE

Oh, What a Beautiful Mornin', CURLY

The Surrey With the Fringe on Top, CURLY, LAUREY, AUNT ELLER

Kansas City, WILL, with AUNT ELLER and BOYS

I Cain't Say No, ADO ANNIE

Many a New Day, LAUREY and GIRLS; danced by SYLVIE, ARMINA, ELLEN

It's a Scandal! It's a Outrage!, ALI HAKIM and BOYS and GIRLS

People Will Say We're in Love, CURLY and LAUREY

SCENE TWO—THE SMOKE HOUSE

Pore Jud Is Daid, CURLY and JUD

Lonely Room, JUD

SCENE THREE—A GROVE ON LAUREY'S FARM

Out of My Dreams, LAUREY and GIRLS

Laurey Makes Up Her Mind Ballet

LAUREY, Katharine Sergava

CURLY, Marc Platt

JUD, George Church

THE CHILD, Bambi Linn

JUD'S POST CARDS: Joan McCracken, Kate Friedlich, Margit DeKova

LAUREY'S FRIENDS: Rhoda Hoffman, Rosemary Schaeffer, Nona Feid, Maria Harriton, Diana Adams, Billie Zay

COWBOYS: Gary Fleming, Erik Kristen, Jack Dunphy, Ray Harrison, Kenneth LeRoy, Eddie Howland, Kenneth Buffet

OTHER POST CARDS: Bobby Barrentine, Vivian Smith

ACT II

SCENE ONE—THE SKIDMORE RANCH

The Farmer and the Cowman, CARNES, AUNT ELLER, CURLY, WILL, ADO ANNIE, FRED and ENSEMBLE; danced by CHALMERS

All er Nothin, ADO ANNIE and WILL; danced by Armina and Sylvie

SCENE TWO—SKIDMORE'S KITCHEN PORCH

Reprise, *People Will Say We're in Love,* CURLY and LAUREY

SCENE THREE—THE BACK OF LAUREY'S FARMHOUSE

Oklahoma, CURLY, LAUREY, AUNT ELLER, IKE, FRED and ENSEMBLE

Reprise, *Oh, What a Beautiful Mornin',* LAUREY, CURLY and ENSEMBLE

Finale, COMPANY

NOTE: *Boys and Girls Like You and Me* cut before New York opening.

Reviews

Lewis Nichols—*New York Times*
". . . truly delightful . . . Wonderful is the nearest adjective for this excursion combines a fresh and infectious gaiety, a charm of manner, beautiful acting, singing and dancing, and a score which does not do any harm either, since it is one of Rodgers' best . . . Mamoulian's best direction . . . deMille's most inspired dances."

Howard Barnes—*New York Herald Tribune*
"*Lilacs to 'Oklahoma!'* . . . Songs, dances and story have been triumphantly blended . . . a jubilant and enchanting musical. The Rodgers score is one of his best, which is saying plenty. Hammerstein has written a dramatically original libretto and a string of catchy lyrics; Agnes de Mille has worked small miracles . . . Mamoulian has directed with great taste and craftsmanship . . . one of the most captivating shows of the season . . . a striking piece of theatrical Americana . . ."

Burns Mantle—*New York Daily News*
"★★★+ . . . the most thoroughly and attractively American musical comedy since *Show Boat*. It has color and rhythm, and harmony plus. It is held to the native idiom and kept sufficiently clean to give it standing in the western country from which it springs. And it has been modestly but handsomely staged . . . The Rodgers score and the Hammerstein lyrics are the really dominant feature of the production . . . *Oklahoma!* is different—beautifully different . . ."

Louis Kronenberger—*PM*
". . . a little more than a musical comedy without being pretentiously so . . . The book is just one of those things, if that, and the comedy is neither subtle nor extensive . . . Rodgers' score is agreeably varied, but the bulk (and the best) of it is well on the romantic side with plenty of melody and warmth . . . Mr. Hammerstein has found very likeable words . . . just different enough to add something special to Broadway's musical life."

George Freedley—*New York Morning Telegraph*
". . . the most beguiling, the most enchanting musical piece in many a long day. It is necessary to go back to *Porgy and Bess* to find anything comparable . . . Rodgers' best score in his long and successful career . . ."

Wilella Waldorf—*New York Post*
"After a mild, somewhat monotonous beginning, it suddenly came to life around the middle of the first act, and grew steadily more

entertaining . . . gay and colorful . . . Rodgers' music is invariably pleasant and will grow on you as it is played and replayed. Hammerstein has done a workmanlike job after that first dull stretch, and his lyrics are often bright and amusing . . . the most original and entertaining production the Guild has sponsored in a considerable time."

Burton Rascoe—*New York World-Telegram*
". . . lovely tunes, and an infectious spirit of gaiety and good humor . . . fresh, lively, colorful and enormously pleasing . . . one of the finest musical scores any musical play ever had . . . Next to Rodgers must stand the amazing Agnes de Mille . . . Among the principals, Celeste Holm simply tucked the show under her arm and just let the others touch it . . . The joy of the production is in the total effect . . . the lyrics are bright and amusing . . ."

Ward Morehouse—*New York Sun*
". . . the result is a happy one. It has great charm. It is fresh and diverting. It is inclined to undue slowness at times and monotony creeps in, but it recovers, and by the time they're singing the lusty title song at the finish, you're under the spell of it . . . It reveals Rodgers in good form indeed . . ."

John Anderson—*New York Journal-American*
". . . a beautiful and delightful show, fresh and imaginative, as enchanting to the eye as Rodgers' music is to the ear. It has, at a rough estimate, practically everything . . . a light and colorful libretto . . . some superb dances . . . But it is Rodgers, I suspect, who puts the spell on the evening with a score that ranks with his best . . ."

Jack Pulaski (Ibee.)—*Variety,* April 7, 1943
". . . It is amusingly romantic, has a superlative score, unusual ensemble dance routines and youthful, clever players to provide a diverting evening . . ."

Wolcott Gibbs—*The New Yorker,* April 10, 1943
". . . a completely enchanting performance—gay, stylish, imaginative, and equipped with some of the best music and dancing in a long time . . . In *Oh, What a Beautiful Mornin'* and *Pore Jud Is Daid,* Rodgers and Hammerstein have turned out two songs that are making the members of my family wish more than ever that I could sing on key . . . I feel nothing but the greatest affection for everybody in it. To the Theatre Guild, my gratitude is practically boundless."

Louis Kronenberger—*Time,* April 12, 1943
"... pretty much deserves its exclamation point ... thoroughly refreshing without being oppressively rustic ... nothing much in the way of a book. But Composer Rodgers has turned out one of his most attractive scores ..."

Joseph Wood Krutch—*The Nation,* April 17, 1943
"... one of the most lively, entertaining and colorful musicals it has ever been my privilege to see ... Hammerstein's lyrics are witty ... Perhaps the most important single element is the music, which has a style all its own ... Only two American operettas of the last two decades have been really remembered widely enough to be frequently mentioned—*Show Boat* and *Porgy and Bess. Oklahoma!* is not so ambitious as the last, and it is not so phenominally slick as the first. But personally I like it quite as well as either."

Stark Young—*The New Republic,* April 19, 1943
"... reminds us at times of a good college show ... Rodgers' songs launch the piece and help wing it along. *Oh, What a Beautiful Mornin'* and *People Will Say We're in Love* are full of well-being and happy health, and a whistling, swinging step, with an air of springing out of the sheer impulse to sing and so I sing. The comic songs are witty and friendly, like turns at a birthday party ..."

Olin Downes—*New York Times,* June 6, 1943
"... delightful show. First because of a number of especially good tunes and excellent lyrics, and tasteful and suggestive decor on Americanesque motives, and, above all, because of the dancing that is so original and so expressive of genuine things that lie deep in the people and the soil. And the thing has style ... the sum of the piece indicates a direction that American opera of native cast might take in the period before us ..."

Bibliography

NEWSPAPERS AND PERIODICALS

In Re "Oklahoma!" by Oscar Hammerstein II.
—*New York Times,* May 23, 1943

"Oklahoma!" —*Life,* May 24, 1943

"Oklahoma!"
Comment and 8 caricatures by Birnbaum. —*Vogue,* June 1, 1943

Mr. Rodgers Insists That It Ain't Luck by Richard Rodgers
—*New York Times,* August 1, 1943

"Oklahoma!" Is Year's Best Success Story by Otis Guernsey, Jr.
—*New York Herald Tribune,* August 1, 1943

"Oklahoma!" —*Life,* March 6, 1944

Oklahoma!" by Gov. Robert Kerr of Oklahoma —*Coronet,* June, 1944

Oh, What a Beautiful Mornin' by Lewis Nichols
—*New York Times Magazine,* March 25, 1945

Birthday Girl —*Time,* April 12, 1948

"Oklahoma!" Ends Broadway Run with 2,500% Net on Investment by Murray Schumach —*New York Times,* May 30, 1948

"Oklahoma!" Seven Years Later by Robert W. Glasgow
—*New York Herald Tribune,* May 7, 1950

"Oklahoma!" Rolls on Like Perennial Brook —*Variety,* May 31, 1950

Nothing the Same After "Oklahoma!" by Richard Rodgers
—*New York Herald Tribune,* May 27, 1951

"Oklahoma!"—the Champ by Paul Gardner and John Friedkin
—*Cosmopolitan,* May, 1953

No Legs No Jokes No Chance by Helene Hanff
—*Harper's Magazine,* March, 1961

Oh, What a Beautiful Musical by Alan Jay Lerner
—*New York Times Magazine,* May 12, 1963

A New Hit Opens at P.S. 28 in Harlem: "Oklahoma!" by M. A. Farber
"Ado Annie Is Gone and Pore Jud Lives in Pupils' Version"
—*New York Times,* February 23, 1966

"Oklahoma!" Introduced New Musical Theatre Form 25 Years Ago by Del Carnes —*Denver Post,* March 17, 1968

"Oklahoma!" by Frank Gagnard
—*New Orleans Times-Picayune,* March 17, 1968

In the Beginning Was "Oklahoma!" by Walter Kerr
—*New York Times,* March 24, 1968

Oh, What a Beautiful 25-Year-Old Musical by William Glover
—*Associated Press,* March 27, 1968

"Oklahoma!" Anniversary Celebrated by Jack Gaver
—*United Press International,* March 27, 1968

"Oklahoma!" Fills Philharmonic in First Concert Performance by Vincent Canby —*New York Times,* March 27, 1968

You're Still Doin' Fine, "Oklahoma!" by Richard Christiansen
—*Chicago Daily News,* March 30, 1968

To "Oklahoma!" by Celeste Holm —*Look,* April 2, 1968

Philharmonic Marks "Oklahoma!" 25th by Robert J. Landry
—*Variety,* April 3, 1968

Oklahoma, OK! —*Newsweek,* April 8, 1968

BOOKS

Oklahoma! (Random House, New York, 1943)
Book and lyrics of the musical.

Awards

Special Pulitzer Prize for Drama, 1944
Original Cast Album, NARAS Hall of Fame, 1976

Tour

Opera House, Boston, May 31, 1948—Auditorium, Barre, Vt., May 21, 1949 (67 cities).

OKLAHOMA!

(Touring Company—1943)

Music director, Arthur Norris

The Cast

AUNT ELLER MURPHY, Mary Marlo
CURLY MC LAIN, Harry Stockwell (danced by Charles Laskey)
LAUREY WILLIAMS, Evelyn Wyckoff (danced by Dania Krupska)
IKE SKIDMORE, Al Webster
FRED, Jack Kilty
SLIM, Victor Young
WILL PARKEP, Walter Donahue
JUD FRY, Lou Polan (danced by Alfred Cibelli)
ADO ANNIE CARNES, Pamela Britton
ALI HAKIM, David Burns
GERTIE CUMMINGS, Katharine Barratt
ELLEN, Dania Krupska
KATE, Mildred Todd
SYLVIE, Sonia Wojcikowska
ARMINA, Katherine Litz
AGGIE, Gemze de Lappe
ANDREW CARNES, David Mallon
CORD ELAM, Eugene Keith
JESS, Robert Early
CHALMERS, Charles Laskey
MIKE, Lloyd Cole
JOE, Jerry Clayton
SAM, Alfred Cibelli
SINGERS: Sonny Daye, Lois Higgins, Rosalind Madison, Miriam Marshall, Bonita Bimrose (Primrose), Phyllis Reed, Claire Stevens, Shirley Winsten

DANCERS: Frances Spelz, Lois Gerard, Patricia O'Bryne, Peggy Campbell, Neville Cummings, Paula Kaye, Harriet Roeder, Bevann Schnebly, Virginia Meyer; Lyle Clark, Harding Blum, Maxwell Coker, Payne Converse, Arthur Filiault, John Miller, Ernest Richman

NOTE: Mr. Stockwell succeeded by John Raitt (June 1944), James Alexander (April 1945), Ridge Bond (Nov. 1947), Ralph Lowe (Aug. 1952), Mr. Bond (Aug. 1953). Miss Wyckoff by Betty Jane Watson (July 1944), Mary Hatcher (Aug. 1945), Peggy Engel (Aug. 1946), Ann Crowley (Oct. 1947), Marilyn Landers (Feb. 1948), Carolyn Adair (Oct. 1948), Patricia Northrop (Aug. 1949), Patricia Johnson (Sept. 1951), Florence Henderson (Aug. 1952). Miss Britton by Dorothea MacFarland (March 1945) Patricia Englund (Dec. 1946), Sara Dillon (Sept. 1949), Jacqueline Sundt (Sept. 1950), Jacqueline Daniels (Aug. 1952), Barbara Cook (Aug. 1953).

Tour

Shubert Theatre, New Haven, October 15, 1943—Convention Hall, Atlantic City, June 11, 1949 (128 cities).

His Majesty's Theatre, Montreal, August 25, 1949—Erlanger Theatre, Chicago, July 22, 1950 (62 cities).

Nixon Theatre, Pittsburgh, September 4, 1950—Auditorium, Rochester, March 15, 1952 (92 cities, incl. Berlin).

Shubert Theatre, New Haven, August 29, 1952—National Theatre, Washington, May 9, 1953 (61 cities).

New York City Center, August 31, 1953—Shubert Theatre, Philadelphia, May 1, 1954 (18 cities).

Tour Reviews

New Haven Journal-Courier
". . . equally as good as the first fine company . . . perhaps a shade better singing in this new group . . . beautiful music . . ."

Nelson B. Bell—*Washington Post*
"Such a musical play as is vouchsafed American audiences only once in a generation—or two, or three . . . fulfilled all the encomiums heaped on it in advance . . . the perfect blending of narrative, music, pungent lyrics and choreography . . ."

Jay Carmody—*Washington Evening Star*
". . . it is simply all that has been said of it . . . amazing, melodious piece of folklore . . . Its every element fuses perfectly with every other . . . fresh and refreshing musical score . . . For once, the whole of an operetta is greater than the sum of its parts . . ."

W. Ward Marsh—*Cleveland Plain Dealer*
". . . I cannot recall a more exuberant play. Or one filled with such springtime colors . . . a Rodgers score of the highest quality, and Hammerstein has composed lyrics which are as dramatic as the best in minstrelsy . . . 'road company' is first rate . . ."

Omar Ranney—*Cleveland Press*
". . . makes you feel good . . . an artfully woven dramatic fabric . . . filled to overflowing with gaiety and freshness and light-heartedness . . . a company that actually tops the New York Company . . . catchy, lilting tunes . . ."

Claudia Cassidy—*Chicago Daily Tribune*
"Fresh and gay and shining, witty and colorful, spilling melody from a lovely score . . . irresistibly entertaining . . . the best musical since *Show Boat* . . . a show with just about everything . . ."

Edward P. Hallins—*Milwaukee Sentinel*
". . . a story of substance . . . Outside of the best operas, the musical stage never has been so packed with sheer excitement . . ."

Len G. Shaw—*Detroit Free Press*
"As breezy and occasionally as sultry as the state from which it derives its title . . . story and song are fused so expertly that each complements the other perfectly to bring forth rollicking down-to-earth diversion . . ."

E. B. Radcliffe—*Cincinnati Enquirer*
". . . an extraordinary musical show that lives up to all the fine things that have been said about it . . . a company whose work is on a par with that of the original . . . just a helluva show . . ."

Linton Martin—*Philadelphia Inquirer*
"There's plenty of reason for hat-tossing, belfry ringing and dancing in the streets . . . fabulous, fantastic musical hit . . ."

Elliot Norton—*Boston Post*
". . . fresh, skillful, tuneful, high spirited, amusing, and in some ways, exciting . . . This is no 'second company.' It is an alternate company which man for man, and girl for girl, can't be topped . . ."

Rudolph Elie, Jr.—*Boston Herald*
". . . nothing tired or shopworn or 'road company' about this one . . . Rodgers' tunes are so good and have caught on so much, a lot of people in the audience feel called upon to hum them along with the cast. I don't know, maybe I was doing it myself."

George L. David—*Rochester Democrat-Chronicle*
". . . mighty well worth all the waitin' and wonderin'. Yes, sirs and madames, no foolin'. This is somethin', plural plus . . . extraordinary entertainment; it is a superb artistic achievement . . . What a show!"

John Hobart—*San Francisco Chronicle*
". . . a wonderful and beautiful show . . . it is being played with all the freshness, skill and enthusiasm that it deserves . . . an enchanting musical score and inspired book and lyrics . . . exhilarating . . ."

Alexander Fried—*San Francisco Examiner*
". . . has the priceless quality of making a person feel good all over . . . the tunes are as captivating as ever . . . a warmly human and comical book . . . the best musical show in American stage history . . ."

Patrick S. Catling—*Baltimore Sun*
". . . the best musical comedy that I have ever seen . . ."

John Rosenfield—*Dallas Morning News*
". . . the cast was young and personable . . . the Hammerstein comedy and lyrics are still laughable, and the Rodgers music still verdant if no longer crisp . . ."

Brooks Atkinson—*New York Times*
". . . If it never had been staged before, it could not have had a fresher performance . . . The songs are classics not merely because they have been sung so often. They are classics because they are romantically true . . . Hammerstein's workmanship has a purity of style that is becoming . . . Everyone deserves a special vote of thanks for preserving the lyrical innocence of a theatrical work that we all have great affection for."

Otis Guernsey, Jr.—*New York Herald Tribune*
". . . stands on its own seemingly timeless merits of melody and gaiety as richly bright as its golden yellow color scheme. Well rehearsed after its three years on the road; with production all spic and span, and with the extra enthusiasm that the company brings to its Broadway appearance, it is as near to a foolproof entertainment as may be seen in our time . . ."

John Chapman—*New York Daily News*
"It is just what it has always been—the perfect musical. It is clean, funny, pretty and fresh, and its tunes and lyrics are among the best in the American theatre . . ."

Vernon Rice—*New York Post*
". . . So much is *Oklahoma!* the show, like Oklahoma the state, we're now using the title song as our state song. Soon we'll be admitting we named the state after the show."

William Hawkins—*New York World-Telegram & Sun*
"One look at it, and you see why it has become a classic. It is still so fresh and strong and bright, and its score so grand, for all the familiarity that tempts you to sing every number aloud . . ."

Robert Garland—*New York Journal-American*
". . . Not even the first cast had more style and substance than the cast now projecting it . . ."

Whitney Bolton—*New York Morning Telegraph*
". . . The theatre is well aware of the debt it owes to Messrs. Rodgers and Hammerstein, but I think one of their shows, like *Oklahoma!,* must be done on occasion to renew awareness of this debt and to revel once again in the lush, rich creations they have made."

Hobe Morrison—*Variety,* June 6, 1951
". . . if the excitement of discovery is now missing, it is offset by the emotional overtones of the by now established popularity of the music and lyrics . . . remains an irresistible show whose appeal is not lessened by familiarity . . ."

Harold Bone—*Variety,* September 3, 1952 (New Haven)
". . . In its fifth local stand, show drew a brand of playgoer, many of whom were seeing the inside of the Shubert for the first time. The sum total of the reaction was highly enthusiastic . . . Castwise, the troupe is on a par with previous national company players . . ."

Walter F. Kerr—*New York Herald Tribune*
"*Eleven Years Young* . . . The balance of the company aren't as exhilarating as Miss Henderson, but they are an agreeable lot . . . It's still a beautiful morning."

Robert Coleman—*New York Daily Mirror*
". . . At a $3 top, it is a real entertainment bargain."

Richard Watts, Jr.—*New York Post*
". . . the songs remain not only as gay and lovely as ever but continue in some oddly touching fashion to sing gallantly of the morning freshness of an innocent world . . . what *Oklahoma!* lacks in smoothness and proficiency, it makes up for in dewy freshness . . ."

John McClain—*New York Journal-American*
". . . it is lacking in ingenuity and laughs; but it is lifted to a high level by the constant brilliance of the music and by the pace of the performance. The current company is excellent . . ."

Tour Bibliography
"Oklahoma!" On Tour by Jack Goodman
—*New York Times*, February 25, 1951

Selected Revivals

St. Louis Municipal Opera, August 16-29, 1954
William Johnson (CURLY); Elise Rhodes (LAUREY); Pamela Britton (ADO ANNIE); Hal LeRoy (WILL); Edith Gresham (ELLER); Jerry Mann (ALI); Norman MacKaye (JUD); Gretchen Wyler (GERTIE).

New York City Center Light Opera, March 19-30, 1958
Herbert Banke (CURLY); Lois O'Brien (LAUREY); Helen Gallagher (ADO ANNIE); Gene Nelson (WILL); Betty Garde (ELLER); Harvey Lembeck (ALI); Gemze de Lappe (SYLVIE); Patricia Birsh (Birch) (DANCER).

Dallas State Fair Music Hall, June 23-July 6, 1958
Rusty Draper (CURLY); Jane Powell (LAUREY); Michele Burke (ADO ANNIE); Jonathan Bush (WILL); Leora Thatcher (ELLER); Mort Marshall (ALI); Lee Cass (JUD).

St. Louis Municipal Opera, August 18-31, 1958
Jack Drummond (CURLY); Dorothy Collins (LAUREY); Helen Gallagher (ADO ANNIE); Hal LeRoy (WILL); Mary Marlo (ELLER); Joey Faye (ALI); Michael Kermoyan (JUD).

San Francisco Civic Light Opera, July 20-August 22, 1959
Los Angeles Civic Light Opera, August 24-October 3, 1959
James Hurst (CURLY); Jacqueline McKeever (LAUREY); Helen Gallagher (ADO ANNIE); Bobby Van (WILL); Reta Shaw (ELLER); Jules Munshin (ALI); Murvyn Vye (JUD); Bruce Yarnell (TOM).

San Juan Drama Festival, Puerto Rico, July 31-August 5, 1961
Stanley Grover (CURLY); Nancy Dussault (LAUREY); Helen Gallagher (ADO ANNIE).

St. Louis Municipal Opera, August 6-12, 1962
Peter Palmer (CURLY); Louise O'Brien (LAUREY); Paula Wayne (ADO ANNIE); Richard France (WILL); Margaret Hamilton (ELLER); Joseph Leon (ALI); Edmund Lyndeck (JUD).

New York City Center Light Opera, Feb. 27-March 10, 1963; May 15-26, 1963
Peter Palmer (CURLY); Louise O'Brien (LAUREY); Ann Fraser (ADO ANNIE); Richard France (WILL); Betty Garde (ELLER); Gabriel Dell (ALI); Daniel P. Hannafin (JUD). For return engagement, Miss Fraser succeeded by Fay DeWitt, Mr. Dell by Barry Newman.

Westbury Music Fair, Long Island, September 17-22, 1963
Fess Parker (CURLY); Joan Weldon (LAUREY); Jayme Mylroie (ADO ANNIE); Michael Dominico (WILL); Lu Leonard (ELLER); Joseph Leon (ALI); Renato Cibelli (JUD).

The White House, Washington, July 27, 1964
Abridged version in honor of President and Mrs. Philbert Tsirnan of the Malagasy Republic. Peter Palmer (CURLY); Shirley Jones (LAUREY); Richard France (WILL); Lu Leonard (ELLER).

New York City Center Light Opera, December 15, 1965-January 2, 1966
John Davidson (CURLY); Susan Watson (LAUREY); Karen Morrow (ADO ANNIE); Richard France (WILL); Ruth Kobart (ELLER); Jules Munshin (ALI); Daniel P. Hannafin (JUD).

Dallas State Fair Music Hall, July 11-23, 1966
Allen Case (CURLY); Linda Michelle (LAUREY); Marilyn Cooper (ADO ANNIE); Joel Warfield (WILL); Mary Loane (ELLER); Phil Leeds (ALI); Gene Rupert (JUD).

St. Louis Municipal Opera, July 25-31, 1966
Robert Horton (CURLY); Marilynn Horton (LAUREY); Gaylea Byrne (ADO ANNIE); Michael Fesco (WILL); Dawna Shove (ELLER); Tim Herbert (ALI); Joshua Hecht (JUD).

Philharmonic Hall, Lincoln Center, New York, March 26, 1968
Concert performance on musical's 25th anniversary. John Davidson (CURLY); Constance Towers (LAUREY); Anita Gillette (ADO ANNIE); Joseph Bova (WILL); Margaret Hamilton (ELLER); Howard DaSilva (JUD); Camarata Singers; New York Philharmonic Symphony Orchestra, Skitch Henderson and Richard Rodgers, cond.

Music Theater of Lincoln Center, June 23-September 6, 1969
Bruce Yarnell (CURLY); Lee Beery (LAUREY); April Shawhan (ADO ANNIE); Lee Roy Reams (WILL); Margaret Hamilton (ELLER); Ted Beniades (ALI); Spiro Malas (JUD).

St. Louis Municipal Opera, July 27-August 2, 1970
Jerry Lanning (CURLY); Susan Watson (LAUREY); Patti Karr (ADO ANNIE); Richard France (WILL); Ruth Gillette (ELLER); Bert Parks (ALI); Daniel P. Hannafin (JUD).

Jones Beach Marine Theatre, Long Island, June 27-August 31, 1975
Thomas McKinney (CURLY); Judith McCauley (LAUREY); Patricia Masters (ADO ANNIE); Harvey Evans (WILL); Nancy Andrews (ELLER); Bruce Adler (ALI); Will Roy (JUD).

St. Louis Municipal Opera, July 17-23, 1978
John McCook (CURLY); Carol Wilcox (LAUREY); Barbara Sharma (ADO ANNIE); Terry Emo (WILL); Mary Wickes (ELLER); Stubby Kaye (ALI); Robert Darnell (JUD).

Miami Beach Theatre of Performing Arts, January 4, 1979
Harve Presnell (CURLY); Betsy Beard (LAUREY); Maureen Moore (ADO ANNIE); David Eric (WILL); Mary Wickes (ELLER); Lewis J. Stadlen (ALI); Alexander Orfaly (JUD). Note: This was beginning of tour.

Pantages Theatre, Los Angeles, May 1, 1979
Laurence Guittard (CURLY); Christine Andreas (LAUREY); Christine Ebersole (ADO ANNIE); Harry Groener (WILL); Mary Wickes (ELLER); Jamie Farr (ALI); Martin Vidnovic (JUD). Directed by William Hammerstein. NOTE: This was beginning of tour that included Kennedy Center, Washington, and Oklahoma City, where, at the invitation of the governor, it was presented in honor of the 72nd anniversary of Oklahoma's statehood. On December 13, 1979, this production opened at the Palace Theatre, New York.

Productions Abroad

Pacific Army Base Tour, February 26-October, 1945
Presented by USO Camp Shows Inc.; supervised by Ted Hammerstein; choreography by Vivian Smith. *Cast:* Robert Lyon (CURLY); Gloria Hamilton (LAUREY); Bonita Bimrose (Primrose) (ADO ANNIE); James Parnell (WILL); Florence Dunlap (ELLER); Jack Starr (ALI); Lou Polan (JUD). *Tour:* Camp Kilmer, New Jersey; Hollandia, Dutch New Guinea; Leyte, Panay, Mindanao, Mindoro, Luzon, all in the Philippines.

Theatre Royal, Drury Lane, London, April 29, 1947-May 27, 1950
(See page 526)

His Majesty's Theatre, Johannesburg, South Africa, December 23, 1948
Presented by African Consolidated Theatres Ltd.; directed by Philip D. Levard; choreography reproduced by Erik Kristen. *Cast:* Robert Lyon (CURLY); LaVerne Burden (LAUREY); Bonita Primrose (ADO ANNIE); Orville Sherman (WILL); Florence Dunlap (ELLER); David Morris (ALI); Bob Nash (JUD). *Tour:* Pretoria, March 28, 1949—Bulawayo, November 12, 1949 (9 cities).

His Majesty's Theatre, Melbourne, Australia, February 19, 1949 (8 months)
Presented by J. C. Williamson Theatres Ltd.; directed by Ted Hammerstein; choreography reproduced by Gemze deLappe. *Cast:* Robert Reeves (CURLY); Carolyn Adair (LAUREY); Louise Bernhardt (ADO ANNIE); William Redd Knight (WILL); Davie Gladstone (ELLER); Harold Gary (ALI); Robert Grandin (JUD). *Tour:* Brisbane, Sydney, New Zealand.

Nørrebros Teater, Copenhagen, Denmark, March 30-December 18, 1949; February 21-March 19, 1950; *228 performances.*
Translated by Holger Bech; directed by Kai Wilton; choreography by Niels Bjørn Larsen. *Cast:* Hans Kurt (CURLY); Else Marie (LAUREY); Grethe Holmer (ADO ANNIE); Poul Bundgaard (WILL); Elga Olga (ELLER); Buster Larsen (ALI); Bjørn Spiro (JUD).

Det Norske Teatret, Oslo, Norway, June 7-Sept. 30, 1949
Translated by Eli Oftedal; directed by Øivind Bergh; choreography by Svenäge Larsen. *Cast:* Gösta Kjellertz (CURLY); Randi Lindtner Naess (LAUREY); Eva Strøm Aastrop (ADO ANNIE); Toms Asbjørn (WILL); Ragnhild Michelsen (ELLER); Harald Heide Steen (JUD); Alf Sommer (ALI).

Lyriska Teater, Göteborg, Sweden, Sept. 29, 1950
Directed by Egon Kjerrman; choreography by Svenäge Larsen. *Cast:* Arne Hasselblad (CURLY); Berit Kjerrman (LAUREY); Maj Lindström (ADO ANNIE); Jackie Söderman (WILL); Märta Ternstedt (ELLER); Claes Jakobsson (JUD); Rutger Nygren (ALI).

Théatre des Champs-Elysées, Paris, June 20-July 3, 1955
ANTA "Salute to France" production; directed by Rouben Mamoulian; choreography by Agnes de Mille. *Cast:* Jack Cassidy (CURLY); Shirley Jones (LAUREY); Pamela Britton (ADO ANNIE); Harrison Muller (WILL); Edith Gresham (ELLER); C. K. Alexander (ALI); Clark Winters (JUD). *Tour:* Rome, Naples, Milan, Venice, July 9-August 16, 1955.

Takarazuka Theatre, Tokyo, September 2-26, 1967
Presented by the Takarazuka Revue Co.; translated by Iwao Mori and Hideyuki Kawai; directed and choreography reproduced by Gemze de Lappe. *Cast:* Noboru Kozuki (CURLY); Jun Hatzukase (LAUREY); Mari Yashioji (ADO ANNIE); Harumi Suga (WILL); Tamamo Mizushiro (ELLER); Harumi Yaye (ALI); Miyako Koshiro (JUD). Note: This was an all-female company.

OKLAHOMA!

(London Production—1947)

Presented by H. M. Tennent Ltd.
Restaged by Jerome Whyte
Miss de Mille's choreography reproduced by Gemze de Lappe
Settings by Lemuel Ayers
Costumes by Miles White
Music director, Salvatore Dell'Isola
Orchestrations by Robert Russell Bennett

London Run

Theatre Royal, Drury Lane, April 29, 1947-May 27, 1950
Stoll Theatre, May 29-October 21, 1950
1,548 performances

NOTE: Until it was overtaken by *My Fair Lady* on January 10, 1962, *Oklahoma!*, with 1,380 performances, was the longest-running production in the history of Drury Lane, which first opened its doors in 1663.

The Cast

AUNT ELLER MURPHY, Mary Marlo
CURLY MCLAIN, Harold (Howard) Keel (danced by Erik Kristen)
LAUREY WILLIAMS, Betty Jane Watson (danced by Gemze de Lappe)

IKE SKIDMORE, Thomas Spencer
FRED, Elliott Martin
SLIM, William Sutherland
WILL PARKER, Walter Donahue
JUD FRY, Henry Clarke (danced by Remington Olmstead, Jr.)
ADO ANNIE CARNES, Dorothea MacFarland
ALI HAKIM, Marek Windheim
GERTIE CUMMINGS, Jacqueline Daniels
ELLEN, Suzanne Lloyd
KATE, Marjorie Austin
SYLVIE, Beatrice Lynn
ARMINA, Isabel Bigley
TERRY, Gemze de Lappe
AGGIE, Margaret Auld Nelson
ANDREW CARNES, William S. McCarthy
CORD ELAM, Leonard Mence
JESS, Remington Olmstead, Jr.
CHALMERS, Erik Kristen
JOE, Walter Peterson
SAM, Robert Patterson
SINGERS: Suzanne Lloyd, Marjorie Austin, Elise Klingerman, Marianne Peterson, Louise Barnhart, Margot Moser, Isabel Bigley, Brender Barker, William Sutherland, Walter Peterson, Robert Patterson, Elliot Martin, Eddie Farrell, Stan Thomason, Earl Young, Peter Evans
DANCERS: George Stecher, Maxwell Coker, Lemoine Ketcham, Eugene Wilson, Payne Converse, Grehan Pearce, William Clarke

NOTE: During run, Miss Marlo succeeded by Jennie Gregson; Mr. Keel by Chris Robinson; Miss Watson by Ann Crowley and Isabel Bigley; Miss MacFarland by Patricia Englund; Mr. Windheim by Harry Ross; Mr. Clarke by Earl MacVeigh.

Musical Numbers

Same as original production.

Reviews

A. V. Cookman—*London Times*

". . . this musical comedy has some things to teach the English light stage . . . a simple, hearty little tale . . . It is remarkable, especially in the long first part, how decoratively the stage is filled with one or two figures, reinforced at exactly the right moment by a modest chorus of half a dozen . . . it would be almost literally true to say that there is never a dull moment."

W. A. Darlington—*London Daily Telegraph*

". . . a terrific show. For drive and vitality, I don't remember to have seen anything like it . . . The Theatre Guild generally has a soul above 'musicals' and it is refreshing to see the highbrows beating the popular managers at their own game."

Leonard Mosley—*London Daily Express*
". . . a gem, a jewel in Drury Lane's crown. It is one of those musical plays, I believe, that will carve a niche in the memories of all who see it and hear its songs . . . What is enchanting in it is the deft, felicitous melange of colour, song and energy, and the way the company has of bringing you in as part of the show . . ."

Lionel Hale—*London Daily Mail*
". . . This smash hit is not an evening of stars—it is color plus music plus wit plus dancing, put together with a sort of inspired single-mindedness to re-create on stage the young people of a youthful part of the earth . . ."

A. E. Wilson—*London Star*
". . . likely to duplicate the astonishing success it has long enjoyed on Broadway . . . It lacks elaborate spectacle and scenery but who misses that when in the music there is such tuneful delight, when there are such good voices and such graceful dancing . . ."

P. L. Mannock—*London Daily Herald*
". . . the most exciting first night Old Drury has known since *Cavalcade* and the best American musical piece for 20 years . . . Rodgers' numbers, artfully blending simplicity and cunning, all have strong appeal and are free from jazz . . ."

James Agate—*London Sunday Times,* May 4, 1947
". . . Bouquet, yes; body, no . . . a whole merchant's venture in shadow without any hint of substance . . . it is best when it has least plot . . . production sizzles with slickness . . ."

J. C. Trewin—*London Observer,* May 4, 1947
". . . deliberately rejects roaring spectacle . . . Everything is very simple—but of what a complex simplicity! . . . For once, all that happens on the stage is significant . . . Rodgers has managed to make an expert, exciting (and how singable!) pastiche . . . The plot is always serviceable . . ."

Bibliography

"Oklahoma!" Wins Ovation in London —*New York Sun,* May 1, 1947

Lend-Lease in the Theatre by W. Macqueen-Pope —*Everybody's Weekly,* June 19, 1947

"Oklahoma!" —*Theatre World,* August, 1947

Ballet in "Oklahoma!" —*Picture Post,* August 9, 1947

"Oklahoma!" by John Courtenay —*The Sketch,* August 20, 1947

"Oklahoma!" Closes in London after 3½ Years Stay with Gross Take of $4,300,000 —*Variety*, October 25, 1950

OKLAHOMA!

(Film Version—1955)

Distributed by Magna Theatre Corporation
Presented by Messrs. Rodgers and Hammerstein
Produced by Arthur Hornblow, Jr.
Directed by Fred Zinnemann
Screenplay by Sonya Levien and William Ludwig
Choreography by Agnes de Mille
Production designed by Oliver Smith
Costumes by Orry Kelly and Motley
Production aide, John Fearnley
Music director, Jay Blackton
Orchestrations by Robert Russell Bennett
Background music adapted by Adolph Deutsch
Photographed by Robert Surtees
Editor, Gene Ruggiero
Filmed in Todd-AO
Color by Eastman Color

Release Date

October 11, 1955

NOTE: On November 1, 1956, the film was rereleased by Twentieth Century-Fox and shown in Cinemascope.

The Cast

CURLY MCLAIN, Gordon MacRae (danced by James Mitchell)
ADO ANNIE CARNES, Gloria Grahame
LAUREY WILLIAMS, Shirley Jones (danced by Bambi Linn)
AUNT ELLER MURPHY, Charlotte Greenwood
ALI HAKIM, Eddie Albert
WILL PARKER, Gene Nelson
ANDREW CARNES, James Whitmore
JUD FRY, Rod Steiger
IKE SKIDMORE, J. C. Flippen
GERTIE CUMMINGS, Barbara Lawrence
MARSHAL, Roy Barcroft
DANCERS: Jenny Workman, Kelly Brown, Lizanne Truex, Virginia Bosler, Evelyn Taylor, Jane Fischer, Marc Platt

Musical Numbers

Same as original production with exception of *It's a Scandal! It's a Outrage!* and *Lonely Room,* which were dropped.

Reviews

Bosley Crowther—*New York Times*
". . . magnifies and strengthens all the charm that it had upon the stage. A full-bodied *Oklahoma!* has been brought forth in this film to match in vitality, eloquence and melody any musical this reviewer has ever seen . . ."

William K. Zinsser—*New York Herald Tribune*
". . . fortunately it is true to the original . . . Todd-AO is best in closeups . . . gay to look at . . ."

Archer Winsten—*New York Post*
". . . the whole entertainment has to rest on those massive and marvelous foundations, the songs. If it weren't for them this would be a very big but ordinary picture . . ."

Alton Cook—*New York World-Telegram & Sun*
". . . News about Todd-AO is less cheery than the report on *Oklahoma!* itself. Fred Zinnemann has directed his players with a determination to be bursting with happy jollity in every tune or step of the way . . . a lush and bountiful version, never allowing its sumptuous trimmings to blot out its basic simplicity."

Fred Hift—*Variety*
". . . There must be reservations registered on the technical end, but otherwise it emerges as a fresh, crisply acted and beautifully sung concoction. It's an outstanding b.o. attraction, of course . . ."

John McCarten—*The New Yorker,* October 22, 1955
"*Act of Todd* . . . has an air of magniloquence hardly suited to the simple rusticity of the theme. The principal reason for this pomposity is that it was filmed in something called Todd-AO . . . The picture does have the virtue of sticking closely to the original script, and there are times when the songs and dances blend together with a kind of noisy charm . . ."

Time, October 24, 1955
". . . one of the biggest musicals ever put on the screen . . . bears about as much relation to the Broadway *Oklahoma!* as a 1956 Cadillac does to the surrey with the fringe on top . . . in spite of its age and the fact that its 145-minute mass is sometimes dragging, it hollers itself home as a handsome piece of entertainment . . . It is as simple and innocent as a birthday cake, in which the songs are set as naturally as candles—and dazzling good songs they still are . . ."

Arthur Knight—*Saturday Review,* November 5, 1955
"*What Hath Todd Wrought?* . . . Its melodies still have their accus-

tomed lilt, the Hammerstein lyrics are still remarkably agile in the comedy numbers, remarkably sweet in the ballads . . . But this *Oklahoma!* insists on the obvious . . . a lumbering and somewhat tedious throwback . . ."

Jesse Zunser—*Cue,* November 19, 1955
"When the movie opened, this department praised the picture but sharply criticized the distortions in the film's print and method of projection . . . These perspective weaknesses have now been largely corrected . . . It is now as beautiful visually as it is aurally—and without reservations, it is now given our highest recommendation."

Bibliography

"Oklahoma!" by Ed Sullivan —*New York Daily News,* March 20, 1955

Biggest Movie News of the Year by Louis Berg —*This Week,* April 24, 1955

Ev'rythin's Up to Date . . . —*Life,* May 2, 1955

"Oklahoma!" in Progress to Screen by Richard Dyer MacCann —*Christian Science Monitor,* May 24, 1955

Awards

Motion Picture Academy Awards, 1955
Best Scoring of a Musical Film, Messrs. Blackton, Russell, Deutsch
Best Sound Recording, Fred Hynes, Todd-AO Sound Dept.

CAROUSEL

(1945)

A musical play with book and lyrics by Oscar Hammerstein II based on the play "Liliom" by Ferenc Molnar, as adapted by Benjamin F. Glazer; music by Richard Rodgers.

Presented by the Theatre Guild
Directed by Rouben Mamoulian
Choreography by Agnes de Mille
Settings by Jo Mielziner
Costumes by Miles White
Music director, Joseph Littau
Orchestrations by Don Walker
Dance arrangements by Trude Rittmann
Production supervised by Theresa Helburn and Lawrence Langner

Tryout
Shubert Theatre, New Haven, March 22-25, 1945
Colonial Theatre, Boston, March 27-April 15, 1945

New York Run
Majestic Theatre, April 19, 1945-May 24, 1947
890 performances

The Story
Julie, a young factory worker, goes to the carnival, meets Billy, a young barker. They fall in love and marry. Billy loses his job, and when Julie is about to have a child, becomes involved in a robbery, and is killed. He goes to heaven. Years later, he is permitted to return to earth to see his daughter graduate from school. Billy gives her a star he has stolen, but she rejects it in fear and mistrust. Billy talks to her at length, and gives the lonely girl a new confidence. He then returns to heaven.

The Cast
CARRIE PIPPERIDGE, Jean Darling
JULIE JORDAN, Jan Clayton
MRS. MULLIN, Jean Casto
BILLY BIGELOW, John Raitt

BESSIE, Mimi Strongin
JESSIE, Jimsie Somers
JUGGLER, Lew Foldes
1ST POLICEMAN, Robert Byrn
DAVID BASCOMBE, Franklyn Fox
NETTIE FOWLER, Christine Johnson
JUNE GIRL, Pearl Lang
ENOCH SNOW, Eric Mattson
JIGGER CRAIGIN, Murvyn Vye
HANNAH, Annabelle Lyon
BOATSWAIN, Peter Birch
ARMINY, Connie Baxter
PENNY, Marilyn Merkt
JENNIE, Joan Keenan
VIRGINIA, Ginna Moise
SUSAN, Suzanne Tafel
JONATHAN, Richard H. Gordon
2ND POLICEMAN, Larry Evers
CAPTAIN, Blaker Ritter
1ST HEAVENLY FRIEND *(Brother Joshua),* Jay Velie
2ND HEAVENLY FRIEND, Tom McDuffie
STARKEEPER, Russell Collins
LOUISE, Bambi Linn
CARNIVAL BOY, Robert Pagent
ENOCH SNOW, JR., Ralph Linn
PRINCIPAL, Lester Freedman
SINGERS: Martha Carver, Iva Withers, Anne Calvert, Connie Baxter, Glory Wills, Josephine Collins, Marilyn Merkt, Joan Keenan, Ginna Moise, Beatrice Miller, Suzanne Tafel, Verlyn Webb; Joseph Bell, Robert Byrn, Tom Duffey, Blake Ritter, Charles Leighton, Louis Freed, Neil Chirico, Lester Freedman, Richard H. Gordon, John Harrold
DANCERS: Pearl Lang, Andrea Downing, Margaret Cuddy, Polly Welch, Diane Chadwicke, Ruth Miller, Lu Lanterbar, Margaretta DeValera, Lynn Joelson, Sonia Joroff, Elena Salamatova, Marjory Svetlik, Ernest Richman, Tom Avera, Larry Evers, Ralph Linn, Tony Matthews, David Ahdar

NOTE: During August, 1945, and from June, to September, 1946, Mr. Raitt replaced by Harold (Howard) Keel. In January 1947, Mr. Raitt succeeded by Henry Michel. In December, 1945, Miss Clayton by Iva Withers. In November, 1946, Mr. Vye by John Conte. In April, 1947, Miss Darling by Connie Baxter. For tour, Miss Baxter by Ann Crowley. During tour, Mr. Michel by Stephen Douglass, Miss Crowley by Margot Moser.

Musical Numbers

TIME: 1873-1888

PRELUDE—AN AMUSEMENT PARK ON THE NEW ENGLAND COAST

Carousel Waltz, ORCHESTRA

ACT I

SCENE ONE—A TREE-LINED PATH ALONG THE SHORE

You're a Queer One, Julie Jordan, CARRIE and JULIE
Mister Snow, CARRIE
If I Loved You, BILLY and JULIE

SCENE TWO—NETTIE FOWLER'S SPA ON THE OCEAN FRONT

June Is Bustin' Out All Over, NETTIE, CARRIE and ENSEMBLE; danced by JUNE GIRL and DANCING ENSEMBLE
Reprise, *Mister Snow,* CARRIE and GIRLS
When the Children Are Asleep, MR. SNOW and CARRIE
Blow High, Blow Low, JIGGER, BILLY and MEN; hornpipe dance led by HANNAH and BOATSWAIN
Soliloquy, BILLY
Finale, BILLY, JIGGER, NETTIE, and CHORUS

ACT II

SCENE ONE—ON AN ISLAND ACROSS THE BAY

A Real Nice Clambake, CARRIE, NETTIE, JULIE, MR. SNOW and ENSEMBLE
Geraniums in the Winder, MR. SNOW
There's Nothin' So Bad for a Woman, JIGGER and ENSEMBLE
What's the Use of Wond'rin', JULIE

SCENE TWO—MAINLAND WATERFRONT

You'll Never Walk Alone, NETTIE

SCENE THREE—UP THERE

The Highest Judge of All, BILLY

SCENE FOUR—DOWN HERE

Ballet
LOUISE, Bambi Linn
A YOUNGER MISS SNOW, Annabelle Lyon
THE BROTHERS AND SISTERS SNOW, Betta Striegler, Lynn Joelson, Sonia Joroff, Fern Whitney, Gisella Svetlik
BADLY BROUGHT UP BOYS, Ralph Linn, Robert Tucker
A YOUNG MAN LIKE BILLY, Robert Pagent
A CARNIVAL WOMAN, Pearl Lang
MEMBERS OF THE CARNIVAL TROUPE: Robert Pagent, Pearl Lang, Beth Nichols, Lawrence Evers, Elena Salamatova, Sidney Stamvaugh, Susan Svetlik, Nathan Baker, Margaret Cuddy, Frank Marasco

SCENE FIVE—OUTSIDE JULIE'S COTTAGE

Reprise, *If I Loved You,* BILLY

SCENE SIX—OUTSIDE A SCHOOLHOUSE

Reprise, *You'll Never Walk Alone,* COMPANY

Reviews

Lewis Nichols—*New York Times*
". . . on the whole, delightful . . . one of the most beautiful Rodgers scores, and some of Hammerstein's best rhymes . . . At the beginning, it moved a little slowly, but as soon as Rodgers has warmed his keyboard and Hammerstein his pen, chance complaints evaporate . . ."

Otis Guernsey, Jr.—*New York Herald Tribune*
". . . with a lovely musical score, a letter-perfect cast, a fine production, and a tale told with sincerity, it is definitely something to see . . . music and real drama can be combined outside the opera with very good entertainment results . . ."

John Chapman—*New York Daily News*
". . . one of the finest musical plays I have ever seen and I shall remember it always. It has everything the professional theatre can give it and something else besides; heart, integrity and an inner glow . . . The score and lyrics are by Rodgers and Hammerstein, and the musical theatre does not have two finer creative artists . . ."

Robert Coleman—*New York Daily Mirror*
". . . beautiful, bountiful, beguiling . . . plays a tune called success—because it is the product of taste, imagination and skill. It will bewitch your senses and race your pulses . . ."

Louis Kronenberger—*PM*
". . . in some small sense an occasion in the theatre . . . sufficiently believes in itself to tell its story with no obeisances to routine musical comedy demands, and sufficiently understands its job not to sacrifice the prevailing mood to the predatory moment. . . Rodgers has once again earned our gratitude for venturing to be different, our gratitude for continuing (on the whole) to be delightful . . . Hammerstein's book is simple without seeming over-simplified; it never shows off; it sticks to humor of character and eschews wisecracks . . ."

Wilella Waldorf—*New York Post*
". . . it is no *Liliom* and also no *Oklahoma!*, but it will doubtless have a nice, hefty run on the strength of both its predecessors' reputations. . . Rodgers' score is more musicianly but less 'pop' than his *Oklahoma!* parade of hits . . . rather a long evening. The *Oklahoma!* formula is becoming a bit monotonous and so are Miss de Mille's ballets. All right, go ahead and shoot!"

Ward Morehouse—*New York Sun*
". . . Rodgers has contributed some of the most beguiling music of his career. Hammerstein has written distinctive lyrics . . . something memorable in the theatre . . . touching and affecting. . ."

Robert Garland—*New York Journal-American*
"Yes, yes, a thousand times yes. . . When somebody writes a better musical play, Rodgers and Hammerstein will have to write it . . . I can't find anything to complain about . . . romantic, melodramatic, fantastical, colorful, comic, tragic, melodic, and an evening of sheer theatrical entertainment."

Abel Green—*Variety*, July 31, 1940
". . . takes its place with *Oklahoma!* as an unqualified Broadway smash musical. . . It has everything from lavish investiture to inspired casting . . . a sentimental, melodious literate adaptation. . ."

Wolcott Gibbs—*The New Yorker*, April 28, 1945
". . . some very fine songs, especially one called *If I Loved You* . . . one of the delights of the season, and one that ought to put everybody connected with it in an income-bracket that I would rather not think about."

George Jean Nathan–*New York Journal-American*, April 30, 1945
". . . welcome in almost every way, and I herewith help to spread out the door mat. . . Its lyrics are delightfully simple. . . It is not afraid of honorable sentiment and does not apologize for it, as is often the case, by incorporating into it a squirt of vaudeville . . . a very good show."

Time, April 30, 1945
". . . All *Oklahoma's* horses and all *Oklahoma's* men have put another charmer together again. But *Carousel* strays pretty far from Oklahoma, just as it shies completely away from Broadway. . . Hammerstein's script is always simple, sometimes touching, never flashy, only here and there a little cute. And Composer Rodgers has swathed it in one of his warmest and most velvety scores. More than a succession of tunes, the music helps interpret the story . . . Hammerstein has caught the spirit with his lyrics. . ."

Joseph Wood Krutch—*The Nation*, May 5, 1945
". . . Rodgers needs some story more buoyant than *Liliom* to provide the occasion for his best music. Despite this, it is still second only to *Oklahoma!* among all the musicals current . . . Rodgers' music is written, not contrived; the story is told, not merely dragged

in from time to time; and Hammerstein's lyrics have freshness and wit . . . the production is extremely lavish, possibly even a little too splendiforous . . ."

Stark Young—*The New Republic,* May 7, 1945
". . . a generous production, lively, amiable and lavish . . . the earlier portion seemed to go somewhat slowly, the rest to pick up. None of the songs seemed inflammably good, but nothing over-boring . . ."

Bibliography

NEWSPAPERS AND PERIODICALS

A New Opera by Olin Downes —*New York Times,* December 24, 1944

Turns on a Carousel by Oscar Hammerstein II —*New York Times,* April 15, 1945

"Carousel" by Helen Ormsbee —*New York Herald Tribune,* April 15, 1945

"Carousel" —*Life,* May 14, 1945

Words and Music by Amy Porter —*Collier's,* May 26, 1945

The Vertical "Carousel" by Richard Rodgers —*New York Herald Tribune Magazine,* August 8, 1965

BOOKS

Carousel (Random House, New York; 1945)
Book and lyrics of the musical.

Awards

N.Y. Drama Critics Circle Award Best Musical, 1944-45
Donaldson Awards, 1944-45
- Best Musical
- Best Performance in Musical (male), John Raitt
- Best Direction, Rouben Mamoulian
- Best Dancer (male), Peter Birch
- Best Dance Direction, Agnes deMille
- Best Book, Oscar Hammerstein II
- Best Lyrics, Oscar Hammerstein II
- Best Score, Richard Rodgers

Tour

Shubert Theatre, Chicago, May 29, 1947—Majestic Theatre, New York, March 5, 1949 (55 cities).

Tour Reviews

Linton Martin—*Philadelphia Inquirer*
"A deluxe delight—musically, dramatically, decoratively, in its dances and other details . . ."

R.E.P. Sensenderfer—*Philadelphia Bulletin*
". . . the performance has become mechanical . . . magnificent score . . . brilliant lyrics . . . a conventional road performance of a worthy musical . . ."

John Rosenfield—*Dallas Morning News*
". . . a tale of tears as well as laughter, heightened by music and staging of rich emotional range . . ."

Lewis Funke—*New York Times*
". . . charming . . . There are things to be desired about this *Carousel* but they are to be overlooked. Its finest virtue is Rodgers' music . . ."

John Chapman—*New York Daily News*
". . . the best performance of *Carousel* I have ever seen—and I've seen many . . . seems to have grown as a work of art . . . The book and lyrics are remarkable for their skill, grace and showmanship . . . Rodgers' most musicianly score to date . . ."

Richard Watts, Jr.—*New York Post*
"It always was a comfort and joy, but it grows even more delightful with familiarity . . . seemed better than ever . . . it is the music and lyrics that make chiefly for the exceptional excellence of *Carousel,* but everyone concerned deserves credit for the remarkable teamwork which makes for a rare achievement of the American theatre."

William Hawkins—*New York World-Telegram*
". . . one of the true classics of the musical theatre . . . aside from its lyrical perfection, the basic story is fine, touching and unforgettable . . . an evening studded with beautiful melodies . . ."

Ward Morehouse—*New York Sun*
". . . fragile beauty and enchanting score . . ."

Robert Garland—*New York Journal-American*
". . . one of the American theatre's most successful dramas-set-to-music. The incoming cast works affectionately together . . . The score is as fresh, if not as unfamiliar, as it first was . . ."

Hobe Morrison—*Variety,* February 2, 1949
". . . seems even more effective than in its smash opening . . . the present cast is excellent . . . Not a commonplace number in the show . . ."

Selected Revivals

St. Louis Opera, August 21-September 3, 1950
Jack Kilty (BILLY); Virginia Haskins (JULIE); Dorothea MacFarland (CARRIE); Mario DeLaval (JIGGER); Winifred Heidt (NETTIE).

Los Angeles Civic Light Opera, May 4-30, 1953
San Francisco Civic Light Opera, June 1, 1953
William Johnson (BILLY); Jan Clayton (JULIE); Kaye Connor (CARRIE); Murvyn Vye (JIGGER); Muriel O'Malley (NETTIE).

New York City Center Light Opera, June 2-August 8, 1954
Chris Robinson (BILLY); Jo Sullivan (JULIE); Barbara Cook (CARRIE); John Conte (JIGGER); Jean Handzlik (NETTIE); Bambi Linn (LOUISE). Note: After first two weeks, Mr. Robinson succeeded by David Atkinson, Miss Linn by Gemze de Lappe.

Dallas State Fair Music Hall, July 21-31, 1955
Gordon MacRae (BILLY); Paula Stewart (JULIE); Susan Johnson (CARRIE); Rosemary Kuhlmann (NETTIE); Andrew Gainey (JIGGER); Reid Shelton (SNOW).

New York City Center Light Opera, September 11-29, 1957
Howard Keel (BILLY); Barabara Cook (JULIE); Pat Stanley (CARRIE); James Mitchell (JIGGER); Marie Powers (NETTIE); Bambi Linn (LOUISE); Victor Moore (STARKEEPER); Russell Nype (SNOW); Kay Medford (MRS. MULLIN); Patricia Birch (DANCER).

San Juan Drama Festival, Puerto Rico, July 17-22, 1961
Bill Walker (BILLY); Carolyn Maye (JULIE); Betty Oakes (CARRIE); Scott Merrill (JIGGER); Helon Blount (NETTIE); Dale Malone (SNOW).

San Francisco Civic Light Opera, April 22-June 8, 1963
Los Angeles Civic Light Opera, June 10, 1963
John Raitt (BILLY); Jan Clayton (JULIE); Pat Stanley (CARRIE); Claramae Turner (NETTIE); Gerald Price (JIGGER); Frank Porretta (SNOW).

Music Theater of Lincoln Center, New York, August 10-September 18, 1965
John Raitt (BILLY); Eileen Christy (JULIE); Susan Watson (CARRIE); Jerry Orbach (JIGGER); Katherine Hilgenberg (NETTIE); Reid Shelton (SNOW); Edward Everett Horton (STARKEEPER); Benay Venuta (MRS. MULLIN); Dixie Carter (ARMINY). *Tour:* September 21, 1965-February 5, 1966. Note: For tour, Mr. Raitt succeeded by Harve Presnell, Miss Watson by Dran Seitz.

New York City Center Light Opera, December 15, 1966-January 7, 1967
Bruce Yarnell (BILLY); Constance Towers (JULIE); Nancy Dussault (CARRIE); Michael Kermoyan (JIGGER); Patricia Neway (NETTIE); Jack DeLon (SNOW); Sandy Duncan (LOUISE); Parker Fennelly (STARKEEPER).

Dallas State Fair Music Hall, July 2-14, 1968
St. Louis Municipal Opera, July 15-21, 1968
John Davidson (BILLY); Barbara Williams (JULIE); Vicki Lawrence (CARRIE); Walter McGinn (JIGGER); Jack DeLon (SNOW).

Jones Beach Marine Theatre, Long Island, June 22-September 22, 1973
John Cullum (BILLY); Barbara Meister (JULIE); Bonnie Franklin (CARRIE); Alfred Toigo (JIGGER); Eileen Schauler (NETTIE); Reid Shelton (SNOW).

Kansas City Starlight Theatre, June 16-August 24, 1975
Ed Ames (BILLY); Patti Davis (JULIE); Suellen Estey (CARRIE); Robert Darnell (JIGGER); Eileen Schauler (NETTIE); Harry Danner (SNOW).

Television Production

ABC Network, May 7, 1967
Produced by Norman Rosemont; adaptation by Sidney Michaels; directed by Paul Bogart; choreography by Edward Villella; music director, Jack Elliott; sponsored by Armstrong Cork. *Cast:* Robert Goulet (BILLY); Mary Grover (JULIE); Marlyn Mason (CARRIE); Pernell Roberts (JIGGER); Patricia Neway (NETTIE); Marge Redmond (MRS. MULLIN); Jack DeLon (SNOW); Charlie Ruggles (STARKEEPER); Barnard Hughes (BASCOMBE).

Productions Abroad

Theatre Royal, Drury Lane, London, June 7, 1950-October 13, 1951
(See below)

U.S. Pavilion, Brussels Exposition, June 4-22, 1958
Presented by the N.Y. City Center Light Opera (Jean Dalrymple, director); directed by John Fearnley; choreography restaged by Robert Pagent. *Cast:* David Atkinson (BILLY); Jan Clayton (JULIE); Jean Hovis (CARRIE); Felice Orlandi (JIGGER); Ruth Kobart (NETTIE); Gemze de Lappe (LOUISE); Russell Nype (SNOW); Ernest Truex (STARKEEPER); John Fearnley (HEAVENLY FRIEND); Kay Medford (MRS. MULLIN).

Princess Theatre, Melbourne, Australia, June 5, 1964
Presented by Garnet H. Carroll; directed by Milton Lyon; choreography by Ernest Parham. *Cast:* Gordon Boyd (BILLY); Susan Swinford (JULIE); Patricia Vivian (CARRIE); Bill Yule (JIGGER); Rosina Raisbeck (NETTIE); David Williams (SNOW); Patricia Cox (LOUISE).

CAROUSEL

(London—1950)

Presented by Prince Littler
in association with the Theatre Guild
Restaged by Jerome Whyte

Choreography by Agnes de Mille
Settings by Jo Mielziner
Costumes by Miles White
Music director, Frederick Dvonch
Orchestrations by Don Walker

London Run
Theatre Royal, Drury Lane, June 7, 1950-October 13, 1951
566 performances

The Cast
CARRIE PIPPERIDGE, Margot Moser
JULIE JORDAN, Iva Withers
MRS. MULLIN, Marjorie Mars
BILLY BIGELOW, Stephen Douglass
BESSIE, Sandra Hartley
JUGGLER, Eddie Le Roy
1ST POLICEMAN, Vincent Charles
DAVID BASCOMBE, W. Thorpe Devereux
NETTIE FOWLER, Marion Ross
JUNE GIRL, Mavis Ray
ENOCH SNOW, Eric Mattson
JIGGER CRAIGIN, Morgan Davies
HANNAH, Jane Evans
BOATSWAIN, Robert Pagent
ARMINY, Dorothy Laroque
PENNY, Rosemary Warren
JENNIE, Muriel Cooke
VIRGINIA, June Powell
SUSAN, Diana Dove
JONATHAN, William Thorburn
2ND POLICEMAN, Bernard Quinn
CAPTAIN, John Sinclair
HEAVENLY FRIEND, *(Brother Joshua)*, Jack Melford
STARKEEPER, William Sherwood
LOUISE, Bambi Linn
CARNIVAL BOY, Robert Pagent
ENOCH SNOW, JR., Edward Monson
PRINCIPAL, Vincent Charles
DR. SELDON, William Sherwood
SINGERS: Pamela Healey, Joan Danson, Diana Dove, Beryl Foley, Dorina Gregory, Sandra Hartley, Enid Heard, Dorothy Laroque, Rosemary Warren, Sylvia Vowles, Audrey Brice; Robert Burns, Vincent Charles, Robert Duval, Gordon Keyes, Donald McLisky, Bernard Quinn, Ken Sandford, Dennis Sears, John Sinclair, John Hughes, Conway Dixon
DANCERS: Silvia Ashmole, Julie Chadwicke, Hermione Harvey, Judy Gold, Clandine Goodfellow, Margaret Jackson, Jean King, Gillian Moran,

Sonya Raven, Margaret Scrimshaw, Lillian Jarvis, Wendy Brandon; Michael Facer, Edward Monson, Matt Winston, Andre Cordova, Harry Cordwell, Raymond Ray, Roy Gunson

NOTE: During run, Mr. Douglass succeeded by Edmund Hockridge; Miss Withers by LaVerne Burden.

Musical Numbers
Same as original production.

Reviews
A. V. Cookman—*London Times*
". . . may slip into excessive sentimentality, but we would be ungrateful to complain of a piece that so liberally adds song and dance to a bizarre story that is not always so dramatic as when Molnar told it . . . as a musical play it has very much to recommend it . . ."

W. A. Darlington—*London Daily Telegraph*
"It is possible to enjoy a great deal of it without taking the story too profoundly . . . The best thing about it is the music . . . a real successor to *Oklahoma!* . . ."

Alan Dent—*London News-Chronicle*
". . . in spite of the conventional cheers at the end, it is a well staged, well sung, colorful, self-repetitive and wishy-washy 'wash-out' . . ."

Cecil Wilson—*London Daily Mail*
". . . in some respects, it is a better show than *Oklahoma!* . . . The music, if less hummable, has more of an operatic quality. The lyrics are cleverer, but there may be mixed feelings about *Liliom* as a theme . . ."

Beverley Baxter, M.P.—*London Evening Standard*
". . . while it lacks the vitality of *Oklahoma!* it is fashioned in the same mould . . . inevitably repetition blunts the edge of spontaneity, and we are more able to note the faults . . . too often Hammerstein achieves tenderness without beauty and frustration without tragedy . . ."

Harold Hobson—*London Sunday Times*, June 11, 1950
". . . a combination of circus and Sunday School, with Sunday School winning in a strong gallop at the end in the most surprising episode I have ever known in any musical comedy on any stage. The first half of the play may not give satisfaction to the judicious, but there are many things in it in which the judicious will find satisfaction . . ."

J. C. Trewin—*London Observer,* June 11, 1950
"... *Carousel* is not another *Oklahoma!* Often it loiters. There is no wind across the wheat ... The June song is the most exhilarating thing in a generous score ... Is *Carousel* good of its kind—that queer kind of sophistication crossed with bland innocence? The answer is Yes ..."

Frances Stephens—*Theatre World,* July, 1950
"... superb technique and lovely music ... The story inclines to impinge too much on the smooth running of the show, particularly in the second act, when the sentiment is also inclined to clog ..."

J. C. Trewin—*Illustrated London News,* July 1, 1950
"... hardly another *Oklahoma!* ... If *Carousel*—the title is American for a merry-go-round—had come first, I think its qualities would have been more generally honoured ... Rodgers' score has half a dozen numbers that flash in remembrance and at least one, *June Is Bustin' Out All Over,* that is bustin' its way far beyond Drury Lane ... The trouble is that it has too much plot—of the wrong kind ... *Liliom* is a disconcerting basis for a musical play ..."

Bibliography

"Carousel" —*Theatre World,* October, 1950

CAROUSEL

(Film Version—1956)

A Twentieth Century-Fox Picture
Produced by Henry Ephron
Directed by Henry King
Screenplay by Henry and Phoebe Ephron
Choreography by Rod Alexander
Louise's ballet from original by Agnes de Mille
Art directors, Lyle Wheeler, Jack Martin Smith
Costumes by Mary Wills
Music director, Alfred Newman
Photographed by Charles G. Clarke
Editor, William Reynolds
Filmed in CinemaScope 55
Color by DeLuxe

Release Date
February 16, 1956

The Cast

BILLY BIGELOW, Gordon MacRae
JULIE JORDAN, Shirley Jones
JIGGER CRAIGIN, Cameron Mitchell
CARRIE PIPPERIDGE, Barbara Ruick
COUSIN NETTIE FOWLER, Claramae Turner
ENOCH SNOW, Robert Rounsville
STARKEEPER, Gene Lockhart
MRS. MULLIN, Audrey Christie
LOUISE, Susan Luckey
HEAVENLY FRIEND, William Le Massena
DAVID BASCOMBE, John Dehner
LOUISE'S DANCING PARTNER, Jacques D'Amboise
CAPTAIN WATSON, Frank Tweddell
CONTORTIONIST, Sylvia Stanton
FAT WOMAN, Mary Orozco
STRONG MAN, Tor Johnson
JUGGLER, Harry "Duke" Johnson
SWORD SWALLOWER, Marion Dempsey
FIRE EATER, Ed Mundy
MIDGET, Angelo Rossito
ENOCH SNOW, JR., Dee Pollock

NOTE: Frank Sinatra, who was to have played BILLY, quit as the shooting was about to start.

Musical Numbers

Same as original production, except for following omissions: *Geraniums in the Window,* and *The Highest Judge of All.*

Reviews

Bosley Crowther—*New York Times*

". . . a beautifully turned out film, crisply played and richly sung by a fine cast that is fully worthy of the original musical show . . . Seldom has a musical comedy been made to look more handsome on the screen . . . The only considerable exception is the rather startling confusion of pictorial styles . . ."

William K. Zinsser—*New York Herald Tribune*

". . . it's unfortunate that the first two Rodgers and Hammerstein musicals—*Oklahoma!* and *Carousel*—have come to the screen in new processes that strive for utmost realism of sight and sound . . . *Carousel* has the most lyrical score that Rodgers and Hammerstein ever wrote, and many of its songs—like *What's the Use of Won'drin'?*—express an emotion with unusual poignance. But in the movie, songs like this are tricked up in Cinemascope 55 . . . a rich movie in many ways . . ."

Archer Winsten—*New York Post*
"... a distinct technical advance in the field of projection ... The screenplay does no violence to the essentials of the stage play ... solely for the story it tells in narrative and beautiful song, it is extremely touching ..."

Fred Hift—*Variety,* February 22, 1956
"A great score, imaginative dance sequences, and the pre-sold reputation of the work, combined with the freshly colored backgrounds make this screen adaptation a major contender for important grosses ... The stars remain Rodgers and Hammerstein. Their songs keep fresh and appealing ..."

John McCarten—*The New Yorker,* March 3, 1956
"... tolerable divertissement ... the latest development in stereophonic sound assaults the ears with such volume that it's hard to lean back and enjoy all the splendid tunes ..."

Jesse Zunser—*Cue,* March 3, 1956
"... a grand and glorious entertainment—among the finest musicals ever to fill a motion picture screen. Its visual and aural beauties have been enlarged and enriched in their transposition from stage to screen ..."

Hollis Alpert—*Saturday Review,* March 15, 1956
"... a fulsome musical score that many already regard as the highpoint of the work of Richard Rodgers ... I suspect that when future historians try to decide what consituted native American opera in our time they'll have to give some careful consideration to *Carousel.* In that case this movie version should be very helpful."

Time, March 19, 1956
"... The melodies have all their clovered freshness still, but if film fans lick their lips over anything else it will be because they can't tell sweet from saccharine ... In a word: goo ..."

Thomas H. Wenning—*Newsweek,* March 19, 1956
"... a musical play that has become an American classic ... At all times it is good to look at and even better to listen to ... The score, of course, is the loveliest, bar none, of the R & H collection ..."

Bibliography

Another Ride on a "Carousel" by Seymour Peck
—*New York Times Magazine,* January 8, 1956

"Carousel" Is Movie Clambake Too —*Life,* February 6, 1956

Awards

Gold Record (sales over $1 million), Capitol soundtrack album

STATE FAIR

(Film—1945)

A musical film with screenplay and lyrics by Oscar Hammerstein II, adaptation by Sonya Levien and Paul Green, based on the novel by Phil Stong; music by Richard Rodgers

A Twentieth Century-Fox Picture
Produced by William Perlberg
Directed by Walter Lang
Art directors, Lyle R. Wheeler and Lewis Creber
Costumes by Rene Hubert
Music directors, Alfred Newman and Charles Henderson
Orchestrations by Edward Powell
Photographed by Leon Shamroy
Editor, J. Watson Webb
Color by Technicolor

Release Date
August 20, 1945

The Story
The Frake family goes to the Iowa State Fair. While there, they win many prizes and ribbons; daughter Margy becomes engaged to Pat Gilbert; son Wayne has a brief romance with singer Emily.

NOTE: The story was originally filmed by Fox in 1933, with Will Rogers as ABEL; Janet Gaynor as MARGY; Lew Ayres as PAT; Sally Eilers as EMILY.

The Cast
MARGY FRAKE, Jeanne Crain (sung by Louanne Hogan)
PAT GILBERT, Dana Andrews
WAYNE FRAKE, Dick Haymes
EMILY EDWARDS, Vivian Blaine
ABEL FRAKE, Charles Winninger
MELISSA FRAKE, Fay Bainter
HIPPENSTAHL, Donald Meek
MC GEE, Frank McHugh
MILLER, Percy Kilbride
BARKER, Henry Morgan
ELEANOR, Jane Nigh

MARTY, William Marshall
HARRY WARE, Phil Brown
HANK, Paul Burns
EPH, Tom Fadden
PAPPY, William Frambes
BARKER, Steve Olson
MRS. METCALFE, Josephine Whittell
SIMPSON, Paul Harvey
ANNOUNCER, John Dehner
JUDGES, Harlan Briggs, Will Wright, Alice Fleming

Musical Numbers

Our State Fair, MILLER, ABEL, MELISSA
It Might as Well Be Spring, MARGY
That's for Me, EMILY
It's a Grand Night for Singing, MARTY, WAYNE and CHORUS
Reprise, *That's for Me,* MARGY and PAT
Reprise, *It's a Grand Night for Singing,* EMILY, MARTY and CHORUS
Isn't It Kinda Fun?, WAYNE and EMILY
All I Owe Ioway, MARTY, EMILY, MELISSA, HIPPENSTAHL, and CHORUS

Reviews

Bosley Crowther—*New York Times*
". . . no more than an average screen musical with a nice bucolic flavor here and there . . . Best of the numbers are a cute one called *It Might as Well Be Spring* and two pictorially unrealized chorales, *It's a Grand Night for Singing* and *All I Owe Ioway* . . ."

Howard Barnes—*New York Herald Tribune*
". . . bright and tuneful . . . Rodgers is one of the most distinctive of musical comedy stylists . . . Hammerstein has arranged a series of joyous passages in his screenplay . . . the team is on its toes . . ."

Alton Cook—*New York World-Telegram*
"The gentlemen of *Oklahoma!* have worked their zestful magic on another rustic story . . . The music and general high spirits have transformed the old vehicle so ecstatically you won't bother about any comparison . . . will remain bountifully full of pleasure through visit after visit."

Archer Winsten—*New York Post*
". . . a honey of a picture . . . it is to movie musicals what *Oklahoma!* is to stage musicals. There is that same quality of a bright and wonderful morning . . . an operetta of the kind that only Hammerstein can create . . ."

Eileen Creelman—*New York Sun*
". . . as fresh as spring, as enchanting as moonlight . . . Blessed with a Rodgers and Hammerstein score . . ."

Nat Kahn—*Variety,* August 22, 1945
". . . Coupled with an excellent cast, it retains the old charm and yet adds some of its own. It is an excellent entertainment and should do boff b.o. . . . The tunes are whammo from both lyrical and melody content . . ."

James Agee—*Time,* September 3, 1945
". . . meant to be as happy as a hayride down the middle aisle of *Oklahoma!* . . . fine tunes . . . Hammerstein has written a screenplay as pleasing and deft as his lyrics. If it had delicacy and imagination to match its competence and good humor—and if its pastoral charm had real outdoor authenticity—it might have become an entertainment classic . . ."

John McCarten—*The New Yorker,* September 15, 1945
". . . a long way from *Oklahoma!* Life on the farm, obviously, is hardly as bouncy as life on the ranch, but it must be a lot more vigorous than *State Fair* would lead you to believe . . . the best song is probably *It Might as Well Be Spring.* 'Nice,' I believe, would be the word for it; I don't think you could consider anything stronger."

James Agee—*The Nation,* September 29, 1945
". . . pretty tunes, graceful lyrics. Otherwise lacking any real delicateness, vitality, or imagination, and painfully air-conditioned-looking, for a bucolic film; it is nevertheless good-natured and pleasant."

Bibliography

"State Fair" –*Life,* September 17, 1945

It's One of the Top Songs of the Year
The writing of *It Might as Well Be Spring.*
—*Boston Daily Record,* April 3, 1946

Awards

Motion Picture Academy Award, 1945
Best song, *It Might as Well Be Spring*

Stage Revival

St. Louis Municipal Opera, June 2, 1969
Ozzie Nelson (ABEL); Harriet Nelson (MELISSA); Jerry Lanning (WAYNE); Carol Richards (MARGY); Ron Husmann (PAT). Stage adaptation by Lucille Kallen.

STATE FAIR

(Film Remake—1962)

A Twentieth Century-Fox Picture
Produced by Charles Brackett
Directed by José Ferrer
Screenplay by Richard Breen
Art directors, Jack Martin Smith and Walter M. Simonds
Costumes by Marjorie Best
Choreography by Nick Castle
Music director, Alfred Newman
Associate music director, Ken Darby
Photographed by William C. Mellor
Editor, David Bretherton
Filmed in Cinemascope
Color by DeLuxe

Release Date

March 15, 1962

The Story

Basically the same as original, except that locale was moved to Dallas, Texas.

The Cast

WAYNE FRAKE, Pat Boone
JERRY DUNDEE, Bobby Darin
MARGIE FRAKE, Pamela Tiffin (sung by Anita Gordon)
EMILY, Ann-Margret
ABEL FRAKE, Tom Ewell
MELISSA FRAKE, Alice Faye
HIPPLEWAITE, Wally Cox
HARRY, David Brandon
DOC CRAMER, Clem Harvey
SQUAT JUDGE, Robert Foulk
BETTY JEAN, Linda Henrich
RED HOERTER, Edward "Tap" Canutt
LILYA, Margaret Deramee

Musical Numbers

Songs retained from original film: *Our State Fair; It Might as Well Be Spring, That's for Me, Isn't It Kinda Fun?*, and *It's a Grand Night for Singing.*

Songs written specially for film (music and lyrics by Mr. Rodgers):
More Than Just a Friend, ABEL
Willing and Eager, WAYNE and EMILY

Never Say No to a Man, MELISSA
This Isn't Heaven, JERRY
It's the Little Things in Texas, ABEL and MELISSA

Reviews

A. H. Weiler—*New York Times*
". . . as wonderful as Texas is to Texans and as pretty as that famed 'beautiful morning' of the lyrics in *Oklahoma!* But it is a basically obvious and, for the most part, dull fare. This *Fair* is, at best, only fair. For all of its good intentions, it seems to be a parody of moviemaking of the past . . . the five original songs by Rodgers and Hammerstein continue to be more enchanting than the five new numbers . . ."

Paul V. Beckley—*New York Herald Tribune*
"Aside from a few glib lines and a song or two, it has a limp and empty look . . . Corn ought to be fresh-picked and quick-cooked and hot-served; if, as here, it is boiled to a watery tastelessness, it is unappetizing . . . The whole thing has the air of something made by people who can't believe a bit of it . . ."

Kate Cameron—*New York Daily News*
"★★★½ . . . The new as well as the old tunes are enticing rhythms . . . a warm, 'corny-as-Kansas-in-August' film that is suitable for all the family."

Justin Gilbert—*New York Mirror*
". . . Its substance is about as sturdy as a fair flimsy (prop), and its significance as gooey as the confections peddled on fair grounds. But it's Americana . . . the older R&H tunes are captivating . . . just plain old U.S. hominy, mush and grit—in a colorful package."

Archer Winsten—*New York Post*
". . . if there's one thing better than another in this classic, it's the Rodgers and Hammerstein songs. Some of the additional songs don't hit the same high standard, but it might be simply that they are less familiar . . . The essential thing about *State Fair* is its long popularity and lasting music, its standard story of tested appeals, and the fact that it has been produced well but without excessive decoration . . ."

Alton Cook—*New York World-Telegram & Sun*
". . . a joyous charmer . . . Prettiness with a leaning toward the garish is the keynote of the whole picture . . . exactly the sort of prettiness and sweetness you expect to find in a popcorn ball."

Larry Tubell—*Variety,* March 14, 1962
". . . still as American as mom's apple pie, but the pie is stale after 17 years in the pantry . . . adheres too rigidly to old style filmusical techniques . . . The old songs are still charming . . . The new ditties aren't bad . . . there's something crass and antiseptic about the atmosphere—a significant loss . . ."

Brendan Gill—*The New Yorker,* April 14, 1962
". . . the sort of picture that goes on being made over and over, on purpose, and I don't suppose it's any better or worse this time around than it was in 1945 . . ."

Time, April 27, 1962
". . . It may not win any Oscars, but durn if it don't take the blue ribbon for the country corn . . . the color is louder and the picture is wider than ever . . . the script and the playing are lively . . ."

ALLEGRO

(1947)

A musical play with book and lyrics by Oscar Hammerstein II, music by Richard Rodgers.

Presented by the Theatre Guild
Directed and choreographed by Agnes de Mille
Assistant to Miss de Mille, Dania Krupska
Settings and lighting by Jo Mielziner
Costumes by Lucinda Ballard
Music director, Salvatore Dell'Isola
Orchestrations by Robert Russell Bennett
Dance arrangements by Trude Rittmann
Choral director, Crane Calder
Director of choral speech, Josephine Callan
Production supervised by Theresa Helburn and Lawrence Langner

Tryout
Shubert Theatre, New Haven, September 1-6, 1947
Colonial Theatre, Boston, September 8-October 4, 1947

New York Run
Majestic Theatre, October 10, 1947-July 10, 1948
315 performances

The Story
The life of Joseph Taylor, Jr., from the cradle, through college and medical school, to his renunciation of his big city practice and neurotic patients, and his return to the small town whence he came.

The Cast
MARJORIE TAYLOR, Annamary Dickey
DR. JOSEPH TAYLOR, William Ching
MAYOR, Edward Platt
GRANDMA TAYLOR, Muriel O'Malley
FRIENDS OF JOEY, Ray Harrison, Frank Westbrook
JENNIE BRINKER, Roberta Jonay
PRINCIPAL, Robert Byrn
MABEL, Evelyn Taylor
BICYCLE BOY, Stanley Simmons

GEORGIE, Harrison Muller
HAZEL SKINNER, Kathryn Lee
CHARLIE TOWNSEND, John Conte
JOSEPH TAYLOR, JR., John Battles
MISS LIPSCOMB, Susan Svetlik
CHEER LEADERS, Charles Tate, Sam Steen
COACH, Wilson Smith
NED BRINKER, Paul Parks
ENGLISH PROFESSOR, David Collyer
CHEMISTRY PROFESSOR, William McCully
GREEK PROFESSOR, Raymond Keast
BIOLOGY PROFESSOR, Robert Byrn
PHILOSOPHY PROFESSOR, Blake Ritter
SHAKESPEARE STUDENT, Susan Svetlik
BERTRAM WOOLHAVEN, Ray Harrison
MOLLY, Katrina Van Oss
BEULAH, Gloria Wills
MINISTER, Edward Platt
MILLIE, Julie Humphries
DOT, Sylvia Karlton
ADDIE, Patricia Bybell
DR. BIGBY DENBY, Lawrence Fletcher
MRS. MULHOUSE, Frances Rainer
MRS. LANSDALE, Lily Paget
JARMAN, *a butler,* Bill Bradley
MAID, Jean Houloose
EMILY WEST, Lisa Kirk
DOORMAN, Tom Perkins
BROOK LANSDALE, Stephen Chase
HARRY BUCKLEY, Wilson Smith

SINGERS: Mary O'Fallon, Charlotte Howard, Lily Paget, Helen Hunter, Sylvia Karlton, Priscilla Hathaway, Gay Lawrence, Josephine Lambert, Julie Humphries, Patricia Bybell, Yolanda Renay, Devida Stewart, Nanette Vezina, Mia Stenn, Lucille Udovick; Glenn Scandur, Gene Tobin, Walter Kelvin, Bernard Green, David Collyer, Joseph Caruso, Tommy Barragan, Victor Clarke, Edward Platt, Robert Reeves, Wilson Smith, Tom Perkins, James Jewell, David Poleri, Robert Neukum, Raymond Keast, Wesley Swails, Clarence Hall, Blake Ritter, Ralph Patterson, Robert Byrn, William McCully, Robert Arnold

DANCERS: Jean Tachau, Evelyn Taylor, Mariane Oliphant, Patricia Gianinoto, Andrea Downing, Jean Houloose, Therese Miele, Frances Rainer, Susan Svetlik, Ruth Ostrander, Patricia Barker; William Bradley, Daniel Buberniak, Bob Herget, John Laverty, Ralph Linn, Harrison Muller, Stanley Simmons, Charles Tate, Frank Westbrook, Ralph Williams, Sam Steen

NOTE: During tour, Mr. Battles succeeded by James Jewell.

Musical Numbers

The three major locations of action are Joseph Taylor, Jr.'s home town, his college town, and a large city, all in the same midwestern state. There are no stage "sets" in the conventional sense, but backgrounds for action are achieved by small scenic pieces on a moving stage, by light projections, and by drops. The singing chorus is used frequently to interpret the mental and emotional reactions of the principal characters, after the manner of a Greek chorus.

ACT I

MARJORIE TAYLOR'S BEDROOM
Joseph Taylor, Jr., CHORUS
I Know It Can Happen Again, GRANDMA
One Foot, Other Foot, MARJORIE, GRANDMA, CHORUS; danced by Kathryn Lee, Patricia Barker, Bob Herget and DANCERS

JOEY'S ROOM
Winters Go By, GRANDMA and CHORUS

IN FRONT OF JENNIE'S HOUSE
Poor Joe, CHORUS

THE TAYLOR'S PORCH
A Fellow Needs a Girl, JOE SR. and MARJORIE

THE COLLEGE GYM–FRESHMAN DANCE
*Mountain Greenery,** danced by Evelyn Taylor, Harrison Muller and DANCERS
A Darn Nice Campus, JOE

THE FOOTBALL FIELD
Wildcats, FRESHMEN

THE CAMPUS

JENNIE'S GARDEN

JOE'S STUDY

CLASSROOM

WOODLAND
So Far, BEULAH

JENNIE'S GARDEN
You Are Never Away, JOE and CHORUS

THE TAYLOR'S PORCH

OUTSIDE THE CHURCH
What a Lovely Day for a Wedding, NED and GUESTS
It May Be a Good Idea, CHARLIE

*Originally in *Garrick Gaieties (1926)*

INSIDE THE CHURCH–THE WEDDING
To Have and to Hold, CHORUS
Wish Them Well, CHORUS

ACT II

BACKYARD OF THE TAYLOR HOME
Money Isn't Ev'rything, JENNIE HAZEL, ADDIE, DOT, MILLIE; danced by HAZEL

BEDROOM
Reprise, *You Are Never Away,* JOE

DR. TAYLOR'S OFFICE

JENNIE'S SALON IN CHICAGO
Yatata, Yatata, Yatata, CHARLIE and GUESTS

FOYER OF THE TAYLOR APARTMENT

STREET ENTRANCE OF THE APARTMENT HOUSE
The Gentleman Is a Dope, EMILY

DR. BIGBY DENBY'S PRIVATE OFFICE
Allegro, EMILY, JOE, CHARLIE, and CHORUS

JOE'S OFFICE
Come Home, MARJORIE

THE LOBBY OF THE NEW PRIVATE PAVILION
Finale Ultimo, COMPANY

Reviews

Brooks Atkinson—*New York Times*
". . . something of magnificence in these early years of American life. The story has style and character; the music enriches it; the staging has the eloquent simplicity of genuine art. Until the disaster of 1929 overtakes it, it has the lyric rapture of a musical masterpiece. Even after 1929, it is a musical play of superior quality . . . it has made history on Broadway. Before the mood breaks after the first act it is full of a kind of unexploited glory. If this review sounds ungratefully reluctant it is because Rodgers and Hammerstein have just missed the final splendor of a perfect work of art."

Howard Barnes—*New York Herald Tribune*
"A musical play of rare distinction . . . a show to be remembered with *Show Boat* and *Oklahoma!* . . . a consummate theatrical achievement and an electrifying entertainment . . . Much of the

music is subordinated to a plot of depth and emotional power . . . At the same time the gifted composer has written such eloquent tunes as *A Fellow Needs a Girl, You Are Never Away* and *So Far* . . . a cohesive libretto and pertinent lyrics . . . a memorable musical comedy."

John Chapman—*New York Daily News*
". . . *An Elaborate Sermon* . . . They have set *Allegro* to an andante beat . . . Much of what they have done is notable for its imagination and sensitivity. Their songs seem rigidly stylized to fit mood and story; and, although many of them are lovely, not many bust loose and make a bid for immediate popular acceptance . . . moments of gaiety may be found in *Allegro.* But in the show itself they seem to disapprove of levity . . ."

Robert Coleman—*New York Daily Mirror*
"*Perfect and Great* . . . a stunning blending of beauty, integrity, intelligence, imagination, taste and skill. It races the pulses and puts lumps in the throat . . . should be embraced affectionately by discriminating playgoers. It lends new stature to the American musical stage."

Richard Watts, Jr.—*New York Post*
". . . a distinguished musical play, beautiful, imaginative, original, and honestly moving . . . a notable achievement in its field and another landmark in pushing back the frontier of the American music drama . . . an emotional honesty that brightens the music, the lyrics and the dancing . . . Mr. Rodgers, in the interest of the purity of his music, has been a little afraid of getting a really tuneful song into his skillful score, falling back on his wonderful *Mountain Greenery* in the scene in which such a song is needed . . ."

William Hawkins—*New York World-Telegram*
". . . a vast disappointment. The early conception of the work has a worthy beauty, but its realization crosses the stage like an impoverished sophomore class production. It lacks consistency of mood, visual excitement and theatrical stimulation . . . In the end it seems like the creation of a pretentious passé costumer who has nothing but cambric to work with . . ."

Ward Morehouse—*New York Sun*
". . . distinguished and tumultuous . . . excitingly unconventional in form and it takes its place alongside of *Oklahoma!* and *Carousel* as a theatrical piece of taste, imagination and showmanship . . . some hypnotic music, the lyrics are pungent, and the story, if somewhat trite, is at least compact . . . a simple story but it becomes frequently

touching and occasionally exalted . . . a musical play of beauty and dignity, produced with perception and imagination . . ."

Robert Garland—*New York Journal-American*
". . . went its slow, unhurried way telling a simple run-of-the-U.S.A. biography. It's as if the story of Dr. Foster, who went to Gloucester, were blown up out of Mother Goose and into the Metropolitan Opera House . . . at its winning best when the machinery has slowed down and the shrewdly selected cast is singing Rodgers' more musical-comedy-minded tunes . . . *Allegro* is bigger than anything Rodgers and Hammerstein have written. But I do wish it had more consistently lived up to its title."

George Freedley—*New York Morning Telegraph*
". . . The great combination which was responsible for *Oklahoma!* and *Carousel* has come up with a masterpiece which surpasses the others by far in its conception . . . a good deed superbly done."

Jack Pulaski (Ibee.)—*Variety,* October 15, 1947
". . . impressive . . . the new season's most unusual attraction . . . creates a virtually new theatre form . . . Music and drama are so integrated that there is no special emphasis on the melodies."

Wolcott Gibbs—*The New Yorker,* October 18, 1947
". . . In describing it as a shocking disappointment, with almost nothing to recommend it except two or three nice songs and quite a lot of attractive performances, I feel sure that I am presenting a minority report . . ."

Time, October 20, 1947
". . . gets too big for its roots and too elaborate to have an honest *Our Town* warmth . . . But with all its faults, it is an impressive effort in a good cause; it is the latest sortie in the well-nigh-won revolution against cloak-and-daguerreotype operetta and June-moon musi-comedy . . ."

Thomas H. Wenning—*Newsweek,* October 20, 1947
"*Allegro con Moto* . . . 'celebration' is the word for the occasion. . . . It is often as deliberately serious as it is amusing. The second act isn't quite as good as the first. But even the second act is so far ahead of its field that the total comes close to greatness . . . Rodgers' score doesn't quite measure up to the scores of *Oklahoma!* and *Carousel,* but such numbers as *A Fellow Needs a Girl, So Far* and *The Gentleman Is a Dope* are out of his top drawer and much too good for the jukeboxes . . ."

George Jean Nathan—*New York Journal-American,* October 27, 1947
". . . as pretentious as artificial jewelry and just about as valuable . . . a combination of the poorer elements of Andreyev's *The Life of a Man* and Wilder's *Our Town,* with an old D. W. Griffith going-forth-to-meet-the-dawn ending tacked on for extra dull measure . . . several passable songs . . . The impression one gets is of a poor little yokel in a calico dress and with a rhinestone tiara on her head optimistically riding a rocking horse in a race with Assault."

Irwin Shaw—*The New Republic,* October 27, 1947
". . . All I can conclude is that Rodgers and Hammerstein bitterly regret being the richest and most successful people in the American theatre, and wish they could go back to some suitable, small, simple community, and there devote their talents to playing the organ for the glee club and composing songs for the high-school football team . . . After saying that I believe the authors have built their play on a sugar-coated lie, I must admit I had a good time. Even the almost solid cloud of sentimentality cannot obscure entirely the sharp, satiric wit of the two masters . . ."

Bibliography

NEWSPAPERS AND PERIODICALS

Birth of "Allegro" —*Cue,* August 16, 1947

An Idea Grows Up by Elliot Norton —*New York Times,* October 5, 1947

Rodgers-Hammerstein Have Season's Big Opening —*Life,* October 13, 1947

Broadway Sortie by Kyle Crichton —*Collier's,* October 20, 1947

A Couple of Stage-Struck Guys by Charles D. Rice and Ben Feiner, Jr. —*This Week,* November 9, 1947

Broadway's Popular "Allegro" Extends New Trend in Musical Drama by John Beaufort —*Christian Science Monitor,* December 5, 1947

A Show Is Born by Carolyn Rolland —*Seventeen,* January, 1948

BOOKS

Allegro (Random House, New York 1948)
Book and lyrics of the musical.

Awards

Donaldson Awards, 1947-48
- Best Book, Oscar Hammerstein II
- Best Lyrics, Oscar Hammerstein II
- Best Score, Richard Rodgers

Tour

Shubert Theatre, Philadelphia, November 5, 1948—Great Northern Theatre, Chicago, June 11, 1949 (16 cities).

Selected Revivals

Lambertville Music Circus, New Jersey, September 16-21, 1952
James Jewell (JOE); Eleanor Lutton (MARJORIE); Roberta Jonay (JENNIE); Kaye Connor (EMILY); Robert Shafer (JOE SR.); Muriel O'Malley (GRANDMA).

St. Louis Municipal Opera, August 1-7, 1955
Bob Shaver (JOE); Terry Saunders (MARJORIE); Christine Mathews (JENNIE); Jen Nelson (EMILY); Edwin Steffe (JOE SR.); Peter Turgeon (CHARLIE); Erik Rhodes (DENBY).

Goodspeed Opera House, East Haddam, Connecticut, July 22, 1968
Jay Gregory (JOE); Virginia Vestoff (MARJORIE); Sheila Sullivan (JENNIE); Stanley Grover (JOE SR.); Muriel Birkhead (GRANDMA).

SOUTH PACIFIC

(1949)

A musical play with book by Oscar Hammerstein II and Joshua Logan, adapted from "Tales of the South Pacific" by James A. Michener; music by Richard Rodgers; lyrics by Mr. Hammerstein.

Presented by Messrs. Rodgers and Hammerstein
in association with Leland Hayward and Mr. Logan
Book and musical numbers directed by Mr. Logan
Settings and lighting by Jo Mielziner
Costumes by Motley
Music director, Salvatore Dell'Isola
Orchestrations by Robert Russell Bennett

Tryout
Shubert Theatre, New Haven, March 7-12, 1949
Shubert Theatre, Boston, March 15-April 2, 1949

New York Run
Majestic Theatre, April 7, 1949-May 16, 1953
(Opera House, Boston, May 18-June 27, 1953)
Broadway Theatre, June 29, 1953-January 16, 1954
1,925 performances

The Story
During World War II, American sailors and Marines have taken over an island in the South Pacific. Abetting them is planter Emile de Becque, who had come to the island from France, lived with a native woman, and fathered two children. Ensign Nellie Forbush, an American nurse, falls in love with Emile, who is much older than she, but until the dangers of war make her realize how much he means to her, she finds it difficult overcoming her doubts about their eventual union.

The Cast
NGANA, Barbara Luna
JEROME, Michael DeLeon or Noel DeLeon
HENRY, Richard Silvera
ENSIGN NELLIE FORBUSH, Mary Martin

EMILE DE BECQUE, Ezio Pinza
BLOODY MARY, Juanita Hall
BLOODY MARY'S ASSISTANT, Musa Williams
ABNER, Archie Savage
STEWPOT, Henry Slate
LUTHER BILLIS, Myron McCormick
PROFESSOR, Fred Sadoff
LT. JOSEPH CABLE, U.S.M.C., William Tabbert
CAPT. GEORGE BRACKETT, U.S.N., Martin Wolfson
COMDR. WILLIAM HARBISON, U.S.N., Harvey Stephens
YEOMAN HERBERT QUALE, Alan Gilbert
SGT. KENNETH JOHNSON, Thomas Gleason
SEABEE RICHARD WEST, Dickinson (Richard) Eastham
SEAMAN TOM O'BRIEN, Bill Dwyer
SEABEE MORTON WISE, Henry Michel
R. O. BOB MC CAFFREY, Biff McGuire
MARINE CPL. HAMILTON STEEVES, Jim Hawthorne
STAFF SGT. THOMAS HASSINGER, Jack Fontan
SEAMAN JAMES HAYES, Beau Tilden
LT. GENEVIEVE MARSHALL, Jacqueline Fisher
ENSIGN DINAH MURPHY, Roslyn Lowe
ENSIGN JANET MAC GREGOR, Sandra Deel
ENSIGN CORA MAC RAE, Bernice Saunders
ENSIGN SUE YAEGER, Pat Northrop
ENSIGN LISA MINELLI, Gloria Meli
ENSIGN CONNIE WALEWSKA, Mardi Bayne
ENSIGN PAMELA WHITMORE, Evelyn Colby
ENSIGN BESSIE NOONAN, Helena Schurgot
LIAT, Betta St. John
MARCEL, *Henry's assistant,* Richard Loo
LT. BUZZ ADAMS, Don Fellows
ISLANDERS, OFFICERS, SAILORS, MARINES: Mary Ann Reeve, Chin Yu, Alex Nicol, Eugene Smith, Richard Loo, William Ferguson

NOTE: Miss Martin succeeded by Martha Wright (June 1951). In October 1952, Miss Wright replaced by Cloris Leachman for three weeks. Mr. Pinza succeeded by Ray Middleton (Aug. 1950), Roger Rico (July 1951), George Britton (Jan. 1952). Miss Hall by Diosa Costello (June 1951), Odette Myrtil (June 1952), Musa Williams (Feb. 1953). Mr. Stephens by Bartlett Robinson (Feb. 1953), Miss St. John by Irma Sandre (October 1951). Mr. Eastham by Webb Tilton (April 1950). Miss Fisher by Betty Gillett (March 1951), Patricia Marand (March 1952), Dorothy Richards (May 1952). Miss Lowe by Mimi Kelly (March 1952). Miss Deel by Billie Worth (May 1950), Mimi Kelly (March 1951), Leigh Allen (March 1952). Miss Saunders by Betty Gillett (March 1952). Miss Northrop by Melle Matthews (May 1950), Betty O'Neil (March 1951), Roberta MacDonald (March 1952), Shirley Jones (Feb. 1953). Miss Schorgut by Virginia Martin (Feb. 1953).

In 1951, role of SEAMAN GUSTL SCHULTZ, played by William Diehl, added to cast.
In 1952, role of PVT. VICTOR MOULTON, played by Arthur Hammond, added to cast.

Musical Numbers

The action takes place on two islands in the South Pacific, during World War II.

ACT I

SCENE ONE—EMILE DEBECQUE'S PLANTATION HOME
Dites-moi, NGANA and JEROME
A Cockeyed Optimist, NELLIE
Twin Soliloquies, NELLIE and EMILE
Some Enchanted Evening, EMILE
Reprise, *Dites-moi,* NGANA and JEROME

SCENE TWO—ANOTHER PART OF THE ISLAND
Bloody Mary, SAILORS, SEABEES, MARINES

SCENE THREE—THE EDGE OF A PALM GROVE NEAR THE BEACH
There Is Nothin' Like a Dame, WISE, STEEVES, JOHNSON, BILLIS, WEST, MC CAFFREY, STEWPOT, ADAMS, QUALE
Bali Ha'i, BLOODY MARY, BILLIS, CABLE

SCENE FOUR—THE COMPANY STREET

SCENE FIVE—INSIDE THE ISLAND COMMANDER'S OFFICE

SCENE SIX—THE COMPANY STREET

SCENE SEVEN—THE BEACH
I'm Gonna Wash That Man Right Outa My Hair, NELLIE and NURSES
Reprise, *Some Enchanted Evening,* EMILE and NELLIE
A Wonderful Guy, NELLIE and NURSES

SCENE EIGHT—INSIDE THE ISLAND COMMANDER'S OFFICE

SCENE NINE—ANOTHER PART OF THE ISLAND
Reprise, *Bali Ha'i,* FRENCH GIRLS

SCENE TEN—INTERIOR OF NATIVE HUT ON BALI HA'I
Younger Than Springtime, CABLE

SCENE ELEVEN—NEAR THE BEACH OF BALI HA'I
Reprise, *Bali Ha'i,* FRENCH GIRLS

SCENE TWELVE—EMILE'S TERRACE
Reprise, *A Wonderful Guy,* NELLIE and EMILE
This Is How It Feels, NELLIE and EMILE
Reprise, *A Cockeyed Optimist,* NELLIE and EMILE
Reprise, *I'm Gonna Wash That Man Right Outa My Hair,* EMILE
Finale, NELLIE and EMILE

ACT II

SCENE ONE—THE STAGE DURING A PERFORMANCE OF "THE THANKSGIVING FOLLIES"
Soft shoe dance, NURSES and SEABEES

SCENE TWO—IN BACK OF THE STAGE
Happy Talk, BLOODY MARY
Reprise, *Younger Than Springtime,* CABLE

SCENE THREE—THE STAGE
Honey Bun, NELLIE, BILLIS and ENSEMBLE

SCENE FOUR—IN BACK OF THE STAGE
You've Got to Be Carefully Taught, CABLE
This Nearly Was Mine, EMILE

SCENE FIVE—THE COMMUNICATIONS OFFICE

SCENE SIX—ANOTHER PART OF THE ISLAND

SCENE SEVEN—THE COMMUNICATIONS OFFICE

SCENE EIGHT—THE COMPANY STREET

SCENE NINE—THE BEACH
Reprise, *Some Enchanted Evening,* NELLIE

SCENE TEN—THE COMPANY STREET
Reprise, *Honey Bun,* SAILORS, SEABEES, MARINES

SCENE ELEVEN—EMILE'S TERRACE
Finale Ultimo, reprise, *Dites-moi,* NELLIE, EMILE, NGANA, JEROME

NOTE: *Loneliness of Evening* and *My Girl Back Home* cut before New York opening.

Reviews

Brooks Atkinson—*New York Times*
". . . magnificent . . . a tenderly beautiful idyll of genuine people . . . If the country still has the taste to appreciate a masterly love song, *Some Enchanted Evening* ought to become reasonably immortal. For Rodgers' music is a romantic incarnation; and as usual Hammerstein's verses are both fervent and simple . . . Since it is not an assembled show, but a thoroughly composed musical drama, you will find high standards of characterization and acting throughout . . . as lively, warm, fresh and beautiful as we had all hoped it would be."

Howard Barnes—*New York Herald Tribune*
"*Pearls, Pure Pearls* . . . rare enchantment. It is novel in texture and treatment, rich in dramatic substance, and eloquent in song . . . a book of variety and color . . . The Rodgers music is not his finest, but it fits the mood and pace so felicitously that one does not miss a series of hit tunes. In the same way, the lyrics are part and parcel of a captivating musical unity . . . a musical play to be cherished."

John Chapman—*New York Daily News*
". . . a big, beautiful musical . . . a remarkable venture . . . the authority of a superb musician is at once apparent . . ."

Robert Coleman—*New York Daily Mirror*
". . . another smash hit . . . a score to rival *Oklahoma!'s* . . . The cast is terrific . . . truly great musical . . . beguiling, heart-warming, amusing and rewarding . . ."

Richard Watts, Jr.—*New York Post*
". . . an utterly captivating work of theatrical art . . . a work of great style and loveliness that is yet gay, vigorous and vital . . . both strangely touching and richly entertaining . . . the rarest and most tasteful showmanship . . ."

William Hawkins—*New York World-Telegram*
". . . soared exquisitely over the Majestic stage . . . the ultimate modern blending of music and popular theatre to date, with the finest kind of balance between story and song, and hilarity and heartbreak . . . Every song has something to say that immediately advances the story or the characters' relationships . . ."

Ward Morehouse—*New York Sun*
". . . combines superb music and lyrics with first-rate book material; fine performances with skillful showmanship. It serves to bring fresh vitality to our soaring musical stage . . . some exhilirating song hits . . . Hammerstein's lyrics were never sharper . . . Great men of the theatre, Rodgers, Hammerstein and Logan. It is a thrilling and exultant musical play. Let Broadway enjoy it for a couple of years."

Robert Garland—*New York Journal-American*
". . . pretty nearly everything for pretty nearly everybody . . . fine and seldom high falutin' score . . . smooth and tops-when-earthy verses . . . The American theatre has a reputation for the worthiness of its musicals. *South Pacific* will, in the long run, enhance it. It has already! . . ."

Thomas H. Wenning—*Newsweek,* April 11, 1949
". . . distinguished, original and eminently entertaining . . . the music remains a brilliant and richly varied catch, from the melodic beauty of *Some Enchanted Evening* and *This Nearly Was Mine* to the earthy, bawling GI plaint, *There Is Nothin' Like a Dame* . . . Pinza's de Becque is a figure of immense personal appeal . . . Martin is a persuasive actress and a remarkably talented performer . . ."

Hobe Morrison—*Variety,* April 13, 1949
"Rodgers and Hammerstein have not only done it again—they've

topped themselves. Their *South Pacific* lives up to all the advance build-up, and then some. It's one of the most enjoyable and satisfying musicals in theatre history . . . Its score is one of Rodgers' finest—possibly *the* finest . . . Its book is excellent . . . Hammerstein's lyrics are among his most graceful and moving . . ."

Wolcott Gibbs—*The New Yorker,* April 16, 1949
". . . Rodgers' score, if not his best, certainly isn't far from it, and Hammerstein's lyrics with one or two exceptions, are just as successful . . . the plot is admirably handled . . . the performances, especially those of Ezio Pinza and Mary Martin, are practically flawless . . . Altogether, it is a fine show . . ."

Louis Kronenberger—*Time,* April 18, 1949
". . . a magnificently effective production . . . Mary Martin gives the performance of her career . . . In quality, the show is by no means up to the production. But it is surefire popular stuff, filled with surefire popular stuffing . . . a shrewd mixture of tear-jerking and ribtickling, of sugar and spice and everything twice . . . has genuine story value, but it is not the integrated work that *Carousel* was . . . The score has its decided merits . . . however, Rodgers' fine talent seemed far more individual in the days when his musicals had crunchy centers rather than gooey ones."

Joseph Wood Krutch—*The Nation,* April 23, 1949
". . . Not since *Oklahoma!* have Rodgers and Hammerstein had so good a book or so happy a score . . . standard ingredients but superficially novel enough not to seem standard, and they have been handled with smooth expertness . . . some very rollicking lyrics, and Rodgers was inspired to find for them bright, swinging tunes. As one has come to expect in his case, the whole musical texture is fuller and richer than what one commonly finds in musical comedies . . ."

Harold Clurman—*The New Republic,* April 25, 1949
". . . a good musical. Others call it great. They mean what I do when I call it good . . . As a score and a book, it is highly efficient. Rodgers' tunes are craftsmanlike and pleasant . . . Hammerstein's lyrics and his book are simple, easy, engaging, not startlingly original but honorably liberal and decent throughout. The real triumph, aside from its unerring sense of trim unity, is the cast . . . Mary Martin tells us with radiant good nature, 'I'm in love, I'm in love with a wonderful guy,' one doesn't murmur 'Who cares?' but 'Congratulations, congratulations, congratulations to you both' . . ."

John Mason Brown—*Saturday Review of Literature,* April 30, 1949
". . . a memorable contribution to this country's musicals. Its excellences are such that it must be bracketed with *Show Boat* and *Oklahoma!* . . . a book almost sturdy enough to stand by itself as a drama without music . . . The proof of Hammerstein's and Logan's expertness is the way they manage to keep heavy material light . . . it would be hard to imagine a better company . . . these cottoned ears found the music beguiling . . ."

George Marek—*Good Housekeeping,* December, 1949
". . . a play in which popular music has been used with operatic skill. Rodgers uses his music as an operatic composer does, to express the play through the music, to create a consistent dramatic mood and delineate the characters musically . . ."

Bibliography

NEWSPAPERS AND PERIODICALS

The Tale of "South Pacific" by Irving Kolodin
—*The Saturday Review of Literature,* March 26, 1949

"South Pacific" —*New York Times Magazine,* March 27, 1949

"South Pacific" by Richard Rodgers —*New York Herald Tribune,* April 3, 1949

Success Travelogue: Oklahoma to Pacific by Lewis Funke
—*New York Times Magazine,* April 10, 1949

"South Pacific" —*Life,* April 18, 1949

How to Make a Small Fortune on Broadway —*Business Week,* June 18, 1949

Miracle on 44th Street: Standing Room Forms Before Dawn by Helen Ormsbee —*New York Herald Tribune,* September 18, 1949

"Pacific," 1 Year by Don Ross —*New York Herald Tribune,* April 2, 1950

My First Year of Playing in "South Pacific" by Mary Martin
—*New York Times,* April 7, 1950

"South Pacific" by John Bartlow Martin —*Cosmopolitan,* May, 1950

Pulitzer Prizes (editorial) —*New York Herald Tribune,* May 3, 1950

"South Pacific" Rolls Along —*Life,* January 29, 1951

My Second Year of Playing in "South Pacific" by Mary Martin
—*New York Times,* April 1, 1951

"South Pacific" Feat: Two Years Without a Seat in House Empty
—*New York Herald Tribune,* April 1, 1951

Mary Martin Free, Even to Wash Her Hair by Lewis Funke
—*New York Times,* June 3, 1951

An Actor Celebrates a 1,000 Birthday by Myron McCormick
—*New York Herald Tribune,* September 16, 1951

Goodbye to "South Pacific" by Charles D. Rice
—*This Week,* January 11, 1954

"Lang Syne" Finale at "South Pacific" by J. P. Shanley
—*New York Times,* January 17, 1954

"South Pacific" Closes (editorial)
—*New York Herald Tribune,* January 18, 1954

"South Pacific" vs. "My Fair Lady" by James A. Michener
—*New York Times,* September 23, 1956

BOOKS
South Pacific (Random House, New York, 1949)
Book and lyrics of the musical.

Awards

Pulitzer Prize in Drama, 1950

N.Y. Drama Critics Circle Award Best Musical, 1949-50

Antoinette Perry "Tony" Awards, 1949-50
- Best Musical
- Best Performance in Musical (male), Ezio Pinza
- Best Performance in Musical (female), Mary Martin
- Best Supporting Performance in Musical (male), Myron McCormick
- Best Supporting Performance in Musical (female), Juanita Hall
- Best Direction, Joshua Logan
- Best Book, Oscar Hammerstein II and Joshua Logan
- Best Score, Richard Rodgers

Donaldson Awards, 1948-49
- Best Musical
- Best Performance in Musical (female), Mary Martin
- Best Supporting Performance in Musical (male), Myron McCormick
- Best Supporting Performance in Musical (female), Juanita Hall
- Best Debut Performance (male), Ezio Pinza
- Best Direction, Joshua Logan
- Best Book, Oscar Hammerstein II and Joshua Logan
- Best Lyrics, Oscar Hammerstein II
- Best Score, Richard Rodgers

Gold Record (sales over $1 million), Columbia original-cast album

SOUTH PACIFIC

(Touring Company—1950)

Music director, Franz Allers

The Cast

NGANA, Maria Migenes or Julia Migenes
JEROME, John Migenes
HENRY, Arsenio Trinidad
ENSIGN NELLIE FORBUSH, Janet Blair
EMILE DE BECQUE, Richard Eastham
BLOODY MARY, Diosa Costello
BLOODY MARY'S ASSISTANT, Jeanette Migenes
ABNER, Arleigh Peterson
STEWPOT, Lee Krieger
LUTHER BILLIS, Ray Walston
PROFESSOR, Bill Mullikan
LT. JOSEPH CABLE, U.S.M.C., Robert Whitlow
CAPT. GEORGE BRACKETT, U.S.N., Robert Emmett Keane
COMDR. WILLIAM HARBISON, U.S.N., Alan Baxter
YEOMAN HERBERT QUALE, Len Dressler
SGT. KENNETH JOHNSON, Bob Held
SEABEE RICHARD WEST, Chris Robinson
SEABEE MORTON WISE, Sam Kirkham
SEAMAN TOM O'BRIEN, Bill Bloxsom
R. O. BOB MC CAFFREY, Stephen Ferry
MARINE CPL. HAMILTON STEEVES, Hobart Streiford
STAFF SGT. THOMAS HASSINGER, William Kester
PVT. SVEN LARSEN, William Ambler
SEAMAN JAMES HAYES, Ross Bowman
LT. GENEVIEVE MARSHALL, Muriel Bullis
ENSIGN DINAH MURPHY, Dody Heath
ENSIGN JANET MAC GREGOR, Laurel Shelby
ENSIGN SUE YAEGER, Florence Wyatt
ENSIGN LISA MINELLI, Louise McMullen
ENSIGN CONNIE WALEWSKA, Pat Finch
ENSIGN PAMELA WHITMORE, Pat Brand
ENSIGN BESSIE NOONAN, Elaine Barrow
LIAT, Norma Calderon
MARCEL, Perry Lopez
LT. BUZZ ADAMS, Warren Brown
CHIN YU, Tauni

NOTE: During August 1951, Miss Blair replaced by Connie Russell, and during October 1952, by Martha Wright. She was succeeded by Jeanne Bal (July 1953), Iva Withers (July 1954). Mr. Eastham succeeded by Webb Tilton (October 1952), Alan Gerard (December 1954). Miss Costello by Irene Bordoni (June 1951), Dorothy

Franklin (September 1952). Mr. Walston by David Burns (September 1951), Benny Baker (September 1952). Mr. Whitlow by Stanley Grover (September 1952). Mr. Keane by Russ Brown (August 1954).

Musical Numbers
Same as original production.

Tour
Hanna Theatre, Cleveland, April 24, 1950—Opera House, Chicago, March 26, 1955 (118 cities).

Tour Reviews
John Rosenfield—*Dallas Morning News*
". . . put together with the close weave of a Debussy-Maeterlinck *Peleas et Melisande.* Without the music, the plot fails to move, without the plot, the music stands as a somewhat lesser, more derivative contribution. The two elements together make a new and stunning effect for the theatre . . ."

Robert Pollak—*Chicago Sun-Times*
". . . within its defined limits, it is the perfect thing of its kind. Its music is close to Rodgers' best . . ."

Ray M. Fevers—*Variety,* October 29, 1952 (Oregon)
". . . It has been a long time since a show created as much comment and interest in this area . . . could have played to SRO for another week . . ."

Elliot Norton—*Boston Post*
"One of the greatest of all musicals . . . still has the lustre of greatness. It is still richly emotional and heartily gay . . . an enchanted evening . . ."

Herman Lowe—*Variety,* May 19, 1954 (Washington)
". . . opus is swept along by its incomparable music and by a generally strong supporting cast . . ."

Tour Bibliography
Road Troupe a Hit in "South Pacific" by William F. McDermitt
—*New York Times,* April 26, 1950

Selected Revivals
New York City Center Light Opera, May 4-17, 1955
Sandra Deel (NELLIE); Richard Collett (EMILE); Sylvia Syms (BLOODY MARY); Henry Slate (LUTHER); Herbert Banke (CABLE); Carol Lawrence (LIAT); Gene Saks (PROFESSOR). Produced by William Hammerstein.

St. Louis Municipal Opera, August 14-28, 1955
Kyle MacDonald (NELLIE); Richard Eastham (EMILE); Dorothy Franklin (BLOODY MARY); Benny Baker (LUTHER); Herbert Banke (CABLE).

New York City Center Light Opera, April 24-May 12, 1957
Mindy Carson (NELLIE); Robert Wright (EMILE); Juanita Hall (BLOODY MARY); Harvey Lembeck (LUTHER); Allen Case (CABLE); Alan Baxter (HARRISON); Dick Button (ADAMS).

San Francisco Civic Light Opera, June 3-July 6, 1957
Los Angeles Civic Light Opera, July 8-August 10, 1957
Mary Martin (NELLIE); Giorgio Tozzi (EMILE); Dorothy Franklin (BLOODY MARY); Myron McCormick (LUTHER); Herbert Banke (CABLE); Barbara Luna (LIAT).

Kansas City Starlight Theatre, June 24-July 7, 1957
Martha Wright (NELLIE); Howard Keel (EMILE); Gloria Lane (BLOODY MARY); Benny Baker (LUTHER); Jim Hawthorne (CABLE); George S. Irving (HARBISON).

Dallas State Fair Music Hall, August 5-18, 1957
Patrice Munsel (NELLIE); Earl Wrightson (EMILE); Sylvia Syms (BLOODY MARY); Lou Parker (LUTHER); Frank Porretta (CABLE).

New York City Center Light Opera, April 20-May 14, 1961
Allyn Ann McLerie (NELLIE); William Chapman (EMILE); Rosetta LeNoire (BLOODY MARY); Dort Clark (LUTHER); Stanley Grover (CABLE); Penny Fuller (CORA); Wesley Addy (HARBISON).

Dallas State Fair Music Hall, August 27-September 9, 1962
Dorothy Collins (NELLIE); Richard Torigi (EMILE); Katherine Graves (BLOODY MARY); Gabriel Dell (LUTHER); Reid Shelton (CABLE).

New York City Center Light Opera, June 3-19, 1965
Betsy Palmer (NELLIE); Ray Middleton (EMILE); Honey Sanders (BLOODY MARY); Alan North (LUTHER); Richard Armbruster (CABLE); Murvyn Vye (BRACKETT).

Music Theater of Lincoln Center, New York, June 12-September 9, 1967
Florence Henderson (NELLIE); Giorgio Tozzi (EMILE); Irene Byatt (BLOODY MARY); David Doyle (LUTHER); Justin McDonough (CABLE); Lyle Talbot (BRACKETT); Bobbi Baird (DINAH).

Jones Beach Marine Theatre, Long Island, June 27-September 2, 1968
Jones Beach Marine Theatre, Long Island, July 3-September 1, 1969
Kathleen Nolan (NELLIE); Jerome Hines (EMILE); Martha Larrimore (BLOODY MARY); Barney Martin (LUTHER); Richard Fredricks (CABLE). NOTE: For second season, Miss Nolan succeeded by Nancy Dussault; Mr. Martin by Jerry Lester; Mr. Fredricks by Nolan Van Way.

St. Louis Municipal Opera, July 29-August 3, 1968
Gisele MacKenzie (NELLIE); Giorgio Tozzi (EMILE); Mokihana (BLOODY MARY); Alan North (LUTHER); Robert Tananis (CABLE).

Valley Forge Music Fair, Pennsylvania, September 3-8, 1973
Janet Blair (NELLIE); Ricardo Montalban (EMILE); Honey Sanders (BLOODY MARY); Jay Garner (LUTHER); Hal Watters (CABLE). NOTE: This was part of tour.

O'Keefe Center, Toronto, July 11-16, 1977
Jane Powell (NELLIE); Howard Keel (EMILE); Queen Yahna (BLOODY MARY); Brandon Maggart (LUTHER); James Ferrier (CABLE). NOTE: This production toured during the summer, reopened in Los Angeles, October 12, 1977, and toured until February, 1978.

Productions Abroad

Theatre Royal, Drury Lane, London, November 1, 1951-September 26, 1953
(See below)

Her Majesty's Theatre, Melbourne, Australia, September 13, 1952
Presented by J. C. Williamson Theatres, Ltd.; directed by Charles Atkin. *Cast:* Mary LaRoche (NELLIE); Richard Collett (EMILE); Virginia Paris (BLOODY MARY); Leonard Stone (LUTHER); David Welsh (CABLE).

Oscarsteatren, Stockholm, September 16, 1952-January 5, 1953

Teatro de la Zarzuela, Madrid, 1955
Presented by Luis Sagi-Vela; translated by José López Rubio. *Cast:* Marta Santa-Olalla (NELLIE); Luis Sagi-Vela (EMILE); Gustavo Rojo (CABLE); Maria Rey (LIAT).

Istanbul, Turkey, 1962
Presented by Haldun Dormen.

Shinjuki Koma Stadium, Tokyo, May 1-29, 1966
Presented by the Toho Co., Ltd.; translated by Iwao Mori and Yohko Takada; directed by Kazuo Kikuta; choreography by Shuny Palmisano. *Cast:* Fubuki Koshiji (NELLIE); Tadao Takashima (EMILE); Sumiko Sakamoto (BLOODY MARY); Kiyoshi Atsumi (LUTHER); Masumi Okada (CABLE); Terumi Niki (LIAT).

Alhambra Theatre, Capetown, South Africa, February 28-March 11, 1968; March 18-23, 1968,
Presented by the Eoan Group; directed by David Bloomberg. NOTE: This was performed by a non-white cast.

SOUTH PACIFIC

(London—1951)

Presented by Williamson Music Ltd.
Directed by Joshua Logan
Settings and lighting by Jo Mielziner

Costumes by Motley
Music director, Reginald Burston
Orchestrations by Robert Russell Bennett
Production supervised by Jerome Whyte

London Run
Theatre Royal, Drury Lane, November 1, 1951-September 26, 1953
802 performances

The Cast
NGANA, Patricia Lowi or Valerie Braithwaite
JEROME, John Levitt or Stanley Blackman
HENRY, Michael Mellinger
ENSIGN NELLIE FORBUSH, Mary Martin
EMILE DE BECQUE, Wilbur Evans
BLOODY MARY, Muriel Smith
BLOODY MARY'S ASSISTANT, Evelyn Dove
ABNER, Archie Savage
STEWPOT, Bill Nagy
LUTHER BILLIS, Ray Walston
PROFESSOR, Wally Peterson
LT. JOSEPH CABLE, U.S.M.C., Peter Grant
CAPT. GEORGE BRACKETT, U.S.N., Hartley Power
COMDR. WILLIAM HARBISON, U.S.N., John McLaren
YEOMAN HERBERT QUALE, Larry Hagman
SGT. KENNETH JOHNSON, Ivor Emanuel
SEABEE RICHARD WEST, Henry Goodier
SEABEE MORTON WISE, A. J. Powell Bristow
SEAMAN TOM O'BRIEN, Raymond Buckingham
R. O. BOB MCCAFFREY, David Williams
MARINE CPL. HAMILTON STEEVES, Paul Dobson
STAFF SGT. THOMAS HASSINGER, Glen Fontane
PVT. SVEN LARSEN, Andrew Cole
PVT. VICTOR JEROME, Desmond D'Arcy
SGT. WATERS, Hayes Nicholas
LT. GENEVIEVE MARSHALL, Patricia Hartley
ENSIGN DINAH MURPHY, Barbara Whiting
ENSIGN JANET MACGREGOR, Deidre De Peyer
ENSIGN CORA MACCRAE, Eileen Sands
ENSIGN SUE YAEGER, June Whitfield
ENSIGN LISA MINELLI, Joyce Blair
ENSIGN CONNIE WALEWSKA, June Charlier
ENSIGN PAMELA WHITMORE, Dorothy Laroque
ENSIGN BESSIE NOONAN, Patricia Hall
ENSIGN BETTY PITT, Rosalie Whitham
LIAT, Betta St. John
MARCEL, Neville Crabbe

LT. BUZZ ADAMS, Gerald Metcalfe
ISLANDERS, SAILORS, MARINES, OFFICERS: Stanley Howlett, Victor Harman

NOTE: Miss Martin succeeded by Julie Wilson in November 1952. Mr. Walston by Fredd Wayne in April 1952.

Musical Numbers
Same as original production.

Reviews
A. V. Cookman—*London Times*
". . . Our celebrated guest is very foreign. The story touches our own experience at few points . . . its pace is something between the deliberate and the ponderous . . . the musical and the narrative parts are not much more closely integrated than in the average English musical . . . All the songs are delightful . . . Miss Martin gives the heroine the jaunty air of a virile Peter Pan . . ."

W. A. Darlington—*London Daily Telegraph*
". . . Mary Martin made the greatest kind of personal success, and deserved it well . . . The music has a haunting charm, and is most expertly handled by composer and performers. That is the piece's guarantee—that and Mary Martin."

John Barber–*London Daily Express*
"My goodness, it isn't. It isn't the sensational show that they said. We HOPED it would be worth £10 a seat. We GOT a fiendishly clever rehash of all the old stuff. We HOPED for a musical *play*. We GOT a 42nd Street *Madame Butterfly* . . . the weakest of all the Hammerstein-Rodgers musicals . . . If this were a film story, you'd say 'Phooey.' Still, these solemn doings are speeded by high spirited antics and by the lilting tunes . . . Nice show, I thought, yawning. Quite. But only a moderately enchanting evening . . ."

Alan Dent—*London News Chronicle*
". . . certainly a lively musical . . . very much all right in its way, though much more conventional than I expected. It has a little wit. It has a great deal of fetching melody. It has both insouciance and assurance . . ."

Cecil Wilson—*London Daily Mail*
". . . It was difficult, after all the preliminary excitement, not to expect a miracle and a disappointment to discover just a musical play—a colourful one, but still just a musical play . . . I had expected dynamic American hustle, and instead the play moved so slowly between its songs that it seemed to be more like *South Soporific.* So

far then, not so good, but approach it as a new show without any preconceived prejudice, and you will find much to applaud . . . Rodgers and Hammerstein have rarely given us a wittier or more tuneful selection of songs . . ."

A. E. Wilson—*London Star*
". . . the show lives up to all that was expected of it, and has enough romantic charm, sentiment and beauty as well as musical delight to succeed with a star of half Miss Martin's talent. Its prospect of success is doubled by her animated presence . . . The score is one of the composer's haunting best . . . Altogether an evening of varied delight."

Beverley Baxter, M.P.—*London Evening Standard*
". . . some good fun here and there, but no wit and little beauty. Again and again, the music came to the rescue, but the story creaks like an old tanker in distress . . . Fortunately, the second act was shorter and much more lively . . . I would not place it in the same street as *Oklahoma!* It is contrived—skillfully but laboriously—whereas *Oklahoma!* just came bursting out all over . . ."

Harold Hobson—*London Sunday Times,* November 4, 1951
". . . one of the best of American musicals . . . the music is as singable and as haunting as *Oklahoma!* . . . an air of civilisation broods over much of Hammerstein's text . . . Miss Martin is a remarkable creature . . ."

Ivor Brown—*London Observer,* November 4, 1951
". . . after all the ballyhoo, what? A number of tunes of most infectious and enchanting quality; a lively and victorious performance by Mary Martin; some agreeable humour by Ray Walston; the American Navy with gleaming torsos . . . Beyond that is Michener's story, adapted by Hammerstein and Logan, whose touch is more heavy than bright . . ."

Robert Ottaway—*London Sunday Graphic,* November 4, 1951
". . . Forget the ballyhoo. Don't compare it with *Oklahoma!*—it doesn't. It's an excellent man-made musical—not the last word of the prophet."

Kenneth Tynan—*The Spectator,* November 24, 1951
"I wept, and there is nothing in criticism harder than to convey one's gratitude for that . . . the first musical romance which was seriously involved in an adult subject . . . the real *raison d'ëtre* are the pleasant graces of Rodgers' music and the boldness of Hammerstein's lyrics . . . The settings are undistinguished, and in the second half, you

may balk at such a steady flow of plot. But these flaws noted, I have nothing to do except thank Logan, Rodgers and Hammerstein and climb up from my knees, a little cramped from the effort of typing in such an unusual position."

Bibliography

Mary Martin Wins Cheers in Britain —*New York Times*, November 2, 1951

"Pacific" or "Soporific" It's Still Terrific for Martin in London —*Variety*, November 7, 1951

Rodgers and Hammerstein —*The Sketch*, October 21, 1951

Evening With Martin Enchants Londoners —*Life*, November 19, 1951

SOUTH PACIFIC

(Film Version—1958)

Twentieth Century-Fox Release
A Magna Theatre Corp. Production
Produced by Buddy Adler
Directed by Joshua Logan
Screenplay by Paul Osborn
Choreography by LeRoy Prinz
Art directors, Lyle R. Wheeler, John DeCuir, Walter M. Scott and Paul S. Fox
Costumes by Dorothy Jeakins
Music director, Alfred Newman
Associate music director, Ken Darby
Orchestrations by Edward B. Powell, Pete King, Bernard Mayers, Robert Russell Bennett
Photographed by Leon Shamroy
Editor, Robert Simpson
Filmed in Todd-AO
Color by Technicolor

Release Date

March 19, 1958

The Cast

EMILE DEBECQUE, Rossano Brazzi (sung by Giorgio Tozzi)
NELLIE FORBUSH, Mitzi Gaynor
LT. JOSEPH CABLE, John Kerr (sung by Bill Lee)
LUTHER BILLIS, Ray Walston

BLOODY MARY, Juanita Hall (sung by Muriel Smith)
LIAT, France Nuyen
CAPT. GEORGE BRACKETT, Russ Brown
PROFESSOR, Jack Mullaney
STEWPOT, Ken Clark (sung by Thurl Ravenscroft)
COMDR. WILLIAM HARBISON, Floyd Simmons
NGANA, Candace Lee (sung by Marie Greene)
JEROME, Warren Hsieh (sung by Betty Wand)
LT. BUZZ ADAMS, Tom Laughlin
SUB CHEF, Galvan de Leon
CO-PILOT, Ronald Ely
COMMUNICATIONS MAN, Robert Jacobs
NATIVE CHIEF, Archie Savage
NURSE, Darleen Engle
ADMIRAL KESTER, Richard Cutting
NURSES: Jan Hanrahan, Muffett Webb, Beverly Johnson, May Fewell, Mary Jo Flanders, Phyllis Butcher, Anna James, Jane Lucas

Musical Numbers

Same as original production, plus *My Girl Back Home* (sung by CABLE and NELLIE), which had been dropped before New York opening.

Reviews

Bosley Crowther—*New York Times*

"*An Enchanted Evening* . . . a large, luxurious film, glowing with literal scenic detail, bursting with a grand romantic story and brimming with stereophonic songs . . . what it lacks in the more subtle values the show had upon the stage is balanced by frank spectacular features that will probably fascinate folks who go to films . . . The picture does not have the tempo and the bounce it should have in some scenes. But let's not be too analytical, for it does have, by and large, a wonderful surge of charm and gusto that just keeps coming for hours and hours . . ."

William K. Zinsser—*New York Herald Tribune*

". . . 20th Century-Fox has wrapped a fancy package—and lost the story inside. Of course it is still quite a spectacle, and it may appeal to people who missed the Broadway show . . . The songs are graceful and tender, even at shattering volume. But the movie is a victim of an old Hollywood fallacy: that if a production is 'big' enough, it's bound to be great . . ."

Archer Winsten—*New York Post*

". . . a clear-cut example of what can be done by over-production to blur character outlines, to wash away reality in fuzzy blurs of bright color, to reduce songs to recurrent themes, lose all emotion in massive group movements, and end in the boredom of a three-hour ruin of a magnificent musical . . ."

Alton Cook—*New York World-Telegram & Sun*
". . . keeps all its delightful bounce and vivacity and has picked up a lot of lavish movie treatment along the way . . . The spectacular scenes are huge and colorful without ever becoming lushly excessive. The comedy remains joyous and hilarious . . . little monkeying with the original story and music . . . The color device may be hailed as a marvelous advance in cinematic art or as an annoying distraction . . ."

Abel Green—*Variety*, March 26, 1958
". . . a boxoffice smash. It should mop up. It's a compelling entertainment . . . Nothing is perfect . . . *South Pacific* isn't. Sometimes there's too much to digest . . . the 'expansion' of the original libretto may give cause to ponder the values where the visualization eclipses the imagination . . . those sepia and other colored filter shots have effective moments but become disconcerting . . . probably the greatest galaxy of popular musical favorites from a single show in the history of musical comedy . . ."

John McCarten—*The New Yorker*, March 29, 1958
". . . full of technical razzle-dazzle, but it never comes anywhere near expressing the simple charm of the work from which it stems . . . yet another example of Hollywood's notion that size can always serve as a profitable substitute for content."

Time, March 31, 1958
". . . almost impossible to make a bad movie out of it—but the moviemakers appear to have tried . . . They gave it every last alarum and excursion of the play's somewhat too ployful plot . . . some of the smoothest Technicolor that has ever creamed a moviegoer's eyeballs; but then they decided to smear 'mood' all over the big scenes by shooting them through filters . . ."

Michael MacKay—*Newsweek*, March 31, 1958
". . . Logan's nine-year love affair with the story plus his infatuation with the beauties of the setting, have bewitched him into tossing very little footage onto the cutting-room floor. As a result the pace is about as fast as Saturday night on Bali Ha'i . . . Chief assets are the voluble love songs and rowdy chanties . . . Summing Up: Musically enchanting, visually fascinating, dramatically slow."

Bibliography

NEWSPAPERS AND PERIODICALS

More Enchanted Evenings by Seymour Peck
—*New York Times Magazine,* September 1, 1957

The Seeable Songs of "South Pacific" —*Life,* March 14, 1958

"South Pacific" by Walter Winchell —*New York Mirror,* March 30, 1958

Nellie Forbush in Rhodesia by Frederic Fox
—*New York Times Magazine,* March 11, 1962

BOOKS

The Tale of "South Pacific" edited by Thana Skouras (Lehmann, New York, 1958).

Awards

Motion Picture Academy Award, Best Sound Recording, Fred Hynes
Gold Record (sales over $1 million), RCA Victor soundtrack album.

THE KING AND I

(1951)

A musical play with book and lyrics by Oscar Hammerstein II, based on the novel, "Anna and the King of Siam" by Margaret Landon; music by Richard Rodgers

Presented by Messrs. Rodgers and Hammerstein
Directed by John van Druten
Choreography by Jerome Robbins
Settings and lighting by Jo Mielziner
Costumes by Irene Sharaff
Music director, Frederick Dvonch
Orchestrations by Robert Russell Bennett
Dance arrangements by Trude Rittmann

Tryout
Shubert Theatre, New Haven, February 26-March 3, 1951
Shubert Theatre, Boston, March 5-24, 1951

New York Run
St. James Theatre, March 29, 1951-March 20, 1954
1,246 performances

The Story
In the 1860s to the court of the King of Siam, comes Anna Leonowens, a proper Victorian lady, to become teacher to the royal princes and princesses. There she encounters many crises, both in the classroom and in the realm of the King's affairs. The longer she stays, the more influential she becomes, and after the King's death, Anna decides to remain in Siam.

The Cast
CAPTAIN ORTON, Charles Francis
LOUIS LEONOWENS, Sandy Kennedy
ANNA LEONOWENS, Gertrude Lawrence
THE INTERPRETER, Leonard Graves
THE KRALAHOME, John Juliano
THE KING, Yul Brynner
PHRA ALACK, Len Mence

TUPTIM, Doretta Morrow
LADY THIANG, Dorothy Sarnoff
PRINCE CHULALONGKORN, Johnny Stewart
PRINCESS YING YAOWALAK, Baayork Lee
LUN THA, Larry Douglas
SIR EDWARD RAMSAY, Robin Craven
PRINCESSES AND PRINCES: Crisanta Cornejo, Andrea del Rosario, Margie James, Barbara Luna, Nora Baez, Corinne St. Denis, Bunny Warner, Rodolfo Cornejo, Robert Cortazal, Thomas Griffin, Alfonso Maribo, James Maribo, Orlando Rodriguez
THE ROYAL DANCERS: Jamie Bauer, Lee Becker, Mary Burr, Gemze de Lappe, Shellie Farrell, Marilyn Gennaro, Evelyn Giles, Ina Kurland, Nancy Lynch, Michiko, Helen Murielle, Prue Ward, Dusty Worrall, Yuriko
WIVES: Stephanie Augustine, Marcia James, Ruth Korda, Suzanne Lake, Gloria Marlowe, Carolyn Maye, Helen Merritt, Phyllis Wilcox
AMAZONS: Geraldine Hamburg, Maribel Hammer, Norma Larkin, Miriam Lawrence
PRIESTS: Duane Camp, Joseph Caruso, Leonard Graves, Jack Matthews, Ed Preston
SLAVES AND MUSICIANS: Doria Avila, Raul Celada, Beau Cunningham, Tommy Gomez

NOTE: From July 30 to August 11, 1952, Miss Lawrence replaced by Celeste Holm. After Miss Lawrence's death, she was succeeded by Constance Carpenter (September 1952), Annamary Dickey (January 1954), and Patricia Morison (February 1954). From April 6 to June 22, 1952, Mr. Brynner replaced by Alfred Drake. In April 1952, Miss Morrow succeeded by Stephanie Augustine, who was replaced by Gloria Marlowe during May and June, 1952. In June 1952, Miss Sarnoff succeeded by Terry Saunders. In August 1955, during tour, Mr. Brynner succeeded by Leonard Graves.

Musical Numbers

The action takes place in and around the King's Palace, Bangkok, Siam. Time: early 1860's.

ACT I

SCENE ONE—DECK OF THE CHOW PHYA AS IT APPROACHES BANGKOK
I Whistle a Happy Tune, ANNA and LOUIS

SCENE TWO—A PALACE CORRIDOR

SCENE THREE—THE KING'S STUDY IN THE PALACE
My Lord and Master, TUPTIM
Hello, Young Lovers, ANNA
March of the Royal Siamese Children, acted by ANNA, THE KING, HIS WIVES, CHILDREN

SCENE FOUR—IN THE PALACE GROUNDS
A Puzzlement, THE KING

SCENE FIVE—THE SCHOOLROOM
The Royal Bangkok Academy, ANNA, KING'S WIVES, CHILDREN

Getting to Know You, ANNA, KING'S WIVES, CHILDREN; danced by Michiko
We Kiss in a Shadow, TUPTIM and LUN THA

SCENE SIX—A PALACE CORRIDOR
Reprise, *A Puzzlement,* PRINCE CHULALONGKORN and LOUIS

SCENE SEVEN—ANNA'S BEDROOM
Shall I Tell You What I Think of You?, ANNA
Something Wonderful, LADY THIANG

SCENE EIGHT—A PALACE CORRIDOR

SCENE NINE—THE KING'S STUDY
Finale, COMPANY

ACT II
SCENE ONE—THE SCHOOLROOM
Western People Funny, LADY THIANG and KING'S WIVES

SCENE TWO—IN THE PALACE GROUNDS
I Have Dreamed, TUPTIM and LUN THA
Reprise, *Hello, Young Lovers,* ANNA

SCENE THREE—THE THEATRE PAVILION
The Small House of Uncle Thomas Ballet
NARRATOR, Doretta Morrow
UNCLE THOMAS, Dusty Worrall
TOPSY, Ina Kurland
LITTLE EVA, Shellie Farrell
ELIZA, Yuriko
KING SIMON OF LAGREE, Gemze de Lappe
ANGEL, Michiko

SCENE FOUR—THE KING'S STUDY
Song of the King, THE KING
Shall We Dance?, ANNA and THE KING

SCENE FIVE—IN THE PALACE GROUNDS

SCENE SIX—A ROOM IN ANNA'S HOUSE

SCENE SEVEN—A PALACE CORRIDOR

SCENE EIGHT—THE KING'S STUDY
Reprise, *I Whistle a Happy Tune,* ANNA
Finale, COMPANY

NOTE: *Waiting, Who Would Refuse?* and *Now You Leave* cut before New York opening.

Reviews
Brooks Atkinson—*New York Times*
". . . no match for *South Pacific* which is an inspired musical drama . . . Strictly on its own terms, it is an original and beautiful excursion

into the rich splendors of the Far East, done with impeccable taste by two artists and brought to life with a warm, romantic score, idiomatic lyrics and some exquisite dancing . . . *Something Wonderful* is one of Rodgers' most exuberant numbers. Probably the most glorious is *I Have Dreamed* . . . This time Rodgers and Hammerstein are not breaking any fresh trails. But it is a beautiful and lovable musical play."

Otis L. Guernsey, Jr.—*New York Herald Tribune*
"*They Do It Again* . . . has everything that one has a right to expect from these two talented collaborators, including a libretto that stands on its own merits, music that transposes emotion into melody and a handsome production . . . has not the masterpiece's brilliance but it glows with its own softer lights of consistent entertainment . . . theatre music of a uniformly superior quality. Its most radiant number is a catchy one called *Getting to Know You* . . . blessed with the presence of Gertrude Lawrence and Yul Brynner . . ."

John Chapman—*New York Daily News*
". . . a distinguished musical play . . . something different. It is beautifully set and sumptuously, excitingly costumed . . . In it is an enchanting ballet. In it is some interesting music. But the most important work of this big, long show is the work of Mr. Hammerstein . . . an intricate and expert piece of showmanship . . ."

Robert Coleman—*New York Daily Mirror*
". . . has heart, drama, comedy and eye-filling spectacle. The Rodgers score has been fashioned to follow the action of the book rather than to shine forth in individual segments. The lyrics are among the best ever penned by Hammerstein . . . They, along with their libretto, offer a philosophy that is decent and enlightening . . . The play sets a new high standard for the musical stage . . ."

Richard Watts, Jr.—*New York Post*
"*Another Triumph for the Masters* . . . a beautiful and fascinating musical play, a splendid successor to *South Pacific* . . . has color, beauty and a strange kind of sweetness, a good story, characteristically fine music and lyrics, a delightful ballet, some of the most charming children in the history of the stage, a remarkably believable performance by Yul Brynner, and the magic of Gertrude Lawrence. In a word, it is a show of rare quality . . . a great and resounding credit to its distinguished authors and the American theatre . . ."

William Hawkins—*New York World-Telegram & Sun*
". . . you expect novelty from Rodgers and Hammerstein. They have achieved it once more, a balance between drama and music which is quite different from their earlier efforts . . . The music is not so much an addition as it is an illumination . . . I cannot help feeling that if it were to do complete justice to its startling narrative, the outcome would have to approximate a popular form of grand opera. As it is, remaining palatable for its intended public, it is often lovely, occasionally languid and stays fragrantly on the surface."

John McClain—*New York Journal-American*
"*Another Great Hit for Dick and Oscar* . . . There has rarely been a better mounted show . . . it is not a great score according to Rodgers' standards . . . I mean there were no musical moments which made you almost jump out of the seat, knowing you were hearing a great hit for the first time, as there have been in most of his successes . . ."

Hobe Morrison—*Variety,* April 4, 1951
". . . an impressive show. It is obviously one of the most beautiful in memory and also tasteful, colorful, sentimental, melodic and generally entertaining. If it is not absolutely top Rodgers-Hammerstein, it is still vastly superior to the best of almost anyone else . . . Hammerstein's lyrics are another of his characteristic blends of apparently effortless grace, pictorial beauty and irresistible sentiment . . ."

John Lardner—*The New Yorker,* April 7, 1951
"*The Surefire Boys in Siam* . . . The touches of character drawing, and its faithfulness to a reasonably adult and literary story, make this at least as novel and effective a musical as *South Pacific* . . . the most beguiling ballet I have ever seen—A Siamese interpretation of *Uncle Tom's Cabin* . . . I liked the music a little better than *South Pacific* . . ."

George Jean Nathan—*New York Journal-American,* April 9, 1951
". . . Aside from the score, which is one of Rodgers' best, the show gives us Hammerstein in his usual happy lyric trim, and the pair once again establishes themselves as the best team in their line that our theatre presently offers . . . numerous points of interest, but indicates some forcing and strain to fit the original to the requirements of the stage . . ."

Louis Kronenberger—*Time,* April 9, 1951
". . . may not quite be Rodgers and Hammerstein at their best, but it is musicomedy at its most charming . . . sometimes touching, and far less insipid than the usual musicomedy romance . . . The score is

thoroughly pleasant . . . it would do better with a less solemn ending. Otherwise, it is all scent and glitter, ritualized movement and high barbaric style."

Thomas H. Wenning—*Newsweek,* April 9, 1951
". . . handsome, tuneful, affectionate, and rather special in its pattern of enchantment . . . has unusually intellectual overtones for a Broadway musical. But it also has an honest understanding of the real people involved, a wistful charm, and an exotic background . . . the matching excellences of Gertrude Lawrence and Yul Brynner give the libretto its full dramatic authority . . . Rodgers songs are in his most ingratiating mood, and, if anything, a little more deceptively simple . . ."

John Mason Brown—*The Saturday Review,* April 14, 1951
"*Another Enchanted Evening* . . . the kind of perfect taste which characterizes the staging, the dancing, the performances, the settings, the costumes, and the writing of both the music and the book of *The King and I* is one of the most uncommon attributes. One of the most delightful, too . . . Rodgers and Hammerstein have never worked together more skillfully as master showmen or offered a production warmer in its feelings or more beguiling in its beauties . . ."

Harold Clurman—*The New Republic,* April 16, 1951
". . . a pleasant affair. Its story is most unusual for a Broadway musical. It has color, sentiment and a quality of good will which seems to me is the source of Hammerstein's appeal as a song writer. Musically, it is probably the weakest of the Rodgers scores . . . for me the star of the evening is Hammerstein telling us modestly that nothing in this world is certain but that it is still wonderful for men to try to learn and for children to begin where their fathers left off."

Richard Watts, Jr.—*New York Post,* August 2, 1951 (follow-up)
". . . I was struck by the way we otherwise enthusiastic reviewers were lacking in appreciation of Rodgers' score . . . On second hearing, I realize that it is brilliant and beautiful . . . and filled with delightful songs . . ."

Bibliography

NEWSPAPERS AND PERIODICALS

Miss Lawrence and "The King and I" by William Hawkins
—*New York World-Telegram & Sun,* March 24, 1951

About "The King and I" by Richard Rodgers and Oscar Hammerstein II
—*New York Times,* March 25, 1951

The Background Is Siam, the Music Pure Broadway by Richard Rodgers
—*New York Herald Tribune,* March 25, 1951

Gertie and the King of Siam by James Poling —*Collier's,* April 7, 1951

A Show Gets Dressed –*This Week,* April 15, 1951

Van Druten in Unique Role as Director by Irving Drutman
—*New York Herald Tribune,* April 22, 1951

Latest Rodgers-Hammerstein Triumph Comes Up With New Star as Monarch Who Met a Schoolmarm –*Life,* April 23, 1951

"The King and I" –*Life,* June 11, 1951

The King of Siam's Children and I by Margaret Landon
—*Vogue,* August 15, 1951

Amateur offering of "The King and I" Acclaimed by Nairobi audiences
—*New York Times,* March 19, 1961

BOOKS

The King and I (Random House, New York, 1951)
Book and lyrics of the musical.

Awards

Antoinette Perry "Tony" Awards, 1951-52
- Best Musical
- Best Performance in Musical (female), Gertrude Lawrence
- Best Score, Richard Rodgers
- Best Book, Oscar Hammerstein II

Donaldson Awards, 1950-51
- Best Performance in Musical (male), Yul Brynner
- Best Supporting Performance (female), Doretta Morrow
- Best Dance Direction, Jerome Robbins
- Best Scenic Designer, Jo Mielziner
- Best Costume Designer, Irene Sharaff

Tour

Community Theatre, Hershey, Pa., March 22, 1954—Shubert Theatre, Philadelphia, December 17, 1955 (30 cities).

Selected Revivals

St. Louis Municipal Opera, August 8-15, 1954
Annamary Dickey (ANNA); Darren McGavin (KING); Terry Saunders (THIANG); Stephanie Augustine (TUPTIM); Tony Bavaar (LUN THA); Erik Rhodes (KRALAHOME).

New York City Center Light Opera, April 18-May 6, 1956
Jan Clayton (ANNA); Zachary Scott (KING); Muriel Smith (THIANG); Christine Matthews (TUPTIM); Philip Wentworth (LUN THA); Yuriko (ELIZA). Produced by William Hammerstein.

Kansas City Starlight Theatre, August 20-September 2, 1956
Jeanette MacDonald (ANNA); Leonard Graves (KING); Terry Saunders (THIANG).

Los Angeles Civic Light Opera, April 21-May 24, 1958
San Francisco Civic Light Opera, May 26-June 28, 1958
Gisele MacKenzie (ANNA); Cameron Mitchell (KING); Rosalind Nadell (THIANG); Beverly Allyson (TUPTIM); Herbert Banke (LUN THA).

St. Louis Municipal Opera, June 11-21, 1959
Patricia Morison (ANNA); Tony Dexter (KING); Terry Saunders (THIANG); Beverly Allyson (TUPTIM); Richard Banke (LUN THA).

New York City Center Light Opera, May 11-19, 1960
Barbara Cook (ANNA); Farley Granger (KING); Anita Darian (THIANG); Joy Clements (TUPTIM); Seth Riggs (LUN THA); Yuriko (ELIZA); Gemze deLappe (SIMON).

Mineola Playhouse, New York, April 16-May 12, 1963
Betsy Palmer (ANNA); William Chapman (KING); Jean Sanders (THIANG); Olga James (TUPTIM); Paul Richards (LUN THA); Murvyn Vye (KRALAHOME).

New York City Center Light Opera, June 2-23, 1963
Eileen Brennan (ANNA); Manolo Fabregas (KING); Anita Darian (THIANG); Joy Clements (TUPTIM); L.D. Clements (LUN THA); Yuriko (ELIZA).

St. Louis Municipal Opera, July 29-August 4, 1963
Betty White (ANNA); Charles Korvin (KING); Jean Sanders (THIANG); Janet Pavek (TUPTIM); Reid Shelton (LUN THA).

Westbury Music Fair, Long Island, August 6-18, 1963
Jane Morgan (ANNA); J. D. Cannon (KING); Melisande Congden (THIANG); Carolyn Maye (TUPTIM); Michael Davis (LUN THA).

Music Theater of Lincoln Center, New York, July 6-August 8, 1964
Risë Stevens (ANNA); Darren McGavin (KING); Patricia Neway (THIANG); Lee Venora (TUPTIM); Frank Porretta (LUN THA); Michael Kermoyan (KRALAHOME); Eric Brotherson (RAMSAY).

Los Angeles Civic Light Opera, April 19-June 5, 1965
San Francisco Civic Light Opera, June 8-July 24, 1965
Florence Henderson (ANNA); Ricardo Montalban (KING); Jean Sanders (THIANG); Lee Venora (TUPTIM); Frank Porretta (LUN THA); Michael Kermoyan (KRALAHOME). NOTE: This was the first production at the Pavilion of the Los Angeles Music Center.

St. Louis Municipal Opera, August 21-September 3, 1967
Ann Blyth (ANNA); Pernell Roberts (KING); Jean Sanders (THIANG); Lee Venora (TUPTIM); Montes de Oca (LUN THA).

New York City Center Light Opera, May 23-June 9, 1968
Constance Towers (ANNA); Michael Kermoyan (KING); Anita Darian (THIANG); Eleanor Calbes (TUPTIM); Stanley Grover (LUN THA); Christopher Hewett (RAMSAY).

St. Louis Municipal Opera, August 23-29, 1971
Roberta Peters (ANNA); James Shigeta (KING); Eileen Schauler (THIANG); Udana Power (TUPTIM); Dean Rhodus (LUN THA).

Jones Beach Marine Theatre, Long Island, June 28-September 3, 1972
Constance Towers (ANNA); John Cullum (KING); Eileen Schauler (THIANG); Patricia Arnell (TUPTIM); John Stewart (LUN THA).

Los Angeles Civic Light Opera, April 30-June 23, 1974
San Francisco Civic Light Opera, June 25, 1974
Sally Ann Howes (ANNA); Ricardo Montalban (KING); Helena Bliss (THIANG); Emily Yancy (TUPTIM); David Cryer (LUN THA).

Productions Abroad

Theatre Royal, Drury Lane, London, October 8, 1953-January 14, 1956
(See page 588)

Princess Theatre, Melbourne, Australia, December 22, 1962-July 6, 1963
Presented by Garnet H. Carroll; directed by Charles Hickman; choreography by Bill Yule. *Cast:* Sheila Bradley (ANNA); Jeff Warren (KING); Lina Denison (THIANG); Geraldene Morrow (TUPTIM); John Rickard (LUN THA). *Tour:* July 17, 1963-April 11, 1964.

Gaiety Theatre, Dublin, Ireland, June 22, 1965
Presented by Louis Elliman; directed by Gerard Phillips; choreography by Alice Delgarno. *Cast:* Ann Martin (ANNA); Peter Elliott (KING); Ida Shepley (THIANG); Catherine Lancaster (TUPTIM); Phillip Hinton (LUN THA).

Takarazuka Theatre, Tokyo, Japan, December 2-27, 1965; January 11-February 4, 1966
Presented by the Toho Co., Ltd.; book translated by Iwao Mori and Yohko Takada; lyrics translated by Tokiko Iwatani; directed by Kazuo Kikuta; choreography by Shuny Palmisano and Kanna Ishii. *Cast:* Fubuki Koshiji (ANNA); Somegoro Ichikawa (KING); Yoshie Minami (THIANG); Kaoru Yodo (TUPTIM); Samito Tachikawa (LUN THA).

Staatstheater, Munich, Germany, April 17, 1966
Translated by Janne Furch; music director, Franz Allers. *Cast:* Liselotte Ebnet (ANNA); Hans Putz (KING); Eva-Maria Görgen (THIANG); Dorothea Chryst (TUPTIM); Ernst Schütz (LUN THA).

Alhambra Theatre, Tel Aviv, Israel, May, 1, 1966; 3 months
Presented by Giora Godik; book translated by Yoram Kaniuk; lyrics translated by Naomi Shemer; directed by James Hammerstein; choreog-

raphy reproduced by Yuriko. *Cast:* Rivka Raz (ANNA); Aric Lavie (KING); Ofra Diron (THIANG); Michal Peres (TUPTIM); Dany Ben-Israel (LUN THA).

Imperial Theatre, Tokyo, Japan, November 1-27, 1968
Presented by the Toho Co. Ltd. *Cast:* Wataru Nachi (ANNA); Somegoro Ichikawa (KING); Yoshie Minami (THIANG); Takeshi Kato (TUPTIM); Samito Tachikawa (LUN THA).

Adelphi Theatre, London, October 10, 1973-May 25, 1974; *260 performances*
Presented by Harold Fielding; directed by Roger Redfarn; choreography by Sheila O'Neill. *Cast:* Sally Ann Howes (ANNA); Peter Wyngarde (KING); Moyna Cope (THIANG); Pauline Antony (TUPTIM); Valentine Palmer (LUN THA); David Davenport (KRALAHOME).

Palladium, London, June 12, 1979
Presented by Tom Arnold Associates & Ross Taylor, in association with Lee Guber & Shelly Gross; directed by Yuriko; choreography reproduced by Susan Kikuchi. *Cast:* Yul Brynner (KING); Virginia McKenna (ANNA); Hye-Young Choi (THIANG); June Angela (TUPTIM); Marty Rhone (LUN THA). NOTE: This production based on 1977 New York revival (see page 594).

THE KING AND I

(London Production—1953)

Presented by Williamson Music Ltd.
Directed by John van Druten
Choreography reproduced by June Graham
Settings and lighting by Jo Mielziner
Costumes by Irene Sharaff
Music director, Reginald Burston
Orchestrations by Robert Russell Bennett
Production supervised by Jerome Whyte

London Run

Theatre Royal, Drury Lane, October 8, 1953-January 14, 1956
926 performances

The Cast

CAPTAIN ORTON, John Harvey
LOUIS LEONOWENS, Roy Grant
ANNA LEONOWENS, Valerie Hobson
THE INTERPRETER, Shaym Bahudur
THE KRALAHOME, Martin Benson
THE KING, Herbert Lom
PHRA ALACK, Thomas Hare

TUPTIM, Doreen Duke
LADY THIANG, Muriel Smith
PRINCE CHULALONGKORN, Timothy Brooking
PRINCESS YING YAOWALAK, Virginia Tarleton
LUN THA, Jan Mazarus
SIR EDWARD RAMSAY, Ronald Leigh Hunt
PRINCESSES AND PRINCES: Souti Anthony, Ann Dickens, Daphne Long, Joyce Long, Florence Meyer, Linda Mooney, Philomena Morgan-Jones, Tamba Allen, Barry Barnett, Ali Houssein, Pat McEwan, Clive Bunyan, Tony Coletti, Michael Cove, Clarence Gordon, Dereck Rozario, Ronald Singer
THE ROYAL DANCERS: Sonya Hana (ELIZA), Joan Elvin (ANGEL), Jean Johnston (TOPSY), Elizabeth Parks, Silvia Herklots, Josephine Spaull, Patricia Hawkes, Denise Merrum, Joan Boyd (UNCLE THOMAS), Maureen Webster, Patricia Colbourne, Dorothy Fraser, Gladys Allgood, Julie Musgrove, Ann Roberts (EVA), Joan Turner (KING SIMON), Brigitte Kelly, Sheila Kennedy
SLAVES: Ivor Meggido, Rikki Septimus, Barrie Irwin, Gilbert Brunett
WIVES: Danutta Karel, Barbara Lewis, Joan Drummond, Nan Williams, Delia Manon, Hilde du Toit, Phyllis Anderson, Dorina Gregory, Joan Merritt, Maureen Hartley
AMAZONS: Mary Midwinter, Ann Pidgeon, Merle Arundale, Lee Vernon
PRIESTS: Henry Goodier, Ivor Emmanuel, James Appleby, Frank O'Connor, Joe McBride, Andrew Cole

NOTE: In May 1955, Miss Hobson succeeded by Eve Lister; Mr. Lom by George Pastell.

Musical Numbers
Same as original production.

Reviews
London Times
". . . finds the authors matching up their melodies and their wit to a Gilbert and Sullivan situation . . . The genuineness in the theme gives the piece a quality of unexpectedness . . . it is an evening of tunes that echo in the mind and of scenes which, though imposingly set, have always a hint of quiet humour in their romantic sentiment. At its best, the pieces takes on the rhythm of a dream-fantasy . . . Altogether, a pleasing affair, if a little unexpected in its quietness."

Paul Holt—*London Daily Herald*
"How fine it is to come across a show as pleasing as this . . ."

Milton Shulman—*London Evening Standard*
". . . Rodgers and Hammerstein are middleaged wizards . . . English audiences may find their latest offering even more irresistible than anything they have done before . . ."

Stephen Williams—*London Evening News*
"... the dialogue is acceptable to adult minds without the insane bawling and hooting we've learned to dread ..."

Harold Hobson—*London Sunday Times,* October 11, 1953
"The enthusiasm of the audience was boundless, and it is easy to understand why. The redoubtable author and composer think in terms of tunes and tales with a unison not matched since Gilbert and Sullivan, and this story provides an unceasing stream of very competent music, a clever ballet, a series of colourful and glittering costumes, and a softly muted love theme ..."

Kenneth Tynan—*London Observer,* October 11, 1953
"... probably comes closer than any of the other Rodgers and Hammerstein shows to the sentimental-genteel spirit of our sick friend, English musical comedy ... sure of a huge popular success ..."

Eric Keown—*Punch,* October 14, 1953
"... goes back unashamedly to a story of simple sentiment; bolder even than that, it has a sad ending. All this must be a welcome change, even if in spite of its undoubted charms, it is sometimes slow in entertainment ... needs a sharper edge."

Harold Myers—*Variety,* October 28, 1953
"... more than justified the grapevine reports. It is sock boxoffice in any language and can be rated one of the outstanding American contributions to the British musical stage ... songs and lyrics may not compare too favorably with earlier Rodgers and Hammerstein successes, but they become a definite, integral part of the production ..."

Bibliography

"The King and I" (cover story) —*Theatre World,* January, 1954

THE KING AND I

(Film Version—1956)

A Twentieth Century-Fox Picture
Produced by Charles Brackett
Directed by Walter Lang
Screenplay by Ernest Lehman
Choreography by Jerome Robbins

Art directors, Lyle R. Wheeler and John De Cuir
Costumes by Irene Sharaff
Music director, Alfred Newman
Associate music director, Ken Darby
Orchestrations by Edward B. Powell, Gus Levene, Bernard Mayers and Robert Russell Bennett
Photographed by Leon Shamroy
Editor, Robert Simpson
Filmed in Cinemascope 55
Color by DeLuxe

Release Date
June 28, 1956

The Cast
ANNA LEONOWENS, Deborah Kerr (sung by Marni Nixon)
THE KING, Yul Brynner
TUPTIM, Rita Moreno
THE KRALAHOME, Martin Benson
LADY THIANG, Terry Saunders
LOUIS LEONOWENS, Rex Thompson
LUN THA, Carlos Rivas (sung by Reuben Fuentes)
PRINCE CHULALONGKORN, Patrick Adiarte
BRITISH AMBASSADOR, Alan Mowbray
SIR EDWARD RAMSAY, Geoffrey Toone
ELIZA, Yuriko
SIMON LEGREE, Marion Jim
KEEPER OF THE DOGS, Robert Banas
UNCLE THOMAS, Dusty Worrall
SPECIALTY DANCER, Gemze de Lappe
TWINS, Thomas and Dennis Bonilla
ANGEL IN BALLET, Michiko
SHIP'S CAPTAIN, Charles Irwin
INTERPRETER, Leonard Strong
SIAMESE GIRL, Irene James
AMAZONS, Jadin and Jean Wong
GUARDS, Fuji and Weaver Levy

Musical Numbers
Same as original production except for following omissions: *My Lord and Master, Shall I Tell You What I Think of You?, I Have Dreamed,* and *Western People Funny.*

The Reviews
Bosley Crowther—*New York Times*
". . . It has the full content of that charmingly droll and poignant

book that Mr. Hammerstein crystallized so smartly . . . It has, too, the ardor and abundance of Mr. Rodgers' magnificent musical score . . . Also, it has the advantage of a handsome and talented cast . . . However, it is the pictorial magnificance of the appropriately regal production that especially distinguishes this film . . . a grand and moving thing."

William K. Zinsser—*New York Herald Tribune*
". . . Rodgers' bewitching melodies and Hammerstein's sensitive lyrics are completely intertwined with the characters . . . The art department has done its job almost too well . . . When the director ranges his camera across the very wide screen, the colors seem to swim, and it's almost impossible to find Anna and the king. This treatment makes the first half distracting and slow . . . Brynner gives the movie its animal spark . . ."

Archer Winsten—*New York Post*
". . . extraordinarily beautiful . . . the original songs have withstood the tests of time, popularity and repetition better than most . . . Yul Brynner is beyond cavil . . . *The Small House of Uncle Thomas* is a creation of such striking visuals and movement that it lingers in the memory . . . Nevertheless, it fell short of expectation . . . The real weakness stems from the negative relationship of the king and Anna . . ."

Saul Levinson—*New York World-Telegram & Sun*
". . . Surely one of the most beautiful pictures ever put on film, it is further enhanced by an excellent cast . . . The melodies and lyrics are of the best . . . This remarkable blending of story, cast, score and setting causes it not to matter if the story is so familiar . . . 'Tis a rare movie that brings no negative criticism, but that's the way this one is."

Hy Hollinger—*Variety*, July 4, 1956
". . . pictorially exquisite, musically exciting, and dramatically satisfying. It's undoubtedly the best celluloid rendition of the R & H creation. It should be the king-sized money-maker of the year . . . a visual and aural triumph . . ."

Ted Robinson, Jr.—*Newsweek*, July 9, 1956
". . . What was one of Broadway's best productions has now become one of Hollywood's best. The screen's extra-added magnificence in this instance intensifies rather than obscures the special qualities of the story . . . There is loveliness in the famous songs (which sound fresh once again) . . . Summing Up: Humor, charm, splendor, excitement."

John McCarten—*The New Yorker,* July 14, 1956
". . . includes a ballet about *The Small House of Uncle Thomas* that goes on longer than all the editions of Harriet Beecher Stowe . . . the various tableaux are altogether delightful. Once you've got on to the basic joke, though, you may find this quaint view of the East just a trifle too extensive. At any rate, it's all pretty and harmless."

Time, July 16, 1956
". . . has no surprises . . . The biggest and best production number is the Siamese version of *Uncle Tom's Cabin* . . . the jokes are pleasant, the children cute, and the songs, though familiar, have the springtime bounciness that mark Rodgers and Hammerstein's work."

Hollis Alpert—*Saturday Review,* July 21, 1956
". . . done up a good deal more handsomely than it was on the stage . . . some pleasant tunes . . . the sets are some of the most lavish ever produced . . . The story has undeniable charm, sometimes a little too thickly sugared . . . there is magnificence in this movie . . ."

Bibliography

"The King and I" in Movies by Thomas Wood
—*New York Herald Tribune,* February 5, 1956

The King, His Camera and a Film Triumph (cover story) —*Life,* May 28, 1956

"The King and I" by Jesse Zunser (cover story) —*Cue,* June 23, 1956

Awards

Motion Picture Academy Awards, 1956
- Best Male Performance, Yul Brynner
- Best Scoring for Musical Film, Alfred Newman and Ken Darby
- Best Set Decoration (color), Walter M. Scott and Paul S. Fox
- Best Art Direction (color), Lyle R. Wheeler and John De Cuir
- Best Costume Design (color), Irene Sharaff
- Best Sound Recording, Carl Faulkner

Film Daily Poll, Best Film of the Year, 1956

Gold Record (sales over $1 million), Capitol soundtrack album

THE KING AND I

(New York—1977)

Presented by Lee Guber and Shelly Gross
Directed by Yuriko
Original choreography by Jerome Robbins
Settings by Peter Wolf
Costumes recreated by Stanley Simmons
Lighting by Thomas Skelton
Music director, John Lesko
Music supervisor, Milton Rosenstock
Orchestrations by Robert Russell Bennett

Tryout

Starlight Theatre, Indianapolis, July 26-August 1, 1976
Municipal Theatre, St. Louis, August 2-8, 1976
Theatre of Stars, Atlanta, August 9-15, 1976
Starlight Theatre, Kansas City, August 16-22, 1976
Theatre of Performing Arts, Miami Beach, August 24-28, 1976
Valley Forge Music Fair, Devon, Pa., August 31-September 12, 1976
Painters Mill Music Fair, Owings Mill, Md., September 14-19, 1976
Westbury Music Fair, N.Y., September 21-October 2, 1976

New York Run

Uris Theatre, May 2, 1977-December 30, 1978
695 performances.

The Cast

CAPTAIN ORTON, Larry Swansen
LOUIS LEONOWENS, Alan Amick
ANNA LEONOWENS, Constance Towers
INTERPRETER, Jae Woo Lee
THE KRALAHOME, Michael Kermoyan
THE KING, Yul Brynner
TUPTIM, June Angela
LADY THIANG, Hye-Young Choi
PRINCE CHULALONGKORN, Gene Profanato
PRINCESS YING YAOWALAK, Julie Woo
LUN THA, Martin Vidnovic
SIR EDWARD RAMSAY, John Michael King
ROYAL DANCERS AND WIVES: Su Applegate, Jessica Chao, Lei-Lynne Doo, Dale Harimoto, Pamela Kalt, Susan Kikuchi, Faye Fujisaki Mar, Sumiko Murashima, Libby Rhodes, Cecile Santos, Hope Sogawa, Mary Ann Teng, Patricia K. Thomas
PRINCESSES AND PRINCES: Ivan Ho, Clark Huang, Annie Lam, Connie Lam,

Jennifer Lam, Paul Siu, Tim Waldrip, Kevan Weber, Kym Weber, Julie Woo, Mary Woo

NURSES AND AMAZONS: Sydney Smith, Marianne Tatum, Patricia K. Thomas, Rebecca West

PRIESTS AND SLAVES: Kaipo Daniels, Barrett Hong, Jae Woo Lee, Ric Ornellas, Simeon Den, Chandra Tanna, Robert Vega

NOTE: From April 11 to May 5, 1978, Miss Towers replaced by Angela Lansbury, Mr. Brynner by Mr. Kermoyan, Mr. Kermoyan by Mr. Lee.

Reviews

Clive Barnes—*New York Times*
". . . the musical returned with a pleasant patina of age, but, even more, as a reminder of what the Broadway musical was like in its Golden Age of Efficiency . . . the new production has been handsomely staged . . . A lovely musical for either memories or drama . . ."

Douglas Watt—*New York Daily News*
". . . a magnificent revival. It is far and away the most beautiful show in town, musically and in all other respects . . . one of the masterpieces of the Rodgers and Hammerstein canon, equipped with one of Rodgers' most masterly scores and perhaps Hammerstein's most secure and appealing libretto. It moves like silk . . . Brynner seems even better than before . . . the finest performance I've ever seen Constance Towers give . . ."

Martin Gottfried—*New York Post*
". . . a virtually flawless collection of Richard Rodgers songs . . . The show has too many flaws of stagecraft . . . But they can't take away what it has, either, and what it has is indeed quality . . . Hammerstein's adaptation most certainly captures the elements of a great story . . . still the best of the Rodgers and Hammerstein musicals, class itself."

John Beaufort—*Christian Science Monitor*
"The next best thing to seeing and hearing *The King and I* for the first time is the pleasure of seeing it and hearing it again. The lush melodies are as irresistibly melting as ever, and the book and lyrics are potently sentimental . . . the elements of musical theatre all blend marvelously . . . This superbly performed, gorgeously designed production is indeed something wonderful."

Hobe Morrison—*Variety*, May 4, 1977
". . . The Rodgers and Hammerstein masterpiece is one of the gems of the golden era of musical shows and 26 years has not lessened its dramatic and emotional impact . . . Brynner is just as dynamic and

perhaps more compelling than ever . . . show is a marvel of shrewd theatrical touches of the sort that invariably delights audiences . . . songs that never miss . . ."

Brendan Gill—*The New Yorker,* May 14, 1977
". . . offers a very pleasant evening indeed . . . a model specimen of the Rodgers and Hammerstein musical; to a degree that I hadn't expected, I find that it has become precious to me not only because it is admirable in itself but because it appears impossible for anyone to write musicals of a similar nature nowadays . . . let your heart be lifted at the Uris . . ."

Marilyn Stasio—*Cue,* May 14, 1977
"Some things wear remarkably well after a quarter century, and an ageless Rodgers and Hammerstein score is one of them. Yul Brynner is another . . . this scrupulously faithful revival transports us into the magical world of the musical theatre at its inspired best. It's a dazzlement . . . Its beauties are timeless, beginning with the enchanting score . . ."

Walter Kerr—*New York Times,* May 15, 1977
". . . obviously born of a tradition that is gradually being replaced, just as obviously studded with matched melodies and lyrics so irresistible that we're going to cling to them for dear life no matter what turns our sluggishly changing theatre may take . . . While we're being literally enveloped by sounds rich enough to surprise us even when we are remembering them, aren't we bothered by what is dated in the book, in the styling? Very, very rarely . . ."

Charles Michener—*Newsweek,* May 16, 1977
"*Long Live the King* . . . a sumptuous revival . . . an embarrassment of riches . . . the most tender avalanche of melodies composed for a Broadway show since the heyday of Jerome Kern . . . a Hammerstein lyric invariably attaches its honest sentiments to a Rodgers tune in a graceful, untricky way that only seems to propel the melodic flight . . . now seems a gracefully tough-minded battle of the sexes . . . there is a new depth to Brynner's performance . . ."

Alan Rich—*New York Magazine,* May 16, 1977
". . . slovenly, vulgar, and dull beyond my most pessimistic expectations . . . a fuzzy, disorganized piece in which both creators sadly overreached themselves . . . It has come in looking dangerously like an economy touring package . . ."

George Oppenheimer—*Newsday,* May 20, 1977
"*Long Live the King* . . . by all odds the best revival of Rodgers and

Hammerstein's show . . . Constance Towers is the most enchanting 'I' you are apt to see in many a day . . . the whole production is a delight . . . a rich and lovely show."

Julius Novick—*Village Voice,* June 1977
". . . it looks fine and sounds fine, too . . . For all its inch-thick orientalism, all its safe liberal platitudes, all its Norman Rockwell sentimentalizing, all its skirting of problems it raises, *The King and I* takes you on a voyage to a place of special vividness, and brings you back stirred, livened, moved, changed from the way you were before . . . produced with taste as well as money . . . a lush and beautiful escapist fantasy . . ."

Bibliography

Once and Future King Revealeth Royal Wrath by Bernard Carragher
—*New York Daily News,* September 19, 1976

Yul Brynner: Long Live the King by Fern Marja Eckman
—*New York Post,* April 23, 1977

King Yul of Siam: At Last the Crown Fits by Tom McMorrow
—*New York Daily News,* May 1, 1977

Tour

Arie Crown Theatre, Chicago, January 4, 1979—Pantages Theatre, Los Angeles, April 22, 1979 (2 cities).

VICTORY AT SEA

(Television Film—1952)

A television documentary series written by Henry Salomon and Richard Hanser; music by Richard Rodgers.

Presented by the NBC-TV Network and the U.S. Navy
Produced by Mr. Salomon
Directed by M. Clay Adams
Narrated by Leonard Graves
Edited by Isaac Kleinerman
Music director, Robert Russell Bennett
conducting the NBC Symphony Orchestra
Orchestrations by Mr. Bennett

Television
NBC-TV Network, Sunday, 3:00-3:30 PM, EST, Oct. 26, 1952-April 26, 1953
26 weeks (13 hours)

NOTE: On May 20, 1954, United Artists released an abridged version of *Victory at Sea* edited to be shown in motion-picture theatres. It was narrated by Alexander Scourby.

Project
A documentary of World War II, covering the period from the Axis ascendancy in 1939 to the end of the war in 1945, with emphasis on naval engagements. Comprises 60,000,000 feet of film from the files of 10 nations.

Musical Themes
Song of the High Seas (Main Theme)
Submarines in a Calm Sea
Beneath the Southern Cross
Guadalcanal March
Theme of Growing and Building
Fiddlin' Off Watch
The Sunny Pacific Islands
The Approaching Enemy
Death and Debris
Hymn of Victory

NOTE: *Beneath the Southern Cross* has same music as *No Other Love (Me and Juliet).*

Reviews
Jack Gould—*New York Times,* October 27, 1952
". . . rare power and poetry. With a superlative score, the series is

not alone history but a drama told with moving simplicity and restrained majesty . . . Especially in the portions accompanying scenes of the sea and the tension of battle, Mr. Rodgers' work has a compelling beauty and vigor that adds incalculably to the emotional intensity of the series . . ."

Eric Larrabee (Mr. Harper)—*Harper's Magazine,* October, 1952
". . . Technically speaking, Richard Rodgers and Robert Russell Bennett have composed the longest symphony ever written . . . It is all so clear, so convincing, that it made me more conscious than I had previously been of documentary's terrible power."

Harriet Van Horne—*New York World-Telegram & Sun,* Nov. 4, 1952
". . . Another distinguishing feature is the original score. Not being a music critic, I lack tongue to praise it. I only know that it's music one feels. And it's music that's exactly right for each scene . . ."

Time, November 10, 1952
". . . boasts a brilliant 13-hour score by composer Richard Rodgers, whose music is often the only description the action needs. A new sort of musical language was developed for the series. Robert Russell Bennett gives an example: 'All airplanes fly in F minor.' "

Newsweek, November 19, 1952
". . . The series is costing NBC $500,000, and it has cost producer Henry Salomon some four years of work. With little narration and a powerful score, the programs are much more than newsreels . . ."

Bluebook, November, 1952
". . . demonstrates again TV's terrific potential as a fascinating, exciting reporter of historic events . . . It's the first time a major composer has done a score tailor-made for a television show . . ."

Bernard DeVoto—*Harper's Magazine,* June, 1954
". . . evokes the most powerful and profound emotions . . . it is a drama, a work of the imagination, art of a high order. And it is new under the sun . . . Mr. Rodgers' score could no more be separated from the film or the narrative than Stravinsky's score could be separated from Diaghilev in *The Firebird* . . . We know now, as we did not know before, that given an artist of proper size, television is one of the arts."

Awards

U.S. Navy Distinguished Public Service Award to Mr. Rodgers.
Television Academy "Emmy" Award, Best Public Affairs Program 1953
Gold Record (sales over $1 million), RCA Victor album (Vol. 1)

ME AND JULIET

(1953)

A musical comedy with book and lyrics by Oscar Hammerstein II; music by Richard Rodgers.

Presented by Messrs. Rodgers and Hammerstein
Directed by George Abbott
Choreography by Robert Alton
Settings and lighting by Jo Mielziner
Costumes by Irene Sharaff
Music director, Salvatore Dell'Isola
Orchestrations and vocal arrangements by Don Walker
Dance arrangements by Roger Adams

Tryout
Hanna Theatre, Cleveland, April 20-May 2, 1953
Shubert Theatre, Boston, May 6-23, 1953

New York Run
Majestic Theatre, May 28, 1953-April 3, 1954
358 performances

The Story
Larry, an assistant stage manager of a new musical, *Me and Juliet,* falls in love with Jeanie, a singer in the show's chorus, and they secretly marry. Threatening their happiness is Bob, a stage electrician, who also loves Jeanie and, in a drunken rage, even tries to kill them. A contrasting romance, involving Mac, the stage manager, and Betty, the principal dancer, is complicated by Mac's credo never to fall for a girl who's in a show he's working on. This dilemma is solved when he is transferred to another show. Scenes from *Me and Juliet* are shown during the production.

The Cast
GEORGE, *2nd assistant stage manager,* Randy Hall
SIDNEY, *electrician,* Edwin Philips
JEANIE, *chorus singer,* Isabel Bigley
HERBIE, *candy counter boy,* Jackie Kelk
CHRIS, *rehearsal piano player,* Barbara Carroll
MILTON, *drummer,* Herb Wasserman

STU, *bass fiddle player,* Joe Shulman
MICHAEL, *chorus boy,* Michael King
BOB, *electrician,* Mark Dawson
LARRY, *assistant stage manager,* Bill Hayes
MAC, *stage manager,* Ray Walston
MONICA, *chorus dancer,* Patty Ann Jackson
RUBY, *company manager,* Joe Lautner
CHARLIE CLAY, ("Me"), *featured lead,* Arthur Maxwell
DARIO, *conductor,* George S. Irving
LILY ("Juliet") *singing principal,* Helena Scott
JIM ("Don Juan"), *principal dancer,* Bob Fortier
SUSIE ("Carmen"), *principal dancer,* Svetlana McLee
VOICE OF BEN HARRISON, *producer,* Henry Hamilton
VOICE OF MISS DAVENPORT, *choreographer,* Deborah Remsen
HILDA, *aspirant for dancing part,* Norma Thornton
MARCIA LAVAL, *another aspirant for dancing part,* Thelma Tadlock
BETTY LORAINE, *successor to Susie as principal dancer,* Joan McCracken
BUZZ, *principal dancer,* Buzz Miller
RALPH, *alley dancer,* Ralph Linn
MISS OXFORD, *bit player,* Gwen Harmon
SADIE, *usher,* Francine Bond
MILDRED, *another usher,* Lorraine Havercroft
THEATRE PATRONS, Barbara Lee Smith, Susan Lovell
DANCING ENSEMBLE: Francine Bond, Betty Buday, Penny Ann Green, Lorraine Havercroft, Patty Ann Jackson, Helene Keller, Lucia Lambert, Harriet Leigh, Sonya Lindgren, Elizabeth Logue, Shirley MacLaine, Cheryl Parker, Dorothy Silverherz, Thelma Tadlock, Norma Thornton, Janyce Ann Wagner, Rosemary Williams; Lance Avant, Grant Delaney, John George, Jack Konzal, Ralph Linn, Eddie Pfeiffer, Augustine Rodriguez, Bob St. Clair, Bill Weber
SINGING ENSEMBLE: Adele Castle, Gwen Harmon, Susan Lovell, Theresa Mari, Georgia Reed, Deborah Remsen, Thelma Scott, Barbara Lee Smith; Jack Drummond, John Ford, Henry Hamilton, Richard Hermany, Warren Kemmerling, Michael King, Larry Laurence, Jack Rains

Musical Numbers

The entire action takes place in and around the theatre in which *Me and Juliet* is playing.

ACT I

SCENE ONE—BACKSTAGE
A Very Special Day, JEANIE and TRIO
That's the Way It Happens, JEANIE and TRIO
Reprise, *That's the Way It Happens,* LARRY
Dance impromptu, CHORUS, GEORGE and TRIO

SCENE TWO—THE ORCHESTRA PIT
Overture to *Me and Juliet,* DARIO and ORCHESTRA

SCENE THREE—FIRST SCENE OF "ME AND JULIET"
Opening, LILY, JIM, SUSIE, CHARLIE
Marriage Type Love, CHARLIE, LILY and SINGERS

SCENE FOUR—THE LIGHT BRIDGE
Keep It Gay, BOB

SCENE FIVE—DURING PERFORMANCE OF "ME AND JULIET"
Keep It Gay, danced by JIM and CHORUS

SCENE SIX—BACKSTAGE
Keep It Gay, danced by BETTY, BUZZ and CHORUS
The Big Black Giant, LARRY
No Other Love, JEANIE and LARRY

SCENE SEVEN—THE ALLEY LEADING TO THE STAGE DOOR
Dance, RALPH, Francine Bond, Elizabeth Logue
Reprise, *The Big Black Giant,* RUBY

SCENE EIGHT—BETTY'S DRESSING ROOM
It's Me, BETTY and JEANIE

SCENE NINE—THE LIGHT BRIDGE

SCENE TEN—NIGHT CLUB SCENE IN "ME AND JULIET" AND BACKSTAGE
Reprise, *No Other Love,* LILY
First Act Finale of *Me and Juliet,* LILY, BETTY, CHARLIE, JIM, JEANIE and CHORUS

ACT II

SCENE ONE—DOWNSTAIRS LOUNGE IN THE THEATRE
Intermission Talk, HERBIE and CHORUS

SCENE TWO—THE BAR ACROSS THE STREET
It Feels Good, BOB

SCENE THREE—A SECOND ACT SEQUENCE OF "ME AND JULIET"
Opening, CHARLIE, JIM, LILY and DANCERS
The Baby You Love, LILY and DANCERS
We Deserve Each Other, BETTY, JIM and CHORUS

SCENE FOUR—THEATRE MANAGER'S OFFICE
I'm Your Girl, JEANIE and LARRY

SCENE FIVE—THE ORCHESTRA PIT
Change Music of Last Scene of *Me and Juliet,* DARIO and ORCHESTRA

SCENE SIX—LAST SCENE OF "ME AND JULIET"
Finale, CHARLIE, LILY, BETTY, JIM, and CHORUS

SCENE SEVEN—BACKSTAGE
Finale, COMPANY

NOTE: *The Baby You Love* dropped in June. *No Other Love* has same music as *Beneath the Southern Cross (Victory at Sea).*

Reviews

Brooks Atkinson—*New York Times*

". . . has just about everything except an intelligible story. Mr. Rodgers has written one of his most melodious scores in the endless variety of form that makes him a musician. *No Other Love* has the warmth and richness of his most popular works. But his *The Big Black Giant* is his most original song . . . looks better than a million dollars: it is gayer and more entrancing . . . the form of Mr. Hammerstein's backstage legend is cumbersome . . ."

Walter F. Kerr—*New York Herald Tribune*

"Mechanically, the show is pure magic . . . Musically, it is good basic Rodgers . . . *Marriage Type Love, No Other Love* and *I'm Your Girl* are all run-of-the-gold-mine Rodgers—fresh, sweet and infinitely singable . . . a dizzying collection of independently attractive fragments, so eager to embrace everything that half its treasures slip through its outstretched arms . . . Rodgers and Hammerstein have come perilously close to writing a show-without-a-show . . . seems more deeply in earnest and a lot less lighthearted than their more significant works."

John Chapman—*New York Daily News*

". . . big and beautiful . . . My own enthusiasm for show business leads me to applaud many lovely and miraculous things . . . Yet it does not strike me as a major work because its story is either too involved or incapable of competing with the remarkable scenic plot . . ."

Richard Watts, Jr.—*New York Post*

". . . if it is far from a peak achievement, it still has its pleasant virtues. For one thing, it isn't a bore. It is lively, vigorous and filled with the showmanlike craftsmanship of its makers. It has a number of attractive songs, its lyrics are bright and intelligent . . . But for all the creative professionalism of the show, there is a curious and surprising air of the commonplace hanging over the evening . . ."

William Hawkins—*New York World-Telegram & Sun*

". . . often a fascinating use of theatre. Sometimes you think they have bitten off more than anybody alive could chew . . . The scheme asks for the fluidity of a movie camera, but demands the operation be in realistic terms. If this is carping, it is done so with admiration for the courage to experiment, and regret that it does not aim in a happy direction."

Hobe Morrison—*Variety*, June 3, 1953

". . . the wonder boys of show biz aren't setting the world on fire with it, but they haven't pulled a clinker either . . . a complex, ponderous book. Thus what is so manifestly meant to be lively, funny and touching, seems deliberate, humorous rather than comic, and confusing as often as it is affecting . . . The book is believable and interesting. The Rodgers music, while perhaps not his best, is better than most composers' best. And the Hammerstein lyrics have his virtuoso touch . . ."

Wolcott Gibbs—*The New Yorker,* June 6, 1953
". . . The chief fault undoubtedly lies with Hammerstein, but part of the blame must be attributed to Rodgers, whose tunes certainly lack his customary verve . . . it is hard to believe that there is enough to entertain the public forever, which is the established tradition of this firm . . . Abbott gets as much fun as possible out of an unpromising script."

Louis Kronenberger—*Time,* June 8, 1953
". . . as an insight into show business, it is merely glib, goes constantly behind the scenes and never below the surface . . . mistakes a lot of whirling motion for excitement, and trick technique for originality . . . a workmanlike score . . . If the evening largely lacks lure, it is perhaps because Rodgers & Hammerstein have gone at show business with no pungency or point of view . . ."

Thomas H. Wenning—*Newsweek,* June 8, 1953
". . . a lively and entertaining show, but also a markedly disappointing one . . . Unfortunately, the matching love affairs generate little more than a tepid emotional interest . . . If Hammerstein's book is neither inspired nor compensatingly witty, his lyrics, as always, are intelligent and remarkably singable. Rodgers' music, a little harsher and brassier than usual, offers any number of first-rate tunes . . ."

John Mason Brown—*Saturday Review,* June 13, 1953
". . . The inner sanctum of make believe is brilliantly materialized by Jo Mielziner . . . it can claim its other and abundant virtues. Moreover, they are of a very high order of excellence and are captivating in their quality . . . Rodgers' music is lively, fresh and charming . . . Hammerstein's lyrics are warmhearted, witty and skillful . . . exceptionally entertaining and beautifully professional musical . . ."

George Jean Nathan—*New York Journal-American,* June 14, 1953
"*A Show Without a Show* . . . Hammerstein's book has the effect of hanging idly around waiting for an idea to come to him . . . What interest the show projects lies solely in two or three Rodgers songs,

in the skill of Mielziner's settings, and in the performances of a few of the principals . . . All the necessary externals for a good show are there, but missing, sadly missing, are the internals."

Freda Kirchwey—*The Nation,* June 20, 1953
". . . the play and the play-within-the-play, though parallel in theme, were just different enough to create an air of mild confusion and dislocation . . . thus tunes all through—barring *The Big, Black Giant*—are good, but they are not rare, magical, wonderful, any of them. Similarly, the lyrics, while smooth, deftly phrased, and amusing or romantic, are not thrilling or very funny or very witty . . . the show is still one that makes a cheerful evening . . ."

George Freedley—*New York Morning Telegraph,* June 22, 1953
". . . far and away the best musical of the season . . . It has a glorious score which we will be hearing for years to come . . . Hammerstein has caught the true spirit of the theatre . . . *Intermission Talk* boasts the best lyrics . . ."

Bibliography

NEWSPAPERS AND PERIODICALS

"Me and Juliet —*New York Times Magazine,* May 24, 1953

A Backstage Music Drama —*Life,* June 15, 1953

"Me and Juliet" —*Look,* June 16, 1953

All the Theatre's a Stage by Richard Rodgers and Oscar Hammerstein II —*Theatre Arts,* September, 1953

BOOKS

Me and Juliet (Random House, New York, 1953)
Book and lyrics of the musical.

Chicago Run

Shubert Theatre, Chicago, April 7-May 29, 1954

PIPE DREAM

(1955)

A musical play with book and lyrics by Oscar Hammerstein II, based on the novel "Sweet Thursday" by John Steinbeck; music by Richard Rodgers.

Presented by Messrs. Rodgers and Hammerstein
Directed by Harold Clurman
Choreography by Boris Runanin
Settings and lighting by Jo Mielziner
Costumes by Alvin Colt
Music director, Salvatore Dell'Isola
Orchestrations by Robert Russell Bennett
Dance arrangements by John Morris

Tryout
Shubert Theatre, New Haven, October 22-29, 1955
Shubert Theatre, Boston, November 1-26, 1955

New York Run
Shubert Theatre, November 30, 1955-June 30, 1956
246 performances

The Story
Doc, a marine biologist, is something of a hero to the citizens of Cannery Row. Among them are Fauna, the madam of the Bear Flag Cafe, and Mac and Hazel, who live in the Palace Flophouse. Into Doc's laboratory comes Suzy, a girl of the road, and Doc's friends are convinced that she would make the perfect wife for him. Although Suzy has some doubts about her own worthiness, she falls in love with Doc, and various schemes are devised to bring them together. Finally, Doc realizes that he too is in love.

The Cast
DOC, William Johnson
HAZEL, Mike Kellin
MILLICENT HENDERSON, Jayne Heller
MAC, G. D. Wallace
SUZY, Judy Tyler
FAUNA, Helen Traubel

JIM BLAIKEY, Rufus Smith
RAY BUSCH, John Call
GEORGE HERMAN, Guy Raymond
BILL, Steve Roland
RED, Keith Kaldenberg
WHITEY, Hobe Streiford
DIZZY, Nicolas Orloff
EDDIE, Warren Kemmerling
ALEC, Warren Brown
JOE, *the Mexican,* Kenneth Harvey
PANCHO, *a wetback,* Ruby Braff
AGNES, Temple Texas
MABLE, Jackie McElroy
EMMA, Marilyn Bradley
BEULAH, Mildred Slavin
MARJORIE, Louise Troy
CHO CHO SEN, Pat Creighton
SUMI, Sandra Devlin
SONNY BOY, Joseph Leon
ESTEBAN, *a wetback,* Jerry LaZarre
A WAITER, Kazimir Kokich
HARRIET, Patricia Wilson
HILDA, Ruth Kobart
FRED, Marvin Krauter
SLICK, Gene Kevin
SLIM, Don Weissmuller
BASHA, Signy
BUBBLES, Marsha Reynolds
SONYA, Annabelle Gold
KITTY, Jenny Workman
WEIRDE, Patti Karkalits
JOHNNY CARRIAGRA, Scotty Engel
PEDRO, Rudolfo Cornejo
DR. ORMONDY, Calvin Thomas

NOTE: In June, Miss Traubel succeeded by Nancy Andrews.

Musical Numbers

The action takes place in Cannery Row, Monterey County, California

ACT I

SCENE ONE—THE WESTERN BIOLOGICAL LABORATORY
All Kinds of People, DOC and HAZEL
The Tide Pool, DOC, HAZEL, MAC
Reprise, *All Kinds of People,* JIM
Ev'rybody's Got a Home but Me, SUZY

SCENE TWO—CANNERY ROW

SCENE THREE—THE PALACE FLOPHOUSE
A Lopsided Bus, MAC, HAZEL, KITTY, SONYA, and FLOPHOUSE GANG
Bums' Opera, FAUNA, JOE, PANCHO, and FLOPHOUSE GANG

SCENE FOUR—CANNERY ROW ON A SWEET THURSDAY

SCENE FIVE—THE WESTERN BIOLOGICAL LABORATORY
The Man I Used to Be, DOC; danced by Don Weissmuller
Sweet Thursday, FAUNA

SCENE SIX—CANNERY ROW

SCENE SEVEN—A ROOM IN THE BEAR FLAG CAFE
Suzy Is a Good Thing, FAUNA and SUZY

SCENE EIGHT—CANNERY ROW

SCENE NINE—SONNY BOY'S PIER RESTAURANT
All at Once You Love Her, DOC, SUZY, ESTEBAN

ACT II

SCENE ONE—A ROOM IN THE BEAR FLAG CAFE
The Happiest House on the Block, FAUNA and GIRLS

SCENE TWO—CANNERY ROW
The Party That We're Gonna Have Tomorrow Night, MAC and ENSEMBLE

SCENE THREE—THE PALACE FLOPHOUSE
Masquerade Brawl at the Flophouse
The Party Gets Going, COMPANY
I Am a Witch, FAUNA, AGNES, MARJORIE, BEULAH, MABLE
Will You Marry Me?, SUZY, FAUNA, DOC

SCENE FOUR—CANNERY ROW
Thinkin', HAZEL

SCENE FIVE—THE BEAR FLAG CAFE
Reprise, *All at Once You Love Her,* FAUNA

SCENE SIX—CANNERY ROW
How Long?, FAUNA, DOC, FLOPHOUSE GANG, BEAR FLAG GIRLS

SCENE SEVEN—INSIDE "THE PIPE"
The Next Time It Happens, SUZY and DOC

SCENE EIGHT—CANNERY ROW

SCENE NINE—THE WESTERN BIOLOGICAL LABORATORY
Reprise, *Sweet Thursday,* COMPANY
Finale, COMPANY

NOTE: *Sitting on the Back Porch* cut before New York.

Reviews

Brooks Atkinson—*New York Times*
". . . tender and entertaining . . . a beautiful score . . . *All at Once You Love Her* is especially captivating. It is a typical Rodgers song of richness and feeling . . . Hammerstein has written his usual effortless verses . . . represents Rodgers and Hammerstein in a minor key. Being professional writers and men of taste, they have made it sweet, pleasant and enjoyable."

Walter F. Kerr—*New York Herald Tribune*
". . . light, deft, sometimes wonderfully melodic improvisations. And sometimes the music is able to take such firm hold of the proceedings that genuine gaiety rears its welcome head . . . But the frolicsome moments are rare . . . The people are capable, the material keeps promising to turn into a party. But someone seems to have forgotten to bring along that gallon jug of good, red wine."

John Chapman—*New York Daily News*
". . . combines some of the best and some of the least effective efforts of the famous team . . . a couple of grand songs—*All At Once You Love Her* and *The Man I Used to Be* . . . a big show—big enough to be unwieldy—and for a surprising amount of time, it is dull . . . perhaps Hammerstein and Rodgers are too gentlemanly to be dealing with Steinbeck's sleazy and raffish denizens . . ."

Robert Coleman—*New York Daily Mirror*
". . . less than Rodgers and Hammersteins' very best . . . no masterpiece. It's just a pretty good musical . . . some vivid and hilarious episodes . . . a score that we are certain is better than it sounded . . ."

Richard Watts, Jr.—*New York Post*
". . . the songs are usually fresh, pleasant and happily tuneful . . . Rodgers demonstrates his notable touch in such matters, while Hammerstein's talent for getting a kind of gay colloquial poetry into his lyrics is almost always in evidence . . . The show is clearly the work of theatre men who know their business. It merely appears oddly lacking in the sense of excitement that had been hoped for . . ."

William Hawkins—*New York World Telegram & Sun*
". . . Much of the show is leisurely. The songs are gentle. The action is casual except for a few outbursts . . . When the story cuts loose it has an offbeat charm that is unforgettable . . . good humored, never

brashly comical. It is gentle, never maudlin. It is like swinging in a hammock that keeps going up, the way a hammock can only do in a good pipe dream."

John McClain—*New York Journal-American*
". . . Only at rare intervals did the sense of mockery come through . . . a story which could never keep close enough to the central theme to be engrossing . . . a good Rodgers and Hammerstein score: they have good numbers in *All Kinds of People, Sweet Thursday* and *All at Once You Love Her* . . . a far cry from the exalted talents of the team that produced *South Pacific.* They must be human, after all."

Hobe Morrison—*Variety,* December 7, 1955
". . . bulges with individualist characters, a colorful and lively locale, and offers at least a half dozen stand-out songs . . . After an impressive start, however, the show subsides into a fairly heavy second act and actually drags to a close . . . Like all R&H musicals, it is done with unerring taste—possibly too much so for the tatterdemalion characters involved . . . many cuts above *Allegro* and probably superior to *Me and Juliet* . . ."

Wolcott Gibbs—*The New Yorker,* December 10, 1955
"*R-H Negative* . . . The tunes supplied by Rodgers are sometimes right up there with his best, and Hammerstein's lyrics, though they contain no rhymes or messages that are likely to stick long in your head, are apt and genial. These blessings, however, are not quite enough to offset the innocent languors of the script, and I'm afraid that it will have to go down, with *Allegro,* as an occasion when an unfortunate book kept an otherwise meritorious show from ever getting off the ground . . ."

Louis Kronenberger—*Time,* December 12, 1955
". . . Except for nice music, it is pretty much of a bust. It is so warmhearted about a cold world, so highminded about its lowlifes as to emerge more hootch-coated butterscotch . . . what is meant to be low-down seems more like a hoedown . . . some attractive Hammerstein lyrics and the Rodgers score ranges pleasantly from the lilt of *A Lopsided Bus* to the schmalz of *All at Once You Love Her* . . ."

Thomas H. Wenning—*Newsweek,* December 12, 1955
"*The Masters Miss* . . . while no one may ever write another *Carousel,* Rodgers and Hammerstein miss that goal by a mile . . . the pattern is not only familiar but a little tiresome . . . Summing Up: Proficient, professional and disappointing."

George Jean Nathan—*New York Journal-American,* Dec. 17, 1955
". . . it somehow is made to give off a periodic suggestion of romantic atmosphere despite the sordid nature of its setting and characters, who would seem to have been much more accurately susceptible to the old, frank Harrigan and Hart treatment . . . The show's assets? Some of Rodgers' songs and some of Hammerstein's characteristic pleasantly simple lyrics . . ."

Robert Hatch—*The Nation,* December 17, 1955
". . . good taste and good humor, a seductive score, lovely sets and a host of attractive people behaving with an easy self-confidence that is almost unprecedented on the musical stage . . . probably the most remarkable thing is Clurman's successful assumption that competent acting is entirely possible on the musical stage . . . Hammerstein's book is sensible and it is sensibly performed, the dialogue being plausible and the mass jollifications being spontaneous outbursts rather than production extravaganzas . . ."

Bibliography

NEWSPAPERS AND PERIODICALS

Dreams Piped from Cannery Row by John Steinbeck
—*New York Times,* November 27, 1955

"Pipe Dream" by Richard Rodgers and Oscar Hammerstein II
—*New York Herald Tribune,* November 27, 1955

BOOKS

Pipe Dream (Viking, New York, 1956)
Book and lyrics of the musical.

Revival

South Shore Music Circus, Cohasset, Mass., July 15-20, 1957
Polyna Stoska (FAUNA); Ted Scott (DOC); Mildred Slavin (SUZY).

CINDERELLA

(Television—1957)

A television musical with book and lyrics by Oscar Hammerstein II, adapted from the fairy tale "Cendrillon, ou la Petite Pantoufle de Vair," by Charles Perrault; music by Richard Rodgers.

Presented by the CBS-TV Network
Produced by Richard Lewine
Directed by Ralph Nelson
Choreography by Jonathan Lucas
Settings and costumes by William and Jean Eckart
Technical director, Lou Tedesco
Lighting by Robert Barry
Music director, Alfredo Antonini
Orchestrations by Robert Russell Bennett
Sponsored by Shulton Inc. and Pepsi-Cola

Television Performance
CBS-TV Network, 8:00-9:30 PM, EST, March 31, 1957

The Story
Cinderella, a drudge at the home of her stepmother and two stepsisters, is given her wish to attend the royal ball by her godmother. There she and the Prince fall in love, but she must leave by midnight. In her haste, she loses her slipper, which provides the means whereby the Prince is able to find her.

The Cast
CINDERELLA, Julie Andrews
THE KING, Howard Lindsay
THE QUEEN, Dorothy Stickney
THE STEPMOTHER, Ilka Chase
STEPSISTER PORTIA, Kaye Ballard
STEPSISTER JOY, Alice Ghostley
FAIRY GODMOTHER, Edith Adams
THE PRINCE, Jon Cypher
TOWN CRIER, Robert Penn
CAPTAIN OF THE GUARDS, Alec Clarke
CHEF, Iggie Wolfington
STEWARD, George Hall

COURT TAILOR, David F. Perkins
TOWNSPEOPLE: Eleanor Phelps, Martha Greenhouse, Jerome Collamore, Julius J. Bloom, Jacqueline Paige, John Call
CHILDREN: Kathy Kelly, Karen Lock, Leland Mayforth, Johnny Towsen, Karen Waters
SINGERS: Charles Aschmann, Herb Banke, Grace Dorian, Pat Finch, Marvin Goodis, Margot Moser, Earl Rogers
DANCERS: Donald Barton, Hank Brunjes, Robert Burland, Jean Cotes, Sally Crane, Richard Crowley, Bill Damian, Debbie Douglas, Jose Falcion, Gloria Hamilton, Dorothy Hill, Stuart Hodes, Diana Hunter, Joseph Layton, Giselle Orkin, Hazel Patterson, Alec Polermo, John Smolko, Tao Strong, Jayne Turner

Musical Numbers

ACT I
SCENE ONE—THROUGHOUT THE KINGDOM
The Prince Is Giving a Ball, TOWN CRIER and ENTIRE POPULACE

SCENE TWO—A STREET
Where Is Cinderella? (instrumental march), CINDERELLA, STEPMOTHER, STEPSISTERS

SCENE THREE—INSIDE CINDERELLA'S HOME
In My Own Little Corner, CINDERELLA

ACT II
SCENE ONE—THE PALACE DRESSING ROOM

ACT III
SCENE ONE—THROUGHOUT THE KINGDOM

SCENE TWO—INSIDE CINDERELLA'S HOME
Impossible, CINDERELLA and FAIRY GODMOTHER

SCENE THREE—INSIDE THE CARRIAGE GOING TO THE BALL
It's Possible, CINDERELLA and FAIRY GODMOTHER

ACT IV
THE BALL
Gavotte, danced by GUESTS
Ten Minutes Ago, CINDERELLA and PRINCE
Stepsisters' Lament, PORTIA and JOY
Waltz for a Ball, danced by CINDERELLA, PRINCE and GUESTS
Do I Love You Because You're Beautiful? PRINCE and CINDERELLA

ACT V
INSIDE CINDERELLA'S HOME
When You're Driving Through the Moonlight, CINDERELLA
A Lovely Night, CINDERELLA, STEPMOTHER, STEPSISTERS

ACT VI
SCENE ONE—THE SEARCH THROUGHOUT THE KINGDOM
The Search (instrumental), ENTIRE POPULACE

SCENE TWO—THE WEDDING IN THE MAIN BALLROOM OF THE PALACE
Finale, COMPANY

NOTE: *If I Weren't King* cut before rehearsals.

Reviews
Jack Gould—*New York Times*
". . . produced with characteristic skill, dexterity and lilt. The whole was a love story of often enormous charm . . . But it can hardly be denied that it was wanting in some respects. Call it that elusive quality of fragile spirit that makes a fairy tale universally loved. Cinderella was lovely to look at but that is not quite the same thing as sharing her enchanting transition from a drab kitchen maid to the radiant princess . . ."

Marie Torre—*New York Herald Tribune*
". . . warm, melodious and pictorially beautiful . . . a polished, thoughtfully conceived presentation which was capable of capturing the fancy of the entire family most of the time. Despite minor flaws and a few dull stretches, it emerged as fine entertainment, due mainly to the musical genius of its creators and a superb cast . . ."

Ben Gross—*New York Daily News*
". . . the best original musical in television's history . . . However, this long awaited work did not quite live up to all expectations in its writing end. Hammerstein's book veered to the stodgy side and, save in a few instances, Rodgers' music, gay and tuneful as it was in its innocent simplicity, lacked the surges of inspiration found in *Oklahoma!*, *Carousel* and *South Pacific* . . ."

Gerald Duncan—*New York Daily Mirror*
"There was magic in what they did with *Cinderella*—as though a fairy's wand had touched it all and made it sing and shine. For it was sheer delight, and the 90 minutes were all too short. This was a spectacular worthy of the name . . . dream stuff for eye and ear . . ."

Harriet Van Horne—*New York World-Telegram & Sun*
". . . superb . . . It had a gossamer beauty, a tender grace, plus the incomparable sheen of a child's dream world . . . One naturally expects high quality from Rodgers and Hammerstein. One also expects a TV spectacular to take the eye—if not always the heart—

with beauty. But I was unprepared for the surpassing loveliness of *Cinderella* . . . Rodgers has written some of the most graceful and touching melodies of his career . . ."

Jack O'Brian—*New York Journal-American*
". . . a perfectly beautiful play, full of pretty scenery and costumes and lovely music to match. If there is any exception to take, it would be in the casting, perhaps a little in the direction . . . It was all a little too absolutely lush and plush, perhaps, with *Cinderella* having almost none of the grimy little gamine quality of the storybook tale . . . The score had the tinkly simplicity the story deserves, and the libretto stuck to the traditional almost all the way . . ."

George Rosen—*Variety,* April 3, 1957
". . . a whale of a show . . . if it wasn't the perfect show, or even the nearly perfect show, there was always Miss Andrews to lend it a special enchantment and to make the most of the 90 minutes a delight . . . artistry of the first order, bespeaking the high professional talents of the R&H combo, which were executed for the most part with finesse and exacting skill . . . unquestionably the finest original cleffing for tv yet . . . The lyrics were clever, yet remained romantic and sweet . . . a class show."

John Crosby—*New York Herald Tribune,* April 3, 1957
". . . Rodgers and Hammerstein modernized the hell out of it . . . All the changes added modernity, humor, humaneness and rather tighter motivation to the ancient story, but there's no evading the fact that it also drained away some of the magic, too . . . Apart from that, though, I have few complaints. Rodgers and Hammerstein, the old pros, have turned out a truly lovely score . . . The *Impossible* number is a beautifully staged and timed dramatic scene . . ."

Irving Kolodin—*Saturday Review,* April 13, 1957
". . . It is in large part high-grade Rodgers and Hammerstein, with such cleverly rhymed lyrics as *Impossible, A Lovely Night* and *In My Own Little Corner* set to music which attests to Rodgers' continued success in wooing the muse and improving the 'inspirational' elements by many skilful devices . . . the debut of Miss Andrews with Rodgers and Hammerstein was an experience to cherish."

Lester Bernstein—*Time,* April 15, 1957
". . . The hero of the evening was Composer Rodgers, who even imitating Rodgers gives a better imitation than anyone else. At least two songs—*Do I Love You Because You're Beautiful?* and *Ten Minutes Ago*—had the lilt to last for a while . . . the score has warmth and

plenty of whirl to propel dancers through Choreographer Lucas' gay patterns in a slick production handsomely set and costumed . . . Hammerstein's script kept shifting uneasily between the sentimental and the sophisticated, and made each seem lamer than the other . . ."

Bibliography

"Eliza" into "Cinderella" —*New York Times,* March 24, 1957

Rear View
A report of a rehearsal of the musical. —*Time,* March 25, 1957

R&H's "Cinderella" TV'er "Opens in New Haven" Via Tryout Technique by Bob Chandler —*Variety,* March 27, 1957

"Cinderella" on a Coaxial Cable by Stanley Green (cover story) —*Saturday Review,* March 30, 1957

"Cinderella": No Time for Geniuses by Faye Emerson —*New York World-Telegram & Sun,* March 30, 1957

Couple of Newcomers by Richard F. Shepard —*New York Times,* March 31, 1957

CBS-TV Claims Over 100,000,000 Viewers for R&H "Cinderella" —*Variety,* April 3, 1957

Uncindery Cinderella —*Life,* April 15, 1957

Stage Revivals

Adaptation by Donn Driver.

Cleveland Musicarnival, June 5-18, 1961
Monte Amundsen (CINDERELLA); Tommy Rall (PRINCE).

St. Louis Municipal Opera, August 14-20, 1961
Marie Santell (CINDERELLA); Harry Snow (PRINCE); Jack Gilford (KING); Hal LeRoy (PORTIA).

St. Louis Municipal Opera, July 19-25, 1965
Judith McCauley (CINDERELLA); William Lewis (PRINCE); Jack Harrold (KING); Hal LeRoy (PORTIA).

CINDERELLA

(London Pantomime—1958)

Presented by Harold Fielding
Directed by Freddie Carpenter
Choreography by Tommy Linden

Settings and costumes by Loudon Sainthill
Lighting by Michael Northen
Music director, Bobby Howell
Orchestrations by Robert Russell Bennett and Ronnie Hanmer
Choral arrangements, Bill Shepherd

London Run

Coliseum, December 18, 1958

The Cast

PORTIA } *the Baron's stepdaughters* { Kenneth Williams
JOY } { Ted Durante
FAIRY GODMOTHER, Betty Marsden
CINDERELLA, *the Baron's daughter,* Yana
BABY BEAR, Maryon Leslie
BUTTONS, *servant to the Baron,* Tommy Steele
DANDINI, *Aide-de-Camp to the Prince,* Godfrey James
THE PRINCE, Bruce Trent
THE KING, Jimmy Edwards
LORD CHANCELLOR, Robin Palmer
THE BARON, Graham Squire
THE QUEEN, Enid Lowe
THE CRYSTAL FAIRY, Prudence Rodney
PRINCIPAL MALE DANCER, Tom Merrifield
VILLAGERS, COURTIERS, LADIES-IN-WAITING, HUNTSMEN, FAIRIES, ETC.
THE BILL SHEPHERD SINGERS: Shelagh Aldrich, Carolyn Gray, June Jay, Pearl Lane, Maeve Leslie, Alison McGuire, Pamela Penfold, Lita Tovey; Donald Cleaver, John Clifford, Barry Daniels, Hugh Elton, Peter Hudson, John Lucas, Tony Marshall, Bill Richards
DANCERS: Diana Atherton, Linda Blackledge, Sheila Browning, Sylvia Cardew, Elaine Carr, Jean Cragg, Sidonie Darrell, Jane Don, Irene Dunn, Ann Edgar, Sylvia Ellis, Susanne Foster, Ann Gotelee, Annette Hylton, Merle Lee, Maryon Leslie, Jill Love, Virginia Minoprio, Vicki Mitchell, Margot Pritchard, Christine Reynolds, Maureen Rudd, Kaye Sargent, Christine Skilton, Marilyn Stevenson; Michael Ashlin, Larry Haider, George Lucas, Ron Lucas, Perry McCann, Larry Oaks
ATTENDANTS: Frank Raymond, Richard Wakeley

Musical Numbers

Same as television production, with following additions: *A Very Special Day, Marriage Type Love,* and *No Other Love,* which were originally in *Me and Juliet,* plus *You and Me* (music and lyrics by Tommy Steele).

Reviews

London Times

". . . may long be remembered as the pantomime which Mr.

Loudon Sainthill decorated so beautifully . . . The tunes and the words are uniformly pleasant, but they are not particularly exciting . . . *Impossible* was one of the wittiest of Mr. Hammerstein's lyrics . . ."

Harold Hobson—*London Sunday Times,* December 21, 1958
". . . the best thing of its kind that I have seen . . . The virtues are numerous. Loudon Sainthill's scenery is sensational, Yana can actually sing, the music is by Richard Rodgers, and Jimmy Edwards is a shining joy . . ."

Angus Wilson—*London Observer,* December 21, 1958
"I enjoyed *Cinderella* immensely . . . The tunes and lyrics were catchy and pleasant, but no more . . . the top, to me, was Tommy Steele . . . Having not seen pantomime since the early days of the war, I was fascinated to note how far along the road of sophistication we have travelled. Mr. Edwards says 'bloody' twice . . . the fun is on enough levels to give all the family a good laugh."

London Revival

Adelphi Theatre, December 22, 1960-March 18, 1961; *101 performances.* Jimmy Edwards, Joan Heal, Arthur Howard, Gillian Lynne.

CINDERELLA

(Television Remake—1965)

Presented by the CBS-TV Network
Executive producer, Richard Rodgers
Produced and directed by Charles S. Dubin
Teleplay by Joseph Schrank
Choreography by Eugene Loring
Art director, Edward Stevenson
Costumes by George Whittaker
Technical director, Ray Swenson
Lighting by Edwin S. Hill
Music director, John Green
Orchestrations by Robert Russell Bennett and Mr. Green
Sponsored by the Procter and Gamble Co.

Television Performance

CBS-TV Network, 8:30-10:00 PM, EST, February 22, 1965

NOTE: Also telecast February 23, 1966; January 18, 1967; February 22, 1968; April 17, 1969; April 3, 1970; January 6, 1971; December 31, 1971; February 3, 1974.

The Cast

THE QUEEN, Ginger Rogers
THE KING, Walter Pidgeon
FAIRY GODMOTHER, Celeste Holm
THE STEPMOTHER, Jo Van Fleet
THE PRINCE, Stuart Damon
PRUNELLA, Pat Carroll
ESMERELDA, Barbara Ruick
CINDERELLA, Lesley Ann Warren
PRINCE'S AIDE, Joe E. Marks
THE HERALD, Don Heitgerd
SMALL BOY, Butch Sherwood
FATHER, Bill Lee
MOTHER, Betty Noyes
DAUGHTER, Trudie Ames
GRANDMOTHER, Alice Mock
MAGIC GROOMS: Jack Tygett, Paul Gleason
MAIDENS: Myra Stephens, Linda Howe, Francesca Bellini, Alicia Adams, Rosemarie Rand, Jackie Ward, Debbie Megowan, Robin Eccles

Musical Numbers

Same as original, plus addition of *Loneliness of Evening*, sung by THE PRINCE.

Reviews

Jack Gould—*New York Times*
". . . richly costumed and sumptuously mounted . . . Since any Rodgers and Hammerstein musical is a novelty on television, the viewers had other reasons to appreciate *Cinderella.* Two numbers in the score, *Ten Minutes Ago* and *Do I Love You?*, haunt the ear, and Lesley Ann Warren was an enchanting vision . . . But the book always was very slow, and the efforts of Joseph Schrank to improve upon the original script were not too successful . . . *Cinderella* was wholesomely pleasant in spots . . ."

Kay Gardella—*New York Daily News*
". . . Unfortunately, the new version, despite its lovely little score, remained grounded, with the exception of an occasionally rewarding scene . . ."

Bob Williams—*New York Post*
". . . the glittering new CBS production of its very own Rodgers and Hammerstein work provided a pleasant TV interlude . . ."

Jack O'Brian—*New York Journal-American*
". . . The music and lyrics remain wonderful in this recreation . . . a somewhat stolid, static, studio-imprisoned production, it lacks the

spun-candy lightness to waft it and its viewers into the rosier nostalgia which helps suspend the power of disbelief showbiz psychologists always aim at in kid-type tales . . ."

Arthur Patureau—*Newsday*
". . . handsomely mounted, a fresh and frequently lilting 90 minutes . . . the acid test of a *Cinderella* is: Does your heart swell and your face smile when the prince fits the glass slipper and they exit into happy ever-after? They do. Enough said."

Rex Polier—*Philadelphia Evening Bulletin*
"One couldn't have asked for a more satisfactory 90 minutes on TV than CBS provided last night with its beautiful, tuneful new color version of *Cinderella* . . . A brilliant cast and some of the most opulent settings ever seen on TV . . . sparkling tunes . . ."

Fred Storm—*San Francisco News Call Bulletin*
". . . provided a tuneful, nostalgic evening. The Rodgers music left nothing to be desired . . ."

Anthony LaCamera—*Boston Record American*
". . . a welcome barrage of fresh air. Its lilting music was exceedingly pleasant; its long-familiar story was filled with unembarrassed sentiment not common to these cynical times; its lavish settings were fittingly eye-catching . . ."

Cynthia Lowery—*Associated Press*
". . . full of Rodgers and Hammerstein music, old fashioned romance and charm . . . The magic of the childhood classic was impeccably preserved . . ."

Murray Horowitz—*Variety,* February 24, 1965
"The magic of the Cinderella story hovered over this vidversion but only upon occasion was it truly captured . . . The fresh production was beautifully mounted and the staging occasionally was breathtaking. Some of the songs, notably *Impossible, In My Own Little Corner,* and *Do I Love You?* were fetching . . ."

Bibliography

"Cinderella" a Hit by Richard K. Doan
—*New York Herald Tribune,* February 24, 1965

FLOWER DRUM SONG

(1958)

A musical play with book by Oscar Hammerstein II and Joseph Fields, based on the novel by C. Y. Lee; music by Richard Rodgers; lyrics by Mr. Hammerstein.

Presented by Messrs. Rodgers and Hammerstein
in association with Mr. Fields
Directed by Gene Kelly
Choreography by Carol Haney
Settings by Oliver Smith
Costumes by Irene Sharaff
Lighting by Peggy Clark
Music director, Salvatore Dell'Isola
Orchestrations by Robert Russell Bennett
Dance arrangements by Luther Henderson, Jr.

Tryout
Shubert Theatre, Boston, October 27-November 29, 1958

New York Run
St. James Theatre, December 1, 1958-May 7, 1960
600 performances

The Story
Mei Li, a "picture bride," has come from China to San Francisco to marry Sammy Fong, a night club owner. Sammy, however, loves Linda Low, a stripper at his club, and his friend, Wang Ta, is urged to marry Mei Li. Although Wang Ta also thinks he loves Linda, at the end he eventually realizes that the shy immigrant is really the one for him.

The Cast
MADAM LIANG, Juanita Hall
LIU MA, Rose Quong
WANG SAN, Patrick Adiarte
WANG TA, Ed Kenney
WANG CHI YANG, Keye Luke
SAMMY FONG, Larry Blyden

DR. LI, Conrad Yama
MEI LI, Miyoshi Umeki
LINDA LOW, Pat Suzuki
MR. LUNG, *the tailor,* Harry Shaw Lowe
MR. HUAN, *the banker,* Jon Lee
HELEN CHAO, Arabella Hong
PROFESSOR CHENG, Peter Chan
FRANKIE WING, Jack Soo
HEAD WAITER, George Young
NIGHT CLUB SINGER, Anita Ellis
DR. LU FONG, Chao Li
MADAM FONG, Eileen Nakamura
DANCING ENSEMBLE: Fumi Akimoto, Paula Chin, Helen Funai, Pat Griffith, Mary Huie, Marion Jim, Betty Kawamura, Baayork Lee, Wonci Lui, Jo Anne Miya, Denise Quan, Vicki Racimo, Shawnee Smith, Maureen Tiongco, Mabel Wing, Yuriko; José Ahumada, Victor Duntiere, George Li, David Lober, Robert Lorca, George Minami, David Toguri, George Young
CHILDREN: Linda Ribuca, Yvonne Ribuca, Susan Lynn Kikuchi, Luis Robert Hernandez

NOTE: During tryout, SAMMY FONG played by Larry Storch. In December 1959, Mr. Blyden succeeded by Mr. Soo, Mr. Soo by Larry Leung, Miss Hong by Anita Darian. In January, 1960, Miss Umeki succeeded by Cely Carrillo; in February, Miss Ellis by Baayork Lee; in May, Miss Suzuki by Elaine Dunn. On tour, Miss Hall succeeded by Nancy Andrews, Mr. Kenney by Jon Lee, Miss Dunn by Arlene Fontana.

Musical Numbers

The action takes place in San Francisco's Chinatown. Time: The Present.

ACT I

SCENE ONE—THE LIVING ROOM IN THE HOUSE OF MASTER WANG CHI YANG
You Are Beautiful, WANG TA and MADAM LIANG
A Hundred Million Miracles, MEI LI, DR. LI, WANG CHI YANG, MADAM LIANG LIU MA

SCENE TWO—A HILL OVERLOOKING SAN FRANCISCO BAY
I Enjoy Being a Girl, LINDA and DANCERS

SCENE THREE—THE WANG LIVING ROOM
I Am Going to Like It Here, MEI LI

SCENE FOUR—WANG CHI YANG'S BEDROOM
Like a God, WANG TA

SCENE FIVE—THE GARDEN OF THE WANG HOUSE
Chop Suey, MADAM LIANG, WANG SAN and ENSEMBLE
Don't Marry Me, SAMMY and MEI LI
Grant Avenue, LINDA and ENSEMBLE

SCENE SIX—LINDA'S DRESSING ROOM AT THE CELESTIAL BAR
Love Look Away, HELEN

SCENE SEVEN—THE CELESTIAL BAR
Fan Tan Fannie, NIGHT CLUB SINGER and GIRLS
Gliding Through My Memoree, FRANKIE and GIRLS
Finale, *Grant Avenue,* COMPANY

ACT II
SCENE ONE—HELEN CHAO'S ROOM
Ballet,
WANG TA, Ed Kenney
MEI LI, Yuriko
LINDA LOW, Jo Anne Miya
DANCERS
Reprise, *Love Look Away,* HELEN

SCENE TWO—THE WANG LIVING ROOM
The Other Generation, MADAM LIANG and WANG CHI YANG

SCENE THREE—SAMMY FONG'S PENTHOUSE APARTMENT
Sunday, LINDA and SAMMY

SCENE FOUR—THE THREE FAMILY ASSOCIATION
Reprise, *The Other Generation,* WANG SAN and CHILDREN

SCENE FIVE—SAMMY FONG'S PENTHOUSE APARTMENT

SCENE SIX—GRANT AVENUE
Wedding Parade, MEI LI and DANCERS

SCENE SEVEN—THE THREE FAMILY ASSOCIATION
Finale, COMPANY

NOTE: During tryout, *You Are Beautiful* known as *She Is Beautiful. My Best Love* cut before New York opening.

Reviews

Brooks Atkinson—*New York Times*
". . . Although it is beautiful to look at and is populated by many winning young people, it does not have the vitality of *South Pacific* or *The King and I* . . . Everything is done with ease, taste, and pride in the theatre . . . a pleasant score . . . Hammerstein's lyrics sustain the melodies perfectly . . . *Flower Drum Song* is not one of their master works. It is a pleasant interlude among some most agreeable people.

Walter Kerr—*New York Herald Tribune*
". . . placid, unruffled, cheerfully confident . . . a modest and engaging leaf from a very full album . . . The atmosphere is attractive, the score ingratiating, and the company good."

John Chapman—*New York Daily News*
". . . lavishly colorful, delightfully tuneful and thoroughly senti-

mental . . . another notable work by the outstanding craftsmen of our musical theatre, and it is unlike anything they have attempted before . . . a lovely show, an outstanding one in theme and treatment. But I shouldn't go to it expecting to be bowled over by sensation; it is a sweet, gentle story, sweetly and gently treated."

Robert Coleman—*New York Daily Mirror*
". . . Rodgers has composed one of his more persuasive scores, and Hammerstein has written lyrics that are moody and amusing . . . a show worth the digging and the waiting for. We found it a delight . . . everything about it is just right . . ."

Richard Watts, Jr.—*New York Post*
". . . surprisingly filled with conventional Broadway showmanship . . . colorful, tuneful and lively, and its cast contains some pleasant and talented performers, but with all its Oriental exoticism, it is astonishingly lacking in distinction . . . attractive songs and there is much that is excellent in Hammerstein's lyrics . . ."

Frank Aston—*New York World-Telegram & Sun*
". . . sumptuous, tuneful and a dance fan's dream . . . The parts fit together precisely, shiningly elegant, guaranteed to give satisfaction, resoundingly true to the mechanical idea. But there was true heart to the proceedings, as became catchingly apparent in *Don't Marry Me* . . . Much of the success is traced to the direction of Gene Kelly . . . a walloping hit."

John McClain—*New York Journal-American*
". . . a big, fat Rodgers and Hammerstein hit . . . remarkably good, but not stupendous musical. It has style and consistent good taste, reasonable humor, enough story to string it together and a score that will probably grow in stature . . . Everything is fine, nothing is sensational . . . certain songs from the show, not immediately contagious, will grow: *You Are Beautiful, Don't Marry Me, Love Look Away* and *Grant Avenue* . . ."

Hobe Morrison—*Variety,* December 3, 1958
". . . an unusually lively and appealing plot . . . Rodgers has written one of his melodious scores, and although the music sounds at moments vaguely reminiscent of some of his memorable past successes, it still has a lush texture and depth that no other contemporary legit composer can match. Hammerstein has provided warm and graceful lyrics . . . *Flower Drum Song* is not absolutely top-quality Rodgers-Hammerstein . . . But it has what it takes for average audiences and hefty box-office . . ."

Kenneth Tynan—*The New Yorker,* December 13, 1958
". . . it was something of a shock, and rather more of a bore, to find the country that cradled Lao-tse, Confucius and Zen Buddhism treated as if our only clues to its way of life were those provided by the lyrics of *Limehouse Blues* and *Chinatown, My Chinatown* . . . a stale Broadway confection wrapped up in spurious Chinese trimmings . . . Perhaps as a riposte to *The World of Suzie Wong,* Rodgers and Hammerstein have given us what, if I had any self-restraint at all, I would refrain from describing as a world of woozy song."

Louis Kronenberger—*Time,* December 15, 1958
". . . thoroughly professional . . . here proof of a jolly Rodgers and there a dreamy one. As purely popular musical fare, the show should fare handsomely . . . passably pleasant in its way, but its way is strictly routine . . . makes Chinatown almost indistinguishable from Broadway . . ."

Thomas H. Wenning—*Newsweek,* December 15, 1958
". . . a score that, if only their middling best, is a musically literate and agreeable illustration of their story . . . an admirable salute to the old world and the new. Summing Up: Another R&H winner."

Harold Clurman—*The Nation,* December 27, 1958
". . . another variation of Rodgers-Hammerstein light-hearted optimism, assuring us with a Dutch-uncle confidence that 'a hundred million miracles happen every day.' This might prove cloying if it were not for the people we see before us: the actors . . . all of them are gracious human beings . . ."

Marya Mannes—*The Reporter,* January 8, 1959
". . . the Chinese in San Francisco cannot be quite as quaint as Rodgers and Hammerstein make them; it is pretty to look at and pleasant to listen to; and it is very reminiscent, in a faded way, of Rodgers and Hammerstein. The critical sprite lay quiet all through, lulled into apathy . . ."

Bibliography

NEWSPAPERS AND PERIODICALS

R. & H. Brand on a Musical by Joanne Stang
—*New York Times Magazine,* November 23, 1958

Almost the Diary of a Musical Production by Joseph Fields
—*New York Herald Tribune,* November 30, 1958

Back In Lights (cover story) —*Newsweek,* December 1, 1958

The Girls on Grant Avenue (cover story) —*Time,* December 22, 1958

Mark of the Music Masters —*Life*, December 22, 1958

BOOKS

Flower Drum Song (Farrar, Straus, & Cudahy, New York, 1959)
Book and lyrics of the musical.

Tour

Riviera Theatre, Detroit, May 11, 1960—Hanna Theatre, Cleveland, October 14, 1961 (22 cities).

Awards

Gold Record (sales over $1 million), Columbia original-cast album

Selected Revivals

Kansas City Starlight Theatre, August 21-September 3, 1961
Fran Warren (LINDA); Christine Mathews (LEI LI); Kevin Scott (WANG TA); Johnny Haymer (SAMMY).

St. Louis Municipal Opera, August 21-September 3, 1961
Devra Korwin (LINDA); Yau Shan Tung (MEI LI); James Stevenson (WANG TA); Tim Herbert (SAMMY); Juanita Hall (MME. LIANG).

St. Louis Municipal Opera, August 9-15, 1965
Maureen Cannon (LINDA); Cely Carrillo (MEI LI); Alvin Ing (WANG TA); Jack Soo (SAMMY).

FLOWER DRUM SONG

(London—1960)

Presented by Williamson Music, Ltd.
Restaged by Jerome Whyte
Choreography restaged by Dierdre Vivian
Settings by Oliver Smith
Costumes by Irene Sharaff
Music director, Robert Lowe
Orchestrations by Robert Russell Bennett

London Run

Palace Theatre, March 24, 1960-April 29, 1961
464 performances

The Cast

MADAM LIANG, Ida Shepley
LIU MA, Mei Juan Chang
WANG SAN, George Minami, Jr.
WANG TA, Kevin Scott

WANG CHI YANG, George Pastell
SAMMY FONG, Tim Herbert
DR. LI, Zed Zakari
MEI LI, Yau Shan Tung
LINDA LOW, Yama Saki
MR. LUNG, *the tailor,* John A. Tinn
MR. HUAN, *the banker,* Michael Kan
HELEN CHAO, Joan Pethers
PROFESSOR CHENG, Mhicheil Kennedy
FRANKIE WING, Leon Thau
HEAD WAITER, David Toguri
NIGHT CLUB SINGER, Ruth Silvestre
DR. LU FONG, Thomas Hare
MADAM FONG, Marie Yang
MEI LI *(in ballet),* Sonya Hana
LINDA LOW *(in ballet),* Naomi Kimura
DANCING ENSEMBLE: Sally Bradley, Valerie Breeze, Su Chin, Annette Clair, Jo Dobson, Sylvia Ellis, Kathleen Eu, Sandra Hampton, Jennifer Mee, Zorenah Osborne, Diane Smith, Elsita Villanueva, Chesterina Sim Zecha; Alan Angel, John MacDonald, Willie Martin, Ken Robson, Charles Schuller, David Toguri, Brian Tucker, Peter Wright
CHILDREN: Nicholette Hicks, Alexandria Jelec, Raymond Moon, Georgina Sibley, Virginia Tarleton, Mary Willis

Musical Numbers
Same as original production.

Reviews
London Times
". . . English audiences have come to feel an almost proprietary pride in the work of Mr. Richard Rodgers and Mr. Oscar Hammerstein, and many who, visiting this show, believe they have caught them both below form, will feel a pang of personal disappointment . . ."

W. A. Darlington—*London Daily Telegraph*
". . . lacking anything that can be called a story, it has to rely for its appeal on exotic charm and incidental decorations . . ."

Harold Hobson—*London Sunday Times,* March 27, 1960
". . . an improvement on some of the semi-Orientalised nonsense we have had on the stage in recent years. The Rodgers music is less tuneful than of yore, but Mr. Hammerstein has written some neat lyrics . . . The story is not in itself interesting nor is it interestingly told, but it becomes the excuse for some dances and stage grouping effects that it would be churlish not to admit to enjoy . . ."

Alan Pryce-Jones—*London Observer,* March 27, 1960
". . . some hummable and perfunctory numbers . . . The story proceeds by a process of disintegration rather than growth, and the cast reacted to their labours either with manic vitality or gentle incompetence. But what freezes the marrow is that somebody has clearly thought the whole thing up as an amusing and original idea . . ."

Dick Richards—*Variety,* March 30, 1960
". . . On the whole this struck the locals as a pleasant and undemanding evening."

Bibliography

Jerome Whyte Colonizes Europe for Rodgers and Hammerstein by John Allen
—*New York Herald Tribune,* March 13, 1960

FLOWER DRUM SONG

(Film Version—1961)

A Universal-International Picture
Produced by Ross Hunter in association with Joseph Fields
Directed by Henry Koster
Screenplay by Joseph Fields
Choreography by Hermes Pan
Art director, Joseph Wright
Costumes by Irene Sharaff
Music director, Alfred Newman
Associate music director, Ken Darby
Photographed by Russell Metty
Editor, Milton Carruth
Filmed in Panavision
Color by Eastman Color

Release Date
November 9, 1961

The Cast
LINDA LOW, Nancy Kwan (sung by B. J. Baker)
WANG TA, James Shigeta
MEI LI, Miyoshi Umeki
MADAM LIANG, Juanita Hall
WANG CHI YANG, Benson Fong
SAMMY FONG, Jack Soo

FRANKIE WING, Victor Sen Yung
HELEN CHAO, Reiko Sato (sung by Marilyn Horne)
DR. LI, Kam Tong (sung by John Dodson)
WANG SAN, Patrick Adiarte
MADAM FONG, Soo Yong

Musical Numbers
Same as original production with exception of *Like a God,* which was cut.

Reviews
Bosley Crowther—*New York Times*
". . . fairly blossoms anew on the vast Panavision color panel . . . nothing subtle or fragile . . . gaudy and gaggy and quite melodic. Along those lines, it is quite a show."

Paul V. Beckley—*New York Herald Tribune*
". . . the basic material has enough charm to give the film a delicate appeal in spots . . . The song, *Don't Marry Me,* is the high spot of the affair . . . one must characterize the film as corn, picked a little late and cooked a little slow but salted and peppered and shiny with butter . . ."

Wanda Hale—*New York Daily News*
"★★★ . . . a big, elaborate spectacle in Panavision color, lush settings, stunning costumes, lovely music, imaginative choreography, and amusing characters. The film has a fault. It runs too long for what it has to offer . . ."

Alton Cook—*New York World-Telegram & Sun*
". . . a sumptuous spectacle . . . This is not the most rewarding example of Rodgers and Hammerstein in either music or comedy so the picture has wisely concentrated on pleasing the eye with gay and lavish costumes, imaginative settings and fanciful ballets . . . certainly ranks as the prettiest musical we have had all year."

Larry Tubell—*Variety,* November 8, 1961
"Much of the fundamental charm, grace and novelty has been 'overwhelmed' by the sheer opulence and glamour with which Ross Hunter has translated it to the screen . . . curiously unaffecting, unstable and rather undistinguished . . . the meat is in the musical numbers. There are some bright spots, but even here the effect isn't overpowering . . ."

Brendan Gill—*The New Yorker,* November 18, 1961
". . . it's still preposterous and still occasionally tuneful and pretty

. . . phony Chinese apothegms flow like tiger-bone wine, and the settings are every bit as authentic as Fu Manchu . . ."

Time, November 24, 1961
". . . offers the U.S. moviegoer roughly the same sensation he would get if he sat down with a single pair of chopsticks before a tun of Sook Muy Dahn Faah Tong (corn soup) . . . nothing of value has been eliminated from the play, but nothing of interest has been added . . . clearly photographed and brightly colored. But the songs, except for a charming little villanelle *(I Am Going to Like It Here),* don't exactly ring the gong . . ."

Richard Lemon—*Newsweek,* November 27, 1961
". . . a musical fairy tale that makes plain that all Chinese are cute as little dolls and most of them as rich as Mme. Chiang . . . two nice songs *(I Enjoy Being a Girl* and *Don't Marry Me)* and a graceful dream ballet . . ."

THE SOUND OF MUSIC

(1959)

A musical play with book by Howard Lindsay and Russel Crouse, suggested by "The Trapp Family Singers" by Maria Augusta Trapp; music by Richard Rodgers; lyrics by Oscar Hammerstein II.

Presented by Leland Hayward, Richard Halliday,
and Messrs. Rodgers and Hammerstein
Directed by Vincent J. Donehue
Musical numbers staged by Joe Layton
Settings by Oliver Smith
Costumes by Lucinda Ballard
Miss Martin's clothes by Mainbocher
Lighting by Jean Rosenthal
Music director, Frederick Dvonch
Orchestrations by Robert Russell Bennett
Choral arrangements by Trude Rittmann

Tryout
Shubert Theatre, New Haven, October 3-10, 1959
Shubert Theatre, Boston, October 13-November 6, 1959

New York Run
Lunt-Fontanne Theatre, November 16, 1959-November 3, 1962
Mark Hellinger Theatre, November 6, 1962-June 15, 1963
1,443 performances

The Story
Maria Rainer, a postulant at Nonnberg Abbey in Austria, is sent to the home of a widower, Capt. Georg Von Trapp, to serve as a governess for his seven children. Although the captain is engaged to wealthy Elsa Schraeder, both he and Maria find themselves falling in love with each other. After their marriage their happiness is short-lived because the Germans, who have invaded Austria, want Von Trapp to serve in their navy. He and his family manage to escape after they have given a concert of songs at a local music festival.

The Cast

MARIA RAINER, *a postulant at Nonnberg Abbey,* Mary Martin
SISTER BERTHE, *Mistress of Novices,* Elizabeth Howell
SISTER MARGARETTA, *Mistress of Postulants,* Muriel O'Malley
THE MOTHER ABBESS, Patricia Neway
SISTER SOPHIA, Karen Shepard
CAPTAIN GEORG VON TRAPP, Theodore Bikel
FRANZ, *the butler,* John Randolph
FRAU SCHMIDT, *the housekeeper,* Nan McFarland

children of Capt. Von Trapp

LIESL — Lauri Peters
FRIEDRICH — William Snowden
LOUISA — Kathy Dunn
KURT — Joseph Stewart
BRIGITTA — Marilyn Rogers
MARTA — Mary Susan Locke
GRETL — Evanna Lien

ROLF GRUBER, Brian Davies
ELSA SCHRAEDER, Marion Marlowe
URSULA, Luce Ennis
MAX DETWEILER, Kurt Kasznar
HERR ZELLER, Stefan Gierasch
BARON ELBERFELD, Kirby Smith
A POSTULANT, Sue Yaeger
ADMIRAL VON SCHREIBER, Michael Gorrin
NEIGHBORS, NUNS, NOVICES, POSTULANTS, FESTIVAL CONTESTANTS: Joanne Birks, Patricia Brooks, June Card, Dorothy Dallas, Ceil Delly, Luce Ennis, Cleo Fry, Barbara George, Joey Heatherton, Lucas Hoving, Patricia Kelly, Maria Kova, Shirley Mendonca, Kathy Miller, Lorna Nash, Keith Prentice, Nancy Reeves, Bernice Saunders, Connie Sharman, Gloria Stevens, Tatiana Troyanos, Mimi Vondra

NOTE: Miss Martin succeeded by Martha Wright (October 1961), Jeannie Carson (July 1962), and Nancy Dussault (September 1962). In October 1961, Mr. Bikel succeeded by Donald Scott, Miss Neway by Elizabeth Howell, Miss Marlowe by Lois Hunt, Miss Peters by Marissa Mason, and Mr. Davies by Jon Voight. In July 1962, Mr. Kasznar succeeded by Paul Lipson, Miss Hunt by Jen Nelson, Miss Mason by Imelda DeMartin, and Mr. Voight by Peter Van Hattum.

Musical Numbers

The story is laid in Austria early in 1938.

ACT I

SCENE ONE—NONNBERG ABBEY
Preludium, NUNS

SCENE TWO—MOUNTAINSIDE NEAR THE ABBEY
The Sound of Music, MARIA

SCENE THREE—THE OFFICE OF THE MOTHER ABBESS, THE NEXT MORNING
Maria, MOTHER ABBESS, SISTERS MARGARETTA, BERTHE, SOPHIA
My Favorite Things, MARIA and MOTHER ABBESS

SCENE FOUR—A CORRIDOR IN THE ABBEY

SCENE FIVE—THE LIVING ROOM OF THE TRAPP VILLA
Do-Re-Mi, MARIA and CHILDREN

SCENE SIX—OUTSIDE THE TRAPP VILLA, THAT EVENING
Sixteen Going on Seventeen, LIESL and ROLF

SCENE SEVEN—MARIA'S BEDROOM
The Lonely Goatherd, MARIA and CHILDREN

SCENE EIGHT—HALLWAY IN THE TRAPP VILLA

SCENE NINE—TERRACE OF TRAPP VILLA, SIX WEEKS LATER
How Can Love Survive?, ELSA, MAX, CAPTAIN
Reprise, *The Sound of Music,* MARIA, CAPTAIN, CHILDREN

SCENE TEN—HALLWAY IN THE TRAPP VILLA

SCENE ELEVEN—THE LIVING ROOM
Laendler, dance by MARIA and CAPTAIN
So Long, Farewell, CHILDREN

SCENE TWELVE—A CORRIDOR IN THE ABBEY

SCENE THIRTEEN—THE OFFICE OF THE MOTHER ABBESS, THREE DAYS LATER
Climb Ev'ry Mountain, MOTHER ABBESS

ACT II

SCENE ONE—THE TERRACE
No Way to Stop It, CAPTAIN, MAX, ELSA
An Ordinary Couple, MARIA and CAPTAIN

SCENE TWO—A CORRIDOR IN THE ABBEY, TWO WEEKS LATER

SCENE THREE—THE OFFICE OF THE MOTHER ABBESS

SCENE FOUR—A CLOISTER OVERLOOKING THE CHAPEL
Processional, ENSEMBLE
Reprise, *Maria,* ENSEMBLE

SCENE FIVE—THE LIVING ROOM, ONE MONTH LATER
Reprise, *Sixteen Going on Seventeen,* MARIA and LIESL
Reprise, *Do-Re-Mi,* MARIA, CAPTAIN, CHILDREN

SCENE SIX—THE CONCERT HALL, THREE DAYS LATER
Edelweiss, CAPTAIN, MARIA, CHILDREN
Reprise, *So Long, Farewell,* MARIA, CAPTAIN, CHILDREN

SCENE SEVEN—THE GARDEN OF NONNBERG ABBEY
Reprise, *Climb Ev'ry Mountain,* COMPANY

Reviews

Brooks Atkinson—*New York Times*

". . . The best of *The Sound of Music* is Rodgers and Hammerstein in good form. Mr. Rodgers has not written with such freshness of style since *The King and I.* Mr. Hammerstein has contributed lyrics that also have the sentiment and dexterity of his best work . . . It is disappointing to see the American musical stage succumbing to the clichés of operetta. The revolution of the Forties and Fifties has lost its fire. But the play retains some of the treasures of those golden days—melodies, rapturous singing and Mary Martin. The sound of music is always moving. Occasionally it is also glorious."

Walter Kerr—*New York Herald Tribune*

". . . The show is handsome, it has a substantial plot, and it is going to be popular . . . But before the play is halfway through its promising chores it becomes not only too sweet for words but almost too sweet for music . . . The people on stage have all melted long before our hearts do. The upshot? What might have been an impressive and moving entertainment will be most admired by people who have always found Sir James M. Barrie pretty rough stuff."

John Chapman—*New York Daily News*

". . . much that is admirable, stunning and exciting . . . The music and lyrics are splendid . . . The cast is incomparable . . . A sequel to it might be even more satisfying . . . The show is, inconclusive as it may be, a lovely piece of theatre . . ."

Robert Coleman—*New York Mirror*

"*Sounds Like Cash* . . . heart-warming . . . For the magnificent Martin and her gifted associates, Rodgers and Hammerstein have written a charming score . . . a serviceable book . . . There's no doubt that it is a titanic hit . . ."

Richard Watts, Jr.—*New York Post*

". . . warmhearted, unashamedly sentimental and strangely gentle charm that is wonderfully endearing . . . strives for nothing in the way of smash effects, substituting instead a kind of gracious and unpretentious simplicity, and, aided by Rodgers' most beguiling recent score, a pleasant book, a tasteful and attractive production, and a fine cast headed by Mary Martin at her best, the result is a most winning musical entertainment . . . both the score and the lyrics are particularly rich in freshness and imagination . . ."

Frank Aston—*New York World-Telegram & Sun*
". . . the loveliest musical imaginable. It places Rodgers and Hammerstein back in top form. The dialogue is vibrant and amusing in a plot that rises to genuine excitement . . . *Climb Ev'ry Mountain* represents the best of Rodgers and Hammerstein . . . Miss Martin and the children spread a glow and a warmth . . ."

John McClain—*New York Journal-American*
". . . the most mature product of the Rodgers-Hammerstein team. It has style, distinction, grace and persuasion; it may not have the popular appeal of *Oklahoma!* or *South Pacific,* but it has more importance. It seemed to me to be the full ripening of these two extraordinary talents . . . the whole production has exquisite good taste. The music, which at times becomes almost operatic, is wonderfully in the mood of the story . . ."

Hobe Morrison—*Variety,* November 18, 1959
". . . warm and pleasant and frequently affecting . . . should keep audiences in a sentimental glow for months and months, and give the public more tunes to hum for years and years . . . a serviceable book . . . Rodgers has composed the sort of richly melodious score for which he's famous, and Hammerstein has provided some of his most graceful lyrics . . . a major hit . . . if there's not much zing or bounce in it, there's plenty of warmth and genuine sentiment . . ."

Kenneth Tynan—*The New Yorker,* November 28, 1959
"*The Case for Trappism* . . . one begins to suspect that the collaborators have succumbed to a sort of joint amnesia and forgotten everything that Broadway learned, partly under their tutelage, in the forties and fifties . . . The book is damp and dowdy . . . Rodgers has written three or four tunes that abound in childlike lilt, and Hammerstein has equipped them with sweetly pubescent lyrics . . . To sum up uncontroversially, it is a show for children of all ages, from six to about eleven and a half."

Louis Kronenberger—*Time,* November 30, 1959
". . . combines the cloister and the kindergarten, nursery rhymes and Nazi salutes. Rodgers meets the challenge best . . . But, in general, the show's virtues are marred by its weaknesses . . . instead of offsetting sweetness with lightness, it turns sticky with sweetness and light . . . ends by making its warmheartedness as cloying as a lollipop, as trying as a lisp."

Thomas H. Wenning—*Newsweek,* November 30, 1959
". . . expert book . . . the very sound of music is the heart and

substance and often even the plot itself . . . Summing Up: A fine new songbag for Mary Martin."

Harold Clurman—*The New Republic,* December 5, 1959
". . . a bundle of sugar . . . The candy is prettily packaged. The cast is proficient and Mary Martin is perennially bright . . . as the performance went on, I lost my sense of taste. The absence of contrast paralyzed my capacity for specific response to what I was being fed . . . The tunes and lyrics are not among the masters' best."

Henry Hewes—*Saturday Review,* December 5, 1959
". . . crushingly unexciting . . . drowns in perfection and tastefulness . . . emerges as an ideal Easter show for Radio City Music Hall, and is eminently suitable for the kiddies."

Bibliography

NEWSPAPERS AND PERIODICALS

Broadway Recipe: Music and Mary Martin by Seymour Peck
—*New York Times Magazine,* November 1, 1959

They Made "The Sound of Music" by Seymour Peck
—*New York Times,* November 15, 1959

Mary Martin Stars in New Musical by Don Ross
—*New York Herald Tribune,* November 15, 1959

Smash-Hit Reunion (cover story) —*Life,* November 23, 1959

The Trapps—After "The Sound of Music" by John S. Wilson
—*New York Times Magazine,* December 13, 1959

Baroness Trapp's Royalties Going to Church by Trudy Goth
—*Variety,* December 16, 1959

Second Year of "Music" in All-Part Harmony by Arlene Wolf
—*New York World-Telegram & Sun,* July 8, 1961

Life Stages a Sequel to "The Sound of Music" by Michael Iachetta
—*New York Sunday News,* July 15, 1962

BOOKS

The Sound of Music (Random House, New York, 1960)
Book and lyrics of the musical.

Awards

Antoinette Perry "Tony" Awards, 1959-60
Best Musical
Best Performance in Musical (female), Mary Martin
Best Supporting Performance in Musical (female), Patricia Neway
Best Music Direction, Frederick Dvonch

Best Book, Howard Lindsay and Russel Crouse
Best Score, Richard Rodgers
Gold Record (sales over $1 million), Columbia Original-cast album
Variety Critics Poll, Best Score 1959-60
NARAS "Grammy" Award, Best Original-Cast Album 1960
National Catholic Theatre Conference Award, 1961

THE SOUND OF MUSIC

(Touring Company—1961)

Presented by Messrs. Rodgers and Hammerstein
Music director, Salvatore Dell'Isola

The Cast

MARIA RAINER, Florence Henderson
SISTER BERTHE, Graziella Polacco
SISTER MARGARETTA, Karen Ford
MOTHER ABBESS, Beatrice Krebs
SISTER SOPHIA, Grace Olsen
CAPTAIN GEORG VON TRAPP, John Myhers
FRANZ, Shev Rodgers
FRAU SCHMIDT, Jane Rose

children of Capt. Von Trapp:
LIESL, Imelda de Martin
FRIEDRICH, Ricky Wayne
LOUISA, Melanie Dana
KURT, Richard Carafa
BRIGITTA, Nita Novy
MARTA, Linda Ross
GRETL, Christopher Norris

ROLF GRUBER, Peter Van Hattum
ELSA SCHRAEDER, Lynn Brinker
URSULA, Betsy Hepburn
MAX DETWEILER, Jack Collins
HERR ZELLER, Larry Swanson
BARON ELBERFELD, Kenneth Mars
POSTULANT, Jyll Alexander
ADMIRAL VON SCHREIBER, Jay Velie
NEIGHBORS, NUNS, NOVICES, POSTULANTS, FESTIVAL CONTESTANTS: Jyll Alexander, Adele Baker, Jeremy Brown, Alice Cannon, Alice Evans, Maxine Foster, Barbara Gregory, Betsy Hepburn, Grace Ann Hays, Evelyn Keller, Beverly Morrison, Barbara Newborn, Ann Nunnally, Gloria Shepherd, Sally Ann Sherrill

NOTE: In June 1962, Miss Henderson succeeded by Barbara Meister; Miss Brinker by Marthe Errolle; Miss de Martin by Jane Zachary.

Tour

Riviera Theatre, Detroit, February 27, 1961—O'Keefe Center, Toronto, November 23, 1963 (35 cities).

Tour Bibliography

The Other "Sound of Music" —*New York Herald Tribune,* February 26, 1961

Selected Revivals

Palm Beach Musicarnival, February 18-23, 1964
Judith McCauley (MARIA); Lawrence Brooks (CAPTAIN); Fran Stevens (MOTHER ABBESS); Alfred Dennis (MAX).

San Fernando Valley Music Theatre, July 7-18, 1964
Janet Blair (MARIA); John Myhers (CAPTAIN); Katherine Hilgenberg (MOTHER ABBESS); Werner Klemperer (MAX).

Kansas City Starlight Theatre, August 24-September 6, 1964
Nancy Dussault (MARIA); Webb Tilton (CAPTAIN); Katherine Hilgenberg (MOTHER ABBESS); Alan Kass (MAX); Marthe Errolle (ELSA).

Oakdale Musical Theatre, Wallingford, Conn., August 9-14, 1965
Gisele MacKenzie (MARIA); Stephen Elliott (CAPTAIN); Nadine Lewis (MOTHER ABBESS); Boris Aplon (MAX); Terry Saunders (ELSA).

Westbury Music Fair, Long Island, June 14-25, 1966
Shirley Jones (MARIA); Stephen Elliott (CAPTAIN); Helon Blount (MOTHER ABBESS); Mitchell Jason (MAX). NOTE: This was part of tour.

New York City Center Light Opera, April 26-May 14, 1967
Constance Towers (MARIA); Bob Wright (CAPTAIN); Eleanor Steber (MOTHER ABBESS); Christopher Hewett (MAX); M'el Dowd (ELSA); Sandy Duncan (LIESL).

St. Louis Municipal Opera, August 19-September 1, 1968
Florence Henderson (MARIA); Bob Wright (CAPTAIN); Claramae Turner (MOTHER ABBESS); Wally Griffin (MAX); Marthe Errolle (ELSA).

Jones Beach Marine Theatre, Long Island, July 1-September 6, 1970
Jones Beach Marine Theatre, Long Island, July 8-September 5, 1971
Constance Towers (MARIA); John Michael King (CAPTAIN); Beatrice Krebs (MOTHER ABBESS); Christopher Hewett (MAX); Nancy Eaton (ELSA). NOTE: For 1971 season, Miss Krebs succeeded by Maggie Task.

San Francisco Civic Light Opera, July 4-August 19, 1972

Los Angeles Civic Light Opera, August 22, 1972
Sally Ann Howes (MARIA); Bob Wright (CAPTAIN); Jean Sanders (MOTHER ABBESS); Werner Klemperer (MAX); Patricia Morison (ELSA).

St. Louis Municipal Opera, August 28-September 3, 1972
Jane Powell (MARIA); Joseph Campanella (CAPTAIN); Joann Grillo (MOTHER ABBESS); Cliff Norton (MAX); Marthe Errolle (ELSA).

Dallas State Fair Music Hall, June 21, 1977
Shirley Jones (MARIA); H. M. Wynant (CAPTAIN); Karen Looze (MOTHER ABBESS); William LeMassena (MAX); Sheila Smith (ELSA). NOTE: This was beginning of 11-week tour.

Cape Cod Melody Tent, August 7-12, 1978
Ann Blyth (MARIA); Jean-Pierre Aumont (CAPTAIN); Eileen Schauler (MOTHER ABBESS); Woody Romoff (MAX); Sara Dillon (ELSA). NOTE: This was part of tour.

Los Angeles Civic Light Opera, September 5-October 21, 1978
San Francisco Civic Light Opera, October 24-December 2, 1978
Florence Henderson (MARIA); Edward Mulhare (CAPTAIN); Jean Fenn (MOTHER ABBESS); Joe Ross (MAX); Jan Lacey (ELSA).

U.S. Military Academy, West Point, September 23, 1978
Sally Ann Howes (MARIA); Earl Wrightson (CAPTAIN); Terry Saunders (MOTHER ABBESS); Lois Hunt (ELSA). NOTE: This was beginning of 27-week tour.

Productions Abroad

Palace Theatre, London, May 18, 1961-January 14, 1967
(See page 640)

Princess Theatre, Melbourne, Australia, October 20, 1961
Presented by Garnet H. Carroll; directed by Charles Hickman; musical numbers staged by Ernest Parham. *Cast:* June Bronhill (MARIA); Peter Graves (CAPTAIN); Rosina Raisbeck (MOTHER ABBESS); Eric Reiman (MAX); Lola Brooks (ELSA).

Brooke Theatre, Johannesburg, South Africa, 1963
Presented by Brian Brooke. Heather Lloyd-Jones (MARIA).

Geijutsu-za Theatre, Tokyo, Japan, January 2-February 28, 1965
Presented by the Toho Co., Ltd.; book translated by Simiko Takeuchi; lyrics translated by Kazuko Wakatani; directed by Kazuo Kikuta; choreography by Momoko Tani and Yukio Sekiya. *Cast:* Kaoru Yodo (MARIA); Tadao Takashima (CAPTAIN); Kimiko Saegusa (MOTHER ABBESS); Munenori Oyamada (MAX); Chikako Urashima (ELSA).

Theater Carré, Amsterdam, The Netherlands
Presented by Rene Sleeswijk and Karel Wunnink; book translated by Alfred Pleiter; lyrics translated by Pleiter and Louis Dusée; directed by Ton Lutz. *Cast:* Mieke Bos (MARIA); Johan Heesters (CAPTAIN); Maria Ballings (MOTHER ABBESS); Guus Verstaete (MAX); Teddy Scholten (ELSA).

THE SOUND OF MUSIC

(London—1961)

Presented by Williamson Music, Ltd.
Restaged by Jerome Whyte
Musical numbers staged by Joe Layton
Settings by Oliver Smith
Costumes by Lucinda Ballard
Lighting by George Wright
Music director, Robert Lowe
Orchestrations by Robert Russell Bennett
Choral arrangements by Trude Rittmann

London Run

Palace Theatre, May 18, 1961-January 14, 1967
2,385 performances

NOTE: To date, *The Sound of Music* is the longest running American musical ever to play in London.

The Cast

MARIA RAINER, Jean Bayless
SISTER BERTHE, Sylvia Beamish
SISTER MARGARETTA, Olive Gilbert
MOTHER ABBESS, Constance Shacklock
SISTER SOPHIA, Lynn Kennington
CAPTAIN GEORG VON TRAPP, Roger Dann
FRANZ, Jay Denyer
FRAU SCHMIDT, Diana Beaumont

children of Capt. Von Trapp:
LIESL, Barbara Brown
FRIEDRICH, John Coxall
LOUISA, Janet Ware
KURT, John Bosch
BRIGITTA, Susan Whitnell
MARTA, Ann Dyer
GRETL, Melanie Parr

ROLF GRUBER, Nicholas Bennett
ELSA SCHRAEDER, Eunice Gayson
URSULA, Betty Wood
MAX DETWEILER, Harold Kasket
HERR ZELLER, Peter Swanwick
BARON ELBERFELD, Jack Lorenzo
POSTULANT, Marilyn Dougan
ADMIRAL VON SCHREIBER, Hilary Wontner

NEIGHBORS, NUNS, NOVICES, POSTULANTS, FESTIVAL CONTESTANTS: Patricia Brooke-Greene, Irene Cole, May Cunningham, Marilyn Dougan, Marie Fidock, Elaine Howells, Patricia Kilgarriff, Joan Lilley, Marie Lorraine, Alison McGuire, Georgina Pearce, Sonia Peters, Patricia Ridgway, Tina Ruta, Lita Tovey, Betty Wood, Christina Wren

NOTE: During run, Miss Bayless succeeded by Sonia Rees, Mr. Dann by Donald Scott.

Musical Numbers
Same as original production.

Reviews
London Times
". . . as pretty and sentimental as an Ivor Novello musical . . . The piece must make its way by its songs rather than by its romantic story, for that, truth to tell, never really gets going till the final scenes. And the best of the songs are songs for children . . ."

W. A. Darlington—*London Daily Telegraph*
"Take the basic story of *The King and I,* scrape the oriental spicing, and substitute Austrian sugar-icing an inch thick. Add a little bit of drama at the end. Serve—and sit back and listen to the praises of the flavor . . ."

Robert Muller—*London Daily Mail*
". . . production has a freshness lacking in the Broadway show . . . Nobody in the cast can conceal the archness of the libretto . . ."

Bernard Levin—*London Daily Express*
". . . Only Rodgers' almost infallible ear for a tune saves the evening from foundering in a marsh of treacle bathed in a dim religious light . . ."

Harold Hobson—*London Sunday Times,* May 21, 1961
". . . It is a mistake to treat the Von Trapps as heroes . . . This falsity of feeling undermines the whole entertainment . . . Far and away the best thing in the evening is Rodgers' music. It is like Moody and Sankey soused in sugar . . . *The Sound of Music* is going to be one of the biggest successes of all time . . ."

Irving Wardle—*London Observer,* May 21, 1961
". . . The plot assumes more importance than is usual in musicals . . . only one number, *My Favorite Things,* stands out in the lush and unmemorable score. What remains is an attempt to impose an American stereotype on a European situation; 'hybrid' is a mild word for the absurdity of the result . . ."

Dick Richards—*Variety*, May 19, 1961
". . . drew a mixed, sometimes patronizing morning press. But it received a tumultuous first night welcome . . . The book is old-fashioned stuff, veering from the frankly dull to the cloyingly sentimental . . . But a musical is sometimes as good as its songs and there are enough that are tunefully hummable in the batch to satisfy most customers . . . an entertainment which will not let down those in search of an escapist night out."

Bibliography

London "Sound" Longevity Champ —*Variety*, November 9, 1966

THE SOUND OF MUSIC

(Film Version—1965)

A Twentieth Century-Fox Picture
Produced and directed by Robert Wise
Screenplay by Ernest Lehman
Associate producer, Saul Chaplin
Choreography by Marc Breaux and Dee Dee Wood
Production designed by Boris Leven
Costumes by Dorothy Jeakins
Music director, Irwin Kostal
Orchestrations by Mr. Kostal
Photographed by Ted McCord
Editor, William Reynolds
Filmed in Todd-AO
Color by DeLuxe

Release Date

March 2, 1965

NOTE: From 1966 through 1969, according to *Variety's* survey, *The Sound of Music* was the All-Time Boxoffice Champion in rentals received in the U.S.-Canadian market. To date, its total rental is $79,000,000.00.

The Cast

MARIA RAINER, Julie Andrews
CAPTAIN GEORG VON TRAPP, Christopher Plummer (sung by Bill Lee)
ELSA SCHRAEDER, Eleanor Parker
MAX DETWEILER, Richard Haydn
THE MOTHER ABBESS, Peggy Wood (sung by Margery McKay)

LIESL	children of Capt. Von Trapp	Charmian Carr
LOUISA		Heather Menzies
FRIEDRICH		Nicolas Hammond
KURT		Duane Chase
BRIGITTA		Angela Cartwright
MARTA		Debbie Turner
GRETL		Kym Karath

SISTER MARGARETTA, Anna Lee
SISTER BERTHE, Portia Nelson
HERR ZELLER, Ben Wright
ROLF GRUBER, Daniel Truhitte
FRAU SCHMIDT, Norma Varden
FRANZ, Gil Stuart
SISTER SOPHIA, Marni Nixon
SISTER BERNICE, Evadne Baker
BARONESS ELBERFELD, Doris Lloyd
The Bil Baird Marionettes

Musical Numbers
Same as original production except for the following omissions: *How Can Love Survive?*, *No Way to Stop It*, and *An Ordinary Couple*. Songs written specially for film (music and lyrics by Mr. Rodgers):
I Have Confidence in Me, MARIA
Something Good, MARIA and CAPTAIN

Reviews
Bosley Crowther—*New York Times*
". . . a cheerful abundance of *kirche-küche-kinder* sentiment . . . generally melodic felicity of the musical score . . . Julie Andrews provides the most apparent and fetching innovation in the film . . . her role is always in peril of collapsing under its weight of romantic nonsense and sentiment . . . staged by Mr. Wise in a cosy-cum-corny fashion that even theatre people know is old hat . . ."

Judith Crist—*New York Herald Tribune*
". . . everything so icky sticky purely ever-lovin' that even Constant Andrews Admirer will get a wittle woozy long before intermission time . . . The movie is for the five to seven set and their mommies who think their kids aren't up to the stinging sophistication and biting wit of *Mary Poppins* . . ."

Kate Cameron—*New York Daily News*
"★★★★ . . . a magical film in which Julie Andrews gives an endearing performance . . . unfolded on the screen in as rosy sentimental a manner as it was presented on the Broadway stage . . . Rodgers' two

new songs add a fresh note to the film's action . . . Wise's direction is excellent . . ."

Archer Winsten—*New York Post*
". . . has the incomparable Julie Andrews, the actual location in beautiful mountainous Austrian Salzburg, and a marvelous, indestructibly appealing story no matter how much it is reorganized to 'musical' dimensions . . . the songs may not be the best Rodgers and Hammerstein, but they certainly do stand the test of time . . . It is not a picture that can fail of popularity . . ."

Alton Cook—*New York World-Telegram & Sun*
". . . The film's charm grows and sentiment becomes unabashed and naively sweet but never cloying. The romantic doings remain hearty and sincere . . . The dominant force of Julie Andrews' presence certainly is demonstrated . . . exquisite scenic treats, dazzling the eye with both mountains and architecture . . . *The Sound of Music* is also the sound of mirth and sheer enjoyment . . ."

Whitney Williams—*Variety,* March 3, 1965
". . . one of the top musicals to reach the screen . . . a warmly-pulsating, captivating drama set to the most imaginative use of the R-H tunes, magnificently mounted, and with a brilliant cast . . . bears the mark of assured lengthy runs, and should be one of the season's most successful entries . . ."

Bruce Williamson—*Time,* March 5, 1965
"*R-H Positive* . . . satisfies nearly all the requirements for what movie-makers tout as wholesome family entertainment. It is tuneful, cheerful and colorful . . . Though Director Wise has made capital of the show's virtues, he can do little to disguise its faults . . . *Music* still contains too much sugar, too little spice . . ."

Brendan Gill—*The New Yorker,* March 6, 1965
". . . a huge, tasteless blowup of the celebrated musical . . . even the handful of authentic location shots have a hokey studio sheen . . . I felt myself slowly drowning in a pit of sticky-sweet whipped cream not of the first freshness . . ."

William Wolf—*Cue,* March 6, 1965
". . . in addition to the utterly delightful Miss Andrews, co-starring with some breathtaking Austrian settings, we are being served a most appealing screen version . . . The improvements over what transpired on stage are notable . . . adds up to a wonderful production job—handsome, in beautiful color, life-like, melodic,

and an object lesson in how to make a film that a family can enjoy seeing together."

Arthur Knight—*Saturday Review*
". . . conveys not only the look of the landscape, but the very smell and feel of the warm and bracing air. And above all, there is Julie Andrews to cast her own special radiance . . . the material cried aloud for a little roughness and earthiness to make it a bit less cloying and its people a lot more believable . . . My own apathy is based on its knowing manipulation of shopworn but sure-fire materials . . ."

Bibliography

Julie Andrews's Star Rises Higher with "The Sound of Music"
—*Look,* January 26, 1965

Sounds of (Movie) Music by Richard Rodgers
—*New York World-Telegram & Sun,* February 27, 1965

A Joyous Julie and Her Sound of Music by Thomas Thompson (cover story)
—*Life,* March 12, 1965

Biggest Money-Making Movie of All Time—How Come? by Joan Barthel
—*New York Times Magazine,* November, 20, 1966

Awards

Motion Picture Academy Awards, 1965
- Best Film of the Year
- Best director, Robert Wise
- Best Film Editing, William Reynolds
- Best Sound Recording, James P. Cocoran, Fred Hynes
- Best Scoring of Music (adaptation), Irwin Kostal

Film Daily Poll, Best Film of the Year
Foreign Correspondents Assn. Golden Globe, Best Film of the Year
National Council of Churches, Best Film of the Year
National Catholic Office, Best Film of the Year
Trophy of the Five Continents, Best Film of the Year
Gold Record (sales over $1 million), RCA soundtrack album

RICHARD RODGERS

"No Strings" (1962) with Diahann Carroll and Richard Kiley.

WINSTON CHURCHILL–THE VALIANT YEARS

(Television Film—1960)

A television documentary series based on "The Second World War," the memoirs of Winston Churchill; scripts by Quentin Reynolds, William L. Shirer, Richard Tregaskis, Victor Wolfson, Sir Arthur Bryant, Beirne Lay, Jr., Robert Pirosh; music by Richard Rodgers.

Presented by the ABC-TV Network
in association with Jack LeVien International Productions
and Columbia Pictures' Screen Gems
Executive producer, Robert D. Graff
Produced by Ben Feiner, Jr.
Churchill's speeches read by Richard Burton
Narration by Gary Merrill
Music director, Robert Emmett Dolan
Orchestrations by Mr. Dolan,
Hershy Kay, Eddie Sauter
Sponsored by Bell & Howell and Mead Johnson & Co.

Television
ABC-TV Network, Sunday, 10:30-11:00 PM, EST, November 27-December 11, 1960; 9:30-10:30 PM, EST, January 1, 1961; 10:30-11:00 PM, EST, January 8-May 21, 1962
26 weeks (13 hours)

Project
A documentary of World War II, covering the period between 1931 and 1945, with emphasis on the role played by Winston Churchill.

Reviews
Jack Gould—*New York Times*
"... short-order history, interesting to a limited extent but hardly a provocative or especially stimulating undertaking . . . Rodgers has written an original score and, as with the series as a whole, it is still too early to tell how it will rank with his memorable work for *Victory at Sea . . .*"

Ibid., December 5, 1960 (follow-up)
"After the misgivings expressed over the initial installment, this corner is happy to report that the second chapter came off most successfully . . . the score beautifully implemented moods ranging from the excitement of the cornering of the Graf Spee to the crowding together of civilians in subway shelters . . ."

Ben Gross—*New York Daily News*
". . . a tremendous feature, epic in scope . . . Rodgers' score is a magnificent one, with the sweep and emotional fervor evoked by his mighty theme . . . Don't fail to see it."

Jack O'Brian—*New York Journal-American*
". . . exciting, fascinating, entertaining . . . a marvelous set of melodies and moods ranging the big, noble, heroic themes for war and courage and as a contrapuntal pedestal for Churchill's words, deeds, actions, moods, memories . . . the contribution of the musical score is part of the skillful whole, and helps the series rise to the top of its special television category; in fact, just a bit above it . . ."

Larry Wolters—*Chicago Tribune*
". . . promises to be one of the finest ventures ever undertaken by television . . . a magnificent musical score . . . It does more than reflect the action. It underscores it superbly. This series proves once again that television can do great programs."

George E. Condon—*Cleveland Plain Dealer*
". . . a blue ribbon feature which promises to be a candidate for public service honors . . . Rodgers has made another monumental contribution . . ."

Percy Shain—*Boston Globe*
"Eloquence in words and pictures—and even in the musical background—is the hallmark of this magnificent series . . . This may be the best that ABC has ever done . . ."

Buffalo Courier Express
". . . Hardly outshone by Churchill is Richard Rodgers, whose music is a real star of the program. The wedding of films, words and music is complete when Rodgers, a real musical giant, projects his score into the action . . ."

Cynthia Lowery—*Associated Press*
". . . dramatic, thoughtfully and lovingly constructed and deeply moving . . . a magnificent score welded the bits and pieces of the giant jigsaw into an emotion-tapping whole . . ."

Fred Danzig—*United Press International*
". . . If the American Broadcasting Corporation lasts for a thousand years, men will say this was their finest half hour."

George Rosen—*Variety,* November 30, 1960
". . . A little less frantic pace, allowing for a more probing, analytical documentation and *The Valiant Years* could yet fulfill its intentions. Rodgers' score was unobtrusive almost to the point of the viewer (and listener) hardly being conscious of this singular musical dimension . . ."

Time, December 5, 1960
". . . if the story has dramatic continuity and a controlled sense of authority, it is because the producers have hired an impressive list of writers. And firmly, but unobtrusively in the background, is the suitably martial, original musical score . . ."

Bibliography

Rodgers' Task: Set Churchill's Words to Music by Sally Hammond
—*New York Post,* August 18, 1960

Story of Churchill to Music by Rodgers by John P. Shanley
—*New York Times,* November 20, 1960

Churchill's War Memoirs in TV Bow by Jim Doyle
—*North American Newspaper Alliance,* November 26, 1960

Rodgers Joins Churchill by Cynthia Lowery
—*Associated Press,* November 27, 1960

Their Finest Half Hours —*Newsweek,* November 28, 1960

Awards

Radio-TV Editors' Awards, 1960-61
Best Documentary Series
Best New Program Idea
Television Academy "Emmy" Award, Best Score, 1962

NO STRINGS

(1962)

A musical with book by Samuel Taylor; music and lyrics by Richard Rodgers.

Presented by Mr. Rodgers
in association with Mr. Taylor
Directed and choreographed by Joe Layton
Associate choreographer, Buddy Schwab
Settings and lighting by David Hays
Costumes by Fred Voelpel and Donald Brooks
Music director, Peter Matz
Orchestrations by Ralph Burns
Dance arrangements by Mr. Matz

Tryout
Fisher Theatre, Detroit, January 15-February 3, 1962
O'Keefe Center, Toronto, February 6-17, 1962
Hanna Theatre, Cleveland, February 19-24, 1962
Shubert Theatre, New Haven, February 27-March 10, 1962

New York Run
54th Street Theatre, March 15-September 29, 1962
Broadhurst Theatre, October 1, 1962-August 3, 1963
580 performances

The Story
Barbara Woodruff, an American model, and David Jordan, a former Pultizer Prize winning novelist, meet and fall in love in Paris. Although David has given up his writing for the indolent life of being a "Europe bum" sponging off rich American tourists, Barbara tries hard to make him return to his profession. But David cannot resist the easy life. Finally, he realizes that he will have to return home, alone, to Maine if he is ever to make anything of himself again. Reluctantly—with no strings—the lovers part.

The Cast
BARBARA WOODRUFF, Diahann Carroll
DAVID JORDAN, Richard Kiley

JEANETTE VALMY, Noelle Adam
LUC DELBERT, Alvin Epstein
MOLLIE PLUMMER, Polly Rowles
MIKE ROBINSON, Don Chastain
LOUIS DE POURTAL, Mitchell Gregg
COMFORT O'CONNELL, Bernice Massi
GABRIELLE BERTIN, Ann Hodges
MARCELLO AGNOLOTTI, Paul Cambeilh
DANCERS: Alan Johnson; Susanne Cansino, Julie Drake, Jean Eliot, Ginny Gan, Ellen Graff, Kay Hudson, Ann Hodges, Diana Hrubetz, Sandy Leeds, Anna Marie Moylan, Patti Pappathatos, Janet Paxton, Dellas Rennie, Bea Salten, Carol Sherman, Mary Zahn; Gene Gebauer, Scott Hunter, Larry Merritt, Michael Maurer, David Neuman, Wakefield Poole, Calvin Von Reinhold
INSTRUMENTAL CHARACTERS: Walter Wegner (flute), Aaron Sachs (clarinet), Ernest Mauro (oboe), James Sedler (trumpet), James Dahl (trombone), Ronnie Bedford (drums), Walter Kane (bassoon)

NOTE: In December, 1962, Miss Adam succeeded by Yvonne Constant. In June, 1963, Miss Carroll succeeded by Barbara McNair; Mr. Kiley by Howard Keel.

Musical Numbers

The action of the play takes place in Paris, Monte Carlo, Honfleur, Deauville, and St. Tropez.

ACT I

The Sweetest Sounds, BARBARA and DAVID
How Sad, DAVID
Loads of Love, BARBARA
The Man Who Has Everything, LOUIS
Be My Host, DAVID, COMFORT, MIKE, LUC, GABRIELLE, and DANCERS
La La La, JEANETTE and LUC
You Don't Tell Me, BARBARA
Love Makes the World Go, MOLLIE, COMFORT and DANCERS
Nobody Told Me, DAVID and BARBARA

ACT II

Look No Further, DAVID and BARBARA
Maine, DAVID and BARBARA
An Orthodox Fool, BARBARA
Eager Beaver, COMFORT, MIKE and DANCERS
No Strings, DAVID and BARBARA
Reprise, *Maine,* BARBARA and DAVID
Reprise, *The Sweetest Sounds,* DAVID and BARBARA

NOTE: *Yankee, Go Home* cut before New York opening.

Reviews

Howard Taubman—*New York Times*

"Richard Rodgers is still a magician of the musical theatre . . . a score full of romance and vivacity . . . enchanted music . . . his lines have a touch of the wholesome ease of Hammerstein and a soupçon of the peppery impertinence of Hart . . . Matching the unspoiled flow of Rodgers' songs is the imagination of the production . . . Taylor's book is at best a fragile sentimental fable, but styled in gay, inventive stage garb it has been wafted into a shimmering and delightful never-never land . . . Rodgers has lost neither his zest nor his art."

Walter Kerr—*New York Herald Tribune*

"The nicest thing to be said about *No Strings* is Diahann Carroll . . . Otherwise, the musical is a show in which the actors never have to go anywhere. Everything comes to them. Everything except an idea . . . The libretto either lazes or moves in circles for much of its talkative length . . . Rodgers' lyrics are perfectly satisfactory—no less, but no more . . . The tunes are a shade more reserved, more constricted, than usual, and double-duty may well be the culprit . . ."

John Chapman—*New York Daily News*

"A somber offbeat affair . . . I do wish somebody had thought of some jokes . . ."

Robert Coleman—*New York Mirror*

". . . has some of Dick Rodgers' best tunes and the magnetic Miss Carroll to sell them. In our books, that spells a hot ticket."

Richard Watts, Jr.—*New York Post*

". . . a particularly lovely score . . . an attractive physical production, and the leading roles are excellently played. The serious difficulty is that the book is heavy-handed and sluggish . . . beautiful and haunting songs . . . Rodgers' gift for melody is at one of its memorable peaks . . . His lyrics have a simple and attractive style of their own, and they fit perfectly with the notable beauty of the music . . ."

Norman Nadel—*New York World-Telegram & Sun*

". . . The persistence of the book's inadequacy undermines what otherwise might have been an impressively original and occasionally striking musical . . . *The Sweetest Sounds* is the loveliest music and words of all that Rodgers has fashioned . . ."

John McClain—*New York Journal-American*
". . . Richard Rodgers can go it alone; we all knew he wrote great music and now he has established himself as his own very gifted lyricist . . . stylish and enlightened musical . . . an accomplished blending of an intelligent story (for a change), a first class score, and an imaginative job of choreography bound together in a most ingenious production package . . . a legalized nuclear cataclysm, an unqualified crowd-pleaser . . ."

Hobe Morrison—*Variety,* March 21, 1962
". . . tantalizingly imperfect . . . has a provocative theme and a fascinating style of presentation . . . songs are generally good; not equal to Rodgers' incomparable best, perhaps, but satisfyingly above Broadway average . . . lyrics are workmanlike . . . a book that is at best adequate . . . except for Rodgers' music and Miss Carroll's presence, it's better for its style than its content."

Theodore E. Kalem—*Time,* March 26, 1962
". . . To bolster this piffling book, Rodgers has fashioned a score of romantic witchery—most hauntingly, *The Sweetest Sounds* . . ."

Edith Oliver—*The New Yorker,* March 31, 1962
"In every way that matters most—music, dancing, singing, staging, sets, costumes, lighting, and charm—Rodgers' new musical is as original and stylish as can be . . . The weakness of the show is in the book and the characters . . . Aurally and visually, it is a delightful show. If musical comedy were an abstract art (which it isn't), it would be a perfect one."

Henry Hewes—*Saturday Review,* March 31, 1962
"It's sophisticated. It's chic. It's inventive. And it's pleasant to the eye and ear . . . a boldly inventive work that establishes Miss Carroll as the top musical-comedy girl of the season, and reveals that Mr. Rodgers can write high-quality lyrics in the style of both Hart and Hammerstein . . ."

Harold Clurman—*The Nation,* April 14, 1962
". . . There is something real in this story . . . I liked the fact that the affair between the lovers of two 'races' (or colors) is taken as a matter of course; it is socially fraudulent but healthy in terms of our stage. The story, however, did not reach me even in the sentimental sense that a musical like *Show Boat* does . . . There is one melody—the theme song, called *The Sweetest Sounds*—which lingers . . . In brief, *No Strings* is a display of cash, skill, modern decoration, adumbrations of talent and meaning without entrails . . ."

Bibliography

NEWSPAPERS AND PERIODICALS

Rodgers Lyrics Join His Melodies for First Time by Stuart W. Little
—*New York Herald Tribune,* December 15, 1961

"No Strings" Is Down on Paper and Rodgers Is Feeling Fine by Jack Gaver —*United Press International,* December 30, 1961

Rodgers & Rodgers by William K. Zinsser —*Life,* March 9, 1962

Man Running Scared by Lewis Funke —*New York Times,* March 11, 1962

A Look at Richard Rodgers Taking a Chance on Himself by Don Ross
—*New York Herald Tribune,* March 11, 1962

A Love Letter—With "No Strings" by Dorothy Kilgallen
—*New York Journal-American,* March 16, 1962

Rodgers & Carroll by Richard Warren Lewis
—*Show Business Illustrated,* April, 1962

BOOKS

No Strings (Random House, New York, 1962)
Book and lyrics of the musical.

Awards

Antoinette Perry "Tony" Awards, 1961-62
Best Score, Richard Rodgers
Best Performance in Musical (female), Diahann Carroll
Best Choreographer, Joe Layton
NARAS "Grammy" Award, Best Original-Cast Album 1962
Outer Circle Award Best Musical, 1961-62

NO STRINGS

(Touring Company—1963)

Supervised by Jerome Whyte
Music director, Jack Lee

The Cast

BARBARA WOODRUFF, Barbara McNair
DAVID JORDAN, Howard Keel
JEANETTE VALMY, Beti Seay
LUC DELBERT, Juki Arkin
MOLLIE PLUMMER, Jane Van Duser
MIKE ROBINSON, Robert Goss
LOUIS DE POURTAL, Ferdinand Hilt
COMFORT O'CONNELL, Kit Smythe
GABRIELLE BERTIN, Ann Hodges
MARCELLO AGNOLOTTI, Marc Scott

DANCERS: Rita Agnese, Annette Bachich, Donna Baccala, Eileen Casey, Martha Cutrufello, Grace Davidson, Jean Duguid, Mary Grace Ezell, Linda Rae Hager, Ann Hodges, Darla Fessler, April Nevins, Helene Parker, Louise Auick, Karen Yaffe; Jere Admire, Hamp Dickens, Jim Hovis, Marc Scott, Keith Stewart, Ron Tassone, Vernon Wendorf

INSTRUMENTAL CHARACTERS: Spencer Sinatra (flute, clarinet), Bobby Nichols (trumpet), Paul Selden (trombone), Bill Price (drums), Ronald Janelli (bassoon, saxophone)

Tour

Shubert Theatre, Boston, August 5, 1963—Curran Theatre, San Francisco, January 4, 1964 (7 cities).

Selected Revivals

Oakdale Music Theatre, Wallingford, Conn., August 3-8, 1964
Barbara McNair (BARBARA); Stuart Damon (DAVID); Edith Meiser (MOLLIE).

Westbury Music Fair, Long Island, August 18-23, 1964
Diahann Carroll (BARBARA); Walter Farrell (DAVID); Harold Lang (LUC).

NO STRINGS

(London—1963)

Presented by Williamson Music Ltd.
Restaged and choreographed by Wakefield Poole
Settings and lighting by David Hays
Costumes by Fred Voelpel and Donald Brooks
Music director, Johnnie Spence
Orchestrations by Ralph Burns
Dance arrangements by Peter Matz
Production supervised by Jerome Whyte

London Run

Her Majesty's Theatre, December 30, 1963-May 9, 1964
135 performances

The Cast

BARBARA WOODRUFF, Beverly Todd
DAVID JORDAN, Art Lund
JEANETTE VALMY, Erica Rogers
LUC DELBERT, Geoffrey Hutchings
MOLLIE PLUMMER, Hy Hazell
MIKE ROBINSON, David Holliday
LOUIS DE POURTAL, Ferdy Mayne
COMFORT O'CONNELL, Marti Stevens
GABRIELLE BERTIN, Meg Walter

MARCELLO AGNOLOTTI, Elwyn Hughes
PRINCIPAL DANCER, Tommy Merrifield
DANCERS: Paula Bell, Sonia Brindle, Patricia Cassie, Sylvia Ellis, Christine Harrington, Patricia Hawks, Wynne Jarman, Valerie Lloyd, Patricia Lovette, Sarah Martin, Janet Matthews, Merle Maxim, Patsy Porter, Vicky Udall, Maureen Willsher; Neil Fitzwilliam, Ian Garry, Louis Godfrey, David Moffatt, Harry Naughton, Ross Parkes, Bryan Payne
INSTRUMENTAL CHARACTERS: Johnny Martine (flute); Bill Jackman (clarinet); Les Baldwin (oboe); Ronnie Hughes (trumpet); Harry Roche (trombone); Paul Brodie (drums); Roy East (alto saxophone)

Musical Numbers
Same as original production.

Reviews
London Times
". . . There is certainly a breath of fresh air—possibly from Off-Broadway—blowing through it . . . for once, music and dance are given dramatic extension . . . In this show there are no bared teeth, nervous cascades of bad jokes or automatic dance routines to soften the audience up . . . Mr. Taylor's handling of his society and his romance has sophistication and unforced charm . . . Rodgers' score varies between the gently lyrical and the blazingly profane . . ."

London Daily Telegraph
". . . the people in the story are dehumanized . . . Rodgers' lyrics serve his purpose well enough . . ."

Manchester Guardian
". . . has its dull and slow patches—which American musical has not? But it has a certain chic and a certain native bounce which should carry it . . ."

J. W. Lambert—*London Sunday Times,* January 5, 1964
"A band box musical, an amiable period piece with contemporary trimmings . . . Rodgers has supplied a handful of pleasant tunes . . . to give the loose-limbed little piece its due, it does not shrink from a gently downbeat ending . . ."

Bamber Gascoigne—*London Observer,* January 5, 1964
". . . The story ambled along with some nice tunes and soon lulled me into a pleasant enough stupor, though there was nothing much to lift me out of it again except the wide-eyed and wide-mouth appeal of Beverly Todd."

Harold Myers—*Variety,* January 29, 1964
". . . looks set for a long stay . . . The score has a succession of hit numbers. The book serves its purpose more than adequately."

DO I HEAR A WALTZ?

(1965)

A musical with book by Arthur Laurents, based on his play "The Time of the Cuckoo"; music by Richard Rodgers; lyrics by Stephen Sondheim.

Presented by Richard Rodgers
Directed by John Dexter
Choreography by Herbert Ross
Settings and costumes by Beni Montresor
Lighting by Jules Fisher
Music director, Frederick Dvonch
Orchestrations by Ralph Burns
Dance arrangements by Richard de Benedictis

Tryout

Shubert Theatre, New Haven, February 1-February 13, 1965
Shubert Theatre, Boston, February 16-March 13, 1965

New York Run

46th Street Theatre, March 18-September 25, 1965
220 performances

The Story

While on vacation in Venice, Leona Samish, an American tourist, has an affair with Renato di Rossi, an Italian shopkeeper. Their brief romance is doomed when Leona becomes too emotionally involved. A secondary plot involves a young bickering couple, Jennifer and Eddie Yaeger, and Eddie's brief fling with Signora Fioria, the owner of their pensione.

The Cast

LEONA SAMISH, Elizabeth Allen
MAURO, Christopher Votos
SIGNORA FIORIA, Carol Bruce
EDDIE YAEGER, Stuart Damon
JENNIFER YAEGER, Julienne Marie
MRS. MC ILHENNY, Madeleine Sherwood
MR. MC ILHENNY, Jack Manning
GIOVANNA, Fleury D'Antonakis
VITO, James Dybas

RENATO DI ROSSI, Sergio Franchi
MAN ON BRIDGE, Michael Lamont
MRS. VICTORIA HASLAM, Helon Blount
SINGERS: Darrell Askey, Sydnee Balaber, Bill Berrian, Helon Blount, Rudy Challenger, Pat Kelly, Liz Lamkin, Michael Lamont, James Luisi, Jack Murray, Carl Nicholas, Candida Pilla, Casper Roos, Bernice Saunders, Liza Stuart
DANCERS: Jere Admire, Bob Bishop, Wayne De Rammelaere, Steve Jacobs, Sandy Leeds, Joe Nelson, Janice Peta, Walter Stratton, Nancy Van Rijn, Mary Zahn

Musical Numbers

ACT I

SCENE ONE—VENICE
Someone Woke Up, LEONA

SCENE TWO—GARDEN OF PENSIONE FIORIA
This Week Americans, FIORIA
What Do We Do? We Fly!, LEONA, MRS. MCILHENNY, MR. MCILHENNY, EDDIE, JENNIFER

SCENE THREE—DI ROSSI'S SHOP
Someone Like You, DI ROSSI
Bargaining, DI ROSSI

SCENE FOUR—PIAZZA SAN MARCO
Here We Are Again, LEONA; danced by VITO and RAGAZZI (Steve Jacobs, Sandy Leeds, Joe Nelson, Nancy Van Rijn, Mary Zahn)

SCENE FIVE—INTERIOR OF PENSIONE FIORIA
Thinking, DI ROSSI AND LEONA

SCENE SIX—GARDEN OF PENSIONE FIORIA
No Understand, FIORIA, EDDIE, GIOVANNA
Take the Moment, DI ROSSI

ACT II

SCENE ONE—FAÇADE OF PENSIONE FIORIA
Moon in My Window, JENNIFER, FIORIA, LEONA

SCENE TWO—OUTSIDE THE GARDEN OF PENSIONE FIORIA
We're Gonna Be All Right, EDDIE, JENNIFER
Do I Hear a Waltz? LEONA, COMPANY

SCENE THREE—PIAZZA SAN MARCO
Stay, DI ROSSI

SCENE FOUR—GARDEN OF PENSIONE FIORIA
Perfectly Lovely Couple, LEONA, DI ROSSI, MR. MCILHENNY, MRS. MCILHENNY, JENNIFER, EDDIE, GIOVANNA, FIORIA

SCENE FIVE—THE SAME
Reprise, *Take the Moment,* DI ROSSI
Thank You So Much, DI ROSSI and LEONA

NOTE: *Philadelphia, Perhaps, Two by Two,* and *Everybody Loves Leona* cut before New York opening.

Reviews

Howard Taubman—*New York Times*
". . . The authors have accomplished their conversion of the play with tact and grace . . . At the same time one cannot suppress a regret that they failed to be bolder. There are times, particularly in the early stages, when the songs are merely a decoration . . . The musical begins to distill a charm of its own midway in the first act . . . *Do I Hear a Waltz?* has the courage to abjure garishness and stridency. It speaks and sings in a low key. It is faithful to the sentimental tale that is its source."

Walter Kerr—*New York Herald Tribune*
". . . an entirely serious and very dry musical . . . it is careful, deliberate, and in a way quite honest about carrying out its earnest intentions . . . a straight play, played at straight play pace, virtually unrelieved by either dancing or comedy, soberly acted, economically directed, and depending for its life upon Richard Rodgers' thoughtful songs . . ."

Ibid., April 4, 1965 (follow-up)
". . . Mr. Rodgers in particular is to be congratulated upon his restiveness, his continued unwillingness to re-do the last show that succeeded, his voluntary surrender of the devices traditionally used to wake customers up . . . *Moon in My Window, No Understand, Stay,* and the title song all serve as reminders that Mr. Rodgers is still king of the hill . . ."

John Chapman—*New York Daily News*
". . . a rueful musical romance . . . I admired very much the playing of the leading roles by Elizabeth Allen and Sergio Franchi . . . except for a couple of musical capers at the beginning, the songs are a pretty solemn lot . . ."

Richard Watts, Jr.—*New York Post*
". . . so winning in its score, lyrics, setting, cast, production, spirit and general atmosphere that it offers an evening of charming and tasteful entertainment despite certain strong reservations I have concerning the libretto . . . the score is tuneful and thoroughly

appealing. The lyrics are deft and intelligent . . . handsome, atmospheric and imaginative settings . . . The score is filled with pleasures, including the haunting title song, the charming *Moon in My Window,* and the brightly sardonic *Perfectly Lovely Couple* . . ."

Norman Nadel—*New York World-Telegram & Sun*
". . . a mellow, sunshine-yellow musical, of less than epic proportions . . . never less than artful even when the material descended to the conventional level, which happened occasionally. Its story is both romantic and honest, a combination which goes wonderfully well when set to music—especially Richard Rodgers music . . . Rodgers has managed to combine the airy consonance and gentle lyricism of Italian music with his own penchant for chromatics alternating with augmented intervals. It works quite well . . ."

John McClain—*New York Journal-American*
". . . at least two spectacular things . . . One of them is the scenery . . . and the other is the portrait of a slipshod maid by Fleury D'Antonakis. Otherwise, this is not by any means a bell ringer . . . some good and probably popular numbers, like the title song and *Stay, Someone Like You* and *Take the Moment* . . ."

William Glover—*Associated Press*
"A musical that glows with lyrical luster . . . a score brimming with that recent Broadway rarity, grand melody, and a host of other quality elements have gone into the production. With so much to praise, however, the show is good rather than great . . . the main difficulty is that the story has been chopped to fit musical requirements in rather arbitrary fashion . . ."

Jack Gaver—*United Press International*
"A light-hearted, melodious Richard Rodgers score and a sensitive, bittersweet love story have been blended into a charming and eye-filling musical . . . a fragile but nevertheless dramatically effective story . . . Rodgers' melodies, fitted with generally friendly lyrics by Stephen Sondheim, are light, tuneful and embrace this love story affectionately . . ."

Hobe Morrison—*Variety,* March 24, 1965
". . . has another beautiful Rodgers score, but the other elements are spotty, and the general effect is uneven—occasionally amusing or moving, but frequently unsatisfying . . . When it ignores the incidentals and concentrates on the basic characters and the Rodgers music, *Do I Hear a Waltz?* is a transiently enjoyable show."

Emory Lewis—*Cue,* March 27, 1965
"... Rodgers has flooded the stage with lilting melody ... Sondheim is at his wittiest in a sardonic ode, *What Do We Do? We Fly!* ... Everything about this musical is tasteful. Quality is stamped on everything and everybody. And yet—a blandness pervades and mars the evening ..."

Henry Hewes—*Saturday Review,* April 3, 1965
"... lyrics are frequently ingenious ... If Rodgers' score is less catchy and haunting than we have come to expect, it somewhat compensates by the way it works to fulfil the playwright's intention. Particularly interesting and amusingly sung is *Bargaining* ... *No Understand* is quite delightful ... Much talent and good intention have arrived at only a modest result and at a disappointingly low amount of emotion-involving interchange in such a highly romantic city."

Bibliography

Rodgers and Sondheim Preparing a Musical by Louis Calta
—*New York Times,* November 6, 1964

Leona Kicks Up Heels in "Waltz" by Arthur Laurents
—*New York World-Telegram & Sun,* March 13, 1965

Richard Rodgers' Boston Overhaul by Stuart W. Little
—*New York Herald Tribune Magazine,* March 14, 1965

A New Word Man for Rodgers by Tom Prideaux —*Life,* March 19, 1965

Selected Revivals

Paper Mill Playhouse, New Jersey, May 31-June 26, 1966
Dorothy Collins (LEONA); Ronald Holgate (RENATO); Dorothy Stinnette (FIORIA); Fleury D'Antonakis (GIOVANNA).

St. Louis Municipal Opera, June 26-July 2, 1967
Dorothy Collins (LEONA); Enzo Stuarti (RENATO); Monique Van Vooren (FIORIA).

Packard Music Hall, Warren, Ohio, August 15-20, 1967
Anita Bryant (LEONA); Bob Wright (RENATO); Carol Bruce (FIORIA).

ANDROCLES AND THE LION

(Television—1967)

A television musical with book by Peter Stone, based on the play by George Bernard Shaw; music and lyrics by Richard Rodgers.

Presented by the NBC-TV Network
Executive producer, Marc Merson
Directed by Joe Layton
Settings by Tom John
Costumes by Theoni Aldredge
Lighting by Phil Hymes
Music director, Jay Blackton
Orchestrations by Robert Russell Bennett
Dance arrangements by David Baker
Sponsored by the American Gas Association

Television Performance
NBC-TV Network, 7:30-9:00 PM, EST, November 15, 1967

The Story
Androcles, a Greek tailor living in ancient Rome, loves animals. Once, while traveling through the woods with his wife, Megaera, he finds a lion with a thorn stuck in his paw, and removes it. Later, because he is a Christian, Androcles is taken with other Christians to the arena to be torn to bits by the lions. When the lion he helped recognizes him, they both dance off together arm in arm.

The Cast
LION, Geoffrey Holder
MEGAERA, Patricia Routledge
ANDROCLES, Norman Wisdom
CAPTAIN, John Cullum
LAVINIA, Inga Swenson
LENTULUS, Brian Bedford
METELLUS, Clifford David
FERROVIUS, Ed Ames
SPINTHO, William Redfield
MANAGER OF GLADIATORS, Kurt Kasznar
ROMAN CENTURION, George Mathews
KEEPER OF LIONS, Bill Hickey

CAESAR, Noel Coward
RETIARIUS, Bill Starr
SECUTOR, George Reeder
THREE LIONS: Steve Bookvar, Bill Starr, George Reeder

Musical Numbers

ACT I
A JUNGLE
Velvet Paws, ANDROCLES; dance by ANDROCLES and LION

ACT II
OUTSKIRTS OF ROME
Follow in Our Footsteps, CHRISTIANS
Strangers, CAPTAIN and LAVINIA

ACT III
A SQUARE IN ROME
A Fine Young Man, FERROVIUS
Strength Is My Weakness, FERROVIUS and ANDROCLES

ACT IV
THE COLISEUM ARENA
Dance, GLADIATORS

ENTRANCE TO ARENA, BEHIND EMPEROR'S BOX
The Emperor's Thumb, CAESAR

ACT V
ENTRANCE TO ARENA
No More Waiting, LAVINIA and CAPTAIN

ACT VI
THE ARENA
Dance, ANDROCLES and LION

ENTRANCE TO ARENA
Don't Be Afraid of an Animal, ANDROCLES and CAESAR
Reprise, *Velvet Paws,* ANDROCLES and LION

Reviews

Jack Gould—*New York Times*
". . . wavered disconcertingly in its indecision over whether to be serious or to have fun . . . the score . . . contained hints of melodic pleasures in the numbers entitled *Strangers, No More Waiting* and *Follow in Our Footsteps* . . ."

Ben Gross—*New York Daily News*
". . . proved that on television, at least, martyrdom and musical

comedy do not mix . . . Rodgers' music, as always, had a fetching quality and one of his numbers, *Follow in Our Footsteps,* might well become a standard hymn of many denominations . . . The book was a workmanlike job . . . Norman Wisdom made Androcles an appealing, loveable figure . . .''

Bob Williams—*New York Post*
''. . . modest theatrical results. The themes and lyrics of Richard Rodgers were not without some charms, but the production was on the ponderous side . . . *Don't Be Afraid of an Animal* was the brightest of the Rodgers' tunes. *Strangers* was also easy on the ears . . .''

Rex Polier—*Philadelphia Evening Bulletin*
''*Music by Rodgers Turns 'Androcles' into 'My Fair Lion'* . . . a bright, colorful musical adaptation . . . Its success was due to a fine blend of many talents . . . *Strangers, The Emperor's Thumb* and *No More Waiting* were the most enjoyable numbers . . . But it was Norman Wisdom's evening . . .''

Eleanor Roberts—*Boston Herald-Traveler*
''What a joy this adaptation was! . . . excellent television fare—handsomely choreographed—laced with wit and humor—yet getting its message across . . . Under the skilled direction of Joe Layton the entire 90 minutes—with Rodgers' wonderful songs—was superior TV entertainment.''

Jerry Coffey—*Fort Worth Star-Telegram*
''. . . quite probably the best TV-originated musical ever made . . . the score was tuneful and inventive . . . a thoroughly delightful and engaging 90 minutes of television. It is certain to be counted a TV classic and to be repeated again and again, and it deserves to be.''

George Friedman—*Variety,* November 22, 1967
''. . . disappointing . . . some entertaining bits, but their presence couldn't offset the general lack of presence of the Shavian spirit . . . some of the Rodgers' numbers were pleasant . . . The best song was *Strangers,* a lovely love song . . .''

Bibliography

Androcles's Lion to Roar to Music by Val Adams
—*New York Times,* September 6, 1966

Shaw Did Write ''Tootsie-Wootsie'' by Gloria Steinem
—*New York Times,* November 12, 1967

TWO BY TWO

(1970)

A musical play by Peter Stone, based on "The Flowering Peach" by Clifford Odets; music by Richard Rodgers; lyrics by Martin Charnin.

Presented by Richard Rodgers
Directed by Joe Layton
Settings by David Hays
Costumes by Fred Voelpel
Lighting by John Gleason
Projections by Cris Alexander
Music director, Jay Blackton
Orchestrations by Eddie Sauter
Dance and vocal arrangements by Trude Rittmann

Tryout
Shubert Theatre, New Haven, September 14-26, 1970
Shubert Theatre, Boston, September 29-October 25, 1970

New York Run
Imperial Theatre, November 10, 1970-October 11, 1971
343 performances

The Story
Despite the derision of others, Noah heeds the voice of God and builds the ark, thus saving his family and the animal twosomes from the flood. But they cannot be saved from such domestic concerns as the romance between son Japheth and Rachel, the wife of his brother, Shem, and the death of Noah's wife, Esther.

The Cast
NOAH, Danny Kaye
ESTHER, Joan Copeland
JAPHETH, Walter Willison
SHEM, Harry Goz
LEAH, Marilyn Cooper
HAM, Michael Karm
RACHEL, Tricia O'Neil
GOLDIE, Madeline Kahn

NOTE: In February 1971, Mr. Kaye was hospitalized for two weeks because of a torn ligament. He was temporarily replaced by Mr. Goz. In August, Miss Kahn was succeeded by Caryl Jeanne Tenney, Mr. Willison by John Stewart; in September, Mr. Goz was succeeded by Jack Davison.

Musical Numbers

TIME: Before, during and after the Flood

ACT I

IN AND AROUND NOAH'S HOME

Why Me?, NOAH
Put Him Away, SHEM, HAM, LEAH
The Gitka's Song, THE GITKA
Something, Somewhere, JAPHETH, FAMILY
You Have Got to Have a Rudder on the Ark, NOAH, SHEM, HAM, JAPHETH
Something Doesn't Happen, RACHEL, ESTHER
An Old Man, ESTHER
Ninety Again!, NOAH
Two by Two, NOAH, FAMILY
I Do Not Know a Day I Did Not Love You, JAPHETH
Reprise, *Something, Somewhere*, NOAH

ACT II

ON THE ARK AND ATOP MT. ARARAT, FORTY DAYS AND FORTY NIGHTS LATER

When It Dries, NOAH, FAMILY
Reprise, *Two by Two*, NOAH, ESTHER
You, NOAH
The Golden Ram, GOLDIE
Poppa Knows Best, NOAH, JAPHETH
Reprise, *I Do Not Know a Day I Did Not Love You*, RACHEL, JAPHETH
As Far as I'm Concerned, SHEM, LEAH
Hey Girlie, NOAH
The Covenant, NOAH

NOTE: *Everything That's Gonna Be Has Been, Getting Married to a Person, Forty Nights, The Brother Department* (same music as *As Far As I'm Concerned*), *The Death of Me, I Can't Complain,* and *Without My Money* were cut before New York opening.

Reviews

Clive Barnes—*New York Times*

". . . Kaye is such a totally ingratiating actor that for me at least he can do no wrong . . . The show seems so long that at times you feel it ought to be called *Three by Three* . . . some very good numbers . . . Rodgers can still write a ballad better than anyone around . . . In Charnin he has found a very serviceable lyricist, with a properly light touch and ear for sinuous rhythms. Of course, the trouble is the story . . . Stone's writing is ponderous here, striking quite the wrong tone, I thought, for the musical theatre . . ."

John Chapman—*New York Daily News*
". . . a musical to be loved, to be cherished . . . it moved me profoundly . . . a magnificent portrayal by Danny Kaye . . . beguiling melodies . . . absorbing libretto . . . Who wants a conventional song-and-dance show with such as this around?"

Richard Watts Jr.—*New York Post*
". . . an ambitious work with many virtues, but just a bit disappointing . . . Kaye is altogether brilliant . . . All of the songs are pleasant, and there are several particularly appealing numbers, among which I would single out the title song, *I Do Not Know a Day I Did Not Love You, As Far as I'm Concerned,* and *Hey, Girlie* . . ."

William Glover—*Associated Press*
". . . one of Rodgers' finest musicals. Kaye is merely magnificent in a show for anyone, rich in comedy, full of melody and that rare ingredient—heart . . . Among the songs there are at least eight which ripple with that infectious magic which Rodgers has been dispensing for a half century . . ."

Hobe Morrison—*Variety,* November 18, 1970
". . . has the sort of music only Rodgers can write and in Danny Kaye one of the great stars of his time . . . the best Rodgers has had in some years—probably since *The Sound of Music* . . . a supple, good book . . . lyrics seem serviceable and the staging appears admirably fluid . . . It's the best musical—or at least has the best music—in some time and maybe for some time to come . . ."

Brendan Gill—*The New Yorker,* November 21, 1970
". . . as nearly dead as a musical can be, and Danny Kaye's attempt to make his own superb vitality mask the lack of it in the book, music, and lyrics is heroic and in vain . . ."

Marilyn Stasio—*Cue,* November 21, 1970
". . . So broadly directed that not a drop of the vulgarity escapes, the show might be dismissed as schlock-kultur were it not for Rodgers' score, which is studded with lovely, melodic songs, and the presence of Danny Kaye . . ."

Walter Kerr—*New York Times,* November 22, 1970
". . . A musical comedy should be able to walk on music, as this one does . . . Rodgers seems to know precisely the quality of sound that will cleave the gathering air . . . *Something Doesn't Happen* penetrates the atmosphere like an arrow halving the sky . . . *I Do Not Know a Day I Did Not Love You* is one of the very best, surely, that Rodgers has ever written . . . the best music (and I count at least five

examples of first-rate Rodgers) is of a quality capable of cracking a whip on the evening . . . too much of the libretto is uneasily poised between the simple vernacular of Odets and a vulgar opportunism . . ."

John Simon—*New York Magazine,* November 23, 1970
". . . The main trouble here are all those clean dirty jokes and cautiously blasphemous God gags, which produce few yoks and fewer shocks . . . three mouth-watering songs—*An Old Man, I Do Not Know a Day I Did Not Love You, As Far as I'm Concerned*—and one almost as good, the title song. The rest are fair to piddling . . . lyrics are not exactly dazzling in their command of language, but generally spunky and peppy . . . Kaye is quietly likable . . . *Two by Two* is not half bad—only two-fifths."

Theodore E. Kalem—*Time,* November 23, 1970
"*Genesis Nemesis* . . . arch, vulgar, lumbering, stale . . . lasts forty days and forty nights, with only one fifteen-minute intermission . . . its characters are unreal and underdeveloped . . . Except for one beguiling ballad, *I Do Not Know a Day I Did Not Love You,* Rodgers' score is almost barren of melodic appeal, and Charnin's lyrics could have been ticked off by a metronome . . ."

Henry Hewes—*Saturday Review,* November 28, 1970
". . . turns a legendary voyage into a squabble-ridden family cruise . . . The show simply neglects to create Danny Kaye's special world. Without it, *Two by Two* emerges as competent but depressingly ordinary and uninspired."

Tom Prideaux—*Life,* December 18, 1970
"*All at Sea Aboard the Ark* . . . The show arches with effort, trying to satisfy too many tastes and meet too many requirements, artistic and commercial . . . Kaye is clearly equally fit to run the ship and star in the sundeck cabaret . . . Rodgers' lovely ballad, *I Do Not Know a Day I Did Not Love You,* with flawless lyrics by Martin Charnin, is exactly what a musical-comedy love song should be, and seldom is . . ."

Bibliography

A Talk with Danny Kaye by Jerry Talmer
—*New York Post,* November 7, 1970

Just a Guy Who Can't Say Noah by Tom Burke
—*New York Times,* November 8, 1970

Danny Kaye, as Noah, Is Hailed on Broadway by McCandlish Phillips
—*New York Times*, November 11, 1970

Revival

St. Louis Municipal Opera, August 2-8, 1971
Milton Berle (NOAH); Kathryn Hays (RACHEL); Nancy Andrews (ESTHER); Rick Podell (JAPHETH).

RODGERS & HART

(1975)

"A musical celebration" with concept by Richard Lewine and John Fearnley; music by Richard Rodgers; lyrics by Lorenz Hart.

Presented by Lester Osterman and Richard Horner
In association with Worldvision Enterprises Inc.
Directed by Burt Shevelove
Choreography by Donald Saddler
Settings by David Jenkins
Costumes by Stanley Simmons
Lighting by Ken Billington
Music director, Buster Davis
Orchestrations by Luther Henderson

New York Run
Helen Hayes Theatre, May 13-August 16, 1975
111 performances

The Cast

Barbara Andres	Mary Sue Finnerty
Jimmy Brennan	Laurence Guittard
Wayne Bryan	Stephen Lehew
David-James Carroll	Jim Litten
Jamie Donnelly	Virginia Sandifur
Tovah Feldshuh	Rebecca York

Musical Numbers
96 Rodgers and Hart songs performed in two acts.

Reviews
Clive Barnes—*New York Times*
". . . a champagne-fizz of an evening . . . what sheer fun to have Rodgers and Hart back, wise, mocking, lovely, tuneful, serious, and, above all, eternally sweet but never sickly . . . smooth, seamless choreography . . . inventive, imaginative staging . . . It is always bewitching, sometimes bewildering, but never bothersome . . . the kind of songs that make you feel great when you just feel good, the pretty good even if you feel terrible. Play it again, Rodgers and Hart!"

Ernest Leogrande—*New York Daily News*
". . . an exuberant couple of hours . . . There was so much gee-gosh puppy-dog energy and beaming youthful smiles that at first I was afraid I would die of the cutes, but they soon won me over . . . The spirit of the evening is one of good clean fun . . ."

Martin Gottfried—*New York Post*
". . . the show's emphasis has been placed on the obscure rather than the familiar. As a result, what the audience has come to hear is not what the audience gets. This violates a basic rule and because of that violation, *Rodgers & Hart* fights an uphill battle . . . has more aplomb than flair. It isn't unpleasant. It merely is what it is—a staged concert."

Allan Wallach—*Newsday*
". . . no creative men of the theatre deserve a tribute more than these two men, but I don't think *Rodgers & Hart* is quite the tribute they deserve . . . an engaging and generally talented cast, but there is a crowded quality to the evening as the songs hurry by . . . the format suggests too often that the songs are machine-processed rather than the hand-crafted gems that an astonishing number are . . ."

Hobe Morrison—*Variety*, May 21, 1975
". . . tends to be a pleasant show for approximately the first half, and a progressively enjoyable and rewarding experience for the concluding portion . . . should be an emotionally satisfying evening for those who treasure the songs from the golden age of the musical stage . . . impressive talent is evident among the singer-dancers . . ."

Walter Kerr—*New York Times*, May 25, 1975
". . . if we are given a fair chance to detect the uniqueness of Hart's work, we are given almost none to chart the highly sophisticated changes Rodgers wrought . . . The show might have been a great deal more exciting if it had spent less time moving its people about on stage—to no very illuminating purpose—and more to displaying Rodgers' own movement, his stubborn, exhilarating growth."

Gerald Nachman—*New York Daily News*, May 25, 1975
". . . everyone who has touched this new show has perfect pitch. The whole thing sings . . . this remarkable revelry has been fashioned out of wit, insight and affection by people who not only like Rodgers and Hart but understand what they are about . . . there's not a camp, coy or embarrassing moment in the show . . . Understatement is its overall style . . . When it's over, you just don't want to leave . . ."

Brendan Gill—*The New Yorker,* May 26, 1975
". . . it may be that the very relentlessness of this procession of instantly recognizable favorites is in part to blame for the show's failure . . . not a show at all but rather a sort of oral catalogue . . ."

John Simon—*New York Magazine,* June 2, 1975
". . . basically a capacious grab bag . . . One big difficulty is all that unrelieved singing . . . A further problem is that so many fine but comparatively seldom heard items get only a couple of bars' worth of hearing . . . But as a musicale, *Rodgers & Hart* is the most tuneful thing in town."

Revival

Westwood Playhouse, Los Angeles, December, 1975.
Leland Palmer, Harve Presnell, Marcia Rodd, Constance Towers, Ed Evanko, David Thomé.

REX

(1976)

A musical play with book by Sherman Yellen; music by Richard Rodgers; lyrics by Sheldon Harnick.

Presented by Richard Adler
In association with Roger Berlind and Edward R. Downe, Jr.
Directed by Edwin Sherin
Choreography by Dania Krupska
Settings and costumes by John Conklin
Lighting by Jennifer Tipton
Music director, Jay Blackton
Orchestrations by Irwin Kostal
Dance arrangements by David Baker

Tryout
Playhouse, Wilmington, February 23-29, 1976
Kennedy Center Opera House, Washington, March 4-20, 1976
Shubert Theatre, Boston, March 23-April 10, 1976

New York Run
Lunt-Fontanne Theatre, April 25-June 5, 1976
49 performances

The Story
In his determination to have a male heir, King Henry VIII weds and beds—and in two cases beheads—a succession of wives. But it is his daughter by Anne Boleyn who proves as willful as he and succeeds to the throne as Queen Elizabeth I.

The Cast
NORFOLK, Charles Rule
CARDINAL WOLSEY, William Griffis
WILL SOMERS, Tom Aldredge
HENRY VIII, Nicol Williamson
MARK SMEATON, Ed Evanko
PRINCESS MARY, Glenn Close
QUEEN CATHERINE, Barbara Andres
LADY JANE SEYMOUR, April Shawhan

KING FRANCIS, Stephen D. Newman
ENGLISH HERALD, Danny Ruvolo
FRENCH HERALD, Jeff Phillips
QUEEN CLAUDE, Martha Danielle
ANNE BOLEYN } Penny Fuller
PRINCESS ELIZABETH } Penny Fuller
DAUPHIN, Keith Koppmeier
COMUS, Merwin Goldsmith
GUARDS: Ken Henley, Dennis Daniels
LADY MARGARET, Martha Danielle
LADY IN WAITING, Melanie Vaughan
PRINCESS ELIZABETH (as child), Sparky Shapiro
NURSE, Lillian Shelby
THOMAS CROMWELL, Gerald R. Teijelo
CATHERINE HOWARD, Valerie Mahaffey
PRINCE EDWARD, Michael John
QUEEN KATHERINE PARR, Martha Danielle
LADIES AND GENTLEMEN OF THE COURTS: Dennis Daniels, Harry Fawcett, Paul Forrest, Pat Gideon, Ken Henley, Dawn Herbert, Robin Hoff, Don Johanson, Jim Litten, Craig Lucas, Carol Jo Lugenbeal, Valerie Mahaffey, G. Eugene Moose, Jeff Phillips, Charles Rule, Danny Ruvolo, Lillian Shelby, Jo Speros, Gerald R. Teijelo, Candace Tovar, John Ulrickson, Melanie Vaughan
SWORD AND MORRIS DANCERS: Dennis Daniels, Ken Henley, Don Johanson, Jim Litten, Jeff Phillips, Danny Ruvolo

Musical Numbers

ACT I

SCENE ONE—GREENWICH PALACE
Te Deum, COMPANY

SCENE TWO—KING HENRY'S TENT
No Song More Pleasing, SMEATON

SCENE THREE—THE FIELD OF CLOTH OF GOLD
Where Is My Son?, HENRY
The Field of Cloth of Gold, COMPANY

SCENE FOUR—FRENCH PAVILLION
Basse Dance, COMPANY

SCENE FIVE—COMUS' CHAMBERS

SCENE SIX—HEVER CASTLE
The Chase, COMUS, WILL, SMEATON, GENTLEMEN OF THE COURT

SCENE SEVEN—HAMPTON COURT PALACE
Away from You, HENRY

SCENE EIGHT—CHAPEL
As Once I Loved You, CATHERINE

SCENE NINE—THE THRONE ROOM

SCENE TEN—HAMPTON COURT CORRIDOR

SCENE ELEVEN—QUEEN ANNE'S BEDROOM
Elizabeth, SMEATON, LADY MARGARET, LADY IN WAITING

SCENE TWELVE—COMUS' LABORATORY
Why?, HENRY

SCENE THIRTEEN—THE PALACE
Reprise, *No Song More Pleasing,* JANE, HENRY
Reprise, *Away from You,* ANNE

SCENE FOURTEEN—THE TOWER OF LONDON

SCENE FIFTEEN—THE CORONATION

SCENE SIXTEEN—THE CITY OF LONDON
Reprise, *Te Deum,* COMPANY

ACT II
SCENE ONE—HAMPTON COURT PALACE, TEN YEARS LATER
Christmas at Hampton Court, ELIZABETH, EDWARD, MARY

SCENE TWO—THE GREAT HALL AT HAMPTON COURT PALACE
The Wee Golden Warrior, WILL, EDWARD, ELIZABETH, MARY
Sword Dance and Morris Dance, SWORD AND MORRIS DANCERS
The Masque, LADIES AND GENTLEMEN OF THE COURT

SCENE THREE—THE THRONE ROOM
From Afar, HENRY

SCENE FOUR—HAMPTON COURT CORRIDOR
In Time, ELIZABETH, WILL

SCENE FIVE—COMUS' LABORATORY

SCENE SIX—HENRY'S BEDROOM

SCENE SEVEN—THE THRONE ROOM
Reprise, *In Time,* ELIZABETH, EDWARD
Reprise, *Te Deum,* COMPANY

NOTE: *I'll Miss You, Tell Me, Dear Jane, So Much You Loved Me,* (same music as *From Afar*), *I Brought You a Gift, Rex,* and *The Pears of Anjou* cut before New York opening.

Reviews
Clive Barnes—*New York Times*
". . . has almost everything not going for it . . . one of the most

interminable musicals in years . . . Williamson walks through the musical like Gulliver through Toytown . . . seems more of an abdication ceremony than a musical celebration."

Douglas Watt—*New York Daily News*
". . . a rather solemn affair, handsome to look at but dull in the telling . . . Williamson makes a pleasantly tempestuous Henry . . . The songs are neatly fashioned . . . one lovely number, *No Song More Pleasing* . . . a cheery, tuneful trio, *Christmas at Hampton Court* . . ."

Martin Gottfried—*New York Post*
". . . Rodgers has provided his finest score since *No Strings.* Here, once more, were lilting, surprising melodies, singing out with no apologies to current musical-theatre sophistication, nor any need for them. The first act is more than bearable . . . the second act played as if it couldn't wait to get itself over with. *Rex* isn't a disaster but, as a musical, it is a bad idea with half a salvage job . . ."

Howard Kissel—*Women's Wear Daily*
". . . you can't help leaving *Rex* humming several of Rodgers' beautiful songs . . . the book rarely probes very deeply into these complex characters . . . clean, attractive lyrics . . . two songs worthy of inclusion in the canon of Rodgers classics—*Away from You* and *As Once I Loved You* . . . *No Song More Pleasing* shows Rodgers is still the master of the long, haunting melodic line . . . a score with integrity . . ."

Emory Lewis—*The Record*
". . . not Rodgers' best score, but it has moments of rare magic . . . Harnick and Rodgers are a perfect team . . . The tunes are delightful, including *Away from You, In Time* and *Elizabeth* . . . *No Song More Pleasing* is a gem . . . The major problem is the sprawling book . . ."

William A. Raidy—*Long Island Press*
". . . lively, colorful entertainment . . . The score has a vaguely Elizabethan quality . . . Of the songs I found *As Once I Loved You* and *Away from You* the most appealing . . . an unforgettable musical portrait of a monumental monarch made memorable by the presence of the incredible Nicol Williamson . . . Such very good company!"

William Glover—*Associated Press*
". . . If opulent glitter, lavish costumes and nice songs that remind you of earlier Rodgers melodies were enough, Broadway's Lunt-Fontanne Theatre would have a palpable hit. But the production

suffers direly from an ungainly story . . . such numbers as *Away from You, As Once I Loved You, From Afar* and *In Time* are charming assets . . . Pageantry aside, *Rex* is a vex."

Hobe Morrison—*Variety,* April 28, 1976
". . . a moderately pleasant, unspectacular show . . . Visually, *Rex* is impressive but the story is slow and humorless . . . Harnick's lyrics are serviceable and sporadically ingenious. The score occasionally suggests the melodic richness of Rodgers' greatest works . . . hardly royal entertainment."

Marilyn Stasio—*Cue,* April 28, 1976
". . . a musical biography whose subject and historical period impose hefty inhibitions on all stylistic fronts . . . the most flavorful songs are the gentle love ballads most unrelated to the show's historical reality . . . a few spoonfuls of wit in the book but it all gets swallowed up by the oceans of factual material . . ."

Brendan Gill—*The New Yorker,* May 3, 1976
"The star is unquestionably John Conklin, who designed the sumptuous sets and the even more sumptuous costumes . . . none of the tunes resembles those of Rodgers' long prime, and the best that one can say for the lyrics is that they are neatly rhymed and occasionally touching. The book is harmless hackwork . . . A star second only to Mr. Conklin is Nicol Williamson . . ."

Walter Kerr—*New York Times,* May 9, 1976
". . . at least two sweet songs that seem to have escaped the show's textbook blight . . . *No Song More Pleasing,* and the title is accurate . . . The other is *Elizabeth* . . . It's a history trot for a high school exam, crammed with factual background too familiar to be of fresh interest or so arcane it'll be forgotten by the morrow."

George Oppenheimer—*Newsday,* May 9, 1976
". . . I found myself overwhelmed . . . show with melody, drama, comedy, wit, tenderness, beauty, action, spectacle, and entertainment such as we have not had in many months . . . a joy to learn, to watch and to hear . . . Rodgers' score was supremely melodic, helped enormously by the literate lyrics of Sheldon Harnick . . . the finest music Rodgers has composed since *The Sound of Music* . . ."

Theodore E. Kalem—*Time,* May 10, 1976
". . . research-soaked tedium . . . Rodgers is incapable of writing an uningratiating tune. But several of the numbers seem more suited to rocking a cradle than stirring a realm, and Harnick's lyrics confuse spareness with childishness . . ."

Bibliography

Rex—The Making of a Musical by Marilyn Stasio —*Cue,* April 24, 1976

Hal Prince's Rx for "Rex" by Caryl Rivers —*New York Times,* April 25, 1976

I REMEMBER MAMA

(1979)

A musical play with book by Thomas Meehan, based on play by John Van Druten and stories by Kathryn Forbes including "Mama's Bank Account"; lyrics by Martin Charnin; additional lyrics by Raymond Jessel; music by Richard Rodgers.

Presented by Alexander H. Cohen & Hildy Parks
Directed by Cy Feuer
Choreography by Danny Daniels
Settings by David Mitchell
Costumes by Theoni V. Aldredge
Lighting by Roger Morgan
Music director, Jay Blackton
Orchestrations by Philip J. Lang
Vocal arrangements by Mr. Blackton

Tryout

Shubert Theatre, Philadelphia, March 9-April 21, 1979

NOTE: Mr. Charnin, the original director, was replaced during tryout.

New York Run

Majestic Theatre, May 31, 1979-September 2, 1979
108 performances

NOTE: Previews ran from April 26-May 30, 1979. For information on Mr. Van Druten's play, *I remember Mama,* produced by Messrs. Rodgers and Hammerstein, see page 701.

The Story

The Hansens are a Norwegian immigrant family living in San Francisco early in the century. Papa, a ship's carpenter, loses his job in the shipyards and returns to Norway for work. Mama takes in washing to help support her five children. One of them, Katrine, has literary ambitions which Mama helps her achieve with the help of a titled English author. On the day Mama is to leave San Franciso and rejoin her husband, Papa returns and they buy their house with the money Katrine earns from the sale of her first published story.

The Cast

KATRINE HANSEN, Maureen Silliman
CHRISTINE HANSEN, Carrie Horner
JOHANNE HANSEN, Kristen Vigard
DAGMAR HANSEN, Tara Kennedy
NILS HANSEN, Ian Ziering
MARTA HANSEN (MAMA), Liv Ullmann
LARS HANSEN (PAPA), George Hearn
MR. MCGUIRE, Dick Ensslen
AUNT TRINA, Elizabeth Hubbard
AUNT JENNY, Dolores Wilson
AUNT SIGRID, Betty Ann Grove
MR. THORKELSON, Armin Shimerman
UNCLE CHRIS, George S. Irving
LUCIE, Janet McCall
NURSE, Sigrid Heath
DOCTOR ANDERSON, Stan Page
DAME SYBIL FITZGIBBONS, Myvanwy Jenn
NEIGHBORS, LITERARY ADMIRERS: Austin Colyer, John Dorrin, Mickey Gunnersen, Daniel Harnett, Danny Joel, Jan Kasni, Kevin Marcum, Richard Maxon, Marisa Morell, Frank Pietrí, Elissa Wolfe

NOTE: During tryout, KATRINE originally played by Kate Dezina.

Musical Numbers

The action takes place in and near San Francisco.
I Remember Mama, KATRINE

ACT I
Summer and Fall, 1910

KITCHEN OF THE HANSEN HOUSE, STEINER STREET
A Little Bit More (Jessel), MAMA, PAPA and CHILDREN
A Writer Writes at Night, KATRINE and MAMA

PARLOR OF THE HANSEN HOUSE
Ev'ry Day (Comes Something Beautiful), MAMA, PAPA, FAMILY and GUESTS; *The Hardangerfjord* danced by The Company

FRONT PORCH OF THE HANSEN HOUSE
You Could Not Please Me More, PAPA and MAMA (choreography by Graciela Daniele)

THE KITCHEN
Uncle Chris (Jessel), AUNT JENNY, AUNT SIGRID, AUNT TRINA, MR. THORKELSON

THE HOSPITAL
Lullaby, MAMA

THE PARLOR
Easy Come, Easy Go (Jessel), UNCLE CHRIS and FRIENDS; danced by DAGMAR and UNCLE CHRIS.

THE KITCHEN
It Is Not the End of the World, PAPA, MAMA and CHILDREN

ACT II
Spring, 1911

BACK PORCH OF THE HANSEN HOUSE
Mama Always Makes It Better, CHILDREN

THE PARLOR
Lars, Lars (Jessel), MAMA

PALACE HOTEL LOBBY
Fair Trade, DAME SYBIL, MAMA and ADMIRERS

UNCLE CHRIS' RANCH
It's Going to Be Good to Be Gone, UNCLE CHRIS

THE KITCHEN
Time, MAMA

NOTE: Cut during tryout: *Maybe, Maybe, Maybe; Midsummer Night; A Most Disagreeable Man; An Old City Boy at Heart; When; A Fam'ly We Will Be; Such Good Fun.* Added and cut during New York previews: *Where We Came From* and *I Don't Know How* (both lyrics by Jessel). *Mama Always Makes It Better* has same music as *Getting Married to a Person* (cut from *Two by Two).*

Reviews

Richard Eder—*New York Times*
". . . the result is not a marriage but a divorce of talents . . . Liv Ullmann and five young actors as her children are badly chosen in the first instance and badly employed in the second . . . The song, *Fair Trade,* is both pretty and witty . . . Rodgers' score includes several nice pieces . . . an interesting bitten-off melody matching Charnin's lyric in *It Is Not the End of the World,* and one or two others . . ."

Douglas Watt—*New York Daily News*
". . . the outlines are inviting but the color's missing . . . attractive tunes are better on the whole than those from either of Rodgers' last two shows . . . a tasteful period musical in the R&H idiom, but almost totally lacking in the R&H energy . . . book is literate and direct, but it is too gentle and sketchy . . . Liv Ullmann is an enchanting actress . . . *Easy Come, Easy Go,* with a delightful child, Tara Kennedy, and George S. Irving, is a high spot . . ."

Clive Barnes—*New York Post*
". . . embellished with the ageless freshness of Rodgers, a few decent lyrics, some moments of honest fun and feeling, and an exquisite performance by Miss Ullmann . . . finds Rodgers, one of the supreme artists of our musical theatre, back in superbly lyrical vein . . . I loved the score . . . It is simple on the mind, but easy on the heart . . . Liv Ullmann is not a singer but she is a song . . . this is a warm-souled, family musical with a good and proper Rodgers score and a lady of glorious luminosity, the kind of mama we would all want to remember."

Allan Wallach—*Newsday*
". . . a pleasant family show that has been assembled with professional skill . . . Rodgers' score is characterized by the melodic simplicity and directness of his collaboration with Oscar Hammerstein . . . Meehan's book, though too sweet for my taste, serves the musical's demands adequately . . . Rodgers' prettiest song is a charming ballad called *You Could Not Please Me More* . . ."

Emory Lewis—*The Record*
"Liv Ullmann lights up the stage with her luminous beauty . . . an unforgettable portrait . . . Meehan's book is properly old-fashioned . . . *You Could Not Please Me More* is a lovely, soft-focus ode to marriage . . . The children are delightful, particularly Tara Kennedy . . ."

William A. Raidy—*Newark Star-Ledger*
". . . arrived with courage, determination and the luminous presence of Liv Ullmann . . . two fine Rodgers melodies to take out of the theatre with you: *You Could Not Please Me More* and *Ev'ry Day (Comes Something Beautiful)* . . . While *I Remember Mama* is hardly bankrupt, a hefty deposit of vigor and uninhibited imagination would have added greatly to its balance . . . *Mama,* nevertheless, has her charms . . ."

Dennis Cunningham—*CBS-TV*
". . . some wonderful moments, some fine performances, a couple of exceptional tunes by the amazing Richard Rodgers . . . Liv Ullmann is triumphant and a joy to behold . . ."

Joel Siegel—*ABC-TV*
". . . Liv Ullmann is a mama you'll remember . . . The theme is a beautiful one but as theatre it doesn't always work . . . lacks the focus and the depth to make it an *I Remember Mama* you'll never forget. Still, this is fine family theatre . . . on balance, a good show . . ."

John Beaufort—*Christian Science Monitor,* June 4, 1979
"There is a warmly endearing quality to much of *I Remember Mama.* The appeal centers around the strong performance of Liv Ullmann, and the aura of good feeling extends to the production as a whole . . . Mama's virtues never cloy. Genuine devotion is always there . . . The score contains several choice numbers . . . The musical revels in a kind of upbeat good cheer that is enhanced in the outgoing performance . . ."

Hobe Morrison—*Variety,* June 6, 1979
". . . based on a credible, colorful locale, situation and characters. It also has a richly melodic score by a Richard Rodgers in fine form. And it has an incandescent, believable and winning title star in Liv Ullmann . . . the book's limitations are particularly disappointing . . . Rodgers remains an indomitably creative composer . . ."

Walter Kerr—*New York Times,* June 10, 1979
". . . the ambience is as neighborly and as soothing as the soft outlines of the streetlamps that manage to penetrate a San Francisco fog . . . in spite of the Rodgers imprint on at lease three freshly melodic songs, in spite of the sturdy, energetic, ever-so-willing comings and goings of Miss Ullmann . . . the mama whose memory is reported as so indelible is nowhere very clearly—or at least emphatically—defined . . ."

Charles Michener—*Newsweek,* June 11, 1979
". . . brimming with good intentions but devoid of dramatic conviction . . . Rodgers is comfortably back on the terrain that he has always understood better than anyone else: the land of milk and cookies . . . With her great radiance, Liv Ullmann is utterly persuasive . . ."

Bibliography

Only Twice Was It Easy by Harry Haun
—*New York Daily News,* May 13, 1979

Remembering "I Remember Mama" by Lillian Africano
—*New York Magazine,* May 14, 1979

The Doctoring of "Mama" by Ralph Tyler
—*New York Times,* May 27, 1979

On the Bumpy Road to Staging "Mama" by Ernest Leogrande
—*New York Daily News,* May 29, 1979

MISCELLANEOUS WORKS

Richard Rodgers and Lorenz Hart

RICHARD RODGERS

All lyrics by Lorenz Hart unless otherwise noted

1916 *Dear Old Wigwam* (lyric by Rodgers)
Camp Fire Days
The first songs by Mr. Rodgers, composed when he was 14 and a camper at Camp Wigwam, Harrison, Maine.

1917 *Auto Show Girl* (lyric by David Dyrenforth)
Mr. Rodgers' first copyrighted song (June 30, 1917), it was later interpolated in an amateur musical, *One Minute, Please* (December 29, 1917).

1919 *Any Old Place with You*
Sung by Alan Hale and Eve Lynn in Lew Fields musical, *A Lonely Romeo,* after it had been added to score August 26, 1919. It was the first Rodgers and Hart song in a Broadway show, and was the team's first published song (copyright date: December 19, 1919). NEW YORK RUN: Shubert Theatre, June 10-July 26; Casino Theatre, July 28-October 11, 1919; *128 performances.*

1921 *Shakespeare of 1921* (lyric with Morrie Ryskind)
Written for Georgie Price who introduced it in vaudeville.

1925 *Terpsichore and Troubadour*
Written for Renée Robert and Jay Velie who introduced it in vaudeville at the Palace Theatre, January 4, 1925.

Anytime, Anywhere, Anyhow
Sung by Elizabeth Hines and Roy Royston in musical comedy, *June Days.* NEW YORK RUN: Astor Theatre, August 6-October 17, 1925; *84 performances*

1926 *Sentimental Me*
(Originally in *The Garrick Gaieties,* 1925.) Introduced in London by Cyril Ritchard, Mimi Crawford, J. H. Roberts and Joyce Barbour in revue, *R.S.V.P.* LONDON RUN: Vaudeville Theatre, February 23-November 9, 1926; *297 performances.*

I'm Crazy 'Bout the Charleston (lyric by Donovan Parsons)
(Same music as *Maybe It's Me,* originally in *The Fifth Avenue Follies,* 1926.) This version sung in London by Billy Bradford and Marion Hamilton in *Cochran's Revue of 1926.* Song dropped from show shortly after opening to be replaced on bill by Will Rogers in his first appearance on the English stage. LONDON RUN: London Pavilion, April 29-September 7, 1926; *149 performances.*

1927 *If I Were You*
Sing
(Both originally in *Betsy,* 1926.) Introduced in London in musical

comedy *Lady Luck.* Former sung by Phyllis Monkman and Leslie Henson; latter by Cyril Ritchard, Laddie Cliff and Mr. Henson. LONDON RUN: Carlton Theatre, April 27, 1927-February 4, 1928; *324 performances.*

Blue Room
The Girl Friend
What's the Use of Talking?
Mountain Greenery
(First two songs originally in *The Girl Friend,* 1926; last two originally in *The Garrick Gaieties,* 1926.) All songs introduced in London in musical comedy *The Girl Friend* (not the same as the New York musical). *Blue Room* and *Mountain Greenery* were sung by Louise Brown and Roy Royston (though both songs were dropped during the run); *What's the Use of Talking?* by Flora LeBreton and Bernard Clifton; *The Girl Friend* by Emma Haig and George Gee. LONDON RUN: Palace Theatre, September 8, 1927-September 8, 1928; *421 performances.*

1929 *I Love You More than Yesterday*
Sing
(Latter originally in *Betsy,* 1926.) Both songs in musical comedy *Lady Fingers.* Former, which was dropped during run, was sung by Louise Brown and John Price Jones; latter by Dorothy and Margaret McCarthy, and later during run by Marjorie White. NEW YORK RUN: Vanderbilt Theatre, January 31-March 30, 1929; Liberty Theatre, April 1-May 30, 1929; *132 performances.*

1930 *With a Song in My Heart*
(Originally in *Spring Is Here,* 1929.) Introduced in London by Eric Marshall, Gunda Mordhorst, Roy Royston and Ada May in *Cochran's 1930 Revue.* LONDON RUN: London Pavilion, March 27-October 26, 1930; *245 performances.*

Lullaby
(Originally in *She's My Baby,* 1928, in which it was called *A Baby's Best Friend.*) Introduced in London by Beatrice Lillie in *Charlot's Masquerade.* LONDON RUN: Cambridge Theatre, September 4, 1930.

I'm Hard to Please
It Never Happened Before
Softer than a Kitten
All three songs written for Paramount film, *Follow Through.* RELEASE DATE: September 14, 1930.

Opening Number (lyric by E. Y. Harburg)
The Three Musketeers
Rose of Arizona
(First song had same music as *Six Little Plays,* originally in *The Garrick Gaieties,* 1926; second originally in *The Garrick Gaieties,* 1925; third

originally in *The Garrick Gaieties,* 1926). All three songs sung in touring edition of *The Garrick Gaieties,* 1930. *Opening Number* sung by Rosalind Russell, Sterling Holloway, James Norris, Neal Caldwell and Roger Stearns; *The Three Musketeers* by Philip Loeb, Mr. Holloway and Mr. Caldwell; *Rose of Arizona* performed by Miss Russell, Ruth Chorpenning, Katherine Carrington, Mr. Norris, Doris Vinton, Mr. Holloway, Mr. Caldwell, Mr. Stearns, and William Holbrook. NEW YORK RUN (prior to tour): Guild Theatre, October 16-25, 1930; *12 performances.*

Sky City
(Originally intended for *Heads Up!* but cut before New York opening.) Sung by Alfred Chigi in *Corned Beef and Roses,* a revue presented by Billy Rose that did not open in New York. PHILADELPHIA RUN: Shubert Theatre, October 27, 1930.

1931 *Rest Room Rose*
Sung by Fanny Brice soon after opening of Billy Rose revue, *Crazy Quilt.* NEW YORK RUN: 44th Street Theatre, May 19-July 24, 1931; *79 performances.*

1933 *That's the Rhythm of the Day*
Sung by Nelson Eddy in M-G-M film, *Dancing Lady.* RELEASE DATE: November 1, 1933.

Rhythm
A Baby's Best Friend
(Latter originally in *She's My Baby,* 1928). Both songs were sung in London by Beatrice Lillie in André Charlot revue, *Please!* LONDON RUN: Savoy Theatre, November 16, 1933-February 15, 1934; *108 performances.*

1934 *That's Love*
Sung by Anna Sten in Samuel Goldwyn film, *Nana.* RELEASE DATE: February 1, 1934.

The Bad in Every Man
(Same music as *Prayer,* cut from *Hollywood Party,* 1934.) Sung by Shirley Ross in M-G-M film, *Manhattan Melodrama.* RELEASE DATE: May 2, 1934. With different lyric song had been intended as title song of the film (also called *It's Just that Kind of a Play*).

Blue Moon
(Same music as *Prayer, The Bad in Every Man* and *Manhattan Melodrama.*) This was the only successful Rodgers and Hart song that was not associated with the stage or films.

1935 *What Are You Doing in Here?*
Sung by chorus of *Anything Goes* to introduce *The Post-Depression Gaieties,* a revue produced by Marc Connelly for benefit of the Authors League Fund and the Stage Relief Fund. NEW YORK RUN: New Amsterdam Theatre, February 24, 1935. *1 performance.*

Little Dolores
Originally written with different lyric and called *The Muchacha.*

You Are So Lovely and I'm So Lonely
Sung by Walter Pidgeon in non-musical play, *Something Gay.* NEW YORK RUN: Morosco Theatre, April 29-June 29, 1935; *72 performances.*

Please Make Me Be Good
I'll Take a Little of You on Toast
You've Got That
All three songs sung by Helen Morgan and Ken Murray in radio musical comedy, *Let's Have Fun.* BROADCAST DATE: October 22, 1935.

1936 *All Points West*
A "symphonic narrative" written for and performed by Paul Whiteman and the Philadelphia Orchestra at the Academy of Music, Philadelphia, November 27 and 28, 1936. Ray Middleton was soloist, orchestration was by Adolph Deutsch. Work was also performed by Mr. Whiteman and his own orchestra, with Mr. Middleton as soloist, at the Hippodrome, New York, December 1, 1936; later performed at the Radio City Music Hall, June 1939.

Rhythm
(Originally in *Please!,* 1933.) Revised version introduced in New York by Beatrice Lillie in the Shuberts' revue, *The Show Is On,* accompanied by Reginald Gardiner. NEW YORK RUN: Winter Garden, December 25, 1936-July 17, 1937; *237 performances.*

1938 *Rhythm*
My Heart Stood Still
Dancing on the Ceiling
(First song originally in *Please!,* 1933; second originally in *One Dam Thing After Another,* 1927; third originally in *Ever Green,* 1930.) All three songs sung in Charles B. Cochran London revue, *Happy Returns. Rhythm* sung by Beatrice Lillie; *My Heart Stood Still* by Patricia Burke and Edward Matthews; *Dancing on the Ceiling* by Constance Carpenter. LONDON RUN: Adelphi Theatre, May 19, 1938.

Nursery Ballet
Orchestral work in three movements: *March of the Clowns, A Doll Gets Broken,* and *Little Girls Don't Fight.* First performed by Paul Whiteman and his Orchestra at Carnegie Hall, New York, December 25, 1938. Orchestration by Roy Bargy.

1939 *Have You Met Miss Jones?*
(Originally in *I'd Rather Be Right,* 1937.) Introduced in London by Bobby Howes in H. M. Tennent revue, *All Clear.* LONDON RUN: Queen's Theatre, December 20, 1939-May 9, 1940; *162 performances.*

1940 *This Can't Be Love*
Sing for Your Supper

Falling in Love with Love
(All originally in *The Boys from Syracuse,* 1938.) Introduced in London in Firth Shepard revue, *Up and Doing. This Can't Be Love* sung by Graham Payn and Patricia Burke; *Sing for Your Supper* by Miss Burke, Cyril Ritchard and Enid Lowe; *Falling in Love with Love* by Binnie Hale. LONDON RUN: Saville Theatre, April 17-September 12, 1940; *171 performances.* Reopened: May 20, 1941-February 28, 1942; *332 performances.*

Now That I Know You
(Same music as original title song for *I'd Rather Be Right,* 1937, which had been cut before New York opening.) Sung by Marie Nash and Earl Oxford in Ted Fetter-Richard Lewine summer revue, *Two Weeks With Pay.* WHITE PLAINS RUN: Ridgeway Theatre, June 19-July 1, 1940; *two weeks.*

1941 *My Romance*
(Originally in *Jumbo,* 1935.) Introduced in England in Jack Hulbert revue, *Hulbert's Follies.* Toured provinces during February, but did not open in London owing to lack of suitable theatre.

1942 *Keep 'Em Rolling*
Sung by Jan Peerce in film short, *Keep 'Em Rolling,* distributed by Universal. RELEASE DATE: May 1942.

Off The Record
(Originally in *I'd Rather Be Right,* 1937.) Sung by James Cagney in Warner Bros. film, *Yankee Doodle Dandy,* in recreation of scene from *I'd Rather Be Right.* RELEASE DATE: June 1, 1942.

Bombardier Song
All royalties went to Army Air Force Aid Society.

1943 *The Girl I Love to Leave Behind*
Sung by Ray Bolger in Sol Lesser film, *Stage Door Canteen.* RELEASE DATE: May 12, 1943.

OSCAR HAMMERSTEIN II

1917 *Make Yourself at Home* (music by Silvio Hein)
Sung by chorus in musical comedy, *Furs and Frills,* produced by Arthur Hammerstein. This was the first Broadway song with an Oscar Hammerstein II lyric, though he received no program credit. NEW YORK RUN: Casino Theatre, October 9, 1917; *32 performances.*

1923 *I Wonder Why the Glow-Worm Winks His Eye* (music by Herbert Stothart)
Sung by Colin Campbell and Irene Olsen in *Hammerstein's 9 o'Clock Revue,* produced by Arthur Hammerstein. NEW YORK RUN: Century Theatre Roof, October 4-13, 1923; *12 performances.* Also sung by Irene Delroy in revue, *Round the Town,* produced by Herman J. Mankiewicz and S. Jay Kaufman. NEW YORK RUN: Century Theatre Roof, May 21-31, 1924; *13 performances.*

1926 *In Araby with You* (music by Jerome Kern; lyric with Otto Harbach)
Sung by Dorothy Francis in musical comedy, *Criss-Cross,* produced by Charles Dillingham. NEW YORK RUN: Globe Theatre, October 12, 1926-April 9, 1927; *206 performances.*

1930 *No Wonder I'm Blue* (music by Louis Alter)
I'm One of God's Children (music by Louis Alter)
Both songs in musical comedy, *Ballyhoo,* produced by Arthur Hammerstein, directed by Oscar Hammerstein II. Former sung by Grace Hayes; latter (whose title was suggested by Harry Ruskin) by Janet Reade with Ted Black's Band. NEW YORK RUN: Hammerstein's Theatre, December 22, 1930-February 21, 1931; *68 performances.*

1935 *Reckless* (music by Jerome Kern)
Sung by Virginia Verrill (for Jean Harlow), Allan Jones and Nina Mae McKinney, then danced by Miss Harlow and Carl Randall in M-G-M film, *Reckless.* RELEASE DATE: April 17, 1935.

When I've Got the Moon (music by Jerome Kern)
Also called *Banjo Song.* Written for unproduced M-G-M film, *Champagne and Orchids.*

1937 *I'll Take Romance* (music by Ben Oakland)
Sung by Grace Moore in Columbia film, *I'll Take Romance.* RELEASE DATE: December 17, 1937.

1939 *The Sweetest Sight that I Have Seen* (music by Jerome Kern)

1940 *Havana for a Night* (music by Gonzalo Curiel)

Your Dream (music by Jerome Kern; lyric with Otto Harbach)
(Originally in *Gentlemen Unafraid,* 1938.) Sung by Allan Jones and uncredited singer (for Nancy Kelly) in Universal film, *One Night in the Tropics.* RELEASE DATE: November 1, 1940.

The Last Time I Saw Paris (music by Jerome Kern)
Dedicated to Noël Coward. Later sung by Ann Sothern in M-G-M film, *Lady, Be Good,* and won Academy Award as best film song of the year. RELEASE DATE: July 15, 1941.

1941 *Serenade to a Pullman Porter* (music by Harry Ruby)

1946 *All Through the Day* (music by Jerome Kern)
Sung by Larry Stevens, Cornel Wilde and Louanne Hogan (for Jeanne Crain) in 20th Century-Fox film, *Centennial Summer.* RELEASE DATE: May 29, 1946.

1951 *A Kiss to Build a Dream On* (music by Harry Ruby; lyric with Bert Kalmar).
(Originally written by Kalmar and Ruby alone and called *Moonlight on the Meadow;* rewritten with Hammerstein for Marx Brothers film, *A Night at the Opera,* but not used.) Sung by Kay Brown in M-G-M film, *The Strip.* RELEASE DATE: August 6, 1951.

RODGERS AND HAMMERSTEIN

1943 *The P.T.Boat Song (Steady as You Go)*
Dedicated to the Officers and Men of the Motor Torpedo Boats. All royalties went to the Navy Relief Society.

1944 *Dear Friend*
Written for the 5th War Loan Drive.

We're on Our Way
Dedicated to the United States Army Infantry.

1946 *I Haven't Got a Worry in the World*
Sung by Helen Hayes in play, *Happy Birthday,* produced by Rodgers and Hammerstein, (See page 701).

1952 *Happy Christmas, Little Friend*
First published in *Life Magazine,* December 29, 1952.

1953 *There's Music in You*
Sung by Mary Martin in Lester Cowan film, *Main Street to Broadway,* released by M-G-M. Rodgers and Hammerstein appeared in the scene. RELEASE DATE: July 29, 1953.

RICHARD RODGERS

1960 *Salute to the Seaway*
Orchestral work in honor of the St. Lawrence Waterway. First performed by the Milwaukee Symphony Orchestra, Alfredo Antonini cond., January 29, 1960. Orchestration by Robert Russell Bennett.

1963 *The Great Adventure*
Orchestral theme for CBS-TV series, *The Great Adventure.*

1964 *Barnard! Barnard!* (lyric by Rodgers)
In honor of the 75th anniversary of Barnard College.

Fair Is Fair (lyric by Rodgers)
Official song of the 1964 New York World's Fair.

1968 *I'd Rather Be Right*
(Originally in *I'd Rather Be Right,* 1937.) Sung by Joel Grey in *George M!* imitating George M. Cohan in *I'd Rather Be Right.* NEW YORK RUN: Winter Garden, April 10, 1968-April 26, 1969; *427 performances.*

Slaughter on Tenth Avenue
(Originally in *On Your Toes,* 1936.) Ballet performed by the New York City Ballet, featuring Arthur Mitchell (HOOFER); Suzanne Farrell (STRIP-TEASE GIRL); Michael Steele (BIG BOSS). Choreography by George Balanchine; orchestrations by Hershy Kay. NEW YORK RUN: New York State Theater, Lincoln Center, April 30, May 2, 8, 10, June 1, 2, 8, 1968. Also performed Saratoga Springs, July 17, 1968, with Mr. Mitchell succeeded by Richard Rapp.

Saturday Night
Orchestral theme for unproduced NBC-TV special, *Saturday Night Around the World.*

1971 *The Regents March*
Commissioned by Board of Regents, University of the State of New York.

Father of the Man (lyric by Rodgers)
All royalties to UNICEF.

1973 *The American Idea—The Land*
Orchestral theme for *The Land,* first program of projected ABC-TV series, *The American Idea,* televised March 18, 1973.

1974 *The Lagoon*
Orchestral work with narration written by James Michener. First performed by André Kostelanetz and his Orchestra, with Douglas Fairbanks Jr. as narrator; Avery Fisher Hall, New York, on May 22, 1974.

PRODUCTION ACTIVITIES

Howard Keel and cast in the opening scene of "Carousel" (1945).

RODGERS AND HAMMERSTEIN

1944 I Remember Mama

A play by John Van Druten, based on book, *Mama's Bank Account*, by Kathryn Forbes.

Directed by Mr. Van Druten; settings and lighting by George Jenkins; costumes by Lucinda Ballard. NEW YORK RUN: Music Box Theatre, October 19, 1944-June 29, 1946; *714 performances*. TOUR: September 26-December 7, 1946

Cast included: Mady Christians, Oscar Homolka, Joan Tetzel, Frances Heflin, Marlon Brando, Raymond Bishop, Oswald Marshall.

1946 Annie Get Your Gun

A musical comedy with book by Herbert and Dorothy Fields; music and lyrics by Irving Berlin.

Directed by Joshua Logan; choreography by Helen Tamiris; settings and lighting by Jo Mielziner; costumes by Lucinda Ballard; music director Jay S. Blackton; orchestrations by Philip J. Lang, Robert Russell Bennett, Ted Royal. NEW YORK RUN: Imperial Theatre, May 16, 1946-February 12, 1949; *1,147 performances*.

Cast included: Ethel Merman, Ray Middleton, Marty May, Lea Penman, Kenny Bowers, Betty Anne Nyman, William O'Neal, Lubov Roudenko, Daniel Nagrin, Harry Bellaver, George Lipton, Marjorie Crossland, Art Barnett, Warren Berlinger, Ellen Hanley, Beau Tilden, Leon Bibb, Milton Watson, Christina Lind, Ellen Hanley, Franca Baldwin.

TOUR: Dallas State Fair Auditorium, October 3, 1947-Cass Theatre, Detroit, May 28, 1949.

Cast included: Mary Martin, Earl Covert, Donald Burr, Jean Cleveland, Tommy Wonder, Billie Worth, Jack Rutherford, Tessie Carrano, Barton Mumaw, Zachary Charles, Bernard Hoffman, Reta Shaw, Edwin Clay, Tommy Rettig, Heller Halliday, Sandra Deel.

Happy Birthday

A comedy by Anita Loos.

Directed by Joshua Logan; setting and lighting by Jo Mielziner; Costumes by Lucinda Ballard; interpolated song by Rodgers and Hammerstein; incidental music by Robert Russell Bennett. NEW YORK RUN: Broadhurst Theatre, October 31, 1946-March 13, 1948; *564 performances*.

Cast included: Helen Hayes, Louis Jean Heydt, Enid Markey, Musa Williams, Dort Clark, Grace Valentine, Ralph Theodore.

1947 John Loves Mary

A comedy by Norman Krasna.

Directed by Joshua Logan; setting and lighting by Frederick Fox;

costumes by Lucinda Ballard. NEW YORK RUN: Booth Theatre, February 4-March 16, 1947; Music Box Theatre, March 17, 1947-February 7, 1948; *421 performances.* TOUR: February 9-October 16, 1948.
Cast included: William Prince, Nina Foch, Tom Ewell, Loring Smith, Ann Mason, Harry Bannister, Pamela Gordon, Max Showalter, Ralph Chambers.

Show Boat
(See page 373)

1950 **The Happy Time**
A comedy by Samuel Taylor, based on the novel by Robert Fontaine. Directed by Robert Lewis; settings and costumes by Aline Bernstein. NEW YORK RUN: Plymouth Theatre, January 24, 1950-July 14, 1951; *614 performances.*
Cast included: Claude Dauphin, Richard Hart, Leora Dana, Kurt Kasznar, Edgar Stehli, Eva Gabor, Johnny Stewart, Mary Aurelius, Gage Clarke, Oliver Cliff.

TOUR: Nixon Theatre, Pittsburgh, September 24, 1951—Blackstone Theatre, Chicago, January 12, 1952
Cast included: Helmut Dantine, Francis Bethencourt, Mary Fickett, Jacques Aubuchon, Joe E. Marks, Marya Saunders, Warren Berlinger, Alice Lee Edwards, Gage Clarke, Henry Wadsworth.

The Heart of the Matter
A play by Graham Greene and Basil Dean, based on the novel by Mr. Greene.
Directed by Mr. Dean; settings by Samuel Leve; costumes by David Ffolkes. NEW YORK RUN: None (closed during Boston tryout, Wilbur Theatre, February 20-March 4, 1950).
Cast included: Ian Hunter, Colin Keith-Johnston, Norah Howard, Robin Craven, Leslie Barrie.

Burning Bright
A play by John Steinbeck.
Directed by Guthrie McClintic; settings and lighting by Jo Mielziner; costumes by Aline Bernstein. NEW YORK RUN: Broadhurst Theatre, October 19-27, 1950; *13 performances.*
Cast included: Barbara Bel Geddes, Kent Smith, Howard DaSilva, Martin Brooks.

RICHARD RODGERS (LINCOLN CENTER)

Mr. Rodgers was President and Producing Director of the Music Theater of Lincoln Center, at the New York State Theater, during its entire existence. Asterisk indicates musical by Rodgers and/or Hammerstein.

1964 The King and I*

Directed by Edward Greenberg; choreography reproduced by Yuriko; settings by Paul C. McGuire; costumes by Irene Sharaff; music director, Franz Allers. NEW YORK RUN: July 6-August 8, 1964; *40 performances.*

Cast included: Risë Stevens, Darren McGavin, Patricia Neway, Lee Venora, Frank Porretta, Michael Kermoyan, Eric Brotherson.

The Merry Widow

An operetta with book by Milton Lazarus, based on adaptation by Edwin Lester of libretto by Victor Leon and Leo Stein; music by Franz Lehar; lyrics by Forman Brown.

Directed by Edward Greenberg; choreography by Zachary Solov; settings by Rouben Ter Arutunian; costumes by Rene Hubert; music director, Franz Allers. NEW YORK RUN: August 17-September 19, 1964; *40 performances.* TOUR: September 22, 1964-January 9, 1965.

Cast included: Patrice Munsel, Bob Wright, Frank Porretta, Mischa Auer, Joan Weldon, Sig Arno, Dixie Carter.

1965 Kismet

A musical play with book by Charles Lederer and Luther Davis, based on the play by Edward Knoblock; music and lyrics by Robert Wright and George Forrest, based on themes by Alexander Borodin.

Directed by Edward Greenberg; choreography by Jack Cole; settings by Lemuel Ayers; costumes by Frank Thompson; lighting by Peter Hunt; music director, Franz Allers. NEW YORK RUN: June 22-July 31, 1965; *48 performances.* TOUR: August 2-December 18, 1965.

Cast included: Alfred Drake, Lee Venora, Anne Jeffreys. Richard Banke, Don Beddoe, Henry Calvin, Beatrice Kraft.

Carousel*

Directed by Edward Greenberg; choreography by Agnes de Mille; Settings by Paul C. McGuire; costumes by Stanley Simmons; lighting by Peter Hunt; music director, Franz Allers. NEW YORK RUN: August 10-September 18, 1965; *48 performances.* TOUR: September 21, 1965-February 5, 1966.

Cast included: John Raitt, Eileen Christy, Susan Watson, Reid Shelton, Benay Venuta, Katherine Hilgenberg, Edward Everett Horton, Dixie Carter.

1966 **Annie Get Your Gun**

A musical comedy with book by Herbert and Dorothy Fields; music and lyrics by Irving Berlin.

Directed by Jack Sydow; choreography by Danny Daniels; settings by Paul C. McGuire; costumes by Frank Thompson; lighting by Peter Hunt; music director, Franz Allers. NEW YORK RUN: May 21-July 9, 1966; *47 performances.* TOUR: July 12-November 26, 1966.

Cast included: Ethel Merman, Bruce Yarnell, Jerry Orbach, Benay Venuta, Rufus Smith, Jack Dabdoub, Bobbi Baird.

Show Boat*

Directed by Lawrence Kasha; choreography by Ronald Field; settings by Oliver Smith; costumes by Stanley Simmons; lighting by Jean Rosenthal; music director, Franz Allers. NEW YORK RUN: July 19-September 10, 1966; *64 performances.* TOUR: September 12-November 5, 1966.

Cast included: David Wayne, Barbara Cook, Stephen Douglass, Constance Towers, William Warfield, Eddie Phillips, Allyn Ann McLerie, Margaret Hamilton, Rosetta LeNoire.

1967 **South Pacific***

Directed by Joe Layton; settings and costumes by Fred Voelpel; lighting by Jules Fisher; music director, Jonathan Anderson. NEW YORK RUN: June 12-September 9, 1967; *104 performances.*

Cast included: Florence Henderson, Giorgio Tozzi, David Doyle, Justin McDonough, Eleanor Calbes, Irene Byatt, Lyle Talbot, Bobbi Baird.

1968 **West Side Story**

A musical play with book by Arthur Laurents, based on a conception of Jerome Robbins; music by Leonard Bernstein; lyrics by Stephen Sondheim.

Directed and choreographed by Lee Theodore, based on original by Jerome Robbins; settings by Oliver Smith; costumes by Winn Morton; lighting by Peter Hunt; music director, Maurice Peress. NEW YORK RUN: June 24-September 7, 1968; *89 performances.*

Cast included: Kurt Peterson, Victoria Mallory, Avind Harum, Barbara Luna, Alan Castner, Martin Wolfson, Robert LuPone.

1969 **Oklahoma!***

Directed by John Kennedy; choreography by Gemze deLappe; settings and lighting Paul C. McGuire; costumes by Miles White; music director, Jay Blackton. NEW YORK RUN: June 23-September 6, 1969; *88 performances.*

Cast included: Bruce Yarnell, Lee Beery, April Shawhan, Margaret Hamilton, Lee Roy Reams, Spiro Malas, Ted Beniades, Judith McCauley.

ADDITIONAL FACTS

The wedding scene of "The Sound of Music" (1959) with Mary Martin and Theodore Bikel.

SPECIAL EVENTS

1929 *Masters of Melody*
Two-reel film short in which Rodgers and Hart appeared as themselves and explained to a magazine interviewer how they allegedly wrote three of their most famous songs: *Manhattan* (sung by Ruth Teste and Allan Gould); *The Girl Friend* (Inez Courtney and Allan Gould); *Blue Room* (Kathryn Reece and Robert Cloy). Film was produced by Paramount-Famous-Lasky Corp.; screenplay and direction by S. Jay Kaufman.

1948 *Rodgers and Hammerstein Night,* Lewisohn Stadium, N.Y.
An annual event on the closing night of the Lewisohn Stadium Summer Concerts, which was inaugurated in July, 1948. Mr. Rodgers has frequently appeared as guest conductor.

1951 *An Evening for Richard Rodgers,* NBC-TV Network, March 4.
An hour program honoring Mr. Rodgers' first 25 years in the theatre.

1952 *The Richard Rodgers Story,* CBS-TV Network, June 15 and June 22.
Two one-hour programs on the Ed Sullivan Show devoted to Mr. Rodgers' career.

1953 *St. Louis Symphony Concert,* conducted by Mr. Rodgers. Convention Hall, St. Louis, Mo., February 22.

Rodgers and Hammerstein Week, New York, August 31-Sept. 6. By proclamation of Mayor Vincent R. Impelliteri on the occasion of 4 Rodgers and Hammerstein musicals running simultaneously—*Oklahoma!, South Pacific, The King and I,* and *Me and Juliet.*

1954 *New York Philharmonic Symphony Concert,* conducted by Mr. Rodgers. Carnegie Hall, New York, November 15.

General Foods 25th Anniversary Show, NBC-TV, CBS-TV, ABC-TV, and Dumont-TV Networks, March 28.
An hour and one-half program honoring Rodgers and Hammerstein. Featured Mary Martin, Ezio Pinza, Gordon MacRae, Florence Henderson, John Raitt, Jan Clayton, Bill Hayes, Janice Rule, Patricia Morison, Yul Brynner, Tony Martin, Rosemary Clooney, Edgar Bergen and Charlie McCarthy, Jack Benny, Ed Sullivan, Groucho Marx, Richard Rodgers and Oscar Hammerstein II.

1955 *Rodgers and Hammerstein Festival,* St. Louis, Mo., July 18-August 27. Presented by the St. Louis Municipal Opera Assn. which devoted a week each to a Rodgers and Hammerstein symphony concert, productions of *Carousel, Allegro,* and *The King and I,* and a two-week production of *South Pacific.*

1957 *Philadelphia Orchestra Concert,* conducted by Mr. Rodgers. Academy of Music, Philadelphia, January 22. Pension Fund benefit concert.

1962 *A Tribute to Richard Rodgers,* CBS-TV Network, November 4.
An hour program on the Ed Sullivan Show emanating from Carnegie Hall.

1963 *Richard Rodgers Festival,* New York, May 15-June 23.
Presented by the New York City Center, which offered two-week productions of *Oklahoma!, Pal Joey,* and *The King and I.*

1966 *The Broadway of Rodgers and Hammerstein,* Dade County Auditorium, Miami, Fla., January 4.
Concert revue touring Miami, St. Petersburg, Jacksonville, Orlando. Presented by Mana Productions, Inc. Featured Earl Wrightson, Lois Hunt.

1967 *Rodgers and Hart Today,* ABC-TV Network, March 2; also telecast May 11, 1967.
An hour-long program shown as part of the *Stage '67* series. Produced and conceived by Richard Lewine. Featured Petula Clark, Bobby Darin, Count Basie, Doodletown Pipers, Peter Gennaro, The Mamas and the Papas, The Supremes.

1976 *America Salutes Richard Rodgers—The Sound of His Music.* CBS-TV Network, December 9; also telecast June 3, 1978.
A two-hour program produced by Gary Smith and Dwight Hemion. Featured Diahann Carroll, Vic Damone, Sammy Davis Jr., Sandy Duncan, Lena Horne, Cloris Leachman, Peggy Lee, John Wayne, and Gene Kelly (as Oscar Hammerstein II) and Henry Winkler (as Lorenz Hart).

1978 *The Young Americans Salute to Richard Rodgers,* October 22-May 15, 1979.
Cross-country tour by vocal group.

GENERAL BIBLIOGRAPHY

Newspapers and Periodicals

Oscar Hammerstein II Arrives
—*New York Dramatic Mirror,* August 21, 1920

Voices Versus Feet by Oscar Hammerstein II
—*Theatre Magazine,* May, 1925

Rodgers, Fields and Hart Win Prolific Prizes
—*New York Herald Tribune,* May 23, 1926

What Makes a Song a Big Hit? (interview with Mr. Rodgers)
—*New York Morning Telegraph,* May 9, 1928

One Hart Would Not Stand Still by Ted Goldsmith
—*Theatre Magazine,* April, 1931

Words and Music by Henry F. Pringle (about Rodgers and Hart)
—*Collier's,* February 18, 1933

Words and Music by Margaret Case Harriman (about Rodgers and Hart)
—*The New Yorker,* May 28 and June 4, 1938

The Boys from Columbia (cover story about Rodgers and Hart)
—*Time,* September 26, 1938

How to Write Music in No Easy Lessons by Richard Rodgers
—*Theatre Arts,* October, 1939

Perfect Union Essential in Lyrics and Music by Richard Rodgers and Lorenz Hart
—*Variety,* July 31, 1940

Why Do I Love You? (Meaning Music) by Oscar Hammerstein II
—*Variety,* July 31, 1940

This Can't Be Corn by Gilbert Seldes (about Rodgers and Hart)
—*Esquire,* October, 1941

Case History of a Non-Combatant by Richard Rodgers
—*The Playbill,* March, 1943

Music for the American Theatre by Richard Rodgers
—*Music Publishers' Journal,* September, 1943

Dear Joe: by Oscar Hammerstein II (letter to an imaginary soldier)
—*PM,* October 24, 1943

Song Writer (editorial on death of Lorenz Hart)
—*New York Times,* November 23, 1943

Hammerstein, a Broadway Stage Dynasty by Otis Guernsey, Jr.
—*New York Herald Tribune,* December 12, 1943

Hammerstein II by William Jennings O'Brien —*PM,* January 7, 1944

Four Ways to Make a Song Hit by Gertrude Samuels (about Mr. Rodgers) —*New York Times Magazine,* May 14, 1944

Oscar Hammerstein II by Francis Sill Wickware —*Life,* May 29, 1944

Theatre Music by Richard Rodgers —*The American Mercury,* September, 1944

Richard Rodgers by George Beiswanger —*Theatre Arts,* December, 1944

Success Story Set to Music by Gertrude Samuels (about Mr. Rodgers) —*New York Times Magazine,* January 21, 1945

Our Future Musical Theatre by Stephen West (about Rodgers and Hammerstein) —*The Etude,* February, 1945

No. 1 U.S. Lyricist by Louis Kronenberger (about Mr. Hammerstein) —*Time,* April 30, 1945

Words and Music by Amy Porter (about Rodgers and Hammerstein) —*Collier's,* May 26, 1945

The Theatre's No. 1 Songwriters by Lewis Funke (about Rodgers and Hammerstein) —*Stage Pictorial,* Autumn, 1945

Oscar Hammerstein II by John K. Hutchens —*Theatre Arts,* January, 1946

The Theatre and Theatre Parties by Richard Rodgers and Oscar Hammerstein II —*New York Times,* February 10, 1946

Hammerstein the Second by S.J. Woolf —*New York Times Magazine,* March 31, 1946

How to Make $4,000,000 on Broadway by David G. Wittels (about Mr. Hammerstein) —*The Saturday Evening Post,* October 4 and 11, 1947

The Careful Dreamer by Henry Anatole Grunwald and Louis Kronenberger (cover story about Mr. Hammerstein) —*Time,* October 20, 1947

R & H Co. by Lewis Nichols —*Saturday Review of Literature,* October 25, 1947

What Makes Songs Popular by Oscar Hammerstein II —*'48,* March, 1948

Where the Song Begins by Oscar Hammerstein II —*Saturday Review,* December 3, 1949

An Optimistic Appraisal of Our Theatre by Richard Rodgers and Oscar Hammerstein II —*New York Times,* January 1, 1950

The Pleasures of Producing by Richard Rodgers and Oscar Hammerstein II —*New York Times,* March 5, 1950

Mr. and Mrs. Richard Rodgers by John Keating —*Cue,* May 6, 1950

Rodgers Has Share in Pulitzer Prize —*Life,* May 15, 1950

Richard Rodgers, Man of the Theatre by Patricia Feldman —*Seventeen,* July, 1950

Broadway's Miracle Man by Allen Churchill (about Mr. Rodgers) —*Nation's Business,* August, 1950

With Songs in His Heart by Lincoln Barnett (about Mr. Rodgers) —*Ladies Home Journal,* November, 1950

The Commercial Aspects of the Art Musical by Richard Rodgers —*Theatre Arts,* November, 1950

Getting Off the Pyramid by Oscar Hammerstein II (article in support of world federalism) —*Saturday Review,* December 23, 1950

Richard Rodgers: Master of Melody by Carol Hughes —*Coronet,* January, 1951

One Man's Way with a Melody by John M. Willig (about Mr. Rodgers) —*New York Times Magazine,* March 18, 1951

The Perfect Glow by Philip Hamburger (about Mr. Hammerstein) —*The New Yorker,* May 12 and 19, 1951

R & H Shows Are Pushing $8-Million (cover story) —*Business Week,* August 11, 1951

Rodgers and Hammerstein—They're Proving that Broadway Is Still Paved with Gold —*Pageant,* October, 1951

Reaching Back into the Files for Those Real Old Rodgers and Hart Tunes by Robert Baral —*Variety,* January 2, 1952

Hammerstein Takes a Look at Theatre—And Likes It (excerpts from a speech) —*New York Herald Tribune,* April 6, 1952

The Rodgers and I by Deems Taylor —*House and Garden,* June, 1952

Happy Birthday, Dear Dick by Oscar Hammerstein II —*Town and Country,* June, 1952

In Defense of Sense by Richard Rodgers —*New York Times,* June 29, 1952

The Magic Light by Oscar Hammerstein II (eulogy of Gertrude Lawrence) —*New York Herald Tribune,* September 10, 1952

Oscar Hammerstein Down on the Farm by Ward Morehouse —*New York World-Telegram & Sun,* December 29, 1952

Do Composers Resent Distortions? by Richard Rodgers
—*New York Herald Tribune,* April 19, 1953

Richard Rodgers: Composer without a Key by Eckart Goodman (cover story)
—*Harper's Magazine,* August, 1953

Happy Birthday, Dear Oscar by Richard Rodgers
—*Town and Country,* August 1953

Musical Keystone: An Expert Writes About the Importance of the Book of Stage Productions by Oscar Hammerstein II
—*New York Times,* August 2, 1953

Revivals Emphasize Hammerstein's Power by Louis Biancolli
—*New York World-Telegram & Sun,* June 12, 1954

Do Go Into the Theatre! by Oscar Hammerstein II
—*Seventeen,* July, 1954

It Feels Good by Oscar Hammerstein II (about song writing)
—*Variety,* October 20, 1954

Double Motive: Rodgers Does Good and Pleases Himself in Activities Aiding Serious Music by Howard Taubman
—*New York Times,* October 31, 1954

Million Dollar Music by Eleanor Harris (about Mr. Rodgers)
—*The American Weekly,* March 6, 1955

Dick and Oscar—Partners in Song by Charles P. Arnot
—*INS,* October 9, 10, 11, 12, 1955

A Kind of Grandfather by Oscar Hammerstein II
—*Saturday Review,* March 17, 1956

Dancing in Musicals by Oscar Hammerstein II
—*Dance Magazine,* April, 1956

The G. and S. of Broadway (about Rodgers and Hammerstein)
—*New York Times,* April 5, 1956

I'll Always Remember—a Pair of Tapestries by Richard Rodgers
—*Parade,* July 15, 1956

Song Is Wedding to Story in Our Musical Dramas by Richard Rodgers
—*New York Herald Tribune,* July 29, 1956

Richard Rodgers' Filmusic by Stanley Green
—*Films in Review,* October, 1956

Hammerstein's Film Career by Stanley Green
—*Films in Review,* February, 1957

ASCAP vs. BMI by Oscar Hammerstein II
—*Saturday Review,* February 23, 1957

Cancer? I've Had It! by Richard Rodgers
—*This Week,* March 17, 1957

Tribute to Yankee Doodle Dandy by Oscar Hammerstein II (about George M. Cohan) —*New York Times Magazine,* May 5, 1957

Is It Really YOUR Hit Parade? by Oscar Hammerstein II
—*New York Herald Tribune,* August 26, 1957

When Rodgers Made His Bow by David Ewen
—*New York Times,* September 15, 1957

Controversy by Oscar Hammerstein II (about radio discrimination of ASCAP songs) —*New York Herald Tribune,* October 11, 1957

Jokes a "Must"?—But How Many? Let Musicals Set Own Rules by Oscar Hammerstein II —*Variety,* January 8, 1957

Want to Write a Hit Song? by Mercury Robbins (about Mr. Hammerstein)
—*Today's Living,* April 6, 1958

Mr. Words and Mr. Music by Jon Whitcomb (about Rodgers and Hammerstein) —*Cosmopolitan,* August 1958

They Light the Musical Stage by Joseph N. Bell (about Rodgers and Hammerstein) —*Family Weekly,* August 24, 1958

Oscar Hammerstein's First Job by Phyllis Cerf
—*Good Housekeeping,* September, 1958

Music for Television by Richard Rodgers —*Variety,* September 10, 1958

Notes on Lyrics by Oscar Hammerstein II —*Variety,* January 7, 1959

The Nicest Guys in Show Business by Cleveland Amory
—*Holiday,* February, 1959

The Legend of Rodgers and Hammerstein by Phyllis Battelle
—*New York Journal-American,* November 11, 12, 13, 1959

U.S. Cain't Say No to R&H; $65-Mil in Albums Since 1943 by Mike Gross
—*Variety,* February 24, 1960

The Rodgers and Hammerstein Story by Hunter Barnell
—*Diners' Club Magazine,* March, 1960

Hammerstein: Words by Rodgers by Richard Rodgers
—*New York Times Magazine,* July 10, 1960

Oscar Hammerstein II (editorial on death of Mr. Hammerstein)
—*New York Times,* August 24, 1960

Oscar Hammerstein and His Songs (editorial)
—*New York Herald Tribune,* August 24, 1960

The Oscar Hammerstein Story —*New York Post,* August 24, 1960

Going to Miss Him (editorial)
—*San Francisco News-Call Bulletin,* August 25, 1960

Happy Talk by Arthur Gelb (about Mr. Hammerstein)
—*New York Times,* August 28, 1960

Paeans of Praise by John Crosby (about Mr. Hammerstein)
—*New York Herald Tribune,* August 29, 1960

Oscar Hammerstein an Immortal Who Followed Credo of Own Lyrics by Abel Green —*Variety,* August 31, 1960

A Healing Guy (about Mr. Hammerstein) —*Time,* September 5, 1960

A Truly Wonderful Guy by Robert Ruark (about Mr. Hammerstein)
—*New York World-Telegram & Sun,* September 6, 1960

Oscar Hammerstein by Howard Lindsay—*Saturday Review,* September 7, 1960

The Book Had Better Be Good by Oscar Hammerstein II
—*Theatre Arts,* November, 1960

The "Unknown" Songs of Oscar Hammerstein II by Stanley Green
—*Variety,* January 4, 1961

Opera and Broadway by Richard Rodgers —*Opera News,* February 25, 1961

As Richard Rodgers Sees It by Richard Gehman —*Theatre Arts,* May, 1961

The Life and Death of Broadway's Gentle Giant by Edward Jablonski and Martin Abramson (about Mr. Hammerstein) —*Coronet,* September, 1961

Rodgers Without Hammerstein by Barbara and Arthur Gelb
—*Esquire,* September, 1961

You Can't Force It by Winthrop Sargeant (about Mr. Rodgers)
—*The New Yorker,* November 18, 1961

Richard Rodgers, a Genius in Melody, to Get Another Award Tomorrow by Brooks Atkinson —*New York Times,* December 5, 1961

Poet on Broadway by Colin MacInnes (about Lorenz Hart)
—*London Sunday Times,* February 18, 1962

Words and Music by Richard Rodgers by Charlie Rice
—*This Week,* March 4, 1962

The Lyrics of Oscar Hammerstein II Reflect His Concern for Mankind by Brooks Atkinson —*New York Times,* March 13, 1962

Show Business in Our Time: The Legend of Richard Rodgers by Richard Gehman (complete issue) —*The American Weekly,* July 22, 1962

How to Get Started in the Theatre by Richard Rodgers
—*Seventeen,* August, 1962

Richard Rodgers: Serious Popular or Popular Serious by Stanley Green
—*Musical America,* February, 1963

Rodgers Is a Festival (editorial) —*New York Times,* May 20, 1963

A Conversation with Richard Rodgers by Samuel Chotzinoff
—*Holiday,* December, 1963

Oscar Hammerstein—"A Healing Sort of Guy" by Russel Crouse
—*Reader's Digest,* January, 1964

Richard Rodgers Remembers New York —*McCall's,* May, 1964

Now the Musical Theatre Is Enshrined by Richard Rodgers (about the Music Theater of Lincoln Center) —*New York Times Magazine,* June 21, 1964

Rodgers Is Giving Theatre to City by Samuel Zolotow (about theatre at Mt. Morris Park) —*New York Times,* July 15, 1964

A Man Named Rodgers by Gerald Nachman —*New York Post,* July 21, 1964

The Night They Sang Rodgers' First Song by Richard Maney
—*New York Herald Tribune Magazine,* August 16, 1964

Stardust and Sweat by Richard Rodgers —*Writer's Yearbook,* 1965

Music by Richard Rodgers by May Okon
—*New York Sunday News Magazine,* February 21, 1965

Number One Melody Man by Gilbert Millstein
—*Saturday Evening Post,* March 13, 1965

Closeup: Rodgers' Legacy—Tunes for World to Whistle by Hope Johnson
—*New York World Telegram & Sun,* April 21, 1966

To the Love Song—with Love by Richard Rodgers
—*Saturday Evening Post,* January 28, 1967

Richard Rodgers: Who Cares Where or When? by Roberta Brandes Gratz
—*New York Post,* February 25, 1967

A Composer Looks at His Lyricists by Richard Rodgers
—*Dramatists Guild Quarterly,* Spring, 1967

Encore, Mr. Rodgers by Howard Taubman —*New York Times,* July 4, 1967

Ode to Richard Rodgers by Walter Wager (cover story)
—*ASCAP Today,* Autumn, 1967

Richard Rodgers Recalls Hart and Hammerstein by Richard Rodgers
—*United Press International,* November 12, 1967

Beethoven—and R. Rodgers by Harold C. Schoenberg
—*New York Times,* March 10, 1968

Richard Rodgers by Frances Swaebly —*Miami Herald,* April, 1970

When Rodgers Scores a Hit by John Barber
—*London Daily Telegraph,* April 17, 1972

Carousel, Pal Joey, South Pacific, The King and I by Robert Sobel
—*Billboard,* May 4, 1974

The Split Personality of Richard Rodgers by Dale Harris
—*New York Times,* July 14, 1974

Richard Rodgers by Glenne Currie
—*United Press International,* October 26, 1975

Composer Richard Rodgers Likes His H's; Hart, Hammerstein and Now "Fiddler's" Harnick by Christopher P. Anderson —*People,* November 17,1975

Richard Rodgers, Man for All Theatre Seasons by David Richards
—*Washington Star,* February 29, 1976

Life's Just a Song for Mr. Music —*Brisbane Courier-Mail,* March 28, 1976

Richard Rodgers: "Work Is a Matter of Survival" by Noel Coppage
—*Family Weekly,* April 18, 1976

Sounds of Music and Richard Rodgers by Emory Lewis
—*The Record,* May 1976

Richard Rodgers by Arthur Unger
—*Christian Science Monitor,* December 8, 1976

Rodgers Nears 75 Years in a Life of Music by Richard Severo
—*New York Times,* June 22, 1977

Still a Song in His Heart as Rodgers Turns 75 by Hugh A. Mulligan
—*Associated Press,* June 28, 1977

Happy Birthday, Richard Rodgers! by James Roos
—*Miami Herald,* June 28, 1977

Richard Rodgers: Dean of the American Musical Theatre by James Goodfriend (cover story) —*Stereo Review,* February, 1978

Richard Rodgers: His Songs Are Part of America's Heritage by Ernest V. Heyn (cover story) —*Family Weekly,* July 9, 1978

With Song in His Heart by Richard L. Coe (about Mr. Rodgers)
—*Washington Post,* December 3, 1978

Richard Rodgers with "Nothing in Mind" by Richard F. Shepard
—*New York Times,* June 12, 1979

Books

AUTOBIOGRAPHY

Rodgers, Richard: *Musical Stages* (Random House, New York, 1975; Literary Guild, 1975; W. H. Allen, London, 1976; Jove paperback, New York, 1978)

Review Excerpts

". . . this cheerful and informative book is worth the attention of all musical-comedy enthusiasts."—Elliot Norton, *Boston Herald-American*

". . . What makes the book a special pleasure are the reminiscences of those thriving days when songwriting seemed like the headiest occupation in the world . . ."—Mel Gussow, *New York Times Book Review*

". . . This is no ordinary 'and-then-I-wrote' narrative or a 'tell-all' account of scandals and human frailties . . . This book, like Rodgers' music and shows, is distinguished by its 'class' . . ."—Clayton Hay, *Seattle Times*

". . . a lot of fun in this book, all warm, witty and wise."—Arnold Gingrich, *Chicago Tribune*

". . . To read his book is to listen for 300-odd pages to a gifted conversationalist explaining with enormous clarity the techniques and processes of his profession . . ."—Pertinax Surly, *St. Louis Post-Dispatch*

"*Some Enchanted Reading* . . . provides an insight into his trade that is both revealing and informative . . ."—Tony Mastroianni, *Cleveland Press*

". . . the reader feels exhilaration at being, even vicariously, part of the glamorous world . . . has a great deal to say about creativity and professionalism."—Robert Kirsch, *Los Angeles Times*

". . . the kind of book you'll read, reread and then use repeatedly for reference."—Robert Stearns, *Pittsburgh Press*

". . . Not only is it well-written, but it contains such an abundance of sheer joy that it leaves the reader feeling warm and grateful . . ."—Monica Ramos, *El Paso Times*

". . . There is no need to be an American musical buff to relish the excitement of Mr. Rodgers' showbiz life, seen with discerning clarity and a refreshing lack of maudlin nostalgia."—Rosemary Say, *London Sunday Telegraph*

". . . full of musical insights and refreshingly free from the sniping that usually mars this sort of memoir, and will provide many an enchanting evening . . ."—Len Capeling, *Liverpool Daily Post*

BIOGRAPHIES

Ewen, David: *Richard Rodgers* (Holt, New York, 1957).
———: *With a Song in His Heart* (Holt, Rinehart and Winston, New York, 1963). Biography of Mr. Rodgers.
Fordin, Hugh: *Getting to Know Him* (Random House, New York, 1977). Biography of Mr. Hammerstein.
Green, Stanley: *The Rodgers and Hammerstein Story* (John Day, New York, 1963).
Marx, Samuel and Jan Clayton: *Rodgers and Hart* (G. P. Putnam's Sons, New York, 1976).
Nolan, Frederick: *The Sound of Their Music* (Walker, New York, 1978) Biography of Rodgers and Hammerstein.
Taylor, Deems: *Some Enchanted Evenings* (Harper, New York, 1953). Biography of Rodgers and Hammerstein.

REFERENCE

Abbott, George: *"Mister Abbott"* (Random House, New York, 1963).
Aldrich, Richard: *Gertrude Lawrence as Mrs. A* (Greystone, New York, 1954).
Anderson, John Murray: *Out Without My Rubbers* (Library Publishers, New York, 1954).
Armitage, Merle, ed.: *George Gershwin* (Longmans, New York, 1938). Contains poem, *To George Gershwin* by Mr. Hammerstein.
Arnold, Elliott: *Deep in My Heart* (Duell, Sloan and Pearce, New York, 1949). Biography of Sigmund Romberg.
Barnett, Lincoln: *Writing on Life* (Sloane, New York, 1951). Contains chapter on Mr. Rodgers.
Bordman, Gerald: *American Musical Theatre* (Oxford, New York, 1978).
Chotzinoff, Samuel: *A Little Nightmusic* (Harper, New York, 1964). Contains chapter on Mr. Rodgers.
Cochran, Charles B.: *Cock-a-Doodle-Do* (Dent, London, 1941).
deMille, Agnes: *Dance to the Piper* (Little, Brown, Boston, 1951).
———: *And Promenade Home* (Little, Brown, Boston, 1958).
Engel, Lehman: *The American Musical Theatre* (CBS Legacy, New York, 1967).
———: *Words with Music* (Macmillan, New York, 1972).
———: *Their Words Are Music* (Crown, New York, 1975). Contains evaluation of Mr. Hammerstein's lyrics.
Ewen, David: *The World of Jerome Kern* (Holt, New York, 1960).
———: *Composers for the American Musical Theatre* (Dodd, Mead, New York, 1968). Contains chapter on Mr. Rodgers.
———: *Great Men of American Popular Song* (Prentice-Hall, New Jersey, 1970). Contains chapters on Rodgers and Hart and Rodgers and Hammerstein.

———: *New Complete Book of the American Musical Theater* (Holt, New York, 1970).
Gordon, Max: *Max Gordon Presents* (Bernard Geis, New York, 1963).
Graves, Charles: *The Cochran Story* (W. H. Allen, London).
Green, Stanley: *Ring Bells! Sing Songs!* (Arlington, New York, 1971). Broadway musicals in the 1930s.
———: *The World of Musical Comedy* (A. S. Barnes, New Jersey, 1980). Contains chapters on Rodgers and Hart and Rodgers and Hammerstein.
———: *Encyclopaedia of the Musical Theatre* (Da Capo, New York, 1980).
Guernsey, Otis, Jr., ed.: *Playwrights, Lyricists, Composers on Theatre* (Dodd, Mead, New York, 1974). Contains *A Composer Looks at His Lyricists* by Mr. Rodgers.
Hamburger, Philip: *Mayor Watching and Other Pleasures* (Rinehart, New York, 1958). Contains chapter on Mr. Hammerstein.
Harriman, Margaret Case: *Take Them Up Tenderly* (Knopf, New York, 1944). Contains chapters on Rodgers and Hart and Mr. Hammerstein.
Hart, Dorothy: *Thou Swell, Thou Witty* (Harper, New York, 1976). Text-and-picture book on Mr. Hart.
Higham, Charles: *Ziegfeld* (Regnery, Chicago, 1972).
Langner, Lawrence: *The Magic Curtain* (Dutton, New York, 1951).
Laufe, Abe: *Broadway's Greatest Musicals* (Funk and Wagnalls, New York, 1969).
Lewine, Richard, and Alfred Simon: *Songs of the American Theatre* (Dodd, Mead, New York, 1973).
Logan, Joshua: *Josh* (Delacorte, New York, 1976).
Martin, Mary: *My Heart Belongs* (Morrow, New York, 1976).
Matthews, Jessie: *Over My Shoulder* (W. H. Allen, London, 1974).
Maxwell, Gilbert: *Helen Morgan* (Hawthorn, New York, 1974).
McCabe, John: *George M. Cohan* (Doubleday, New York, 1973).
Milne, Tom: *Mamoulian* (Indiana University Press, Bloomington, 1969).
Morehouse, Ward: *George M. Cohan* (Lippincott, Philadelphia, 1943).
Oppenheimer, George, ed.: *The Passionate Playgoer* (Viking, New York, 1958) Contains *Reflections on Musical Comedy* by Clifton Fadiman; *Hart Never Stood Still* by Mr. Rodgers; *The Trouble with "Oklahoma!"* by Deems Taylor.
Pinza, Ezio: *An Autobiography* (Rinehart, New York, 1958).
Schmidt-Joos Siegfried: *Das Musical* (Deutscher Taschenbuch Verlag, Munich, 1965). Contains chapters on Rodgers and Hart and Rodgers and Hammerstein.
Sheean, Vincent: *Oscar Hammerstein I* (Simon and Schuster, New York, 1956). Preface by Oscar Hammerstein II.
Skinner, Cornelia Otis: *Life with Lindsay and Crouse* (Houghton Mifflin, Boston, 1976.
Smith, Cecil: *Musical Comedy in America* (Theatre Arts, New York, 1950).
Spaeth, Sigmund: *A History of Popular Music in America* (Random House, New York, 1948).

Thornton, Michael: *Jessie Matthews* (Hart-Davis, London, 1974).
Wallace, Mike: *Mike Wallace Asks . . .* (Simon and Schuster, New York, 1958). Contains excerpts from interview with Mr. Hammerstein.
Wilder, Alec: *American Popular Song* (Oxford, New York, 1972). Contains evaluation of Mr. Rodgers' music.
Wilk, Max: *They're Playing Our Song* (Atheneum, New York, 1973). Contains chapters on Messrs. Hart, Rodgers and Hammerstein.

DISCOGRAPHY

Productions

Allegro (R-H, 1947)
RCA CBM1 2758 (formerly RCA Victor LOC 1099)
Original cast.

Androcles and the Lion (R-R, 1967)
RCA Victor LSO 1141
Original cast.

Babes in Arms (R-Hart, 1937)
Columbia AOS 2570 (formerly Columbia ML 4488)
Mary Martin, Mardi Bayne, Jack Cassidy, with chorus and orchestra, Lehman Engel cond.

Boys from Syracuse, The (R-Hart, 1938)
Columbia COS 2580 (formerly Columbia ML 4837)
Jack Cassidy, Portia Nelson, Bibi Osterwald, Stanley Prager, Holly Harris, Bob Shaver, with chorus and orchestra, Lehman Engel cond.
Capitol STAO 1933
Original New York cast, 1963.
Stet DS 15017 (formerly English Decca SKL 4564)
Original London cast, 1963.

By Jupiter (R-Hart, 1942)
Roulette S 25278
Jackie Cain and Roy Kral.
RCA Victor LSO 1137
Original New York cast, 1967.

Carmen Jones (H-Bizet, 1943)
MCA 2054 (formerly Decca DL 8014)
Original cast.
RCA Victor LM 1881
Film soundtrack, 1954.

Carousel (R-H, 1945)
MCA 2033 (formerly Decca DL 8003)
Original cast.
RCA Victor LPM 1048
Patrice Munsel, Robert Merrill, Florence Henderson, Gloria Lane, Herbert Banke, George S. Irving, with chorus and orchestra, Lehman Engel cond.
Epic BN 563
Lois Hunt, Harry Snow, Charmaine Harma.
Command RS 843 SD
Alfred Drake, Roberta Peters, Claramae Turner, Lee Venora, with chorus and orchestra, Jay Blackton cond.

Capitol SW 694
Film soundtrack, 1956.
Buena Vista STER 3317
Jan Clayton, with orchestra, Camarata cond.
RCA Victor LSO 1114
Lincoln Center cast, 1965.
CBS CSM 479
Original television cast, 1967.

Chee-Chee (R-Hart, 1928)
Ava AS 26
Betty Comden, Richard Lewine (piano).

Cinderella (R-H, 1957)
Columbia OS 2005
Original television cast.
Columbia OS 2730
Television cast, 1965.
RCA Victor LPM 2012
Mary Martin, with The Little Orchestra, Thomas Sherman cond.

Connecticut Yankee, A (R-Hart, 1927)
RCA Victor LK 1026
Earl Wrightson, Elaine Malbin, with Al Goodman Orchestra.

Deep in My Heart (H-Romberg, 1954)
MGM 2 SES 54 ST (formerly MGM E 3153)
Film soundtrack. (Six songs with Hammerstein lyrics.)

Desert Song, The (H-Harbach, Romberg, 1926)
Columbia ACL 831 (formerly Columbia ML 4636)
Nelson Eddy, Doretta Morrow, Wesley Dalton, Lee Cass, David Atkinson, Wilton Clary, with chorus and orchestra, Lehman Engel cond.
Capitol P 384
Gordon MacRae, Lucille Norman, Bob Sands, Thurl Ravenscroft, with chorus and orchestra, George Greeley cond.
RCA Victor LK 1013
Earl Wrightson, Frances Greer, Jimmy Carroll, with Al Goodman Orchestra.
Angel S 37319 (formerly Capitol SW 1842)
Gordon MacRae, Dorothy Kirsten, Roger Wagner Chorale, with orchestra, Van Alexander cond.
RCA Victor LSO 1000
Giorgio Tozzi, Kathy Barr, Peter Palmer, Warren Galjour, Eugene Morgan, with chorus and orchestra, Lehman Engel cond.
RCA Victor LSC 2440
Mario Lanza, Judith Raskin, Raymond Murcell, Donald Arthur, with chorus and orchestra, Constantine Callinicos cond.

Angel S 35905
Edmund Hockridge, June Bronhill, Julie Dawn, Leonard Weir, Inia Wiata, Bruce Forsyth, The Williams Singers, with Michael Collins Orchestra.
Reader's Digest RDS 40-4
Anna Moffo, Richard Fredricks, William Lewis, Kenneth Smith, with chorus and orchestra, Lehman Engel cond.
Monmouth-Evergreen MES 7054
Original London cast, 1927.

Do I Hear a Waltz? (R-Sondheim, 1965)
Columbia AKOS 2770
Original cast.

Ever Green (R-Hart, 1930)
Monmouth-Evergreen MES 7049
Jessie Matthews; Jack Payne and BBC Dance Orchestra; Van Phillips and Orchestra.

Flower Drum Song (R-H, 1958)
Columbia OS 2009
Original cast.
Angel S 35886
Original London cast, 1960.
MCA 2069 (formerly Decca 7-9098)
Film soundtrack, 1961.

Ghost Town (R, 1939)
DRG 6102
Richard Rodney Bennett (piano).

Jumbo (R-Hart, 1935)
Columbia AOS 2260
Film soundtrack, 1962.

King and I, The (R-H, 1951)
MCA 2028 (formerly Decca DL 9008)
Original cast.
Stet DS 15014 (formerly Philips BBL 7002)
Original London cast, 1953.
Capitol SW 740
Film soundtrack, 1956.
RCA Victor LSO 1092
Lincoln Center cast, 1964.
Epic BN 564
Lois Hunt, Samuel Jones, Charmaine Harma.
Columbia OS 2640
Barbara Cook, Theodore Bikel, Anita Darian, Jeanette Scovotti, Daniel Ferro, with chorus and orchestra, Lehman Engel cond.

Philips 838.908 SY (sung in German)
Original Munich cast, 1966.
CBS S 70023 (sung in Hebrew)
Original Israeli cast, 1966.
RCA ABL1 2610
Original New York cast, 1977.

Me and Juliet (R-H, 1953)
RCA Victor LSO 1098
Original cast.

Mississippi (R-Hart, 1935)
Decca DL 4250
Bing Crosby, with George Stoll Orchestra.

Music in the Air (H-Kern, 1932)
RCA Victor LK 1025
Jane Pickens, with Al Goodman Orchestra.

New Moon, The (H-Romberg, 1928)
RCA Victor LK 1011
Earl Wrightson, Frances Greer, Donald Dame, Earl Oxford, with Al Goodman Orchestra.
Capitol T 219
Gordon MacRae, Lucille Norman, with orchestra, Paul Weston cond.
Angel S 37320 (formerly Capitol SW 1842)
Gordon MacRae, Dorothy Kirsten, Richard Robinson, Jeannine Wagner, Earle Wilkie, James Tippey, Roger Wagner Chorale, with orchestra, Van Alexander cond.
Columbia P 13878 (formerly Columbia ML 2164)
Nelson Eddy, Eleanor Steber, with chorus and orchestra, Leo Arnaud cond.
Monmouth-Evergreen MES 7051
Original London cast, 1929.
Reader's Digest RDS 407
Jeanette Scovotti, Peter Palmer, Arthur Rubin, with chorus and orchestra, Lehman Engel cond.

No Strings (R-R, 1962)
Capitol SO 1695
Original cast.
Stet DS 15013 (formerly English Decca SKL 4576)
Original London cast, 1963.
Atlantic S 1383
LeVern Baker, Chris Connor, Herbie Mann, Bobby Short, with groups conducted by Al Cohn, Herbie Mann and Bobby Scott.

Oklahoma! (R-H, 1943)
MCA 2030 (formerly Decca DL 8000)
Original cast.

Stanyan 10069
Original London cast, 1947.
Capitol SWAO 595
Film soundtrack, 1955.
Harmony 11164 (formerly Columbia CS 8739)
Nelson Eddy, Virginia Haskins, Portia Nelson, Kaye Ballard, Wilton Clary, David Atkinson, David Morris, Lee Cass, with chorus and orchestra, Lehman Engel cond.
Epic BN 562
Stuart Foster, Lois Hunt, Fay DeWitt.
Columbia OS 2610
John Raitt, Florence Henderson, Phyllis Newman, Jack Elliott, with chorus and orchestra, Franz Allers cond.
Ariola S 70627 IU (sung in German)
Christine Görner, Benno Kusche, Fifi Brix, Heinz Maria Linz, with FFB Orchester, Hans-Georg Arlt cond.

On Your Toes (R-Hart, 1936)
Columbia COS 2590
Portia Nelson, Jack Cassidy, Laurel Shelby, Zamah Cunningham, Robert Eckles, Ray Hyson, with chorus and orchestra, Lehman Engel cond.
Stet DS 15014 (formerly Decca DL 9015)
Original New York cast, 1954.
Monmouth-Evergreen MES 7049
Jack Whiting, Carroll Gibbons Savoy Hotel Orpheans

Pal Joey (R-Hart, 1940)
Columbia COL 4364
Vivienne Segal, Harold Lang, Beverly Fite, Barbara Ashley, Kenneth Remo, Jo Hurt, with chorus and orchestra, Lehman Engel cond.
Capitol S 310
Original New York cast, 1952, with exception of Jane Froman for Vivienne Segal and Dick Beavers for Harold Lang.
Capitol DW 912
Film soundtrack, 1957.

Pipe Dream (R-H, 1955)
RCA Victor LSO 1097
Original cast.

Rex (R-Harnick, 1976)
RCA ABL1 1683
Original cast.

Rose-Marie (H-Harbach, Friml, Stothart, 1924)
RCA Victor LK 1012
Charles Fredericks, Marion Bell, Christina Lind, Guild Choristers, with Al Goodman Orchestra.
MGM 2 SES 41 ST (formerly MGM E 3228)
Film soundtrack, 1954.

RCA Victor LSO 1001
Julie Andrews, Giorgio Tozzi, Meier Tzelniker, Frances Day, Marion Keene, Frederick Harvey, John Hauxvell, Tudor Evans, Michael Sammes Singers, with New Symphony Orchestra of London, Lehman Engel cond.
Columbia P 13878 (formerly Columbia ML 2164)
Dorothy Kirsten, Nelson Eddy, with chorus and orchestra, Leon Arnaud cond.
World Records SHB 37
Original London cast, 1925.
Reader's Digest RDS 40-5
Anna Moffo, Rosalind Elias, Richard Fredricks, William Chapman, with chorus and orchestra, Lehman Engel cond.
Pathé DTX 151 (sung in French)
Lina Dachary, Guy Fontagnere, Rogers, Gise May, Duvaleix, Raymond Saint-Paul Chorus, with orchestra, Paul Bonneau cond.

Show Boat (H-Kern, 1927)
Columbia AC 55
Helen Morgan, Paul Robeson, Countess Albani, Frank Munn, with orchestra, Victor Young cond.
Columbia OL 4058
Original New York cast, 1946.
RCA Victor LM 9002
Dorothy Kirsten, Robert Merrill, with orchestra, John Scott Trotter cond.
MGM 2 SES 44 ST (formerly MGM E 3230)
Film soundtrack, 1951.
RCA Victor LM 2008
Patrice Munsel, Robert Merrill, Risë Stevens, Katherine Graves, Janet Pavek, Kevin Scott, with chorus and orchestra, Lehman Engel cond.
RCA Victor LSO 1505
Gogi Grant, Howard Keel, Anne Jeffreys, with Henri Rene Orchestra.
Columbia OS 2220
John Raitt, Barbara Cook, William Warfield, Anita Darian, Fay DeWitt, Louise Parker, Jack Dabdoub, Merrill Staton Singers, with orchestra, Franz Allers cond.
Reader's Digest RDS 40-7
Anna Moffo, Mary Ellen Pracht, Rosalind Elias, Richard Fredricks, Valentine Pringle, with chorus and orchestra, Lehman Engel cond.
RCA Victor LSO 1126
Lincoln Center cast, 1966.
Stanyan 10048
Original London cast, 1971.
RCA Victrola AMV1 1741
Robert Merrill, Patrice Munsel, Paul Robeson, Helen Morgan, Janet Pavek, Howard Keel, Gogi Grant, Kevin Scott, Dorothy Kirsten, Risë Stevens.

Sound of Music, The (R-H, 1959)
Columbia S 32601 (formerly Columbia KOS 2020)
Original cast.
Regal SRA 5003 (formerly HMV CLP 1453)
Original London cast, 1961.
Philips 625 821 QL (sung in Dutch)
Original Amsterdam cast.
Warner Bros. S 1377
Trapp Family Singers.
Disneyland DQ 1296
Mary Martin
RCA Victor LSOD 2005
Film soundtrack, 1965.
RCA Victor 430.696 S (sung in French)
Film soundtrack, 1965.
RCA Victor LPM S 10056 (sung in German)
Film soundtrack, 1965.
RCA Victor ALPM 10171 (sung in Italian)
Film soundtrack, 1965.
RCA Victor LPM 10309 (sung in Spanish)
Film soundtrack, 1965.

South Pacific (R-H, 1949)
Columbia S 32604 (formerly Columbia OS 2040)
Original cast.
RCA Victor LSO 1032
Film soundtrack, 1958.
Columbia, OS 3100
Lincoln Center cast, 1967.

State Fair (R-H, 1945)
Dot 29011
Film remake soundtrack, 1962.

Sunny (H-Kern, 1925)
Stanyan 10035
Original London cast, 1926.

Till the Clouds Roll By (H-Kern, 1946)
MGM 2 SES 45 ST (formerly MGM E 3231)
Film soundtrack. (Six songs with Hammerstein lyrics.)

Too Many Girls (R-Hart, 1939)
Painted Smiles PS 1368
Nancy Andrews, Johnny Desmond, Estelle Parsons, Anthony Perkins, with chorus and orchestra, Dennis Deal cond.

Two by Two (R-Charnin, 1970)
Columbia S 30338
Original cast.

Victory at Sea (R, 1952)
RCA Victor LSC 2335 (Vol. 1)
RCA Victor LSC 2226 (Vol. 2)
RCA Victor LSC 2523 (Vol. 3)
All RCA Victor Symphony Orchestra, Robert Russell Bennett cond.

Wildflower (H-Harbach, Youmans, Stothart, 1923)
Monmouth-Evergreen MES 7052
Original London cast, 1926.

Winston Churchill—The Valiant Years, (R, 1960)
ABC Paramount S 387
ABC Symphony Orchestra, Robert Emmett Dolan cond.

Words and Music (R-Hart, 1948)
MGM 2 SES 54 ST (formerly MGM E 3233)
Film soundtrack.

Collections

BEN BAGLEY SERIES
Rodgers and Hart Revisited Vol. 1
Painted Smiles PS 1341 (formerly RIC M 3001)
Dorothy Loudon, Charlotte Rae, Danny Meehan, Cy Young, Arthur Siegel, with Norman Paris music director.
Garrick Gaieties Opening; Come and Tell Me; This Funny World; Send for Me; I Must Love You; Morning Is Midnight; Don't Tell Your Folks; At the Roxy Music Hall; I Still Believe in You; Singing a Love Song; I Blush; How Was I to Know?; Why Do You Suppose?; Everybody Loves You; Like Ordinary People Do.

Rodgers and Hart Revisited Vol. 2
Painted Smiles PS 1343 (formerly Crewe CR 1343)
Blossom Dearie, Gloria DeHaven, Dorothy Loudon, Bibi Osterwald, Charles Rydell, Bobby Short, with Norman Paris music director.
Any Old Place with You; A Tree in the Park; From Another World; A Baby's Best Friend; Blue Moon; Prayer; Sleepyhead; You're the Cats; Disgustingly Rich; Can't You Do a Friend a Favor?; A Ship without a Sail; A Lady Must Live; Angel without Wings; Bye and Bye; I Like to Recognize the Tune.

Jerome Kern Revisited
Painted Smiles PS 1363 (formerly Columbia OS 2840)
Nancy Andrews, Barbara Cook, Harold Lang, Cy Young, with Norman Paris music director.
Lyrics by Mr. Hammerstein: I Have the Room Above Her; Heaven in My Arms; In Egern on the Tegern See; In the Heart of the Dark.

Oscar Hammerstein Revisited
Painted Smiles PS 1365
Cab Calloway, Blossom Dearie, Alfred Drake, E. Y. Harburg, Dorothy Loudon, Patrice Munsel, Elaine Stritch, Gloria Swanson, with Norman Paris music director.

We've Got Something; Lonely Feet; No Wonder I'm Blue; Totem Tom-Tom; Somebody Wants to Go to Sleep; Eleven Levee Street; The Sweetest Sight that I Have Seen; I'm One of God's Children; Toodle-oo; Little Hindoo Man; We Were So Young; When I've Got the Moon; My Best Love; That's Love (by Rodgers and Hart); All in Fun; Dance, My Darlings; Medley.

Rodgers and Hart Revisited Vol. 3
Painted Smiles PS 1366
Nancy Andrews, Blossom Dearie, Johnny Desmond, Estelle Parsons, Anthony Perkins, Lynn Redgrave, Arthur Siegel, with Dennis Deal music director.

It's a Lovely Day for a Murder; Morning's at Seven; How's Your Health?; Someone Should Tell Them; The Damsel who Done All the Dirt; Life Was Monotonous; Why Do I?; I'm a Fool, Little One; The Letter Song; We'll Be the Same; Where the Hudson River Flows; I'd Like to Hide It; The Hermits; Are You My Love?; Nothing to Do but Relax; He Was Too Good to Me; Women; Who Are You?; It's Just that Kind of a Play; Sky City; I've Got to Get Back to New York.

Rodgers and Hart Revisited Vol. 4
Painted Smiles PS 1367
Nancy Andrews, Blossom Dearie, Johnny Desmond, Anthony Perkins, Lynn Redgrave, Elaine Stritch, with Dennis Deal music director.

Knees; It Must Be Heaven; Me for You; I Love You More than Yesterday; I Can Do Wonders with You; Queen Elizabeth; Now That I Know You; Did You Ever Get Stung?; A Twinkle in Your Eye; How to Win Friends and Influence People; Take and Take and Take; I'd Rather Be Right; Sweet Sixty-Five; I'm Talking to My Pal; Fool Meets Fool; A Little Souvenir; You're the Mother Type; Moon of My Delight; Medley.

Tony Bennett: 10 Rodgers and Hart Songs
Improv 7113

This Can't Be Love; Blue Moon; The Lady Is a Tramp; Lover; Manhattan; Spring Is Here; Have You Met Miss Jones?; Isn't It Romantic?; Wait Till You See Her; I Could Write a Book.

Tony Bennett: More Great Rodgers and Hart
Improv 7120

Thou Swell; The Most Beautiful Girl in the World; There's a Small Hotel; I've Got Five Dollars; You Took Advantage of Me; I Wish I Were in Love Again; This Funny World; My Heart Stood Still; My Romance; Mountain Greenery.

Dave Brubeck Quartet: My Favorite Things
Columbia CS 9237
My Favorite Things; Over and Over Again; Why Can't I?; Little Girl Blue; This Can't Be Love; My Romance; The Circus Is on Parade; The Most Beautiful Girl in the World.

Louise Carlyle, Bob Shaver, with John Morris Trio: Rodgers and Hart
Walden 304
Did You Ever Get Stung?; Nobody's Heart; A Tree in the Park; Sentimental Me; To Keep My Love Alive; Wait Till You See Her; A Ship Without a Sail; Any Old Place With You; Easy to Remember; I've Got Five Dollars.

Barbara Cook, with Arthur Harris Orchestra: From the Heart
Urania UR 9026/USD1026
You Have Cast Your Shadow on the Sea; I Didn't Know What Time It Was; My Funny Valentine; Nobody's Heart; A Ship Without a Sail; Dancing on the Ceiling; Little Girl Blue; It Never Entered My Mind; There's a Small Hotel; Glad to Be Unhappy; She Was Too Good to Me; Where or When.

David Daniels, Christina Lind, with Ben Ludlow Orchestra: The Melodies of Jerome Kern Vol. 2
Walden 309
Lyrics by Mr. Hammerstein; All Through the Day; Will You Marry Me Tomorrow, Maria?; The Folks who Live on the Hill; Here Am I; The Sweetest Sight that I Have Seen.

Matt Dennis, with orchestra, Harry Geller cond.: She Dances Overhead
RCA Victor LPM 1065
Dancing on the Ceiling; Mimi; Nobody's Heart; Blue Moon; Isn't It Romantic?; I Married an Angel; Mountain Greenery; Give Her a Kiss; Wait Till You See Her; I Didn't Know what Time It Was; This Funny World; Have You Met Miss Jones?

June Ericson, Warren Galjour, Jay Harnick, with John Morris Trio: The Melodies of Jerome Kern Vol. 1
Walden 308
Lyrics by Mr. Hammerstein: High, Wide and Handsome; All in Fun; All the Things You Are; Don't Ever Leave Me; In the Heart of the Dark.

Ella Fitzgerald, with Buddy Bregman Orchestra: Rodgers and Hart Songbook
Verve VEZ 2519 (2 LPs)
Have You Met Miss Jones?; You Took Advantage of Me; Ship Without a Sail; To Keep My Love Alive; Dancing on the Ceiling; The Lady Is a Tramp; With a Song in My Heart; Manhattan; Johnny One Note; I Wish I Were in Love Again; Spring Is Here; It Never Entered My Mind; This Can't Be Love; Thou Swell; My Romance; Where or When; Little Girl Blue; Give It Back to the Indians; Ten Cents a Dance; There's a Small

Hotel; I Didn't Know What Time It Was; Everything I've Got; I Could Write a Book; Blue Room; My Funny Valentine; Bewitched; Mountain Greenery; Wait Till You See Her; Lover; Isn't It Romantic?; Here in My Arms; Blue Moon; My Heart Stood Still; I've Got Five Dollars.

Sergio Franchi, with orchestra, Marty Manning cond.: The Songs of Richard Rodgers
RCA ANL1 2463 (formerly RCA Victor LSP 3365)
If I Loved You; Bali Ha'i; People Will Say We're in Love; Spring Is Here; This Nearly Was Mine; My Funny Valentine; Someone Like You; Falling in Love With Love; My Romance; I Didn't Know What Time It Was; Blue Moon; My Heart Stood Still.

Marty Gold Orchestra: Music of Rodgers and Hart
RCA Victor LSP 2535
Where or When; My Funny Valentine; I Could Write a Book; Dancing on the Ceiling; There's a Small Hotel; I Didn't Know What Time It Was; Spring Is Here; Manhattan; My Heart Stood Still; Everything I've Got; Bewitched; Falling in Love With Love.

André Kostelanetz Orchestra: Columbia Album of Richard Rodgers
Columbia EN2 13725
How Was I to Know?; A Ship Without a Sail; You Took Advantage of Me; Soliloquy; Wait Till You See Her; The Most Beautiful Girl in the World; Lover; Carousel Waltz; Do I Love You Because You're Beautiful?; Ev'ry Sunday Afternoon; Have You Met Miss Jones?; Over and Over Again; Little Girl Blue; Thou Swell; I Could Write a Book; It's a Grand Night for Singing; Loneliness of Evening; Oklahoma!; Out of My Dreams; The Surrey With the Fringe on Top; Oh, What a Beautiful Mornin'; Where's That Rainbow?; My Funny Valentine; Mimi; My Romance; You Have Cast Your Shadow on the Sea; Some Enchanted Evening; A Wonderful Guy; Younger Than Springtime; Happy Talk; Dites-moi; Quiet Night; Dancing on the Ceiling; With a Song in My Heart.

Michel Legrand Orchestra Plays Richard Rodgers
Philips 600074
Falling in Love With Love; People Will Say We're in Love; Bali Ha'i; Have You Met Miss Jones?; It Might as Well Be Spring; This Can't Be Love; Some Enchanted Evening; There's a Small Hotel; Getting to Know You; My Funny Valentine; The Lady Is a Tramp.

Mary Martin, Richard Rodgers (piano), with orchestra, John Lesko cond.: Mary Martin Sings—Richard Rodgers Plays
RCA Victor LPM 1539
Getting to Know You; You're Nearer; I Could Write a Book; Sleepyhead; It Might as Well Be Spring; My Funny Valentine; To Keep My Love Alive; It Never Entered My Mind; Moon of My Delight; You Are Never Away; There's a Small Hotel; Some Enchanted Evening.

Melachrino Orchestra: Music of Rodgers and Hammerstein
RCA Victor LSP 2513
No Other Love; Bali Ha'i; Hello, Young Lovers; It Might as Well Be Spring; The Sound of Music; Climb Ev'ry Mountain; Carousel Waltz; If I Loved You; Love, Look Away; Some Enchanted Evening; Out of My Dreams; The Surrey With the Fringe on Top; Oklahoma!

Anita O'Day, with Billy May Orchestra: Rodgers and Hart
Verve (6)2141
Johnny One Note; Little Girl Blue; Falling in Love With Love; Bewitched; I Could Write a Book; Have You Met Miss Jones?; Lover; It Never Entered My Mind; Ten Cents a Dance; I've Got Five Dollars; To Keep My Love Alive; Spring Is Here.

Cyril Ornadel and Starlight Symphony: Musical World of Rodgers and Hammerstein
MGM (S) 3817
Some Enchanted Evening; I'm in Love With a Wonderful Guy; There Is Nothin' Like a Dame; Younger Than Springtime; Bali Ha'i; Oh What a Beautiful Mornin'; The Surrey With the Fringe on Top; People Will Say We're in Love; June Is Bustin' Out All Over; Do-Re-Mi; Climb Ev'ry Mountain; If I Loved You; Soliloquy; You'll Never Walk Alone; Something Wonderful; I Whistle a Happy Tune; Hello, Young Lovers; You Are Beautiful; Love, Look Away.

Oscar Peterson: Richard Rodgers Song Book
Verve 6088
This Can't Be Love; It Might as Well Be Spring; Johnny One Note; The Surrey With the Fringe on Top; The Lady Is a Tramp; Blue Moon; Manhattan; Isn't It Romantic?; Lover; I Didn't Know What Time It Was; Bewitched; My Funny Valentine.

Richard Rodgers conducts the New York Philharmonic Symphony Orchestra
Odyssey Y 35213 (formerly Columbia CL 810)
Waltz Medley; March of the Siamese Children; Carousel Waltz; Slaughter on Tenth Avenue; Victory at Sea.

Richard Rodgers and Oscar Hammerstein II in Conversation with Arnold Michaelis
DRG Archive DARC 2-1121 (2 LPs) (formerly MGM 2E4)

Reid Shelton, Susan Watson, Danny Carroll, with Ted Auletta Orchestra: Jerome Kern/All the Things You Are
Monmouth-Evergreen MES 6808
Lyrics by Mr. Hammerstein: All the Things You Are; In Other Words, Seventeen; All in Fun; That Lucky Fellow; Heaven in My Arms; In the Heart of the Dark; Your Dream; All Through the Day; Nobody Else but Me.

Bobby Short Celebrates Rodgers and Hart
Atlantic SD 2-610 (2 LPs)
On Your Toes; Hollywood Party; You Mustn't Kick It Around; Where or When; Have You Met Miss Jones?; Hallelujah, I'm a Bum; Johnny One Note; With a Song in My Heart; I Didn't Know What Time It Was; My Romance; Wait Till You See Her; There's a Small Hotel; Soon; Spring Is Here; Ev'ry Sunday Afternoon; Glad to Be Unhappy; I Still Believe in You; Nobody's Heart; You're What I Need; No Place but Home; You Took Advantage of Me; It's Got to Be Love; Isn't It Romantic?; Ev'rything I've Got; Bewitched; I Wish I Were in Love Again.

Frank Sinatra Sings Rodgers and Hart
Capitol W 1825
Little Girl Blue; My Funny Valentine; Wait Till You See Her; Spring Is Here; Dancing on the Ceiling; The Lady Is a Tramp; I Wish I Were in Love Again; Lover; Easy to Remember; It Never Entered My Mind; Glad to Be Unhappy; Blue Moon.

The Supremes: Rodgers and Hart
Motown S 6599
The Lady Is a Tramp; This Can't Be Love; Where or When; Lover; My Funny Valentine; My Romance; My Heart Stood Still; Falling in Love with Love; Thou Swell; Dancing on the Ceiling; Blue Moon.

Ronny Whyte and Travis Hudson: It's Smooth, It's Smart! It's Rodgers, It's Hart!
Monmouth-Evergreen MES 7069
I Feel at Home with You; You're Nearer; Nothing but You; I'll Tell the Man in the Street; What's the Use of Talking?; You Always Love the Same Girl; This Is My Night to Howl; The Girl Friend; Where's That Rainbow?; Atlantic Blues; You Have Cast Your Shadow on the Sea; On a Desert Island with Thee; I'd Like to Poison Ivy; Nobody's Heart; Sing.

Lee Wiley Sings Rodgers and Hart
Monmouth-Evergreen MES 6807
Baby's Awake Now; Here in My Arms; You Took Advantage of Me; A Little Birdie Told Me So; A Ship without a Sail; I've Got Five Dollars; Glad to Be Unhappy; As Though You Were There.

Teddy Wilson Revamps Rodgers and Hart
Chiaroscuro CR 168
Manhattan; Thou Swell; My Heart Stood Still; You Took Advantage of Me; Isn't It Romantic?; There's a Small Hotel; My Funny Valentine; Where or When; The Lady Is a Tramp; Have You Met Miss Jones?; Bewitched; Ev'rything I've Got.

LONGEST RUNNING MUSICALS
(All engagements of over 500 performances)

New York

Oklahoma! (R-H) (1943)	2,212
South Pacific (R-H) (1949)	1,925
The Sound of Music (R-H) (1959)	1,443
The King and I (R-H) (1951)	1,246
Carousel (R-H) (1945)	890
The King and I (R-H) (1977)	695
Flower Drum Song (R-H) (1958)	600
No Strings (R-R) (1962)	580
Show Boat (H-Kern) (1927)	572
Rose-Marie (H-Friml) (1924)	557
Pal Joey (R-Hart) (1952)	542
Sunny (H-Kern) (1925)	517
The New Moon (H-Romberg) (1928)	509
Boys from Syracuse, The (R-Hart) (1963)	502
Carmen Jones (H-Bizet) (1943)	502

NOTE: As a writing team, Rodgers and Hammerstein established a Broadway record with four musicals running over 1,000 performances.

London

The Sound of Music (R-H) (1961)	2,385
Oklahoma! (R-H) (1947)	1,548
The King and I (R-H) (1953)	926
Show Boat (H-Kern) (1971)	910
Rose-Marie (H-Friml) (1925)	851
South Pacific (R-H) (1951)	802
Carousel (R-H) (1950)	566

NOTE: In London, from April 29, 1947 through January 14, 1956, four Rodgers and Hammerstein musicals—*Oklahoma!, Carousel, South Pacific,* and *The King and I*—were the only productions shown at the Theatre Royal, Drury Lane.

BIRTHDAY GREETINGS TO RICHARD RODGERS

On June 28, 1967, in celebration of Mr. Rodgers' 65th birthday, the American Society of Composers, Authors and Publishers (ASCAP) hosted a luncheon on the stage of the Alvin Theatre in New York. The following are excerpts from the messages read on the occasion:

Stanley Adams (president, ASCAP): ". . . Dick Rodgers is not only a musical, but a medical magician who has consistently diagnosed and interpreted the musical pulse and heart of the nation . . . To talk of his talent is to tell you that the Mona Lisa is a work of art, and all of those whose hearts react to the magic of music will attest to his greatness . . ."

Cleveland Amory (author, lecturer): "The sweetest sounds we've ever heard are those he's written—but think of this! At 65, the sweetest sounds he's ever heard are still inside his head."

Brooks Atkinson (former drama critic, *N.Y. Times*): ". . . He is the greatest. And everyone knows it because his music is in the air every day of our lives."

Betty Comden and Adolph Green (co-lyricists and librettists): ". . . he is still just a growing boy, with no time to think of himself as a monument as he keeps gloriously turning out the music of everyone's future . . ."

Robert Crichton (author, *The Secret of Santa Vittoria*): ". . . I feel strongly that the reason so much of Rodgers' music so perfectly fits the words for which it was written—so perfectly that at times it is impossible to imagine that the words and the music weren't born at the same instant so much a part of each other are they—is as much a tribute to his literary talent as to his musical talent . . ."

Peter DeVries (author, *The Tunnel of Love; Reuben, Reuben*): ". . . this must be one of the exceptions—an artist who seems wholly unreliant on drawbacks, a nice guy who finished first . . . Milestone year indeed! One more milestone around his neck won't mean anything at all."

Sen. Everett McKinley Dirksen: ". . . Frankly, I do not know how we would measure the inestimable debt that I think the country owes to Richard Rodgers and his associates for all those tuneful melodies and those entrancing things in the whole field of performing arts that have made life in America so real . . ."

Bob Hope: "Congratulations on No. 65. In addition to your Pulitzer Prize, your Emmy and your Oscar, it's wonderful that you have at last achieved the truly significant award, Social Security . . ."

Vice President Hubert H. Humphrey: ". . . You've helped America to sing and whistle and laugh and sometimes cry in rich sentiment; but most of all you have given us happy music to happy talk . . ."

Fannie Hurst (author, *Humoresque; Back Street*): "Richard Rodgers is an enrichment to his country as a musician and a person. His music so brilliantly written in the idiom of the American people is built into the nation . . ."

Sidney Kingsley (author, *Dead End; Detective Story):* "In an age of unprecedented horror, cruelty and inhumanity—that one man could fill the world with such beauty—to make life worth the living—attests to the miracle of the human spirit."

Howard Lindsay (co-author, *Life with Father; The Sound of Music*): "There is no greater talent in the American musical theatre than Richard Rodgers. It is a talent disciplined by character and a sound musical education, enriched by humanity and mother wit."

James A. Michener (author, *Tales of the South Pacific; The Source*): "You have me all confused. According to the youthful brilliance of your music you must be about 26 years old. According to the number of world accepted classics you must have been writing for about 80 years . . ."

Gov. Nelson A. Rockefeller: "If, as the poets say, 'music is the speech of angels' then—at the very least—you, Richard Rodgers, must be classified as a very heavenly body . . ."

Samuel A. Taylor (author, *The Happy Time; No Strings*): ". . . At the opening night of *The Boys from Syracuse* in New Haven, at the very first public performance, *Sing for Your Supper* stopped the show. Stopped it cold. The applause went on and on. And Dick turned to me impassively and said, 'There's only one other feeling like this and this is better . . .' "

Howard Teichman (co-author, *The Solid Gold Cadillac*): "In the theatre, the label, 'Genius,' is used almost as often as 'Bayer' on bottles of aspirin. It is difficult to believe, therefore, that an immaculately dressed, closely shaven, soft spoken, exquisitely mannered gentleman without visible temper tantrums and constant needs for ego gratification should be the one, the only, the genuine guaranteed genius of twentieth century music . . ."

TRIBUTES TO OSCAR HAMMERSTEIN II

On April 8, 1962, the United World Federalists sponsored a musical tribute to the memory of Mr. Hammerstein at the 46th Street Theatre in New York. The following are excerpts from letter received on the occasion regarding his activities in behalf of this cause:

The Rt. Hon. Earl Attlee (former British Prime Minister): ". . . Oscar Hammerstein's vision was not limited by the boundless, yet confined, area of the theatre. He was deeply aware of the world in which he lived and deeply sensitive equally to human emotion and to human folly. Hatred was his chief abomination . . . If the world is to be made one, we have to see ourselves as Oscar did, as individual members of a great human family . . ."

Norman Cousins (Editor, *Saturday Review*): ". . . years ago, Oscar Hammerstein was one of the first starry-eyed and divinely discontented astronomers to bring the Federalist concept to our attention and urge its importance on us . . . Many men have responded to the intellectual pull of this concept, but Oscar also reacted to it as a man; and he made it impossible for others to sidestep its human implications . . ."

Russel Crouse (co-author, *Life with Father; The Sound of Music*): ". . . He had the courage to believe in and urge for the entire world a concept which today holds our fifty states united in peaceful federation. Oscar died too soon to see the Common Market demonstrate on a small scale and in a limited way, that European nations, all extremely nationalistic, once even enemies, could work together to solve problems. Let us hope that we will all live to learn that real men of vision, as Oscar was, are not just dreamers."

John Hersey (author, *A Bell for Adano; Hiroshima*): "To honor a memory of Oscar's devotion to the cause of world government is easy and pleasant, for the memory is of an unstinting warmth, a love of mankind and concern for its future, poured out with all the urgency he gave to every side of life . . ."

Dore Schary (author, *Sunrise at Campobello*): "Oscar Hammerstein was a rare man who wrote rare words and accomplished rare deeds. His legacy includes not only the hundreds of lyric words that are part of our lives but also the burning conviction that there can be a better future for us than the atomization of the world . . ."

Sir Percy Claude Spender (President, International Court of Justice at The Hague): ". . . His profound belief in the worth and dignity of all men and women directed his mind constantly to their welfare and happiness and in particular to the problem of how his fellow humans could dwell in peace together . . . His talents were indeed great, his love of his fellow man greater still, and his vision was rare . . ."

John Steinbeck (author, *The Grapes of Wrath*): ". . . It is interesting to me that people like Oscar, whose thoughts and wills set the direction of a changing world, are invariably called romantics and dreamers when in the light of futures, they turn out to be the only realists. Such dreams are the propulsive force of every plunge ahead the world has known. When Oscar threw his resources behind world federation it was not as a wild idealistic dream but as a necessity and an inevitability . . ."

Rex Stout (novelist): ". . . the cause of world peace through world law was closest to Oscar's heart . . . With his lucid and honest mind he perceived the problem and its only workable solution. With his courage, his vigor, and his extraordinary mental and material resources, he did all he could to make that solution possible . . ."

Index

Songs

Includes titles of works written by Rodgers (R) and Hammerstein (H) both together and with other collaborators.

Productions

Includes titles of stage, film and television productions that contain works written by Rodgers (R) and Hammerstein (H), both together and with other collaborators.

CATEGORICAL LISTING OF SONGS

(Includes songs written by Rodgers (R) and Hammerstein (H), both together and with other collaborators.)

Age

All at Once (R-Hart), *Babes in Arms*
Babes in Arms (R-Hart), *Babes in Arms*
Hello, Young Lovers (R-H), *The King and I*
In Other Words, Seventeen (H-Kern), *Very Warm for May*
Ninety Again (R-Charnin), *Two by Two*
Old Enough to Love (R-Hart), *Dearest Enemy*
Old Man, An (R-Charnin), *Two by Two*
One Day When We Were Young (H-Strauss), *The Great Waltz*
Sixteen Going on Seventeen (R-H), *The Sound of Music*
Sweet Sixty-Five (R-Hart), *I'd Rather Be Right*
Sweetest Sight that I Have Seen, The (H-Kern)
'Twas Not So Long Ago (H-Kern), *Sweet Adeline*
We Were So Young (H-Kern), *Sweet Adeline*
When I Grow Too Old to Dream (H-Romberg), *The Night Is Young*
Younger than Springtime (R-H), *South Pacific*

Animals and Birds

Don't Be Afraid of an Animal (R-R), *Androcles and the Lion*
Eager Beaver (R-R), *No Strings*
Get a Horse, Get a Mule (H-Youmans), *Rainbow* (cut)
Golden Ram, The (R-Charnin), *Two by Two*
More than Just a Friend (hog) (R-R), *State Fair*
Softer than a Kitten (R-Hart), *Follow Through*
Two by Two (miscellaneous) (R-Charnin), *Two by Two*
Two Little Blue Birds (H-Kern), *Sunny*
Velvet Paws (lion) (R-R), *Androcles and the Lion*
Why Do You Suppose? (miscellaneous) (R-Hart), *Heads Up!*

Avenues, Squares, Streets

Eleven Levee Street (H-Romberg), *Sunny River* (cut)
Grant Avenue (R-H), *Flower Drum Song*
Little Flat in Soho, A (R-Hart), *Lido Lady*
Slaughter on Tenth Avenue (R), *On Your Toes*
Way Out West (on West End Avenue) (R-Hart), *Babes in Arms*

Ballets

Ghost Town (R)
Nursery Ballet (R)
Slaughter on Tenth Avenue (R), *On Your Toes*
Small House of Uncle Thomas (R-H), *The King and I*

Circus

Circus Is on Parade, The (R-Hart), *Jumbo*
Little Girl Blue (R-Hart), *Jumbo*
My Beautiful Circus Girl (H-Kern), *Three Sisters*
Over and Over Again (R-Hart), *Jumbo*
Song of the Roustabouts (R-Hart), *Jumbo*

Cities

New York
Give It Back to the Indians (R-Hart), *Too Many Girls*
I Gotta Get Back to New York (R-Hart), *Hallelujah, I'm a Bum*
Manhattan (R-Hart), *The Garrick Gaieties* (1925)
Sky City (R-Hart), *Heads Up!* (cut)
Where the Hudson River Flows (R-Hart), *Dearest Enemy*

Paris
Last Time I Saw Paris, The (H-Kern)
Paree (H-Romberg), *The New Moon* (cut)
Paris Is Really Divine (R-Hart), *One Dam Thing After Another*
That Week in Paris (H-Oakland), *The Lady Objects*
That's the Song of Paree (R-Hart), *Love Me Tonight*

Vienna
I'm in Love with Vienna (H-Strauss), *The Great Waltz*
Tales of the Vienna Woods (H-Strauss), *The Great Waltz*
You Will Remember Vienna (H-Romberg), *Viennese Nights*

Others
Amarillo (R-Hart), *They Met in Argentina*
Chicago (R-Hart), *Pal Joey*
Dear Old Syracuse (R-Hart), *The Boys from Syracuse*
Havana (R-Hart), *Peggy-Ann*
Havana for a Night (H-Curiel)
Hollywood Party (R-Hart), *Hollywood Party*
In Egern on the Tegern See (H-Kern), *Music in the Air*
Kansas City (R-H), *Oklahoma!*
Someone Woke Up (Venice) (R-Sondheim), *Do I Hear a Waltz?*

Colors
Big Black Giant, The (R-H), *Me and Juliet*
Blue Moon (R-Hart)
Blue Ocean Blues (R-Hart), *Present Arms*
Blue Room (R-Hart), *The Girl Friend*
Bride Was Dressed in White, The (H-Youmans), *Rainbow*
Brown Eyes (H-Harbach, Friml), *The Wild Rose*
Field of Cloth of Gold, The (R-Harnick), *Rex*
Golden Ram, The (R-Charnin), *Two by Two*
Little Girl Blue (R-Hart), *Jumbo*
Mountain Greenery (R-Hart), *The Garrick Gaieties* (1926)
One Golden Hour (H-Harbach, Friml), *The Wild Rose*
That Terrific Rainbow (R-Hart), *Pal Joey*

Comic
(For comic love songs, see general heading of "Love Songs")

At the Roxy Music Hall (R-Hart), *I Married an Angel*
Baby's Best Friend, A (R-Hart), *She's My Baby*
Bambalina (H-Harbach, Youmans), *Wildflower*
Bargaining (R-Sondheim), *Do I Hear A Waltz?*
Chop Suey (R-H), *Flower Drum Song*
Damsel who Done All the Dirt, The (R-Hart), *The Girl Friend*
Dear Old Syracuse (R-Hart), *The Boys from Syracuse*
Den of Iniquity (R-Hart), *Pal Joey*
Disgustingly Rich (R-Hart), *Higher and Higher*
Don't Be Afraid of an Animal (R-R), *Androcles and the Lion*
Emperor's Thumb, The (R-R), *Androcles and the Lion*
Flower Garden of My Heart, The (R-Hart), *Pal Joey*
Give It Back to the Indians (R-Hart), *Too Many Girls*

Hard-Boiled Herman (H-Harbach, Stothart), *Rose-Marie*
Heart Is Quicker than the Eye, The (R-Hart), *On Your Toes*
How Sad (R-R), *No Strings*
I Blush (R-Hart), *A Connecticut Yankee* (cut)
I Like to Recognize the Tune (R-Hart), *Too Many Girls*
Intermission Talk (R-H), *Me and Juliet*
It (H-Harbach, Romberg), *The Desert Song*
It's a Scandal! It's a Outrage! (R-H), *Oklahoma!*
It's Me (R-H), *Me and Juliet*
Johnny One Note (R-Hart), *Babes in Arms*
Kansas City (R-H), *Oklahoma!*
Lady Is a Tramp, The (R-Hart), *Babes in Arms*
Life Upon the Wicked Stage (H-Kern), *Show Boat*
Life with Father (R-Hart), *By Jupiter*
Little Birdie Told Me So, A (R-Hart), *Peggy-Ann*
Lonely Goatherd, The (R-H), *The Sound of Music*
Mary, Queen of Scots (R-Fields), *Poor Little Ritz Girl*
Mountain Greenery (R-Hart), *The Garrick Gaieties* (1926)
Old-Fashioned Girl, An (R-Meiser), *The Garrick Gaieties* (1925)
Other Generation, The (R-H), *Flower Drum Song*
Paris Is Really Divine (R-Hart), *One Dam Thing After Another*
Pore Jud (R-H), *Oklahoma!*
Queen Elizabeth (R-Hart), *The Garrick Gaieties* (1926)
Rhythm (R-Hart), *Please*
So Long, Farewell (R-H), *The Sound of Music*
Strength Is My Weakness (R-R), *Androcles and the Lion*
Take Him (R-Hart), *Pal Joey*
That Terrific Rainbow (R-Hart), *Pal Joey*
There Is Nothin' Like a Dame (R-H), *South Pacific*
Thinkin' (R-H), *Pipe Dream*
This Week Americans (R-Sondheim), *Do I Hear a Waltz?*
Three B's, The (R-Hart), *On Your Toes*
Three Musketeers, The (R-Hart), *The Garrick Gaieties* (1925)
Twinkle in Your Eye, A (R-Hart), *I Married an Angel*
Vodka (H-Harbach, Gershwin, Stothart), *Song of the Flame*
What Do We Do? We Fly! (R-Sondheim), *Do I Hear a Waltz?*
Where the Hudson River Flows (R-Hart), *Dearest Enemy*
Yatata Yatata Yatata (R-H), *Allegro*
Zip (R-Hart), *Pal Joey*

Countries
For Jupiter and Greece (R-Hart), *By Jupiter*
In Araby with You (H-Harbach, Kern), *Criss-Cross*
Never Go to Argentina (R-Hart), *They Met in Argentina*
Poncho de Panther from Brazil (H-Bizet), *Carmen Jones*

Dancing

Bambalina (H-Harbach, Youmans), *Wildflower*
Beat Out dat Rhythm on a Drum (H-Bizet), *Carmen Jones*
Camelot Samba (R-Hart), *A Connecticut Yankee*
Dance Away the Night (H-Kern), *Show Boat*
Dance, My Darlings (H-Romberg), *May Wine*
Dancing on the Ceiling (R-Hart), *Ever Green*
Heaven in My Arms (H-Kern), *Very Warm for May*
I Haven't Got a Worry in the World (R-H), *Happy Birthday*
I Won't Dance (H-Kern), *Three Sisters*
I'm Crazy 'Bout the Charleston (R-Parsons), *Cochran's Revue of 1926*
In the Cool of the Evening (R-Hart), *Ever Green*
Lonely Feet (H-Kern), *Three Sisters*
Minuet of the Minute, The (H-Harbach, Stothart), *Rose-Marie*
Morning's at Seven (R-Hart), *Higher and Higher*
Never Go to Argentina (R-Hart), *They Met in Argentina*
On with the Dance (R-Hart), *The Garrick Gaieties* (1925)
One More Dance (H-Kern), *Music in the Air*
Shall We Dance? (R-H), *The King and I*
Ten Cents a Dance (R-Hart), *Simple Simon*
Totem Tom-Tom (H-Harbach, Friml, Stothart), *Rose-Marie*
Try Again Tomorrow (R-Hart), *Lido Lady*
Try Her Out at Dances (H-Romberg), *The New Moon*
Virginia Hoe Down (H-Harbach, Kern), *Gentlemen Unafraid*
What's the Use of Talking? (R-Hart), *The Garrick Gaieties* (1926)
When You're Dancing the Waltz (R-Hart), *Dancing Pirate*

Day, Morning, Afternoon, Night

All Through the Day (H-Kern), *Centennial Summer*
Dance Away the High (H-Kern), *Show Boat*
Ev'ry Day (Comes Something Beautiful) (R-Charnin) *I Remember Mama*
Ev'ry Sunday Afternoon (R-Hart), *Higher and Higher*
Havana for a Night (H-Curiel)
In the Cool of the Evening (R-Hart), *Ever Green*
It's a Grand Night for Singing (R-H), *State Fair*
Let's Say Goodnight Till It's Morning (H-Harbach, Kern), *Sunny*
Loneliness of Evening (R-H), *South Pacific* (cut)
Love Me Tonight (R-Hart), *Love Me Tonight*
Lovely Night, A (R-H), *Cinderella*
Many A New Day (R-H), *Oklahoma!*
Midnight Bells (H-Harbach, Gershwin), *Song of the Flame*
Morning Is Midnight (R-Hart), *Lido Lady* (cut)
Morning's at Seven (R-Hart), *Higher and Higher*
Night Flies By (H-Kern), *Music in the Air*
Night Is Young, The (H-Romberg), *The Night Is Young*

Oh, What a Beautiful Mornin' (R-H), *Oklahoma!*
One Day When We Were Young (H-Strauss), *The Great Waltz*
Quiet Night (R-Hart), *On Your Toes*
Shortest Day of the Year, The (R-Hart), *The Boys from Syracuse*
Some Enchanted Evening (R-H), *South Pacific*
This Is My Night to Howl (R-Hart), *A Connecticut Yankee*
Very Special Day, A (R-H), *Me and Juliet*

Days of the Week
E'vry Sunday Afternoon (R-Hart), *Higher and Higher*
Sunday (R-H), *Flower Drum Song*
Sweet Thursday (R-H), *Pipe Dream*

Dreams
Baby Dreams (H-Harbach, Stothart), *Jimmie*
Call It a Dream (H-Romberg), *Sunny River*
Door of Her Dreams (H-Harbach, Friml), *Rose-Marie*
Dream a Dream (H-Harbach, Kern), *Sunny* (cut)
Dreaming Alone (H-Gensler), *Queen o' Hearts*
Dreaming in Paradise (H-Harbach, Romberg), *The Desert Song* (cut)
Everybody Loves You (R-Hart), *I'd Rather Be Right*
Happy Talk (R-H), *South Pacific*
I Built a Dream One Day (H-Romberg), *May Wine*
I Have Dreamed (R-H), *The King and I*
In My Own Little Corner (R-H), *Cinderella*
In the Heart of the Dark (H-Kern), *Very Warm for May*
Kiss to Build a Dream On, A (H-Kalmar, Ruby), *The Strip*
Out of My Dreams (R-H), *Oklahoma!*
Sleepyhead (R-Hart), *The Garrick Gaieties* (1926)
This Nearly Was Mine (R-H), *South Pacific*
When I Grow Too Old to Dream (H-Romberg), *The Night Is Young*
When the Children Are Asleep (R-H), *Carousel*
You Never Can Blame a Girl for Dreaming (H-Harbach, Youmans), *Wildflower*
Your Dream (H-Harbach, Kern), *Gentlemen Unafraid*

Family
Babes in Arms (R-Hart), *Babes in Arms*
Baby's Best Friend, A (R-Hart), *She's My Baby*
Father of the Man (R-R)
Folks who Live on the Hill, The (H-Kern), *High, Wide and Handsome*
I Remember Mama (R-Charnin), *I Remember Mama*
Life with Father (R-Hart), *By Jupiter*
Mama Always Makes It Better (R-Charnin), *I Remember Mama*
Ordinary Couple, An (R-H), *The Sound of Music*

Poppa Knows Best (R-Charnin), *Two by Two*
Soliloquy (R-H), *Carousel*
Stepsisters' Lament (R-H), *Cinderella*
Time (R-Charnin), *I Remember Mama*
When the Children Are Asleep (R-H), *Carousel*
Where Is My Son? (R-Harnick), *Rex*
You Could Not Please Me More (R-Charnin), *I Remember Mama*

Flowers

April Blossoms (H-Harbach, Stothart), *Wildflower*
Dainty Wisp of Thistledown (H-Romberg), *The New Moon*
Dis Flower (H-Bizet), *Carmen Jones*
Edelweiss (R-H), *The Sound of Music*
Flower Garden of My Heart, The (R-Hart), *Pal Joey*
Geraniums in the Winder (R-H), *Carousel*
Goodbye, Little Rosebud (H-Harbach, Stothart), *Wildflower*
One Flower Grows Alone in Your Garden (H-Harbach, Romberg), *The Desert Song*
One Flower that Blooms for You (H-Stothart), *Daffy Dill*
Thistledown (H-Harbach, Stothart), *Mary Jane McKane*
Wild Rose (H-Harbach, Friml), *The Wild Rose*
Wildflower (H-Harbach, Youmans), *Wildflower*

Food & Drink

Bottoms Up (R-Hart), *By Jupiter*
'Cause We Got Cake (R-Hart), *Too Many Girls*
Chop Suey (R-H), *Flower Drum Song*
It Feels Good (drink) (R-H), *Me and Juliet*
Real Nice Clambake, A (R-H), *Carousel*
Sing for Your Supper (R-Hart), *The Boys from Syracuse*
Tavern Song (Red Wine) (H-Romberg), *The New Moon*
Tennessee Fish Fry (H-Schwartz), *American Jubilee*
Vodka (H-Harbach, Gershwin, Stothart), *Song of the Flame*

Foreign Flavor

French

Dites-moi (R-H), *South Pacific*
La, La, La (R-R), *No Strings*
Mimi (R-Hart), *Love Me Tonight*
Paree (H-Romberg), *The New Moon* (cut)
Poor Apache, The (R-Hart), *Love Me Tonight*
That's Love (R-Hart), *Nana*
That's the Song of Paree (R-Hart), *Love Me Tonight*

Italian

No Understand (R-Sondheim), *Do I Hear a Waltz?*

Latin American
Camelot Samba (R-Hart), *A Connecticut Yankee*
Cutting the Cane (R-Hart), *They Met in Argentina*
Havana (R-Hart), *Peggy-Ann*
Havana for a Night (H-Curiel)
Little Dolores (R-Hart)
Lolita (R-Hart), *They Met in Argentina*
No Other Love (R-H), *Me and Juliet*
Pablo, You Are My Heart (R-Hart), *Mississippi* (cut)
She Could Shake the Maracas (R-Hart), *Too Many Girls*
Simpatica (R-Hart), *They Met in Argentina*
Spic and Spanish (R-Hart), *Too Many Girls*

Middle European
Bambalina (H-Harbach, Youmans), *Wildflower*
Edelweiss (R-H), *The Sound of Music*
I'm in Love with Vienna (H-Strauss), *The Great Waltz*
In Egern on the Tegern See (H-Kern), *Music in the Air*
Lonely Goatherd, The (R-H), *The Sound of Music*
Tales of the Vienna Woods (H-Strauss), *The Great Waltz*
You Will Remember Vienna (H-Romberg), *Viennese Nights*

Oriental
Bali Ha'i (R-H), *South Pacific*
Happy Talk (R-H), *South Pacific*
Hundred Million Miracles, A (R-H), *Flower Drum Song*
I Am Going to Like It Here (R-H), *Flower Drum Song*
March of the Siamese Children (R), *The King and I*
Moon of My Delight (R-Hart), *Chee-Chee*
Puzzlement, A (R-H), *The King and I*
Tartar Song (R-Hart), *Chee-Chee*
You Are Beautiful (R-H), *Flower Drum Song*

Russian
Cossack Love Song, The (H-Harbach, Gershwin, Stothart), *Song of the Flame*

Heart

Flower Garden of My Heart, The (R-Hart), *Pal Joey*
Heart Is Quicker than the Eye, The (R-Hart), *On Your Toes*
In the Heart of the Dark (H-Kern), *Very Warm for May*
My Heart Stood Still (R-Hart), *One Dam Thing After Another*
Nobody's Heart (R-Hart), *By Jupiter*
Pablo, You Are My Heart (R-Hart), *Mississippi* (cut)
Something New Is in My Heart (H-Romberg), *May Wine*
With a Song in My Heart (R-Hart), *Spring Is Here*

Holidays

Christmas at Hampton Court (R-Harnick), *Rex*
Happy Christmas, Little Friend (R-H)
My Funny Valentine (R-Hart), *Babes In Arms*

Home

All I Want Is a Home (H-Abraham), *Ball at the Savoy*
Blue Room (R-Hart), *The Girl Friend*
Come Home (R-H), *Allegro*
Den of Iniquity (R-Hart), *Pal Joey*
Eleven Levee Street (H-Romberg), *Sunny River* (cut)
Ev'rybody's Got a Home but Me (R-H), *Pipe Dream*
Folks who Live on the Hill, The (H-Kern), *High, Wide and Handsome*
Happiest House on the Block, The (R-H), *Pipe Dream*
In Egern on the Tegern See (H-Kern), *Music in the Air*
I'll Build a Bungalow (H-Stothart), *Daffy Dill*
In My Own Little Corner (R-H), *Cinderella*
In Our Parlor on the Third Floor Back (R-Hart), *Betsy*
Little Flat in Soho (R-Hart), *Lido Lady*
Lonely Room (R-H), *Oklahoma!*
No Place but Home (R-Hart), *Ever Green*

Inspirational

Climb Ev'ry Mountain (R-H), *The Sound of Music*
Follow in Our Footsteps (R-R), *Androcles and the Lion*
You'll Never Walk Alone (R-H), *Carousel*

Instrumental

Carousel Waltz, *Carousel*
Gavotte, *Cinderella*
Ghost Town
Great Adventure, *The Great Adventure*
Lagoon
March of the Siamese Children, *The King and I*
Nursery Ballet
Salute to the Seaway
Slaughter on Tenth Avenue, *On Your Toes*
Victory at Sea
Waltz for a Ball, *Cinderella*
Where Is Cinderella?, *Cinderella*
Winston Churchill—The Valiant Years

Islands

Bali Ha'i (R-H), *South Pacific*

Guadalcanal March (R), *Victory at Sea*
On a Desert Island with Thee (R-Hart), *A Connecticut Yankee*

Kisses

Give Her a Kiss (R-Hart), *The Phantom President*
Here's a Kiss (R-Hart), *Dearest Enemy*
I Want a Kiss (H-Harbach, Romberg), *The Desert Song*
Kiss to Build a Dream On, A (H-Kalmar, Ruby), *The Strip*
One Kiss (H-Romberg), *The New Moon*
Only a Kiss (H-Harbach, Stothart), *Rose-Marie*
There's So Much More (R-Hart), *America's Sweetheart*
We Kiss in a Shadow (R-H), *The King and I*

Locations

Miscellaneous

All Points West (Grand Central Station) (R-Hart)
At the Roxy Music Hall (R-Hart), *I Married an Angel*
Christmas at Hampton Court (R-Harnick), *Rex*
Dancing on the Ceiling (R-Hart), *Ever Green*
Dere's a Café on de Corner (H-Bizet), *Carmen Jones*
Eleven Levee Street (H-Romberg), *Sunny River* (cut)
Harlemania (R-Hart), *Ever Green*
Memories of Madison Square Garden (R-Hart), *Jumbo*
Mountain Greenery (R-Hart), *The Garrick Gaieties* (1926)
There's a Boy in Harlem (R-Hart), *Fools for Scandal*
There's a Small Hotel (R-Hart), *On Your Toes*
Tree in the Park, A (R-Hart), *Peggy-Ann*
Winter in Central Park (H-Kern), *Sweet Adeline*

Multiple

Any Old Place with You (R-Hart), *A Lonely Romeo*
No Place but Home (R-Hart), *Ever Green*

Love Songs

Romantic and Sincere

All at Once You Love Her (R-H), *Pipe Dream*
All in Fun (H-Kern), *Very Warm for May*
All the Things You Are (H-Kern), *Very Warm for May*
All Through the Day (H-Kern), *Centennial Summer*
April Blossoms (H-Harbach, Stothart), *Wildflower*
Are You My Love? (R-Hart), *Dancing Pirate*
Away from You (R-Harnick), *Rex*
Blue Moon (R-Hart)
Blue Room (R-Hart), *The Girl Friend*
Boys and Girls Like You and Me (R-H), *Oklahoma!* (cut)

Bye and Bye (R-Hart), *Dearest Enemy*
Can I Forget You? (H-Kern), *High, Wide and Handsome*
Can't Help Lovin' dat Man (H-Kern), *Show Boat*
Careless Rhapsody (R-Hart), *By Jupiter*
Come and Tell Me (R-Hart), *Peggy-Ann* (cut)
Cossack Love Song (H-Harbach, Gershwin), *Song of the Flame*
Dancing on the Ceiling (R-Hart), *Ever Green*
Dear, Oh Dear (R-Hart), *Chee-Chee*
Desert Song, The (H-Harbach, Romberg), *The Desert Song*
Dis Flower (H-Bizet), *Carmen Jones*
Do I Hear You Saying "I Love You"? (R-Hart), *Present Arms*
Do I Love You Because You're Beautiful? (R-H), *Cinderella*
Don't Ever Leave Me (H-Kern), *Sweet Adeline*
D'Ye Love Me? (H-Kern), *Sunny*
Embrace Me (H-Romberg), *East Wind*
Fellow Needs a Girl, A (R-H), *Allegro*
From Another World (R-Hart), *Higher and Higher*
Have You Met Miss Jones? (R-Hart), *I'd Rather Be Right*
Hello, Young Lovers (R-H), *The King and I*
Here in My Arms (R-Hart), *Dearest Enemy*
Here's a Hand (R-Hart), *By Jupiter*
Here's a Kiss (R-Hart), *Dearest Enemy*
How Can I Ever Be Alone? (H-Schwartz), *American Jubilee*
How Was I to Know? (R-Hart), *She's My Baby* (cut)
I Bring a Love Song (H-Romberg), *Viennese Nights*
I Can Do Wonders with You (R-Hart), *Simple Simon*
I Could Write a Book (R-Hart), *Pal Joey*
I Didn't Know What Time It Was (R-Hart), *Too Many Girls*
I Do Not Know a Day I Did Not Love You (R-Charnin), *Two by Two*
I Have Dreamed (R-H), *The King and I*
I Have the Room Above Her (H-Kern), *Show Boat*
I Love You More than Yesterday (R-Hart), *Lady Fingers*
I Must Love You (R-Hart), *Chee-Chee*
I'd Like to Hide It (R-Hart), *Dearest Enemy*
If a Wish Could Make It So (H-Harbach, Stothart), *Tickle Me*
If I Loved You (R-H), *Carousel*
I'll Take Romance (H-Oakland), *I'll Take Romance*
I'll Tell the Man in the Street (R-Hart), *I Married an Angel*
I'm Your Girl (R-H), *Me and Juliet*
Indian Love Call (H-Harbach, Friml), *Rose-Marie*
Isn't It Romantic? (R-Hart), *Love Me Tonight*
It Must Be Heaven (R-Hart), *Heads Up!*
I've Told Ev'ry Little Star (H-Kern), *Music in the Air*
Kiss to Build a Dream On, A (H-Kalmar, Ruby), *The Strip*
Let Me Give All My Love to Thee (H-Youmans), *Rainbow*
Lolita (R-Hart), *They Met in Argentina*

Look No Further (R-R), *No Strings*
Love Me Tonight (R-Hart), *Love Me Tonight*
Lover (R-Hart), *Love Me Tonight*
Make Believe (H-Kern), *Show Boat*
Marianne (H-Romberg), *The New Moon*
Marriage-Type Love (R-H), *Me and Juliet*
Most Beautiful Girl in the World, The (R-Hart), *Jumbo*
My Boy and I (H-Duncan, Youmans), *Mary Jane McKane*
My Funny Valentine (R-Hart), *Babes in Arms*
My Heart Stood Still (R-Hart), *One Dam Thing After Another*
My Romance (R-Hart), *Jumbo*
No More Waiting (R-R), *Androcles and the Lion*
No Other Love (R-H), *Me and Juliet*
No Strings (R-R), *No Strings*
Nothing but You (R-Hart), *Higher and Higher*
Now that I Know You (R-Hart), *Two Weeks with Pay*
One Alone (H-Harbach, Romberg), *The Desert Song*
One Kiss (H-Romberg), *The New Moon*
Ordinary Couple, An (R-H), *The Sound of Music*
People Will Say We're in Love (R-H), *Oklahoma!*
Quiet Night (R-Hart), *On Your Toes*
Rose-Marie (H-Harbach, Friml), *Rose-Marie*
Send for Me (R-Hart), *Simple Simon*
Shortest Day of the Year, The (R-Hart), *The Boys from Syracuse*
Simpatica (R-Hart), *They Met in Argentina*
So Far (R-H), *Allegro*
Some Enchanted Evening (R-H), *South Pacific*
Someone Like You (R-Sondheim), *Do I Hear a Waltz?*
Something Good (R-R), *The Sound of Music*
Song Is You, The (H-Kern), *Music in the Air*
Soon (R-Hart), *Mississippi*
Stay (R-Sondheim), *Do I Hear a Waltz?*
Strangers (R-R), *Androcles and the Lion*
Sweetest Sounds, The (R-R), *No Strings*
Take the Moment (R-Sondheim), *Do I Hear a Waltz?*
Ten Minutes Ago (R-H), *Cinderella*
That Lucky Fellow (H-Kern), *Very Warm for May*
That's for Me (R-H), *State Fair*
Then You Will Know (H-Harbach, Romberg), *The Desert Song*
There's a Small Hotel (R-Hart), *On Your Toes*
There's So Much More (R-Hart), *America's Sweetheart*
This Isn't Heaven (R-R), *State Fair*
Tree in the Park, A (R-Hart), *Peggy-Ann*
Wait Till You See Her (R-Hart), *By Jupiter*
Wanting You (H-Romberg), *The New Moon*
We Kiss in a Shadow (R-H), *The King and I*

We Were So Young (H-Kern), *Sweet Adeline*
When I Grow Too Old to Dream (H-Romberg), *The Night Is Young*
Where or When (R-Hart), *Babes in Arms*
Who? (H-Harbach, Kern), *Sunny*
Who Are You? (R-Hart), *The Boys from Syracuse*
Why Do I Love You? (H-Kern), *Show Boat*
Wildflower (H-Harbach, Youmans), *Wildflower*
Willing and Eager (R-R), *State Fair*
With a Song in My Heart (R-Hart), *Spring Is Here*
Wonderful Guy, A (R-H), *South Pacific*
You Are Beautiful (R-H), *Flower Drum Song*
You Are Love (H-Kern), *Show Boat*
You Are Never Away (R-H), *Allegro*
You Are So Fair (R-Hart), *Babes in Arms*
You Are Too Beautiful (R-Hart), *Hallelujah, I'm a Bum*
You Could Not Please Me More (R-Charnin), *I Remember Mama*
You Have Cast Your Shadow on the Sea (R-Hart), *The Boys from Syracu*
You Need Someone (H-Gensler), *Queen o' Hearts*
You Talk Just Like My Maw (H-Bizet), *Carmen Jones*
Younger than Springtime (R-H), *South Pacific*
You're Nearer (R-Hart), *Too Many Girls*
You're What I Need (R-Hart), *She's My Baby*
Yours Sincerely (R-Hart), *Spring Is Here*

COMIC AND RHYTHMIC
All at Once (R-Hart), *Babes in Arms*
All er Nothin' (R-H), *Oklahoma!*
Any Old Place with You (R-Hart), *A Lonely Romeo*
April Fool (R-Hart), *The Garrick Gaieties* (1925)
As Far as I'm Concerned (R-Charnin), *Two by Two*
Better Be Good to Me (R-Hart), *Chee-Chee*
Boy I Left Behind Me (R-Hart), *By Jupiter*
Come on and Pet Me (H-Duncan, Youmans), *Mary Jane McKane* (cut)
Dear, Dear (R-Hart), *Ever Green*
Dat's Love (H-Bizet), *Carmen Jones*
Did You Ever Get Stung? (R-Hart), *I Married an Angel*
Do It the Hard Way (R-Hart), *Pal Joey*
Don't Tell Your Folks (R-Hart), *Simple Simon*
Ev'ry Sunday Afternoon (R-Hart), *Higher and Higher*
Ev'rything I've Got (R-Hart), *By Jupiter*
Girl Friend, The (R-Hart), *The Girl Friend*
Gorgeous Alexander (H-Romberg), *The New Moon*
He and She (R-Hart), *The Boys from Syracuse*
Honey Bun (R-H), *South Pacific*
How About It? (R-Hart), *America's Sweetheart*
How Can Love Survive? (R-H), *The Sound of Music*

How's Your Health? (R-Hart), *Higher and Higher*
I Cain't Say No (R-H), *Oklahoma!*
I Feel at Home with You (R-Hart), *A Connecticut Yankee*
I Might Fall Back on You (H-Kern), *Show Boat*
I Might Grow Fond of You (H-Kern), *Sunny*
I Wish I Were in Love Again (R-Hart), *Babes in Arms*
I'm Gonna Wash That Man Right Outa My Hair (R-H), *South Pacific*
Imagine (R-Hart), *Babes in Arms*
Isn't It Kinda Fun? (R-H), *State Fair*
It's Got to Be Love (R-Hart), *On Your Toes*
It's the Little Things in Texas (R-R), *State Fair*
I've Got Five Dollars (R-Hart), *America's Sweetheart*
June Is Bustin' Out All Over (R-H), *Carousel*
Love Makes the World Go (R-R), *No Strings*
Love Never Went to College (R-Hart), *Too Many Girls*
Manhattan (R-Hart), *The Garrick Gaieties* (1925)
Mimi (R-Hart), *Love Me Tonight*
More than Just a Friend (R-R), *State Fair*
My Man Is on the Make (R-Hart), *Heads Up!*
Never Say No to a Man (R-R), *State Fair*
Now that I've Got My Strength (R-Hart), *By Jupiter*
Old Enough to Love (R-Hart), *Dearest Enemy*
On a Desert Island with Thee (R-Hart), *A Connecticut Yankee*
One Good Man Gone Wrong (H-Harbach, Romberg), *The Desert Song*
Sentimental Me (R-Hart), *The Garrick Gaieties* (1925)
She Could Shake the Maracas (R-Hart), *Too Many Girls*
Sixteen Going on Seventeen (R-H), *The Sound of Music*
Tempt Me Not (R-H), *Too Many Girls*
This Can't Be Love (R-Hart), *The Boys from Syracuse*
Thou Swell (R-Hart), *A Connecticut Yankee*
To Keep My Love Alive (R-Hart), *A Connecticut Yankee*
We Deserve Each Other (R-H), *Me and Juliet*
We'll Be the Same (R-Hart), *America's Sweetheart*
What Can You Do with a Man? (R-Hart), *The Boys from Syracuse*
Why Do I? (R-Hart), *The Girl Friend*
Why Do You Suppose? (R-Hart), *Heads Up!*
Why Shouldn't We? (H-Harbach, Stothart), *Rose-Marie*
You Took Advantage of Me (R-Hart), *Present Arms*

Disenchanted and Unrequited
As Once I Loved You (R-Harnick), *Rex*
Bad in Every Man, The (R-Hart), *Manhattan Melodrama*
Bewitched (R-Hart), *Pal Joey*
Bill (H-Wodehouse, Kern), *Show Boat*
Can't You Do a Friend a Favor? (R-Hart), *A Connecticut Yankee*
Easy to Remember (R-Hart), *Mississippi*
Falling in Love with Love (R-Hart), *The Boys from Syracuse*

Fool Meets Fool (R-Hart), *By Jupiter* (cut)
Gentleman Is a Dope, The (R-H), *Allegro*
Glad to Be Unhappy (R-Hart), *On Your Toes*
He Was too Good to Me (R-Hart), *Simple Simon*
How Can You Forget? (R-Hart), *Fools for Scandal*
I Built a Dream One Day (H-Romberg), *May Wine*
I Still Believe in You (R-Hart), *Simple Simon*
I Want a Man (H-Youmans), *Rainbow*
I'm a Fool, Little One (R-Hart), *Present Arms*
I'm One of God's Children (H-Ruskin, Alter), *Ballyhoo*
In the Heart of the Dark (H-Kern), *Very Warm for May*
It Never Entered My Mind (R-Hart), *Higher and Higher*
Just Once Around the Clock (H-Romberg), *May Wine*
Little Girl Blue (R-Hart), *Jumbo*
Lonely Feet (H-Kern), *Three Sisters*
Love, Look Away (R-H), *Flower Drum Song*
Lover, Come Back to Me (H-Romberg), *The New Moon*
My Joe (H-Bizet), *Carmen Jones*
No Wonder I'm Blue (H-Alter), *Ballyhoo*
Nobody Told Me (R-R), *No Strings*
Nobody's Heart (R-Hart), *By Jupiter*
Ship Without a Sail, A (R-Hart), *Heads Up!*
Singing a Love Song (R-Hart), *Chee-Chee*
So Much You Loved Me (R-Harnick), *Rex*
Softly, as in a Morning Sunrise (H-Romberg), *The New Moon*
Somebody Ought to Be Told (H-Romberg), *May Wine*
Something Doesn't Happen (R-Charnin), *Two by Two*
Spring Is Here (R-Hart), *I Married an Angel*
Ten Cents a Dance (R-Hart), *Simple Simon*
Thank You So Much (R-Sondheim), *Do I Hear a Waltz?*
That's Love (R-Hart), *Nana*
This Nearly Was Mine (R-H), *South Pacific*
Where's That Rainbow? (R-Hart), *Peggy-Ann*
Why Can't I? (R-Hart), *Spring Is Here*
Why Was I Born? (H-Kern), *Sweet Adeline*

Lullabies
Elizabeth (R-Harnick), *Rex*
Everybody Loves You (R-Hart), *I'd Rather Be Right* (cut)
Sleepyhead (R-Hart), *The Garrick Gaieties* 1926
Slumber Song (H-Whiting), *Free For All*
Somebody Wants to Go to Sleep (H-Kern), *Three Sisters*

Marches
At the Field of Cloth of Gold (R-Harnick), *Rex*
Babes in Arms (R-Hart), *Babes in Arms*

Bombardier Song (R-Hart)
Cheerio (R-Hart), *Dearest Enemy*
Circus Is on Parade, The (R-Hart), *Jumbo*
Come with Me (R-Hart), *The Boys from Syracuse*
Fair Is Fair (R-R)
Follow In Our Footsteps (R-R), *Androcles and the Lion*
French Military Marching Song (H-Harbach, Romberg), *The Desert Song*
Good Fellow, Mine (R-Hart), *The Girl Friend*
Guadalcanal March (R), *Victory at Sea*
Here's a Hand (R-Hart), *By Jupiter*
High, Wide and Handsome (H-Kern), *High, Wide and Handsome*
How Can Love Survive? (R-H), *The Sound of Music*
Like a God (R-H), *Flower Drum Song*
March of the Siamese Children (R), *The King and I*
Mounties, The (H-Harbach, Friml, Stothart), *Rose-Marie*
One Foot, Other Foot (R-H), *Allegro*
One Girl, The (H-Youmans), *Rainbow*
Our State Fair (R-H), *State Fair*
Riff Song, The (H, Harbach, Romberg), *The Desert Song*
Stan' Up and Fight (H-Bizet), *Carmen Jones*
Stouthearted Men (H-Romberg), *The New Moon*
There Is Nothin' Like a Dame (R-H), *South Pacific*
There's a Hill Beyond a Hill (H-Kern), *Music in the Air*
Two by Two (R-Charnin), *Two by Two*
We're on Our Way (R-H)
Where Is Cinderella? (R), *Cinderella*

Marriage
Blue Room (R-Hart), *The Girl Friend*
Bride Was Dressed in White, The (H-Youmans), *Rainbow*
Don't Marry Me (R-H), *Flower Drum Song*
Folks who Live on the Hill, The (H-Kern), *High, Wide and Handsome*
I Married an Angel (R-Hart), *I Married an Angel*
It Must Be Heaven (R-Hart), *Heads Up!*
Like Ordinary People Do (R-Hart), *The Hot Heiress*
Marriage-Type Love (R-H), *Me and Juliet*
Mister Snow (R-H), *Carousel*
My Best Love (R-H), *Flower Drum Song* (cut)
Ordinary Couple, An (R-H), *The Sound of Music*
This Is My Night to Howl (R-Hart), *A Connecticut Yankee*
To Have and to Hold (R-H), *Allegro*
To Keep My Love Alive (R-Hart), *A Connecticut Yankee*
We Two (H-Harbach, Kalman, Stothart), *Golden Dawn*
Wedding Knell, The (H-Harbach, Kern), *Sunny*
What a Lovely Day for a Wedding (R-H), *Allegro*
Will You Marry Me? (R-H), *Pipe Dream*

Will You Marry Me Tomorrow, Maria? (H-Kern), *High, Wide and Handsome*
Wish Them Well (R-H), *Allegro*

Money

Disgustingly Rich (R-Hart), *Higher and Higher*
How Can Love Survive? (R-H), *The Sound of Music*
I've Got Five Dollars (R-Hart), *America's Sweetheart*
Loads of Love (R-R), *No Strings*
Money Isn't Everything (R-H), *Allegro*
Ten Cents a Dance (R-Hart), *Simple Simon*

Months

April Blossoms (H-Harbach, Stothart), *Wildflower*
April Fool (R-Hart), *The Garrick Gaieties* (1925)
June Is Bustin' Out All Over (R-H), *Carousel*
Melodies of May (H-Beethoven, Kern), *Music in the Air*
Something in the Air of May (H-Romberg), *May Wine*

Moon

Blue Moon (R-Hart)
Mist Is Over the Moon, A (H-Oakland), *The Lady Objects*
Moon in My Window (R-Sondheim), *Do I Hear a Waltz?*
Moon of My Delight (R-Hart), *Chee-Chee*
When I've Got the Moon (H-Kern)
When You're Driving Through the Moonlight (R-H), *Cinderella*

Music

General

Allegro (R-H), *Allegro*
Careless Rhapsody (R-Hart), *By Jupiter*
Creole Crooning Song (R-Hart), *The Girl Friend*
Do I Hear a Waltz? (R-Sondheim), *Do I Hear a Waltz?*
Do Re Mi (R-H), *The Sound of Music*
Heaven in My Arms (H-Kern), *Very Warm for May*
I Bring a Love Song (H-Romberg), *Viennese Nights*
I Like to Recognize the Tune (R-Hart), *Too Many Girls*
No Song More Pleasing (R-Harnick), *Rex*
Rhythm (R-Hart), *Please*
Song of the Flame (H-Harbach, Gershwin, Stothart), *Song of the Flame*
Song Is You, The (H-Kern), *Music in the Air*
Sound of Music, The (R-H), *The Sound of Music*
Sweetest Sounds, The (R-R), *No Strings*
That's the Rhythm of the Day (R-Hart), *Dancing Lady*

That's the Song of Paree (R-Hart), *Love Me Tonight*
There's a Boy in Harlem (R-Hart), *Fools for Scandal*
There's Music in You (R-H), *Main Street to Broadway*
Three B's, The (R-Hart), *On Your Toes*
With a Song in My Heart (R-Hart), *Spring Is Here*

INSTRUMENTS
Bambalina (fiddle) (H-Harbach, Youmans), *Wildflower*
Beat Out dat Rhythm on a Drum (H-Bizet), *Carmen Jones*
Happy Hunting Horn (R-Hart), *Pal Joey*
Pipes of Pansy (R-Hart), *Dearest Enemy* (cut)
Red Hot Trumpet (R-Hart), *Spring Is Here*
She Could Shake the Maracas (R-Hart), *Too Many Girls*

SINGING AND WHISTLING
I Whistle a Happy Tune (R-H), *The King and I*
It's a Grand Night for Singing (R-H), *State Fair*
Johnny One Note (R-Hart), *Babes in Arms*
Sing (R-Hart), *Betsy*
Sing for Your Supper (R-Hart), *The Boys from Syracuse*
Singing a Love Song (R-Hart), *Chee-Chee*

Nature

It's a Grand Night for Singing (R-H), *State Fair*
June Is Bustin' Out All Over (R-H), *Carousel*
Oh, What a Beautiful Mornin' (R-H), *Oklahoma!*
Oklahoma (R-H), *Oklahoma!*
Mountain Greenery (R-Hart), *The Garrick Gaieties* (1926)
Nothing to Do but Relax (R-Hart), *By Jupiter* (cut)
Sound of Music, The (R-H), *The Sound of Music*
Sweet Thursday (R-H), *Pipe Dream*
Tree in the Park, A (R-Hart), *Peggy-Ann*

Occupations and Professions

MILITARY
Bombardier Song, The (R-Hart)
Cossack Love Song, The (H-Harbach, Gershwin, Stothart), *Song of the Flame*
Good Luck, Mr. Flyin' Man (H-Bizet), *Carmen Jones*
My Mother Told Me Not to Trust a Soldier (H-Youmans), *Rainbow*
Mounties, The (H-Harbach, Friml, Stothart), *Rose-Marie*
Tell It to the Marines (R-Hart), *Present Arms*
Three Musketeers, The (R-Hart), *The Garrick Gaieties* (1925)
What Kind of Soldier Are You? (H-Harbach, Kern), *Gentlemen Unafraid*
Why Did We Marry Soldiers? (H-Harbach, Romberg), *The Desert Song*

MISCELLANEOUS
Bambalina (fiddler) (H-Harbach, Youmans), *Wildflower*
Country Needs a Man, The (president) (R-Hart), *The Phantom President*
Cutting the Cane (R-Hart), *They Met in Argentina*
Farmer and the Cowman, The (R-H), *Oklahoma!*
Hallelujah, I'm a Bum (R-Hart), *Hallelujah, I'm a Bum*
Hermits, The (R-Hart), *Dearest Enemy*
Johnny One Note (opera singer) (R-Hart), *Babes in Arms*
Ladies of the Evening (R-Hart), *The Boys from Syracuse*
Life Upon the Wicked Stage (H-Kern), *Show Boat*
Lonely Goatherd, The (R-H), *The Sound of Music*
Mr. Snow (fisherman) (R-H), *Carousel*
Nobody Loves a Riveter (R-Hart), *The Hot Heiress*
Over and Over Again (aerialists) (R-Hart), *Jumbo*
Puzzlement, A (king) (R-H), *The King and I*
Stan' Up an' Fight (H-Bizet), *Carmen Jones*
Till Good Luck Comes My Way (gambler) (H-Kern), *Show Boat*
When I Go on the Stage (R-Hart), *She's My Baby*

Oceans, Rivers, Seas
Atlantic Blues (R-Hart), *Lido Lady*
Blow High, Blow Low (R-H), *Carousel*
Blue Ocean Blues (R-Hart), *Present Arms*
Down by the River (R-Hart), *Mississippi*
In Egern on the Tegern See (H-Kern), *Music in the Air*
Ol' Man River (H-Kern), *Show Boat*
Roll, Mississippi (R-Hart), *Mississippi*
Salute to the Seaway (R)
Ship without a Sail, A (R-Hart), *Heads Up!*
Sunny River (H-Romberg), *Sunny River*
Tide Pool, The (R-H), *Pipe Dream*
Where the Hudson River Flows (R-Hart), *Dearest Enemy*
You Have Cast Your Shadow on the Sea (R-Hart), *The Boys from Syracuse*

People's Names

MEN
Abe Lincoln Has Just One Country (H-Harbach, Kern), *Gentlemen Unafraid*
Allegheny Al (H-Kern), *High, Wide and Handsome*
Bambalina (H-Harbach, Youmans), *Wildflower*
Bill (H-Wodehouse, Kern), *Show Boat*
Hard-Boiled Herman (H-Harbach, Stothart), *Rose-Marie*
Gorgeous Alexander (H-Romberg), *The New Moon*
Johnny One Note (R-Hart), *Babes in Arms*
Joseph Taylor, Jr. (R-H), *Allegro*

Jupiter Forbid (R-Hart), *By Jupiter*
Lak Jeem (H-Harbach, Friml), *Rose-Marie*
Mister Snow (R-H), *Carousel*
My Joe (H-Bizet), *Carmen Jones*
Pablo, You Are My Heart (R-Hart), *Mississippi* (cut)
Pal Joey (R-Hart), *Pal Joey*
Poncho de Panther from Brazil (H-Bizet), *Carmen Jones*
Pore Jud (R-H), *Oklahoma!*
Sweet Peter (R-Hart), *Dearest Enemy*

WOMEN
Bloody Mary (R-H), *South Pacific*
Dawn (H-Harbach, Stolz, Stothart), *Golden Dawn*
Elizabeth (R-Harnick), *Rex*
Everybody Loves Leona (R-Sondheim), *Do I Hear a Waltz?* (cut)
Fan Tan Fannie (R-H), *Flower Drum Song*
Gateway of the Temple of Minerva (R-Hart), *By Jupiter*
I'd Like to Poison Ivy (R-Hart), *The Melody Man*
Jimmie (H-Harbach, Stothart), *Jimmie*
Little Dolores (R-Hart)
Lolita (R-Hart), *They Met in Argentina*
Margot (H-Harbach, Romberg), *The Desert Song*
Maria (R-H), *The Sound of Music*
Marianne (H-Romberg), *The New Moon*
Mary, Queen of Scots (R-Fields), *Poor Little Ritz Girl*
Mimi (R-Hart), *Love Me Tonight*
Mollie O'Donahue (H-Kern), *Sweet Adeline*
Pipes of Pansy (R-Hart), *Dearest Enemy* (cut)
Queen Elizabeth (R-Hart), *The Garrick Gaieties* (1926)
Rose-Marie (H-Harbach, Friml), *Rose-Marie*
Sunny (H-Harbach, Kern), *Sunny*
Suzy Is a Good Thing (R-H), *Pipe Dream*
Will You Marry Me Tomorrow, Maria? (H-Kern), *High, Wide and Handsome*
You're a Queer One, Julie Jordan (R-H), *Carousel*

Philosophical

Ah Still Suits Me (H-Kern), *Show Boat*
All Kinds of People (R-H), *Pipe Dream*
Allegro (R-H), *Allegro*
Big Black Giant, The (R-H), *Me and Juliet*
Boys and Girls Like You and Me (R-H), *Oklahoma!* (cut)
Bum's Opera (R-H), *Pipe Dream*
Chop Suey (R-H), *Flower Drum Song*
Climb Ev'ry Mountain (R-H), *The Sound of Music*
Cockeyed Optimist, A (R-H), *South Pacific*

Come Home (R-H), *Allegro*
Dat Ol' Boy (H-Bizet), *Carmen Jones*
Dat's Love (H-Bizet), *Carmen Jones*
Do I Love You Because You're Beautiful? (R-H), *Cinderella*
Do It the Hard Way (R-Hart), *Pal Joey*
Every Day (Comes Something Beautiful) (R-Charnin), *I Remember Mama*
Ev'rybody's Got a Home but Me (R-H), *Pipe Dream*
Falling in Love with Love (R-Hart), *The Boys from Syracuse*
Father of the Man, The (R-R)
Getting to Know You (R-H), *The King and I*
Hallelujah, I'm a Bum (R-H), *Hallelujah, I'm a Bum*
Happy Talk (R-H), *South Pacific*
Hello, Young Lovers (R-H), *The King and I*
How Sad (R-R), *No Strings*
Hundred Million Miracles, A (R-H), *Flower Drum Song*
I Can Always Find Another Partner (H-Harbach, Youmans), *Wildflower*
I Enjoy Being a Girl (R-H), *Flower Drum Song*
I Have Confidence in Me (R-R), *The Sound of Music*
I Whistle a Happy Tune (R-H), *The King and I*
Impossible (R-H), *Cinderella*
In Time (R-Harnick), *Rex*
Keep It Gay (R-H), *Me and Juliet*
Lady Is a Tramp, The (R-Hart), *Babes in Arms*
Lady Must Live, A (R-Hart), *America's Sweetheart*
Let Love Come (H-Harbach, Romberg), *The Desert Song*
Little Bit More, A (R-Jessel), *I Remember Mama*
Little Workaday World (R-Wright, Forrest), *I Married an Angel*
Loads of Love (R-R), *No Strings*
Love Is Quite a Simple Thing (H-Romberg), *The New Moon*
Man I Used to Be, The (R-H), *Pipe Dream*
Man who Has Everything, The (R-R), *No Strings*
Money Isn't Everything (R-H), *Allegro*
My Favorite Things (R-H), *The Sound of Music*
My Romance (R-Hart), *Jumbo*
Never Say No to a Man (R-R), *State Fair*
Next Time It Happens, The (R-H), *Pipe Dream*
No Strings (R-R), *No Strings*
Ol' Man River (H-Kern), *Show Boat*
On Your Toes (R-Hart), *On Your Toes*
One Flower Grows Alone in Your Garden (H-Harbach, Romberg), *The Desert Son*
Other Generation, The (R-H), *Flower Drum Song*
Puzzlement, A (R-H), *The King and I*
Reckless (H-Kern), *Reckless*
Soliloquy (R-H), *Carousel*
Some Enchanted Evening (R-H), *South Pacific*

Something Wonderful (R-H), *The King and I*
Sound of Music, The (R-H), *The Sound of Music*
Sweetest Sounds, The (R-R), *No Strings*
That's Love (R-Hart), *Nana*
There's Nothin' So Bad for a Woman (R-H), *Carousel*
There's So Much More (R-Hart), *America's Sweetheart*
This Can't Be Love (R-Hart), *The Boys from Syracuse*
This Funny World (R-Hart), *Betsy*
Till Good Luck Comes My Way (H-Kern), *Show Boat*
Twin Soliloquies (R-H), *South Pacific*
Twinkle in Your Eye, A (R-Hart), *I Married an Angel*
We'll Be the Same (R-Hart), *America's Sweetheart*
We're Gonna Be All Right (R-Sondheim), *Do I Hear a Waltz?*
What Is a Man? (R-Hart), *Pal Joey*
What's the Use of Wond'rin'? (R-H), *Carousel*
Where's the Mate for Me? (H-Kern), *Show Boat*
Wild Rose (H-Harbach, Kern), *Sunny*
You Always Love the Same Girl (R-Hart), *A Connecticut Yankee*
You'll Never Walk Alone (R-H), *Carousel*
You've Got to Be Carefully Taught (R-H), *South Pacific*

Seasons

Autumn
Heroes in the Fall (R-Hart), *Too Many Girls*

Spring
Hermits, The (R-Hart), *Dearest Enemy*
It Might as Well Be Spring (R-H), *State Fair*
Now that I Have Springtime (H-Kern), *Three Sisters*
Spring Is Here (R-Hart), *I Married an Angel*
Spring Is Here (R-Hart), *Spring Is Here*
When the Spring Is in the Air (H-Kern), *Music in the Air*
Younger that Springtime (R-H), *South Pacific*

Summer
June is Bustin' Out All Over (R-H), *Carousel*
Nothing to Do But Relax (R-Hart), *By Jupiter* (cut)

Winter
Winter in Central Park (H-Kern), *Sweet Adeline*
Winters Go By (R-H), *Allegro*

Singers

For Choral Groups
All I Owe Ioway (R-H), *State Fair*
Babes in Arms (R-Hart), *Babes in Arms*

Bombardier Song, The (R-Hart)
Bloody Mary (R-H), *South Pacific*
Blow High, Blow Low (R-H), *Carousel*
'Cause We Got Cake (R-Hart), *Too Many Girls*
Cheerio (R-Hart), *Dearest Enemy*
Chicago (R-Hart), *Pal Joey*
Circus Is on Parade (R-Hart), *Jumbo*
Climb E'vry Mountain (R-H), *The Sound of Music*
Do Re Mi (R-H), *The Sound of Music*
Edelweiss (R-H), *The Sound of Music*
Farmer and the Cowman, The (R-H), *Oklahoma!*
Field of Cloth of Gold, The (R-Harnick), *Rex*
Follow in Our Footsteps (R-R), *Androcles and the Lion*
French Military Marching Song (H-Harbach, Romberg), *The Desert Song*
Getting to Know You (R-H), *The King and I*
Grant Avenue (R-H), *Flower Drum Song*
High, Wide and Handsome (H-Kern), *High, Wide and Handsome*
Hollywood Party (R-Hart), *Hollywood Party*
It's a Grand Night for Singing (R-H), *State Fair*
June Is Bustin' Out All Over (R-H), *Carousel*
Jupiter Forbid (R-Hart), *By Jupiter*
Lonely Goatherd (R-H), *The Sound of Music*
Lopsided Bus, A (R-H), *Pipe Dream*
Maria (R-H), *The Sound of Music*
Marianne (H-Romberg), *The New Moon*
Money Isn't Everything (R-H), *Allegro*
Mounties, The (H-Harbach, Friml, Stothart), *Rose-Marie*
Oh, What a Beautiful Mornin' (R-H), *Oklahoma!*
Oklahoma (R-H), *Oklahoma!*
One Foot, Other Foot (R-H), *Allegro*
Our State Fair (R-H), *State Fair*
Over and Over Again (R-Hart), *Jumbo*
Prince Is Giving a Ball, The (R-H), *Cinderella*
Real Nice Clambake, A (R-H), *Carousel*
Riff Song (H-Harbach, Romberg), *The Desert Song*
So Long, Farewell (R-H), *The Sound of Music*
Sound of Music, The (R-H), *The Sound of Music*
Stouthearted Men (H-Romberg), *The New Moon*
Sunny (H-Harbach, Kern), *Sunny*
Sweet Peter (R-Hart), *Dearest Enemy*
Sweet Thursday (R-H), *Pipe Dream*
There Is Nothin' Like a Dame (R-H), *South Pacific*
There's a Hill Beyond a Hill (H-Kern), *Music in the Air*
There's Nothin' So Bad for a Woman (R-H), *Carousel*
To Have and to Hold (R-H), *Allegro*
Totem Tom-Tom (H-Harbach, Friml, Stothart), *Rose-Marie*

What a Lovely Day for a Wedding (R-H), *Allegro*
Wish Them Well (R-H), *Allegro*
Yatata Yatata Yatata (R-H), *Allegro*

For Duets
All er Nothin' (R-H), *Oklahoma!*
April Blossoms (H-Harbach, Stothart), *Wildflower*
April Fool (R-Hart), *The Garrick Gaieties* (1925)
Away from You (R-Harnick), *Rex*
Blue Room (R-Hart), *The Girl Friend*
Bye and Bye (R-Hart), *Dearest Enemy*
Careless Rhapsody (R-Hart), *By Jupiter*
Dear, Dear (R-Hart), *Ever Green*
Den of Iniquity (R-Hart), *Pal Joey*
Desert Song, The (H-Harbach, Romberg), *The Desert Song*
Don't Tell Your Folks (R-Hart), *Simple Simon*
Every Sunday Afternoon (R-Hart), *Higher and Higher*
Ev'rything I've Got (R-Hart), *By Jupiter*
Girl Friend, The (R-Hart), *The Girl Friend*
He and She (R-Hart), *The Boys from Syracuse*
How Can Love Survive? (R-H), *The Sound of Music*
I Could Write a Book (R-Hart), *Pal Joey*
I Feel at Home with You (R-Hart), *A Connecticut Yankee*
I Have Dreamed (R-H), *The King and I*
I Might Fall Back on You (H-Kern), *Show Boat*
I Might Grow Fond of You (H-Kern), *Sunny*
If I Give in to You (R-Hart), *Ever Green*
If I Loved You (R-H), *Carousel*
If I Were You (R-Hart), *Betsy*
Impossible (R-H), *Cinderella*
Indian Love Call (H-Harbach, Friml), *Rose-Marie*
Isn't It Kinda Fun? (R-H), *State Fair*
It's Got to Be Love (R-Hart), *On Your Toes*
It's the Little Things in Texas (R-R), *State Fair*
I've Got Five Dollars (R-Hart), *America's Sweetheart*
La, La, La (R-R), *No Strings*
Let's Say Goodnight 'Til It's Morning (H-Harbach, Kern), *Sunny*
Life with Father (R-Hart), *Jupiter Forbid*
Like Ordinary People Do (R-Hart), *The Hot Heiress*
Look No Further (R-R), *No Strings*
Maine (R-R), *No Strings*
Make Believe (H-Kern), *Show Boat*
Manhattan (R-Hart), *The Garrick Gaieties* (1925)
Me for You (R-Hart), *Heads Up!*
Morning Is Midnight (R-Hart), *Lido Lady* (cut)
Mountain Greenery (R-Hart), *The Garrick Gaieties* (1926)

My Heart Stood Still (R-Hart), *One Dam Thing After Another*
On a Desert Island with Thee (R-Hart), *A Connecticut Yankee*
People Will Say We're in Love (R-H), *Oklahoma!*
Pore Jud (R-H), *Oklahoma!*
Sentimental Me (R-Hart), *The Garrick Gaieties* (1925)
Sixteen Going on Seventeen (R-H), *The Sound of Music*
Strangers (R-R), *Androcles and the Lion*
Sunday (R-H), *Flower Drum Song*
Sweet Sixty-Five (R-Hart), *I'd Rather Be Right*
Take Him (R-Hart), *Pal Joey*
Then You Will Know (H-Harbach, Romberg), *The Desert Song*
There's So Much More (R-Hart), *America's Sweetheart*
Thou Swell (R-Hart), *A Connecticut Yankee*
Twin Soliloquies (R-H), *South Pacific*
Wanting You (H-Romberg), *The New Moon*
Way Out West (R-Hart), *Babes in Arms*
We Belong Together (H-Kern), *Music in the Air*
We Deserve Each Other (R-H), *Me and Juliet*
We Kiss in a Shadow (R-H), *The King and I*
We're Gonna Be All Right (R-Sondheim), *Do I Hear a Waltz?*
When the Children Are Asleep (R-H), *Carousel*
Where the Hudson River Flows (R-Hart), *Dearest Enemy*
Who? (H-Harbach, Kern), *Sunny*
Why Do I Love You? (H-Kern), *Show Boat*
Why Do You Suppose? (R-Hart), *Heads Up!*
Why Shouldn't We? (H-Harbach, Stothart), *Rose-Marie*
You Are Love (H-Kern), *Show Boat*

For Female Solos
As Once I Loved You (R-Harnick), *Rex*
As Though You Were There (R-Hart), *Heads Up!* (cut)
Baby's Awake Now (R-Hart), *Spring Is Here*
Baby's Best Friend (R-Hart), *She's My Baby*
Bad in Every Man, The (R-Hart), *Manhattan Melodrama*
Better Be Good to Me (R-Hart), *Chee-Chee*
Bewitched (R-Hart), *Pal Joey*
Bill (H-Wodehouse, Kern), *Show Boat*
Boy I Left Behind Me (R-Hart), *By Jupiter*
Can't Help Lovin' dat Man (H-Kern), *Show Boat*
Dat's Love (H-Bizet), *Carmen Jones*
Don't Ever Leave Me (H-Kern), *Sweet Adeline*
Falling in Love with Love (R-Hart), *The Boys from Syracuse*
Gentleman Is a Dope, The (R-H), *Allegro*
Glad to Be Unhappy (R-Hart), *On Your Toes*
He Was Too Good to Me (R-Hart), *Simple Simon*
Heart Is Quicker than the Eye, The (R-Hart), *On Your Toes*

Hello, Young Lovers (R-H), *The King and I*
I Blush (R-Hart), *A Connecticut Yankee* (cut)
I Cain't Say No (R-H), *Oklahoma!*
I Didn't Know What Time It Was (R-Hart), *Too Many Girls*
I Enjoy Being a Girl (R-H), *Flower Drum Song*
I Want a Man (R-Hart), *America's Sweetheart*
I Want a Man (H-Youmans), *Rainbow*
I'll Be a Buoyant Girl (H-Harbach, Romberg), *The Desert Song*
I'm Gonna Wash That Man Right Outa My Hair (R-H), *South Pacific*
I'm One of God's Children (H-Ruskin, Alter), *Ballyhoo*
I'm Your Girl (R-H), *Me and Juliet*
In My Own Little Corner (R-H), *Cinderella*
It Never Entered My Mind (R-Hart), *Higher and Higher*
It's Me (R-H), *Me and Juliet*
Lady Is a Tramp, The (R-Hart), *Babes in Arms*
Lady Must Live, A (R-Hart), *America's Sweetheart*
Lak Jeem (H-Harbach, Friml), *Rose-Marie*
Little Birdie Told Me So, A (R-Hart), *Peggy-Ann*
Loads of Love (R-R), *No Strings*
Many a New Day (R-H), *Oklahoma!*
Mister Snow (R-H), *Carousel*
My Boy and I (H-Duncan, Youmans), *Mary Jane McKane*
My Funny Valentine (R-Hart), *Babes in Arms*
My Joe (H-Bizet), *Carmen Jones*
My Lord and Master (R-H), *The King and I*
My Man Is on the Make (R-Hart), *Heads Up!*
My Prince (R-Hart), *Too Many Girls*
Never Say No to a Man (R-R), *State Fair*
No Wonder I'm Blue (H-Alter), *Ballyhoo*
Nobody's Heart (R-Hart), *By Jupiter*
Old-Fashioned Girl, An (R-Meiser), *The Garrick Gaieties* (1925)
Pretty Things (H-Harbach, Friml), *Rose-Marie*
Romance (H-Harbach, Romberg), *The Desert Song*
So Much You Loved Me (R-Harnick), *Rex*
Ten Cents a Dance (R-Hart), *Simple Simon*
That's Love (R-Hart), *Nana*
This Is My Night to Howl (R-Hart), *A Connecticut Yankee*
To Keep My Love Alive (R-Hart), *A Connecticut Yankee*
We Were So Young (H-Kern), *Sweet Adeline*
What Is a Man? (R-Hart), *Pal Joey*
What's the Use of Wond'rin'? (R-H), *Carousel*
Where's That Rainbow? (R-Hart), *Peggy-Ann*
Why Can't I? (R-Hart), *Spring Is Here*
Why Was I Born? (H-Kern), *Sweet Adeline*
Wild Rose (H-Harbach, Kern), *Sunny*
Wonderful Guy, A (R-H), *South Pacific*

You Never Can Blame a Girl for Dreaming (H-Harbach, Youmans), *Wildflower*
Zip (R-Hart), *Pal Joey*

For Male Solos
All at Once (R-Hart), *Babes in Arms*
All at Once You Love Her (R-H), *Pipe Dream*
Dawn (H-Harbach, Stolz, Stothart), *Golden Dawn*
Dis Flower (H-Bizet), *Carmen Jones*
Don't Marry Me (R-H), *Flower Drum Song*
Fellow Needs a Girl, A (R-H), *Allegro*
Gateway to the Temple of Minerva (R-Hart), *By Jupiter*
Hallelujah, I'm a Bum (R-Hart), *Hallelujah, I'm a Bum*
Happy Hunting Horn (R-Hart), *Pal Joey*
Have You Met Miss Jones? (R-Hart), *I'd Rather Be Right*
Here's a Hand (R-Hart), *By Jupiter*
How Sad (R-R), *No Strings*
I Married an Angel (R-Hart), *I Married an Angel*
I'd Rather Be Right (R-Hart), *I'd Rather Be Right*
I'm Talking to My Pal (R-Hart), *Pal Joey* (cut)
It Feels Good (R-H), *Me and Juliet*
It Must Be Heaven (R-Hart), *Heads Up!*
It's a Scandal! It's a Outrage! (R-H), *Oklahoma!*
Kansas City (R-H), *Oklahoma!*
Like a God (R-H), *Flower Drum Song*
Lolita (R-Hart), *They Met in Argentina*
Lonely Room (R-H), *Oklahoma!*
Man I Used to Be, The (R-H), *Pipe Dream*
Man who Has Everything, The (R-R), *No Strings*
Marriage-Type Love (R-H), *Me and Juliet*
Mimi (R-Hart), *Love Me Tonight*
Most Beautiful Girl in the World, The (R-Hart), *Jumbo*
My Beautiful Circus Girl (H-Kern), *Three Sisters*
My Bicycle Girl (H-Schwartz), *American Jubilee*
My Girl and I (H-Romberg), *Sunny River*
My Girl Back Home (R-H), *South Pacific* (cut)
Ol' Man River (H-Kern), *Show Boat*
One Girl, The (H-Youmans), *Rainbow*
Puzzlement, A (R-H), *The King and I*
Rose-Marie (H-Harbach, Friml), *Rose-Marie*
Soliloquy (R-H), *Carousel*
Surrey with the Fringe on Top, The (R-H), *Oklahoma!*
That Lucky Fellow (H-Kern), *Very Warm for May*
This Isn't Heaven (R-R), *State Fair*
Till Good Luck Comes My Way (H-Kern), *Show Boat*
Wait Till You See Her (R-Hart), *By Jupiter*

We Two (H-Harbach, Kalman, Stothart), *Golden Dawn*
Where's the Mate for Me? (H-Kern), *Show Boat*
Wild-Flower (H-Harbach, Youmans), *Wildflower*
You Always Love the Same Girl (R-Hart), *A Connecticut Yankee*
You Are Beautiful (R-H), *Flower Drum Song*
You Are My Woman (H-Romberg), *East Wind*
You Are So Fair (R-Hart), *Babes in Arms*
You Are Too Beautiful (R-Hart), *Hallelujah, I'm a Bum*
You Talk Just Like My Maw (H-Bizet), *Carmen Jones*
Younger than Springtime (R-H), *South Pacific*

States
All I Owe Ioway (R-H), *State Fair*
Fly Away to Ioway (R-Hart), *Hollywood Party* (cut)
Hawaii (R-Hart), *Present Arms*
In Californ-i-a (R-Hart), *America's Sweetheart*
It's the Little Things in Texas (R-R), *State Fair*
Maine (R-R), *No Strings*
Oklaho. ıa (R-H), *Oklahoma!*
Tennessee Fish Fry (H-Schwartz), *American Jubilee*
Virginia Hoe Down (H-Harbach, Kern), *Gentlemen Unafraid*

Teaching
All at Once (R-Hart), *Babes in Arms*
Getting to Know You (R-H), *The King and I*
Love Never Went to College (R-Hart), *Too Many Girls*
Try Again Tomorrow (R-Hart), *Lido Lady*
You've Got to Be Carefully Taught (R-H), *South Pacific*

Theatre
At the Roxy Music Hall (R-Hart), *I Married an Angel*
Big Black Giant, The (R-H), *Me and Juliet*
Innocent Chorus Girls of Yesterday (R-Hart), *America's Sweetheart*
Intermission Talk (R-H), *Me and Juliet*
Life Upon the Wicked Stage (H-Kern), *Show Boat*
Two-a-Day for Keith (R-Hart), *On Your Toes*
When I Go on the Stage (R-Hart), *She's My Baby*

Time
I Didn't Know What Time It Was (R-Hart), *Too Many Girls*
In Time (R-Harnick), *Rex*
Just Once Around the Clock (H-Romberg), *May Wine*
One Golden Hour (H-Harbach, Friml), *The Wild Rose*

Take the Moment (R-Sondheim), *Do I Hear a Waltz?*
Ten Minutes Ago (R-H), *Cinderella*
There'll Come a Time (H-Strauss), *The Great Waltz*
Time (R-Charnin), *I Remember Mama*
Time Is Standing Still (H-Romberg), *Sunny River*
Where or When (R-Hart), *Babes in Arms*

Transportation and Travel
All Points West (R-Hart)
Any Old Place with You (R-Hart), *A Lonely Romeo*
Girl on the Prow, The (H-Romberg), *The New Moon*
Keep 'Em Rolling (R-Hart), *Keep 'Em Rolling*
Lopsided Bus, A (R-H), *Pipe Dream*
My Bicycle Girl (H-Schwartz), *American Jubilee*
No Place but Home (R-Hart), *Ever Green*
Ship Without a Sail, A (R-Hart), *Heads Up!*
Surrey with the Fringe on Top, The (R-H), *Oklahoma!*
What Do We Do? We Fly! (R-Sondheim), *Do I Hear a Waltz?*
When You're Driving Through the Moonlight (R-H), *Cinderella*
Whizzin' Away Along de Track (H-Bizet), *Carmen Jones*
You Have Got to Have a Rudder on the Ark (R-Charnin), *Two by Two*

Waltzes
And Love Was Born (H-Kern), *Music in the Air*
Carousel Waltz (R), *Carousel*
Do You Love Me? (R-Hart), *The Garrick Gaieties* (1925)
Door of Her Dreams (H-Harbach, Friml), *Rose-Marie*
D'Ye Love Me? (H-Harbach, Kern), *Sunny*
Edelweiss (R-H), *The Sound of Music*
Falling in Love with Love (R-Hart), *The Boys from Syracuse*
Girl on the Prow, The (H-Romberg), *The New Moon*
Goodbye, Little Rosebud (H-Harbach, Stothart), *Wildflower*
Happiest House on the Block, The (R-H), *Pipe Dream*
Hello, Young Lovers (R-H), *The King and I*
Here's a Kiss (R-Hart), *Dearest Enemy*
I Am So Eager (H-Kern), *Music in the Air*
I Blush (R-Hart), *A Connecticut Yankee* (cut)
I Built a Dream One Day (H-Romberg), *May Wine*
I Mean to Say I Love You (H-Korngold), *Give Us This Night*
I Want a Kiss (H-Harbach, Romberg), *The Desert Song*
I'll Take Romance (H-Oakland), *I'll Take Romance*
I'm in Love with Vienna (H-Strauss), *The Great Waltz*
It's a Grand Night for Singing (R-H), *State Fair*
Lopsided Bus, A (R-H), *Pipe Dream*
Love Makes the World Go (R-R), *No Strings*

Lover (R-Hart), *Love Me Tonight*
Memories of Madison Square Garden (R-Hart), *Jumbo*
Money Isn't Everything (R-H), *Allegro*
More than Just a Friend (R-R), *State Fair*
Most Beautiful Girl in the World (R-Hart), *Jumbo*
My Beautiful Circus Girl (H-Kern), *Three Sisters*
My Boy and I (H-Duncan, Youmans), *Mary Jane McKane*
My Bwana (H-Harbach, Kalman, Stothart), *Golden Dawn*
My Favorite Things (R-H), *The Sound of Music*
Never Say No to a Man (R-R), *State Fair*
Night Flies By (H-Kern), *Music in the Air*
Nothing but You (R-Hart), *Higher and Higher*
Oh, What a Beautiful Mornin' (R-H), *Oklahoma!*
One Day When We Were Young (H-Strauss), *The Great Waltz*
One Golden Hour (H-Harbach, Friml), *The Wild Rose*
One Kiss (H-Romberg), *The New Moon*
One Kiss Is Waiting for One Man (H-Romberg), *The New Moon* (cut)
One More Dance (H-Kern), *Music in the Air*
Out of My Dreams (R-H), *Oklahoma!*
Over and Over Again (R-Hart), *Jumbo*
Real Nice Clambake, A (R-H), *Carousel*
Romance (H-Harbach, Romberg), *The Desert Song*
Somebody Wants to Go to Sleep (H-Kern), *Three Sisters*
Something in the Air of May (H-Romberg), *May Wine*
Something New Is in My Heart (H-Romberg), *May Wine*
Sun About to Rise, The (H-Kern), *Sweet Adeline*
Tales from the Vienna Woods (H-Strauss), *The Great Waltz*
Ten Minutes Ago (R-H), *Cinderella*
There'll Come a Time (H-Strauss), *The Great Waltz*
This Nearly Was Mine (R-H), *South Pacific*
Thistledown (H-Harbach, Stothart), *Mary Jane McKane*
Velvet Paws (R-R), *Androcles and the Lion*
Wait Till You See Her (R-Hart), *By Jupiter*
Waltz for a Ball (R), *Cinderella*
Wander Away (H-Harbach, Stothart), *Song of the Flame*
Wanting You (H-Romberg), *The New Moon*
When I Grow Too Old to Dream (H-Romberg), *The Night Is Young*
When You're Dancing the Waltz (R-Hart), *Dancing Pirate*
Wonderful Guy, A (R-H), *South Pacific*
You Are Love (H-Kern), *Show Boat*
You Talk Just Like My Maw (H-Bizet), *Carmen Jones*

Yesterday and Tomorrow
I Love You More than Yesterday (R-Hart), *Lady Fingers*
Party that We're Gonna Have Tomorrow Night, The (R-H), *Pipe Dream*
Try Again Tomorrow (R-Hart), *Lido Lady*

Stop-Press Addendum

The 1979 production of OKLAHOMA! (see page 525) opened at the Palace Theatre, New York, on December 13, and was greeted by the following reviews:

Walter Kerr—*New York Times*
"...freshly revived...As I went up the aisle at intermission, I noticed one and all were beaming. Some were smiling because they remember. The others were smiling because they will...*Oklahoma!* remains the gently enchanting sampler it is because it is utterly un-self-conscious about what it is doing...owns the best of both worlds, old and new...a winning and welcome evening...I have a hunch some snipping might well be done in Ali Hakim's later, noticeably anticlimactic scenes. No one should touch the music, though. All that incredible music."

Douglas Watt—*New York Daily News*
"'*Oklahoma!' is OK*...Such a lovely outpouring of song! Such profligacy of talent as the master lyricist and master composer leaned over the same piano for the first time! The revival is first-class...What more could one ask? Less. Not less songs. No, never that, not with those gems. But, surprisingly, less dancing...William Hammerstein has staged the classic brightly and lovingly...Forget the 'landmark musical' cachet, however accurate. See it for the fun of it, for its freshet of great songs, and for its splendid cast."

Clive Barnes—*New York Post*
"...a spanking new production...What music! What sheer good fun! And what wonderfully assertive innocence, what an asseveration of America the proud, America the beautiful, America the unlimited!...Virtually every number is a hit...But what was more important, and what made *Oklahoma!* such a landmark, was its new homogenity, its specific blend of music, drama and dance, and its new seriousness...directed with a sort of traditional pizzazz...DeMille's contribution was, and is, essential...Perhaps the best news is that this *Oklahoma!* has the zest of an original...a show to freshen your heart and make your next morning wonderful..."

William A. Raidy—*Newhouse newspapers*
"Oh, what a beautiful musical...Still!...A delightful revival of a truly great musical..."

Emory Lewis—*The Record*
"...pure enchantment...The music is immortal...The direction is lively and witty. William Hammerstein has assembled the best cast since the original production..."

Allan Wallach—*Newsday*
"A sparkling new production that is an occasion for some words of celebration... A loving and lovely version, with a talented cast bringing freshness to the score and dances..."

Pia Lindstrom—*NBC-TV*
"...cheered a new generation with its warmth... a beautiful, spirited musical... every song is a classic... the choreography is as witty and clever as it was decades ago. I cannot imagine anyone leaving the theatre not humming the songs."

Rex Reed—*New York Daily News*, December 19, 1979
"...magical revival... Broadway at its best, with fabulous sets, great voices, expert dances... *Oklahoma!* is the star on top of Broadway's tree and I hope it lights up the seasons for years to come."

Theodore E. Kalem—*Time*, December 24, 1979
"*A-yip-i-o-ee-ay!*... Its endearing score is indestructible, and the new production is finely cast and admirably polished... The songs are a Comstock lode of golden oldies... You won't just be humming the tunes as you leave the theatre. You will hum them for the rest of your life."

Jack Kroll—*Newsweek*, December 24, 1979
"*Beautiful Evening*... almost the first thing that hits you is Hammerstein's poetic gift. His lyrics are as pellucid, firm and bright as pebbles shining under water. The amazing score is a triumph of inspired simplicity. You think, my God, the Broadway musical really used to *sing!*... a buoyant and winning show..."

Martin Gottfried—*Cue*, January 4, 1980
"...superbly directed by William Hammerstein with emphasis on precision of speech, clarity of lyrics, discipline, and trueness of singing... reproduced honestly... a rollcall of glorious showtunes... pure Broadway gold. Dramatically and musically the company is marvelous..."